朗文
外研社

新概念英语

NEW CONCEPT ENGLISH

New Edition 新 版

Practice & Progress
实践与进步

2

亚历山大（L. G. ALEXANDER）何其莘　著

 外语教学与研究出版社

PEARSON　LONGMAN

京权图字：01-2004-4973

图书在版编目（CIP）数据

朗文·外研社新概念英语：新版. 2 ／（英）亚历山大（L. G. Alexander），何其莘著. ——
北京：外语教学与研究出版社，1997.10（2019.4 重印）
ISBN 978-7-5600-1347-3

Ⅰ. ①朗… Ⅱ. ①亚… ②何… Ⅲ. ①英语－自学参考资料 Ⅳ. ①H31

中国版本图书馆 CIP 数据核字（2017）第 118479 号

出 版 人　蔡剑峰
出版发行　外语教学与研究出版社
社　　址　北京市西三环北路 19 号（100089）
网　　址　http://www.fltrp.com
印　　刷　河北鹏盛贤印刷有限公司
开　　本　787×1092　1/16
印　　张　30
版　　次　1997 年 10 月第 1 版 2019 年 4 月第 208 次印刷
印　　数　15524000—15624000 册
书　　号　ISBN 978-7-5600-1347-3
定　　价　38.90 元

购书咨询：（010）88819926　电子邮箱：club@fltrp.com
外研书店：https://waiyants.tmall.com
凡印刷、装订质量问题，请联系我社印制部
联系电话：（010）61207896　电子邮箱：zhijian@fltrp.com
凡侵权、盗版书籍线索，请联系我社法律事务部
举报电话：（010）88817519　电子邮箱：banquan@fltrp.com
物料号：113470003

记载人类文明
沟通世界文化
www.fltrp.com

朗文
外研社
新概念英语（新版）

NEW CONCEPT ENGLISH (*New Edition*)
PRACTICE AND PROGRESS *Students' Book* 实践与进步　学生用书2

English edition © L. G. Alexander 1967
Original English material © Addison Wesley Longman Ltd. 1997
This revised edition of New Concept English with the addition of Chinese material is
published by arrangement with Addison Wesley Longman Limited, London and
Longman Asia Limited, Hong Kong.

Licensed for sale in the mainland territory of the People's Republic of China only

This simplified Chinese characters edition first published
in 1997 jointly by Foreign Language Teaching and Research Press
and Longman Asia Ltd.

双语版出版人：沈维贤
合作出版人：李朋义
合作编著者：亚历山大（L. G. Alexander），何其莘
策划编辑：赵嘉文，蔡女良
责任编辑：（朗文）王德厚，梅丹心；（外研社）孙蓓，任小玫
封面设计：梁若基

外语教学与研究出版社
朗文出版亚洲有限公司　联合出版

What's new in this edition?

This is the only new edition ever to be undertaken since *NCE* was originally published. The classic course continues to provide a complete and well-tried system for learning English, enabling students to reach their maximum potential in the four primary skills of understanding, speaking, reading and writing. The sound basic principles which made *NCE* a world-famous course have been retained. However, the following important features have been introduced in the new edition:

- All topical references in the texts and exercises have been brought up to date.
- All outdated texts have been completely replaced and accompanied by new exercises and new artwork.
- The original methodology has been modified to improve communication skills, with active training in listening comprehension right from the very first lesson.
- Drills and written exercises, previously published separately as supplementary materials, have been incorporated into the main coursebooks.
- The following features have been added to help Chinese learners of English: Bi-lingual vocabulary lists; notes in Chinese on texts and exercises and suggested translations of the texts.
- The pages have been enlarged and, where possible, are self-contained, so that lessons are easy to conduct.

本版本有什么新内容？

本版是《新概念英语》首次出版以来第一次推出的新版本。这套经典教材一如既往地向读者提供一个完整的、经过实践检验的英语学习体系，使学生有可能在英语的 4 项基本技能——理解、口语、阅读和写作——方面最大限度地发挥自己的潜能。新版本保留了《新概念英语》得以成为世界闻名英语教程的一整套基本原则，同时又包含了以下重要特色：

- 所有课文和练习中有关时事的内容都已更新。
- 所有过时的课文都已更换，由新课文和配套的新练习、新插图取代。
- 原有的教学法经过调整，以利于提高学生的交际能力。从第一课开始就安排了有效的听力训练。
- 教材更简洁精炼，过去作为补充材料单独出版的句型训练和笔头练习均已取消，其精华纳入主干教程。
- 为了帮助中国的英语学习者，新版增加了英汉对照词汇表、课文注释、简短的练习讲解和课文的参考译文。
- 版面加大，在可能情况下，每课书相对独立，以方便课堂教学。

CONTENTS 目录

To the teacher and student
Language learning at the pre-intermediate level

General principles

Traditional methods of learning a foreign language die hard. As long ago as 1921, Dr. Harold Palmer pointed out the important difference between understanding how a language works and learning how to use it. Since that time, a great many effective techniques have been developed to enable students to learn a foreign language. In the light of intensive modern research, no one would seriously question the basic principles that have evolved since Palmer's day, though there is considerable disagreement about how these principles can best be implemented. Despite the great progress that has been made, teachers in many parts of the world still cling to old-fashioned methods and to some extent perpetuate the systems by which they themselves learnt a foreign language. It may, therefore, not be out of place to restate some basic principles and to discuss briefly how they can best be put into effect in the classroom.

Learning a language is not a matter of acquiring a set of rules and building up a large vocabulary. The teacher's efforts should not be directed at informing his students about a language, but at enabling them to use it. A student's mastery of a language is ultimately measured by how well he can use it, not by how much he knows about it. In this respect, learning a language has much in common with learning a musical instrument. The drills and exercises a student does have one end in sight: to enable him to become a skilled performer. A student who has learnt a lot of grammar but who cannot *use* a language is in the position of a pianist who has learnt a lot about harmony but cannot play the piano. The student's command of a language will therefore be judged not by how much he knows, but how well he can perform in public.

In order to become a skilled performer, the student must become proficient at using the units of a language. And the unit of a language is not, as was once commonly suppose, the word, but the sentence. Learning words irrespective of their function can be a waste of time, for not all words are equal. We must draw a distinction between *structural* words and *lexical* items. Words like *I, you, he,* etc. are *structural*. Their use can be closely defined; they are part of a grammatical system. Words like *tree, plant, flower,* etc. are purely *lexical* items and in no way part of a grammatical system. From the learner's point of view, skill in handling structural words is the key to mastering a language, for the meaning that is conveyed in sentence-patterns depends largely on the function of the structural words that hold them together.

It is possible, though this has yet to be proved scientifically, that every student of a foreign language has what might be called a 'language ceiling', a point beyond which he cannot improve very much. If we accept this supposition, our aim must be to enable every student to learn as much as he is capable of learning in the most efficient way. The old-fashioned translation and grammar-rule methods are extremely wasteful and inefficient, for the student is actually encouraged to make mistakes: he is asked to perform skills before he is adequately prepared. Teachers who use such methods unwittingly create the very problems they seek to avoid. At some point in the course their students inevitably become incapable of going *on*: they have to go *back*. They have become remedial students and the teacher is faced with the problem of remedying what has been incorrectly learnt. No approach could be more ineffective, wasteful and inefficient.

The student should be trained to learn by making as few mistakes as possible. He should never be required to do anything which is beyond his capacity. A well-designed course is one which takes into account what might be called the student's 'state of readiness': the point where he can proceed from easy to difficult. If the student is to make the most of his abilities, he must be trained to adopt correct learning habits.

What has to be learnt

The student must be trained adequately in all four basic language skills: *understanding*, *speaking*, *reading* and *writing*. In many classroom courses the emphasis is wholly on the written language. The student is trained to use his eyes instead of his ears and his inability to achieve anything like correct pronunciation, stress and intonation must be attributed largely to the tyranny of the printed word. If the teacher is to train his students in all four skills, he must make efficient use of the time at his disposal. Efficiency presupposes the adoption of classroom procedures which will yield the best results in the quickest possible time. The following order of presentation must be taken as axiomatic:

Nothing should be spoken before it has been heard.

Nothing should be read before it has been spoken.

Nothing should be written before it has been read.

Speaking and writing are the most important of these skills, since to some extent they presuppose the other two.

Learning to speak

The traditional 'conversation lesson' is of no value at all if the student is not ready for it. It is impossible for any student at the post-elementary level to take part in discussions on topics like 'The cinema today', for his ideas quite outstrip his capacity for expressing them. The student must first be trained to use patterns in carefully graded aural/oral drills. Only in this way will he finally learn to speak.

Before considering how this can be done, it should be noted that the patterns in a language fall into two distinct categories: *progressive* and *static*. For instance, learning how to answer and to ask questions involves the use of *progressive* patterns. They are *progressive* because the student's skill in handling these complex forms must be developed over a long period, beginning with a simple response like 'Yes, it is' and culminating in complex responses like 'Yes, I should, shouldn't I'. A *static* pattern, on the other hand, like the comparison of adjectives can be taught in a limited number of lessons, not over a long period.

Progressive patterns should be practised through comprehension exercises which require the student to answer and to ask questions which become increasingly complex as the course proceeds. The student should be trained to give tag answers; make negative and affirmative statements to answer double questions joined by *or*; answer general questions which begin with question-words like *When, Where, How,* etc.; and at each stage, the student should be trained to ask questions himself. It is obvious that these skills cannot be dealt with in one or two lessons: the student requires practice of this kind in *every* lesson.

At the same time, static patterns should be practised by means of drills which make use of language-laboratory techniques. In each of these drills, the teacher seeks to elicit a particular kind of response. He provides the student with a stimulus to elicit the new pattern in a series of oral drills until the student is able to respond accurately and automatically.

Students may also be trained to speak through oral composition exercises where they are required to reproduce orally a passage of English they are familiar with. At the outset, the student should practise reproducing narrative and descriptive pieces. At a much later stage, he will practise reproducing the substance of an argument. When he can do this well, he will be in a position to converse on set topics which deal with abstract ideas. By this time he will be able to express himself with confidence and will make relatively few mistakes.

The techniques used in speech training at the pre-intermediate level may be summarized as follows:

Drilling in progressive patterns.
Drilling in static patterns.
Practice in oral composition.

Learning to write The same sort of careful grading is required when we attempt to teach students to write. We must again begin with the simplest form of statement. Students are all too often plunged into composition work long before they are ready for it. At some point in a course, the teacher may decide that it is time his students attempted to write a composition, so he sets a short narrative or descriptive piece and hopes for the best. This is a random, hit-or-miss method which creates enormous remedial problems and produces disastrous results. If a student's sole experience of written English has been to fill in blank spaces in tailor-made sentences, it is wildly unreasonable to spring a composition subject on him and then expect him to produce correct and readable prose. As with premature discussions on set topics, all we are doing is to encourage him to make mistakes. And it is no good hoping that after a few years of this (involving massive correction on the part of the teacher) the student will somehow improve on his own. Very few students are sufficiently conscientious or highly motivated to examine in detail their own corrected written work. Even if they did, there is absolutely no guarantee that they will not go on making the same mistakes. Writing skill can best be developed through carefully controlled and graded comprehension/summary writing exercises. Summary writing is not a sterile academic exercise useful only for examination purposes. It can be used effectively to develop a student's writing ability. At the pre-intermediate stage, the student must learn how to write simple, compound, and complex sentences and to connect ideas from notes. Controlled summary writing will enable the student to master each of these difficulties and bring him to a point where he will be capable of writing a composition with a minimum of error.

The main stages in training the student in the written language at the pre-intermediate level may be summarized as follows:

Practice in writing simple sentences through controlled comprehension exercises.

Practice in writing compound sentences through controlled comprehension exercises.

Practice in writing complex sentences through controlled comprehension exercises.

Practice in connecting ideas from notes that have been provided.

The teaching of grammar

In traditional textbooks, all information about sentence patterns is presented in the form of 'rules' which the student applies in a series of disconnected sentences by filling in blank spaces, or by giving the correct form of words in brackets. It has become abundantly clear that this approach to language-learning is highly ineffective. It encourages the teacher to talk *about* the language, instead of training his students to use it. The emphasis is on written exercises. The greatest weakness in this approach is that the student cannot transfer what he has learnt from abstract exercises of this kind to other language skills like understanding, speaking and creative writing.

A new pattern should not be presented as the exemplification of some abstract grammar-rule, but as a *way of saying something*. No further explanation or elucidation is necessary. The student is trained to use correct forms automatically, rather than by applying 'grammar logic'. Where explanation is necessary, it can be done by relating a new pattern to one that has already been learnt. If, for instance, the student has learnt the use of 'must', he can be taught the use of 'have to' by being made to see a meaningful relationship between the two.

Students working at the pre-intermediate level may be given exercises in recall, that is, relating language difficulties to a particular context they know well. In this way they will be trained to use correct forms instinctively. The teacher is, incidentally, saved the trouble of correcting exercises, since, for the most part, the passages do this for him.

Traditional filling-in-the-blank exercises still have a place in a modern course, but with one important difference: they should not be used as a means of teaching new patterns, but as a means of consolidating what has been learnt. They are an end, not a means to an end. In this respect, they are extremely useful in tests and can be employed for diagnostic purposes or to enable the teacher to assess terminal behaviour.

The multi-purpose text

In order to do all the exercises outlined above, the student must work from specially-written texts. Each text must be used to train the student in the following skills:

Listening comprehension.

Oral practice (*progressive* and *static* patterns).

Reading aloud.

Oral composition.

Dictation.

Controlled comprehension, summary writing and composition practice (simple, compound and complex sentences).

Written grammar exercises in recall.

We might call these specially-written passages *multi-purpose texts*, since they are used as the basis for a variety of exercises which aim at developing a number of skills simultaneously.

If these texts are to be suitable for so many purposes, they must be specially devised. The new patterns that are to be taught must be *contextualized*, that is, they must be built into each text. These reiterated patterns should be unobtrusive: their use should strike the listener as being inevitable rather than artificially superimposed. There is also another very important requirement: the texts must be interesting or amusing so that they will entertain the student, hold his attention, and minimize the inevitable drudgery involved in drill work. If the texts are accompanied by illustrations, they will be even more appealing. At the beginner's level, illustrations are more functional than decorative. At this level, the reverse is true: the pre-intermediate stage marks a transition from audio-visual techniques to audio-lingual ones.

Speed and intensity

Traditional courses are often divided into 'lessons', but these 'lessons' do not take into account what can be done in an average teaching period of forty-five minutes or an hour. They simply consist of 'an amount of information' and may run on for a great many pages. In the classroom, one of these 'lessons' might drag on for weeks because so much has to be done.

A lesson must be precisely what the word implies: an amount of material that can reasonably be covered in a teaching period, possibly with additional material which can be done as homework. In other words, a lesson must be considered as a unit of instruction and no more. Now it is extremely difficult for the course designer to decide what can be done in an average period. Obviously a class of bright students will cover more ground than a class of less able ones. This problem can be overcome if the lesson contains material which can be omitted at the discretion of the teacher, providing that these omissions do not hamper the students' progress.

Levels

For purely practical purposes, students attending language schools have to be classified in terms of knowledge and achievement. It might be worth noting that a full-scale course would resolve itself into three parts, each of which would consist of two stages:

Stage 1:   Pre-elementary level.

            Elementary level.

Stage 2:   Pre-intermediate level.

            Intermediate level.

Stage 3:   Pre-advanced level.

            Advanced level.

About this course

From theory to practice: basic aims

This course attempts to put into practice all the theories about language learning outlined above. Briefly, the aims may be stated as follows:

1 To provide a comprehensive course for post-elementary adult or secondary students. The course contains sufficient material for about one and a half academic years' work. It is assumed that the student will receive about four hours' instruction each week i.e. four one-hour lessons on four separate occasions, or two 'double periods' each consisting of two hours or ninety minutes. If we take the academic year to consist of thirty-six weeks, there will be sufficient material in this course for fifty-four weeks' work. The student will receive most of his training in the classroom and will be required to do a little extra work in his own time.

2 To train the student in all four skills: *understanding*, *speaking*, *reading*, and *writing* — in that order. In this respect, the course sets out to do two things: to provide material which will be suitable for aural/oral practice and which can at the same time be used to train the student systematically to write English.

3 To provide the student with a book which will enable him to *use* the language.

4 To provide the teacher with well-co-ordinated and graded material which will enable him to conduct each lesson with a minimum of preparation. As many of the exercises are 'self-correcting', the teacher will, incidentally, be relieved of the arduous task of correcting a great many written exercises.

5 To enable the teacher and the student to work entirely from a single volume without the need for additional 'practice books'.

6 To prepare the ground for students who might, at some future date, wish to sit for academic examinations like the Cambridge First Certificate. This aim must be regarded as coincidental to the main purpose of training students in the four language skills.

7 To provide the teacher and student with recorded material which can be used in the classroom and at home. It must be emphasized, however, that this is in no way a full-scale self-study course. It is essentially a classroom course, with taped material that can be used at home. The recorded drills supplement work done in the classroom.

For whom the course is intended

This course should be found suitable for:

1 Adult or secondary students who have completed *First Things First: an integrated course for beginners*, or who have completed *any* other elementary course.

2 Students in need of remedial work: e.g. students who did English at school and now wish to take it up again; students who have begun English several times and never got beyond the point of no return.

3 Schools and Language Institutes where 'wastage' caused by irregular attendance and late starters is a problem. The course is so designed that it will enable hard-pressed or erratic students to catch up on work they have missed.

4 Post-elementary students who wish to study on their own.

How much knowledge has been assumed	The material in *First Things First*, the beginners' course which precedes this one, has been designed to 'overlap' this course. Students who have completed it will have no difficulty whatever in continuing where they left off.

The material in *First Things First*, the beginners' course which precedes this one, has been designed to 'overlap' this course. Students who have completed it will have no difficulty whatever in continuing where they left off.

Students who have learnt English from other elementary courses and now wish to continue their studies with this course should have a fair working knowledge of the structures listed below. The list may look formidable, but close inspection will reveal that there is nothing in it that would not be found in the average elementary course. In any case, most of the knowledge that has been assumed is revised in the course itself.

It should be noted that a distinction has been drawn in the list between *active* and *passive* knowledge. A student has *active* command of a pattern if he can use it in speech or writing. He has *passive* command of a pattern if he can understand it when he hears or reads it, but is, as yet, incapable of using it. In the list below, this distinction is drawn by the following designations: ability to recognize and to form (*active* knowledge); ability to recognize (*passive* knowledge).

Assumed knowledge

1 Elementary uses of the verbs *be* and *have* in the present and past.
2 The present continuous: ability to recognize and to form.
3 The simple present: ability to recognize; to form with *s*, *es*, or *ies* in the third person.
4 The simple past: ability to recognize and to form with common regular and irregular verbs.
5 The past continuous: ability to recognize.
6 The present perfect (Simple): ability to recognize.
7 The past perfect: ability to recognize.
8 The future: ability to recognize and to form with *going to*, *shall* and *will*.
9 Auxiliary verbs: elementary uses of *can*, *may* and *must*. The ability to recognize the forms *could*, *might* and *would*.
10 The ability to form *questions* and *negatives* with auxiliary verbs including *do/does* and *did*. The use of interrogative pronouns and adverbs.
11 The ability to answer questions beginning with auxiliary verbs and question words.
12 Adverbs: ability to form with *ly* and *ily*. The ability to recognize exceptions like *well*, *hard* and *fast*.
13 Articles: definite and indefinite. Elementary uses of *a/an* and *the*. The use of *some*, *any*, *no*, *much*, *many*, *a lot of* with countable and uncountable nouns.
14 Nouns: the ability to form the plural with *s*, *es*, *ves*; common irregular plurals: *men*, *women*, *children*, *teeth*, etc.
15 Pronouns: personal, possessive, reflexive. Apostrophe 's' ('s).
16 Adjectives: elementary uses. Regular comparison; irregular comparison: *good*, *bad*, *much/many* and *little*.
17 Prepositions: the use of common prepositions of *place*, *time* and *direction*.

18 Relative pronouns: the ability to recognize and to use *who/whom*, *which* and *that*.

Miscellaneous features

19 This/that; these/those.

20 Elided forms: it's, I'm, isn't, didn't, etc.

21 There is/it is; there are/they are.

22 The imperative.

23 The days of the week, dates, seasons, numbers, points of time (today, yesterday, tomorrow, etc.).

24 Telling the time.

The components of the course

The course consists of the following:

- One students' book (to be used by teachers and students in class, or by students working on their own).
- One teacher's book (for use in the classroom by teachers).
- A set of cassettes, on which the multi-purpose texts have been recorded.
- Another set of cassettes, on which 'Repetition drill' in the Teacher's Book has been recorded.

A description of the course

General arrangement of material

This course is divided into four Units each of which is preceded by a searching test. Each unit consists of twenty-four passages which become longer and more complex as the course progresses. Detailed instructions to the student, together with worked examples, precede each unit.

The passage are multi-purpose texts. Each passage will be used to train the student in the following: aural comprehension; oral practice (*progressive* and *static* patterns); reading aloud; oral composition; dictation; controlled comprehension, summary writing and composition practice (simple, compound and complex sentences); written grammar exercises in recall.

Instructions and worked examples

These precede each unit and should be read very carefully. The successful completion of this course depends entirely on the student's ability to carry out the instructions given.

Pre-unit tests

A searching test, based on material already studied, precedes each Unit. This will make it possible for students to find their own level and enable them to begin at any point in the book. At the same time, the student who works through the course systematically from beginning to end is not expected to make too sudden a jump between units. The tests should enable the teacher to assess how much the students have learnt. If they are found to be too long, they should be divided into manageable compartments.

The passages

An attempt has been made to provide the student with passages which are as interesting and as varied in subject-matter as possible. Each passage contains examples of the language patterns the student is expected to master. It will also be used as the basis for all aural/oral and written work. The approximate length of the passages in each unit is as follows:

Unit 1:	100 words.
Unit 2:	140 words.
Unit 3:	160 words.
Unit 4:	180 words.

Oral exercises

Oral exercises are not included in the book itself and must be supplied by the teacher. They may be along the lines suggested in the section on *How to use this course.*

Summary writing

The aim has been to train the student to make statements which are based directly on the passages he has read. The student is required to derive specific information from each passage (comprehension) which he will put together to form a paragraph (summary). The amount of help he is given to do this gradually diminishes. In these exercises, the student will incidentally gain a great deal of experience in coping with one of the biggest difficulties in English: word order. Here is a brief outline of what is required in each unit:

Unit 1: The passages contain mainly compound sentences. The comprehension questions have been designed to elicit *simple* statements which will be put together to form a summary and composition.
Unit 2: The passages contain mainly complex sentences (though not necessarily difficult ones) and the comprehension questions are designed to elicit *simple* and *compound* statements. These will be put together to form a summary of the passage.
Unit 3: The comprehension questions are designed to elicit *simple*, *compound* and *complex* statements. These will be put together to form a summary.
Unit 4: The student will practise writing all three types of statement by using connecting words to join ideas. The ideas are derived from each passage and will be joined together to form a summary.

Composition

Composition exercises, which are introduced in Unit 2, run closely parallel to work that is being done in summary writing. From Unit 3 onwards, these exercises are based on ideas suggested by the passages. This will relieve the student of the added burden of having to find something to say when he is struggling to express himself. The arrangement is as follows:

Unit 2: Exercises in writing compound statements.
a Passages 25–36: selecting correct verbs and joining words.
b Passages 37–48: joining simple statements to make compound statements.

Unit 3: Alternating exercises.
a Joining ideas to make compound or complex statements.
b Joining simple statements to make compound or complex statements.
Unit 4: Joining ideas to write two short paragraphs (a total of about 150 words).

Letter writing
Work in letter writing is begun in Unit 2 and difficulties concerning layout and subject-matter are introduced gradually. This course deals with personal letters only. The exercises have been graded as follows:

Unit 2:   The Heading.
Unit 3:   The Salutation and the opening paragraph.
Unit 4:   The Body, the Subscription, the Signature and the Postscript.

Key structures and Special difficulties
A distinction has been drawn between absolutely essential grammar (Key structures) and difficulties in usage (Special difficulties). No attempt has been made to deal with every aspect of grammar. All information about Key structures and Special difficulties is derived directly from each passage. Grammatical terminology has not been used at all. New items are presented in the form of sentence patterns. Where explanations are necessary, this has been done by relating a new pattern to one which the student already knows and by providing numerous examples, not by abstract description and 'grammar rules'.

Filling-in-the-blank exercises are given to consolidate what the student has already learnt and practised orally. They cannot be used to teach new patterns. There are also numerous exercises in recall where the student is required to relate language difficulties to a passage he knows well. These grammar exercises are presented as part of a real context, not in disconnected sentences. By referring to the passage, the student can find out immediately whether he has grasped the new patterns. The teacher is also saved the trouble of correcting exercises of this type, since, for the most part, the passages do this for him.

The way the Key structures have been arranged is one of the most important features of this course. The Key structures have been presented in what might be called 'concentric cycles', the basic idea being that no new concept should be introduced without reference to what has been learnt so far. This concentric arrangement makes provision for constant revision of the most difficult sentence patterns. The following outline will make this clear:

Unit 1 (Passages 1–24): Key structures are dealt with at an elementary level.
Unit 2 (Passages 25–48): Exactly the same ground is covered at a slightly more difficult level.
Unit 3 (Passages 49–72): The same ground is covered yet again at a still more difficult level.
Unit 4 (Passages 73–96): The Key structures are revised.

Cross-references

Cross-references have been included to enable the student to refer to material he has already learnt and to draw useful comparisons. In the text, cross-references are indicated in the following manners:

1 **KS (= KEY STRUCTURES).** These letters are followed by a lesson number and sometimes a paragraph reference: e.g. **KS 18b.**
2 **SD (= SPECIAL DIFFICULTIES).** These letters are also followed by a lesson number and sometimes a paragraph reference: e.g. **SD 20c.**

The tapes

Two sets of tapes accompany the course for use in the classroom and for home study.

1 The first set of cassettes.

On these, the ninety-six multi-purpose texts have been recorded at slightly less than normal speed (120 words per minute). These cassettes are intended for use in the classroom when the teacher is working through the nine steps when presenting each text. However, students studying at home may also make use of these cassettes to improve their listening comprehension.

2 The second set of cassettes.

On these, selected drills have been recorded for use in the classroom or at home. There are ninety-six drills in all, each of which lasts approximately for three and a half minutes. They are intended for teachers to use in the classroom and for students who decide to do the drills on their own with the aid of a cassette player at home.

The drills are three-phase: stimulus/*student response*/correct response. They are based entirely on the Key structures and Special difficulties introduced in each lesson. The vocabulary used in the drills is drawn from the course itself. The tapescript of the drills is included in the Teacher's Book.

Vocabulary range

Structures permitting, the vocabulary in Units 1 and 2 is based largely on the General Service List of English Words, compiled and edited by Dr. Michael West. From then on, the range is unrestricted — within, of course, reasonable limits, and gradually becomes more difficult.

How to use this course

TEACHERS! PLEASE READ THIS INTRODUCTION CAREFULLY!

Allocation of time

Ideally, two classroom lessons of approximately 50 minutes each should be spent on each text. The first lesson should be devoted to Guided Conversation; the second to Composition and Language Study. This means that there is enough material in this book for 200 lessons (including tests). However, you may choose to spend only *one* classroom lesson on each text — in which case, *every* lesson may be devoted to Guided Conversation and a selection of exercises may be set as homework. Your first task is to decide how much time you have in your programme in relation to the material available in the course.

The suggestions given below outline the basic steps in each lesson. You may decide to follow them closely, adapt them to suit your style of teaching, or reject them altogether — BUT PLEASE READ THEM FIRST!

Lesson 1 : Guided conversation

Books required:

Practice and Progress (for teachers and students)

The stages of the Lesson

1 Listening comprehension	about 15 minutes
2 Comprehension questions	about 5 minutes
3 Asking questions	about 5 minutes
4 Pattern drill	about 5 minutes
5 Tell the story	about 10 minutes
6 Topics for discussion	about 10 minutes

Let's see what each step involves:

1 Listening comprehension
There are nine recommended steps for presenting each text which will train students to understand spoken English. The steps are as follows:
a Introduce the story
b Understand the situation
c Listening objective
d Play the tape or read the text
e Answer the question
f Intensive reading
g Play the tape or read the text again
h Repetition
i Read aloud

Every one of these steps must be very brief:

a Introduce the story
The teacher introduces the text with a few words, so the student clearly understands what's going on and is not obliged to guess. English should be used entirely as far as possible. For example (Text 1):

Today we'll listen to a story about some people in a theatre.

NCE Teacher's Book 2 always provides a brief introduction to each text.

b Understand the situation
The students are asked to look at the cartoon to see if they can understand what is going on in the text. The teacher may ask a few questions in English to help the students to understand the picture.
For example (Text 1):

What do you think is happening in the picture?
What is the man in front doing? Why?

NCE Teacher's Book 2 always provides a few questions of this kind.

c Listening objective
The teacher gives the students 'a listening objective', by setting them a question they will try to find the answer to. This means, the students will listen to the text *actively* rather than *passively*.
For example (Text 1):

Listen to the story, then tell me: Why did the writer complain to the people behind him?

NCE Teacher's Book 2 always provides a question of this kind.

d Play the tape or read the text
The teacher plays the tape or reads the text just once while the students simply listen without interruption. They should try to 'hear' the answer to the question given in *c* above.

e Answer the question
Now the teacher asks the question (*c* above) again and the students try to answer it: *Now you've heard the story, why did the writer complain to the people behind him?* Don't let students shout out the answer. Train them to raise their hands if they think they know the answer. Get one student to answer, then ask the others, *How many of you agree with him/her? Put up your hands if you agree with him/her. You don't agree* (to another student) *so what do you think the answer is? How many of you agree with him/her? Put up your hands.* This keeps the students guessing and involves *the whole class*. Students should be trained to listen right from the start without 'preparation' or 'translation'. They will soon get used to the sound of English and to understanding the meaning of what they hear.

f Intensive reading
Now the teacher plays the tape or reads the text again, pausing after every sentence to check the students understand. This is an extremely

important part of the lesson as the students must fully understand the text at the end of the presentation. Rather than give direct explanations, try to get as much information as possible from the students (think of it as 'a corkscrew operation'!). Explanations should be given entirely in English, but don't carry direct-method teaching to absurd lengths. Use gesture and mime where possible. If some of your students still don't understand, ask the best students in the class for a 'confirmatory translation' of a particular word or phrase for the benefit of other students who haven't grasped the meaning. Remember, if you don't translate a particular difficulty, then someone in the class will. However, translation should always be regarded as a last resort.

g Play the tape or read the text again

Play the tape or read the text again right through without interruption. This time, the students will understand it without difficulty because of the careful explanation you provided in *f* above.

h Repetition

Repetition is an *optional* activity at this level, and in any case should be confined to (say) the first cycle of 24 lessons only. If you conduct repetition exercises, first ask the *whole* class to repeat the text after you. Next divide the class into three groups and repeat the text once more. Finally, ask individual students round the class to repeat the text. When conducting chorus and group repetition, make sure the students repeat all together after you give them a clear signal. You can give such a signal simply by nodding or with a pencil in your hand. Imagine you're conducting an orchestra!

i Read aloud

Ask a few students to read the text aloud, taking turns round the class. You will be able to tell from this how well particular students can pronounce correctly the English they have already heard.

This presentation should not take more than about fifteen minutes.
DON'T SPEND TOO MUCH TIME ON ANY ONE ACTIVITY!

Students working at home on their own should listen to the recording of each text as often as is necessary for them to become completely familiar with it.

2 Comprehension questions

After presenting the text (the nine steps above), the teacher asks individual students questions rapidly round the class. Think of this as a bombardment phase! If a student fails to answer, move quickly on to another student, so that this part of the lesson has *pace*. The students are asked two kinds of questions which are presented in any order: yes/no questions and wh-questions. All the questions you will ask (with brief answers) are printed for you in NCE Teacher's Book 2. Of course, you can ask additional questions of your own if you want to. Note these observations about yes/no questions and wh-questions:

a Yes/No questions

It is generally considered rude to answer a question with just 'Yes' or 'No'. The student is trained to listen to the first word in the yes/no question and to use the same word in the answer:

TEACHER : *Did* you have a good seat? (The first word in the question is *Did*)

STUDENT : Yes, I *did*. (*did* forms part of the answer)

TEACHER : *Did* you enjoy the play?

STUDENT : No, I *didn't*.

b Wh-questions and questions with How

The student is trained to answer questions beginning with When, Where, Which, How, etc. The student provides short natural answers.

TEACHER : Where did you go last week?

STUDENT : (To) the theatre, etc.

In this way, the student is trained over a period to associate When? with time, Where? with place, Why? with reason, Who? with identity, Whose? with possession, Which? with choice, What? with choice, identity or activity, How? with manner, etc.

3 Asking questions

In order to prevent incorrect forms like *Where he went?*, students are trained to ask two questions at a time. The first of these is a yes/no question and the second a Wh- question. For example:

TEACHER : Ask me if I went to the theatre last week.

STUDENT : Did you go to the theatre last week?

TEACHER : When …?

STUDENT : When did you go to the theatre? (Not *When you went to the theatre?* or *When you go to the theatre?*)

All the Asking questions exercises are printed for you in the Teacher's Book. You can add some of your own if you want to.

4 Pattern drill

In addition to the exercise on tape (printed in the Teacher's Book under the heading **Repetition drill**), there are pattern drills for each lesson. These are all 'stimulus-response' exercises. You provide a 'stimulus' and two students respond. Always give a clear example first with your best students, so students know exactly what to do before attempting each exercise. Here is a typical example.

TEACHER :   hear the radio

STUDENT 1 :   I can hear the radio now. Can you?

STUDENT 2 :   Of course, I can. I can hear it perfectly well.

(Further prompts are listed in the Teacher's Book, so you can conduct the exercise round the class.)

Remember, material recorded on tape is given for each lesson under the heading **Repetition drill**. See below in Lesson 2.

5 Tell the story

Write a number of brief notes ('key words') on the blackboard summarizing the subject-matter of the text. Now invite individual students to reconstruct the text by referring to the notes. The students should be encouraged to speak without interruption for up to a minute at a time and should try to use as many as possible of the expressions, structures, etc. of the original story. Here, for instance, are some notes which relate to Text 4:

(1) just – letter – brother – Tim
(2) in Australia
(3) there – six months
(4) Tim – engineer
(5) big firm – already – number – places
(6) bought – Australian car – Alice Springs – small town – centre
(7) soon – Darwin
(8) From there – fly – Perth
(9) never before – trip – exciting

In the NCE Teacher's Book 2, you will find notes like this for every text.

6 Topics for discussion

The final part of the guided conversation lessons should be devoted to free conversation. Where the text immediately suggests a subject or subjects for general discussion, individual students should be invited to speak impromptu. Here, for instance, are a few talking points suggested by Text 4:

(1) Do you know anyone who lives or works abroad? Tell us about him/her.
(2) Which country would you like to visit? Why?
(3) Have you got a pen friend? Do you think pen friends are a good idea? Why?

**Lesson 2:
Composition and
language study**

As has already been indicated, this entire lesson may be omitted and a selection of written exercises may, instead, be set as homework. If this approach is adopted, then the Summary and Composition exercises *must always be set*. Needless to say, more satisfactory results will be obtained where a complete classroom lesson can be devoted to written exercises.

Books required:

Practice and Progress (for teachers and students)

The stages of the Lesson

1 Summary writing/Composition/Letter writing
2 Key structures
3 Repetition drill
4 Exercises
5 Special difficulties
6 Exercises
7 Dictation
8 Multiple choice questions

No specific suggestions are made regarding the amount of time to be spent on each part of the lesson as this will be found to vary greatly.

1 Summary writing/Composition/Letter writing

These exercises must never be omitted as they are part of a carefully planned guided summary and composition programme which evolves progressively through *Practice and Progress* and *Developing Skills*. As the exercises are largely self-correcting, it will be sufficient to check that they have been done. Go round the class while the students are writing and help individuals.

2 Key structures

This part of the lesson should be devoted to a *brief* explanation of the main grammar points that were presented in the text. Grammatical information should be considered a means to an end, not an end in itself. Technical terms have been deliberately excluded: it has been left to the teacher to decide how to present the grammar. This, in turn, will depend wholly on the class. In the case of students who are familiar with the grammar of their own language, there is no reason why the teacher should not make use of technical terms. In the case of students who are wholly unfamiliar with grammatical concepts, no technical terms should be used at all. The aim behind all the explanation should be to reinforce theoretically what the student has already practised orally. It is best to avoid sweeping 'rules' and to confine the study of grammar to the points presented. Additional information can be obtained from any standard grammar practice book.

3 Repetition drill

The students practise the taped drill. They may do this with the aid of a cassette player in the classroom, or at home if they are working on their own. Alternatively, the teacher may conduct the drill 'live' from the tapescript printed in the lesson.

4 Exercises (in grammatical structure)

These should be tackled in writing. They will provide further reinforcement of the grammar that has just been presented.

5 Special difficulties

A brief explanation regarding the special lexical/structural difficulties should now be given. This section concentrates on words and structures often misused and confused as a result of interference from the students' mother tongue. Where appropriate, you may draw a brief contrast between the problem presented in the text and a similar problem in the mother tongue.

6 Exercises (in special difficulties)

These should be tackled in writing to reinforce what has just been presented.

7 Dictation

Depending on the amount of time available, dictations should be given frequently. A few sentences taken from a passage the students have already studied may be dictated. The students may correct their own work by comparing their version with the passage. Dictation is an excellent exercise in syntax, spelling and listening comprehension.

8 Multiple choice exercises

Multiple choice is a *testing* device, not a *teaching* device. Its purpose here is to train students for the kind of objective testing which is usual in public examinations. Multiple choice exercises cover the following: reading comprehension, structure and vocabulary. Multiple choice exercises are usually followed by an exercise in sentence structure.

Homework

The written exercises become more demanding and time-consuming as the student progresses through the course. At a later stage, exercises which have not been completed in class may be set as homework.

Pre-unit tests

These should always be set before the students move on to a new unit.

Future work

If the student wishes to proceed further, he may go on to the following books after completing this one. They are designed to 'overlap' each other so that the student can continue without difficulty:

Developing Skills:
An integrated course for intermediate students

Fluency in English:
An integrated course for advanced students

致教师和学生

中级以下水平的语言学习

基本原理

学习外语的传统方法根深蒂固。早在 1921 年,哈罗德·帕尔默博士就指出,理解一种语言是如何运作的与学会如何使用这种语言之间存在着重大的差别。从那时以来,人们已经找到了许多卓有成效的方法教授学生外语。根据现代所作的深入细微的研究,没有人会对自帕尔默以来发展而成的学习外语的基本原理提出重大质疑,尽管在如何才能最好地贯彻这些原理方面仍有相当大的分歧。虽然在外语教学上取得了重大的进步,但是世界上许多地方的教师依然眷恋着过时的教学方法,在一定程度上,他们是用当年自己学外语的方法使旧的教学体系永久化。因此,重述一遍其中一些基本原理,简要探讨如何在课堂上有效地实施这些原理,大概不算不合时宜吧。

学习一门语言,不仅仅是掌握一套规则,积累大量词汇。教师工作的重点不应是告诉学生关于一门语言的知识,而应是使学生能够使用这门语言。衡量学生是否掌握一门语言,最终是要看他运用如何,而不是懂了多少。在这方面,学习语言与学习乐器十分相似。学生所做的操练与练习都是为了达到一个明确的目标,使他成为一个熟练的操作者。一个学生学了许多语法知识却不会运用语言,就像一个弹钢琴的学了许多有关和声的知识却不会弹钢琴一样。因此,衡量学生是否掌握语言并不看他懂了多少,而要看他在众人面前语言运用得如何。

学生要想成为熟练的语言运用者,就必须能够熟练地使用语言单位,而语言单位并不是人们曾经普遍认为的单词,而是句子。学习单词而不考虑它们的作用可能会白白浪费时间,因为单词并不都是同样重要的。我们必须把**结构词**和**词项**加以区别。像 I, you, he 等词便是**结构词**,它们的作用可以准确地加以界定,它们是语法体系的一部分; 而像 tree, plant, flower 等词则是单纯的**词项**,与语法体系毫无关系。就学生而言,运用结构词的技巧是掌握一门语言的关键,因为由句型表达的含义主要依靠把句子联结起来的结构词所起的作用。

虽然以下一点仍有待于科学地论证,但每个学习外语的学生可能都有一个也许可以称为"语言极点"的地方,即过了这点他的水平不可能有很大的提高。如果我们接受这一假设,那么,我们的目标就必须是用最有效的方法使学生在其能力范围内尽量多学到一点东西。过时的翻译-语法教学法极端浪费时间而且效率很低,因为这种方法实际上是鼓励学生犯错误: 让学生在没有充分准备的情况下运用语言技能。使用这种方法的教师无意中制造了他们企图避免的问题。他们的学生在学到一定程度后会不可避免地无法继续**往下学**,他们不得不**回过头来重新开始**。他们成了需要补课的学生,教师面临的问题是为学生补课,纠正他们所学到的错误内容。同别的教学方法相比,这是一种最无益,最浪费时间和效率最低的方法。

应该训练学生学会尽量少犯错误。决不应该要求学生去做力所不及的事情。一本精心设计的教材应考虑到学生所谓的"准备状况",即可以使他从易到难循序渐进的那个交接点。要使学生最充分地发挥自己的能力,必须训练他从一开始就采用正确的学习方法。

学什么

学生必须在语言的 4 项基本技能方面得到充分的训练。这些技能是**理解、口语、阅读和写作**。在课堂教学中,许多教师把重点完全放在书面文字上。学生接受的训练是如何用眼而不是如何用耳来学习。学生不能掌握正确的发音,重音和语调,这不得不主要归罪于书面文字的束缚。教师若想培养学生全面的 4 项基本技能, 就必须有效地利用自己的时间。要做到有效, 首先就要采用能在最短时间内产生最佳效果的课堂教学法。下列讲课顺序务必作为格言来遵循:

听到的再说;

说过的再读;

读过的再写。

上述技能中, 口语与写作是最重要的。在某种程度上, 它们是以另外两项技能为前提的。

学着说

在学生的口语能力还不成熟的情况下上传统的 "口语课" 是毫无意义的。让一个刚学完初级语言课程的学生来参加诸如 "今日之电影艺术" 这类内容的讨论是不可能的, 因为他想表达的思想远远超出了他的表达能力。首先必须训练学生通过做精心设计的循序渐进的听/说练习学会使用句型, 只有这样才能使他最终学会表达。

在考虑如何实现这一目标之前, 应该注意到语言中的句型可以分成两种截然不同的类型: **渐进型的**和**静态型的**。例如, 学习回答问题和提出问题就涉及了**渐进型**的句型。它们属于**渐进型**, 这是因为学生运用这些复杂形式的技能要在很长的一段时间里才能培养起来: 从一开始的简单回答, 如 "Yes, it is", 发展到复杂回答, 如 "Yes, I should, shouldn't I"。而**静态型**的句型, 如形容词的比较级, 可以在有限的几课课文中讲授, 不必占用很长时间。

渐进型句型必须在检查学生理解能力的练习中进行训练。这种练习要求学生回答问题并提出问题, 而问题的难度则随着教程的进展而不断加深。必须训练学生用简略形式回答一般疑问句, 用肯定形式和否定形式来回答用 or 连结的选择疑问句, 回答用 When, Where, How 等疑问词开头的问句。而在每一个阶段, 必须训练学生自己提问题。很明显, 这些技能不可能在一两课书中学会: 在**每课书**中都必须有这种练习。

与此同时, 静态型句型必须在利用语言实验室技术的练习中得到训练。在每一个录音练习中, 教师试图引出某一特定的回答。他在一系列口头练习中给学生某种诱导以引出新句型, 直到学生可以准确地、下意识地作出反应。

培养学生说的能力也可以通过做口头作文练习的途径来达到目的。这种练习要求学生口头复述一段他所熟悉的英语短文。一开始应该要求学生练习复述叙述性与描写性的文字, 待学到相当程度之后, 再让他练习复述实质性的论说文。一旦他能够很好地完成这种练习, 他便有能力就一些涉及抽象观点的指定的话题同别人交谈了。到了这个时候, 他就能够有把握地表达自己的思想, 犯的错误也会相对减少。

中级以下水平口语训练所用技巧大概可以归纳如下:

反复训练渐进型句型;

反复训练静态型句型;

练习口头作文。

学着写

在试图教学生写作时, 我们同样需要这种精心的分级训练。仍然必须从最简单的陈述句开始。学生常常是在写的能力还不成熟的情况下便要匆匆提笔写作文。在课程的某一阶段, 教师会认为是该由他的学生试着写作文的时候了。于是, 他规定写一篇短的叙述文章或描写文章, 盼望着会得到最好的结果。这种随心所欲、漫无目标的方法会制造大量的补课难题, 产生灾难性的后果。如果一个学生在英语写作方面只在专门编写的句子中做过一些句型填空练习，那么突然塞给他一个作文题目，并期待他能写出一篇语言准确、有可读性的文章来，那实在是太不合情理了。同在不成熟的情况下就规定题目进行讨论一样，我们在这儿做的只是鼓励他犯错误。指望如此这般几年之后（加上教师大量的纠正错误）学生就可以自己提高水平，那是毫无把握的。仅有少数学生具有足够的自觉性和高度的主动性，在书面作业批改后认真地检查一遍。即使他们检查了，也绝对无法保证今后他们不会继续犯类似的错误。培养写作技能的最佳途径是做一些精心设计的、有指导的、循序渐进的理解/摘要练习。摘要写作并不是仅仅适用于考试目的的、枯燥无味的学究式练习。它可以用来很有效地提高学生的写作能力。在中级以下阶段，学生务必学会造简单句、并列句、复合句，并能根据要点把意思连成文。有指导的摘要写作练习能使学生逐一克服上述难点，并使他在写作文时尽量少犯错误。

中级以下水平学生的写作训练，其主要阶段大概可以归纳如下：

通过有指导的理解练习进行简单句写作训练；
通过有指导的理解练习进行并列句写作训练；
通过有指导的理解练习进行复合句写作训练；
根据给出的要点进行把意思连成文的训练。

教授语法

在传统教材中，所有有关句型的信息都是以"规则"的形式来介绍的，学生将这些规则用于相互没有关联的句子的填空练习或填上括号中所列词的正确词形的练习之中，这种学习语言的方法收效甚微，这点现在已经变得非常清楚。这种方法鼓励教师**谈论**语言，而不是训练他的学生去使用语言。侧重点是在书面练习上。这种方法的最大弱点是，学生不能将他从这种抽象的练习中所学到的知识转化成其他语言技能，如理解、口语和创作性写作。

每个新句型不应作为某一种抽象的语法规则的范例来介绍，而应**作为表达某种思想的方法**，也不需要进一步的说明和解释。学生在训练中学会下意识地运用正确的句型，而不是用"语法逻辑"去进行推理。如果需要解释，可以把新句型与已经学会的旧句型联系起来。举例来说，如果学生已经学会了 must 的用法，那么在讲授 have to 的用法时，可以让学生领会这两个句型之间有机的联系。

对中级以下水平的学生可以布置一些回顾练习，即把语言难点同他们熟悉的特定的上下文联系起来。这样可以训练他们凭直觉使用正确的句型。这在无意中也可为教师免去批改作业之苦，因为在大多数情况下，课文本身就可以代劳了。

在现代教程中，传统的填空练习仍有它的一席之地，但有一点重大的区别，即填空练习不应作为教授新句型的一种手段，而应作为巩固已学知识的途径。它们是目的，而不是达到目的的一种手段。从这个意义上讲，填空练习在测验中尤其有用，可以用来分析学生的错误，或让教师评估学生最终的成果。

多功能课文

为了进行上述各项练习，学生务必学习专门编写的课文。每课课文务必可以用来使学生在下列技能方面得到训练：

听力理解；
口语训练（**渐进型**句型和**静态型**句型）；
朗读；
口头作文；

听写；

有指导的理解、摘要写作和作文练习（简单句、并列句、复合句）；

回顾语法的书面练习。

这些专门编写的课文大概可以称作**多功能课文**，因为它们可用来提供各类练习，旨在同时培养多种技能。

要使这些课文适应如此众多的目的，就必须进行特殊的设计。凡是要讲的新句型都必须融合进**有上下文的语境**中，也就是说，必须组织进每篇课文里。这些反复出现的句型应该贴切自然，要使听者觉得使用这些句型是不可避免的，而不是人工堆砌在一起的。另外还有一条非常重要的标准，即课文务必饶有趣味，引人入胜，使学生感到愉悦，能吸引住他的注意力，从而把反复训练带来的无法避免的厌烦减少到最低限度。如果课文配上插图，那就更加吸引人了。在初学阶段，插图的功能性大于装饰性；而在现阶段，则是装饰性大于功能性：中级以下阶段标志着听/视教学法向听/写教学法的过渡。

速度和深度

传统的教程往往分为"课"，而这些"课"却没有考虑一般长度为 45 分钟或 1 小时的课中可以做些什么。它们只是简单地包含"一定量的信息"，而且常常是洋洋洒洒好几页。在课堂教学中，这些"课"可能讲上好几周，因为要做的事情太多了。

"课"应该名符其实：教学内容一般可以在一个课时内完成，可能再加上一些补充的内容在课下作为作业。换句话说，一课书应被视作一个教学单位，仅此而已。现在，让教程设计者决定一个课时内可以做些什么是极其困难的。显然，由聪明学生组成的一个班所完成的内容要多于由不太聪明的学生组成的另一个班。如果课文中含有可以由教师决定取舍的内容，这个问题就可以迎刃而解，当然这种删节不应妨碍学生水平的提高。

程度

纯粹出于教学实际的需要，上语言学校的学生必须按其知识和成绩来分班。值得注意的是，一个完整的教程一般分为 3 个阶段，而每个阶段又分成两个级别：

第 1 阶段　初级以下
　　　　　　初级
第 2 阶段　中级以下
　　　　　　中级
第 3 阶段　高级以下
　　　　　　高级

关于本教材的说明

从理论到实践：基本目的

这本教材试图将上面简述的关于语言学习的理论付诸实践。现将目的简述如下：

1 为完成初级水平英语学习的成年学习者和中学生提供一本教材。这本教材的内容足够一年半使用。我们设想学生每周上课约 4 个课时，即互不相连的 4 个课时，每课时为 1 小时，或两个"双课时"，每个双课时为 2 小时或 90 分钟。如果 1 学年有 36 周的话，那么这本教材中有足够 54 周使用的材料。学生主要在课上接受训练，在课下仅做一点额外的作业。

2 全面训练学生的 4 项技能：**理解、口语、阅读、写作**——按此顺序进行训练。从这方面来讲，这本教材准备做两件事：为听/说练习提供适合的材料，同时，这些材料也可用于系统地训练学生的写作能力。

3 为学生提供一本令他能够**使用**语言的教材。

4 为教师提供配合得当、循序渐进的教材，使他们在上课前只需做极少的准备。由于许多练习有"自动纠错"的功能，因此，教师也就相应地免去了批阅大量书面练习的负担。

5 为教师和学生提供一本单卷本的教材，而不必增加"练习册"。

6 为今后准备参加诸如剑桥初级证书考试的学生打下一个基础。必须认识到这个目标与训练学生的 4 项语言技能的主要目标是一致的。

7 为教师提供可在课堂使用的录音材料，学生也可在家中使用这些材料。然而，必须强调的是，这不是一本全面供自学使用的教程。从根本上来说，这是一本供课堂使用的教材，但其录音材料也可在家中使用。录音练习是为补充课堂教学而准备的。

适用对象

本教材应能适用于：

1 已经学完初学者综合教材《英语初阶》或其他**任何**一种初级教程的成年人或中学生。

2 需要补课的学生，即在学校曾经学过英语现又想重新捡起来的人；学英语屡次中途而废而终未学成者。

3 那些由于学生上课出勤率不高、英语起步较晚而造成"损失"的中学及语言学校。本教材的设计使那些学习有困难或上课时断时续的学生能够赶上他们落下的课程。

4 学完初级课程后而又想自学的学生。

应具备的知识范围

本教材的前一册是初学者教材《英语初阶》，其内容编排与本册有所"重叠"。学完前一册的学生接着学本册，根本不会有什么困难。

学完其他英语教程而想接着学本教材的学生，应对下列语言结构具有扎实的知识，并能运用。这些内容看来或许吓人，但仔细观察便可发现这些内容在一般初级教程中均可找到。总之，那些应该具备的知识中的大部分在本教材都得到了温习。

应该指出，在下表中有**积极知识**与**消极知识**之分。如果学生能够在口语与作文中运用一个句型，那他就是**积极地**掌握了这个句型。如果学生在听到或看到一个句型时能够理解，却还没学会运用，那他就是**消极地**掌握了这个句型 。在下表中, 可用以下标准来加以区分, 能够识别并懂得如何构成 (**积极知识**); 只能够识别 (**消极知识**)。

应有的知识

1　动词 be 与 have 现在时与过去时的基本用法 。

2　现在进行时: 能够识别并懂得如何构成 。

3　一般现在时: 能够识别; 懂得在动词第 3 人称单数上添加 s, es, 或 ies 后缀 。

4　一般过去时: 能够识别并会运用常见的规则动词与不规则动词的一般过去时形式 。

5　过去进行时: 能够识别 。

6　现在完成时 (一般): 能够识别 。

7　过去完成时: 能够识别 。

8　将来时: 能够识别并运用 going to, shall 与 will 构成的将来时 。

9　助动词: can, may 与 must 的基本用法; 能够识别 could, might 与 would 的形式 。

10　能够用 do/does/did 等助动词造疑问句与否定句; 能运用疑问代词与副词 。

11　能够回答以助动词与疑问词开头的问句 。

12　副词: 能够用 ly 与 ily 后缀组成副词; 能够识别 well, hard, fast 等特例 。

13　冠词: 定冠词与不定冠词 。懂得 a/an/the 的基本用法; some, any, no, much, many, a lot of 接可数、不可数名词的用法 。

14　名词: 能够用 s, es, ves 后缀组成名词复数形式; 会用常见的不规则复数形式: men, women, children, teeth 等 。

15　代词: 人称代词、所有格代词 、反身代词; 所有格符号 "'" 加 s ('s) 。

16　形容词: 基本用法; 规则的比较级; 不规则的比较级 good, bad, much, many 与 little 。

17　介词: 常见的地点、时间、方位介词的用法 。

18　关系代词: 能够识别并使用 who/whom, which/that 。

杂项

19　this/that; these/those 。

20　省略形式 it's, I'm, isn't, didn't 等 。

21　There is/it is; there are/they are 。

22　祈使句 。

23　一周 7 天的名称 、日期、季节 、数字、时辰 (今天 、昨天 、明天等)。

24　报时 。

教材内容

这本教材由以下各部分组成:

• 学生用书 (教师和学生在课堂上使用, 或学生自学时使用)

• 教师用书 (教师在课堂上使用)

• 一组录有多功能课文的盒式磁带

• 一组录有教师用书中的 "重复训练" 的盒式磁带

教材介绍

材料的总安排

本书分为 4 个单元, 每个单元前各有一个摸底测验。每一单元有 24 篇课文, 其长度和难度逐渐加大。每一单元前均有详尽的学生须知和实例示范。

课文均为多功能课文, 每篇课文均可用来对学生进行下列训练: 听力理解; 口头练习(**渐进型**句型及**静态型**句型); 朗读; 口头作文; 听写; 有指导的理解、摘要写作和作文练习(简单句、并列句、复合句); 回顾语法的书面练习。

学生须知和实例示范

应认真阅读每一单元前的学生须知和实例示范。学生能否学好本教材, 完全要看学生能否照须知去做。

单元前测验

每一单元前都有一份根据已学内容编制的摸底测验, 使学生得以了解自己的程度以便从教材中的某一点开始学习。与此同时, 从头到尾系统地学习本教材的学生不宜从一个单元突然跳到另一个单元。测验也可使教师评估学生学得如何。如果认为测验内容太多, 可以分为长短适宜的几部分, 分几次进行。

课文

为学生提供的课文力求做到富有趣味性, 题材多样化。每篇课文含有要求学生掌握的语言句型的实例。这些课文也作为进行听力/口语与笔头训练的原始材料。各单元课文的长度大致如下:

第 1 单元: 100 个词
第 2 单元: 140 个词
第 3 单元: 160 个词
第 4 单元: 180 个词

口头练习

本书没有编排口头练习, 须由教师提供。这些练习原则上可以参照《本教材使用说明》中的有关建议进行编写。

摘要写作

此练习旨在训练学生直接根据读过的课文进行造句的能力。要求学生从每篇课文中获取具体信息(理解), 然后将这些信息集中起来形成一个段落(摘要)。学生在做此项练习时得到的帮助将逐渐减少。在完成这些练习的过程中, 学生可同时学习如何对付英语学习中的一大难题——词序的问题, 并在这方面积累丰富的经验。每个单元的具体要求简列如下:

第 1 单元: 本单元课文以并列句为主。编写理解性问题的目的是引导学生说出**简单句**, 然后把这些句子组织起来形成摘要和作文。

第 2 单元: 本单元课文以复合句为主(不一定很难)。编写理解性问题的目的是引导学生说出**简单句与并列句**, 然后把这些句子组织起来形成每课的摘要。

第 3 单元: 编写理解性问题的目的是引导学生说出**简单句**、**并列句**和**复合句**, 然后把这些句子组织起来形成摘要。

第 4 单元: 学生通过使用连结词把想表达的意思串连起来, 从而练习写出上述 3 种类型的句子。原始材料取之于每篇课文, 串起来后形成摘要。

作文

从第 2 单元开始的作文练习与摘要写作密切配合, 同时进行。从第 3 单元往后, 作文练习根据课文的内容编排。这样一来, 本来表达就有困难的学生不必煞费苦心地去另外寻找表达的内容了。具体安排如下:

第 2 单元: 并列句练习
a   25~36 课: 选择正确的动词, 连词成句。
b   37~48 课: 把简单句串连起来组成并列句。

第 3 单元: 句型替换练习
a   把想表达的意思连起来组成并列句或复合句。
b   把简单句连起来组成并列句或复合句。

第 4 单元: 把想表达的意思连起来写出两个小段落 (合计 150 个词左右)。

书信练习

书信练习从第 2 单元开始, 格式与题材方面的问题逐步解决。本教材仅练习私人信件的写作, 练习编排如下:

第 2 单元: 信头。
第 3 单元: 称呼语, 信文的第 1 段。
第 4 单元: 正文, 署名, 签名, 附言。

关键句型和难点

本书对于必不可少的语法知识 (关键句型) 与惯用法中的语言难点 (难点) 加以区分。对语法的讲解不准备面面俱到。关键句型和难点中的所有材料均取自于各篇课文, 语法术语一概弃之不用。新的语法现象以句型的形式进行介绍。在必须解释的地方, 就让学生将新的语法现象同已经学过的语法现象联系起来作比较, 并列举大量实例, 而不作抽象的讲解或搬出 "语法规则"。

填空练习用以巩固学生口头学到或练习过的句型, 不能用来教授新的语言现象。还有大量回顾练习, 要求学生在做这些练习时将语言难点同自己熟悉的课文进行对照。这种语法练习是在有语境的真实的上下文中出现, 而不是一些互不相关的句子。学生通过对照课文, 可以立即发现自己是否已经掌握了一种新的句型。老师也可省去批改这类作业的麻烦, 因为在大多数情况下, 课文为他代劳了。

关键句型的安排方式是本教材最重要的特色之一。关键句型是以一种或许可以称为 "同心圆" 的方法进行介绍的。其基本构想是, 凡要引入新的概念, 必须要同学生已经学过的知识联系起来。这种同心圆式的安排使学生可以不断地复习一些最为困难的句型。这点看了下列要点即可明白:

第 1 单元 (1~24课): 关键句型以初级难度材料介绍。
第 2 单元 (25~48课): 同样的关键句型重新出现, 材料难度略微加深。
第 3 单元 (49~72课): 同样的关键句型再度出现, 材料难度进一步加深。
第 4 单元 (73~96课): 复习上述关键句型。

参见

本书加入了互相参见的提示, 为的是便于学生参考学过的内容, 并进行有益的对比。书中参见的具体标记如下:

1   **KS**（= **KEY STRUCTURES**）后面紧跟着的是某课书的序号，有时还标出段落的序号，例如：**KS18b** 。

2   **SD**（= **SPECIAL DIFFICULTIES**）后面也紧跟着某课书的序号，有时还标出段落的序号，例如：**SD20c** 。

录音带

与教程配套的两组录音磁带，可用于教室，也可在家中使用 。

1   第 1 组录音磁带

录有 96 篇多功能课文，朗读速度比正常速度稍慢（每分钟 120 词），可供教师在课堂上根据建议的 9 个教学步骤介绍课文时使用 。但在家中自学的学生也可利用这些录音带来提高自己的听力理解能力 。

2   第 2 组录音磁带

录有精选的练习题，供课堂教学或在家中自学使用 。共有 96 组练习，每组长约 3 分半钟，供教师在课堂上使用，也供那些想在家中听录音做练习的学生自学时使用 。

练习分成 3 个步骤：引导——**学生回答**——正确答案 。这些练习是根据每课介绍的关键句型和难点而编写的，所用词汇来自本教材 。练习的书面材料刊印在教师用书上 。

词汇量

在内容允许的前提下，第 1、2 单元的词汇大体不超过由迈克尔·韦斯特博士编撰的《英语常用词汇总表》的范围 。从第 3 单元往后，对词汇量不加限制——当然，控制在合理的范围之内，而且难度逐渐加大 。

本教材使用说明

请各位教师仔细阅读本说明!

时间分配

    理想的安排是, 每篇课文用两个课时, 每课时 50 分钟左右。第 1 课时用于教师引导下的会话, 第 2 课时用于作文和语言学习。这样, 本书内容足够约 200 课时使用 (包括测验)。但是, 每篇课文也可只用 **1** 个课时——在这种情况下, 上课时间便完全用于教师引导下的对话, 另选一部分书面练习让学生作为课外作业。因此, 教师的首要任务是根据教学计划规定的时间确定如何运用教材。

    下列建议简要地说明了每堂课的讲课步骤。你可以遵照执行, 并加以修订以适应你的教学方式, 但也可以拒之不用——不过, **请你先读一下本说明!**

第 1 课时: 教师引导下的会话

所需书目

Practice and Progress 《实践与进步》 (师生均用此书)

讲课步骤

1	听力理解	约 15 分钟
2	理解性问题	约 5 分钟
3	学生提问题	约 5 分钟
4	句型训练	约 5 分钟
5	复述故事	约 10 分钟
6	讨论题	约 10 分钟

现把 6 个步骤分别说明如下:

1   听力理解

我们推荐介绍课文的 9 个步骤, 以训练学生听懂英语口语的能力。这 9 个步骤为:

a	介绍故事
b	了解情景
c	听力训练目标
d	播放录音或朗读课文
e	回答问题
f	精读
g	再次播放录音或朗读课文
h	重复
i	大声朗读

每一个步骤都必须简洁:

a   介绍故事

教师用几句话介绍课文, 这样学生就能清楚课文中发生的是什么事情, 而不需要去猜测。只要有可能, 应全部使用英语。以第 1 课为例:

Today we'll listen to a story about some people in a theatre. （今天我们要听一个故事, 讲的是在剧场中的几个人。）

《新概念英语》第 2 册的教师用书中对每课书都提供一个简要的介绍。

b   了解情景

要求学生看插图, 以便检查学生是否了解课文中所发生的事情。教师可以用英语向学生提几个问题, 以引导学生理解图意。仍以第 1 课为例:

What do you think is happening in the picture? （你认为图中正在发生什么事情?）

What is the man in front doing? Why? （前面那个男子在做什么? 为什么?）

《新概念英语》第 2 册的教师用书总是提供几个这类的问题。

c   听力训练目标

通过给学生提个问题, 让他们寻找答案, 教师为学生确立一个"听力训练目标"。这就意味着学生**会积极地**而不是**消极地**去听课文。

以第 1 课为例:

Listen to the story, then tell me: Why did the writer complain to the people behind him? （听故事, 然后告诉我: 为什么作者抱怨坐在他身后的人?）

《新概念英语》第 2 册教师用书总是提供这样的问题。

d   播放录音或朗读课文

教师播放录音或朗读课文, 在不停顿的情况下让学生静听一遍课文。他们应试图找到 c 项中所列问题的答案。

e   回答问题

现在教师再一次问第 3 步骤（即上述 c 项）中的问题, 让学生试着回答"现在你听了这个故事, 为什么作者抱怨坐在他身后的人?"不要让学生高声集体回答。如果他们认为自己知道答案, 请他们举手。问一个学生, 然后问其他的人: " 你们中有多少人同意他/她的回答?"" 如果你们同意, 请举起手来。""[对另一个学生]如果你不同意, 那么你认为答案是什么?"" 你们中有多少人同意他/她的回答?"" 同意的请举起手来。"这样就能让学生不断地猜测, 而且把**全班学生**都调动起来。从一开始就要训练学生不做任何准备地去听, 也不要通过翻译来听。他们很快会适应英语的语音, 并理解他们所听到的内容。

f   精读

现在教师重放录音或重读课文, 每句话后停顿, 以检查学生是否理解。这是课堂教学中非常重要的一个环节, 因为在介绍课文结束时, 学生应该彻底理解课文的意思。教师不要直接讲解, 而应尽量从学生那里获取信息（可以把这种方法看作是"用螺丝起子拔瓶塞的行动"!）。讲解全部要用英文, 但不要把直接教学法弄到一种荒唐的绝对程度, 在可能情况下, 使用手势和模拟动作。如果班上仍有学生不理解, 教师应该请班上学得最好的学生给出一个单词或词组的译文, 以照顾尚未理解词义的学生。请记住, 如果你不把一个难点译成中文, 班上的其他人会这样做的。但是, 翻译始终应被看成是最后一着。

g   再次播放录音或朗读课文

不停顿地再次播放录音或朗读课文, 因为有了 f 项中的精心解释, 这次学生会很容易听懂。

h 重复

在这个阶段，重复是一项**可供选择**的课堂活动。而在任何情况下，这项活动也应该限制在——比如说——第 1 单元的 24 课课文之内。如果你进行这项训练，首先让**全班**跟着你朗读课文。然后，把全班分成 3 个组，再次重复课文。最后，在全班范围内让个别学生重复课文。当你让学生全体或小组重复时，要求学生在看到你的明确信号后才一起开始。你可用点头或手中的铅笔当信号，想象自己是在指挥一个交响乐团！

i 大声朗读

在班上让学生轮流大声朗读课文。从朗读中你可以看出不同的学生是否能够准确地读出他们已听过的英语。

介绍课文的全过程不应超过 15 分钟的时间。

不要在任何一项活动中花费太多的时间！

在家里自学的学生应尽量多听课文录音，使自己非常熟悉课文。

2 理解性问题

按照以上 9 个步骤介绍完课文后，教师应在班上向不同的学生快速地提问题。可以把它看作是"轰炸阶段"！如果一个学生没能回答出来，很快转向另一个学生，因此，这部分练习应注意**节奏**。教师问两类问题：一般疑问句和以 Wh- 开头的疑问句。所有的问题和简要的回答都刊印在《新概念英语》第 2 册教师用书上。当然，如果你愿意，还可以问额外的问题。请注意以下有关一般疑问句和以 Wh- 开头的疑问句的事项：

a 一般疑问句

一般来说，仅用"是"或"不"来回答一个问题是不礼貌的。要训练学生注意听一般疑问句的第 1 个单词，并在回答时用同样的词。

教师：*Did* you have a good seat?（你有一个好座位吗？）（问题中的第 1 个词是 Did）
学生：Yes, I *did*.（是的，我有。）（*did* 是回答的一部分）
教师：*Did* you enjoy the play?（你喜欢这个剧吗？）
学生：No, I *didn't*.（不，我不喜欢。）

b 以 Wh- 和以 How 开头的疑问句

训练学生回答以 When, Where, Which, How 等词开头的疑问句。学生可以简短的，较自然的方式回答。

教师：Where did you go last week?（上周你去了什么地方？）
学生：(To) the theatre, etc.（去了剧场等。）

就这样，经过一段时间的训练，学生就会把 When 和时间、Where 和地点、Why 和原因、Who 和身份、Whose 和所有权、Which 和选择、What 和选择、身份或活动、How 和方式联系起来。

3 学生提问题

为了防止类似 *Where he went?* 的错误问句，需要训练学生同时问两个问题。第 1 个是一般疑问句，第 2 个是以 Wh- 开头的特殊疑问句。例如：

教师：Ask me if I went to the theatre last week.（问我上周是否去过剧场。）
学生：Did you go to the theatre last week?（上周你去剧场了吗？）
教师：When...?（什么时间……？）

学生: When did you go to the theatre?（你是什么时候去剧场的?）（而不是 *When you went to the theatre?* 或 *When you go to the theatre?*）

所有这类提问题练习都刊印在教师用书中。如果愿意,你可以增加一些你自己的问题。

4　句型练习

除了录音带上的练习（在教师用书中刊印在 **Repetition drill** 这一部分）,每课书还有句型练习。这些练习属于"提示－回答"这一类型。你说出一个提示,两个学生回答。每次先和学得最好的学生一起作出明确的示范,以便学生在开始练习之前就明确要做什么。以下是一个典型的例子:

教师:　　hear the radio（听收音机）
学生 1:　I can hear the radio now. Can you?（我可以听见收音机了,你能吗?）
学生 2:　Of course, I can. I can hear it perfectly well.（当然,我能。我能听得非常清楚。）
　　　　（在教师用书中还有进一步的提示,因此,你可以在全班进行这个练习。）
记住,录音带上每课练习的文字材料都刊印在 **Repetition drill** 之下。见下面第 2 课时。

5　复述故事

归纳课文的主题,用简短的要点（"关键词"）的形式把它们写在黑板上。让学生借助这些要点来复述课文。鼓励学生不停顿地连续讲一分钟,并要他们尽量使用原有课文中的词组、结构等等。例如: 下面是与第 4 课有关的一些要点:

(1)　just — letter — brother — Tim
(2)　in Australia
(3)　there — six months
(4)　Tim — engineer
(5)　big firm — already — number — places
(6)　bought — Australian car — Alice Springs — small town — centre
(7)　soon — Darwin
(8)　From there — fly — Perth
(9)　never before — trip — exciting

在《新概念英语》第 2 册的教师用书中可以找到每课课文的要点。

6　讨论题

由教师引导的会话课的最后一部分应用于自由会话。如果可以从课文中找出一个或几个与课文有关的题目供讨论,就应鼓励学生单独即席发言。例如,下面是第 4 课中找出的几个讨论题:

(1)　你是否认识某个在国外居住或工作的人? 给我们讲讲这个人。
(2)　你希望到哪一个国家去访问? 为什么?
(3)　你有笔友吗? 你认为交笔友是一个好主意吗? 为什么?

第 2 课时: 作文和语言学习

如上所述,这第 2 课时可以完全不上,而将一部分笔头练习作为课外作业。如采用这种方法,那么,在课外作业中**必须布置**摘要写作与作文练习。当然,如果能把一整课时用来做笔头练习,效果必定更为理想。

所需书目
Practice and Progress 《实践与进步》（师生均用此书）

讲课步骤
1 摘要写作/作文/书信练习
2 关键句型
3 重复训练
4 练习
5 难点
6 练习
7 听写
8 选择题

对本课每一步骤所用时间不作具体建议, 因为这会因人因地而异。

1 摘要写作/作文/书信练习
这些练习不论在什么情况下都不应删去, 因为它们是经过精心设计的、循序渐进的、在教师指导下进行摘要写作和学习作文的教学计划的一部分, 贯穿于《实践与进步》、《培养技能》两本书的始终。由于这些练习大部分可由学生自行批改, 教师只需检查学生是否做了这些作业即可。学生做练习时, 教师可在班中巡视, 给予个别辅导。

2 关键句型
在这一部分应**简要**解释一下课文中出现的语法现象。语法知识应视作达到目的的一种手段, 本身并不是目的。语法术语故意剔除了, 语法如何讲, 由教师决定。而反过来这又完全取决于班上学生的情况。如果班上学生熟悉母语的语法, 那么教师不妨用些语法术语, 如果学生对语法概念一无所知, 那么, 教师连一个语法术语都不应使用。解释语法的目的在于从理论上巩固学生在口头练习中获得的知识。最好避免面面俱到地讲"规则", 而应以课文中讲到的语法现象为限。若想增加语法知识, 可以参考任何一本标准的语法练习册。

3 重复训练
学生用磁带上录好的练习进行训练。他们可以用录音机在课堂上进行, 或在家里自学时这样做。另一种选择是, 教师利用书中印出的录音材料在课堂上"现场"口头指导学生进行训练。

4 （语法结构的）练习
此项练习应以书面形式完成, 以便巩固刚刚教过的语法知识。

5 难点
对于词汇/语法结构上的特殊难点现在应作出简要的解释。这一部分的重点集中在由于学生的母语干扰而造成误用和混用的词和结构上。在适当的时机, 可将课文里出现的问题与学生母语中的类似问题作一简单的比较。

6 （难点的）练习
此项练习应以书面形式完成, 以便巩固刚刚教过的内容。

7　听写

只要时间允许, 听写练习应经常进行。可从学生刚刚学过的课文中摘取个别句子作为听写内容。学生可对照课文自行批改。听写是训练句法, 拼写和听力的一项极好的练习。

8　选择练习

选择练习是一种**测试**手段, 而不是一种**教学**手段。目的是为了培养学生应付公共测试中常见的客观试题的能力。选择题包含以下方面的练习: 阅读理解、结构、词汇。选择练习之后一般都有一项有关句子结构的练习。

课外作业

随着学习的不断深入, 笔头作业会越来越难, 越来越费时间。学到本教材后面几课时, 凡在课堂上完不成的作业可留作课外作业。

单元前的测验

此项测验必须在学生开始新的一个单元学习之前进行。

继续深造

凡想继续深造的学生, 学完本书后, 可以接着学习以下各册。教材各册之间的内容互相"重叠", 学生继续学习不会觉得困难:

Developing Skills 《培养技能》: 中级水平综合教材
Fluency in English 《流利英语》: 高级水平综合教材

PRE-UNIT TEST 1
测试 1

IF YOU CAN DO THIS TEST GO ON TO UNIT 1
如果你能完成以下测验，请开始第1单元的学习

A Look at this example:
   阅读以下例句：

> I am tired.
> He *is* tired.

Write these sentences again. Begin each sentence with *He*.
改写下面的句子，用He作句子的主语。

1 I am busy.
2 I am learning English.
3 I have a new book.
4 I live in the country.
5 I shall see you tomorrow.
6 I can understand you.
7 I must write a letter.
8 I may come next week.
9 I do a lot of work every day.
10 I did a lot of work yesterday.
11 I played football yesterday.
12 I bought a new coat last week.
13 I have had a letter from Tom.
14 I was busy this morning.
15 I could play football very well when I was younger.
16 I always try to get up early.
17 I might see you next week.
18 I always enjoy a good film.
19 I had finished my work before you came.
20 I watch television every night.

B Look at these examples:
   阅读以下例句：

> I want *a* biscuit.   I want *a* cup of coffee.
> I want *some* biscuits.   I want *some* coffee.
> Do you want *any* biscuits?   Do you want *any* coffee?
> I don't want *any* biscuits.   I don't want *any* coffee.

Write these sentences again. Put in *a*, *some* or *any*.
用a, some 或 any填空。

1 There are _____ books on the desk.
2 I drank _____ glass of beer.
3 Do you want _____ butter?

4 There aren't _____ people in the street.

5 Tom has just bought _____ new car.

6 We have _____ apple trees in our garden.

7 Can I have _____ bar of chocolate, please?

8 There isn't _____ bread in that tin.

9 Is there _____ ink in that bottle?

10 Are there _____ eggs in that basket?

C Look at these examples:

阅读以下例句:

I haven't any eggs.	I haven't *got many* eggs.
He hasn't any coffee.	He hasn't *got much* coffee.

Do these in the same way:

模仿例句, 改写下面的句子:

1 I haven't any butter.

2 You haven't any cigarettes.

3 We haven't any milk.

4 She hasn't any biscuits.

5 They haven't any stationery.

D Look at this example:

阅读以下例句:

She goes to town every day.	She *went* to town yesterday.

Do these in the same way:

模仿例句, 完成下面的句子:

1 He buys a new car every year.   He _____ a new car last year.

2 She airs the room every day.   She _____ it this morning.

3 He often loses his pen.   He _____ his pen this morning.

4 He always listens to the news.   He _____ to the news yesterday.

5 She empties this basket every day.   She _____ it yesterday.

E Look at these examples:

阅读以下例句:

	He went to the cinema yesterday.
Question:	Did he go to the cinema yesterday?
Question:	Where did he go yesterday?
Negative:	He didn't go to the cinema yesterday.

Do these in the same way:

模仿例句提问, 并作出否定的回答:

1 He bought a new car.
Q: _____
Q: What _____
N: _____

2 She can come tomorrow.
Q: _____
Q: When _____
N: _____

3 They were here yesterday.
Q: _____
Q: When _____
N: _____

4 He must leave early.
Q: _____
Q: Why _____
N: _____

5 He gave you a pen.
Q: _____
Q: What _____
N: _____

6 He lives next door.
Q: _____
Q: Where _____
N: _____

7 You know him well.
Q: _____
Q: How well _____
N: _____

8 He has found his pen.
Q: _____
Q: What _____
N: _____

9 You saw that film.
Q: _____
Q: When _____
N: _____

10 He arrived at two o'clock.
Q: _____
Q: When _____
N: _____

F Look at this example:

阅读以下例句：

> She smiled _____ (pleasant)
> She smiled *pleasantly*.

Do these in the same way:
模仿例句，完成下面的句子：

1 He read the phrase _____ (slow)

2 He worked _____ (lazy)

3 He cut himself _____ (bad)

4 He worked _____ (careful)

5 The door opened _____ (sudden)

G Look at this example:

阅读以下例句：

> *It will* rain tomorrow.
> *It'll* rain tomorrow.

Write these sentences again. Use short forms.
用缩写形式改写下面的句子。

1 *He will* arrive tomorrow morning.

2 *She will* come this evening.

3 *I shall* see you the day after tomorrow.

4 He *will not* believe me.

5 We *shall not* remain here.

H Look at this example:
阅读以下例句:

> This dress belongs to my sister.   It is *hers*.

Do these in the same way:
模仿例句, 完成下面的句子:

1 These things belong to my husband. They are _____ .

2 This coat belongs to me. It is _____ .

3 These shoes belong to my wife. They are _____ .

4 These pens belong to Tom and Betty. The pens are _____ .

5 This suitcase belongs to you. It is _____ .

I Look at this example:
阅读以下例句:

> It is *warm* today, but it was *warmer* yesterday.

Do these in the same way:
模仿例句, 完成下面的句子:

1 It is *cool* today, but it was _____ yesterday.

2 It is *wet* today, but it was _____ yesterday.

3 He's *late* again today, but he was _____ yesterday.

4 This test is *easy*, but that one is _____ .

5 This book is *expensive*, but that one is _____ .

6 This bookcase is *large*, but that one is _____ .

7 That film was *interesting*, but the other one was _____ .

8 Betty is *pretty*, but Jane is _____ .

9 Miss Green is *beautiful*, but Miss White is _____ .

10 Tom is *intelligent*, but Bill is _____ .

J Put in the right word or phrase: *yesterday, last night, tomorrow* etc.
用正确的词或词组填空: yesterday, last night, tomorrow 等。

The date today is Monday, March 5th. 今天的日期是3月5日, 星期一。

1 I saw him _____ (Sunday, March 4th)

2 I shall see him _____ (Tuesday, March 6th)

3 I shall see him _____ (Monday, March 5th)

4 I shall see him _____ (Monday, March 5th—afternoon)

5 I shall see him _____ (Wednesday, March 7th)

6 I saw him _____ (Saturday, March 3rd)

7 I saw him _____ (Sunday, March 4th—night)

8 I shall see him _____ (Tuesday, March 6th—morning)

9 I shall see him _____ (Monday, March 5th—morning)

10 I saw him _____ (Sunday, March 4th—afternoon)

K Put in *at, in,* or *on*:

用 at, in 或 on 填空:

1 He is going to telephone _____ five o'clock.
2 My birthday is _____ May 21st.
3 It is always cold _____ February.
4 My father was there _____ 1984.
5 He is going to arrive _____ Tuesday.

L Put in *across, over, between, off, along, in, on, into, out of,* or *under:*

用 across, over, between, off, along, in, on, into, out of 或 under 填空:

1 The aeroplane is flying _____ the village.
2 The ship is going _____ the bridge.
3 The boy is swimming _____ the river.
4 Two cats are running _____ the wall.
5 My books are _____ the shelf.
6 The bottle of milk is _____ the refrigerator.
7 The boy is jumping _____ the branch.
8 Mary is sitting _____ her mother and her father.
9 It is 9 o'clock. The children are going _____ class.
10 It is 4 o'clock. The children are coming _____ class.

M Put in *Who* or *Which*:

用 Who 或 Which 完成下列句子:

1 _____ hat did you buy?
2 _____ broke this plate?
3 _____ bus did you catch?
4 _____ is knocking at the door?
5 _____ of the two books do you want?

N Look at these examples:

阅读以下例句:

She is the girl.   *She* met me yesterday.
She is the girl *who* met me yesterday.
She is the girl.   I met *her* yesterday.
She is the girl *whom* I met yesterday.
This is the book.   I bought *it* yesterday.
This is the book *which* I bought yesterday.

Join these sentences in the same way. Use *who, whom* or *which.*

模仿例句, 用 who, whom 或 which 连接下面的每组句子。

1 This is the car. The mechanic repaired *it* yesterday.

2 He is the man. I invited *him* to the party.

3 These are the things. I bought *them* yesterday.

4 He is the man. *He* came here last week.

5 He is the policeman. *He* caught the thieves.

6 She is the nurse. *She* looked after me.

7 She is the woman. I met *her* yesterday.

8 I am the person. *I* wrote to you.

9 They are the people. I saw *them* yesterday.

10 They are the trees. We cut *them* down yesterday.

O Look at this example:

阅读以下例句：

> I can see some cups, but I can't see any *glasses*.

Do these in the same way:

模仿例句，完成下面的句子：

1 I can see some spoons, but I can't see any _____ . (knife)

2 I can see some hammers, but I can't see any _____ . (box)

3 I can see some cupboards, but I can't see any _____ . (shelf)

4 I can see Mr. Jones and Mr. Brown, but I can't see their _____ . (wife)

5 I can see some cups, but I can't see any _____ . (dish)

P Read this story carefully:

仔细阅读以下故事：

Last week, I took my four-year-old daughter, Sally, to a children's party. We travelled by train. Sally has never travelled by train before. She sat near the window and asked a lot of questions. Suddenly, a middle-aged lady came into our compartment and sat opposite Sally. 'Hello, little girl,' she said. Sally did not answer, but looked at her curiously. The lady took out her powder compact. She then began to make up her face.

'Why are you doing that?' Sally asked.

'To make myself beautiful,' the lady answered. She put away her compact and smiled kindly.

'But you are still ugly,' Sally said.

Now write answers to these questions:

回答以下问题：

1 Did you take Sally to the park?

2 Did you take Sally to a children's party?

3 Where did Sally sit?

4 Who came into your compartment?

5 Was the lady young or was she middle-aged?

6 Where did the lady sit?

7 Did she say 'Hello' to Sally, or did Sally say 'Hello' to her?

8 Why did the lady make up her face?

9 Did Sally think the lady was beautiful?

10 What did Sally say to the lady?

Unit 1
第 1 单元

Unit 1　第 1 单元

INSTRUCTIONS TO THE STUDENT 致学生

Summary writing 摘要写作

Summary writing is a test of your ability to find the important points in a piece of writing and to put them together. To write a *summary*, you must be able to do two things. You must be able to understand what you read, and to put ideas together. *Comprehension* is a test of your ability to understand what you read. *Writing* is a test of your ability to put ideas together. So *Summary writing* and *Comprehension* are closely related to each other.

"摘要写作"用于检测你发现一篇文章的要点和把这些要点组织起来的能力。要写好一篇摘要,你需要做两方面的工作:你需要理解所读文章和把其中的要点归纳出来。"理解"检测你对文章的理解能力;"写作"检测你把要点归纳表达的能力。因此,"摘要写作"和"理解"是紧密相连的。

Unit 1 contains twenty-four short pieces. There are some questions under each piece. Your answers to these questions will be in short, simple sentences. Put your answers together. In this way, you will make a short paragraph. Your paragraph will be a *summary* of the piece.

第 1 单元共有 24 篇短文。每篇文章之后均有一系列问题。你应该用短小的简单句来回答这些问题,然后把你的回答组成一个段落,这个段落就是一篇摘要。

Before you begin each exercise, read these instructions carefully. Read them each time you begin a new piece. They are very important.

开始每次练习前,请仔细阅读题示,每课开始前都要这样做,因为它们很重要。

How to work 做法

1 Read the piece carefully two or three times. Make sure you understand it.
   细读课文2-3遍,理解全文。

2 Write an answer to each question. Each answer must be *a complete sentence*.
   回答每个问题,每个答案必须是一个完整的句子。

3 Your answers to the questions must follow one another. Together, they will make *a complete paragraph*.
   你的答案应该句句相连,共同组成一个完整的段落。

4 Read through your work and correct your mistakes.
   通读你写的段落,改正错误。

5 Count the number of words in your paragraph. Words like 'the', 'a', etc. count as single words. Words which are joined by a hyphen (e.g. hold-up) also count as single words. Do not go over the word limit. At the end of your paragraph write the number of words that you have used.
   数一下段落的字数。冠词和用连字符相连的词均为一个词。不要超过字数限制。在段落结尾处写上全段的总字数。

Example 范例

Work through this example carefully and then try to do the exercises in Unit 1 in the same way.
仔细研究以下例子，然后用同样的方法完成第1单元的练习。

Granny Forbes

Mrs. Forbes was very old and very poor. Everybody in the neighbourhood called her Granny Forbes and tried to help her. Some neighbours came in each day and cooked meals for her. Others came and cleaned her room. There was little furniture in her room. It was small, dark, and almost empty. There was a bed and a table, and there were two chairs. In winter, neighbours sometimes brought coal and lit a fire, but Granny's room was often very cold. Granny lived in poverty all her life. She died at the age of eighty-four. Then her neighbours got a big surprise. She left £50,000!

Summary writing 摘要写作

Answer these questions *in not more than 50 words*.
回答这些问题，将答案组成一个段落，不要超过50个单词。

1   Did Granny Forbes live in poverty all her life or not?
2   Did her neighbours help her, or did her relations help her?
3   Did they cook meals for her every day or not?
4   Did they clean her small, poorly-furnished room or not?
5   Did they sometimes light a fire for her in winter or not?
6   Did Granny Forbes die at the age of eighty-one, or did she die at the age of eighty-four?
7   Did everyone get a surprise or not?
8   How much did she leave?

Answer 参考答案

Granny Forbes lived in poverty all her life. Her neighbours helped her. They cooked meals for her every day. They cleaned her small, poorly-furnished room. They sometimes lit a fire for her in winter. Granny Forbes died at the age of eighty-four. Everyone got a surprise. She left £50,000!   (49 words)

Key structures and Special difficulties 关键句型和难点

When you finish the exercise in **Summary writing**, go on to the language exercises that follow. The information under the title **Key structures** gives you advice about important problems in grammar. The information under the title **Special difficulties** gives you advice about particular problems. The twenty-four passages in Unit 1 will help you to understand these problems and to do the language exercises.
当你完成"摘要写作"中的练习后，就可以进行紧随其后的语言练习。"关键句型"是有关语法的练习，"难点"则与一些特殊的语言点有关。第1单元的24课书将有助于你理解这些问题并完成有关语言的练习。

Lesson 1 A private conversation 私人谈话

First listen and then answer the question.

听录音，然后回答以下问题。

Why did the writer complain to the people behind him?

'It's none of your business'

Last week I went to the theatre. I had a very good seat. The play was very interesting. I did not enjoy it. A young man and a young woman were sitting behind me. They were talking loudly. I got very angry. I could not hear the actors. I turned round. I looked at
5 the man and the woman angrily. They did not pay any attention. In the end, I could not bear it. I turned round again. 'I can't hear a word!' I said angrily.

'It's none of your business,' the young man said rudely. 'This is a private conversation!'

New words and expressions 生词和短语

private (title) /'praɪvɪt/ adj. 私人的
conversation (title) /ˌkɒnvə'seɪʃən/ n. 谈话
theatre (1.1) /'θɪətə/ n. 剧场, 戏院
seat (1.1) /siːt/ n. 座位
play (1.1) /pleɪ/ n. 戏
loudly (1.3) /'laʊdli/ adv. 大声地

angry (1.4) /'æŋgri/ adj. 生气的
angrily (1.5) /'æŋgrɪli/ adv. 生气地
attention (1.5) /ə'tenʃən/ n. 注意
bear (1.6) /beə/ (bore /bɔː/, borne /bɔːn/) v. 容忍
business (1.8) /'bɪznɪs/ n. 事
rudely (1.8) /'ruːdli/ adv. 无礼地, 粗鲁地

Notes on the text 课文注释

1 go to the theatre, 去看戏。
2 got angry, 生气。
3 turn round, 转身, 也可用 turn around。
4 pay attention, 注意。
5 I could not bear it. 我无法忍受。
  其中的 it 是指上文中的那对男女大声说话又不理会作者的愤怒目光。
6 none of your business, 不关你的事。

参考译文

　　上星期我去看戏。我的座位很好，戏很有意思，但我却无法欣赏。一青年男子与一青年女子坐在我的身后，大声地说着话。我非常生气，因为我听不见演员在说什么。我回过头去怒视着那一男一女，他们却毫不理会。最后，我忍不住了，又一次回过头去，生气地说："我一个字也听不见了！"

　　"不关你的事，"那男的毫不客气地说，"这是私人间的谈话！"

Summary writing 摘要写作

Answer these questions *in not more than 55 words*.

回答下列问题，将答案组成一个段落，不要超过55个单词。

1　Where did the writer go last week?
2　Did he enjoy the play or not?
3　Who was sitting behind him?
4　Were they talking loudly, or were they talking quietly?
5　Could the writer hear the actors or not?

6　Did he turn round or not?
7　What did he say?
8　Did the young man say, 'The play is not interesting,' or did he say, 'This is a private conversation!'?

Key structures 关键句型

Word order in simple statements 简单陈述句的语序

a　A statement tells us about something. All the sentences in the passage are statements. Each of these statements contains one idea. Each statement tells us about *one thing*. A statement that tells us about one thing is a *simple statement*.

陈述句用来叙述一件事情。本段课文中的所有句子都是陈述句。每个句子包含着一个概念，告诉我们一件事情。凡是叙述一件事情的陈述句都是简单陈述句。

b　The order of the words in a statement is very important. Look at these two statements. They both contain the words but they do not mean the same thing:

陈述句中的语序很重要，注意下面两个句子，每句话所用的单词相同，但句子所表达的意思不同：

The policeman arrested the thief. 警察逮捕了小偷。
The thief arrested the policeman. 小偷逮捕了警察。

c　A simple statement can have six parts, but it does not always have so many. Study the order of the words in the following columns. Note that column 6 (When?) can be at the beginning or at the end of a statement.

一个简单陈述句可以由6部分组成，但是并不是每个句子都有这么多组成部分。注意下表中句子的语序。第6栏（表示时间）可以放在句首或句尾。

Exercises 练习

A　Rule seven columns on a double sheet of paper. At the top of each column, write the numbers and the words given in the Table below. Copy out the rest of the passage. Put the words of each statement in the correct column in the way shown in the Table.

在一张大纸上画出7栏，在前两行相应的栏内填入下表中第1、2行的数字和关键词，将课文中其他句子也按同一形式抄入表内。

6	1	2	3	4	5	6
When?	Who? Which? What?	Action	Who? Which? What?	How?	Where?	When?
Last week	I	went			to the theatre.	
	I	had	a very good seat.			
	The play	was		very interesting.		
	I	did not enjoy	it.			
	A young man and a young woman	were sitting			behind me.	
	They	were talking		loudly.		

B Use the seven columns again for this exercise. There is a line under each word or group of words in the statements below. The words are not in the right order. Arrange them correctly in the seven columns. Look at this example:

用同一张表格来完成这个练习。下列陈述句中的每个词或词组下面有一条横线。这些词的语序不对，参照例句在表中重新排列各句的语序。请看以下例句：

I   last year   to America   went.

The correct order is: I (*who*) went (*action*) to America (*where*) last year (*when*).

Or: Last year I went to America.

1 The film   I   enjoyed   yesterday.

2 The news   listened to   I   carefully.

3 Well   the man   the piano   played.

4 Games   played   yesterday   in their room   the children   quietly.

5 Quietly   the door   he   opened.

6 Immediately   left   he.

7 A tree   in the corner   of the garden   he   planted.

8 Before lunch   the letter   in his office   quickly   he   read.

9 This morning   a book   I   from the library   borrowed.

10 The soup   spoilt   the cook.

11 We   at home   stay   on Sundays.

12 There   a lot of   people   are   at the bus stop.

13 The little boy   an apple   this morning   ate greedily   in the kitchen.

14 She   beautifully   draws.

15 Music   I   like   very much.

16 A new school   built   they   in our village   last year.

17 The match   at four o'clock   ended.

18 She   a letter from her brother   last week   received.

Multiple choice questions 选择题

Comprehension 理解

1 The writer turned round. He looked at the man and the woman angrily _____ .

(a) and they stopped talking

(b) but they didn't stop talking

(c) but they didn't notice him

(d) but they looked at him rudely

2 The young man said, 'It's none of your business.'

(a) He was talking to the young woman.

(b) He was talking about the play.

(c) He thought the writer was trying to listen to his conversation with the young woman.

(d) He thought the writer was asking him a question.

Structure 句型

3 Last week the writer went to the theatre. He was _____ the theatre.

(a) to   (b) at   (c) into   (d) on

4 The young man and the young woman were sitting behind him. He was sitting _____ them.

(a) before   (b) above   (c) ahead of   (d) in front of

5 _____ did the writer feel? Angry.

(a) Where   (b) Why   (c) How   (d) When

6 He looked at the man and the woman angrily. He looked at _____ angrily.

(a) them   (b) they   (c) their   (d) us

7 The young man and the young woman paid _____ attention to the writer.

(a) none   (b) any   (c) not any   (d) no

Vocabulary 词汇

8 He had a good seat. He was sitting in a good _____ .

(a) chair   (b) place   (c) armchair   (d) class

9 He was a young man. He wasn't very _____ .

(a) old   (b) big   (c) tall   (d) large

10 The writer looked at the man and the woman angrily. He was very _____ .

(a) sad   (b) unhappy   (c) cross   (d) pleased

11 The writer could not bear it. He could not _____ it.

(a) carry   (b) suffer   (c) stand   (d) lift

12 The young man spoke rudely. He wasn't very _____ .

(a) clever   (b) rude   (c) polite   (d) kind

Sentence structure 句子结构

Arrange these words in their correct order, then check your answer against the text.

按照正确的次序排列以下单词，然后对照课文第2-3行，核对你的答案。

a me young behind man sitting and were a woman young

15

Lesson 2　Breakfast or lunch?　早餐还是午餐?

First listen and then answer the question.

听录音, 然后回答以下问题。

Why was the writer's aunt surprised?

I never get up early

It was Sunday. I never get up early on Sundays. I sometimes stay in
bed until lunchtime. Last Sunday I got up very late. I looked out of
the window. It was dark outside. 'What a day!' I thought. 'It's
raining again.' Just then, the telephone rang. It was my aunt
5　Lucy. 'I've just arrived by train,' she said. 'I'm coming to see
you.'
　　'But I'm still having breakfast,' I said.
　　'What are you doing?' she asked.
　　'I'm having breakfast,' I repeated.
10　'Dear me!' she said. 'Do you always get up so late? It's one o'clock!'

New words and expressions　生词和短语

until (l.2) /ʌn'tɪl/ *prep.* 直到

outside (l.3) /ˌaʊt'saɪd/ *adv.* 外面

ring (l.4) /rɪŋ/ (rang /ræŋ/, rung /rʌŋ/) *v.*（铃、
电话等）响

aunt (l.4) /ɑːnt/ *n.* 姑, 姨, 婶, 舅母

repeat (l.9) /rɪ'piːt/ *v.* 重复

Notes on the text　课文注释

1　on Sundays, 指每个星期日。星期几的前面用介词on。

2　What a day! 多么糟糕的天气! 这是一个省略的感叹句。完整的句子应该是What a day it is! 英语中的感叹
句常用what开头, 后面紧跟一个名词或名词性短语（包括连系动词）, 然后是主语和谓语, 句尾用感叹号。

3　I'm coming to see you. 在这句话中现在进行时用来表示近期按计划或安排要进行的动作。

4　Dear me! 天哪! 这也是一个感叹句。

参考译文

　　那是个星期天, 而在星期天我是从来不早起的, 有时我要一直躺到吃午饭的时候。上个星期天, 我起得很
晚。我望望窗外, 外面一片昏暗。"鬼天气!"我想,"又下雨了。"正在这时, 电话铃响了。是我姑母露西打
来的。"我刚下火车,"她说,"我这就来看你。"

　　"但我还在吃早饭,"我说。

　　"你在干什么?"她问道。

　　"我正在吃早饭,"我又说了一遍。

　　"天啊,"她说,"你总是起得这么晚吗? 现在已经1点钟了!"

Summary writing　摘要写作

Answer these questions *in not more than 50 words*.

回答下列问题，将答案组成一个段落，不要超过50个单词。

1   Does the writer always get up early on Sundays, or does he always get up late?

2   Did he get up early last Sunday, or did he get up late?

3   Who telephoned then?

4   Had she just arrived by train, or had she come on foot?

5   Was she coming to see him or not?

6   Did he say, 'I'm still having breakfast', or did he say, 'I am still in bed'?

7   Was his aunt very surprised or not?

8   What was the time?

Key structures 关键句型

Now, Often and Always 表示现在和经常发生的动作

Study these statements and questions from the passage.

注意以下摘自本课的陈述句和疑问句。

Now

It's raining.

I'm coming to see you.

I'm still having breakfast.

What are you doing?

Often and Always

I never get up early on Sundays.

I sometimes stay in bed until lunchtime.

Do you always get up so late?

Here are some more sentences:

请看其他例句：

He is still sleeping. 他仍在睡觉。

He rarely gets up before 10 o'clock. 他极少在10点以前起床。

We're enjoying our lunch. 我们正在享用午餐。

We frequently have lunch at this restaurant. 我们经常在这家餐馆吃午饭。

I am reading in bed. 我正在床上看书。

Do you ever read in bed? 你有没有在床上看过书？

Exercises 练习

A   Write out these two paragraphs again. Give the right form of the words in parentheses.

用括号中动词的正确形式填空。

1   I am looking out of my window. I can see some children in the street. The children _____ (play) football. They always _____ (play) football in the street. Now a little boy _____ (kick) the ball. Another boy _____ (run) after him but he cannot catch him.

2   I carried my bags into the hall.

'What you _____ (do) ?' my landlady asked.

'I _____ (leave), Mrs. Lynch,' I answered.

'Why you _____ (leave) ?' she asked. 'You have been here only a week.'

'A week is too long, Mrs. Lynch,' I said. 'There are too many rules in this house. My friends never _____ (come) to visit me. Dinner is always at seven o'clock, so I frequently _____ (go) to bed hungry. You don't like noise, so I rarely _____ (listen) to the radio. The heating doesn't work, so I always _____ (feel) cold. This is a terrible place for a man like me. Goodbye, Mrs. Lynch.'

B Note the position of the words in italics in these sentences.

注意以下句子中用斜体印出的词的位置。

My friends *never* come to visit me. 我的朋友们从来不来看我。

I *frequently* go to bed hungry. 我经常空着肚子上床睡觉。

I *rarely* listen to the radio. 我很少听收音机。

I *always* feel cold. 我总是感到冷。

I *never* get up early on Sundays. 星期日我从不早起。

I *sometimes* stay in bed until lunchtime. 我有时一直到午饭时间才起床。

Write these sentences again. Put the words in parentheses in the right place.

改写下列句子, 把括号中的词放在合适的位置。

1　She answers my letters. (rarely)

2　We work after six o'clock. (never)

3　The shops close on Saturday afternoons. (always)

4　Do you go to work by car? (always)

5　Our teacher collects our exercise books. (frequently)

6　We spend our holidays abroad. (sometimes)

7　I buy CDs. (often)

8　Do you buy CDs? (ever)

Special difficulties 难点

在英语中往往可以用what引导的感叹句来表示惊奇、愤怒、赞赏、喜悦等感情。在感叹句中主谓语采用正常语序。如课文中第3行的例句 "What a day!"。注意以下例句:

Instead of saying:

除了这种表述方法外:

It is a terrible day!

This is a beautiful picture!

We can say:

还可以说:

What a terrible day!

What a beautiful picture!

Or:　What a beautiful picture this is!

Exercise 练习

Write these sentences again. Each sentence must begin with *What*.

改写下列句子, 用What来引导下列感叹句。

1　This is a wonderful garden!

2　This is a surprise!

3　He is causing a lot of trouble!

4　They are wonderful actors!

5　She is a hard-working woman!

6　It is a tall building!

7　It's a terrible film!

8　You are a clever boy!

9　She is a pretty girl!

10　He is a strange guy!

Multiple choice questions 选择题

Comprehension 理解

1 When Aunt Lucy telephoned _____ .

(a) the writer was asleep　　　　　　(b) the writer was still in bed

(c) the writer had already got up　　　(d) the writer was having lunch

2 Aunt Lucy was surprised because _____ .

(a) the writer was having lunch　　　(b) it was one o'clock

(c) it was late　　　　　　　　　　(d) the writer was having breakfast at lunchtime

Structure 句型

3 He sometimes _____ in bed until lunchtime.

(a) stay　　　　(b) is staying　　　　(c) stays　　　　(d) staying

4 He stayed in bed until lunchtime. He went _____ bed late last night.

(a) in　　　　　(b) into　　　　　　(c) to　　　　　(d) at

5 He doesn't get up early on Sundays. He gets up _____ .

(a) late　　　　(b) lately　　　　　(c) slowly　　　(d) hardly

6 _____ did Aunt Lucy come? By train.

(a) When　　　(b) How　　　　　　(c) Why　　　　(d) Where

7 The writer can't see Aunt Lucy _____ . He's having breakfast.

(a) still　　　　(b) now　　　　　　(c) often　　　　(d) always

Vocabulary 词汇

8 He _____ out of the window and saw that it was raining.

(a) looked　　　(b) saw　　　　　　(c) remarked　　(d) watched

9 Just then, the telephone rang. It rang _____ .

(a) at once　　　(b) immediately　　(c) again　　　　(d) at that moment

10 She was his aunt, so he was her _____ .

(a) son　　　　(b) grandson　　　　(c) nephew　　　(d) niece

11 Breakfast is the first _____ of the day.

(a) food　　　　(b) dinner　　　　　(c) lunch　　　　(d) meal

12 Aunt Lucy said, 'Dear me!' because she was _____ .

(a) angry　　　(b) surprised　　　　(c) tired　　　　(d) pleased

Sentence structure 句子结构

Rewrite this sentence, then check your answer against the text.

改写下列句子，然后对照课文第5行，核对你的答案。

I arrived by train a moment ago.

I've _____ .

Lesson 3 Please send me a card 请给我寄一张明信片

🔊 **First listen and then answer the question.**

听录音，然后回答以下问题。

How many cards did the writer send?

Postcards always spoil my holidays. Last summer, I went to Italy. I visited museums and sat in public gardens. A friendly waiter taught me a few words of Italian. Then he lent me a book. I read a few lines, but I did not understand a word. Every day I thought about
5 postcards. My holidays passed quickly, but I did not send cards to my friends. On the last day I made a big decision. I got up early and bought thirty-seven cards. I spent the whole day in my room, but I did not write a single card!

I bought thirty-seven cards.

New words and expressions 生词和短语

send (title) /send/ (sent /sent/, sent) v. 寄，送
postcard (l.1) /ˈpəʊstkɑːd/ n. 明信片
spoil (l.1) /spɔɪl/ (spoiled or spoilt /spɔɪlt/)
    v. 使索然无味，损坏
museum (l.2) /mjuːˈziːəm/ n. 博物馆
public (l.2) /ˈpʌblɪk/ adj. 公共的

friendly (l.2) /ˈfrendli/ adj. 友好的
waiter (l.2) /ˈweɪtə/ n. 服务员，招待员
lend (l.3) /lend/ (lent /lent/, lent) v. 借给
decision (l.6) /dɪˈsɪʒən/ n. 决定
whole (l.7) /həʊl/ adj. 整个的
single (l.8) /ˈsɪŋɡəl/ adj. 唯一的，单一的

Notes on the text 课文注释

1 a few words, 几句话。

2 lent me a book 中，lent 是 "借出" 的意思。我们常说 lend sb. sth. 或 lend sth. to sb.。borrow 是 "借入" 的意思，常用的结构是 borrow sth. 或 borrow sth. from sb.。

参考译文

明信片总搅得我假日不得安宁。去年夏天，我去了意大利。我参观了博物馆，还去了公园。一位好客的服务员教了我几句意大利语，之后还借给我一本书。我读了几行，但一个字也不懂。我每天都想着明信片的事。假期过得真快，可我还没有给我的朋友们寄过一张明信片。到了最后一天，我作出了一项重大决定。我早早起了床，买来了37张明信片。我在房间里关了整整一天。然而竟连一张明信片也没写成！

Summary writing 摘要写作

Answer these questions *in not more than 50 words*.

回答下列问题，将答案组成一个段落，不要超过50个单词。

1 Do postcards always spoil the writer's holidays or not?

2 Where did he spend his holidays last summer?

3 What did he think about every day?

4   Did he send any cards to his friends or not?

5   How many cards did he buy on the last day?

6   Where did he stay all day?

7   Did he write any cards or not?

Key structures 关键句型

What happened? 一般过去时

Read this short conversation. Pay close attention to the verbs in italics. Each of these verbs tells us *what happened*.

读一读下面的这段对话，要特别注意用斜体印出的动词，每个动词都告诉我们发生了什么事情。

POLICEMAN: Did you see the accident, sir?

先生，你看到那个事故了吗？

MAN: Yes, I did. The driver of that car *hit* that post over there.

是的，我看到了。那辆车的司机撞到那边的杆子上了。

POLICEMAN: What happened?

发生了什么事情？

MAN: A dog *ran* across the road and the driver *tried to avoid* it. The car suddenly *came* towards me. It *climbed* on to the pavement and *crashed* into that post.

一条狗穿过马路，那位司机企图躲开狗。突然，汽车朝我开过来。它走上人行道，撞到那根杆子上。

POLICEMAN: What did you do?

你做了什么？

MAN: I *ran* across the street after the dog.

我穿过马路去追狗。

POLICEMAN: Why did you do that? Were you afraid of the car?

你为什么这样做呢？你怕汽车吗？

MAN: I wasn't afraid of the car. I was afraid of the driver. The driver *got out* of the car and *began shouting* at me. He was very angry with me. You see, it was my dog.

我不怕汽车，我怕那个司机。他下了车，开始朝我喊了起来。他对我很生气。你知道的，那是我的狗。

Exercises 练习

A   Look at the passage 'Please send me a card'. Put a line under all the verbs which tell us what happened to the writer when he was on holiday in Italy.

重读课文，找出那些说明作者在意大利度假时所发生的事情的动词，在这些动词的下面画上横线。

B   Give the correct form of all the verbs in parentheses. Do not refer to the passage until you finish the exercise.

用括号中动词的正确形式填空，完成练习后再对照课文，核对你的答案。

Last summer, I _____ (go) to Italy. I _____ (visit) museums and _____ (sit) in public gardens. A friendly waiter _____ (teach) me a few words of Italian. Then he _____ (lend) me a book. I _____ (read) a few lines, but I _____ (not understand) a word. Every day I _____ (think) about postcards. My holidays _____ (pass) quickly, but I _____ (not send) cards to my friends. On the last day, I _____ (make) a big decision. I _____ (get) up early and _____ (buy) thirty-seven cards. I _____ (spend) the whole day in my room, but I _____ (not write) a single card!

C Give the correct form of the verbs in parentheses in the passage below. Each verb must tell us *what happened*.
用括号中动词的正确形式填空，每个动词都必须告诉我们发生了什么事情。

My friend, Roy, _____ (die) last year. He _____ (leave) me his CD player and his collection of CDs. Roy _____ (spend) a lot of money on CDs. He _____ (buy) one or two new CDs every week. He never _____ (go) to the cinema or to the theatre. He _____ (stay) at home every evening and _____ (listen) to music. He often _____ (lend) CDs to his friends. Sometimes they _____ (keep) them. He _____ (lose) many CDs in this way.

Special difficulties 难点

英语中有些动词可以带两个宾语，这些动词大多具有"给予"的含义。如课文中第 3 行的句子"He lent me a book"中，动词lent后面带有表示动作结果的直接宾语 (a book) 和表示动作目标的间接宾语 (me)。间接宾语在大多数情况下置于直接宾语之前，如果间接宾语在后，间接宾语前必须加"to"（表示动作对什么人而做）或"for"（表示动作为什么人而做），因此，课文中的句子也可以改写成：He lent a book to me. 注意以下例句。

Instead of saying:
除了这种表述方法外：

He lent me a book.

He sent me a card.

He passed me the salt.

She bought me a tie.

She made me a cake.

We can say:
还可以说：

He lent a book to me.

He sent a card to me.

He passed the salt to me.

She bought a tie for me.

She made a cake for me.

Exercise 练习

Write each of the following sentences in a different way:
改写下列句子：

1 He paid the shopkeeper some money.

2 He handed me the prize.

3 The waiter brought a bottle of beer to the man.

4 He sold all his books to me.

5 The shop assistant found some curtain material for me.

6 He did me a big favour.

7 She showed her husband her new hat.

8 She promised a reward to the finder.

9 He gave his son some advice.

10 His uncle left him some money.

11 He is teaching English to us.

12 I bought this bunch of flowers for you.

13 Bring that book to me please.

14 He offered me a cigarette.

15 Read me the first paragraph.

16 I've ordered some soup for you.

17 I owe him a lot of money.

18 Pass the mustard to your father.

Multiple choice questions 选择题

Comprehension 理解

1 The writer _____ .

  (*a*) doesn't like buying postcards   (*b*) doesn't like receiving postcards

  (*c*) doesn't like writing postcards   (*d*) doesn't like postcards

2 What was the writer's 'big decision'?

  (*a*) He decided to write postcards to his friends.   (*b*) He decided to spend the whole day in his room.

  (*c*) He decided to buy a lot of postcards.   (*d*) He decided not to write a single card.

Structure 句型

3 Last summer he went to Italy. He was _____ Italy last summer.

  (*a*) at   (*b*) to   (*c*) in   (*d*) on

4 _____ him a few words of Italian? The waiter.

  (*a*) Who taught   (*b*) Who did teach   (*c*) What did he teach   (*d*) Whom did he teach

5 He was a friendly waiter. He spoke to the writer _____ .

  (*a*) friend   (*b*) as friends   (*c*) like friends   (*d*) in a friendly way

6 The writer _____ a few lines, but he didn't understand a word.

  (*a*) reads   (*b*) read   (*c*) red   (*d*) reading

7 He spent the whole day in his room. He was in his room _____ day.

  (*a*) the hole   (*b*) the all   (*c*) all   (*d*) all of

Vocabulary 词汇

8 A waiter usually works in a _____ .

  (*a*) public garden   (*b*) shop   (*c*) restaurant   (*d*) private house

9 The waiter lent him a book. He _____ a book from the waiter.

  (*a*) lent   (*b*) borrowed   (*c*) took   (*d*) stole

10 On the last day he made a big decision. It was the _____ day of his holiday.

  (*a*) final   (*b*) end   (*c*) latest   (*d*) bottom

11 He made a big decision. He _____ .

  (*a*) thought about it   (*b*) made up his mind   (*c*) changed his mind   (*d*) made a wish

12 He didn't write a single card. So he _____ .

  (*a*) wrote only one   (*b*) didn't write even one

  (*c*) wrote just one   (*d*) wrote all the cards except one

Sentence structure 句子结构

Rewrite this sentence, then check your answer against the text.

改写以下句子, 然后对照课文第5-6行, 核对你的答案。

I did not send my friends cards.

I did not send _____ .

Lesson 4　An exciting trip　激动人心的旅行

🔊 **First listen and then answer the question.**

听录音，然后回答以下问题。

Why is Tim finding this trip exciting?

an engineer in Australia

I have just received a letter from my brother, Tim. He is in Australia. He has been there for six months. Tim is an engineer. He is working for a big firm and he has already visited a great number of different places in Australia. He has just bought an Australian car and has
5　gone to Alice Springs, a small town in the centre of Australia. He will soon visit Darwin. From there, he will fly to Perth. My brother has never been abroad before, so he is finding this trip very exciting.

New words and expressions　生词和短语

exciting (title) /ɪkˈsaɪtɪŋ/ *adj.* 令人兴奋的
receive (l.1) /rɪˈsiːv/ *v.* 接受，收到
firm (l.3) /fɜːm/ *n.* 商行，公司

different (l.3) /ˈdɪfərənt/ *adj.* 不同的
centre (l.5) /ˈsentə/ *n.* 中心
abroad (l.7) /əˈbrɔːd/ *adv.* 在国外

Notes on the text　课文注释

1　He has been there for six months. 他在那儿已经住了 6 个月了。关于动词的现在完成时，可以参看第 1 册第 83 至 87 课。
2　a great number of ...，许多……，用于修饰复数可数名词。
3　in the centre of ...，在……中部。

参考译文

　　我刚刚收到弟弟蒂姆的来信，他正在澳大利亚。他在那儿已经住了6个月了。蒂姆是个工程师，正在为一家大公司工作，并且已经去过澳大利亚的不少地方了。他刚买了一辆澳大利亚小汽车，现在去了澳大利亚中部的小镇艾利斯斯普林斯。他不久还将到达尔文去，从那里，他再飞往珀斯。我弟弟以前从未出过国，因此，他觉得这次旅行非常激动人心。

Summary writing　摘要写作

Answer these questions *in not more than 50 words*.

回答下列问题，将答案组成一个段落，不要超过50个单词。

1　What has the writer just received from his brother, Tim?
2　Is Tim an engineer, or is he a doctor?
3　How long has he been in Australia?
4　Has he already visited many places or not?
5　Where is he now?
6　Has Tim ever been abroad before or not?
7　Is he enjoying his trip very much or not?

Key structures 关键句型

What has happened? 现在完成时

These sentences are from the passage. Study them carefully. Pay close attention to the words in italics.
下面的这些句子摘自课文, 仔细地研究这些例句, 特别要注意现在完成时句子中表示时间的状语（用斜体印出）。

I have *just* received a letter from my brother, Tim. (l.1)

He has *just* bought an Australian car and has gone to Alice Springs. (ll.4-5)

He has been there *for six months*. (l.2)

He has *already* visited a great number of different places. (ll.3-4)

My brother has *never* been abroad before. (ll.6-7)

Here are some more sentences.
请看其他例句:

He has retired *now*. 他现在已经退休了。

Have you *ever* been to Australia? 你去过澳大利亚吗?

Have you read any good books *lately*? 你最近有没有读到好书?

I haven't been very successful *so far*. 至今我不十分成功。

The train has not arrived *yet*. 火车还没有到。

Exercises 练习

A Write these sentences again. Put the words in parentheses in the right place.
改写以下句子, 将括号中表示时间的状语放在恰当的位置。

1 I have had breakfast. (just)

2 He has been in prison. (for six months)

3 The police have not caught the thief. (yet)

4 You have asked that question three times. (already)

5 Have you been to Switzerland? (ever)

6 I have been to Switzerland. (never)

7 He is a wonderful runner. He has broken two records. (so far)

8 I haven't seen George. (lately)

B Give the correct form of the verbs in parentheses. Do not refer to the passage until you finish the exercise.
用括号中动词的正确形式填空, 完成练习后再对照课文, 核对你的答案。

I just _____ (receive) a letter from my brother, Tim. He is in Australia. He _____ (be) there for six months. Tim is an engineer. He is working for a big firm and he already _____ (visit) a great number of different places in Australia. He just _____ (buy) an Australian car and _____ (go) to Alice Springs ... My brother never _____ (be) abroad before, so he is finding this trip very exciting.

C What is happening? What has happened? 现在进行时与现在完成时
  Read these two statements.
  对比以下两个句子。

  The bell is ringing.   The bell has just rung.

  Complete the following in the same way.
  模仿例句完成以下练习。

1 He is leaving the house.   He has just _____

2 He is having breakfast.   He has _____

3 She is writing a letter.   _____

4 My sister is turning on the radio. _____

5 My mother is making the bed.   _____

6 She is buying a new hat.   _____

D Read these two statements.

对比以下两个句子。

He is still having breakfast. He hasn't had breakfast yet.

Complete the following in the same way.

模仿例句完成以下练习。

1 He is still washing the dishes.   He hasn't _____

2 She is still making the beds.   She _____

3 He is still combing his hair.   _____

4 She is still sweeping the carpet.   _____

5 We are still reading 'Macbeth'.   _____

E Read these two sentences.

注意现在完成时的疑问句形式。

I've already had lunch.

Have you had lunch yet?

Ask questions in the same way.

模仿例句提问。

1 I've already seen the new play at 'The Globe'.   Have you _____

2 I've already taken my holidays.   _____

3 I've already read this book.   _____

4 I've already done my homework.   _____

5 I've already finished my work.   _____

Special difficulties 难点

Words often confused 经常容易混淆的词

Receive and *Take*.

receive: I *have* just *received* a letter from my brother. 我刚从我弟弟那里收到一封信。receive 是 "接收" 的意思。

take: Someone *has taken* my pen. 有人拿走了我的钢笔。take 是 "拿走" 的意思。

Exercise 练习

Choose the correct words in the following.

根据全句的意思选用合适的动词。

1 Yesterday I (took) (received) a present from Aunt Jane.

2 Have you (taken) (received) a letter from him yet?

3 I (took) (received) the letter with me.

4 He has (taken) (received) some flowers to her.

5 Why did you (receive) (take) this book off the shelf?

Multiple choice questions 选择题

Comprehension 理解

1 Only one of these statements is true. Which one?

(*a*) The writer has been in Australia for six months.

(*b*) Tim is a mechanic and he's working in Australia.

(*c*) Tim is working for an Austrian firm.

(*d*) Tim is working for a big firm as an engineer.

2 Only one of these statements is true. Which one?

(*a*) Tim has been in Darwin for six months.

(*b*) It's the first time Tim has ever been to another country.

(*c*) Perth is in the centre of Australia.

(*d*) Tim's brother has never been abroad before.

Structure 句型

3 Tim is in Australia. He went _____ Australia six months ago.

(*a*) to   (*b*) in   (*c*) at   (*d*) into

4 Tim is in Australia. How long _____ there?

(*a*) is he   (*b*) has he been   (*c*) has he   (*d*) was he

5 Tim has been in Australia for six months. His brother hasn't seen him _____ January.

(*a*) for   (*b*) since   (*c*) from   (*d*) by

6 He has just bought an Australian car. He bought one _____ .

(*a*) a short time ago   (*b*) a long time ago   (*c*) last year   (*d*) six months ago

7 He has just gone to Alice Springs. He has never _____ there before.

(*a*) went   (*b*) being   (*c*) been   (*d*) was

Vocabulary 词汇

8 Tim is working for a big firm. He is working for a big _____ .

(*a*) society   (*b*) company   (*c*) factory   (*d*) store

9 He has visited a great number of different places. He hasn't stayed in _____ place.

(*a*) the only   (*b*) a similar   (*c*) the same   (*d*) alike

10 Alice Springs is a small town. A town is usually _____ .

(*a*) bigger than a village but smaller than a city   (*b*) bigger than a city

(*c*) the same size as a city   (*d*) the same size as a village

11 He will soon visit Darwin. He will visit Darwin _____ .

(*a*) quickly   (*b*) for a short time   (*c*) shortly   (*d*) in a hurry

12 He will fly to Perth. He will go there _____ .

(*a*) with air   (*b*) in air   (*c*) by air   (*d*) through air

Lesson 5　No wrong numbers　无错号之虞

... *private 'telephone' service*

First listen and then answer the question.

听录音，然后回答以下问题。

What does 'No wrong numbers' mean?

Mr. James Scott has a garage in Silbury and now he has just bought
another garage in Pinhurst. Pinhurst is only five miles from Silbury,
but Mr. Scott cannot get a telephone for his new garage, so he has
just bought twelve pigeons. Yesterday, a pigeon carried the first
5　message from Pinhurst to Silbury. The bird covered the distance in
three minutes. Up to now, Mr. Scott has sent a great many requests
for spare parts and other urgent messages from one garage to the
other. In this way, he has begun his own private 'telephone'
service.

New words and expressions　生词和短语

pigeon(l.4) /ˈpɪdʒɪn/ *n.* 鸽子
message (l.5) /ˈmesɪdʒ/ *n.* 信息
cover (l.5) /ˈkʌvə/ *v.* 越过
distance (l.5) /ˈdɪstəns/ *n.* 距离

request (l.6) /rɪˈkwest/ *n.* 要求，请求
spare part (l.7) /ˌspeə-ˈpɑːt/ 备件
service (l.9) /ˈsɜːvɪs/ *n.* 业务，服务

Notes on the text　课文注释

1　from Silbury, 介词from作"距……"、"离……"讲，常与away连用。如：
　　It is far (away) from here. 离这里很远。
2　up to now (= up till now), 到现在为止；作时间状语，句子的时态多用现在完成时。
3　a great many, 许多的，其中great表示数量很大；只能同可数名词的复数连用。

参考译文

　　詹姆斯·斯科特先生在锡尔伯里有一个汽车修理部，现在他刚在平赫斯特买了另一个汽车修理部。平赫斯特离锡尔伯里只有5英里，但詹姆斯·斯科特先生未能为他新的汽车修理部搞到一部电话机，所以他买了12只鸽子。昨天，一只鸽子把第一封信从平赫斯特带到锡尔伯里。这只鸟只用了3分钟就飞完了全程。到目前为止，斯科特先生从一个汽车修理部向另一个发送了大量索取备件的信件和其他紧急函件。就这样，他开始了自己的私人"电话"业务。

Summary writing　摘要写作

Answer these questions *in not more than 50 words*.
回答下列问题，将答案组成一个段落，不要超过50个单词。

1　Where has Mr. Scott opened his second garage?
2　Where is his first garage?

3   How far away is Silbury?

4   Can Mr. Scott get a telephone for his new garage or not?

5   What has he bought?

6   In how many minutes do they carry messages from one garage to the other?

Key structures 关键句型

What happened? What has happened? 一般过去时与现在完成时

Study these sentences. Pay close attention to the words in italics.

仔细地研究这些例句, 特别注意用斜体印出的表示时间的状语。

What happened? (**KS3**)（第3课关键句型）

在第3课的"关键句型"部分, 我们讨论了英语中的一般过去时。一般过去时用来表示过去某一特定时间发生的事情或动作, 因此, 句中常有表示过去某一时刻的短语。请注意以下句子中斜体的表示时间的短语。

I wrote to him *last month*. 上个月我给他写了信。

I bought this car *last year*. 去年我买了这辆车。

He came to see me *this morning*. 今天上午他来看我。

I saw him *ten minutes ago*. 我10分钟以前见到了他。

What has happened? (**KS4**)（第4课关键句型）

在第4课的"关键句型"部分, 我们又讨论了现在完成时。现在完成时用来表示发生在过去但对现在仍有影响的一个动作。在现在完成时的句子中常有一些表示时间的词和短语。请注意以下句子中斜体的时间状语。

The train has *just* left the station. 火车刚刚驶离车站。

I've *already* seen that film. 那个电影我已经看过了。

He has been abroad *for six months*. 他在国外已6个月了。

Have you *ever* met him *before*? 你以前见过他吗？

I have *never* met him *before*. 我从未见过他。

I have not finished work *yet*. 我还没有做完工作。

There have been a great number of accidents *lately*. 最近事故极多。

Up till now he has won five prizes. 至今为止他已赢得了5个奖。

Exercises 练习

A   Underline all the verbs in the passage which tell us *what happened* and *what has happened*.
在课文中的所有动词下面画上横线, 并指出哪些是一般过去时, 哪些是现在完成时。

B   Give the correct form of the verbs in parentheses. Do not refer to the passage until you finish the exercise.
用括号中动词的正确形式填空, 完成练习后再对照课文, 核对你的答案。

Mr. James Scott has a garage in Silbury and now he just _____ (buy) another garage in Pinhurst. Pinhurst is only five miles from Silbury, but Mr. Scott cannot get a telephone for his new garage, so he just _____ (buy) twelve pigeons. Yesterday, a pigeon _____ (carry) the first message from Pinhurst to Silbury. The bird _____ (cover) the distance in three minutes. Up to now, Mr. Scott _____ (send) a great many requests for spare parts and other urgent messages from one garage to the other. In this way, he _____ (begin) his own private 'telephone' service.

C Give the correct form of the verbs in parentheses.
　用括号中动词的正确形式填空。

1 What _____ you _____ (buy) yesterday?

2 Up till now, he never _____ (lend) me anything.

3 _____ you (burn) those old papers yet?

4 He _____ (fight) in Flanders in the First World War.

5 They already _____ (leave).

6 When _____ you _____ (lose) your umbrella?

7 _____ you _____ (listen) to the concert last night?

8 We just _____ (win) the match.

Special difficulties 难点

Words often confused or misused 经常容易混淆和误用的词

a Phrases with the word *way*.
　带 way 的短语
　课文的第 8-9 行有这样一句话，"*In this way*, he has begun his own private 'telephone' service." 以下是与 way 这个词组成的短语。

In the way: Please move this chair. It is *in the way*. 请挪一下这把椅子，它把路挡住了。

Do your work *in the way* I have shown you. 按我给你示范的方法来做你的工作。

On the way: *On the way* to the station, I bought some chocolate. 在去车站的路上我买了些巧克力。

In this way: He saves old envelopes. *In this way*, he has collected a great many stamps. 他搜集旧信封，用这种办法他收集了大量的邮票。

By the way: *By the way*, have you seen Harry recently? 顺便问一句，你最近见过哈里吗？

In a way: *In a way*, it is an important book. 在某种意义上，这是一本重要的书。

Exercise 练习

Supply the correct phrases with *way* in the following.
用带有 way 的短语填空。

1 _____ from Athens to London, the plane stopped at Rome.

2 I cooked this _____ you showed me.

3 _____ , where is my coat?

4 Yes, _____ he has been very successful.

5 Children get _____ during the holidays.

b *Spare* and *To Spare* ('spare parts'[l.7]). 形容词 spare 和动词 to spare 的区别
　Note the following.
　细读下面的例句，注意 spare 这个词作形容词和动词用时的不同含义。

I cannot *spare* the time. 我花不起时间。

I have no time to *spare*. 我没有时间。

I cannot buy *spare* parts for this car. 我买不起这辆车的备件。

There is a *spare* room in this house. 在这栋房子里有一间空房。

Caligula *spared* the slave's life. 卡里格勒饶了那个奴隶的命。

Exercise 练习

Rewrite these sentences using *spare* or *to spare* in place of the words or phrases in italics. Make any other necessary changes.
改写下面的句子，用 spare 的形容词形式或动词形式来代替句子中用斜体书写的单词或短语，并对句中的其他部分作必要的改动。

1 There is *an extra* wheel in the back of the car.

2 I always go on excursions in my *free* time.

3 'Have you any old clothes *that you do not want*?' he asked.

4 The guest slept in the room *we do not use*.

5 '*Do not kill* me!' begged the prisoner.

Multiple choice questions 选择题

Comprehension 理解

1 Mr. Scott hasn't got a telephone in his new garage because _____ .

    (*a*) it isn't far from his old garage, so he doesn't need one   (*b*) he has twelve pigeons

    (*c*) he can't get one   (*d*) it's too expensive

2 Mr. Scott keeps pigeons because _____ .

    (*a*) he uses them to send messages   (*b*) it's his hobby

    (*c*) he has two garages   (*d*) he likes them

Structure 句型

3 Mr. Scott has a garage. The garage is _____ .

    (*a*) to him   (*b*) of him   (*c*) of his   (*d*) his

4 Mr. Scott cannot get a telephone for his garage. _____ he has just bought twelve pigeons.

    (*a*) That's so   (*b*) That's why   (*c*) Because   (*d*) For

5 He has just bought twelve pigeons. When did he _____ them?

    (*a*) bought   (*b*) buys   (*c*) buy   (*d*) buying

6 What's the distance from Pinhurst to Silbury? How _____ is Pinhurst _____ Silbury?

    (*a*) long ago ... until   (*b*) long ... away   (*c*) away ... till   (*d*) far ... from

7 The pigeon flew from one garage to the other _____ three minutes.

    (*a*) in   (*b*) into   (*c*) with   (*d*) on

Vocabulary 词汇

8 Mr. Scott has a garage in Silbury. His _____ garage is in Pinhurst.

    (*a*) another   (*b*) other   (*c*) else   (*d*) different

9 Mr. Scott can't get a telephone. Telephones are hard to _____ .

    (*a*) take   (*b*) receive   (*c*) obtain   (*d*) find

10 He has sent requests for spare parts. He has _____ spare parts.

    (*a*) asked   (*b*) asked for   (*c*) begged   (*d*) pleased

11 Urgent messages are important, so they must be sent _____ .

    (*a*) quickly   (*b*) slowly   (*c*) by hand   (*d*) largely

12 Mr. Scott's 'telephone service' is private. It is _____ .

    (*a*) general   (*b*) spare   (*c*) secret   (*d*) his own

Sentence structure 句子结构

Join these sentences together with *but* and *so*. Then check your answer against the text.

用but和so把下列句子连接起来，然后对照课文第2-4行，核对你的答案。

Pinhurst is only five miles from Silbury. Mr. Scott cannot get a telephone for his new garage. He has just bought twelve pigeons.

Lesson 6　Percy Buttons　珀西·巴顿斯

First listen and then answer the question.

听录音，然后回答以下问题。

Who is Percy Buttons?

... *stood on his head and sang songs*

I have just moved to a house in Bridge Street. Yesterday a beggar knocked at my door. He asked me for a meal and a glass of beer. In return for this, the beggar stood on his head and sang songs. I gave

5　him a meal. He ate the food and drank the beer. Then he put a piece of cheese in his pocket and went away. Later a neighbour told me about him. Everybody knows him. His name is Percy Buttons. He calls at every house in the street once a month and always asks for a meal and a glass of beer.

New words and expressions　生词和短语

beggar (1.1) /ˈbegə/ n. 乞丐

food (1.4) /fuːd/ n. 食物

pocket (1.5) /ˈpɒkɪt/ n. 衣服口袋

call (1.7) /kɔːl/ v. 拜访，光顾

Notes on the text　课文注释

1　He asked me for a meal and a glass of beer. 他问我要一顿饭和一杯啤酒。ask sb. for sth., 向某人索要某物。

2　in return for this, 作为回报。句中this指上文的a meal and a glass of beer。

3　stand on one's head, 倒立。

4　He calls at every house in the street, 他光顾街上的每一幢房子。

参考译文

我刚刚搬进了大桥街的一所房子。昨天一个乞丐来敲我的门，问我要一顿饭和一杯啤酒。作为回报，那乞丐头顶地倒立起来，嘴里还唱着歌。我给了他一顿饭。他把食物吃完，又喝了酒。然后把一块乳酪装进衣袋里走了。后来，一位邻居告诉了我他的情况。大家都认识他，他叫珀西·巴顿斯。他每月对这条街上的每户人家光顾一次，总是请求给他一顿饭和一杯啤酒。

Summary writing　摘要写作

Answer these questions *in not more than 55 words*.

回答下列问题，将答案组成一个段落，不要超过55个单词。

1　Has the writer just moved to a house in Bridge Street or not?

2　Who knocked at her door yesterday?

3　Did he sing songs, or did he ask for money?

4　What did the writer give him in return for this?

5　What is the beggar's name?

6　Does he call at every house once a week or once a month?

Key structures 关键句型

A, The and Some

a   *A* and *Some*. 不定冠词和表示不确定数量的some

We can say:

我们可以说:

a pen, some pens; a book, some books; a picture, some pictures; a glass of milk, some milk; a bag of flour, some flour; a bar of soap, some soap.

We can also use some nouns without *a* or *some* in general statements. Read these sentences carefully.

在表示一种笼统概念的陈述句中也可以省略a或some。细读下列句子。

Yesterday I bought *a book*. *Books* are not very expensive. 昨天我买了一本书。书不很贵。

I have just drunk *a glass of milk*. *Milk* is very refreshing. 我刚刚喝了一杯奶, 牛奶很提神。

Mrs. Jones bought *a bag of flour, a bag of sugar* and *some tea*. 琼斯太太买了一袋面粉、一袋糖和一些茶叶。

She always buys *flour, sugar* and *tea* at the grocer's. 她总是在食品店买面粉、糖和茶叶。

b   *A* and *The*. 不定冠词和定冠词

Read this paragraph. Pay close attention to the words *a* and *the*:

注意以下段落中a和the的用法:

A man is walking towards me. *The* man is carrying *a* parcel. *The* parcel is full of meat. *The* man has just bought some meat. *A* dog is following *the* man. *The* dog is looking at *the* parcel. 一个男人朝我走来。他拿着一个包。包里装满了肉。他刚刚买了些肉。一条狗跟着他, 它正盯着他的那个包。

c   Names. 姓名

We cannot put *a* or *the* in front of names.

姓名前不能用不定冠词或定冠词。

John lives in England. He has a house in London. His house is in Duke Street. Last year he went to Madrid. John likes Spain very much. He goes there every summer. 约翰住在英国, 他在伦敦有一栋房子。那栋房子在公爵街。去年他去了一趟马德里。约翰很喜欢西班牙, 他每年夏天都去那里。

Exercises 练习

A   Write these words again. Put in *a* or *some* in front of each one.

重抄以下词语, 分别加上a或some。

meat, desk, tobacco, tin of beans, comb, city, cloth, oil, bottle of beer, day, word, student, sugar, rain, orange, rubber.

B   Read the passage again. Put a line under the words *a* and *the*.

重读课文, 画出不定冠词和定冠词。

C   Put in the words *a* or *the* where necessary. Do not refer to the passage until you finish the exercise:

根据需要填上不定冠词或定冠词。完成练习后再对照课文, 核对你的答案:

I have just moved to _____ house in _____ Bridge Street. Yesterday _____ beggar knocked at my door. He asked me for _____ meal and _____ glass of beer. In return for this, _____ beggar stood on his head and sang _____ songs. I gave him _____ meal. He ate _____ food and drank _____ beer. Then he put _____ piece of cheese in his pocket and went away. Later _____ neighbour told me about him. Everybody knows him. His name is _____ Percy Buttons. He calls at every house in _____ street once _____ month and always asks for _____ meal and _____ glass of beer.

D Write sentences using *a, the* or *some* with the following:

用下列词语造句，选用a, the 或some:

1 found/coin/garden.　　　　2 put/sugar/my tea.　　　　3 cut/wood/fire.

4 bought/newspaper.　　　　5 made/coffee.　　　　6 like/curtains in this room.

Special difficulties 难点

Some verbs change in meaning when we put short words after them. Read these sentences. Do you know what the verbs in italics mean?

有些动词的后面加上介词或副词以后就会改变词义。这种新的组合被称作短语动词。读一读下面的句子，句中的动词用斜体印出，你知道这些短语动词的词义吗？

I *put* your book on the shelf. 我把你的书放在书架上。

I *put on* my hat and left the house. 我戴上帽子，离开了屋子。

Who *took* my umbrella? 谁拿走了我的伞？

It was very hot, so I *took off* my coat. 天很热，因此我脱掉了外套。

Come and *look at* my photograph album. 过来，看看我的相册。

I *am looking for* my pen. I lost it this morning. 我正在找我的钢笔，我今天早上把它弄丢了。

Will you *look after* the children for me please? 请你帮我照看一下孩子们，好吗？

Read these sentences. Each one contains the verb *knock*. The verb has a different meaning in each sentence.

读一读下面的句子，每个句中都含有动词knock, 但它们的词义有很大差异。

A beggar *knocked at* my door. (l.2)

I *knocked* the vase *off* the table and broke it. 我把花瓶从桌上碰掉，把它打碎了。

He always *knocks off* at six o'clock. (He finishes his work.) 他总是6点钟下班。

The shop assistant *knocked* 10% *off* the bill. (He reduced the price by 10%.) 售货员给了10%的优惠。

A car *knocked* the boy *over*. (It hit him hard and made him fall.) 汽车把男孩撞倒了。

In the fight, the thief *knocked* the policeman *out*. (The policeman was unconscious for three minutes.) 在搏斗中，小偷把警察打昏了。

Exercises 练习

A Put in the correct words.

根据上下文填上正确的介词或副词。

1 He did not know how to fight, but he knocked the boxer _____ .

2 This flowerpot is broken. Who knocked it _____ ?

3 I knocked _____ early yesterday and went to a football match.

4 Listen! Someone is knocking _____ the window!

B Rewrite the following sentences using the correct form of the verb *knock* in place of the words in italics.

改写以下句子，用含有knock的短语动词来替代以下句子中用斜体印出的词语。

1 The old lady hit the thief over the head with a candlestick and *now he is unconscious*.

2 At what time do you *finish work* every day?

3 The shopkeeper *reduced* the price of all his goods *by 20%*.

Multiple choice questions 选择题

Comprehension 理解

1 Percy Buttons stood on his head and sang songs because _____ .

  (*a*) he wanted a piece of cheese   (*b*) he liked doing this

  (*c*) he was a beggar   (*d*) he wanted to 'pay' for his meal in this way

2 The writer didn't know about Percy Buttons because _____ .

  (*a*) she was new to the neighbourhood   (*b*) he had never called at that house before

  (*c*) he was a beggar   (*d*) he didn't live near her

Structure 句型

3 The writer has just moved to a new house. She was _____ yesterday.

  (*a*) at house   (*b*) to the house   (*c*) at home   (*d*) in the home

4 She gave _____ .

  (*a*) to him a meal   (*b*) a meal for him   (*c*) him to a meal   (*d*) a meal to him

5 A neighbour told me about him. He _____ Percy Buttons was a beggar.

  (*a*) told   (*b*) said me   (*c*) told to me   (*d*) said

6 Everybody knows him. _____ know him.

  (*a*) They all   (*b*) Each   (*c*) Every   (*d*) All they

7 _____ does he call? Once a month.

  (*a*) How seldom   (*b*) How long   (*c*) How soon   (*d*) How often

Vocabulary 词汇

8 A beggar is a person who _____ .

  (*a*) asks for money but doesn't work   (*b*) asks for food

  (*c*) works hard   (*d*) is out of work

9 You can have a meal _____ .

  (*a*) only in the morning   (*b*) at any time   (*c*) only at midday   (*d*) only in the evening

10 She gave him a piece of cheese. He put the _____ of cheese in his pocket.

  (*a*) bit   (*b*) bar   (*c*) block   (*d*) packet

11 He calls at every house in the street. He _____ everyone.

  (*a*) shouts at   (*b*) calls   (*c*) cries out at   (*d*) visits

12 All the houses in our _____ are the same age and size.

  (*a*) street   (*b*) way   (*c*) road   (*d*) route

Sentence structure 句子结构

Arrange these groups of words in the correct order, then check your answer against the text.

按照正确的语序排列以下词组, 然后对照课文第6-8行, 核对你的答案。

and a glass of beer/he calls/for a meal/at every house/and always asks/in the street/once a month

Lesson 7　Too late　为时太晚

First listen and then answer the question.

听录音，然后回答以下问题。

Did the detectives save the diamonds?

The plane was late and detectives were waiting at the airport all morning. They were expecting a valuable parcel of diamonds from South Africa. A few hours earlier, someone had told the police that thieves would try to steal the diamonds. When the plane arrived,
5　some of the detectives were waiting inside the main building while others were waiting on the airfield. Two men took the parcel off the plane and carried it into the Customs House. While two detectives were keeping guard at the door, two others opened the parcel. To their surprise, the precious parcel was full of stones and sand!

Two men took the parcel

New words and expressions　生词和短语

detective (l.1) /dɪˈtektɪv/ *n.* 侦探

airport (l.1) /ˈeəpɔːt/ *n.* 机场

expect (l.2) /ɪkˈspekt/ *v.* 期待，等待

valuable(l.2) /ˈvæljuəbəl/ *adj.* 贵重的

parcel (l.2) /ˈpɑːsəl/ *n.* 包裹

diamond (l.2) /ˈdaɪəmənd/ *n.* 钻石

steal (l.4) /stiːl/ (stole /stəʊl/, stolen /ˈstəʊlən/) *v.* 偷

main (l.5) /meɪn/ *adj.* 主要的

airfield (l.6) /ˈeəfiːld/ *n.* 飞机起落的场地

guard (l.8) /gɑːd/ *n.* 警戒，守卫

precious (l.9) /ˈpreʃəs/ *adj.* 珍贵的

stone (l.9) /stəʊn/ *n.* 石子

sand (l.9) /sænd/ *n.* 沙子

Notes on the text　课文注释

1　detectives were waiting at the airport all morning, 侦探们在机场等了整整一上午。句中的动词时态是过去进行时。过去进行时常用来表示过去某时正在进行的情况或动作。本课课文中有4个句子使用了过去进行时。参看第 1 册第 117-119 等课中的例句。

2　keep guard, 守卫。

3　to their surprise, 使他们吃惊的是。

参考译文

　　飞机误点了，侦探们在机场等了整整一上午。他们正期待从南非来的一个装着钻石的贵重包裹。数小时以前，有人向警方报告，说有人企图偷走这些钻石。当飞机到达时，一些侦探等候在主楼内，另一些侦探则守候在停机坪上。有两个人把包裹拿下飞机，进了海关。这时两个侦探把住门口，另外两个侦探打开了包裹。令他们吃惊的是，那珍贵的包裹里面装的全是石头和沙子!

36

Summary writing 摘要写作

Answer these questions *in not more than 50 words*.
回答下列问题，将答案组成一个段落，不要超过50个单词。

1 How long were detectives waiting at the airport?

2 What were they expecting from South Africa?

3 Where did two men take the parcel after the arrival of the plane?

4 How many detectives opened it?

5 What was the parcel full of?

Key structures 关键句型

What were you doing when I telephoned? 过去进行时

Study these sentences carefully. Pay close attention to the words in italics.
细读这些过去进行时的例句，特别注意用斜体印出的表示时间的状语。

When I was watering the garden, it began to rain. 当我正在花园里浇水时，开始下雨了。

I was having breakfast *when* the telephone rang. 我正在吃早饭时，电话铃响了。

While we were having a party, the lights went out. 当我们正在聚会时，灯熄灭了。

George was reading *while* his wife was listening to the radio. 乔治在看书时，他的妻子在听收音机。

As I was getting on the bus, I slipped and hurt my foot. 当我上公共汽车时，我滑了一下，撞伤了我的脚。

Someone knocked at the door *just as* I was getting into the bath. 就在我要进澡盆洗澡时有人敲门。

The plane was late and detectives were waiting at the airport *all morning*. (ll.1-2) 飞机误点了，侦探们在机场等了整整一上午。

Exercises 练习

A Underline the verbs in the passage which tell us *what was happening*.
选出课文中表示过去某时正在进行的动作的句子，并在下面画上横线。

B What was happening when ... ?
Read the passage again then answer these questions. Write a complete sentence in answer to each question.
重读课文后回答以下问题，回答时写出完整的句子。

1 What was happening when the plane arrived?

2 What was happening when two of the detectives opened the parcel?

C Write sentences of your own in answer to these questions. Each answer must begin with 'I was ... '
根据自己的情况回答以下问题，每句回答均要以 I was 开头。

1 What were you doing when I telephoned you?

2 What were you reading when I saw you in the library this morning?

3 What were you saying when I interrupted you?

D What was happening? What happened? 过去进行时与一般过去时。
Give the correct form of the verbs in parentheses.
用括号中动词的正确形式填空。

1 As my father _____ (leave) the house, the postman _____ (arrive).

Unit 1 Lesson 7

2 Tom _____ (work) in the garden while I _____ (sit) in the sun.

3 As I _____ (walk) down the street, I _____ (meet) Charlie.

4 While he _____ (read) the letter, he _____ (hear) a knock at the door.

5 While mother _____ (prepare) lunch, Janet _____ (set) the table.

6 She _____ (drop) the tray when I _____ (speak) to her.

Special difficulties 难点

Two men took the parcel off the plane. (ll.6-7)

Do you remember these sentences? **(SD6)**

你还记得这些句子吗？（参见第6课的难点）

Come and *look at* my photograph album.

I am *looking for* my pen. I lost it this morning.

Will you *look after* the children for me please?

Now read these sentences:

仔细阅读这些句子：

Instead of saying:	*We can say*:
除了这种表述方法外：	还可以说：
He took off his coat.	He took his coat off. He took it off.
He put out the fire.	He put the fire out. He put it out.
She put on her hat.	She put her hat on. She put it on.

Exercise 练习

We can change the position of the words in italics in some of the sentences below. For instance, we can change the position of the word *out* in this sentence: He put *out* the fire. But we cannot change the position of the word *for* in this sentence: He is looking *for* his pen. Where possible, change the position of the words in italics in the sentences below.

在下面的有些句子中我们可以调换用斜体印出的词的位置。比如说，在 "He put *out* the fire." 这句话中，我们可以变动out的位置(He put the fire *out*.)。但是，在 "He is looking *for* his pen." 中，我们却不能变动for的位置，如有可能，调换下列句子中用斜体印出的词的位置。

1 He gave *away* all his books.

2 She woke *up* the children early this morning.

3 He is looking *for* his umbrella.

4 They cut *off* the king's head.

5 Put *on* your hat and coat.

6 Give it *back to* your brother.

7 Help me to lift *up* this table.

8 Take *off* your shoes and put *on* your slippers.

9 He is looking *at* the picture.

10 Send her *away* or she will cause trouble.

11 They have pulled *down* the old building.

12 Make *up* your mind.

13 He asked *for* permission to leave.

14 She threw *away* all those old newspapers.

Multiple choice questions 选择题

Comprehension 理解

1 The detectives were at the airport _____ .

  (*a*) to meet a plane   (*b*) to prevent a robbery

  (*c*) to watch the building   (*d*) because the plane was late

2 The detectives _____ .

  (*a*) found the diamonds   (*b*) didn't open the parcel

  (*c*) didn't prevent the robbery   (*d*) caught the thieves

Structure 句型

3 _____ were the detectives waiting? At the airport.

  (*a*) Why   (*b*) When   (*c*) Where   (*d*) What

4 _____ were they expecting? A valuable parcel of diamonds.

  (*a*) Why   (*b*) When   (*c*) Where   (*d*) What

5 Someone had told the police that thieves would try to steal the diamonds. This happened _____ the plane arrived.

  (*a*) before   (*b*) after   (*c*) when   (*d*) as soon as

6 The detectives went into the building and waited _____ .

  (*a*) in   (*b*) into   (*c*) inside   (*d*) for

7 Two men took the parcel off the plane. They _____ .

  (*a*) took off it   (*b*) it took off   (*c*) took off   (*d*) took it off

Vocabulary 词汇

8 The detectives were _____ a valuable parcel of diamonds.

  (*a*) expecting   (*b*) waiting   (*c*) expecting for   (*d*) expecting to

9 The parcel was valuable. It was _____ .

  (*a*) worth   (*b*) worthy   (*c*) precious   (*d*) value

10 The thieves wanted to _____ the diamonds.

  (*a*) rob   (*b*) steal   (*c*) take from   (*d*) take to

11 The detectives waited inside the main building. This was the _____ building.

  (*a*) most important   (*b*) smallest   (*c*) first   (*d*) greatest

12 Someone had filled the parcel with stones and sand. It was _____ stones and sand.

  (*a*) full with   (*b*) full of   (*c*) full by   (*d*) full in

Sentence structure 句子结构

Arrange these groups of words in the correct order, then check your answer against the text.

按照正确的语序排列以下词组, 然后对照课文第6-7行, 核对你的答案。

into the Customs House/two men/and carried it/took the parcel/off the plane

Lesson 8　The best and the worst　最好的和最差的

First listen and then answer the question.

听录音，然后回答以下问题。

Why is Joe's garden the most beautiful one in the town?

Joe Sanders has the most beautiful garden in our town. Nearly everybody enters for 'The Nicest Garden Competition' each year, but Joe wins every time. Bill Frith's garden is larger than Joe's. Bill works harder than Joe and grows more flowers and vegetables, but
5 Joe's garden is more interesting. He has made neat paths and has built a wooden bridge over a pool. I like gardens too, but I do not like hard work. Every year I enter for the garden competition too, and I always win a little prize for the worst garden in the town!

Joe wins every time

New words and expressions　生词和短语

competition (l.2) /ˌkɒmpəˈtɪʃən/ *n.* 比赛，竞赛

neat (l.5) /niːt/ *adj.* 整齐的，整洁的

path (l.5) /pɑːθ/ *n.* 小路，小径

wooden (l.6) /ˈwʊdn/ *adj.* 木头的

pool (l.6) /puːl/ *n.* 水池

Notes on the text　课文注释

1　Joe Sanders has the most beautiful garden in our town. 乔·桑德斯拥有我们镇上最漂亮的花园。在第1册的第107-112课中，我们讲到了英文中形容词和副词的比较级和最高级。本课的主要句型仍是形容词和副词的比较级和最高级。如果形容词或副词有两个以上的音节，其比较级和最高级是在形容词或副词前加上more或most，如more interesting, the most beautiful。

2　enter for, 报名参加（各种竞赛，考试等活动）。

3　more flowers and vegetables, 更多的花卉和蔬菜。英语中有些形容词或副词的比较级和最高级并不规则，如课文中的good — better — best, bad — worse — worst, many — more — most。

4　for the worst garden in the town是介词短语作定语，修饰prize。

参考译文

　　乔·桑德斯拥有我们镇上最漂亮的花园。几乎每个人都参加每年举办的"最佳花园竞赛"，而每次都是乔获胜。比尔·弗里斯的花园比乔的花园大，他比乔也更为勤奋，种植的花卉和蔬菜也更多，但乔的花园更富有情趣。他修筑了一条条整洁的小路，并在一个池塘上架了一座小木桥。我也喜欢花园，但我却不愿意辛勤劳动。每年的花园竞赛我也参加，但总因是镇上最差的花园而获得一个小奖！

Summary writing　摘要写作

Answer these questions *in not more than 45 words*.

回答下列问题，将答案组成一个段落，不要超过45个单词。

1　Who has the best garden in town?

2   What does he win each year?

3   Who else has a fine garden?

4   Is Joe's better or not?

5   Is the writer's garden beautiful, or is it terrible?

6   What does he always win a prize for?

Key structures 关键句型

The best and the worst 比较

Read these sentences carefully:

仔细阅读这些句子：

Mary is tall, but Jane is taller. Jane is taller than Mary. Caroline is very tall. She is the tallest girl in the class. 玛丽很高，但是简更高。简比玛丽高。卡罗琳非常高，她是班上最高的女孩子。

Jane's handwriting is bad, but Mary's is worse. Caroline's handwriting is very bad. It is the worst handwriting I have ever seen. 简的书写很差，但是玛丽的更差。卡罗琳的书写非常糟糕，这是我见过的最差的书写。

The three girls collect photos of film stars. Mary hasn't many photos, but Jane has more. Jane has more photos than Mary. Caroline has very many. She has the most. 这3个女孩子搜集影星的照片。玛丽的照片不多，但是简要多一些。简的照片比玛丽的多。卡罗琳有很多照片，她的照片最多。

Mary's collection of photos is not very good. Jane's is better. Caroline's collection is the best. 玛丽的影集不太好，简的要好一些，卡罗琳的最好。

Last week the three girls bought expensive dresses. Caroline's dress was more expensive than Jane's. Mary's was more expensive than Caroline's. Mary's dress was the most expensive. 上周这3个女孩子买了很昂贵的连衣裙。卡罗琳的连衣裙比简的贵，玛丽的又比卡罗琳的贵。玛丽的连衣裙是最贵的。

Exercises 练习

A   These questions are about Mary, Jane and Caroline. Answer each question with a complete sentence.
这些问题都是关于玛丽、简和卡罗琳的，用完整的句子来回答以下问题。

1   How does Mary's handwriting compare with Jane's?

2   How does Caroline's handwriting compare with Mary's and Jane's?

3   How does Caroline's dress compare with Jane's?

4   How does Mary's dress compare with Jane's and Caroline's?

B   In the passage 'The best and the worst' there are seven comparisons. Can you find them?
找出本课中7个比较级的例子。

C   Give the correct form of the words in parentheses and make other necessary changes. Do not refer to the passage until you finish the exercise.
用括号中动词的正确形式填空，并对句子作必要的调整，完成练习后再对照课文，核对你的答案。

Joe Sanders has the _____ (beautiful) garden in our town. Nearly everybody enters for 'The _____ (Nice) Garden Competition' each year, but Joe wins every time. Bill Frith's garden is _____ (large) Joe's. Bill works _____ (hard) than Joe and grows _____ (many) flowers and vegetables, but Joe's garden is _____ (interesting). He has made neat paths and has built a wooden bridge over a pool. I like gardens too, but I do not like hard work. Every year I enter for the garden competition too, and I always win a little prize for the _____ (bad) garden in the town!

D Put in *of* or *in*.

用 of 或 in 填空。

1   Which is the longest river _____ the world?

2   This is the finest picture _____ them all.

3   This stereo is the most expensive _____ all the ones in the shop.

4   He is the best boxer _____ our town.

Special difficulties 难点

a Everyone, Everybody, Everything 与 every 一起复合而成的不定代词 (everyone, everybody, everything) 是单数形式

Read these sentences.

注意以下句子中动词的形式。

Everybody enters for 'The Nicest Garden Competition' (l.2)

Everything is ready. 万事俱备。

Everybody has come. 每个人都到了。

Everyone likes ice cream. 每人都喜欢冰激凌。

Exercise 练习

Choose the correct verbs in the following sentences.

选择动词的正确形式。

1   Everybody (believe) (believes) he will win.

2   I heard a noise and went downstairs. I found that everything (were) (was) in order.

3   Everyone(try) (tries) to earn more and work less.

b Enter

Read these sentences.

注意下列句子中动词 enter 和短语动词 enter for 的不同含义。

Everybody enters *for* the competition. (l.2)

Everyone stood up when he *entered* the room. 当他走进房间时每个人都站了起来。

Did you *enter for* this examination? 你有没有参加这次考试？

The lights went out just as we *entered* the cinema. 当我们走进电影院时，灯熄灭了。

How many people have *entered for* the race? 多少人报名参加比赛？

Exercise 练习

Put in the word *for* where necessary.

必要时填上 for。

1   He is very ill. No one is allowed to enter _____ his room.

2   Will you enter _____ this week's crossword competition?

3   Many athletes have entered _____ the Olympic Games this year.

4   No one saw the thief when he entered _____ the building.

5   I have entered _____ the examination but I don't want to take it.

Multiple choice questions 选择题

Comprehension 理解

1 One of these sentences is true. Which one?

(a) Bill Frith's garden is the best and Joe Sanders' is the worst.

(b) Joe Sanders' garden is the best and Bill Frith's is the worst.

(c) The writer's garden is the best and Joe Sanders' is the worst.

(d) Joe Sanders' garden is the best and the writer's is the worst.

2 One of these sentences is true. Which one?

(a) The writer doesn't like gardens.   (b) The writer likes gardens, but he is lazy.

(c) The writer never enters for the competition.   (d) The writer never wins a prize.

Structure 句型

3 Bill Frith's garden is larger than Joe's. It is _____ .

(a) larger garden   (b) a large garden   (c) large garden   (d) largest garden

4 Bill is a hard worker. He works _____ than Joe.

(a) harder   (b) more hard   (c) more hardly   (d) hardier

5 Joe's garden is more interesting _____ Bill's.

(a) by   (b) for   (c) than   (d) from

6 The writer is fond of gardens. _____ .

(a) They like him   (b) They like to him   (c) He likes them   (d) He likes

7 Joe's garden is the best in the town. It's the best _____ them all.

(a) in   (b) of   (c) for   (d) by

Vocabulary 词汇

8 Joe wins every time. He always _____ Bill Frith.

(a) wins   (b) beats   (c) gains   (d) earns

9 Joe grows more flowers. More flowers _____ in his garden.

(a) grow   (b) grow tall   (c) grow up   (d) grow big

10 Joe's garden is interesting. Joe is _____ in gardening.

(a) interesting   (b) interest   (c) interestingly   (d) interested

11 The writer doesn't like hard work. It's _____ to look after a garden.

(a) a hard work   (b) a hard job   (c) hard job   (d) hardly a job

12 Every year the writer enters for the garden competition _____ .

(a) very   (b) also   (c) and   (d) either

Sentence structure 句子结构

Rewrite this sentence, then check your answer against the text.

改写下列句子, 然后对照课文第3行, 核对你的答案。

Joe's garden is not as large as Bill Frith's.

Bill Frith's _____ .

Lesson 9   A cold welcome   冷遇

First listen and then answer the question.

听录音，然后回答以下问题。

What does 'a cold welcome' refer to?

On Wednesday evening, we went to the Town Hall. It was the last day of the year and a large crowd of people had gathered under the Town Hall clock. It would strike twelve in twenty minutes' time. Fifteen minutes passed and then, at five to twelve, the clock stopped.
5   The big minute hand did not move. We waited and waited, but nothing happened. Suddenly someone shouted, 'It's two minutes past twelve! The clock has stopped!' I looked at my watch. It was true. The big clock refused to welcome the New Year. At that moment, everybody began to laugh and sing.

the clock stopped

New words and expressions 生词和短语

welcome (title) /'welkəm/ *n.* 欢迎；(1.8) *v.* 欢迎

crowd (1.2) /kraʊd/ *n.* 人群

gather (1.2) /'gæðə/ *v.* 聚集

hand (1.5) /hænd/ *n.* （表或机器的）指针

shout (1.6) /ʃaʊt/ *v.* 喊叫

refuse (1.8) /rɪ'fjuːz/ *v.* 拒绝

laugh (1.9) /lɑːf/ *v.* 笑

Notes on the text 课文注释

1   Town Hall, 市政厅，地方政府办公之处。

2   a large crowd of ..., 一大群……。

3   in twenty minutes' time, 20分钟之后。

参考译文

　　星期三的晚上，我们去了市政厅。那是一年的最后一天，一大群人聚集在市政厅的大钟下面。再过20分钟，大钟将敲响12下。15分钟过去了，而就在11点55分时，大钟停了。那根巨大的分针不动了。我们等啊等啊，可情况没有变化。突然有人喊道："已经12点零2分了！那钟已经停了！"我看了一下我的手表，果真如此。那座大钟不愿意迎接新年。此时，大家笑了起来，同时唱起了歌。

Summary writing 摘要写作

Answer these questions *in not more than 50 words*.

回答下列问题，将答案组成一个段落，不要超过50个单词。

1   Where did we go on New Year's Eve?

2   Were there a lot of people there or not?

3   In how many minutes would the Town Hall clock strike twelve?

4   At what time did it stop?

44

5 Did it refuse to welcome the New Year or not?

6 What did the crowd do then?

Key structures 关键句型

When did you arrive? I arrived at 10 o'clock.

Read these sentences carefully. Pay close attention to the phrases in italics. We can use phrases like these to answer questions beginning with *When*.

仔细阅读以下句子，特别要注意用斜体印出的词组，我们可以用这些表示时间的短语来回答以When开头的疑问句。

a Phrases with *at*. 带at的短语

I always leave home *at 8 o'clock*. I begin work *at 9 o'clock*. I work all day and often get home late *at night*. 我总是8点钟离家，9点开始工作。我工作一整天，常常是晚上很晚才到家。

b Phrases with *in*. 带in的短语

I'm going out now. I'll be back *in ten minutes* or *in half an hour*. 我现在出去，大概在10分钟或半小时以后回来。

The Second World War began *in 1939* and ended *in 1945*. 第二次世界大战于1939年开始，于1945年结束。

Many tourists come here *in summer*. They usually come *in July* and *in August*. It is very quiet here *in winter*. The hotels are often empty *in January*, *February* and *in March*. 许多旅游者夏天到这里来。他们常在7、8月来。冬天这里很安静。1、2、3月份酒店常常是空的。

I'll see you *in the morning*. I can't see you *in the afternoon* or *in the evening*. 我将在早上见你，下午或晚上不行。

c Phrases with *on*. 带on的短语

I shall see him *on Wednesday*. I'm not free *on Tuesday or Thursday*. 我将在星期三见他，星期二和星期四我都没空。

My brother will arrive from Germany *on April 27th*. He will return *on May 5th*. 我的弟弟将于4月27日从德国到达这里。他将在5月5日返回。

d Other phrases. 其他短语

The shops are open *from 9 till 5*. 商店营业从9点至5点。

It rained heavily *during the night*. 夜里雨下得很大。

He will not arrive *until 10 o'clock*. 他要到10点钟才能到。

Exercises 练习

A Answer these questions on the passage.

根据课文回答以下问题。

1 When did we go to the Town Hall?

2 When would the clock strike twelve?

3 When did the clock stop?

B Supply the correct words in the following sentences.

用正确的介词填空。

1 He has gone abroad. He will return _____ two years' time.

2 _____ Saturdays I always go to the market.

3 I never go to the cinema _____ the week.

4 He ran a hundred metres _____ thirteen seconds.

5 I can't see him _____ the moment. I'm busy.

6 My birthday is _____ November 7th. I was born _____ 1974.

7 The days are very short _____ December.

8 We arrived at the village late _____ night. We left early _____ the morning.

9 I shall not hear from him _____ tomorrow.

C Write sentences using the following.
   用以下词组造句。

1 begin/3 o'clock.

2 bought/1980.

3 shop/from ... till.

4 children/school/morning.

5 finish/two years' time.

6 go for a walk/evening.

7 went to church/Sunday.

Special difficulties 难点

Any, Not ... Any and No

We can answer these questions in two ways. Both answers mean the same thing.
可以用两种不同的方式对以下疑问句作出否定的回答。这两种回答的意思是相同的。

Question	*Answer*
Is there any tea in the pot?	There isn't any tea in the pot.
	There's no tea in the pot.
Is there anyone at the door?	There isn't anyone at the door.
	There's no one at the door.
Is there anybody at the door?	There isn't anybody at the door.
	There's nobody at the door.
Is there anything in the box?	There isn't anything in the box.
	There's nothing in the box.
Did you go anywhere yesterday?	I didn't go anywhere yesterday.
	I went nowhere yesterday.

Exercises 练习

A Write negative answers to these questions in two different ways.
   用两种不同的方式来对以下疑问句作出否定的回答。

1 Have you any money?

2 Did you go anywhere in the holidays?

3 Did you buy anything this morning?

4 Was there anybody present when the accident happened?

B Change the form of these sentences.
   改写以下句子。

He hasn't any hobbies. He does not go anywhere. He does not see anybody. He is not interested in anything — except food!

Multiple choice questions 选择题

Comprehension 理解

1 The crowd gathered under the clock because _____ .

   (*a*) it was twenty to twelve   (*b*) they wanted to welcome the New Year

   (*c*) it was Wednesday evening   (*d*) the clock had stopped

2 They realized the clock had stopped _____ .

   (*a*) before midnight   (*b*) after midnight   (*c*) at midnight   (*d*) just in time

Structure 句型

3 They went to the Town Hall on Wednesday evening. They went _____ .

   (*a*) the evening   (*b*) on the evening   (*c*) evening   (*d*) in the evening

4 The people _____ under the Town Hall clock.

   (*a*) were   (*b*) was   (*c*) is   (*d*) be

5 _____will it strike? In twenty minutes' time.

   (*a*) When   (*b*) How long   (*c*) How long ago   (*d*) How much

6 What time did it stop? _____ five to twelve.

   (*a*) On   (*b*) At   (*c*) In   (*d*) During

7 Did _____ happen? No, nothing happened.

   (*a*) nothing   (*b*) anything   (*c*) any   (*d*) a thing

Vocabulary 词汇

8 How many times did the clock _____?

   (*a*) hit   (*b*) beat   (*c*) knock   (*d*) strike

9 It was fifteen minutes _____ eleven.

   (*a*) pass   (*b*) past   (*c*) passed   (*d*) pasted

10 A clock usually has two hands, a minute hand and _____ hand.

   (*a*) a second   (*b*) an hour   (*c*) a time   (*d*) a big

11 Most people wear or carry _____ .

   (*a*) an alarm clock   (*b*) an alarm   (*c*) a clock   (*d*) a watch

12 It refused to welcome the New Year. It _____ .

   (*a*) denied it   (*b*) wanted to   (*c*) didn't want to   (*d*) wished to

Sentence structure 句子结构

Join these two sentences, then check your answer against the text.

将以下两个简单句改写成为一个句子, 然后对照课文第1行, 核对你的答案。

It was Wednesday evening. We went to the Town Hall.

On _____ .

Lesson 10 Not for jazz 不适于演奏爵士乐

My father was shocked

First listen and then answer the question.

听录音，然后回答以下问题。

What happened to the clavichord?

We have an old musical instrument. It is called a clavichord. It was made in Germany in 1681. Our clavichord is kept in the living room. It has belonged to our family for a long time. The instrument was bought by my grandfather many years ago. Recently it was damaged
5 by a visitor. She tried to play jazz on it! She struck the keys too hard and two of the strings were broken. My father was shocked. Now we are not allowed to touch it. It is being repaired by a friend of my father's.

New words and expressions 生词和短语

jazz (title) /'dʒæz/ n. 爵士音乐
musical (l.1) /'mjuːzɪkəl/ adj. 音乐的
instrument (l.1) /'ɪnstrʊmənt/ n. 乐器
clavichord (l.1) /'klævɪkɔːd/ n. 古钢琴
recently (l.4) /'riːsəntli/ adv. 最近
damage (l.4) /'dæmɪdʒ/ v. 损坏

key (l.5) /kiː/ n. 琴键
string (l.6) /strɪŋ/ n.（乐器的）弦
shock (l.6) /ʃɒk/ v. 使不悦或生气，使震惊
allow (l.7) /ə'laʊ/ v. 允许，让
touch (l.7) /tʌtʃ/ v. 触摸

Notes on the text 课文注释

1 It is called a clavichord. 它被称作古钢琴。这是一个被动语态的句子。本课的许多动词都是被动语态，如："Our clavichord is kept ...", "The instrument was bought ...", "it was damaged ...", "two of the strings were broken" 等。

2 a friend of my father's, 我父亲的一位朋友。在英语中我们通常用 's 和 of 结构来表示所有格。's 的结构通常用在人名和表示人称的名词的末尾，而 of 结构则常与无生命的名词连用。在这个例句中同时使用了 's 和 of 的结构，这被称作双重所有格。

参考译文

我家有件古乐器，被称作古钢琴，是 1681 年德国造的。我们的这架古钢琴存放在起居室里。我们家有这件乐器已经很久了，是我祖父在很多年以前买的。可它最近被一个客人弄坏了，因为她用它来弹奏爵士乐。她在击琴键时用力过猛，损坏了两根琴弦。我父亲大为吃惊，不许我们再动它。父亲的一个朋友正在修理这件乐器。

Summary writing 摘要写作

Answer these questions *in not more than 45 words*.
回答下列问题，将答案组成一个段落，不要超过45个单词。

1 Do we own an old clavichord, or do we own a new piano?

2 When was it made?

3 Who bought the instrument many years ago?

4 Who damaged it recently?

5 What did she try to do?

6 What did she break?

7 Who is repairing it now?

Key structures 关键句型

It was made in Germany in 1681. （一般过去时中的）被动语态

在第 1 册的第 141-144 课中我们接触到了被动语态这一语法现象, 现在我们来对比一下被动语态与主动语态在使用上的区别。

a Read these two questions and answers.

读一读这两个问题和答案。

Who built this bridge? 谁修建的这座桥？

Prisoners of war built this bridge in 1942. 战俘于 1942 年建的这座桥。

When was this bridge built? 桥是什么时候修建的？

This bridge was built in 1942. 桥是 1942 年建的。

In the first question we want to know *who* built the bridge. In the second question we want to learn about *the bridge*.

在第一个问题中我们想知道是谁建了这座桥, 在第二个问题中我们想弄清有关桥的一些情况。因此, 第一句使用了主动语态, 第二句运用了被动语态。

We can still say *who* built it. We can say: 我们也可以讲清是什么人修建的这座桥，用 "by + 动作执行者" 的结构来表示, 我们可以说:

This bridge was built *by prisoners of war* in 1942. 这座桥是战俘于 1942 年修建的。

b Now read these pairs of sentences carefully. The first sentence in each pair tells us about *a person*. (Who) The second tells us about a thing. (What or Which)

仔细地阅读以下几对句子, 每对中的第一句话告诉我们一个人（回答 "谁"）, 第二句话告诉我们一件事（回答 "什么" 或 "哪一个"）。

Workmen are building a new road outside my house. (Who) 工人们正在我的房子外面修一条新路。

A new road is being built outside my house. (What) 我的房子外面有一条新路在建设之中。

The newsagent delivers our papers every morning. (Who) 每天上午送报人来送我们的报纸。

Our papers are delivered every morning. (What) 我们的报纸每天上午送到。

The postman delivered a letter this morning. (Who) 今天上午邮递员送来了一封信。

A letter was delivered this morning. (What) 今天上午来了一封信。

c Now read these sentences:

仔细阅读以下句子:

Instead of saying: *We can say*:

除了这种表述方法外: 还可以说:

The police arrested the thief.   The thief was arrested (by the police).

He gave me a present.   I was given a present.

The headmaster has punished the boy.   The boy has been punished (by the headmaster).

Exercises 练习

A Answer these questions on the passage. Write a complete answer to each question.
回答以下有关课文的问题，写出完整的句子。

1 What is our old musical instrument called?

2 Where was it made?

3 Where is it kept?

4 When was it bought?

5 When was it damaged?

6 How many strings were broken?

7 How did my father feel about this?

8 What aren't we allowed to do?

9 What is being done to the clavichord?

B Change the form of the phrases in italics. Do not refer to the passage until you finish the exercise.
将斜体印出的短语改成被动语态，完成练习后再对照课文核对你的答案。

We have an old musical instrument. *We call it a clavichord. Someone made it* in Germany in 1681. *We keep our clavichord* in the living room. *My grandfather bought the instrument* many years ago. Recently *a visitor damaged it* ... She struck the keys too hard and *broke two of the strings. This shocked my father. Now he does not allow us* to touch it. *A friend of my father's is repairing it.*

Special difficulties 难点

a Made in, Made of, Made from, Made by 与被动语态的 made 连用的几个介词

Made in (a country) 表示产地：It *was made in* Germany. (ll.1-2)

Made of (a material) 表示用某种材料制成：The tea pot *is made of* silver. 这个茶壶是银制的。

Made from (a number of materials) 表示用数种材料制成：Glass *is made from* sand and lime. 玻璃是由沙和石灰制成的。

Made by (someone) 表示制造人：This cake *was made by* my sister. 这块蛋糕是我姐姐做的。

Exercise 练习

Supply the correct words in the following.
用正确的介词填空。

1 Is your watch made _____ gold?

2 These knives were made _____ Sheffield.

3 This cake was made _____ sugar, flour, butter and eggs.

b A friend of my father's (ll.7-8) 见课文中第7-8行的双重所有格

Instead of saying:

除了这种表述方法外：

He is one of my father's friends.

Tom lent me one of his books.

He is one of my friends.

We can say:

还可以说：

He is a friend of my father's.

Tom lent me a book of his.

He is a friend of mine.

Exercise 练习

Change the form of the phrases in italics.
改写以下斜体部分。

1 He borrowed *one of my records*.

2 She showed me *one of John's pictures*.

3 It was *one of her ideas*.

4 *One of your letters* was found on my desk.

5 *Some of their friends* came to see me.

Multiple choice questions 选择题

Comprehension 理解

1 The old musical instrument _____ .

(a) has been in the family for a long time

(b) was bought recently

(c) was sold recently

(d) was repaired recently

2 How did the visitor damage the clavichord?

(a) She played jazz on it.

(b) She played it.

(c) She cut the strings.

(d) She hit the keys too hard.

Structure 句型

3 Our clavichord is kept in the living room. That's where we _____ it.

(a) kept   (b) have kept   (c) are keeping   (d) keep

4 It has belonged to our family for years. It's the _____ .

(a) families   (b) families'   (c) family's   (d) familys'

5 The family have had the clavichord _____ many years.

(a) since   (b) for   (c) from   (d) by

6 Who _____ it? Grandfather did.

(a) buy   (b) was bought   (c) bought   (d) did buy

7 We are not allowed to touch it. We _____ touch it.

(a) mustn't   (b) mustn't to   (c) haven't to   (d) don't have to

Vocabulary 词汇

8 What's it _____ ? A clavichord.

(a) told   (b) said   (c) called   (d) spoken

9 It's kept in the living room. That's where we _____ it.

(a) have   (b) hold   (c) lift   (d) carry

10 The visitor damaged it. She _____ it.

(a) hurt   (b) pained   (c) broke   (d) destroyed

11 Recently it was damaged. She damaged it _____ .

(a) late   (b) lastly   (c) lately   (d) finally

12 A friend of my father's is _____ the clavichord.

(a) mending   (b) making   (c) doing   (d) building

Sentence structure 句子结构

Rewrite this sentence, then check your answer against the text.

改写以下句子, 然后对照课文第 3-4 行, 核对你的答案。

It was my grandfather who bought the instrument many years ago.

The instrument _____ .

Lesson 11   One good turn deserves another   礼尚往来

🔊 **First listen and then answer the question.**

听录音, 然后回答以下问题。

Who paid for Tony's dinner?

'you can pay for my dinner!'

I was having dinner at a restaurant when Tony Steele came in. Tony worked in a lawyer's office years ago, but he is now working at a bank. He gets a good salary, but he always borrows money from his friends and never pays it back. Tony saw me and came and sat at the
5 same table. He has never borrowed money from me. While he was eating, I asked him to lend me twenty pounds. To my surprise, he gave me the money immediately. 'I have never borrowed any money from you,' Tony said, 'so now you can pay for my dinner!'

New words and expressions 生词和短语

turn (title) /tɜːn/ *n.* 行为, 举止
deserve (title) /dɪ'zɜːv/ *v.* 应得到, 值得
lawyer (l.2) /'lɔːjə/ *n.* 律师

bank (l.3) /bæŋk/ *n.* 银行
salary (l.3) /'sæləri/ *n.* 工资
immediately (l.7) /ɪ'miːdiətli/ *adv.* 立刻

Notes on the text 课文注释

1 One good turn deserves another. 这是句谚语, 意思是对于别人的善意或帮助应作出相应的回报。
2 gets a good salary, 有一份很高的薪水。
3 never pays it back, 从不归还。

参考译文

　　我正在一家饭馆吃饭, 托尼·斯蒂尔走了进来。托尼曾在一家律师事务所工作, 而现在正在一家银行上班。他的薪水很高, 但他却总是向朋友借钱, 并且从来不还。托尼看见了我, 就走过来和我坐到一张桌子前。他从未向我借过钱。当他吃饭时, 我提出向他借20英镑。令我惊奇的是, 他立刻把钱给了我。"我还从未向你借过钱," 托尼说道, "所以现在你可以替我付饭钱了!"

Summary writing 摘要写作

Answer these questions *in not more than 50 words*.

回答下列问题, 将答案组成一个段落, 不要超过50个单词。

1 Where were you having dinner?
2 Did you see Tony Steele after a while or not?
3 What does he always borrow from his friends?
4 Did Tony sit at your table, or did he sit somewhere else?
5 How much did you ask him to lend you?
6 Did he give you the money at once or not?

7   What did he want you to do?

Key structures 关键句型

Review KS2-10 复习第2-10课的关键句型

Now, Often and Always **(KS2)**（第2课）

What happened? **(KS3)**（第3课）

What has happened? **(KS4)**（第4课）

What were you doing when I telephoned? **(KS7)**（第7课）

It was made in Germany. **(KS10)**（第10课）

Exercises 练习

A   Which verbs in the passage tell us *a* what is happening now; *b* what always happens; *c* what happened; *d* what has happened; *e* what was happening when/while ...?
在课文中选出表达以下意思的动词：a 现在正在进行的动作；b 通常发生的事情；c 过去发生的事情；d 已经发生的事情；e 过去某一特定时刻正在进行的动作。

B   Give the correct form of the verbs in parentheses. Do not refer to the passage until you finish the exercise.
用括号中动词的正确形式填空，完成练习后再对照课文，核对你的答案。

I _____ (have) dinner at a restaurant when Tony Steele _____ (come) in. Tony _____ (work) in a lawyer's office years ago, but he now _____ (work) at a bank. He _____ (get) a good salary, but he always _____ (borrow) money from his friends and never _____ (pay) it back. Tony _____ (see) me and _____ (come) and _____ (sit) at the same table. He never _____ (borrow) money from me. While he _____ (eat), I _____ (ask) him to lend me twenty pounds. To my surprise he _____ (give) me the money immediately. 'I never _____ (borrow) any money from you,' Tony _____ (say), 'so now you can pay for my dinner!'

C   Give the correct form of the verbs in parentheses.
用括号中动词的正确形式填空。

1   He usually _____ (get) up at 7 o'clock, but this morning he _____ (get) up at 6 o'clock.

2   So far, we not _____ (have) a reply.

3   While he _____ (write) on the blackboard, the children _____ (talk).

4   I can't come now. At the moment I _____ (type) a letter.

5   As the royal visitors _____ (pass), the people cheered.

D   Supply the correct form of the verbs in parentheses.
用括号中动词的正确形式填空，如有问题可参见第10课的关键句型。

The Taj Mahal _____ (build) in the seventeenth century for the emperor Shah Jahan. A few years after he _____ (become) ruler, his wife, Mumtaz-i-Mahal, _____ (die). The Taj Mahal _____ (build) in her honour. Experts _____ (call) in from many parts of the world to construct the domes and to decorate the walls. The Taj Mahal which _____ (begin) in 1632 and _____ (complete) in 1654 _____ (cost) a fortune. Up to the present day, it _____ (visit) by millions of people.

Special difficulties 难点

a   I asked him to lend me twenty pounds. (l.6)

语序：有些动词的后面先加上一个名词或代词作宾语，再加动词不定式作宾语补足语。

Study the word order in these sentences.

注意以下句中的语序，在动词后面均有一个代词或名词（用斜体印出）。

He wants *me* to ask you a question. 他让我问你一个问题。

Frank helped *Tom* to dig this hole. 弗兰克帮助汤姆挖了这个洞。

She taught *her son* to read. 她教儿子读书。

We advised *them* to stay at home. 我们建议他们待在家里。

They did not allow *us* to enter the museum before 9 o'clock. 他们不允许我们在9点之前进博物馆。

Exercises 练习

A   Put the words in parentheses in their correct order.

将括号内的词按正确的语序排好。

1 The officer ordered (to fire, at the enemy, the men).

2 He wants (his wife, this dress, to wear).

3 She wants (us, it, to explain).

4 I cannot allow (the room, him, to enter).

B   Write similar sentences using the following.

模仿以上例句完成以下句子。

1 He asked _____   2 We prefer _____   3 He taught _____

4 My mother wished _____   5 Do you want _____ ?

b   Words often confused 经常容易混淆的词

Salary (l.3) and *Wages*.

Salary: He collects his *salary* at the end of each month. 他每个月末领取工资。

Wages: The workmen collected their *wages* at the end of the week. 工人们每周末领工资。

Borrow and Lend.

Borrow: He has never *borrowed* money from me. (l.5)

Lend: I asked him to *lend* me £20. (l.6)

I asked him to *lend* £20 to me. (**SD3**)（参见第3课的难点）

Exercise 练习

Use any of the above words in the following sentences.

用上面的词填空。

1 He is a bank manager and he gets a good _____ .

2 I _____ him some money and he said he would give it back to me when he got his _____ .

3 Yesterday he _____ my laptop. I hope he returns it soon.

4 The postmen are on strike again. They want higher _____ .

5 Workmen's _____ have gone up a lot in the last year.

Multiple choice questions 选择题

Comprehension 理解

1 Tony sat at the same table as the writer and _____ .

(a) borrowed some money from him   (b) lent some money to him

(c) paid back some money to him   (d) begged for some money

2 Tony wants the writer to pay for his dinner because _____ .

(a) he gave him £20

(b) the writer hasn't ever lent him any money before

(c) the writer has never borrowed any money from Tony before

(d) he hasn't any money

Structure 句型

3 Tony Steele _____ into the restaurant when the writer was having dinner.

(a) was going   (b) went   (c) has gone   (d) did go

4 Tony is working at a bank _____ .

(a) at the moment   (b) a year ago   (c) since last year   (d) for a year

5 _____ he has never borrowed any money from the writer.

(a) Last week   (b) Up till now   (c) Since   (d) A week ago

6 _____ did he ask for? £20.

(a) How many   (b) How   (c) How much   (d) How few

7 I have never borrowed any money from you. I _____ lend me some money.

(a) want to   (b) want   (c) want you to   (d) you want to

Vocabulary 词汇

8 He gets a good salary. His salary is very _____ .

(a) good   (b) well   (c) fine   (d) beautiful

9 Tony usually gets his salary at the end of the _____ .

(a) day   (b) year   (c) month   (d) week

10 Tony must pay the money back. He must _____ .

(a) pay it again   (b) pay it   (c) repay it   (d) pay it once more

11 There aren't enough chairs here for us all. Please bring _____ one.

(a) other   (b) another   (c) extra   (d) a different

12 He gave him the money immediately. He gave him the money _____ .

(a) soon   (b) in a hurry   (c) once more   (d) at once

Sentence structure 句子结构

Rewrite this sentence, then check your answer against the text.

改写以下句子, 然后对照课文第 6-7 行, 核对你的答案。

I was surprised when he gave me the money immediately.

To _____ .

Lesson 12   Goodbye and good luck   再见，一路顺风

First listen and then answer the question.

听录音，然后回答以下问题。

Where is Captain Alison going and how?

Our neighbour, Captain Charles Alison, will sail from Portsmouth tomorrow. We'll meet him at the harbour early in the morning. He will be in his small boat, *Topsail*. *Topsail* is a famous little boat. It has sailed across the Atlantic many times. Captain Alison will set
5 out at eight o'clock, so we'll have plenty of time. We'll see his boat and then we'll say goodbye to him. He will be away for two months. We are very proud of him. He will take part in an important race across the Atlantic.

We'll say goodbye to him

New words and expressions   生词和短语

luck (title) /lʌk/ *n.* 运气，幸运

captain (l.1) /ˈkæptən/ *n.* 船长

sail (l.1) /seɪl/ *v.* 航行

harbour (l.2) /ˈhɑːbə/ *n.* 港口

proud (l.7) /praʊd/ *adj.* 自豪的

important (l.7) /ɪmˈpɔːtənt/ *adj.* 重要的

Notes on the text   课文注释

1   Captain Charles Alison, 查尔斯·艾利森船长。

2   the Atlantic /ət'læntɪk/, 大西洋，全称为 "the Atlantic Ocean"。

参考译文

我们的邻居查尔斯·艾利森船长明天就要从朴次茅斯起航了。明天一大早我们将在码头为他送行。他将乘坐他的"涛波赛"号小艇。"涛波赛"号是艘有名的小艇，它已经多次横渡大西洋。艾利森船长将于8点钟起航，因此我们有充裕的时间。我们将参观他的船，然后和他告别。他要离开两个月，我们真为他感到自豪，他将参加一次重大的横渡大西洋的比赛。

Summary writing   摘要写作

Answer these questions *in not more than 45 words.*

回答下列问题，将答案组成一个段落，不要超过45个单词。

1   Whom shall we meet at Portsmouth Harbour early tomorrow morning?

2   Where will he be?

3   At what time will he leave?

4   Shall we say goodbye to him, or shall we travel with him?

5   What will he take part in?

Key structures 关键句型

I'll see you tomorrow. 一般将来时

These sentences tell us about the future. Read them carefully. Pay close attention to the words in italics.

这些句子讲的是将来要发生的事情。一般将来时用shall或will加上动词原形来表示，shall常用在第一人称的代词 I 或 we 的后面；而 will 则可用于所有人称，在书写时和口语中，常可缩略为'll。仔细读一读以下例句，要特别注意用斜体印出的部分。

I will see you tomorrow. *I'll see* you at 3 o'clock. 明天我会见你，我将在3点钟见你。

We will travel by air. *We'll be* at the airport tomorrow morning. 我们将乘飞机旅行。明天上午我们将在机场。

George will be here this evening. *He'll come* by train. 今晚乔治会到达这里。他将乘火车来。

Alice will meet him at the station. *She'll be* there at 5 o'clock. 艾丽丝会在车站接他。她将在5点到达车站。

The train will arrive at 4.55. *It'll be* here soon. 火车4点55分到达。它很快就要到了。

You will miss the train. *You'll be* late. 你会误了火车的，你会迟到。

They will come here on foot. *They'll walk* from the station. 他们将步行来这里。他们会从车站开始走。

Exercises 练习

A Underline all the verbs in the passage which tell us *what will happen*.
在课文中所有表示将来发生的事情的动词下面画上横线。

B Give the correct form of the verbs in parentheses. Do not refer to the passage until you finish the exercise.
用括号中动词的正确形式填空，完成练习后再对照课文，核对你的答案。

Our neighbour, Captain Charles Alison, _____ (sail) from Portsmouth tomorrow. We _____ (meet) him at the harbour early in the morning. He _____ (be) in his small boat, *Topsail*. *Topsail* is a famous little boat. It has sailed across the Atlantic many times. Captain Alison _____ (set out) at eight o'clock, so we _____ (have) plenty of time. We _____ (see) his boat and then we _____ (say) goodbye to him. He _____ (be) away for two months. We are very proud of him. He _____ (take part) in an important race across the Atlantic.

C In the paragraph below, the verbs in italics tell us *what happened*. Write the passage again. Change the verbs in italics so that they tell us *what will happen*.
在下面这段文章中，用斜体印出的动词表示的是过去发生的事情，改写这些动词，使它们表述将来要发生的动作。

I *went* to the theatre with my friend Reg. Reg and I *saw* the first performance of a play called 'The End of the Road'. After the play, the producer *gave* a short speech. He *spoke* to the audience about the play. The play *was* very successful and I think a great many people *enjoyed* it very much.

Special difficulties 难点

a In each sentence, *be* combines with a different adverb. Each combination has a different meaning.
各句中的be与不同的副词连用，意思各不相同。

He *will be away* for two months. (l.6)

I'm going out now. *I'll be back* at six o'clock. 我要走了，将在6点钟的时候回来。

If anyone telephones, tell them *I'll be out* all morning. 如果有人来电话，告诉他们我一上午都不在。

I went to Ted's house and asked to see him but he *wasn't in*. 我去特德的家，希望能见到他，但他不在。

Why don't you forget about it? *It's all over*. (It is finished.) 你为什么不把它忘掉？事情已经过去了。

Unit 1 Lesson 12

What's on at the local cinema this week?这星期本地的电影院上映什么片子？

She is very ill. She can't start work yet. She *is not up to* it. (She is not capable of it.) 她的病很重，还不能开始工作。她的身体还不能胜任。

b Now look at the verb *set* in these sentences.

注意下面句子中的动词set。

Captain Alison will *set out* at eight o'clock. (ll.4-5) (He will start his journey.) 艾理森船长将于8点出发。

Tom and I *set off* early in the morning. (We started our journey.) 我和汤姆一早就出发了。

Jansen *set up* a new world record for the 400 metres. 珍森为400米跑创造了一个新的世界纪录。

Exercise 练习

Replace the words in italics by the correct phrase with *be* or *set*.

用短语动词be或set来替代下列句子中斜体印出的部分。

1 He *has not yet returned*. He will *return* in ten minutes.

2 A new play is *being performed* at the Globe Theatre.

3 When the concert *ended*, we went home.

4 They will *leave* very early tomorrow morning.

5 You can't take the exam yet. You are not *capable of* it.

6 He will be *absent* from home for two months.

7 She swam across the English Channel and *created* a new world record.

Multiple choice questions 选择题

Comprehension 理解

1 *Topsail* is famous because _____ .

　(*a*) it is a little boat

　(*b*) it belongs to Captain Alison

　(*c*) it is a little boat which has sailed across the Atlantic many times

　(*d*) it will sail from Portsmouth tomorrow

2 *Topsail* _____ .

　(*a*) will win the race across the Atlantic　　(*b*) has won the race across the Atlantic

　(*c*) will be in the race across the Atlantic　　(*d*) was in the race across the Atlantic

Structure 句型

3 Our neighbour, _____ name is Charles Alison, will sail tomorrow.

　(*a*) whose　　　(*b*) whose his　　　(*c*) his　　　(*d*) of whom

4 He will sail from Portsmouth. He is _____ Portsmouth now.

　(*a*) to　　　(*b*) from　　　(*c*) on　　　(*d*) at

5 His boat, _____ is *Topsail,* is famous.

　(*a*) whose the name　　(*b*) the whose name　　(*c*) of whom the name　　(*d*) the name of which

6 We'll have plenty of time. There will be _____ time to see him.

　(*a*) enough　　(*b*) almost enough　　(*c*) less than enough　　(*d*) hardly enough

7 We'll _____ .

　(*a*) say him goodbye　　(*b*) tell him goodbye　　(*c*) tell goodbye to him　　(*d*) say goodbye to him

58

Vocabulary 词汇

8 He's our neighbour so he lives _____ us.

    (*a*) near   (*b*) a long way from   (*c*) in a different town from   (*d*) next door

9 It has sailed across the Atlantic many times. It has sailed across the Atlantic _____ .

    (*a*) sometimes   (*b*) always   (*c*) often   (*d*) usually

10 He will set out at eight o'clock. That's when _____ .

    (*a*) the trip ends   (*b*) the journey ends   (*c*) the voyage stops   (*d*) the journey begins

11 He will take part in a race. He will _____ in it.

    (*a*) be   (*b*) take place   (*c*) act   (*d*) do

12 The Atlantic is _____ .

    (*a*) an ocean   (*b*) a sea   (*c*) a river   (*d*) a lake

Sentence structure 句子结构

Arrange these groups of words in the correct order, then check your answer against the text.

按正确的语序排列以下单词和短语，然后对照课文第2行，核对你的答案。

him/we shall meet/early/in the morning/at the harbour

Lesson 13　The Greenwood Boys　绿林少年

🔊 **First listen and then answer the question.**
听录音，然后回答以下问题。

Why will the police have a difficult time?

The Greenwood Boys are a group of pop singers. At present, they are visiting all parts of the country. They will be arriving here tomorrow. They will be coming by train and most of the young people in the town will be meeting them at the station. Tomorrow
5 evening they will be singing at the Workers' Club. The Greenwood Boys will be staying for five days. During this time, they will give five performances. As usual, the police will have a difficult time. They will be trying to keep order. It is always the same on these occasions.

a group of pop singers

New words and expressions　生词和短语

group (l.1) /gruːp/ *n.* 小组，团体
pop singer (l.1) /ˈpɒp-ˌsɪŋə/ 流行歌手
club (l.5) /klʌb/ *n.* 俱乐部

performance (l.7) /pəˈfɔːməns/ *n.* 演出
occasion (l.9) /əˈkeɪʒən/ *n.* 场合

Notes on the text　课文注释

1　all parts of the country, 全国各地。
2　will be arriving, 将要到达。
　　这句话中的时态被称作将来进行时，用来表示最近的将来正在进行的动作或说话人设想已经安排好的事情。
3　by train, 乘火车（来），以此类推，我们可以说by air, by sea, by bus等。
4　as usual, 和往常一样。
5　keep order, 维持秩序。

参考译文

　　"绿林少年"是一个流行歌曲演唱团。目前他们正在全国各地巡回演出，明天就要到达此地。他们将乘火车来，镇上的大部分青年人将到车站迎接他们。明晚他们将在工人俱乐部演出。"绿林少年"准备在此逗留5天。在此期间，他们将演出5场。同往常一样，警察的日子将不好过，他们将设法维持秩序。每逢这种场合，情况都是这样。

Summary writing　摘要写作

Answer these questions *in not more than 50 words.*
回答下列问题，将答案组成一个段落，不要超过50个单词。

1　Are the Greenwood Boys singers, or are they dancers?
2　When will they be coming here?

60

3　Who will be meeting them at the station?

4　How many performances will they give?

5　What will the police be trying to do as usual?

Key structures 关键句型

What will you be doing tomorrow? 将来进行时

a　Read these sentences carefully. Pay close attention to the verbs in italics.

仔细阅读以下句子，特别注意用斜体印出的动词。

Now	Tomorrow
I *am writing* letters now.	I *shall be writing* letters all day tomorrow.
我现在正在写信。	明天我将整天写信。
We *are decorating* this room.	We *shall be decorating* this room tomorrow.
我们正在布置这个房间。	明天我们将布置这个房间。
He *is working* in the garden.	He *will be working* in the garden tomorrow.
他正在花园里干活。	明天他将在花园里干活。
She *is getting* ready for the party.	She *will be getting* ready for the party tomorrow.
她正在为聚会作准备。	明天她将为聚会作准备。
Are you washing your car?	*Will* you *be washing* your car tomorrow?
你正在洗你的汽车吗?	明天你将洗你的汽车吗?
They *are playing* football.	They *will be playing* football tomorrow.
他们正在踢足球。	明天他们将踢足球。

b　Now read these pairs of sentences. Each pair has the same meaning.

对比以下句子，用一般将来时和将来进行时所表述的含义是一致的。

Instead of:	We can say:
除了这种表述方法外:	还可以说:
I'll come to your house tomorrow.	*I'll be coming* to your house tomorrow.
我明天去你家。	
He'll arrive in a minute.	*He'll be arriving* in a minute.
他马上就到。	
He'll catch the 4 o'clock train.	*He'll be catching* the 4 o'clock train.
他将乘4点钟的火车。	
I'll see you next week.	*I'll be seeing* you next week.
我下周见你。	
She'll meet him at the station.	*She'll be meeting* him at the station.
她将去车站接他。	

Exercises 练习

A　Underline all the verbs in the passage which tell us *what will be happening*.

在课文中所有表示将来进行时的动词下面画上横线。

B　Give the correct form of the verbs in parentheses. Do not refer to the passage until you finish the exercise.

用括号中动词的正确形式填空，完成练习后再对照课文，核对你的答案。

The Greenwood Boys are a group of popular singers. At present, they are visiting all parts of the country. They ＿＿＿＿＿＿ (arrive) here tomorrow. They ＿＿＿＿＿＿ (come) by train and most of the young people in the town

_____ (meet) them at the station. Tomorrow evening they _____ (sing) at the Workers' Club. The Green-wood Boys _____ (stay) for five days. During this time, they will give five performances. As usual, the police will have a difficult time. They _____ (try) to keep order. It is always the same on these occasions.

C Change the form of the verbs in italics so that they tell us what will be happening.
将下列句子中用斜体印出的动词改写为将来进行时。

1 I *am ironing* the clothes.

2 The train *will arrive* in a few minutes.

3 We*'ll see* you in the morning.

4 We *are watching* the match.

5 He *is correcting* exercise books.

Special difficulties 难点

The Workers' Club (l.5) (Compare **SD60**) 名词的所有格（对比第60课的难点）

Read these questions and answers. Pay close attention to the position of the apostrophe (') in each answer.
读一读以下的问句和回答，注意名词所有格的形式。其规则为：(a) 在单数名词及不以s结尾的人名后加's; (b) 在以s结尾的单数名词后加's; (c) 在规则的复数名词的s后面加所有格符号'; (d) 在以s结尾的人名后面既可用's也可用所有格符号'。

Whose is this car?	It is Tom's.	It belongs to Tom.
Whose is this handbag?	It is Susan's.	It belongs to Susan.
Whose is this hammer?	It is the workman's.	It belongs to the workman.
Whose are these exercise books?	They are the students' exercise books.	They belong to the students.
Whose are these toys?	They are the children's.	They belong to the children.
Whose are these tools?	They are the workmen's.	They belong to the workmen.
Whose is this car?	It is James' (*or* James's) car.	It belongs to James.
When will he arrive?	He will arrive in three hours' time.	
How much minced meat do you want?	I want ten pounds' worth of minced meat.	

Exercise 练习

Answer these questions, using the words in parentheses. Put the apostrophe in the right place.
用括号中的词或词组来回答问题，注意所有格符号的位置。

1 Whose is this umbrella? (George)

2 Whose is this idea? (Jean)

3 Whose is this handbag? (That woman)

4 Whose poetry do you like best? (Keats)

5 Whose are these clothes? (The children)

6 Whose are these uniforms? (The soldiers)

7 When will you leave? (In six hours' time)

8 How much damage was there?
   (A hundred pounds worth)

Multiple choice questions 选择题

Comprehension 理解

1 The pop singers will attract _____ in the town.
   (*a*) all the people
   (*b*) mainly the young people
   (*c*) only the old people
   (*d*) no one

2 The police will be there _____ .

(*a*) because there will be trouble

(*b*) because the singers are popular

(*c*) because there will be a lot of young people there

(*d*) to prevent trouble

Structure 句型

3 Most of the young people will be there. _____ the young people will be there.

(*a*) A lot   (*b*) Nearly all   (*c*) Some   (*d*) Many

4 How _____ staying? For five days.

(*a*) long they will be   (*b*) they will be   (*c*) long will they be   (*d*) long they be

5 During this time, they will give five performances. That's what they'll do _____ this time.

(*a*) in   (*b*) on   (*c*) for   (*d*) while

6 The police will have a difficult time _____ .

(*a*) as usually   (*b*) as usual   (*c*) than usual   (*d*) from usual

7 The police _____ expecting the singers to arrive soon.

(*a*) is   (*b*) are   (*c*) will   (*d*) was

Vocabulary 词汇

8 They are pop singers. So _____ .

(*a*) they are folk singers

(*b*) they are public singers

(*c*) everyone likes them

(*d*) no one likes them

9 At present they are visiting all parts of the country. They are doing this _____ .

(*a*) now   (*b*) for a short time   (*c*) in future   (*d*) all the time

10 They are visiting all parts of the country. So they will go _____ .

(*a*) to cities, towns and villages

(*b*) only to towns

(*c*) only to villages

(*d*) only to cities

11 The Greenwood Boys will give five performances. They will give five _____ .

(*a*) recitals   (*b*) executions   (*c*) plays   (*d*) songs

12 It's always the same on these occasions. It's always the same at _____ like this.

(*a*) situations   (*b*) conditions   (*c*) places   (*d*) times

Sentence structure 句子结构

Read this sentence:

读读这句话：

They will be coming and the young people will be meeting them.

Now add the following phrases:

在适当的位置加进以下短语：

at the station, in the town, most of and by train.

Check your answer against the text.

对照课文第3-4行核对你的答案。

Lesson 14   Do you speak English?   你会讲英语吗?

First listen and then answer the question.

听录音, 然后回答以下问题。

Did the young man speak English?

'Do you speak English?'

I had an amusing experience last year. After I had left a small village in the south of France, I drove on to the next town. On the way, a young man waved to me. I stopped and he asked me for a lift. As soon as he had got into the car, I said good morning to him in French and he replied in the same language. Apart from a few
5 words, I do not know any French at all. Neither of us spoke during the journey. I had nearly reached the town, when the young man suddenly said, very slowly, 'Do you speak English?' As I soon learnt, he was English himself!

New words and expressions   生词和短语

amusing (l.1) /əˈmjuːzɪŋ/ *adj.* 好笑的, 有趣的

experience (l.1) /ɪkˈspɪəriəns/ *n.* 经历

wave (l.3) /weɪv/ *v.* 招手

lift (l.4) /lɪft/ *n.* 搭便车

reply (l.5) /rɪˈplaɪ/ *v.* 回答

language (l.5) /ˈlæŋɡwɪdʒ/ *n.* 语言

journey (l.7) /ˈdʒɜːni/ *n.* 旅行

Notes on the text   课文注释

1 I drove on to the next town. 我继续驶往下一个城镇。
句中的副词on有 "继续地", "不停顿地" 的意思。

2 on the way, 在途中。

3 ask for a lift, 要求搭车。

4 apart from, 除了……以外。

5 As I soon learnt, he was English himself! 我很快就知道, 他自己就是个英国人。

参考译文

去年我有过一次有趣的经历。在离开法国南部的一个小村庄后, 我继续驶往下一个城镇。途中, 一个青年人向我招手。我把车停下, 他向我提出要求搭车。他一上车, 我就用法语向他问早上好, 他也同样用法语回答我。除了个别几个单词外, 我根本不会法语。旅途中我们谁也没讲话。就要到达那个镇时, 那青年突然开了口, 慢慢地说道:"你会讲英语吗? "我很快了解到, 他自己就是个英国人!

Summary writing   摘要写作

Answer these questions *in not more than 55 words.*

回答下列问题, 将答案组成一个段落, 不要超过55个单词。

1 Whom did the writer give a lift to in the south of France last year?

2 Did they greet each other in English or in French?

3 Does the writer speak any French or not?

4 Did they sit in silence, or did they talk to each other?

5 What did the young man say at the end of the journey?

6 Was he English himself, or was he French?

Key structures 关键句型

After he had finished work he went home. 过去完成时

在第1册的第119-120课，我们第一次接触到了过去完成时。有人认为，过去完成时是表示"很久以前发生的事情"，这个概念是错误的。过去完成时常常用来表示发生在过去的两个事件、动作中哪一个发生在前。

Read these two sentences.

读一读这两句话。

He finished work. He went home. 他结束了工作。他回家了。

We can join these two sentences together with the word *after*.

我们可以用after把这两句话连在一起。

We can say: 我们可以说:

After he had finished work he went home. 他结束工作后就回家了。

Note how these sentences have been joined. Pay close attention to the words in italics.

注意以下句子是如何连在一起的，要特别注意用斜体印出的词。

The children ran away. They broke the window. 孩子们跑了。他们打碎了玻璃。

The children ran away *after they had broken the window*. 孩子们打碎了玻璃之后跑了。

The sun set. We returned to our hotel. 太阳下山了。我们回到了旅馆。

As soon as the sun had set we returned to our hotel. 太阳一下山我们就回到了旅馆。

He finished lunch. He asked for a glass of water. 他吃完了中午饭。他要一杯水。

When he had finished lunch he asked for a glass of water. 他吃完中午饭后要了一杯水。

I did not understand the problem. He explained it. 我不懂这个问题。他解释了。

I did not understand the problem *until he had explained* it. 在他解释之前我不懂这个问题。

Exercises 练习

A These questions are about the passage. Write a complete sentence in answer to each question.

这些问题都是有关课文的。用一个完整的句子来回答以下每个问题。

1 When did you drive on to the next town?

2 When did you say good morning to him in French?

3 When did the young man say 'Do you speak English?'?

B Join these sentences together. Do not refer to the passage until you finish the exercise.

把以下句子连在一起，完成练习后再对照课文核对你的答案。

1 I left a small village in the south of France. I drove on to the next town.

2 He got into the car. I said good morning to him in French.

3 I nearly reached the town. The young man said, 'Do you speak English?'

C Join these pairs of sentences with the words given in parentheses.

用括号中的词将以下句子连到一起。

1 (After) She wrote the letter. She went to the post office.

2 (After) He had dinner. He went to the cinema.

3 (When) I fastened my seat belt. The plane took off.

4 We did not disturb him. (until) He finished work.

5 (As soon as) He left the room. I turned on the radio.

6 He was very ill. (before) He died.

D Give the correct form of the verbs in parentheses.
   用括号中动词的正确形式填空。

1 The moment he had said this, he _____ (regret) it.

2 It _____ (begin) to rain before she took a taxi.

3 When all the guests had left, Derek _____ (arrive).

Special difficulties 难点

Words often confused 经常容易混淆的词

a *Ask* and *Ask for*. He *asked* me *for* a lift. (ll.3-4)

   Ask (a question) 问（一个问题）: After the lesson, he *asked* me a question. 课后他问了我一个问题。

   Ask for (something) 要求（某样东西）: He *asked for* an apple. 他要一个苹果。

b *Except, except for, apart from. Apart from* a few words ... (ll.5-6)

   When *except* is used at the beginning of a sentence, it is followed by *for*.

   当except用在句首时，常用except for这个词组。

   Read these sentences.

   读一读下面的句子。

   I invited everyone *except* George. 除了乔治之外我请了每一个人。

   Except for/Apart from this, everything is in order. 除此之外，其他都已就绪。

c *Which of, either of, neither of, both of. Neither of* us ... (l.6)

   We use these words when we refer to *two* persons or things.

   这些短语用于两个人或两件事。

   Which of the two do you want? 这两个你要哪一个？

   Either of them will do. 哪一个都行。

   I like *neither of* them. 我哪一个也不喜欢。

   I bought *both of* them. 这两个我都买了。

Exercise 练习

Choose the correct words in these sentences.
选择正确的词或词组。

1 (Except) (Except for) a slight headache, I feel all right now.

2 I liked them very much so I bought (neither of) (both of) them.

3 (Except) (Apart from) being a bit too long, the play was very good.

4 I (asked) (asked for) a question. I did not (ask for) (ask) an answer.

5 He could not answer (neither of) (either of) the questions I (asked) (asked for).

Multiple choice questions 选择题

Comprehension 理解

1 The young man stopped the writer because _____ .

(*a*) he wanted to speak to him
(*b*) he wanted a free ride in the car
(*c*) he recognized him
(*d*) he spoke French

2 The two men didn't speak to each other during the journey because _____ .

(*a*) neither of them spoke French
(*b*) neither of them spoke English
(*c*) they each thought the other was French
(*d*) they each thought the other was English

Structure 句型

3 What kind of car did he _____?

(*a*) drive
(*b*) drove
(*c*) driven
(*d*) driving

4 As soon as he had got into the car, I said good morning. I said good morning _____ he had got into the car.

(*a*) before
(*b*) a long time after
(*c*) just after
(*d*) a moment before

5 'Good morning,' I _____ .

(*a*) spoke
(*b*) talked
(*c*) told
(*d*) said

6 I speak a few words of French. I don't know _____ French.

(*a*) many
(*b*) much
(*c*) plenty of
(*d*) a little

7 Neither of us spoke. We _____ .

(*a*) neither spoke
(*b*) either spoke
(*c*) both didn't speak
(*d*) neither didn't speak

Vocabulary 词汇

8 On the way, a young man waved to me. This happened _____ .

(*a*) before the writer's journey
(*b*) during the writer's journey
(*c*) after the writer's journey
(*d*) a long time ago

9 The young man waved to the writer. He _____ him.

(*a*) saluted
(*b*) greeted
(*c*) signalled to
(*d*) nodded

10 He asked for a lift. He was a _____ .

(*a*) tramp
(*b*) hitch hiker
(*c*) passenger
(*d*) foreigner

11 He replied in French. He _____ the writer in French.

(*a*) responded
(*b*) answered
(*c*) returned
(*d*) remarked

12 The writer had _____ reached the town when the young man spoke.

(*a*) often
(*b*) almost
(*c*) sometimes
(*d*) just as

Sentence structure 句子结构

Rewrite this sentence, then check your answer against the text.

改写以下句子, 然后对照课文第6行, 核对你的答案。

I know no French at all.

I do not _____ .

Lesson 15　Good news　佳音

business was very bad

First listen and then answer the question.

听录音，然后回答以下问题。

What was the good news?

The secretary told me that Mr. Harmsworth would see me. I felt very nervous when I went into his office. He did not look up from his desk when I entered. After I had sat down, he said that business was very bad. He told me that the firm could not afford to pay such
5　large salaries. Twenty people had already left. I knew that my turn had come.

　　'Mr. Harmsworth,' I said in a weak voice.

　　'Don't interrupt,' he said.

　　Then he smiled and told me I would receive an extra thousand pounds a year!

New words and expressions　生词和短语

secretary (l.1) /ˈsekrətəri/ *n.* 秘书
nervous (l.2) /ˈnɜːvəs/ *adj.* 精神紧张的
afford (l.4) /əˈfɔːd/ *v.* 负担得起

weak (l.7) /wiːk/ *adj.* 弱的
interrupt (l.8) /ˌɪntəˈrʌpt/ *v.* 插话，打断

Notes on the text　课文注释

1　look up, 抬头看。
2　could not afford to ..., 不能支付。afford 为 "有能力做……"，常和 can, could 连用。
3　I knew that my turn had come. 我知道这次该轮到我了。my turn 指上文中有人被公司解雇这件事。

参考译文

　　秘书告诉我说哈姆斯沃斯先生要见我。我走进他的办公室，感到非常紧张。我进去的时候，他连头也没抬。待我坐下后，他说生意非常不景气。他还告诉我，公司支付不起这么庞大的工资开支，有20个人已经离去。我知道这次该轮到我了。

　　"哈姆斯沃斯先生，"我无力地说。

　　"不要打断我的话，"他说。

　　然后他微笑了一下告诉我说，我每年将得到1,000英镑的额外收入。

Summary writing　摘要写作

Answer these questions *in not more than 55 words*.

回答下列问题，将答案组成一个段落，不要超过55个单词。

1　Who wanted to see you?
2　How did you feel about this?
3　Where did you go?

4　Did he say that business was bad, or did he say that it was good?
5　Could the firm pay such large salaries or not?

6   How many people had left already?

7   Did he ask you to leave as well or not?

8   What did he offer you?

Key structures 关键句型

He said that ... He told me ... 间接引语

在第1册的第99-102课和第133-136课，我们已经接触到了直接引语和间接引语。在把直接引语改为间接引语时，除了用动词say以外，还可用动词tell, 后面可跟人名或代词作间接宾语，然后是以that引导的引语作直接宾语。

Study these sentences carefully.

仔细阅读以下句子。

'I am busy,' he said. "我忙，" 他说道。

He says that he is busy. 他说他忙。

He said that he was busy. 他说过他忙。

He told me that he was busy. 他告诉过我他忙。

'I never work on Sundays,' she said. "我星期日从不工作，" 她说。

She says that she never works on Sundays. 她说她星期日从不工作。

She said that she never worked on Sundays. 她说过她星期日从不工作。

She told Mr. Harmsworth that she never worked on Sundays. 她告诉过哈姆斯沃斯先生，她星期日从不工作。

'I have just finished work,' Mr. Jones said. "我刚刚完成工作，" 琼斯先生说。

Mr. Jones says that he has just finished work. 琼斯先生说他刚刚完成工作。

Mr. Jones said that he had just finished work. 琼斯先生说过他刚刚完成工作。

Mr. Jones told his wife that he had just finished work. 琼斯先生告诉过他的夫人，他刚刚完成工作。

'I broke that plate,' he said. "我把那个盘子打破了，" 他说道。

He says that he broke that plate. 他说他打碎了那个盘子。

He said that he had broken that plate. 他说过他打碎了那个盘子。

He told me that he had broken that plate. 他告诉我他打碎了那个盘子。

'Mr. Jones will see you now,' she said. "琼斯先生现在要见你，" 她说。

She says that Mr. Jones will see you now. 她说琼斯先生现在要见你。

She said that Mr. Jones would see you now. 她说过琼斯先生现在要见你。

She told me that Mr. Jones would see you now. 她告诉我琼斯先生现在要见你。

'You can go now,' the teacher said. "你现在可以走了，" 老师说。

The teacher says that you can go now. 老师说你现在可以走了。

The teacher said that you could go now. 老师说过你现在可以走了。

The teacher told the pupil that he could go now. 老师告诉过学生他现在可以走了。

Exercises 练习

A These questions are about the passage. Write a complete sentence in answer to each question.
   这些问题都是有关课文的，用一个完整的句子来回答以下每个问题。

1   *a*   What did the secretary tell me?

    b   What were the secretary's exact words?

2 *a* What did Mr. Harmsworth say after I had sat down?

   b What were Mr. Harmsworth's exact words?

3 *a* What did Mr. Harmsworth tell me about the firm?

   b What were Mr. Harmsworth's exact words?

B Supply *said* or *told* in the following sentences. Give the correct form of the verbs in parentheses.
  在下面的句子里填上 said 或 told, 并用括号中动词的正确形式填空。

  1 He _____ me that she _____ (come) tomorrow.

  2 The gardener _____ that he _____ (cut) that tree down yesterday.

  3 I _____ you I _____ (have) never played tennis before.

  4 What _____ he _____ that he _____ (do)?

  5 When _____ he _____ you that he _____ (buy) this car?

  6 He _____ he _____ (cannot) understand me.

  7 He _____ that he _____ (work) all day yesterday.

  8 He _____ me he never _____ (write) letters to anybody.

  9 Why _____ you _____ that you _____ (be) busy?

 10 He _____ that he _____ (will wait) for me.

Special difficulties 难点

Words often confused and misused 经常容易混淆和误用的词

a *Nervous* and *Irritable*. I felt very *nervous*. (ll.1-2)

Nervous 紧张不安的 (restless or uneasy): Examinations make me *nervous*. 考试使我感到紧张。

Irritable 易怒的 (easily made angry): He is such an *irritable* person, you can hardly speak to him. 他这个人如此容易发怒, 你简直没有办法与他讲话。

b *Office* (l.2), *Study, Desk* (l.3).

Study these examples:

细读以下例句:

There are six people in our *office*. 我们办公室有 6 个人。

The living room is next to the *study*. I often read in the *study* when I want peace and quiet. 起居室在书房的隔壁, 当我需要安静时我常在书房里看书。

My *desk* is covered with books. 我的书桌上铺满了书。

c *Afford* (l.4).

Study these examples:

细读以下例句:

Will you buy this car? I can't *afford* it. I can't *afford* £7,000. 你想买这辆车吗? 我买不起, 我掏不出 7,000 英镑。

You can *afford* this model. It's not very expensive. 你能买得起这种型号的, 它不很贵。

I haven't been to the cinema lately, I can't *afford* the time. 最近我一直没去电影院, 我没时间。

Exercise 练习

Supply any of the above words in the sentences below.
用上面的词填空。

  1 We shall use the spare room in our new house as a _____ .

  2 Smith works in a lawyer's _____ .

  3 She felt very _____ before the plane took off.

4 I can only _____ to pay £100 a week in rent.

5 Since his illness he has been very _____ . He is always losing his temper.

Multiple choice questions 选择题

Comprehension 理解

1 The writer felt nervous because _____ .

  (*a*) Mr. Harmsworth wanted to see him

  (*b*) the secretary told him that Mr. Harmsworth wanted to see him

  (*c*) business was very bad

  (*d*) he thought he would lose his job

2 The writer _____ .

  (*a*) expected to receive some extra money   (*b*) was surprised to receive some extra money

  (*c*) wanted to receive some extra money   (*d*) asked for some extra money

Structure 句型

3 'Mr. Harmsworth _____ see you,' the secretary said.

  (*a*) would   (*b*) shall   (*c*) will   (*d*) could

4 _____ did he feel? Very nervous.

  (*a*) What   (*b*) How   (*c*) How much   (*d*) Which

5 The firm couldn't pay _____ large salaries.

  (*a*) so   (*b*) such a   (*c*) such   (*d*) a such

6 _____ turn is it? It's your turn.

  (*a*) Which   (*b*) To whom   (*c*) Whom   (*d*) Whose

7 'Mr. Harmsworth,' I said _____ a weak voice.

  (*a*) in   (*b*) with   (*c*) on   (*d*) under

Vocabulary 词汇

8 Mr. Harmsworth wanted to see me. He wanted to _____ me.

  (*a*) watch   (*b*) look at   (*c*) look for   (*d*) speak to

9 I felt nervous because I felt _____ .

  (*a*) angry   (*b*) cross   (*c*) anxious   (*d*) ill

10 It's your turn. _____ .

  (*a*) It's your line   (*b*) It's your row   (*c*) You're next   (*d*) It's your chance

11 Don't interrupt! Don't _____ .

  (*a*) speak   (*b*) talk   (*c*) talk while I'm talking   (*d*) cut off

12 The writer would receive an extra £1,000 a year. He would get £1,000 a year _____ .

  (*a*) less   (*b*) more   (*c*) over   (*d*) up

Sentence structure 句子结构

Rewrite this sentence, then check your answer against the text.

改写以下句子, 然后对照课文第4-5行, 核对你的答案。

The firm hadn't the money to pay such large salaries.

The firm couldn't _____ .

Lesson 16 A polite request 彬彬有礼的要求

First listen and then answer the question.

听录音，然后回答以下问题。

What was the polite request?

If you park your car in the wrong place, a traffic policeman will soon find it. You will be very lucky if he lets you go without a ticket. However, this does not always happen. Traffic police are sometimes very polite. During a holiday in Sweden, I found this
5 note on my car: 'Sir, we welcome you to our city. This is a "No Parking" area. You will enjoy your stay here if you pay attention to our street signs. This note is only a reminder.' If you receive a request like this, you cannot fail to obey it!

If you receive a request like this . . .

New words and expressions 生词和短语

park (l.1) /pɑːk/ v. 停放（汽车）
traffic (l.1) /'træfɪk/ n. 交通
ticket (l.3) /'tɪkɪt/ n. 交通违规罚款单
note (l.5) /nəʊt/ n. 便条
area (l.6) /'eərɪə/ n. 地段

sign (l.7) /saɪn/ n. 指示牌
reminder (l.7) /rɪ'maɪndə/ n. 提示
fail (l.8) /feɪl/ v. 无视，忘记
obey (l.8) /əʊ'beɪ/ v. 服从

Notes on the text 课文注释

1 if he lets you go without a ticket, 如果他没给你罚款单就放你走。let (someone) go是"放开"的意思。
2 traffic police, 交通警察。police是集合名词，后面用复数动词。
3 "No Parking" area, 禁止停放汽车的地段。
4 street signs, 交通标志。

参考译文

　　一旦你把汽车停错了地方，交通警很快就会发现。如果他没给你罚款单就放你走了，算你走运。然而，情况并不都是这样，交通警有时也很客气。有一次在瑞典度假，我发现我的车上有这样一个字条："先生，欢迎您光临我们的城市。此处是'禁止停车'区。如果您对我们街上的标牌稍加注意，您在此会过得很愉快的。谨此提请注意。"如果你收到这样的恳求，你是不会不遵照执行的！

Summary writing 摘要写作

Answer these questions *in not more than 55 words.*
回答下列问题，将答案组成一个段落，不要超过55个单词。

1 Do traffic police usually give you a ticket if you park your car in the wrong place or not?
2 When did the writer find a polite note on his car?
3 What did the traffic policeman want him to do?
4 Can anyone fail to obey a request like this or not?

Key structures 关键句型

If you open the door you will get a surprise. 条件句

在第1册的第137-138课中我们接触到了if引导的条件句。下面的条件句主要是用来询问或谈论十分可能的事情。在这些条件句中，if从句用现在时，主句用将来时(will)。

Study these sentences. Pay close attention to the words in italics.

仔细阅读以下句子，特别注意用斜体印出的词或词组。

a *If he is out,* I'll call tomorrow. 如果他不在，我明天打电话。

If it rains tomorrow, we'll stay at home. 如果明天下雨，我们将待在家里。

You'll miss the train *if you don't hurry.* 你如果不快一点儿，会误了火车的。

If you see him, will you tell him about it? 如果你见到他，你能告诉他那件事吗?

If he is working, I won't disturb him. 如果他正在干活，我就不打搅了。

If I have time, I'll be writing to him tomorrow. 如果我有时间，我明天给他写信。

He will come tomorrow *if he can.* 如果有可能的话，他明天会来的。

If they can help you they will. 如果他们有可能，他们会帮你的。

b *If you make a mistake,* correct it. 如果你出了一个错，纠正它。

If you don't like the food, don't eat it. 如果你不喜欢，就别吃它了。

Please don't disturb him *if he is busy.* 如果他正忙，请别打搅他。

Exercises 练习

A How many times has the word *if* been used in the passage?

课文中有几个由if引导的条件句?

B Give the correct form of the verbs in parentheses. Do not refer to the passage until you finish the exercise.

用括号中动词的正确形式填空，完成练习后再对照课文，核对你的答案。

1 If you _____ (park) your car in the wrong place, a traffic policeman soon _____ (find) it.

2 You _____ (be) very lucky if he _____ (let) you go without a ticket.

3 You _____ (enjoy) your stay here if you _____ (pay) attention to our street signs.

4 If you _____ (receive) a request like this, you _____ (cannot) fail to obey it!

C Supply the correct form of the verbs in parentheses in these sentences.

用括号中动词的正确形式填空。

1 If it _____ (rain), I shall take an umbrella with me.

2 You never _____ (pass) this test if you don't work hard.

3 If he _____ (be) here before 10 o'clock, I shall see him.

4 If he plays well, he _____ (get) into the team.

5 If he _____ (enjoy) concerts, why doesn't he come with us?

6 Tell him to wait for me if he _____ (be) not in a hurry.

D Supply the correct form of the verbs in parentheses in this paragraph.

用括号中动词的正确形式填空。

A mother received a letter from her eight-year-old daughter. Here is part of it: 'If I _____ (listen) to the radio, don't tell me to do my homework. If I _____ (do) something wrong, _____ (not shout) at me. If the house _____ (be) untidy, _____ (not blame) me. If you _____ (want) me to do something, _____ (not for-get) to say "please" . If I _____ (play) a nice game, _____ (not send) me to bed. If I _____ (ask) for something, don't always say "No!" If it _____ (be) cold, _____ (not put) the cat out. Don't say "don't" so often!'

Special difficulties 难点

Words often confused and misused 经常容易混淆和误用的词

a   *Police*. Traffic police *are* sometimes very polite. (ll.3-4)

Study these examples:

仔细阅读这些例句：

The police *are* looking for him. *They have* not found him. 警察正在找他，他们还没有找到他。

There were police everywhere. 到处都是警察。

b   *Pay attention to, Care, Take care of, Look after*.

Compare the following:

对比以下句子：

Please *pay attention to* the blackboard. 请注意看黑板。

I don't *care* if he breaks his neck! 他就是折断颈骨，我也不在乎！

Don't worry about the garden. I'll *take care of/look after* it while you are on holiday. 别担心花园，你度假的时候我会照顾它的。

Please *take care of/look after* the children for me when I am out. 我出去的时候请代我照看孩子。

c   *Remind and Remember*. This note is only a *reminder*. (l.7)

I *reminded* him to post my letter. 我提醒他替我寄信。

I *remembered* to post your letter. 我没有忘记为你寄信。

Remember me to your mother. 代我向你的母亲问好。

d   *You*. If *you* receive a request like this ... (ll.7-8)

Instead of saying:	*We can say*:
除了这种表述方式外：	还可以说：
One must be careful these days.	You must be careful these days.
One must never tell lies.	You must never tell lies.

'You' can have the sense of 'anyone'.

英语中第二人称代词you还有 "任何人" 的意思。

Exercise 练习

Choose the correct words in the following sentences.

选择正确的词或短语。

1 You can only learn if you (look after) (pay attention).

2 Don't forget to (remind) (remember) me about it tomorrow.

3 The police (is knocking) (are knocking) at the door.

4 Our neighbours will (pay attention to) (look after) our house when we are away.

5 (Remind me) (Remember me) to your wife.

Multiple choice questions 选择题

Comprehension 理解

1 Traffic police are _____ .

(a) occasionally very polite   (b) never very polite

(c) always very polite   (d) seldom very polite

2 In Sweden, the writer _____ .

(a) parked his car in the wrong place and received a polite note from the police

(b) parked his car in the wrong place and received a ticket from the police

(c) parked his car in the wrong place and paid a fine

(d) parked his car in the wrong place and quarrelled with a policeman

Structure 句型

3 If you park your car in the right place you _____ receive a ticket.

(a) will   (b) wouldn't   (c) didn't   (d) won't

4 Traffic police never let you _____ without a ticket.

(a) go   (b) to go   (c) going   (d) have gone

5 We welcome you to our city. You _____ to our city.

(a) welcome   (b) are welcome   (c) have welcomed   (d) are welcoming

6 'No Parking' means _____ .

(a) don't leave your car here   (b) without parking

(c) don't stop   (d) there's no room to park here

7 This note is only a reminder. It's _____ .

(a) nothing   (b) no one   (c) nothing extra   (d) nothing more

Vocabulary 词汇

8 This is a 'No Parking' area. Cars aren't allowed in this _____ .

(a) district   (b) country   (c) surrounding   (d) kingdom

9 You will enjoy your stay. It will _____ you.

(a) amuse   (b) enjoy   (c) laugh at   (d) please

10 You will enjoy your stay. How long will you _____ here?

(a) rest   (b) prevent   (c) sit   (d) remain

11 This note is only a reminder. It will help _____ .

(a) you remind   (b) your souvenir   (c) your remembrance (d) you to remember

12 You cannot fail to obey it. You can't _____ to do this.

(a) refuse   (b) deny   (c) resist   (d) withdraw

Sentence structure 句子结构

Rewrite this sentence, then check your answer against the text.

改写下列句子, 然后对照课文第1-2行, 核对你的答案。

Park your car in the wrong place and a traffic policeman will soon find it.

If _____ .

Lesson 17　Always young　青春常驻

🎞 **First listen and then answer the question.**

听录音，然后回答以下问题。

Why doesn't Aunt Jennifer tell anyone how old she is?

My aunt Jennifer is an actress. She must be at least thirty-five years old. In spite of this, she often appears on the stage as a young girl. Jennifer will have to take part in a new play soon. This time, she will be a girl of seventeen. In the play, she must appear in a bright
5　red dress and long black stockings. Last year in another play, she had to wear short socks and a bright, orange-coloured dress. If anyone ever asks her how old she is, she always answers, 'Darling, it must be *terrible* to be grown up!'

. . . often appears as a young girl

New words and expressions　生词和短语

appear (l.2) /ə'pɪə/ v. 登场, 扮演
stage (l.2) /'steɪdʒ/ n. 舞台
bright (l.4) /'braɪt/ adj. 鲜艳的

stocking (l.5) /'stɒkɪŋ/ n.（女用）长筒袜
sock (l.6) /sɒk/ n. 短袜

Notes on the text　课文注释

1　She must be at least thirty-five years old. 她至少也有35岁了。
　　must be, 一定是, 表示对现在情况的一种推测, 带有一定的肯定程度。at least, 至少。
2　in spite of, 尽管。
3　in a bright red dress, 穿一身鲜红色的裙子。介词in表示"穿着"。
4　orange-coloured, 橘红色的。
5　grown up, 成熟的, 成人的。

参考译文

　　我的姑姑詹妮弗是位演员, 她至少也有35岁了。尽管如此, 她却常在舞台上扮演小姑娘。詹妮弗很快又要参加一个新剧的演出。这一次, 她将扮演一个17岁的少女。演出时她必须穿一条鲜红色的裙子和黑色的长筒袜。去年在演另一个剧时, 她不得不穿短袜和一件鲜艳的橘红色的衣服。一旦有人问起她有多大年纪, 她总是回答: "亲爱的, 长成大人真可怕啊!"

Summary writing　摘要写作

Answer these questions *in not more than 50 words.*
回答下列问题, 将答案组成一个段落, 不要超过50个单词。

1　Is your aunt Jennifer an actress or a nurse?
2　Is she over thirty years old or is she under thirty years old?
3　Does she often appear on the stage as a young girl or not?

76

4   Will Jennifer act the part of a girl of seventeen in a new play soon or not?

5   Does she ever tell anyone how old she really is or not?

Key structures 关键句型

Must

情态动词must常常用来表示不可逃避的义务，这种义务在说话人看来是没有选择余地的。另外，还可以用have to或have got to来代替must。这3种形式就它们所表达的意义而言，一般可以互换。而have to这个短语可以与更多的时态连用。

Study these sentences:

仔细阅读以下句子：

a *Instead of saying:*
除了这种表述方法外：

I must leave now.

He must leave now.

Must you leave now?

We must leave early tomorrow.

He said he must leave early.

We can say:
还可以说：

I have to leave now.

Or: I have got to leave now.

He has to leave now.

Or: He has got to leave now.

Do you have to leave now?

Or: Have you got to leave now?

We have to leave early tomorrow.

Or: We have got to leave early tomorrow.

Or: We shall have to leave early tomorrow.

He said he would have to leave early.

（有关间接引语的时态变化，请参看第15课的关键句型）

b We cannot use *must* in this sentence.
在下列句子中我们不能用must, 也就是说，在过去时的句子中，要用had to来表示"必须"。
She had to go shopping yesterday.

c must用来表示推测。
Instead of saying:
除了这种表述方法外：

I, personally, think he is a fool.

I, personally, think he is mad.

I, personally, think she is over forty.

We can say:
还可以说：

He must be a fool.

He must be mad.

She must be over forty.

Exercises 练习

A Underline the verbs *must* or *have to* in the passage.
挑选出课文中所有must或have to的例子。

B Supply *must* or the correct form of *have to* in the spaces below. Do not refer to the passage until you finish the exercise.
用must或have to来填空，注意相应的时态，完成练习后再对照课文核对你的答案。

My aunt Jennifer is an actress. She _____ be at least thirty-five years old. In spite of this, she often appears on the stage as a young girl. Jennifer will _____ take part in a new play soon. This time, she will be a girl of seventeen.

Unit 1　Lesson 17

In the play, she _____ appear in a bright red dress and long black stockings. Last year in another play, she _____ wear short socks and a bright, orange-coloured dress. If anyone ever asks her how old she is, she always answers, 'Darling, it _____ be *terrible* to be grown up!'

C Write these sentences again using *must* or *have to* in place of the words in italics.

改写下列句子, 用 must 或 have to 来替代斜体印出的部分。

It is necessary for you to work hard.

You *must* (or *have to*) work hard.

1　*It will be necessary for you to* see a doctor.

2　*Is it necessary for you to* make so much noise?

3　She said *it would be necessary for us to* stay here.

4　*It is necessary for me to* have some help.

5　*It was necessary for him to* go out last night.

Special difficulties 难点

Words often confused and misused 经常容易混淆和误用的词

a *As.* She often appears on the stage *as* a young girl. (l.2)

As can have a number of meanings:

As 可以有不同的含义:

I cannot come *as* I am busy. (because) 由于忙, 我不能来。

As I was leaving the house, the postman brought a letter. (at the time when) 在我离开房子的时候, 邮递员送来一封信。

Do *as* you are told. (the thing that) 叫你怎么做你就怎么做。

He works *as* an engineer. (in the position of) 他担任工程师的工作。

b *Dress, Suit, Costume.* She must appear in a bright red *dress*. (ll.4-5)

Study these examples:

仔细阅读这些例句:

My sister bought a new *dress* yesterday. 我的妹妹昨天买了一条新连衣裙。

My brother never wears ready-made *suits*. 我的弟弟从来不穿成衣。

All the actors wore fifteenth-century *costumes*. 所有的演员都穿着15世纪的服装。

c *Grow* and *Grow up.* It must be terrible to be *grown up*! (ll.7-8)

Study these examples:

仔细阅读这些例句:

Children *grow* quickly. The grass has *grown* very high. 孩子们长得很快。草长得很高。

Some people never *grow up*. (mature in mind) 有些人总是成熟不起来。

Exercises 练习

A What does *as* mean in these sentences?

在下列句子中 as 是什么意思?

1　He works *as* a pilot.

2　You mustn't shout so loudly *as* you'll wake up the baby.

3　*As* we were listening to the radio, someone knocked at the door.

78

B Choose the correct words in the following sentences:

选择正确的词：

1 Trees take a long time to (grow) (grow up).

2 My father bought a new (suit) (costume) recently.

3 She hired a (suit) (costume) for the fancy-dress party.

4 Do you like my sister's new (dress) (costume)?

Multiple choice questions 选择题

Comprehension 理解

1 The story about Jennifer suggests that _____ .

  (a) she is not too old to appear on stage as a young girl

  (b) she is too young to appear on stage as a young girl

  (c) she is the right age to appear on stage as a young girl

  (d) she is too old to appear on stage as a young girl

2 One of these statements is true. Which one?

  (a) We know exactly how old Jennifer is.

  (b) We do not know exactly how old Jennifer is.

  (c) Jennifer is thirty-five years old.

  (d) Jennifer is over thirty-five years old.

Structure 句型

3 She must be at least thirty-five years old. In my opinion she _____ .

  (a) has   (b) is   (c) can   (d) must

4 _____ is she? At least thirty-five years old.

  (a) How   (b) How big   (c) How much   (d) How old

5 She must appear in a bright red dress. She will be dressed _____ red.

  (a) with   (b) on   (c) in   (d) by

6 She must appear in a bright red dress. That's what she _____ .

  (a) has done   (b) have to do   (c) has to do   (d) had done

7 She had to wear short socks. It was _____ for her to wear them.

  (a) certain   (b) necessary   (c) important   (d) impossible

Vocabulary 词汇

8 She often appears as a young girl. She _____ on the stage as a young girl.

  (a) is presented   (b) points   (c) shows   (d) seems

9 We went to the theatre to see a _____ .

  (a) play   (b) game   (c) toy   (d) match

10 Jennifer will take part in the play. She _____ it.

  (a) will write   (b) won't be in   (c) will be in   (d) will produce

11 Men usually wear _____ .

  (a) socks instead of stockings   (b) stockings instead of socks

  (c) either socks or stockings   (d) neither socks nor stockings

12 She is grown up. She is _____ .

  (a) very old   (b) an adolescent   (c) a teenager   (d) an adult

Lesson 18   He often does this!   他经常干这种事！

First listen and then answer the question.

听录音，然后回答以下问题。

What had happened to the writer's bag?

'He often does this!'

After I had had lunch at a village pub, I looked for my bag. I had left it on a chair beside the door and now it wasn't there! As I was looking for it, the landlord came in.

'Did you have a good meal?' he asked.

5   'Yes, thank you,' I answered, 'but I can't pay the bill. I haven't got my bag.'

The landlord smiled and immediately went out. In a few minutes he returned with my bag and gave it back to me.

'I'm very sorry,' he said. 'My dog had taken it into the garden. He often does this!'

New words and expressions 生词和短语

pub (l.1) /pʌb/ n. 小酒店

landlord (l.3) /ˈlændlɔːd/ n. 店主

bill (l.5) /bɪl/ n. 账单

Notes on the text 课文注释

1   pay the bill, 付账。

2   He often does this. 他经常干这种事。句中的He是指店主的狗。英语国家人士常用人称代词he或she来指自己喂养的宠物。

参考译文

我在一家乡村小酒店吃过午饭后，就找我的提包。我曾把它放在门边的椅子上，可这会儿不见了！当我正在寻找时，酒店老板走了进来。

"您吃得好吗？"他问。

"很好，谢谢。"我回答，"但我付不了账，我的提包没有了。"

酒店老板笑了笑，马上走了出去。一会儿工夫他拿着我的提包回来了，把它还给了我。

"实在抱歉，"他说，"我的狗把它弄到花园里去了，他经常干这种事！"

Summary writing 摘要写作

Answer these questions *in not more than 40 words.*

回答下列问题，将答案组成一个段落，不要超过40个单词。

1   Did the writer have lunch at a village pub or not?

2   Could she find her bag after her meal or not?

3   Could she pay the bill or not?

4 Who soon found it for her?

5 Where had his dog taken it?

Key structures 关键句型

Have

Study these uses of *have*:

研究一下 have 的多种用法：

a   Have you had lunch yet? 现在完成时 **(KS4)**（参看第 4 课关键句型）

    After he had finished work he went home. 过去完成时 **(KS14)**（参看第 14 课关键句型）

b   *Instead of saying*:   *We can say*:

    除了这种表述方法外：   还可以说：

    He owns a new house.   He *has* a new house.

                                                 Or: He *has got* a new house.

    He possesses a lot of money.   He *has a* lot of money

                                                 Or: He *has got* a lot of money.

    Does he possess a lot of money?   *Has* he a lot of money?

                                                 Or: *Has* he *got* a lot of money?

    He doesn't possess a lot of money.   He *hasn't* a lot of money.

                                                 Or: *He hasn't got* a lot of money.

c   *Instead of saying*:   *We can say*:

    除了这种表述方法外：   还可以说：

    I took a bath before dinner.   I *had* a bath before dinner. 我饭前洗了一个澡。

    Take a biscuit.   *Have* a biscuit. 吃块饼干。

    I enjoyed myself at the party.   I *had* a good time at the party. 我在聚会上玩得很痛快。

    I received a letter from him yesterday.   I *had* a letter from him yesterday. 昨天我收到他的一封信。

Exercises 练习

A   These questions are on the passage. Write a complete sentence in answer to each question.

    以下这些问句都是有关本课课文的，用完整的句子来回答每个问题。

1 When did you look for your bag?

2 What had you done with your bag?

3 What did the landlord ask you?

4 Why can't you pay the bill?

5 What had the dog done with the bag?

B   Supply the correct form of *have* in the following. Do not refer to the passage until you finish the exercise:

    用 have 的正确形式填空，完成练习后再对照课文，核对你的答案。

1 After I _____ lunch at the village pub, I looked for my bag.

2 I _____ left it on a chair beside the door.

3 '_____ a good meal?' he asked.

4 I can't pay the bill. I _____ got my bag.

5 I'm very sorry. My dog _____ taken it into the garden.

C In which of these sentences can we put the verb *got* after *have*?

在下面哪几句话中可用 have got 来代替 have?

1 He had a drink before dinner.

2 Mrs. Sullivan has a lot of money.

3 He had to leave early.

4 We have had a long conversation.

5 My mother has a headache.

6 They had a good time at the party.

7 This sock has a hole in it.

8 She has to be patient with him.

9 I have a bath every day.

10 This room has four windows.

11 He has a farm.

12 We had a letter from Jill yesterday.

Special difficulties 难点

a Read these sentences. Each one contains the verb *give*. The verb has a different meaning in each sentence.

读一读以下句子, 每句话中都有动词give, 但含义不同。

He returned with my bag and *gave* it *back* to me. (1.8).

Give in your exercise books to me. 把你的练习本交给我。

He can't continue fighting. He will soon *give in*. (He will surrender.) 他不能继续战斗了, 很快将投降。

I *gave away* my collection of stamps to the little boy. 我把我搜集的邮票送给了那个小男孩。

I have *given up* smoking. (I have stopped.) 我已戒烟。

Three of our officers *gave* themselves *up* to the enemy. (They surrendered.) 我方的3名军官向敌人投降了。

b Words often confused 经常容易混淆的词

Beside (1.2), *Besides*.

Come and sit *beside* me. (next to me) 过来, 坐到我的身旁。

Besides this photograph, I have a number of others. (in addition to) 除了这张照片外, 我还有好几张其他的照片。

Exercises 练习

A Supply the missing words in the following sentences.

用适当的词填空。

1 Will the person who took my ruler please give it _____ to me?

2 When my children grew up, I gave all their toys _____ .

3 When do we have to give _____ our compositions?

4 We were losing the battle but we did not give _____ .

B Supply *beside* or *besides* in the following.

用 beside 或 besides 填空。

1 _____ football he plays tennis.

2 Can you see that boy standing _____ the tree?

Multiple choice questions 选择题

Comprehension 理解

1 The writer _____ .

  (a) didn't have her bag with her when she went to the pub

  (b) had her bag with her when she went to the pub

  (c) lost her bag on the way to the pub

  (d) lost her bag after she left the pub

2 The landlord _____ .

  (a) was angry because the writer couldn't pay her bill

  (b) was sorry that the writer couldn't pay her bill

  (c) knew that the writer couldn't pay her bill

  (d) knew that the writer could pay her bill

Structure 句型

3 After I had lunch ... After I had _____ it ...

  (a) paid for   (b) eaten   (c) kept   (d) bought

4 She couldn't find her bag. It wasn't _____ .

  (a) their   (b) theirs   (c) they're   (d) there

5 _____ I was looking for it, the landlord came in.

  (a) Because   (b) While   (c) But   (d) Even if

6 I haven't got a bag. I don't _____ one.

  (a) get   (b) buy   (c) own   (d) owe

7 My dog had taken it into the garden. It was _____ the garden.

  (a) to   (b) into   (c) at   (d) in

Vocabulary 词汇

8 I looked for my bag. I _____ it.

  (a) tried to look after   (b) tried to look at   (c) tried to find   (d) tried to see

9 I had left it on the chair. That's where I _____ it.

  (a) put   (b) let   (c) allowed   (d) permitted

10 The chair was beside the door. It was _____ it.

  (a) near   (b) far from   (c) next to   (d) besides

11 The landlord returned with my bag. He _____ quickly.

  (a) turned   (b) turned back   (c) came back   (d) turned round

12 He gave it back to me. He _____ to me.

  (a) turned it   (b) returned it   (c) turned it back   (d) turned it round

Sentence structure 句子结构

Write the words he actually spoke, then check your answer against the text.

将下列间接引语改写成直接引语，然后对照课文第4行，核对你的答案。

He asked me if I had had a good meal.

' _____ ?' he asked.

Lesson 19　Sold out　票已售完

a man hurried to the ticket office

🔊 **First listen and then answer the question.**

听录音，然后回答以下问题。

When will the writer see the play?

　　'The play may begin at any moment,' I said.

　　'It may have begun already,' Susan answered.

　　I hurried to the ticket office. 'May I have two tickets please?' I asked.

5　'I'm sorry, we've sold out,' the girl said.

　　'What a pity!' Susan exclaimed.

　　Just then, a man hurried to the ticket office.

　　'Can I return these two tickets?' he asked.

　　'Certainly,' the girl said.

10　I went back to the ticket office at once.

　　'Could I have those two tickets please?' I asked.

　　'Certainly,' the girl said, 'but they're for next Wednesday's performance. Do you still want them?'

　　'I might as well have them,' I said sadly.

New words and expressions　生词和短语

hurry (l.3) /ˈhʌri/ v. 匆忙

ticket office (l.3) /ˈtɪkɪt ˈɒfɪs/ 售票处

pity (l.6) /ˈpɪti/ n. 令人遗憾的事

exclaim (l.6) /ɪkˈskleɪm/ v. 大声说

return (l.8) /rɪˈtɜːn/ v. 退回

sadly (l.13) /ˈsædli/ adv. 悲哀地，丧气地

Notes on the text　课文注释

1　The play may begin at any moment, 剧马上就要开演了。在这句话中，说话人指的并不是一种确信不疑的事实，而是可能发生的事情，因此用了"may + 动词"的结构。

2　It may have begun already. 可能已经开始了。这句话同样表示可能发生的事情，但与上句的区别在于它指的是可能已经发生的事情，因此，要用"may + 动词的完成时"的结构。

3　we've sold out, 票已售完。

4　What a pity! 真遗憾！

5　at once, 立刻。

6　Could I ... please? 这里could是代替can的一种比较委婉地提出请求的用法。在时间上和can没有区别。

7　might as well ... 作"还是……好""不妨"讲，与may as well的意思完全相同，只是前者更为委婉。

参考译文

　　"剧马上就要开演了，"我说。

　　"也许已经开演了呢，"苏珊回答说。

　　我匆匆赶到售票处，问："我可以买两张票吗？"

　　"对不起，票已售完。"那位姑娘说。

"真可惜!"苏珊大声说。

正在这时,一个男子匆匆奔向售票处。

"我可以退掉这两张票吗?"他问。

"当然可以,"那姑娘说。

我马上又回到售票处。

"我可以买那两张票吗?"我问。

"当然可以,不过这两张票是下星期三的,您是否还要呢?"

"我还是买下的好,"我垂头丧气地说。

Summary writing 摘要写作

Answer these questions *in not more than 50 words*.

回答下列问题,将答案组成一个段落,不要超过50个单词。

1 When was the play going to begin?
2 How many tickets did you ask for?
3 Were there any left or not?
4 Were Susan and you disappointed or not?
5 Who hurried to the ticket office just then?
6 How many tickets did he return?
7 Were they for that day's performance, or were they for next Wednesday's performance?
8 Did you buy them or not?

Key structures 关键句型

Can and May

Study these uses of *can* and *may*:

研究一下can和may的用法:

a 表示请求

Instead of saying:

除了这种表述方法外:

Will you let me use your phone please?

We can say:

还可以说:

Can I use your phone please?

Or: *Could* I use your phone please?

Or: *May* I use your phone please?

Or: *Might* I use your phone please?

b 表示推测

Instead of saying:

除了这种表述方法外:

Perhaps he will come tomorrow.

We can say:

还可以说:

He *may* come tomorrow.

Or: He *might* come tomorrow.

Perhaps he telephoned last night,
but I'm not sure.

He *may have* telephoned last night, but I'm not sure.

Or: He *might have* telephoned last night, but I'm not sure.

c Now study these expressions:

读一读以下表达方式:

Do you want to come to the cinema with me? 你想和我一起去看电影吗?

I haven't got anything to do, so I *may as well* (or: I *might as well*) come with you. 我无事可做，还是和你一起去吧。

Do you think he'll pass that exam? 你认为他这次考试能及格吗？

He'll never pass. He *might as well* give up. 他决不会及格，还不如放弃的好。

Exercises 练习

A Read the passage again. Put a line under the verbs *can, could, may* and *might*.
重读课文，在 can, could, may, might 下面画上横线。

B Use a phrase with *can, could, may or might* in place of the words in italics. Do not refer to the passage until you finish the exercise.
用 can, could, may 或 might 组成的短语来替代句子中的用斜体印出的部分，完成练习后再对照课文，核对你的答案。

'*Perhaps the play will begin* at any moment,' I said.

'*Perhaps it has begun* already,' Susan answered.

I hurried to the ticket office. '*Will you let me have* two tickets, please?' I asked.

'I'm sorry, we've sold out,' the girl said.

Just then, a man hurried to the ticket office.

'*Will you let me return* these two tickets?' he asked.

I went back to the ticket office at once.

'*Will you let me have* those two tickets please?' I asked.

'Certainly,' the girl said, 'but they are for next Wednesday's performance. Do you still want them?'

'*Not really, but I'll have them,*' I said sadly.

Special difficulties 难点

Instead of saying:	*We can say*:
除了这种书写形式外：	我们可用缩略形式：
I am sorry.	I'm sorry. (l.5)
We have sold out.	We've sold out. (l.5)

Exercise 练习

Change the form of the verbs in italics.
将下列用斜体印出的动词改变形式。

1 I *haven't* seen him for three years.

2 There *are not* many people here.

3 He *doesn't* understand what *you're* saying.

4 She *did not* tell me she *had not* seen you.

5 I *shall not* stay a moment longer.

6 He *will not* do as *he is* told.

7 *When'll* I see you?

8 *What've* you done? *You've* broken that bottle!

9 He's in the living room. *He's* just come home.

10 I *cannot* understand why he *hasn't* arrived.

11 You *mustn't* believe him.

12 I *wasn't* expecting you. You *weren't* supposed to arrive until 6 o'clock.

13 That *man's* been in prison.

14 They *hadn't* seen the film before.

Multiple choice questions 选择题

Comprehension 理解

1 The writer couldn't get tickets for the performance that evening because _____ .

   (a) they had all been sold   (b) there were only a few left

   (c) there was no one at the ticket office   (d) the girl at the ticket office wouldn't give him any

2 The writer _____ .

   (a) was very pleased to get tickets for next Wednesday's performance

   (b) didn't buy tickets for next Wednesday's performance

   (c) didn't want tickets for next Wednesday's performance

   (d) wasn't too pleased to get tickets for next Wednesday's performance

Structure 句型

3 The play may begin at any moment. It _____ .

   (a) has begun   (b) won't begin for a long time

   (c) hasn't begun yet   (d) began a long time ago

4 May I have two tickets please? _____ two tickets please?

   (a) You must give me   (b) You have got to give me

   (c) Could I have   (d) You may give me

5 May I have two tickets? Please let me _____ two tickets.

   (a) having   (b) to have   (c) had   (d) have

6 The performance _____ next Wednesday.

   (a) was   (b) will be   (c) shall be   (d) has been

7 I might as well have them. I am _____ to have them.

   (a) very pleased   (b) very glad   (c) not very glad   (d) delighted

Vocabulary 词汇

8 I hurried to the ticket office. I _____ .

   (a) went there   (b) went there quickly   (c) went there slowly   (d) didn't go there

9 'What a pity!' Susan exclaimed. Susan was _____ .

   (a) pleased   (b) glad   (c) sorry   (d) amused

10 Can I return these tickets? I want to _____ .

   (a) give them back   (b) give them in   (c) give them up   (d) give them off

11 'Certainly,' the girl said. '_____ ,' the girl said.

   (a) Off course   (b) Course   (c) Of course   (d) Surely not

12 Do you still want them? Do you want them _____ ?

   (a) yet   (b) even   (c) now   (d) more

Sentence structure 句子结构

Rewrite this sentence, then check your answer against the text.

改写以下句子, 然后对照课文第13行, 核对你的答案。

I don't really want them, but I'll have them.

I might _____ .

Lesson 20 One man in a boat 独坐孤舟

I never catch anything.

First listen and then answer the question.

听录音，然后回答以下问题。

Why is fishing the writer's favourite sport?

Fishing is my favourite sport. I often fish for hours without catching anything. But this does not worry me. Some fishermen are unlucky. Instead of catching fish, they catch old boots and rubbish. I am even less lucky. I never catch anything — not even old boots. After having
5 spent whole mornings on the river, I always go home with an empty bag. 'You must give up fishing!' my friends say. 'It's a waste of time.' But they don't realize one important thing. I'm not really interested in fishing. I am only interested in sitting in a boat and doing nothing at all!

New words and expressions 生词和短语

catch (1.1) /kætʃ/ (caught /kɔːt/, caught) v. 抓到
fisherman (1.2) /'fɪʃəmən/ n. 钓鱼人，渔民
boot (1.3) /buːt/ n. 靴子

waste (1.6) /weɪst/ n. 浪费
realize (1.7) /'rɪəlaɪz/ v. 意识到

Notes on the text 课文注释

1 Fishing is my favourite sport. 钓鱼是我最喜欢的一项运动。在这句话中，主语是fishing，这是一个动名词，由动词加上ing组成。

2 I often fish for hours without catching anything. 我经常一钓数小时却一无所获。这句话中的catching也是动名词，它作介词without的宾语。动名词也有动词的特性，它可以有自己的宾语。

3 After having spent whole mornings on the river, 在河上待了整整一个上午之后。由于作介词after的宾语的动名词所表示的动作发生在谓语动词go之前，因此，动名词要用完成形式，即having spent。

4 be interested in doing sth.，对做某事感兴趣。

参考译文

　　钓鱼是我最喜欢的一项运动。我经常一钓数小时却一无所获，但我从不为此烦恼。有些垂钓者就是不走运，他们往往鱼钓不到，却钓上来些旧靴子和垃圾。我的运气甚至还不及他们。我什么东西也未钓到过——就连旧靴子也没有。我总是在河上待上整整一上午，然后空着袋子回家。"你可别再钓鱼了！"我的朋友们说，"这是浪费时间。"然而他们没有认识到重要的一点，我并不是真的对钓鱼有兴趣，我感兴趣的只是独坐孤舟，无所事事！

Summary writing 摘要写作

Answer these questions *in not more than 50 words*.
回答下列问题，将答案组成一个段落，不要超过50个单词。

1 What is the writer's favourite sport?

2　What do some unlucky fishermen catch?

3　Is the writer as lucky as they are, or is he not so lucky?

4　Does he ever catch anything?

5　Is he really interested in fishing?

6　What is the only thing that interests him?

Key structures 关键句型

You must give up fishing. 动名词

Study these sentences carefully. Pay close attention to the verbs in italics. All these verbs end in *ing*.
细读下面的例句, 特别注意用斜体印出的以 ing 结尾的词。

a　动名词作主语

Eating is always a pleasure. 吃总是一件愉快的事情。

Watching television is my favourite pastime. 看电视是我最喜爱的业余爱好。

Reading in bed is something I always enjoy. 我总是喜欢躺在床上看书。

b　动名词作宾语

I am very keen on *cycling*. 我非常喜欢骑自行车。

She is afraid of *staying* in that house alone. 她害怕单独住在那间屋子里。

He is capable of *doing* anything. 他能胜任任何事情。

c　Note how these sentences have been joined.
注意在以下例句中如何用动名词将两个短句连到一起。

He sat there. He did not say anything. 他坐在那儿, 他什么话也不说。

He sat there without *saying* anything. 他默默无语地坐在那里。

He turned off the radio. He left the room. 他关掉了收音机, 他离开了房间。

Before *leaving* the room, he turned off the radio. 离开房间之前, 他关掉了收音机。

He looked at his watch. He hurried to the station. 他看了一下手表。他匆忙赶往火车站。

After *looking* at his watch, he hurried to the station. 他看了一下手表之后, 就匆忙赶往火车站。

Or: After *having looked* at his watch, he hurried to the station.

I must apologize. I interrupted you. 我得表示道歉。我打断了你的说话（工作）。

I must apologize for *interrupting* you. 由于打断了你的说话（工作）, 我得表示道歉。

Or: I must apologize for *having interrupted* you.

I must apologize. I did not let you know earlier. 我得表示道歉。我没有早一点让你知道。

I must apologize for *not letting* you know earlier. 由于没有早点让你知道, 我得表示道歉。

Or: I must apologize for *not having let* you know earlier.

He congratulated me. I won the competition. 他向我道贺。我赢得了这次比赛。

He congratulated me on *winning* the competition. 在我赢得这次比赛之际, 他向我祝贺。

Or: He congratulated me on *having won* the competition.

Exercises 练习

A　Underline all the verbs in the passage that end in *ing*.
在课文中所有动词加 ing 的例子下面画上横线。

B Give the correct form of the verbs in parentheses. Do not refer to the passage until you finish the exercise.
用括号中动词的正确形式填空，完成练习后再对照课文，核对你的答案。

_____ (Fish) is my favourite sport. I often fish for hours without _____ (catch) anything. But this does not worry me. Some fishermen are unlucky. Instead of _____ (catch) fish, they catch old boots and rubbish. I am even less lucky. I never catch anything — not even old boots. After _____ (have spend) whole mornings on the river, I always go home with an empty bag. 'You must give up _____ (fish)!' my friends say. 'It's a waste of time.' But they don't realize one important thing. I'm not really interested in _____ (fish). I am only interested in _____ (sit) in a boat and _____ (do) nothing at all!

C Join these pairs of sentences with the words given in parentheses. Make any other necessary changes.
用括号中的词来连接下列句子，如需要可对原句进行必要的改动。

1 He went out of the restaurant. (without) He did not pay the bill.

2 She bought a pair of boots. (instead of) She did not get a pair of shoes.

3 She was afraid. (of) She did not spend the night alone.

4 (After) She heard the news. She fainted.

5 Think carefully. (before) Answer my question.

6 (On) I saw the plane coming towards me. I dashed for cover.

Special difficulties 难点

Words often confused 经常容易混淆的词

Study these examples:
细读以下例句：

a *Interested* and *Interesting*. *Excited* and *Exciting*.

  Fishing is not *interesting*. I am not really *interested* in fishing. (ll.7-8)
  钓鱼没意思。我对钓鱼并不真正感兴趣。

  The match was very *exciting*. The crowd got very *excited*. 比赛非常激动人心。观众非常激动。

b *It's* and *Its*. *It's* a waste of time. (ll.6-7)

  It's (= it is) cold today. *It's* raining too. 今天天气冷。而且正在下雨。

  The cat drank *its* milk. 猫喝了它的牛奶。

  This engine has lost *its* power. 这台发动机已失去了动力。

c *Realize* and *Understand*. They don't *realize* ... (l.7)

  I *realized* he was mad. 我意识到他疯了。

  He didn't *realize* that he had made a mistake. 他没有意识到他犯了一个错误。

  I don't *understand* English. 我不懂英语。

Exercise 练习

Choose the correct words in the following.
选择正确的词。

1 I (realized) (understood) he was not telling me the truth.

2 This poem is difficult. (It's) (Its) impossible for you to (understand) (realize) (its) (it's) meaning.

3 There was some (excited) (exciting) news on the radio.

4 He is not an (interesting) (interested) person.

5 He is all explorer. He leads an (excited) (exciting) life.

6 I am not (interesting) (interested) in other people's affairs.

Multiple choice questions 选择题

Comprehension 理解

1 The writer _____ .

(*a*) always catches something   (*b*) never catches anything

(*c*) sometimes pulls up old boots and rubbish   (*d*) never goes home with an empty bag

2 The writer enjoys _____ .

(*a*) catching fish   (*b*) fishing   (*c*) doing nothing   (*d*) swimming in the river

Structure 句型

3 _____ is your favourite sport? Fishing.

(*a*) Who   (*b*) Which   (*c*) Whom   (*d*) Whose

4 He doesn't catch anything. He never catches _____ .

(*a*) nothing   (*b*) anything   (*c*) something   (*d*) everything

5 I am even less lucky. I am _____ lucky.

(*a*) more   (*b*) as   (*c*) not so   (*d*) so

6 His bag is empty. He has _____ .

(*a*) a empty bag   (*b*) an empty bag   (*c*) empty bag   (*d*) one empty bag

7 I am only interested in doing nothing. That's _____ I'm interested in.

(*a*) only   (*b*) the one   (*c*) all   (*d*) the only

Vocabulary 词汇

8 Fishing is my favourite sport. It is _____ .

(*a*) the one I like best   (*b*) prefer   (*c*) my best   (*d*) the best

9 A fisherman usually_____ fish.

(*a*) buys   (*b*) sells   (*c*) tries to catch   (*d*) keeps

10 He never _____ any fish.

(*a*) holds   (*b*) takes hold of   (*c*) catches   (*d*) takes

11 He always goes _____ with an empty bag.

(*a*) to home   (*b*) to house   (*c*) to the house   (*d*) home

12 You must give up fishing. You must _____ .

(*a*) stop   (*b*) begin   (*c*) surrender   (*d*) end

Sentence structure 句子结构

Join these two sentences with *without*, then check your answer against the text.

用without连接下面两个句子, 对照课文第1-2行, 核对你的答案。

I often fish for hours. I don't catch anything.

Lesson 21　Mad or not?　是不是疯了?

听录音, 然后回答以下问题。

Why do people think the writer is mad?

Aeroplanes are slowly driving me mad. I live near an airport and passing planes can be heard night and day. The airport was built years ago, but for some reason it could not be used then. Last year, however, it came into use. Over a hundred people must have been
5　driven away from their homes by the noise. I am one of the few people left. Sometimes I think this house will be knocked down by a passing plane. I have been offered a large sum of money to go away, but I am determined to stay here. Everybody says I must be mad and they are probably right.

Everybody says I must be mad

New words and expressions　生词和短语

mad (l.1) /mæd/ *adj.* 发疯
reason (l.3) /ˈriːzən/ *n.* 原因

sum (l.7) /sʌm/ *n.* 量
determined (l.8) /dɪˈtɜːmɪnd/ *adj.* 坚定的, 下决心的

Notes on the text　课文注释

1　Aeroplanes are slowly driving me mad. 飞机正在逐渐把我逼疯。drive someone mad, 把某人逼疯。

2　passing planes can be heard night and day, 过往飞机日夜不绝于耳。在句中, passing用来修饰名词planes, 起形容词作用, 是一个现在分词。

3　came into use, 启用。

4　Over a hundred people must have been driven away from their homes by the noise. 有100多人肯定是被噪音逼得离家远去。情态动词must +完成时态, 是对过去事情的推测, 猜测某一事情肯定已经发生。drive away, 赶走, 逼走。

参考译文

　　飞机正在逐渐把我逼疯。我住在一个机场附近, 过往飞机日夜不绝于耳。机场是许多年前建的, 但由于某种原因当时未能启用。然而去年机场开始使用了。有100多人肯定是被噪音逼得已经弃家远去, 我是少数留下来的人中的一个。有时我觉得这房子就要被一架飞过的飞机撞倒。他们曾向我提供一大笔钱让我搬走, 但我决定留在这儿。大家都说我肯定是疯了, 也许他们说的是对的。

Summary writing　摘要写作

Answer these questions *in not more than 50 words*.
回答下列问题, 将答案组成一个段落, 不要超过50个单词。

1　Is the writer slowly going mad or not?
2　Where does he live?

3 What can be heard night and day?

4 Have most of his neighbours left their homes or not?

5 Has he been offered money to leave or not?

6 What is he determined to do?

7 What does everyone say?

8 Are they probably right or wrong?

Key structures 关键句型

Passing planes can be heard night and day. 被动语态 (KS10)（参见第10课关键句型）

a Read these pairs of sentences carefully. The first sentence in each pair tells us about a person (Who). The second tells us about a thing (What or Which).

仔细阅读以下句子，每一对中的第1句以人为主（谁），第2句以物品为主（什么，哪一件）。

He *will repair* your watch. (Who) 他会修理你的表。

Your watch *will be repaired*. (What) 你的表会修好的。

He *can repair* your watch. (Who) 他能修你的表。

Your watch *can be repaired*. (What) 你的表能修好。

They *must test* this new car. (Who) 他们必须试试这辆新车。

This new car *must be tested*. (What) 这辆新车必须试一试。

You *have to write* this letter again. (Who) 你必须重写这封信。

This letter *has to be written* again. (What) 这封信必须重写。

I told you he *could do* it. (Who) 我告诉你他能做。

I told you it *could be done*. (What) 我告诉你这件事能做。

I told you he *would do* it. (Who) 我告诉你他会做这件事。

I told you it *would be done*. (What) 我告诉你这件事会干好的。

I can't find my bag. Someone *has stolen* it. (Who) 我找不到我的提包。有人偷走了。

I can't find my bag. It *has been stolen*. (What) 我找不到我的提包。它被偷走了。

I can't find my bag. Someone *must have stolen* it. (Who) 我找不到我的提包。有人肯定把它偷走了。

I can't find my bag. It *must have been stolen*. (What) 我找不到我的提包。它肯定被人偷走了。

b *Instead of saying*:   *We can say*:

除了这种表述方法外：   还可以说：

The police will arrest the thieves.   The thieves will be arrested (by the police).

You must pay me for this.   I must be paid for this.

They cannot find him.   He cannot be found.

Exercises 练习

A There are some verbs in the passage which are like the examples given above. Can you find them?
找出课文中所有被动语态的例子。

B Change the form of the phrases in italics. Do not refer to the passage until you finish the exercise.
将斜体印出的部分改写成被动语态，完成练习后再对照课文核对你的答案。

I live near an airport and *I can hear passing planes* night and day. *They built the airport* years ago, but for some reason *they could not use it* then. Last year, however, it came into use. *The noise must have driven over a hundred people away* from their homes. I am one of the few people left. Sometimes I think *a passing plane will knock down this house*. *They have offered me* a large sum of money to go away, but I am determined to stay here.

C Change the form of these sentences. Your sentences must begin with the words in italics.
改写以下句子, 将斜体印出的词或词组作主语。

1 I will send *a message* immediately.

2 We must sell *all these goods*.

3 I told you he would receive *the parcel* in time.

4 He has to deliver *the letter* by hand.

5 They must have lost *your letter* in the post.

Special difficulties 难点

Words often confused and misused 经常容易混淆和误用的词

Study these examples:
细读以下例句:

a *Drive*. This verb can be used in many ways. 这个动词的词义很多。

Aeroplanes are slowly *driving* me mad. (l.1)

He *drives* his car very badly. 他开车开得很糟糕。

The farmer *drove* the cattle into the field. 农夫把牛赶进田里。

Our army *drove* the enemy back. 我们的军队把敌人撵了回去。

During the war, many people were *driven* out of their homes. 战争期间, 许多人被赶出了家园。

b *Home* (l.5) and *House* (l.6).

After work I always go *home*. I stay at *home* during the weekend. There is no place like *home*. 下班后我总是回家。
周末我待在家里。没有任何地方像家那么好。

They are building many new *houses* in our district. *Houses* are very expensive. I paid a lot of money for a new
house. 他们正在我们这个区修建大量的新房子。住宅很昂贵。我为一栋新房子付了一大笔款。

Exercises 练习

A Write sentences using *drive out of, drive back* and *drive into*.
用 drive out of, drive back 与 drive into 造句。

B Supply *house*(s) or *home* in the following:
用 house(s) 或 home 填空。

1 It was raining heavily and I was glad to get _____ .

2 The government plans to build thousands of _____ next year.

3 He is very rich. He owns a _____ in the country.

4 Most people like to spend their Christmas holidays at _____ .

Multiple choice questions 选择题

Comprehension 理解

1 The airport _____ .

   (*a*) has been used since it was completed

   (*c*) came into use recently

   (*b*) has never been used

   (*d*) has just come into use

2 The writer _____ .

(*a*) will be leaving his house soon   (*b*) has accepted a lot of money for his house

(*c*) likes the noise of passing planes   (*d*) has refused to leave his house

Structure 句型

3 Passing planes can be heard night and day. You _____ them all the time.

(*a*) can heard   (*b*) can to hear   (*c*) can hear   (*d*) can be heard

4 It couldn't be used then. It wasn't _____ to use it.

(*a*) able   (*b*) allowed   (*c*) impossible   (*d*) possible

5 Over a hundred people must have been driven away. _____ they were.

(*a*) I think   (*b*) I'm sure   (*c*) Certain   (*d*) Of course

6 I am one of the few people left. So there _____ .

(*a*) are none left   (*b*) is one left   (*c*) are some left   (*d*) are a lot left

7 How much _____ ? A large sum of money.

(*a*) you have been offered   (*b*) have you been offered

(*c*) you have offered   (*d*) they offered you

Vocabulary 词汇

8 I have been offered some money. They want to _____ me some money.

(*a*) serve   (*b*) give   (*c*) take   (*d*) make

9 I have been offered a large _____ of money.

(*a*) amount   (*b*) number   (*c*) some   (*d*) piece

10 I am determined to stay here. I _____ stay here.

(*a*) am will to   (*b*) want to   (*c*) may   (*d*) am going to

11 Everyone says I must be mad and they are probably right. _____ they are.

(*a*) Of course   (*b*) It's certain   (*c*) Perhaps   (*d*) It's sure

12 Everyone says I must be mad and that is probably _____ .

(*a*) just   (*b*) fair   (*c*) correct   (*d*) equal

Sentence structure 句子结构

Rewrite this sentence, then check your answer against the text.

改写下列句子, 然后对照课文第2-3行, 核对你的答案。

They built the airport years ago, but for some reason they couldn't use it then.

The airport _____ , but for some reason it _____ .

Lesson 22　A glass envelope　玻璃信封

First listen and then answer the question.

听录音, 然后回答以下问题。

How did Jane receive a letter from a stranger?

My daughter, Jane, never dreamed of receiving a letter from a girl of her own age in Holland. Last year, we were travelling across the Channel and Jane put a piece of paper with her name and address on it into a bottle. She threw the bottle into the sea. She never thought
5　of it again, but ten months later, she received a letter from a girl in Holland. Both girls write to each other regularly now. However, they have decided to use the post office. Letters will cost a little more, but they will certainly travel faster.

ten months later, she received a letter

New words and expressions　生词和短语

dream (l.1) /driːm/ v. 做梦, 梦想
age (l.2) /eɪdʒ/ n. 年龄
channel (l.3) /'tʃænl/ n. 海峡

throw (l.4) /θrəʊ/ (threw /θruː/, thrown /θrəʊn/) v. 扔, 抛

Notes on the text　课文注释

1　dreamed of receiving a letter, 想到会收到一封信。dream of 作 "梦想", "幻想" 讲; receiving 是动名词, 作介词 of 的宾语。
2　Last year, we were travelling across the Channel and ..., 去年, 当我们横渡英吉利海峡时……。这是过去进行时的一种用法, 用来叙述故事情节的背景。过去进行时描述背景, 由此引出一般过去时表示的新动作。
3　with her name and address on it 用来进一步说明 a piece of paper。可译作 "写有她姓名和地址的 (一张纸条)"。

参考译文

　　我的女儿简从未想过会接到荷兰一位同龄姑娘的来信。去年, 当我们横渡英吉利海峡时, 简把写有她姓名和住址的一张纸条装进了一只瓶子, 又将瓶子扔进了大海。此后她就再没去想那只瓶子。但10个月以后, 她收到了荷兰一位姑娘的来信。现在这两位姑娘定期通信了。然而她们还是决定利用邮局。这样会稍微多花点钱, 但肯定是快得多了。

Summary writing　摘要写作

Answer these questions *in not more than 55 words*.

回答下列问题, 将答案组成一个段落, 不要超过55个单词。

1　When did Jane cross the Channel?
2　What did she throw into the sea?
3　What did it contain?

4   What did she receive ten months later?

5   Do they write to each other regularly now or not?

6   Do they send their letters by post, or do they send them in bottles?

Key structures 关键句型

Verbs followed by *of, from, in* and *on* 后面可跟 of, from, in 和 on 的动词

We can put *of, from, in,* or *on* after certain verbs:

of, from, in, on 可以用在某些动词的后面:

Jane never dreamed *of* receiving a letter ... (ll.1-2)

She never thought *of* it again. (ll.4-5)

She received a letter *from* a girl in Holland. (ll.5-6)

Use this list for reference:

以下搭配表可供参考:

a   OF: accuse, approve, assure, beware, boast (or about), complain (or about), consist, convince (or about), cure, despair, dream (or about), expect (or from), hear (or from), be/get rid, smell, suspect, think (or about), tire(d), warn (or against).

后接 of 的动词: 控告; 赞成; 让……放心; 谨防; 夸耀; 埋怨; 由……组成; 使信服; 治愈; 丧失……希望; 幻想; 期望; 听到……消息; 摆脱; 闻到; 对……猜疑; 思考; 对……感到厌烦; 警告……有危险。

b   FROM: borrow, defend (or against), demand (or of), differ, dismiss, draw **(SD 64)**, emerge, escape, excuse (or for), hinder, prevent, prohibit, protect (or against), receive, separate, suffer.

后接 from 的动词: 从……借; 保护……使免于; 向……要求; 有别于; 解雇; 从……中得出(参见第64课难点); 从……出现; 从……逃出; 允许不……; 阻止; 妨碍; 不准许; 保护……使免于; 接到; 把……分开; 受难。

c   IN: believe, delight, employ(ed), encourage, engage(d), experience(d), fail, help (or with), include, indulge, instruct, interest(ed), invest, involve(d), persist, share.

后接 in 的动词: 信仰; 喜欢; 从事; 鼓励; 正做; 在……方面有经验; 没有做到; 帮助; 包括; 沉醉; 教导; 对……感兴趣; 投资; 卷入; 坚持; 分享。

d   ON: act, base(d), call **(SD 34)**, comment, concentrate, congratulate, consult (or about), count, decide, depend, economize, embark, experiment, insist, lean (or against), live, operate, perform (or in), pride (oneself), rely, vote (*on* a motion; *for* someone), write (or about).

后接 on 的动词: 遵守; 在……基础上; 拜访(参见第34课难点); 评论; 集中于; 祝贺; 商量; 依赖; 决定; 依靠; 节约; 从事; 尝试; 坚持; 倚靠于……; 靠……为生; 起作用; 扮演; 为……感到自豪; 依靠; 对……表决(投……的票); 写……的事。

Exercise 练习

Supply the missing words (*of, from, in* or *on*) without referring to the above lists as far as possible:

用 of, from, in 或 on 填空, 尽可能不查阅以上搭配表:

1   I withdrew a lot of money _____ the bank yesterday.

2   I refuse to comment _____ his work.

3   The waiter's tip is included _____ the bill.

4   He congratulated me _____ having got engaged.

5 This warm coat will protect you _____ the cold.

6 Did anything emerge _____ your discussion?

7 I dreamt _____ you last night.

8 You can never rely _____ him to be punctual.

9 Nothing will prevent him _____ succeeding.

10 Are you interested _____ music?

11 I suppose I can count _____ you for help _____ this matter?

12 Beware _____ the dog.

13 He persisted _____ asking questions.

14 I insist _____ your telling me the truth.

15 It took me a long time to get rid _____ him.

16 Do you mean to say you have never heard _____ Beethoven?

17 I separated them _____ each other because they were fighting.

18 They can only cure him _____ his illness if they operate _____ him.

19 You can depend _____ me.

20 I haven't accused him _____ anything, but I suspect him _____ having taken it.

21 Whatever made you think _____ such a thing?

22 We expect a great deal _____ you, Smith.

23 My hands smell _____ soap.

24 They differ _____ each other so much.

25 He invested a lot of money _____ shipping.

26 The film was based _____ a novel by Dickens.

27 Don't lean _____ that shelf! You'll regret it.

28 She often suffers _____ colds.

29 We have embarked _____ a new scheme.

30 I believe _____ taking my time.

31 Jones was dismissed _____ the firm.

32 They began by experimenting _____ rats.

33 Please concentrate _____ what you are doing.

34 She prides herself _____ her clean house.

35 The climber failed _____ his attempt to reach the summit.

36 Many people escaped _____ prisons during the last five years.

37 We must economize _____ fuel.

38 He's never done any work. He lives _____ his mother.

39 He was employed _____ a factory before he joined the army.

40 And what does this horrible drink consist _____ ?

41 I shall certainly act _____ your advice.

42 Don't write _____ the desk!

43 You should not boast _____ your success.

44 You must encourage him _____ his efforts.

45 He should be instructed _____ his duties.

46 Two or three people were involved _____ the accident.

47 Children should be prohibited _____ smoking.

48 I can assure you _____ my support.

49 Do you approve _____ hunting?

50 I despair _____ ever teaching him anything!

51 Has this play ever been performed _____ the stage?

52 I warned him _____ the danger, but he wouldn't listen to me.

53 How much have you borrowed _____ me already?

54 He delights _____ annoying me.

Multiple choice questions 选择题

Comprehension 理解

1 Jane never dreamed of receiving a letter from a girl in Holland because _____ .

  (*a*) it is a long way away   (*b*) she has never been abroad

  (*c*) no one in Holland knows her address   (*d*) she didn't expect anyone to find the bottle

2 Both girls _____ .

  (*a*) meet regularly now   (*b*) correspond in the normal way now

  (*c*) send notes to each other in bottles   (*d*) travel regularly now

Structure 句型

3 Jane never dreamed _____ a letter.

  (*a*) to receive   (*b*) to receiving   (*c*) of receive   (*d*) that she would receive

4 She received a letter from a girl of her own age. The girl is _____ she is.

  (*a*) the same age with   (*b*) the same age   (*c*) as old   (*d*) the same age as

5 Did she _____ the bottle into the sea?

  (*a*) threw   (*b*) throw   (*c*) thrown   (*d*) throwing

6 She never thought _____ it again.

  (*a*) for   (*b*) to   (*c*) at   (*d*) about

7 The girls write _____ regularly now.

  (*a*) to one another   (*b*) the one to the other   (*c*) each to other   (*d*) to other

Vocabulary 词汇

8 We were travelling across the Channel. We went on a _____ across the Channel.

  (*a*) sail   (*b*) travel   (*c*) trip   (*d*) run

9 Jane wrote her name and address on a _____ of paper.

  (*a*) lump   (*b*) bar   (*c*) tube   (*d*) sheet

10 Both girls often write to each other now. They write _____ .

  (*a*) frequently   (*b*) occasionally   (*c*) sometimes   (*d*) now and again

11 You can buy _____ at the post office.

  (*a*) sweets   (*b*) stamps   (*c*) apples   (*d*) sugar

12 They will travel faster. They will travel _____ .

  (*a*) sooner   (*b*) more quickly   (*c*) hurriedly   (*d*) shorter

Sentence structure 句子结构

Join these statements together to make one sentence. Then check your answer against the text.

将下列几个句子合成一句话，然后对照课文第2-4行，核对你的答案。

Last year we were travelling across the Channel. Jane put a piece of paper into a bottle. It had her name and address on it.

Lesson 23　A new house　新居

First listen and then answer the question.

听录音，然后回答以下问题。

Why is the new house special?

I had a letter from my sister yesterday. She lives in Nigeria. In her letter, she said that she would come to England next year. If she comes, she will get a surprise. We are now living in a beautiful new house in the country. Work on it had begun before my sister
5 left. The house was completed five months ago. In my letter, I told her that she could stay with us. The house has many large rooms and there is a lovely garden. It is a very modern house, so it looks strange to some people. It must be the only modern house in the district.

the only modern house in the district

New words and expressions　生词和短语

complete (l.5) /kəmˈpliːt/ v. 完成
modern (l.7) /ˈmɒdn/ adj. 新式的，与以往不同的

strange (l.8) /streɪndʒ/ adj. 奇怪的
district (l.9) /ˈdɪstrɪkt/ n. 地区

Notes on the text　课文注释

1　get a surprise 中的surprise在这里作 "使人惊奇、意外的事物" 解，是可数名词。
2　Work on it had begun ...，住宅的建设在……就开始了。work是名词，作主语；it指房屋。
3　The house has many large rooms and there is a lovely garden. 这栋房子里有许多大房间，还有一个漂亮的花园。there is 这个结构在第1册第42-44课中曾经出现过，用来说明人/物的存在。

参考译文

　　昨天我收到了姐姐的一封信，她住在尼日利亚。在信中她说她明年将到英国来。如果她来了，她会感到非常惊奇的。我们现在住在乡间的一栋漂亮的新住宅里。这栋房子在我姐姐离开之前就已动工了，是在5个月以前竣工的。我在信中告诉她，她可以和我们住在一起。这栋房子里有许多大房间，还有一个漂亮的花园。它是一栋非常现代化的住宅，因此在有些人看来很古怪。它肯定是这个地区唯一的一栋现代化住宅。

Summary writing　摘要写作

Answer these questions *in not more than 50 words*.
回答下列问题，将答案组成一个段落，不要超过50个单词。

1　What will your sister do next year?
2　Will she get a surprise if she comes or not?
3　Have you a new house in the country or not?
4　Have you invited your sister to stay with you or not?
5　Is it a very modern house, or is it an old house?
6　Has it got many large rooms and a lovely garden or not?

Key structures 关键句型

Review KS 12-21 复习第12-21课的关键句型

I'll see you tomorrow. **(KS12)**（第12课）

What will you be doing tomorrow? **(KS13)**（第13课）

After he had finished work he went home. **(KS14)**（第14课）

He said that ... He told me ... **(KS15)**（第15课）

If you open the door you will get a surprise. **(KS16)**（第16课）

Must **(KS17)**（第17课）

Have **(KS18)**（第18课）

Can and May **(KS19)**（第19课）

Passing planes can be heard night and day. **(KS21)**（第21课）

Exercises 练习

A Underline all the verbs in the passage. Revise any Key Structures you have forgotten.
画出课文中所有的动词。复习你已忘记的关键句型。

B Give the correct form of the verbs in parentheses. Do not refer to the passage until you finish the exercise:
用括号中动词的正确形式填空，完成练习后再对照课文，核对你的答案：

I _____ (have) a letter from my sister yesterday. She _____ (live) in Nigeria. In her letter, she _____ (say) that she _____ (come) to England next year. If she _____ (come), she _____ (get) a surprise. We now _____ (live) in a beautiful new house in the country. Work on it _____ (begin) before my sister _____ (leave). The house _____ (complete) five months ago. In my letter, I _____ (tell) her that she _____ (can stay) with us. The house _____ (have) many large rooms and there _____ (be) a lovely garden. It _____ (be) a very modern house, so it _____ (look) strange to some people.

C Give the correct form of the verbs in parentheses:
用括号中动词的正确形式填空：

1 After he had read the book, he _____ (write) a review of it.

2 He did not leave his office until he _____ (finish) work.

3 If he _____ (break) his promise, I'll never speak to him again.

4 If the weather is fine, we _____ (go) for a picnic.

D Supply *said* or *told* in the following sentences. Give the correct form of the verbs in parentheses:
用 said 或 told 填空，用括号中动词的正确形式填空：

1 She _____ me she _____ (will) be absent from work.

2 I _____ my mother that I _____ (lose) the key.

3 The manager _____ that he _____ (not like) my work.

Unit 1 Lesson 23

E Which verbs can we use in place of the verbs or phrases in italics? Make any other changes necessary.

选择恰当的动词来替代用斜体印出的词或词组，必要时可作改动。

1 He *owns* a new house.

2 He *possesses* a lot of money.

3 I *took* a bath before dinner.

4 *Take* a biscuit.

5 *Will you let me* use your telephone please?

6 *Perhaps the play will* begin at any moment.

7 *Perhaps it has* begun already.

8 *It is necessary for me to* take a taxi.

Special difficulties 难点

There is and It is

Study these examples:

细读以下例句：

The house has many large rooms and *there is* a lovely garden. *It is* a very modern house, so it looks strange to some people. (ll.6-8)

There is a new school in our neighbourhood. *It was* only built last year. *There are* 250 pupils at the school. Last year *there were* only 180. Next year *there will be* over 300.

在我们这个地区有一所新学校。它是去年才建成的。共有250个学生。去年仅有180人。明年会超过300人。

What's the time? *It is* five o'clock. 现在几点钟？5点。

How far away is the station from here? *It is* five miles away. 车站离这里多远？5英里。

What's the weather like? *It is* very cold. 天气如何？天很冷。

Exercise 练习

Supply *it* or *there* in the following sentences:

用 it 或 there 填空：

1 _____ is a pity that he could not come.

2 _____ is a bus that leaves in ten minutes.

3 _____ were some men digging up the road outside my house.

4 Look at those clouds. I think _____ will be a thunderstorm.

5 _____ is unusual for him to be late.

6 _____ has been very cold this year.

7 _____ has been no news of him.

8 I am sure _____ will be fine tomorrow.

9 After dinner _____ will be a long discussion on politics.

10 When will _____ be convenient for you to come?

Multiple choice questions 选择题

Comprehension 理解

1 The writer's sister will be surprised _____ .

   (*a*) when she sees the writer's new house   (*b*) when she comes to England

   (*c*) when she sees the writer   (*d*) when she leaves Nigeria

2 Some people will find the house strange because _____ .

   (*a*) it is modern   (*b*) it is new   (*c*) it is large   (*d*) it is old

Structure 句型

3 If she _____ she will get a surprise.

   (*a*) comes   (*b*) came   (*c*) has come   (*d*) will come

4 I like my sister's house. It's a _____ .

   (*a*) new beautiful house   (*b*) beautiful house new

   (*c*) beautiful new house   (*d*) new house beautiful

5 The house _____ five months ago.

   (*a*) has completed   (*b*) completed   (*c*) was completed   (*d*) has been completed

6 I told her she could stay with us. That's what I _____ .

   (*a*) said to her   (*b*) said her   (*c*) told to her   (*d*) told

7 The house has many large rooms. _____ many large rooms.

   (*a*) They have   (*b*) They are   (*c*) There have   (*d*) There are

Vocabulary 词汇

8 I had a letter yesterday. I _____ one.

   (*a*) sent   (*b*) took   (*c*) wrote   (*d*) received

9 She will come to England _____ year.

   (*a*) last   (*b*) next   (*c*) the other   (*d*) the last

10 Our house is in the country. It's not in _____ .

   (*a*) Nigeria   (*b*) the city   (*c*) England   (*d*) France

11 Work on it had begun before my sister left. My sister left _____ it had begun.

   (*a*) after   (*b*) without   (*c*) behind   (*d*) soon

12 It is a very modern house. It was built _____ .

   (*a*) lastly   (*b*) late   (*c*) latest   (*d*) recently

Sentence structure 句子结构

Rewrite this sentence, then check your answer against the text.

改写下列句子, 然后对照课文第5-6行, 核对你的答案。

'You can stay with us,' I told her.

I told her that _____ .

Lesson 24　It could be worse　不幸中之万幸

First listen and then answer the question.

听录音, 然后回答以下问题。

Had the writer's money been stolen?

The manager was sympathetic

I entered the hotel manager's office and sat down. I had just lost £50 and I felt very upset. 'I left the money in my room,' I said, 'and it's not there now.' The manager was sympathetic, but he could do nothing. 'Everyone's losing money these days,' he said. He started
5 to complain about this wicked world but was interrupted by a knock at the door. A girl came in and put an envelope on his desk. It contained £50. 'I found this outside this gentleman's room,' she said. 'Well,' I said to the manager, 'there is still some honesty in this world!'

New words and expressions　生词和短语

manager (l.1) /ˈmænɪdʒə/ *n.* 经理
upset (l.2) /ˌʌpˈset/ *adj.* 不安的
sympathetic (l.3) /ˌsɪmpəˈθetɪk/ *adj.* 表示同情的
complain (l.5) /kəmˈpleɪn/ *v.* 抱怨

wicked (l.5) /ˈwɪkɪd/ *adj.* 很坏的, 邪恶的
contain (l.7) /kənˈteɪn/ *v.* 包含, 内装
honesty (l.8) /ˈɒnɪsti/ *n.* 诚实

Notes on the text　课文注释

1　本文的题目可以有几种不同的理解方式: "如果我丢失的不止50英镑", "如果经理没有任何同情心", "如果拾到钱的姑娘没有把钱送回来", 结局会更糟糕。

2　Everyone's losing money these days. 现在大家都在丢钱。
用现在进行时来表示不断重复的动作, 其中常含有埋怨的意思。

参考译文

　　我走进饭店经理的办公室, 坐了下来。我刚刚丢了50英镑, 感到非常烦恼。"我把钱放在房间里," 我说, "可现在没有了。"经理深表同情, 但却无能为力。"现在大家都在丢钱," 他说。他开始抱怨起这个邪恶的世道来, 却被一阵敲门声打断了。一个姑娘走了进来, 把一个信封放在了他桌上。它里面装着50英镑。"这是我在这位先生的房门外捡到的," 她说。"是啊," 我对那位经理说, "这世界上还是有诚实可言的!"

Summary writing　摘要写作

Answer these questions *in not more than 55 words*.

回答下列问题, 将答案组成一个段落, 不要超过55个单词。

1　How much money had you just lost?
2　How did you feel?
3　Did you tell the manager about it or not?

4   Could he do anything or not?

5   What did he begin complaining about?

6   Who came in with the money just then?

7   Where had she found it?

8   Is there still some honesty in this world or not?

Special difficulties 难点

Review SD2-23 复习第2-23课的难点

Exercises 练习

A   Choose the correct words in the following sentences.
   选用正确的词或短语。

1   I (took) (received) a letter from him yesterday. **(SD4)**（第4课）

2   I met Harry (in the) (on the) way to the station. **(SD5)**（第5课）

3   (In the) (On the) way from Athens to London, the plane stopped at Rome. **(SD5)**（第5课）

4   Everybody (believe) (believes) he will win. **(SD8)**（第8课）

5   Is your watch made (of) (from) gold? **(SD10)**（第10课）

6   At the end of the month I received my (salary) (wages). **(SD11)**（第11课）

7   Can you (borrow) (lend) me £5? **(SD11)**（第11课）

8   I (asked) (asked for) an explanation. **(SD14)**（第14课）

9   (Except) (Apart from) that, everything is all right. **(SD14)**（第14课）

10 He is such a(n) (irritable) (nervous) person. He is always bad tempered. **(SD15)**（第15课）

11 The police (is) (are) looking for him. **(SD16)**（第16课）

12 Please (look after) (pay attention to) the blackboard. **(SD16)**（第16课）

13 (Remind) (Remember) me to your mother. **(SD16)**（第16课）

14 Father bought a new (suit) (costume) yesterday. **(SD17)**（第17课）

15 When I (grow) (grow up) I shall be a pilot. **(SD17)**（第17课）

16 He was standing (besides) (beside) the window. **(SD18)**（第18课）

17 (It's) (Its) a very (excited) (exciting) film. **(SD20)**（第20课）

18 He does not (realize) (understand) English. **(SD20)**（第20课）

19 It was raining heavily so I was glad to get (house) (home). **(SD21)**（第21课）

20 (It is) (There is) someone at the door. **(SD23)**（第23课）

B   What a day! 感叹句 **(SD2)**（参见第2课难点）

   英语中的感叹句通常用 What 来引导,用来表示惊奇、愤怒、赞赏、喜悦等感情,结构通常为: What + 形容词 + 名词 + 主语 + 谓语动词（包括连系动词）。

   Write these sentences again. Each sentence must begin with *What*.
   改写以下句子,用What来引导每句话。

1   This is a wonderful garden!

2   He is causing a lot of trouble!

3   It is a tall building!

4   You are a clever girl!

C He lent me a book. He lent a book to me. **(SD3)**

直接宾语与间接宾语（参见第3课难点）

She bought me a tie. She bought a tie for me.

Write each of the following sentences in a different way:

用另一种形式来表示以下句子中的直接宾语和间接宾语：

1 He handed me the prize.

2 The waiter brought a bottle of beer to the man.

3 I've ordered some soup for you.

4 Bring that book to me please.

5 She promised a reward to the finder.

D Is there any tea in the pot? **(SD9)**（参见第9课难点中的 there be 结构）

There isn't any tea in the pot.

There's no tea in the pot.

Write negative answers to these questions in two different ways:

用两种不同的方式写出下列问题的否定回答：

1 Have you any money?

2 Did you go anywhere in the holidays?

3 Was there anybody present when the accident happened?

E Answer these questions. Put the apostrophe in the right place. **(SD13)**

回答以下问题，注意所有格符号的位置。（参见第13课难点）

1 Whose umbrella is this? (George)

2 Whose is this handbag? (That woman)

3 Whose poetry do you like best? (Keats)

4 Whose are these clothes? (The children)

5 Whose are these uniforms? (The soldiers)

F Knock **(SD6)**（第6课难点）; Be **(SD12)**（第12课难点）; Give **(SD18)**（第18课难点）.

Complete these sentences by adding any of the following words: *up, off, over, back, on,* or *away.*
用 up, off, over, back, on 或 away 填空。

1 He usually knocks _____ at 6 o'clock, but today he's working late.

2 I'm going out now, but I'll be _____ in half an hour.

3 I gave _____ smoking last year but I have just started again.

4 The concert was _____ and everybody left the hall.

5 A new play is _____ at the Phoenix.

6 I've given _____ all my old furniture.

G Change the position of the words in italics.

改变斜体印出的词的位置。**(SD6, SD7)**（参见第6、7课的难点）

1 I put *on* my hat.

2 I took *off* my coat.

3 He put *out* the fire.

4 They cut *off* the king's head.

Multiple choice questions 选择题

Comprehension 理解

1 The writer thought _____ .

  (*a*) he had lost his money   (*b*) someone had stolen his money

  (*c*) the manager had the money   (*d*) the girl had stolen the money

2 What had really happened?

  (*a*) The writer had lost the money.   (*b*) The girl had stolen the money.

  (*c*) The manager had taken the money.   (*d*) Someone had stolen the money.

Structure 句型

3 The money _____ in his room.

  (*a*) was   (*b*) were   (*c*) are   (*d*) has

4 He could do nothing. He couldn't do _____ .

  (*a*) something   (*b*) nothing   (*c*) anything   (*d*) everything

5 A knock at the door _____ him.

  (*a*) interrupted   (*b*) was interrupted   (*c*) interrupting   (*d*) was interrupting

6 Where did she find the money? _____ the room.

  (*a*) Outside   (*b*) Out of   (*c*) Out   (*d*) Without

7 _____ room was it? This gentleman's.

  (*a*) To whom   (*b*) Who   (*c*) Whose   (*d*) Of whom

Vocabulary 词汇

8 The writer had lost his money. He felt upset. He must have been _____ .

  (*a*) sick   (*b*) ill   (*c*) worried   (*d*) tired

9 The manager was sympathetic. _____ .

  (*a*) Everyone liked him   (*b*) He liked everyone

  (*c*) He was sorry for the writer   (*d*) He liked the writer

10 He lost his money. His money was _____ .

  (*a*) losing   (*b*) missing   (*c*) going away   (*d*) disappearing

11 You can't post this letter without _____ .

  (*a*) an envelope   (*b*) a packet   (*c*) some string   (*d*) a pen

12 The girl returned the money. She was very _____ .

  (*a*) honourable   (*b*) honest   (*c*) honoured   (*d*) trusting

Sentence structure 句子结构

Rewrite this sentence, then check your answer against the text.

改写下列句子, 然后对照课文第4-6行, 核对你的答案。

When he started to complain about this wicked world, he was interrupted by a knock at the door.

He started _____ .

PRE-UNIT TEST 2
测试 2

IF YOU CAN DO THIS TEST GO ON TO UNIT 2

如果你能完成以下测验，请开始第 2 单元的学习

Key structures 关键句型

A Word order in simple statements 简单陈述句的语序

a There is a line under each word or group of words in the statements below. The words are not in the right order. Arrange them correctly.

下列句子中的每一个词或每一组词的下面均有一条横线。按正常语序排列这些词和词组。

1 <u>The film</u>   <u>I</u>   <u>enjoyed</u>   <u>yesterday</u>.

2 <u>My mother</u>   <u>to market</u>   <u>went</u>.

3 <u>The</u>   <u>children</u>   <u>asked</u>   <u>continuously</u>   <u>questions</u>   <u>in</u>   <u>class</u>   <u>this morning</u>.

4 <u>We</u>   <u>at home</u>   <u>stay</u>   <u>on Sundays</u>.

5 <u>This morning</u>   <u>a book</u>   <u>I</u>   <u>from the library</u>   <u>borrowed</u>.

b Write these sentences again. Put the words in parentheses in the right place.

改写以下句子，将括号中的词置于正确的位置。

1 She answers my letters. (rarely)

2 The shops close on Saturday afternoons. (always)

3 We work after six o'clock. (never)

4 We spend our holidays abroad. (sometimes)

5 Do you buy CDs? (ever)

B Verbs 动词

a Now and Always 表示现在和经常发生的动作

The verbs in parentheses tell us what is happening *now* and what *always* happens. Give the correct form of each verb.

括号中的动词告诉我们现在正在进行和经常发生的动作。给出这些动词的正确形式。

I am looking out of my window. I can see some children in the street. The children (play) football. They always (play) football in the street. Now a little boy (kick) the ball. Another boy (run) after him but he cannot catch him.

b What happened? 一般过去时

The verbs in parentheses tell us *what happened*. Give the correct form of each verb.

括号中的动词告诉我们过去发生的动作，给出这些动词的正确形式。

My friend, Roy, _____ (die) last year. He _____ (leave) me his CD player and his collection of CDs. Roy _____ (spend) a lot of money on CDs. He _____ (buy) one or two new CDs every week. He never _____ (go) to the cinema or to the theatre. He _____ (stay) at home every evening and _____ (listen) to music. He often _____ (lend) CDs to his friends. Sometimes they _____ (keep) them. He _____ (lose) many CDs in this way.

c What has happened? 现在完成时

The verbs in parentheses tell us *what has happened*. Give the correct form of each verb.

括号中的动词告诉我们现在已经完成的动作。给出这些动词的正确形式。

I just _____ (receive) a letter from my brother Tim. He is in Australia. He _____ (be) there for six

110

months. Tim is an engineer. He is working for a big firm and he already _____ (visit) a great number of different places in Australia. He just _____ (buy) an Australian car and _____ (go) to Alice Springs.

d What happened? What has happened? 一般过去时和现在完成时

The verbs in parentheses tell us *what happened* and *what has happened*. Give the correct form of each verb.

括号中的动词告诉我们过去发生和现在已经完成的动作。给出这些动词的正确形式。

1 What _____ you (buy) yesterday?

2 Up till now, he never _____ (lend) me anything.

3 _____ you (burn) those old papers yet?

4 He _____ (fight) in Flanders in the First World War.

5 We just _____ (win) the match.

e What was happening? What happened? 过去进行时和一般过去时

The verbs in parentheses tell us *what was happening* and *what happened*. Give the correct form of each verb.

括号中的动词告诉我们过去正在进行和过去发生的动作。给出这些动词的正确形式。

1 As my father (leave) the house, the postman (arrive).

2 Tom (work) in the garden while I (sit) in the sun.

3 As I (walk) down the street, I (meet) Charlie.

4 While he (read) the letter, he (hear) a knock at the door.

5 She drop the tray when I spoke to her.

f What will happen? 一般将来时

In the paragraph below, the verbs in italics tell us *what happened*. Write the passage again. Change the verbs in italics so that they tell us *what will happen*.

在下面这个段落中，斜体印出的动词告诉我们过去发生的动作。重写这个段落，将斜体印出的动词改为一般将来时。

I *went* to the theatre with my friend Reg. Reg and I *saw* the first performance of a play called 'The End of the Road'. After the play, the producer *gave* a short speech. He *spoke* to the audience about the play. The play *was* very successful and I think a great many people *enjoyed* it very much.

g What will be happening? 将来进行时

Change the form of the verbs in italics so that they tell us *what will be happening*.

将斜体印出的动词改为将来进行时。

1 I *am ironing* the clothes.

2 The train *will arrive* in a few minutes.

3 We'*ll see* you in the morning.

4 We *are watching* the match.

5 He *is correcting* exercise books.

h After he had finished work he went home. 过去完成时

Join these pairs of sentences with the words given in parentheses.

用括号内所给的词连接以下各对句子。

1 (After) She wrote the letter. She went to the post office.

2 (After) He had dinner. He went to the cinema.

3 (When) I fastened my seat belt. The plane took off.

4 We did not disturb him. (until) He finished work.

5 (As soon as) He left the room. I turned on the radio.

i   It was made in Germany in 1681. 被动语态
    Supply the correct form of the verbs in parentheses.
    给出括号内动词的正确形式。
    The Taj Mahal _____ (build) in the seventeenth century for the emperor Shah Jahan. A few years after he _____ (become) ruler, his wife, Mumtaz-i-Mahal, _____ (die). The Taj Mahal _____ (build) in her honour. Experts _____ (call) in from many parts of the world to construct the domes and to decorate the walls. The Taj Mahal which _____ (begin) in 1632 and _____ (complete) in 1654 _____ (cost) a fortune. Up to the present day, it _____ (visit) by millions of people.

j   He said that ... He told me ... 间接引语
    Supply *said* or *told* in the following sentences. Give the correct form of the verbs in parentheses.
    在下列句子中填上 said 或 told, 并给出括号内动词的正确形式。
    1 He _____ me that she _____ (come) tomorrow.
    2 The gardener _____ that he _____ (cut) that tree down yesterday.
    3 I _____ you I _____ (have) never played tennis before.
    4 What _____ he _____ that he _____ (do) last weekend?
    5 When _____ he _____ you that he _____ (buy) this car?

k   If 条件句
    Give the correct form of the verbs in parentheses.
    给出括号内动词的正确形式。
    1 If it _____ (rain) I shall take an umbrella with me.
    2 You never _____ (pass) this test if you don't work hard.
    3 If he _____ (be) here before 10 o'clock, I shall see him.
    4 If he plays well, he _____ (get) into the team.
    5 If he _____ (enjoy) concerts, why doesn't he come with us?

l   Give the correct form of the verbs in parentheses.
    给出括号内动词的正确形式。
    _____ (fish) is my favourite sport. I often fish for hours without _____ (catch) anything. But this does not worry me. Some fishermen are unlucky. Instead of _____ (catch) fish, they catch old boots and rubbish. I am even less lucky. I never catch anything — not even old boots. After _____ (have spend) whole mornings on the river, I always go home with an empty bag. 'You must give up _____ (fish)!' my friends say. 'It's a waste of time.' But they don't realize one important thing. I'm not really interested in _____ (fish). I am only interested in _____ (sit) in a boat and _____ (do) nothing at all!

C Must, Have to, Can and May

a   Write these sentences again using *must* or *have* to in place of the words in italics.
    用 must 或 have to 来代替斜体印出的词组。
    1 *It will be necessary for you to* see a doctor.
    2 *Is it necessary for you to* make so much noise?
    3 She said *it would be necessary for us to* stay here.
    4 *It is necessary for me to* have some help.

5 *It was necessary for him to* go out last night.

b   Write these sentences again in a different way using *must be* in place of the words in italics.
改写以下句子, 用 must be 来代替斜体印出的词组。

1 *I, personally, think he is* a fool.
2 *I, personally, think he is* mad.
3 *I, personally, think she is* over forty.

c   Write these sentences again in a different way using *can* or *may* in place of the words in italics.
改写以下句子, 用 can 或 may 来代替斜体印出的词组。

1 *Will you let me* use your telephone please?
2 *Perhaps he will* telephone tomorrow.
3 *Will you let me* have two tickets please?
4 *Perhaps the play has* begun already.
5 *Will you let me* leave the table please?

D   A, The and Some

a   Write these words again. Put in *a* or *some* in front of each one.
在下列词前加上 a 或 some。

soap, picture, milk, money, woman, window, bus, sand, rice, newspaper, water, cloud, son, coal, secretary, oil.

b   Put in *a* or *the* where necessary in the passage below.
在需要的地方加上 a 或 the。

I have just moved to _____ house in _____ Bridge Street. Yesterday _____ beggar knocked at my door. He asked me for _____ meal and _____ glass of beer. In return for this, _____ beggar stood on his head and sang _____ songs. I gave him _____ meal. He ate _____ food and drank _____ beer. Then he put _____ piece of cheese in his pocket and went away. Later _____ neighbour told me about him. Everybody knows him. His name is _____ Percy Buttons. He calls at every house in _____ street once _____ month and always asks for _____ meal and _____ glass of beer.

E   The best and the worst 形容词的比较级和最高级

Give the correct form of the words in parentheses. Supply *than* where necessary.
给出括号中形容词的正确形式, 必要时加上 than。

1 It is _____ (unusual) film I have ever seen.
2 Mr. Jones is a _____ (good) teacher _____ Mr. Brown.
3 This book is _____ (interesting) _____ that one.
4 She is _____ (lazy) pupil in the class.
5 The weather today is _____ (bad) _____ it was yesterday.

F   When did you arrive? I arrived at ten o'clock.

Supply the correct words in the following sentences.
用正确的词填空。

1 He has gone abroad. He will return _____ two years' time.
2 _____ Saturdays I always go to the market.
3 I never go to the cinema _____ the week.

4 I can't see him _____ the moment. I'm busy.

5 My birthday is _____ November 7th. I was born _____ 1988.

6 The days are very short _____ December.

7 We arrived at the village late _____ night. We left early _____ the morning.

G Verbs followed by *of, from, in* and *on* 带有 of, from, in 和 on 的动词短语

Supply the missing words in the sentences below.

用正确的词填空。

1 Is this included _____ the bill?

2 I received a telephone call _____ him yesterday.

3 You can rely _____ me.

4 I am thinking _____ going abroad next year.

5 Are you interested _____ music?

6 I am tired _____ telling you the same thing again and again.

Special difficulties 难点

A Words often confused 经常混淆的词

Choose the correct words in the following sentences.

选择正确的词或短语。

1 (By the way) (On the way) have you seen Tom lately?

2 I (borrowed) (lent) this book from the library.

3 Can you (ask) (ask for) questions in English?

4 That tree has (grown) (grown up) a lot since I last saw it.

5 (Besides) (Beside) being a teacher, he is also a novelist.

6 The cat has drunk (it's) (its) milk.

7 Have you seen Tom (yet) (still)?

8 I put the papers on your (desk) (office).

9 You can't jump over that fence. (It is) (There is) impossible.

10 I like staying at (house) (home) during the weekend.

B Knock, Give and Be

Supply the missing words in the following.

用正确的词填空。

1 Someone is knocking _____ the door.

2 The doctor told him to give _____ smoking.

3 What's _____ at the cinema this week?

4 You can't see Mr Jones. He is _____ at the moment. He will be _____ in ten minutes.

5 The soldier hit the guard very hard and knocked him _____ .

C Where possible, change the position of the words in italics.

在可能的情况下改变斜体印出的词的位置。

1 Who knocked *over* this vase?

2 She is looking *after* the children.

3 Put *on* your jacket.

4 Bring it *back* quickly.

5 The thieves woke *up* the night watchman.

D Put the words in parentheses in their correct order.

按正确的语序排列括号中的词。

1 The officer ordered (to fire — at the enemy — the men).

2 He wants (his wife — this dress — to wear)

3 She wants (us — it — to explain)

4 I cannot allow (the room — him — to enter).

5 She taught (to read — her son).

E Write these sentences in a different way. Omit the words in italics.

改写以下句子，省略斜体印出的词。

1 She made this dress *for* me.

2 I lent my book *to* him.

3 I showed the letter *to* George.

4 Pass that cup *to* your mother.

5 Johnny gave the doll *to* his sister.

Unit 2
第 2 单元

Unit 2 第 2 单元

INSTRUCTIONS TO THE STUDENT 致学生

In Unit 1 you learned how to write simple statements. In Unit 2 you will learn how to join simple statements together with words like 'and', 'but' and 'so'. You will learn how to write sentences which contain more than one idea.

在第 1 单元你学会了如何组成简单句。在第 2 单元你要学习如何用 "and", "but", "so" 一类词来连接简单句。你要学会组成表达一层以上意思的句子。

Before you begin each exercise, read these instructions carefully. Read them *each time* you begin a new piece. They are very important.

在开始每项练习之前，要细读这些指令。它们很重要，每次开始新课前都要读读指令。

How to work — Summary writing 如何写摘要

Unit 2 contains twenty-four short passages. There are questions under each piece. Your answers to these questions will often contain more than one idea. Put your answers together to make a short paragraph.

第 2 单元共有 24 篇短文。每篇课文下面都有问题。你的回答常常有多层意思。把你的答案组成一个小的段落。

1 Read the passage carefully two or three times. Make sure you understand it.

   细读课文 2 至 3 遍。一定要理解课文。

2 Write a full answer to each question. When you find two or three questions together, join up your answers with the joining words given in parentheses. Each answer you write must be a *complete sentence*.

   给每个问题一个完整的答案。当你发现有 2 或 3 个问题相关联时，用括号中所给的连词把你的答案连成一句话。你写的每一个答案都必须是**一个完整的句子**。

3 Your answers to the questions must follow one another. All your answers together will then make *a complete paragraph*.

   你的答案必须句句相连。所有的答案加起来可组成**一个完整的段落**。

4 Read through your work and correct your mistakes.

   从头至尾读一遍你的答案，纠正其中的错误。

5 Count the number of words in your paragraph. Words like 'the', 'a', etc. count as single words. Words which are joined by a hyphen (e.g. hold-up) also count as single words. Do not go over the word limit. At the end of your paragraph write the number of words that you have used.

   数一下段落的字数。冠词和用连字符连起来的词均为一个词。不要超过字数的限制。在段落的后面注明全段的字数。

Example 范例

Work through this example carefully and then try to do the exercises in Unit 2 in the same way.

仔细研究以下例题，然后用同样的方式完成第 2 单元的练习。

What's the time?

People often collect things. Stamps, books and records are fairly common. But the strangest collection I have ever seen belongs to a man who possesses 1,500 clocks. There are clocks in every room of his house. The living room is lined with shelves which have been filled with clocks. As there is not enough room for so many clocks, the man has filled several trunks and stored them in the garage. His wife complains every day about the work she has to do, for it is not easy to dust several hundred clocks. She also complains about the noise. Each clock keeps its own time, so chimes can be heard almost any time during the day and night. In her opinion, however, there is something even worse than dust and noise. Even with so many clocks around, she never knows what time it is!

Summary writing 摘要写作

Answer these questions *in not more than 70 words*.
回答以下问题, 不要超过 70 个单词。

1 How many clocks has the man collected? Has he put them in every room of his house or not? (*and*)

2 Has he lined his living room with them or not? What else has he filled? (*not only ... but ... as well*)

3 Does his wife have to dust hundreds of clocks or not?

4 Does she complain about the work and the noise or not?

5 Does each clock keep the correct time, or does it keep its own time?

6 What does she hear day and night? Does she ever know the correct time or not? (*Because of this ... not only ... but*)

Answer 答案

A man has collected 1,500 clocks and has put them in every room of his house. He has *not only* lined his living room with them, *but* has filled several trunks *as well*. His wife has to dust hundreds of clocks. She complains about the work and noise. Each clock keeps its own time. *Because of this,* she *not only* hears chimes day and night, *but* never knows the correct time. (70 words)

Composition 如何作文

In Unit 2 Composition has been dealt with separately. This unit contains two types of composition exercise:
在第 2 单元, 作文是单独一项练习。这个单元的作文有两种形式:

1 Learning how to select correct verbs and joining words. (Passages 25-36.)
学会选择正确的动词和连词。

2 Joining simple sentences together. (Passages 37-48.)
连接简单句。

Examples 范例

Work through these examples carefully and then try to do the composition exercises in the same way.
仔细研究以下例题, 然后用同样的方式完成第 2 单元的作文练习。

1 Sample composition 作文范例 1

Rewrite these sentences using the correct verbs and joining words:
用正确的动词和连词改写以下句子。

He never (knows) (understands) the correct time (and) (but) is often late for work. It was his birthday last week (so) (yet) his wife (took) (bought) him a present. She (brought) (bought) him an alarm clock (but) (and) he was (delighted) (enjoyed) with it.

Answer 答案

He never *knows* the correct time *and* is often late for work. It was his birthday last week *so* his wife *bought* him a present. She *bought* him an alarm clock *and* he was *delighted* with it.

2 Sample composition 作文范例 2

Rewrite the following sentences using the joining words in parentheses.
用括号中的连词改写以下句子。

1   His wife tells him he must sell the clocks. He must give them away to a museum. (*either ... or*)

2   He refuses to do so. He spends even more money on clocks. (*not only ... but*)

3   He says he will not sell them. He will not give them away. (*neither ... nor*)

Answer 答案

His wife tells him he must *either* sell the clocks *or* give them away to a museum. He *not only* refuses to do so *but* spends even more money on clocks. He says he will *neither* sell them *nor* give them away.

Letter writing 书信写作

This is begun in Unit 2. Carefully follow the instructions given under each passage.
书信写作从第 2 单元开始，仔细研究每课中的指令。

Key structures and Special difficulties 关键句型和难点

When you finish the **Letter writing** exercise, go on to the language exercises that follow. The **Key structures** deal with exactly the same problems that were considered in Unit 1. You may refer back if you have forgotten anything. A little more new information about the **Key structures** is added here. **Special difficulties** are dealt with after the **Key structures**. The work you do in grammar is based on material contained in the passages. Refer to the passages frequently. They will help you to understand the grammar and to do the exercises.
当你结束"书信写作"后，就可以开始紧随其后的语言练习。"关键句型"的问题与第 1 单元相同。如果你有遗忘的地方，可以在第 1 单元查找。这里增加了有关句型的一点新内容。"关键句型"之后是"难点"。其中的语法练习是以课文中的语言点为基础的。经常查找课文可以帮助你理解语法并完成练习。

Lesson 25　Do the English speak English?　英国人讲的是英语吗?

Then he spoke slowly

First listen and then answer the question.

听录音，然后回答以下问题。

Why does the writer not understand the porter?

I arrived in London at last. The railway station was big, black and dark. I did not know the way to my hotel, so I asked a porter. I not only spoke English very carefully, but very clearly as well. The porter, however, could not understand me. I repeated my question
5　several times and at last he understood. He answered me, but he spoke neither slowly nor clearly. 'I am a foreigner,' I said. Then he spoke slowly, but I could not understand him. My teacher never spoke English like that! The porter and I looked at each other and smiled. Then he said something and I understood it. 'You'll soon learn English!' he said. I wonder. In England,
10　each person speaks a different language. The English understand each other, but *I* don't understand *them*! Do they speak English?

New words and expressions　生词和短语

railway (l.1) /ˈreɪlweɪ/ *n.* 铁路

porter (l.2) /ˈpɔːtə/ *n.* 搬运工

several (l.5) /ˈsevərəl/ *quantifier* 几个

foreigner (l.6) /ˈfɒrɪnə/ *n.* 外国人

wonder (l.9) /ˈwʌndə/ *v.* 感到奇怪

Notes on the text　课文注释

1　at last, 终于。

2　the way to my hotel, 去（我住的那家）饭店的路。

3　not only ... but ... as well, 不但……而且……，与 not only ... but also 是同样意思，所连接的前后两部分的成分必须一致。

4　neither ... nor ..., 既不……又不……，这个结构所连接的两个否定概念也必须是对等的成分。

5　like that, 像那样。介词短语作状语，修饰动词 spoke。

6　the English, 英国人。与定冠词连用，表示一个群体，所跟的动词用复数。

参考译文

　　我终于到了伦敦。火车站很大，又黑又暗。我不知道去饭店的路该怎么走，于是向一个搬运工打听。我的英语讲得不但非常认真，而且咬字也非常清楚。然而搬运工却不明白我的话。我把问话重复了很多遍。他终于听懂了。他回答了，但他讲得既不慢也不清楚。"我是个外国人，"我说。于是他说得慢了，可我还是听不懂。我的老师从来不那样讲英语! 我和搬运工相视一笑。接着，他说了点什么，这回我听懂了。"您会很快学会英语的!"他说。我感到奇怪。在英国，人们各自说着一种不同的语言。英国人之间相互听得懂，可我却不懂他们的话! 他们说的是英语吗?

Summary writing 摘要写作

Answer these questions *in not more than 70 words.*
回答下列问题, 将答案组成一个段落, 不要超过 70 个单词。

1 Did you arrive at a railway station in London or not? Did you ask a porter the way to your hotel or not? Could he understand you or not? (*and ... but*)

2 Did he understand you at last or not? Could you understand his answer? (*but*)

3 Did your teacher ever speak English like that or not?

4 What did the porter say to you?

5 Does each person speak a different language in England or not?

6 Do they understand each other or not? Do you understand them? (*but*)

Letter writing 书信写作

The address appears at the top right-hand corner of the page. It is called 'the Heading'. The address is always followed by the date:
写信人的地址位于信纸的右上角, 被称为 "信头", 地址后面总是接着写日期:

14 Grafton St.,	格拉夫顿大街 14 号
Croydon,	克莱敦市
Surrey,	萨里郡
England.	英格兰
24th April, 19__	19__ 年 4 月 24 日

Exercise 练习

Write your home address. Follow the above pattern carefully.
仔细按照上面的格式, 写出你家的地址。

Key structures 关键句型

Word order in compound statements 并列句中的语序

a　Do you remember the six parts of a simple statement? Refer to **KS 1** if you have forgotten them.
你还记得简单句中的 6 个组成部分吗? 如果记不清, 可以查看第 1 课的关键句型。

b　We can join simple statements together to make *compound statements*. Here are some of the joining words we use:
我们可以将几个简单句连在一起, 组成并列句。我们常用以下连词:
and, but, so, yet, or, both ... and, either ... or, neither ... nor, not only ... but ... as well (or also)。

Study these sentences carefully. Pay close attention to the way they have been joined:
仔细阅读以下句子, 特别注意它们是如何连接起来的:
He finished lunch. He went into the garden. 他吃完午饭。他走进花园。
He finished lunch *and went* into the garden. 他吃完午饭, 走进花园。
I ran to the station. I missed the train. 我跑到车站。我误了火车。
I ran to the station *but missed* the train. 我跑到车站, 但误了火车。
I saw him yesterday. He did not greet me. 我昨天见到了他。他没有理我。
I saw him yesterday *but he* did not greet me. 我昨天见到了他, 但他没有理我。

He teaches English. I teach English. 他教英语。我教英语。

Both he and I teach English. 他和我都教英语。

He teaches English. He teaches French. 他教英语。他教法语。

He teaches *both English and French.* 他既教英语又教法语。

You must tell him. I must tell him. 你必须告诉他。我必须告诉他。

Either you or I must tell him. 或是你或是我必须告诉他。

He plays soccer. He plays rugby. 他踢英式足球。他玩橄榄球。

He plays *either soccer or rugby.* 他或是玩英式足球或是玩橄榄球。

He does not speak English. I do not speak English. 他不讲英语。我不讲英语。

Neither he nor I speak English. 他和我都不讲英语。

He does not speak English. He does not speak French. 他不讲英语。他不讲法语。

He speaks *neither English nor French.* 他既不讲英语也不讲法语。

He cannot read. He cannot write. 他不会读。他不会写。

He can *neither read nor write.* 他既不会读也不会写。

You must wash the dishes. You must sweep the floor. 你必须洗碗。你必须擦地。

You must *not only* wash the dishes *but* sweep the floor *as well.* 你不仅需要洗碗而且还要擦地。

Exercises 练习

A Underline the joining words in the passage.
画出课文中所有连词。

B Join these pairs of sentences. Use the joining words in parentheses. Do not refer to the passage until you finish the exercise.
用括号中的连词将每组句子连到一起，完成练习后再对照课文，核对你的答案。

1 I did not know the way to my hotel. I asked a porter. (*so*)

2 I spoke English very carefully. I spoke very clearly. (*not only ... but ... as well*)

3 I repeated my question several times. At last he understood. (*and*)

4 He answered me. He did not speak slowly. He did not speak clearly. (*but ... neither ... nor*)

5 Then he spoke slowly. I could not understand him. (*but*)

6 Then he said something. I understood it. (*and*)

7 The English understand each other. I don't understand them. (*but*)

C Join these sentences with the words in parentheses:
用括号中的斜体字连接以下句子：

1 I knocked at the door. He did not open it. (*but*)

2 He went on holiday. I went on holiday. (*Both ... and*)

3 He must be mad. He must be very wise. (*either ... or*)

Composition 作文

Join the following sentences using the words in parentheses:
用括号中的词连接下列句子：

1 My sister went shopping. I went shopping. (*Both ... and*)

2 We got very tired. We got very hungry. (*not only ... but ... as well*)

3 It was three o'clock. We could not get lunch. We had a cup of tea. (*and ... so*)

Multiple choice questions 选择题

Comprehension 理解

1 Why couldn't the writer understand the porter?

(*a*) The writer didn't know any English.   (*b*) The porter didn't speak English.

(*c*) The writer couldn't understand the porter's English.   (*d*) The writer was a foreigner.

2 The writer _____ .

(*a*) didn't think the porter was English   (*b*) expected everyone in England to speak like his teacher

(*c*) doesn't think the English speak English   (*d*) thinks that the English speak many different languages

Structure 句型

3 English _____ not a difficult language.

(*a*) are   (*b*) is   (*c*) was   (*d*) has

4 _____ did you repeat your question? Several times.

(*a*) How many times   (*b*) How many   (*c*) How much   (*d*) How

5 He didn't speak slowly and he didn't speak clearly _____ .

(*a*) neither   (*b*) either   (*c*) too   (*d*) nor

6 The porter and I looked at each other. _____ both smiled.

(*a*) I   (*b*) He   (*c*) We   (*d*) They

7 He said something and I understood it. He said something _____ I understood.

(*a*) who   (*b*) whose   (*c*) whom   (*d*) which

Vocabulary 词汇

8 I repeated my question several times. I repeated it _____ times.

(*a*) much   (*b*) a number of   (*c*) only a few   (*d*) three

9 At last he understood. He understood _____ .

(*a*) in the end   (*b*) at least   (*c*) lastly   (*d*) at the finish

10 I come from abroad. I am _____ .

(*a*) a foreigner   (*b*) strange   (*c*) overseas   (*d*) abroad

11 My teacher _____ me English.

(*a*) learnt   (*b*) trained   (*c*) instructed   (*d*) taught

12 'You'll soon learn English,' he said. I wonder. I _____ .

(*a*) am not sure   (*b*) am sure   (*c*) wander   (*d*) know

Sentence structure 句子结构

Rewrite this sentence, then check your answer against the text.

改写下列句子, 然后对照课文第 2 行, 核对你的答案。

Because I did not know the way to my hotel, I asked a porter.

I _____ .

Lesson 26   The best art critics   最佳艺术评论家

First listen and then answer the question.

听录音，然后回答以下问题。

Who is the student's best critic?

I am an art student and I paint a lot of pictures. Many people
pretend that they understand modern art. They always tell you what
a picture is 'about'. Of course, many pictures are not 'about' anything.
They are just pretty patterns. We like them in the same way that we
5 like pretty curtain material. I think that young children
often appreciate modern pictures better than anyone else.
They notice more. My sister is only seven, but she always tells me
whether my pictures are good or not. She came into my room
yesterday.

10   'What are you doing?' she asked.

'I'm hanging this picture on the wall,' I answered. 'It's a new one. Do you like it?'

She looked at it critically for a moment. 'It's all right,' she said, 'but isn't it upside down?'

I looked at it again. She was right! It was!

She looked at it critically

New words and expressions   生词和短语

art (title) /ɑːt/ *n.* 艺术
critic (title) /'krɪtɪk/ *n.* 评论家
paint (l.1) /peɪnt/ *v.* 画
pretend (l.2) /prɪ'tend/ *v.* 假装
pattern (l.4) /'pætən/ *n.* 图案
curtain (l.5) /'kɜːtn/ *n.* 窗帘，幕布
material (l.5) /mə'tɪərɪəl/ *n.* 材料

appreciate (l.6) /ə'priːʃieɪt/ *v.* 鉴赏
notice (l.7) /'nəʊtɪs/ *v.* 注意到
whether (l.8) /'weðə/ *conj.* 是否
hang (l.11) /hæŋ/ (hung /hʌŋ/, hung) *v.* 悬挂，吊
critically (l.12) /'krɪtɪˌkli/ *adv.* 批评地
upside down (l.12) /ˌʌpsaɪd-'daʊn/ 上下颠倒地

Notes on the text   课文注释

1 art student, 学艺术的学生。

2 They always tell you what a picture is 'about'. 他们总是告诉你一张画的"意思"是什么。很明显，作者认为
那些自以为懂得现代艺术的人的评论根本不着边际。因此，把 about（"对画的分析"）这个词放在引号
里，以示一种讽刺的口吻。

3 It's a new one. 这是一幅新画。句中的 one 用来代替前一句中的名词 picture, 以免重复。

参考译文

　　我是个学艺术的学生，画了很多画。有很多人装成很懂现代艺术的样子，总是告诉你一幅画的"意思"是
什么。当然，有很多画是什么"意思"也没有的。它们就是些好看的图案，我们喜爱它们就像我们喜欢漂亮
的窗帘布一样。我觉得小孩子们往往比任何人都更能欣赏现代绘画，他们观察到的东西更多。我的妹妹只有7
岁，但她总能说出我的画是好还是坏。昨天她到我房里来了。

"你在干什么呢?"她问。

"我正把这幅画挂到墙上去。"我回答说,"这是幅新画,你喜欢吗?"

她用挑剔的目光看了一会儿。"还可以吧。"她说,"不过,是不是挂倒了?"

我再次看了看画。她说对了! 是挂倒了!

Summary writing 摘要写作

Answer these questions *in not more than 70 words.*
回答下列问题, 将答案组成一个段落, 不要超过 70 个单词。

1 Does the writer study art, or does he study music? Does he paint a lot of pictures or not? (*and*)

2 Do many people really understand modern art or not?

3 Do paintings always have a meaning or not?

4 Are they sometimes pretty patterns or not?

5 Do young children appreciate modern paintings better than others or not? Do they notice more or not? (*not only ... but*)

6 When did the writer's young sister go into his room? Did she examine his new picture or not? (*and*)

7 Had he hung it upside down, or had he hung it the right way up? Did she notice this immediately or not? (*and*)

Composition 作文

Rewrite these sentences using the correct verbs and joining words:
改写以下句子, 选用正确的动词和连词:

I (looked at) (watched) the picture (but) (and) I could not (understand) (realize) it. It was in black and white and was (called) (named) 'Trees and snow'. I could see (neither) (not only) trees (or) (nor) snow.

Letter writing 书信写作

Which of the following headings is correct?
下列信头中哪一个是正确的?

John Madgewick,	Grafton St., 14,	14 Grafton St.,
14 Grafton St.,	Croydon,	Croydon,
Croydon,	Surrey,	Surrey,
Surrey,	England.	England.
England.	24th April, 19__	24th April, 19__

Key structures 关键句型

These things always happen. 经常发生的事情

a　I am having breakfast. Do you always get up so late? (Now and Always **KS2** 见第 2 课的关键句型)

b　The earth *goes* round the sun. 地球围绕太阳转。

　　The sun *rises* in the east and *sets* in the west. 太阳从东方升起, 在西方落下。

c　We rarely put *ing* at the end of these verbs: 以下动词很少用于进行时态:

　　appear, appreciate, believe, feel, forget, hear, know, like, look like, notice, remember, resemble, see, think (that), understand.

　　These verbs tell us what always happens:
　　这些动词告诉我们经常发生的事情:

　　I *hear* that you *like* classical music. 我听说你喜欢古典音乐。

I *remember* Tom very well. *Do you know* him? 我很清楚地记得汤姆。你认识他吗?

Exercises 练习

A   Underline the verbs in the passage that tell us what *always* happens and those which tell us what is happening *now*.

将课文中描述经常发生的动作和正在发生的动作的动词画出来。

B   What is happening? What always happens? 现在进行时和一般现在时

Give the correct form of the verbs in parentheses:

用括号中动词的正确形式填空:

'Some people still _____ (believe) the world is flat,' he said.

'You _____ (joke),' I replied. 'I _____ (not know) anyone who does.'

'Well, you _____ (know) me,' he replied. 'I _____ (believe) that the earth is flat. I met a man the other day. I _____ (forget) his name now. He said that the earth _____ (look) like a flat dish.'

'_____ you (try) to tell me that you _____ (believe) him?' I asked.

'I certainly do,' he answered. 'I _____ (think) that he is right.'

'And which side of the dish you _____ (live) on?'

'Oh, I _____ (not know). He didn't tell me that!'

Special difficulties 难点

Speech marks 引号

In written conversation, we put speech marks ('...') or ("...") round the words that are actually spoken.

在书面会话中, 我们用引号(单引号或双引号)把实际的对话括起来。

Read this carefully:

细读以下例句:

'What are you doing?' she asked.

'I'm hanging this picture on the wall,' I answered. 'It's a new one. Do you like it?'

She looked at it critically for a moment. 'It's all right,' she said, 'but isn't it upside down?' (l.12)

Some things to notice:

注意事项:

a   The speech marks are above the line. They go outside all other marks like commas (,), full stops (.) and question marks (?).

引号位于一行之上, 它们应在句尾其他标点符号——如逗号、句号、问号——之外。

b   The speaker's first word begins with a capital letter.

引语的第一个词以大写字母开头。

c   Words like 'said' and 'asked' are followed by a comma. We put a full stop after them only when they come at the end of a sentence.

在 said, asked 等词后面用逗号, 只有当它们位于句尾时, 才在它们的后面用句号。

d   When words like 'said' or 'asked' interrupt the speaker, the second half of the sentence begins with a small letter.

当 said, asked 等词置于引语之间时, 句子的后半部分以小写字母开始。

e   We begin a new paragraph each time a new speaker is introduced.

当一个新的说话人开始讲话时, 要另起一个段落。

Exercise 练习

Write this piece of conversation again using speech marks:

用引号改写以下对话:

Look! she said, isn't that man drunk? I think we should cross the road, answered her husband. It's too late now, she replied. Eh, you two. Look where you're going, called the drunk. Can't you walk in a straight line?

Multiple choice questions 选择题

Comprehension 理解

1 The writer thinks _____ .

  (*a*) you can't always 'explain' modern pictures   (*b*) you can always 'explain' modern pictures

  (*c*) modern pictures are always about something   (*d*) we can use modern pictures as curtain material

2 The writer's sister _____ .

  (*a*) paints pictures   (*b*) didn't like her brother's picture

  (*c*) didn't see her brother's picture   (*d*) noticed that her brother had made a mistake

Structure 句型

3 Many people pretend that they _____ modern art.

  (*a*) understood   (*b*) are understanding   (*c*) understand   (*d*) understands

4 What is it about? Tell me _____ .

  (*a*) what is it about   (*b*) what it is about   (*c*) what about it is   (*d*) what about is it

5 She tells me _____ my pictures are good or not.

  (*a*) weather   (*b*) that   (*c*) if   (*d*) unless

6 Do you like my picture? It's _____ .

  (*a*) a new   (*b*) one new   (*c*) new one   (*d*) a new one

7 I looked at it again. She _____ right! It was!

  (*a*) had   (*b*) has   (*c*) is   (*d*) was

Vocabulary 词汇

8 We like them _____ we like pretty curtain material.

  (*a*) just as   (*b*) the same   (*c*) just the same   (*d*) so

9 This curtain material is very good _____ .

  (*a*) clothes   (*b*) cloth   (*c*) substance   (*d*) matter

10 Young children often appreciate modern pictures. They _____ them.

  (*a*) estimate   (*b*) esteem   (*c*) value   (*d*) understand and enjoy

11 They notice more. They _____ more.

  (*a*) remark   (*b*) observe   (*c*) say   (*d*) take care

12 It's upside down. It isn't _____ .

  (*a*) up   (*b*) down   (*c*) the right way down   (*d*) the right way up

Sentence structure 句子结构

Rewrite this sentence, then check your answer against the text.

改写以下句子, 然后对照课文第 7-8 行, 核对你的答案。

Are my pictures good or not?

Please tell me _____ .

Lesson 27　A wet night　雨夜

First listen and then answer the question.

听录音，然后回答以下问题。

What happened to the boys in the night?

Late in the afternoon, the boys put up their tent in the middle of a field. As soon as this was done, they cooked a meal over an open fire. They were all hungry and the food smelled good. After a wonderful meal, they told stories and sang songs by the campfire.
5　But some time later it began to rain. The boys felt tired so they put out the fire and crept into their tent. Their sleeping bags were warm and comfortable, so they all slept soundly. In the middle of the night, two boys woke up and began shouting. The tent was full of water! They all leapt out of their sleeping bags and hurried outside. It was raining heavily and they found that a
10　stream had formed in the field. The stream wound its way across the field and then flowed right under their tent!

a stream had formed in the field

New words and expressions 生词和短语

tent (l.1) /tent/ n. 帐篷

field (l.2) /fi:ld/ n. 田地，田野

smell (l.3) /smel/ (smelled or smelt /smelt/, smelled or smelt) v. 闻起来

wonderful (l.4) /'wʌndəfəl/ adj. 极好的

campfire (l.4) /'kæmpfaɪə/ n. 营火，篝火

creep (l.6) /kri:p/ (crept /krept/, crept) v. 爬行

sleeping bag (l.6) /'sli:pɪŋ-bæg/ 睡袋

comfortable (l.7) /'kʌmfətəbəl/ adj. 舒适的，安逸的

soundly (l.7) /'saʊndli/ adv. 香甜地

leap (l.9) /li:p/ (leapt /lept/, leapt) v. 跳跃，跳起

heavily (l.9) /'hevɪli/ adv. 大量地

stream (l.10) /stri:m/ n. 小溪

form (l.10) /fɔ:m/ v. 形成

wind (l.10) /waɪnd/ (wound /waʊnd/, wound) v. 蜿蜒

right (l.10) /raɪt/ adv. 正好

Notes on the text 课文注释

1　late in the afternoon, 快到傍晚的时候。

2　put up (= set up), 搭起。

3　put out, 熄灭（灯、火）。

4　wake up, 醒来。

参考译文

　　傍晚时分，孩子们在田野中央搭起了帐篷。这件事刚刚做完，他们就在篝火上烧起了饭。他们全都饿了，饭菜散发出阵阵香味。他们美美地吃了一顿饭后，就围在营火旁讲起了故事，唱起了歌。但过了一阵子，天下起雨来。孩子们感到困倦了，于是他们扑灭了篝火，钻进了帐篷。睡袋既暖和又舒服，所以，他们都睡得很香。午夜前后，有两个孩子醒了，大声叫了起来。原来帐篷里到处都是水！他们全都跳出睡袋，跑到外面。雨下得很大，他们发现地上已经形成了一条小溪。那小溪弯弯曲曲穿过田野，然后正好从他们的帐篷底下流过去！

Summary writing 摘要写作

Answer these questions *in not more than 70 words*.
回答下列问题，将答案组成一个段落，不要超过 70 个单词。

1   Where did the boys put up their tent? What did they cook? (*and*)

2   What did they do after their meal? Did it begin to rain or not? Did they creep into their tent or not? (*but ... so*)

3   Did the boys wake up in the middle of the night or not?

4   Was the tent full of water or not? Did they rush outside or did they stay in their tent? (*so*)

5   Where had a stream formed? Where did it flow? (*and*)

Composition 作文

Rewrite these sentences using the correct verbs and joining words:
用正确的动词和连词改写以下句子：

I am very tall (so) (but) I must be careful. Doorways are often low (and) (but) I usually (beat) (knock) my head against them. My head always (hurts) (pains). I have never (met) (recognized) a tall architect. Have you?

Letter writing 书信写作

The order of the heading is as follows: the number of the house, the name of the street, the town or city, the area, the country and the date. Put in the name of the country only when you are writing to someone who lives abroad.
信头各部分的顺序如下：门牌号码、街名、城市名称、地区、国家和日期。只有当你给居住在国外的人写信时，才需要写上国名。

Exercise 练习

Arrange the following heading in the correct order:
按照正确的顺序排列以下信头：

California, Woodside, 21st Feb, 19__, U.S.A., 21 Brook St.,

Key structures 关键句型

What happened? 一般过去时 (KS3) (参见第 3 课的关键句型)

Read these sentences carefully. The verbs in italics tell us what happened:
仔细阅读以下句子，用斜体印出的动词告诉我们过去发生的事件：

I *lost* my umbrella a few days ago. 几天前我把伞丢了。

I *bought* this coat yesterday. 昨天我买了这件外衣。

I *dreamt* of you last night. 昨晚我梦见了你。

She *paid* the bill and *left* the shop. 她交了钱，离开了商店。

Exercises 练习

A   Underline the verbs in the passage that tell us *what happened*
用横线画出所有表示过去发生的事件的动词。

B   Give the correct form of the verbs in parentheses. Do not refer to the passage until you finish the exercise:

用括号中动词的正确形式填空,完成练习后再对照课文,核对你的答案:

Late in the afternoon, the boys _____ (put) up their tent in the middle of a field. As soon as this _____ (do), they _____ (cook) a meal over an open fire. They were all hungry and the food _____ (smell) good. After a wonderful meal, they _____ (tell) stories and _____ (sing) songs by the campfire. But some time later it _____ (begin) to rain. The boys _____ (feel) tired so they _____ (put) out the fire and _____ (creep) into their tent. Their sleeping bags were warm and comfortable, so they all _____ (sleep) soundly. In the middle of the night, two boys _____ (wake) up and _____ (begin) shouting. The tent _____ (be) full of water! They all _____ (leap) out of their sleeping bags and _____ (hurry) outside. It was raining heavily and they _____ (find) that a stream had formed in the field. The stream _____ (wind) its way across the field and then _____ (flow) right under their tent!

Special difficulties 难点

(SD6, SD7) 参见第 6, 7 课的难点

Study these sentences. Each one contains the verb *put*. The verb has a different meaning in each sentence:
细读以下例句,每句均有动词 put, 但词义不同:

... the boys *put up* their tent in the middle of a field. (ll.1-2)。

... they *put out* the fire and crept into their tent. (ll.5-6)。

I *put on* my coat and left the house. 我穿上外衣, 离开房子。

You needn't go back to London tonight. We can *put* you *up* for the night. (We can provide you with a bed). 你今夜不必回伦敦, 我们能为你安排住宿。

The teacher sent the boy to the headmaster. He could not *put up with* him any longer. (He could not stand him.) 教师把那个男孩送到校长那里去, 他已经无法容忍这个孩子了。

Take out your notebooks. *Put down* all the sentences that are on the blackboard. (Write all the sentences ...) 拿出你的笔记本, 抄下黑板上的所有句子。

We cannot have the meeting tonight. We shall have to *put it off* until tomorrow. (We shall have to postpone it.) 今晚我们无法开会, 只好把它推迟到明天。

Close your books and *put* them *away*. 把书合上, 放到一边去。

Exercise 练习

Use the correct expression with *put* in each of the following:
选用正确的带 put 的动词短语:

1 Mrs. Bowers told her children to _____ their toys _____ and go to bed.

2 You can stay here tonight. We can _____ you _____ in the spare room.

3 I'm not ready yet. I haven't _____ my shoes _____ .

4 'Open your exercise books and _____ the following,' the teacher said.

5 Father is _____ the fire he lit in the garden.

6 When they have _____ that new building, it will spoil the view.

7 I have _____ my trip to Japan until next month.

8 I am getting a divorce. I can't _____ him any longer.

Multiple choice questions 选择题

Comprehension 理解

1 The boys went to bed because _____ .

   (*a*) it was late

   (*c*) it began to rain

   (*b*) they had sung songs

   (*d*) it had begun to rain and they felt tired

2 The boys _____ .

   (*a*) had a good night's sleep

   (*c*) had camped in the path of a stream

   (*b*) stayed in their tent all night

   (*d*) had camped beside a stream

Structure 句型

3 Where did they _____?

   (*a*) it put up   (*b*) their tent put up   (*c*) put up it   (*d*) put their tent up

4 _____ this was done, they cooked a meal over an open fire.

   (*a*) As soon   (*b*) Just as   (*c*) Until   (*d*) Just after

5 They cooked a meal because _____ .

   (*a*) they had hunger   (*b*) they had hungry   (*c*) they were hunger   (*d*) they felt hungry

6 They sang songs by the campfire. They sang songs _____ the campfire.

   (*a*) close   (*b*) near   (*c*) besides   (*d*) at

7 Where did the stream _____?

   (*a*) flow   (*b*) flowed   (*c*) flew   (*d*) fly

Vocabulary 词汇

8 They cooked a meal because they wanted to _____ .

   (*a*) sing songs   (*b*) tell stories   (*c*) play   (*d*) eat

9 The boys had put out the campfire. The fire wasn't _____ .

   (*a*) switched on   (*b*) on fire   (*c*) on   (*d*) alight

10 They crept into their tent, so they _____ .

   (*a*) made a lot of noise   (*b*) ran quickly   (*c*) were very quiet   (*d*) were very noisy

11 The boys slept comfortably. Their sleeping bags were _____ .

   (*a*) a comfort   (*b*) in comfort   (*c*) comfortable   (*d*) comfortably

12 They slept soundly. They slept _____ .

   (*a*) noisily   (*b*) fast   (*c*) deeply   (*d*) good

Sentence structure 句子结构

Rewrite this sentence, then check your answer against the text.

改写以下句子, 然后对照课文第 2-3 行, 核对你的答案。

As soon as they did this, they cooked a meal over an open fire.

As soon as this _____ .

Lesson 28   No parking   禁止停车

hopes she will turn cars and
their owners to stone

First listen and then answer the question.

听录音，然后回答以下问题。

What is Jasper White's problem?

Jasper White is one of those rare people who believes in ancient myths. He has just bought a new house in the city, but ever since he moved in, he has had trouble with cars and their owners. When he returns home at night, he always finds that someone has parked a
5 car outside his gate. Because of this, he has not been able to get his own car into his garage even once. Jasper has put up 'No Parking' signs outside his gate, but these have not had any effect. Now he has put an ugly stone head over the gate. It is one of the ugliest faces I have ever seen. I asked him what it was and he told me that it was Medusa, the Gorgon. Jasper hopes
10 that she will turn cars and their owners to stone. But none of them has been turned to stone yet!

New words and expressions 生词和短语

rare (l.1) /reə/ *adj.* 罕见的

ancient (l.1) /'eɪnʃənt/ *adj.* 古代的，古老的

myth (l.2) /mɪθ/ *n.* 神话故事

trouble (l.3) /'trʌbəl/ *n.* 麻烦

effect (l.7) /ɪ'fekt/ *n.* 结果，效果

Medusa (l.9) /mɪ'djuːzə/ *n.* 美杜莎（古希腊神话中
3 位蛇发女怪之一）

Gorgon (l.9) /'gɔːgən/ *n.* （古希腊神话中的）3 位蛇
发女怪之一（凡见其貌者都会变成石头）

Notes on the text 课文注释

1 one of those rare people who believes in ancient myths, 少有的相信古代神话的人之一。其中 who believes in ancient myths 是一个从句，起定语作用，修饰 one; 由于 one 是单数，因此，从句中需用单数动词。of those rare people 是另一个定语，也用来修饰 one。

2 he has not been able to get his own car into his garage even once, 他甚至一次也未能把自己的车开进他的车库。虽然 be able to 这个短语与 can 表达相同的意思，但这个短语可以用在各种不同的时态中。even 用来修饰 once, 加强语气。

3 stone head, 石雕头像。

4 It is one of the ugliest faces I have ever seen. 这是我见过的最丑陋的头像之一。这句话中有一个定语从句 I have ever seen, 关系代词 that 被省略了。

参考译文

贾斯珀·怀特是少有的相信古代神话的人之一。他刚在城里买下一所新房子，但自从搬进去后，就和汽车及车主们发生了摩擦。当他夜里回到家时，总是发现有人把车停在他家大门外。为此，他甚至一次也没能把自己的车开进车库。贾斯珀曾把几块"禁止停车"的牌子挂在大门外边，但没有任何效果。现在他把一个丑陋的石雕头像放在了大门上边，这是我见过的最丑陋的头像之一。我问他那是什么，他告诉我那是蛇发女怪美杜莎。贾斯珀希望她把汽车和车主们都变成石头。但到目前为止还没有一个人变成石头呢！

Summary writing 摘要写作

Answer these questions *in not more than 65 words*.
回答下列问题，将答案组成一个段落，不要超过 65 个单词。

1 What does Jasper White believe in?

2 Where do car owners always park their cars? Has he put up 'No Parking' signs or not? Have they paid any attention to them or not? (*so ... but*)

3 What has he put over his gate now?

4 Whose head is it?

5 What does he want her to do? Has she done so yet or not? (*but*)

Composition 作文

Rewrite these sentences using the correct verbs and joining words:
用正确的动词和连词改写以下句子：

My wife (drives) (leads) a car. She has (driven) (ridden) a car for many years (and) (but) she says that women drivers (do not deserve) (are not worth) their bad reputation. Yet, on the road, she often (criticizes) (judges) other women drivers.

Letter writing 书信写作

I am writing to someone who lives in the same country as I do. Which of these two headings would be correct?
我给同住在英国的人写信，以下哪个信头是正确的？

<table>
<tr><td>19 High Lane,</td><td>19 High Lane,</td></tr>
<tr><td>Newton,</td><td>Newton,</td></tr>
<tr><td>Middlesex,</td><td>Middlesex,</td></tr>
<tr><td>10th September, 19__</td><td>England.</td></tr>
<tr><td></td><td>10th September, 19__</td></tr>
</table>

Key structures 关键句型

What has happened? 现在完成时

Study these sentences carefully. Pay close attention to the words in italics:
仔细阅读以下句子，特别注意用斜体印出的、与现在完成时连用的、表示时间的词或词组：

I have *just* received a letter from my brother, Tim. (**KS4**) (参见第 4 课关键句型)

I have not seen Tim *since* last January. 从 1 月份以来我一直没有见过蒂姆。

I have not seen Tim *since* 1994. 从 1994 年以来我一直没有见过蒂姆。

I have not seen Tim *for* three years. 我有 3 年没有见过蒂姆了。

Tim has been abroad *for* three years. 蒂姆出国已有 3 年。

Up till now he has won five prizes. 至今他已得了 5 次奖。

Up till now I have been to New York *three times*. 至今我已去过纽约 3 次了。

I have been to New York *three times so far*. 迄今为止，我已去过纽约 3 次了。

Have you been to New York? 你去过纽约吗？

Have you seen this film? 你看过这电影吗？

Have you read this book? 你读过这本书吗？

Unit 2　Lesson 28

Exercises 练习

A　Underline the verbs in the passage that tell us *what has happened*.
在课文中所有表示已经发生的事件的动词下面画上横线。

B　Give the correct form of the verbs in parentheses. Do not refer to the passage until you finish the exercise:
用括号中动词的正确形式填空，完成练习后再对照课文，核对你的答案：

Jasper White is one of those rare people who believes in ancient myths. He just _____ (buy) a new house in the city, but ever since he moved in, he _____ (have) trouble with cars and their owners. When he returns home at night, he always finds that someone _____ (park) a car outside his gate. Because of this, he _____ (not be) able to get his own car into his garage even once. Jasper _____ (put) up 'No Parking' signs outside his gate, but these _____ (not have) any effect. Now he _____ (put) an ugly stone head over the gate. It is one of the ugliest faces I ever _____ (see). I asked him what it was and he told me that it was Medusa, the Gorgon. Jasper hopes that she will turn cars and their owners to stone. But none of them _____ (turn) to stone yet!

Special difficulties 难点

Who, Which, That, and Whose

在 whom, which, that 引导的定语从句中，如果关系代词 whom, which, that 充当从句中的宾语，关系代词可以省略。

Instead of saying:
除了这种表述方法外：

The man *whom* you met yesterday is an actor.

The book *which* you lent me is not very interesting.

The flowers *that* I love best are roses.

We can say:
还可以说：

The man you met yesterday is an actor.

The book you lent me is not very interesting.

The flowers I love best are roses.

We *cannot* leave out *who, which, that* or *whose* in these sentences:
在以下句子中，我们不能省略 who, which, that 或 whose 等关系代词：

Jasper White is one of those rare people *who* believes in ancient myths. (ll.1-2)

This is the hotel *which* was built last year. 这是去年建的那个酒店。

This is the island *that* was bought by a millionaire. 这是那个被百万富翁买下来的岛。

The pilot *whose* plane landed in a field was not hurt. 那个把飞机降落在田里的飞行员没有受伤。

Exercise 练习

Supply *who, which, that or whose* only where necessary:
在需要的地方填上 who, which, that 或 whose：

1 The only games _____ I play are football and tennis.

2 He is the only student _____ understands English well.

3 He is a writer _____ books are seldom read.

4 This is the hotel at _____ we are staying.

5 Is this the money _____ you lost?

6 That is the horse _____ won the race.

7 He is the sort of person _____ everyone admires.

Multiple choice questions 选择题

Comprehension 理解

1 Jasper White _____ .

  (a) doesn't like cars and their owners

  (b) doesn't like cars

  (c) is angry with cars and their owners who park in front of his house

  (d) can't get his car out of his garage

2 Jasper White has put Medusa's head over his gate because _____ .

  (a) she turns cars and their owners to stone   (b) she is ugly

  (c) she is made of stone   (d) he believes in ancient myths

Structure 句型

3 How many people _____ in ancient myths?

  (a) believes   (b) believe   (c) are believing   (d) believing

4 He has just bought a new house. He has been in it _____ a short time.

  (a) since   (b) for   (c) about   (d) ago

5 There is always a car outside his gate. _____ he can't get into his garage.

  (a) For this   (b) Because   (c) That's why   (d) Because of

6 It is one of the ugliest faces I have ever seen. I've never seen _____ .

  (a) an ugly one   (b) an ugliest one   (c) the ugliest one   (d) an uglier one

7 _____ of them has been turned to stone.

  (a) No one   (b) Not one   (c) No   (d) Even one

Vocabulary 词汇

8 The myth is an ancient one. Jasper himself isn't _____ .

  (a) an ancient   (b) ancient   (c) an old   (d) old

9 He is a rare person. You _____ meet such people.

  (a) often   (b) never   (c) seldom   (d) sometimes

10 Not all car owners are good _____ .

  (a) guides   (b) conductors   (c) leaders   (d) drivers

11 You can see some _____ outside his gate. They say 'No Parking'.

  (a) labels   (b) notices   (c) signals   (d) notes

12 The signs haven't had any effect. They haven't _____ anyone.

  (a) affected   (b) effected   (c) resulted in   (d) imposed

Sentence structure 句子结构

Rewrite this sentence, then check your answer against the text.

改写以下句子, 然后对照课文第9行, 核对你的答案。

'What is it?' I asked.

I asked him what _____ .

Lesson 29 Taxi! 出租汽车！

First listen and then answer the question.

听录音，然后回答以下问题。

Does Captain Fawcett think any trip is too dangerous?

Captain Ben Fawcett has bought an unusual taxi and has begun a new service. The 'taxi' is a small Swiss aeroplane called a 'Pilatus Porter'. This wonderful plane can carry seven passengers. The most surprising thing about it, however, is that it can land anywhere: on
5 snow, water, or even on a ploughed field. Captain Fawcett's first passenger was a doctor who flew from Birmingham to a lonely village in the Welsh mountains. Since then, Captain Fawcett has flown passengers to many unusual places. Once he landed on the

landed in a deserted car park

roof of a block of flats and on another occasion, he landed in a deserted car park. Captain Fawcett has just
10 refused a strange request from a businessman. The man wanted to fly to Rockall, a lonely island in the Atlantic Ocean, but Captain Fawcett did not take him because the trip was too dangerous.

New words and expressions 生词和短语

taxi (title) /'tæksi/ *n.* 出租汽车
Pilatus Porter (ll.2-3) /'pɪlətəs 'pɔːtə/ 皮勒特斯·波特
　（飞机机名）
land (l.4) /lænd/ *v.* 着陆
plough (l.5) /plaʊ/ *v.* 耕（地）
lonely (l.6) /'ləʊnli/ *adj.* 偏僻的，人迹罕至的

Welsh (l.7) /welʃ/ *adj.* 威尔士的
roof (l.9) /ruːf/ *n.* 楼顶
block (l.9) /blɒk/ *n.* 一座大楼
flat (l.9) /flæt/ *n.* 公寓房
desert (l.9) /dɪ'zɜːt/ *v.* 废弃

Notes on the text 课文注释

1　The most surprising thing about it, however, is that it can land anywhere. 然而，最令人惊奇的是它能在任何地方降落。在这句话中，that it can land anywhere 是一个从句，起表语作用，被称为表语从句。

2　on another occasion, 还有一次。

3　car park, 汽车停车场。

4　a lonely island in the Atlantic Ocean, 大西洋中的一个孤岛。这个短语用来补充说明名词 Rockall。

参考译文

　　本·弗西特机长买了一辆不同寻常的出租汽车，并开始了一项新的业务。这辆"出租汽车"是一架小型瑞士飞机，叫"皮勒特斯·波特"号。这架奇妙的飞机可以载 7 名乘客。然而，最令人惊奇的是它能够在任何地方降落：雪地上，水面上，甚至刚耕过的田里。弗西特机长的第一名乘客是位医生，他从伯明翰飞往威尔士山区一个偏僻的村庄。从那时开始，弗西特机长已经载送乘客到过许多不寻常的地方。一次，他把飞机降落在了一栋公寓楼的屋顶上；还有一次，降落在了一个废弃的停车场上。弗西特机长刚刚拒绝了一位商人的奇怪要求。这个人想要飞往大西洋上的一个孤岛——罗卡尔岛，弗西特机长之所以不送他去，是因为那段飞行太危险了。

Summary writing 摘要写作

Answer these questions *in not more than 60 words*.

回答下列问题，将答案组成一个段落，不要超过 60 个单词。

1 Has Captain Ben Fawcett bought a small Swiss aeroplane, or has he bought an ordinary taxi? Does he use it as a taxi or not? (*and*)

2 What is it called?

3 How many passengers can it carry? Can it land anywhere or not? (*not only ... but*)

4 Has Captain Fawcett taken passengers to many strange places in his plane or not?

5 Did he refuse to fly a businessman to Rockall or not?

6 Was the journey too dangerous or not?

Composition 作文

Rewrite these sentences using the correct verbs and joining words:

用正确的动词和连词改写以下句子：

The plane (not only) (neither) (flew) (threw) close to the river, (but) (or) also flew under a bridge. (Then) (However) it (climbed) (ran) into the air. The people on the bridge (waved) (shook) to the pilot (and) (yet) he did not (notice) (look after) them.

Letter writing 书信写作

I am writing to someone who lives abroad. Which of these two headings would be correct?

我给居住在国外的人写信，以下哪个信头是正确的？

<table>
<tr><td>19 High Lane,</td><td>19 High Lane,</td></tr>
<tr><td>Newton,</td><td>Newton,</td></tr>
<tr><td>Middlesex.</td><td>Middlesex,</td></tr>
<tr><td>10th September, 19__</td><td>England.</td></tr>
<tr><td></td><td>10th September, 19__</td></tr>
</table>

Key structures 关键句型

What happened? What has happened? 对比一般过去时和现在完成时 (KS5)（参见第 5 课关键句型）

Study these pairs of sentences. Pay close attention to the words in italics:

仔细阅读以下句子，特别注意用斜体印出的部分：

I saw him *in 1994*. 我在 1994 年见到了他。

I have not seen him *since 1994*. 从 1994 年以来我一直没有见过他。

I saw him *three years ago*. 我 3 年前见过他。

I have not seen him *for three years*. 我有 3 年没有见到他了。

He stayed at this hotel *last month*. 上个月他住在这个酒店。

Have you *ever* stayed at this hotel? 你在这个酒店住过吗？

I went abroad *last year* 去年我出国了。

Up till now, I have never been abroad *before*. 至今我还没有出过国。

Exercises 练习

A Underline the verbs in the passage that tell us *what happened* and *what has happened*.
   在课文中画出表示过去发生的事件和已经发生的事件的动词。

B Give the correct form of the verbs in parentheses. Do not refer to the passage until you finish the exercise:
   用括号中动词的正确形式填空，完成练习后再对照课文，核对你的答案：

Captain Ben Fawcett _____ (buy) an unusual taxi and _____ (begin) a new service. The 'taxi' is a small Swiss aeroplane called a 'Pilatus Porter'. This wonderful plane can carry seven passengers. ... Captain Fawcett's first passenger _____ (be) a doctor who _____ (fly) from Birmingham to a lonely village in the Welsh mountains. Since then, Captain Fawcett _____ (fly) passengers to many unusual places. Once he _____ (land) on the roof of a block of flats and on another occasion, he _____ (land) in a deserted car park. Captain Fawcett just _____ (refuse) a strange request from a businessman. The man _____ (want) to fly to Rockall, but Captain Fawcett _____ (not take) him because the trip _____ (be) too dangerous.

Special difficulties 难点

Words often confused 经常容易混淆的词

a *Refuse and Deny.*

   Refuse (a request or something offered) 拒绝（一个请求或给予的某种东西）: Captain Fawcett has just *refused* a strange request from a businessman. (ll.9-10)

   Deny (an accusation) 否认（一种指控）: He *denied* that he had stolen the money. 他否认曾偷过钱。

b *Bring, Take,* and *Fetch.* He did not *take* him. (l.11)

   Bring (come from somewhere with something) 带来（由某处带来某物）: He *brought* the book with him when he came to see me. 他来看我时把书带来了。

   Take (go away from somewhere or someone with something) 拿走（从某地或某人处带走）: He *took* the book with him when he left. 他走的时候把书带走了。**(SD4)**（对比第 4 课难点）

   Fetch (go somewhere, pick something up and bring it back) 取来（去某地取某物并带回）: I asked him to go to my room and *fetch* my glasses. 我请他去我的房间取来我的眼镜。

c *Very* and *Too.* The trip was *too* dangerous. (l.11)

   Very 很，非常: I arrived *very* late but I caught the train. 我到得很迟，但赶上了火车。

   Too 太，过于: I arrived *too* late and I missed the train. 我到得太迟，误了火车。

Exercise 练习

Choose the correct words in the following:
选择正确的词：

1 When you go to the kitchen, please (fetch) (bring) me a glass of water.

2 The ball went over the fence and the football player asked a boy to (fetch) (bring) it.

3 When I asked him he (refused) (denied) to tell me.

4 Do you (deny) (refuse) that you have told me a lie?

5 How are you? (Too) (Very) well, thank you.

Multiple choice questions 选择题

Comprehension 理解

1 The most remarkable thing about the 'Pilatus Porter' is that _____ .

   (*a*) it can be used as a taxi   (*b*) it doesn't need a runway to land on

   (*c*) it can carry seven passengers   (*d*) it is a Swiss aeroplane

2 Captain Fawcett _____ .

   (*a*) is prepared to fly passengers anywhere

   (*b*) flies passengers anywhere

   (*c*) will fly passengers anywhere except very dangerous places

   (*d*) will fly passengers anywhere except Rockall

Structure 句型

3 The 'taxi' is a small Swiss aeroplane _____ called a 'Pilatus Porter'.

   (*a*) who is   (*b*) whom is   (*c*) which is   (*d*) whose is

4 This is the most surprising thing about it. It is _____ than anything.

   (*a*) most surprising   (*b*) more surprising   (*c*) more surprised   (*d*) most surprised

5 He flew a doctor to a Welsh village. _____ he has flown to many unusual places.

   (*a*) From then   (*b*) By then   (*c*) By that time   (*d*) Since that time

6 He was asked _____ a businessman to fly to Rockall and he refused.

   (*a*) from   (*b*) by   (*c*) with   (*d*) out of

7 The man wanted to fly to Rockall. _____ to take him there.

   (*a*) He wanted the pilot   (*b*) He wanted   (*c*) The pilot he wanted   (*d*) The pilot the man wanted

Vocabulary 词汇

8 It's an unusual taxi. It isn't very _____ .

   (*a*) accustomed   (*b*) common   (*c*) usually   (*d*) used to

9 The ploughed field is ready for _____ .

   (*a*) sewing   (*b*) sowing   (*c*) seeding   (*d*) growing

10 It's a lonely village. It is _____ .

   (*a*) far   (*b*) far from anywhere   (*c*) alone   (*d*) the only one

11 Captain Fawcett has flown passengers to many unusual _____ .

   (*a*) parts   (*b*) pieces   (*c*) spots   (*d*) sections

12 The car park was deserted. It was _____ .

   (*a*) a desert   (*b*) empty   (*c*) abandoned   (*d*) wasted

Sentence structure 句子结构

Join these sentences, then check your answer against the text.

连接以下两个句子, 然后对照课文第 5-7 行, 核对你的答案。

Captain Fawcett's first passenger was a doctor. The doctor flew from Birmingham to a lonely village.

Lesson 30　Football or polo?　足球还是水球?

nearly fell into the water

First listen and then answer the question.

听录音, 然后回答以下问题。

What happened to the man in the boat?

The Wayle is a small river that cuts across the park near my home.
I like sitting by the Wayle on fine afternoons. It was warm last
Sunday, so I went and sat on the river bank as usual. Some children
were playing games on the bank and there were some people rowing
5　on the river. Suddenly, one of the children kicked a ball very hard
and it went towards a passing boat. Some people on the bank called
out to the man in the boat, but he did not hear them. The ball struck
him so hard that he nearly fell into the water. I turned to look at the
children, but there weren't any in sight: they had all run away! The man laughed when he realized what had
10　happened. He called out to the children and threw the ball back to the bank.

New words and expressions　生词和短语

polo (title) /ˈpəʊləʊ/ *n.* 水球
Wayle (l.1) /weɪl/ *n.* 威尔（河名）
cut (l.1) /kʌt/ (cut, cut) *v.* 穿过
row (l.4) /rəʊ/ *v.* 划（船）

kick (l.5) /kɪk/ *v.* 踢
towards (l.6) /təˈwɔːdz/ *prep.* 朝, 向
nearly (l.8) /ˈnɪəli/ *adv.* 几乎
sight (l.9) /saɪt/ *n.* 眼界, 视域

Notes on the text　课文注释

1　a small river that cuts across the park, 横穿公园的一条小河。其中, 以 that 引导的定语从句用来修饰 a small
river。

2　on fine afternoons, 天气晴朗的下午。当 morning, afternoon, evening 这些词的前面或后面有修饰词时要用
介词 on。

3　as usual, 像往常一样。

4　called out to the man in the boat, 对船上的人高喊。

5　The ball struck him so hard that he nearly fell into the water. 球重重地打在他身上, 使他差点落入水中。"so
+ 形容词 + that 从句" 往往表达 "如此……以至于……" 的意思。

6　in sight, 可以看到。反义词为 out of sight。

参考译文

　　威尔河是横穿过我家附近公园的一条小河。我喜欢在天气晴朗的下午到河边坐坐。上星期日天气很暖
和。于是我和往常一样, 又去河边坐着。河岸上有些孩子正在玩耍, 河面上有些人正在划船。突然, 一个孩子狠
狠地踢了一脚球, 球便向一只划过来的小船飞去。岸上的一些人对着小船上的人高喊, 但他没有听见。球重重
地打在他身上, 使他差点儿落入水中。我转过头去看那些孩子, 但一个也看不见, 他们全都跑了! 当那个人明白
了发生的事情时, 笑了起来。他大声叫着那些孩子, 把球扔回到岸上。

Summary writing 摘要写作

Answer these questions *in not more than 70 words*.

回答下列问题，将答案组成一个段落，不要超过 70 个单词。

1　Did the writer sit by the river last Sunday or not?

2　Were some children playing games nearby or not?

3　Who kicked a ball hard? Where did it go? (*and*)

4　Did the man in the boat see the ball? Did he hear people shouting? (*neither ... nor*)

5　Did the ball hit the man or not? What did the children do? (*and*)

6　Was the man angry or not? Where did he throw the ball? (*However ... and*)

Composition 作文

Rewrite these sentences using the correct verbs and joining words:

用正确的动词和连词改写以下句子：

The wind (threw) (blew) his hat into the river. He (put) (took) out his hand (and) (but) tried to (reach) (catch) it (so) (but)

he could not (so) (but) he (jumped) (fell) into the river (and) (but) got it.

Letter writing 书信写作

Arrange the following heading in the correct order:

接正确的顺序编排以下信头的各个组成部分：

Middlesex, England, 10th September, 19__, 19 High Lane, Newton.

Key structures 关键句型

A, The, Some and Any (KS6) （参见第 6 课关键句型）

a　*Some* and *Any*. （对比第 9 课难点）

Note the use of *some* and *any* in these sentences:

注意以下句子中 some 和 any 的用法：

Is there *any* milk in the bottle? 瓶子里有牛奶吗？

There isn't *any* milk in the bottle, but there is *some* in this jug. 瓶子里没有一点儿奶，但是罐子里有一些。

Is there *any* soap in the bathroom? 卫生间里有肥皂吗？

There isn't *any* soap in the bathroom, but there's *some* in the cupboard. 卫生间里没有肥皂，但橱里有一些。

Are there *any* nails in that tin? 那个罐头盒子里有钉子吗？

There aren't *any* in the tin, but there are *some* in this box. 罐头盒子里没有，但这个盒子里有一些。

b　*Names*. 姓名

We cannot put *a* or *the* in front of names. (KS6c)

在人名和地名前面不加冠词 a 或 the。（参见第 6 课关键句型 c）

John lives in England. He has *a* house in London. 约翰住在英国。他在伦敦有座房子。

But we must put *the* in front of the names of oceans, seas, rivers, mountain ranges and certain countries:

但在海洋、河流、山脉和部分国名前，一定要用定冠词 the:

Who was the first person to sail across *the* Pacific? 谁是第一个横渡太平洋的人？

It can get very rough in *the* Mediterranean. 地中海中可能会非常不平静。

Unit 2　Lesson 30

Many great cities are built on rivers. Paris is on *the* Seine, London is on *the* Thames and Rome is on *the* Tiber. 许多大城市都建在河岸上。巴黎在塞纳河上，伦敦在泰晤士河上，罗马在第伯尔河上。

I know a man who has been on climbing expeditions in many parts of the world. He has climbed in *the* Alps, *the* Himalayas, and *the* Rocky Mountains. 我认识一个参加过世界各地登山探险的人。他曾攀登过阿尔卑斯山、喜马拉雅山和洛矶山。

Instead of saying:	*We can say*:
除了这种表述方法外：	还可以说：
I went to America last year.	I went to *the* United States of America last year.
Would you like to go to China?	Would you like to go to *the* People's Republic of China?

Exercises　练习

A Underline the words *a, the, some* and *any* in the passage.

画出课文中的 a, the, some 和 any。

B Put in the words *a, the, some,* and *any* where necessary. Do not refer to the passage until you finish the exercise.

在必要的地方填上 a, the, some 和 any。完成练习后再对照课文，核对你的答案。

_____ Wayle is _____ small river that cuts across _____ park near my home. I like sitting by _____ Wayle on fine afternoons. It was warm last Sunday, so I went and sat on _____ river bank as usual. _____ children were playing _____ games on _____ bank and there were _____ people rowing on _____ river. Suddenly, one of _____ children kicked _____ ball very hard and it went towards _____ passing boat. _____ people on _____ bank called out to _____ man in _____ boat, but he did not hear them. _____ ball struck him so hard that he nearly fell into _____ water. I turned to look at _____ children, but there weren't _____ in sight.

C Answer these questions in two ways using *some* and *any*:

用 some 和 any 对以下问题作出肯定和否定的答复：

1 Did you take any photographs? Yes, _____ No, _____

2 Did you buy any bread? Yes, _____ No, _____

3 Did you see any people outside the cinema? Yes, _____ No, _____

D Put in *a* or *the* where necessary:

在必要的地方填上冠词 a 或 the：

1 _____ refrigerators are necessary in _____ hot countries.

2 Which river is _____ longest, _____ Nile, _____ Amazon, or _____ Mississippi?

3 Heyerdahl crossed _____ Pacific on _____ raft.

4 Why is _____ Britain sometimes called _____ United Kingdom?

5 We sailed up _____ Red Sea and then went through _____ Suez Canal.

Multiple choice questions 选择题
Comprehension 理解

1 The writer _____ .
  (a) likes sitting on the bank of the river when it's fine
  (b) rarely goes to the river
  (c) likes sitting on the bank of the river all the time
  (d) likes sitting on the bank of the river on Sundays

2 One of these statements is true. Which one?
  (a) Some people tried to warn the man about the ball.
  (b) Some people shouted to the writer, but he didn't hear them.
  (c) The children laughed when they realized what had happened.
  (d) The man was angry with the children and kept their ball.

Structure 句型

3 There is a river near the writer's home. It is called _____ .
  (a) a Wayle   (b) Wayle   (c) this Wayle   (d) the Wayle
4 It cuts across the park. It goes _____ it.
  (a) through   (b) over   (c) round   (d) along
5 Why did they kick the ball so _____ ?
  (a) hardly   (b) hard   (c) hardy   (d) hardily
6 The ball went towards a passing boat. It went _____ of a passing boat.
  (a) forwards   (b) forward   (c) in the direction   (d) in direction
7 There weren't any in sight. They _____ .
  (a) couldn't see   (b) hadn't seen   (c) couldn't be seen   (d) weren't seen

Vocabulary 词汇

8 The man was rowing, so he was using _____ .
  (a) rows   (b) sticks   (c) oars   (d) rudders
9 Some people on the bank _____ the man.
  (a) cried   (b) cried with   (c) cried for   (d) cried to
10 The man in the boat didn't _____ anyone shouting.
  (a) hear   (b) listen to   (c) mind   (d) take care of
11 The ball _____ him very hard.
  (a) knocked at   (b) beat   (c) bounced   (d) hit
12 They had run away, so they had _____ .
  (a) dismissed   (b) disturbed   (c) displaced   (d) disappeared

Sentence structure 句子结构

Join these sentences, then check your answer against the text.
连接以下句子, 然后对照课文第 7-8 行, 核对你的答案。

The ball struck him hard. He nearly fell into the water.

The ball struck him so _____ .

145

Lesson 31 Success story 成功者的故事

🔊 **First listen and then answer the question.**
听录音, 然后回答以下问题。

What was Frank's first job?

Yesterday afternoon Frank Hawkins was telling me about his experiences as a young man. Before he retired, Frank was the head of a very large business company, but as a boy he used to work in a small shop. It was his job to repair bicycles and at that time he used
5 to work fourteen hours a day. He saved money for years and in 1958 he bought a small workshop of his own. In his twenties Frank used to make spare parts for aeroplanes. At that time he had two helpers. In a few years the small workshop had become a large factory which employed seven hundred and twenty-eight people. Frank smiled when he remembered his hard early years
10 and the long road to success. He was still smiling when the door opened and his wife came in. She wanted him to repair their grandson's bicycle!

experiences as a young man

New words and expressions 生词和短语

retire (l.2) /rɪˈtaɪə/ v. 退休
company (l.3) /ˈkʌmpəni/ n. 公司
bicycle (l.4) /ˈbaɪsɪkəl/ n. 自行车
save (l.5) /seɪv/ v. 积蓄

workshop (l.6) /ˈwɜːkʃɒp/ n. 车间
helper (l.7) /ˈhelpə/ n. 帮手, 助手
employ (l.9) /ɪmˈplɔɪ/ v. 雇用
grandson (l.11) /ˈgrænsʌn/ n. 孙子

Notes on the text 课文注释

1 but as a boy he used to work in a small shop, 但他小时候却在一家小铺里工作。used to do 表示过去经常做而现在已经停止、不再做某事。

2 of his own, 自己的。

3 in his twenties, 20 多岁的时候。

参考译文

昨天下午弗兰克·霍金斯向我讲述了他年轻时的经历。在退休前, 弗兰克是一家非常大的商业公司的经理, 但他小时候却在一家小铺里做工。他那时的工作是修理自行车, 并且通常是一天工作 14 个小时。他靠多年积蓄, 于 1958 年买下了自己的一个小铺子。20 多岁的时候, 弗兰克曾生产飞机零配件。那时他有两个帮手。几年之后, 小铺子已经发展成了一个雇有 728 人的大工厂。弗兰克回想着他早年的艰难经历和走过的漫长的成功之路时笑了。他正笑着的时候门开了, 他的妻子走了进来。她叫他去修理孙子的自行车!

Summary writing 摘要写作

Answer these questions *in not more than 80 words*.
回答下列问题, 将答案组成一个段落, 不要超过 80 个单词。

1　What was Frank Hawkins telling the writer about?

2　Where did Frank use to work as a boy?

3　What did he use to do there?

4　When did he buy his own shop? What did he make in his twenties? (*and*)

5　Did he employ a lot of people in a few years or not?

6　Who came into the room after a while?

7　What did she want him to repair?

Composition 作文

Rewrite these sentences using the correct verbs and joining words:

用正确的动词和连词改写以下句子：

Frank (not only) (neither) (repaired) (made) his grandson's bicycle, (but) (also) went for a ride on it (as well) (both). He (said) (told) me later: 'I (make) (do) aeroplanes, (and) (but) I prefer bicycles.'

Letter writing 书信写作

Which of the following headings is correct?

以下的哪一个信头是正确的？

Mr. Bill Howard,	214 Duke St.,	Duke St. 214,
214 Duke St.,	Perth,	14th May, 19__,
Perth,	Western Australia.	Perth,
Western Australia.	14th May, 19__	Western Australia.

Key structures 关键句型

He used to work fourteen hours a day.

Do you remember these sentences? (**KS7**)

你记得这些句子吗？（参见第 7 课关键句型）

When I *was watering* the garden, it *began* to rain.

As I *was getting* on the bus, I *slipped* and *hurt* my foot.

Now compare them with these sentences:

比较以下句子：

used to do

I *used to go* to work by bus. Now I go by car. 我过去常乘公共汽车上班，现在开小车去。

He *used to be* a postman a long time ago. He's a taxi driver now. 很久以前他曾是个邮递员，现在他是个出租车司机。

I have given up smoking. I *used to smoke* very heavily. 我已经戒烟了，过去我吸烟很厉害。

I *used to collect* stamps when I was a boy. 当我还是个小男孩时，我常搜集邮票。

My uncle *used to live* in New Zealand but he's now living in Australia. 我叔叔过去住在新西兰，但他现在住在澳大利亚。

Exercises 练习

A　Underline the verbs in the passage which tell us *what was happening, what happened* and *what used to happen*.

在课文中画出所有过去进行时、一般过去时和含有 used to do 的句子：

B Give the correct form of the verbs in parentheses. Do not refer to the passage until you finish the exercise:

用括号中动词的正确形式填空，完成练习后再对照课文，核对你的答案：

1 Before he retired, Frank was the head of a very large business company, but as a boy he _____ (work) in a small shop. It _____ (be) his job to repair bicycles and at that time he _____ (work) fourteen hours a day. He _____ (save) money for years and in 1958 he _____ (buy) a small workshop.

2 Frank _____ (smile) when he _____ (remember) his hard early years. He still _____ (smile) when the door _____ (open) and his wife _____ (come) in.

C What was happening? What happened? What used to happen?

Give the correct form of the verbs in parentheses:

用括号中动词的正确形式填空：

While my wife _____ (work) in the kitchen, I _____ (sit) in the garden. I _____ (look) at cars which _____ (pass) in the street, when a small car _____ (stop) outside my gate and a man _____ (get) out. I was most surprised to see that the man was Ted Hale. We _____ (be) at the same school years ago. In those days, Ted _____ (come) to our house nearly every day and we often _____ (go) out together. We _____ (be) great friends, but one day we _____ (quarrel) and I never _____ (see) him again. As he _____ (get) out of his car, I _____ (call) my wife and we both _____ (hurry) out to greet an old friend.

Special difficulties 难点

Words often misused and confused 经常容易混淆和误用的词

a *Experience*.

Frank Hawkins was telling me about his *experiences*. (ll.1-2)

This job requires a lot of *experience*. 这种工作需要有丰富的经验。

He is an *experienced* worker. 他是一位有经验的工人。

b *Save*.

He *saved* money for years. (l.5)

The young man dived into the river and *saved* the boy's life. 那位年轻人跳入水中，救了那个男孩的性命。

c *Work* and *Job*.

It was his *job* to repair bicycles. (l.4)

I've just found a new *job*. I begin *work* on Monday. 我找到了一份新的工作，我星期一开始上班。

Exercise 练习

Choose the correct words in the following sentences:

选择正确的词：

1 He is a very (experience) (experienced) doctor.

2 My father enjoys doing (jobs) (works) about the house.

3 I am looking for a new (work) (job).

4 The government is trying to persuade people to (economise) (save) money.

Multiple choice questions 选择题

Comprehension 理解

1 When he was a young man, Frank _____ .

(*a*) owned a small shop

(*b*) made spare parts for aeroplanes

(*c*) made spare parts for bicycles

(*d*) worked hard and saved his money

2 Frank has been very successful _____ .

(*a*) and he still repairs bicycles for a living

(*b*) but he might occasionally repair a bicycle

(*c*) and he would never repair a bicycle now

(*d*) and he is only interested in aeroplanes

Structure 句型

3 Frank used to work in a small shop. He _____ .

(*a*) doesn't anymore

(*b*) still does

(*c*) is now

(*d*) has never done anything else

4 He used to work fourteen hours a day. He did this _____ day.

(*a*) one   (*b*) some

(*c*) each   (*d*) a

5 He had a shop of his own. It was _____ shop.

(*a*) his own   (*b*) his's

(*c*) his' own   (*d*) his'

6 In his twenties, 728 people _____ in the shop.

(*a*) were employed   (*b*) employed

(*c*) are employed   (*d*) employ

7 _____ this bicycle? Their grandson's.

(*a*) Who's is   (*b*) Whoses

(*c*) Who's   (*d*) Whose is

Vocabulary 词汇

8 Frank is the _____ of a business company.

(*a*) director   (*b*) headmaster

(*c*) superior   (*d*) leader

9 He saved money, so he had to _____ .

(*a*) spare it   (*b*) economise

(*c*) keep it   (*d*) rescue it

10 Spare parts for aeroplanes are made in Frank's _____ .

(*a*) industry   (*b*) fabric

(*c*) factory   (*d*) workhouse

11 He employed over seven hundred people. _____ .

(*a*) They worked for him

(*b*) He worked for them

(*c*) They employed him

(*d*) They were in charge

12 He was still smiling when the door opened and his wife _____ .

(*a*) went in   (*b*) entered in

(*c*) entered   (*d*) entered into

Sentence structure 句子结构

Rewrite this sentence, then check your answer against the text.

改写下列句子, 然后对照课文第 10-11 行, 核对你的答案。

She asked him if he would repair their grandson's bicycle.

She wanted _____ .

Lesson 32　Shopping made easy　购物变得很方便

🔊 **First listen and then answer the question.**

听录音，然后回答以下问题。

Who was the thief?

People are not so honest as they once were. The temptation to steal is greater than ever before — especially in large shops. A detective recently watched a well-dressed woman who always went into a large store on Monday mornings. One Monday, there were fewer
5　people in the shop than usual when the woman came in, so it was easier for the detective to watch her. The woman first bought a few small articles. After a little time, she chose one of the most expensive dresses in the shop and handed it to an assistant who wrapped it up for her as quickly as possible. Then the woman simply took the
10　parcel and walked out of the shop without paying. When she was arrested, the detective found out that the shop assistant was her daughter. The girl 'gave' her mother a free dress once a week!

A detective watched a well-dressed woman

New words and expressions 生词和短语

once (1.1) /wʌns/ *adv.* 曾经，以前
temptation (1.1) /temp'teɪʃən/ *n.* 诱惑
article (1.7) /'ɑːtɪkəl/ *n.* 物品，东西

wrap (1.8) /ræp/ *v.* 包裹
simply (1.9) /'sɪmpli/ *adv.* 仅仅
arrest (1.10) /ə'rest/ *v.* 逮捕

Notes on the text 课文注释

1　People are not so honest as they once were. 人们不再像以前那样诚实了。其中的句型 "not so + 形容词 + as ..." 是比较状语从句，可以译成 "不如……那样……"。

2　The temptation to steal is greater than ever before, 偷窃的诱惑力比以往任何时候更强烈。to steal 是动词不定式，用来作 temptation 的定语。

3　well-dressed, 穿着入时的，这是复合形容词。

4　than usual, 比平常。

5　so it was easier for the detective to watch her, 因此，侦探比较容易监视她。在这句话中，it 只是一个先行词，实际主语是后面的不定式短语 for the detective to watch her。

6　wrap up, 包起来。

7　as ... as possible, 尽可能……。

8　without paying, 没有付款，这里用介词短语作状语，表示方式；其中的动名词 paying 作介词 without 的宾语。

参考译文

　　人们不再像以前那样诚实了。偷窃的诱惑力比以往任何时候都更强烈——特别是在大的商店里。一名侦探最近注意上了一位穿着讲究的妇女，她总是在星期一上午进入一家大商场。有一个星期一，当这位妇女走进这家商场时，里面的人比往常少，因此，侦探比较容易监视她。这位妇女先是买了几样小商品。过了一会儿，

她又选了商场里最昂贵的一件衣服，把它递给了售货员。那售货员以最快的速度为她包好了衣服。然后，那妇女拿过包就走出了商场，根本没有付钱。她被逮捕后，侦探发现原来那售货员是她的女儿。那姑娘每星期"送"她母亲一件免费的衣服！

Summary writing 摘要写作

Answer these questions *in not more than 70 words*.

回答下列问题，将答案组成一个段落，不要超过 70 个单词。

1　Whom did a detective watch in a large store one Monday?

2　What did she buy? Did she choose an expensive dress or not? (*and then*)

3　Did the assistant wrap it up for her or not? Did the woman take it with her or not? (*and*)

4　Did she pay for it or not? Did the detective arrest her or not? (*so*)

5　Who was the assistant?

6　What did she give her mother once a week?

Composition 作文

Rewrite these sentences using the correct verbs and joining words:

用正确的动词和连词改写以下句子：

I (came) (arrived at) the office late as usual (so) (but) Mr. Blake (saw) (understood) me (and) (or) he was very angry. 'This is your last day here, Jones,' he said. 'You can (neither) (either) (stay) (sit) here (or) (nor) go home!'

Letter writing 书信写作

Each line of the address is followed by a comma. The last line is followed by a full stop. We do not put a comma or a full stop after the date.

地址的每一行都以逗号结尾，最后一行用句号。在日期后面不用标点符号。

Exercise 练习

Arrange the following heading in the correct order. Put in full stops or commas where necessary:

按正确的顺序排列以下信头，在必要的地方加上逗号和句号：

New York/504 West 94th St./N.Y./24th June, 19__/U.S.A.

Key structures 关键句型

People are not so honest as they once were.

Do you remember these sentences? (**KS8**)

你记得这些句子吗？（参见第 8 课关键句型）

Mary is tall, but Jane is taller. Jane is taller than Mary. Betty is very tall. She is the tallest girl in the class.

Now study these sentences carefully:

仔细阅读以下句子：

a　He is *as old as* I am. 他和我年龄一样大。

　He unlocked the door *as quickly as* he could. 他尽快地打开了门。

　She is not *as intelligent as* we think. 她不像我们想象得那么聪明。

　Or: She is not *so intelligent as* we think.

b *Instead of saying*:

除了这种表述方法外：

There isn't much I can do to help him.

He hasn't got as much work to do *as* I have.

There weren't many people in the shop.

He hasn't as many books *as* I have.

There isn't much whisky in this bottle, but you can have *some* if you want it.

There aren't many apples on the tree, but you can pick *some* if you want to.

We can say:

还可以说：

There is little I can do to help him.

He's got less work to do *than* I have.

There were very few people in the shop.

He has fewer books *than* I have.

There isn't much whisky in this bottle, but you can have *a little* if you want it.

There aren't many apples on the tree, but you can pick *a few* if you want to.

Exercises 练习

A How many comparisons can you find in the passage? Underline them.
在课文中你能找出几种表示比较的方式？在它们下面画上横线。

B Supply the missing words and give the correct form of the words in parentheses. Do not refer to the passage until you finish the exercise.
在空白处填上适当的词，并将括号内词的正确形式填上，完成练习后再对照课文，核对你的答案。

People are not _____ honest _____ they once were. The temptation to steal is _____ (great) than ever before — especially in large shops. A detective recently watched a well-dressed woman who always went into a large store on Monday mornings. One Monday, there were _____ (few) people in the shop than usual when the woman came in, so it was _____ (easy) for the detective to watch her. The woman first bought a _____ small articles. After a _____ time, she chose one of the _____ (expensive) dresses in the shop and handed it to an assistant who wrapped it up for her _____ quickly _____ possible.

Special difficulties 难点

Words often confused 经常容易混淆的词

A and *One*. (**KS6**)（参见第 6 课关键句型）

Study these examples:

细读以下例句：

A detective watched *a* well-dressed woman. (ll.2-3)

One Monday, there were fewer people in the shop. (ll.4-5)

Compare:

对比以下两个句子：

There is *a* boy in the classroom. 教室里有个男孩。

There is only *one* boy in the classroom. (And not two or more.) 教室里仅有 1 个男孩子。

Exercise 练习

Put in *a/an* or *one*: 用 a/an 或 one 填空：

_____ day I received _____ postcard from Harry. He invited me to go on _____ excursion. As he was setting out that afternoon, there was only _____ thing to do. I had to send _____ fax. I went to my desk and picked up _____ form. I wrote _____ fax of _____ word: NO.

Multiple choice questions 选择题

Comprehension 理解

1 The detective saw the woman _____ .

(*a*) every Monday

(*b*) pay the assistant for the dresses

(*c*) buy a few things

(*d*) put the dresses in her bag

2 It was easy for the woman to steal because _____ .

(*a*) she was clever

(*b*) no one ever saw her

(*c*) she was related to one of the assistants

(*d*) an assistant wrapped her parcels

Structure 句型

3 People are not so honest as they once were. They are _____ honest.

(*a*) as

(*b*) so

(*c*) less

(*d*) fewer

4 There were fewer people in the shop than usual. There were _____ .

(*a*) as many as usual

(*b*) not as many as usual

(*c*) as few as usual

(*d*) more than usual

5 The woman bought a few small articles. She bought _____ .

(*a*) a little

(*b*) some

(*c*) one

(*d*) three

6 Which dress did she _____?

(*a*) chosen

(*b*) chose

(*c*) choose

(*d*) choosing

7 It was one of the most expensive dresses _____ the shop.

(*a*) in

(*b*) of

(*c*) from

(*d*) to

Vocabulary 词汇

8 A detective recently watched a well-dressed woman. He _____ her.

(*a*) looked

(*b*) looked for

(*c*) looked after

(*d*) looked at

9 The woman first bought a few small articles. She bought some small _____ .

(*a*) things

(*b*) pieces

(*c*) bits

(*d*) parts

10 The assistant wrapped it. She _____ it.

(*a*) papered

(*b*) turned

(*c*) enveloped

(*d*) made a parcel of

11 She was arrested. She _____ .

(*a*) escaped

(*b*) was caught

(*c*) was stopped

(*d*) was seen

12 The dress was free. It _____ .

(*a*) was priceless

(*b*) was worthless

(*c*) cost nothing

(*d*) was grateful

Sentence structure 句子结构

Join these sentences, then check your answer against the text.

连接以下句子, 然后对照课文第 4-6 行, 核对你的答案。

One Monday, there were fewer people in the shop than usual. The woman came in. It was easier for the detective to watch her.

Lesson 33 Out of the darkness 冲出黑暗

First listen and then answer the question.

听录音，然后回答以下问题。

Why was the girl in hospital?

caught in a storm

Nearly a week passed before the girl was able to explain what had happened to her. One afternoon she set out from the coast in a small boat and was caught in a storm. Towards evening, the boat struck a rock and the girl jumped into the sea. Then she swam to the shore
5 after spending the whole night in the water. During that time she covered a distance of eight miles. Early next morning, she saw a light ahead. She knew she was near the shore because the light was high up on the cliffs. On arriving at the shore, the girl struggled up the cliff towards the light she had seen. That was all she remembered. When she woke up a day later, she
10 found herself in hospital.

New words and expressions 生词和短语

darkness (title) /'dɑːknəs/ n. 黑暗

explain (l.1) /ɪks'pleɪn/ v. 解释，叙述

coast (l.2) /'kəʊst/ n. 海岸

storm (l.3) /stɔːm/ n. 暴风雨

towards (l.3) /tə'wɔːdz/ prep. 向，朝；接近

rock (l.4) /rɒk/ n. 岩石，礁石

shore (l.4) /ʃɔː/ n. 海岸

light (l.7) /laɪt/ n. 灯光

ahead (l.7) /ə'hed/ adv. 在前面

cliff (l.8) /klɪf/ n. 峭壁

struggle (l.8) /'strʌgəl/ v. 挣扎

hospital (l.10) /'hɒspɪtl/ n. 医院

Notes on the text 课文注释

1 set out, 出发，动身。

2 ... was caught in a storm, 遇上了暴风雨。catch 此处作"突然遇上"讲。

3 During that time she covered a distance of eight miles. 在那段时间里，她游了 8 英里。cover 作"行过"、"走过"、"游过"等讲。

4 a light ahead, 前面的一盏灯。ahead 是形容词，此处作定语，放在所修饰的名词的后面。

5 On arriving at the shore ..., 一到岸边……。on + 动名词相当于一个由 as soon as 引导的时间状语从句。

6 That was all she remembered. 她所记得的就是这些。all 是句中的表语，she remembered 是定语从句，用来修饰 all，关系代词 that 因在从句中作宾语而被省略。

参考译文

　　几乎过了一个星期，那姑娘才能讲述自己的遭遇。一天下午，她乘小船从海岸出发，遇上了风暴。天将黑时，小船撞在了一块礁石上，姑娘跳进了海里。她在海里游了整整一夜才游到岸边。在那段时间里，她游了 8 英里。第二天凌晨，她看到前方有灯光，知道自己已经接近岸边了，因为那灯光是在高高的峭壁上。到达岸边后，姑娘朝着她看到的灯光方向挣扎着往峭壁上爬去。她所记得的就是这些。第二天她醒来时，发现自己躺在医院里。

Summary writing 摘要写作

Answer these questions *in not more than 65 words.*
回答下列问题, 将答案组成一个段落, 不要超过 65 个单词。

1   When did the girl set out from the coast? Was she caught in a storm or not? (*and*)

2   Did her boat strike a rock or not? Did she jump into the sea, or did she remain in the boat? (*so*)

3   How many miles did she swim that night?

4   When did she reach the shore?

5   What had she seen high up on the cliffs? Did she climb up or not? (*and*)

6   Where did she find herself a day later?

Composition 作文

Rewrite these sentences using the correct verbs and joining words:
用正确的动词和连词改写以下句子:

On Saturday I (wanted) (needed) to go to a football match. It (not only) (neither) rained all day (or) (but) it was cold as well, (but) (so) I (stayed) (waited) at home (and) (but) (watched) (looked) the match on television.

Letter writing 书信写作

Arrange the following heading in the correct order. Put in full stops or commas where necessary:
按正确的顺序排列以下信头中的各个部分, 在必要的地方加上逗号或句号:

Grimsby/Lincs./17 Howland St./England/18th May, 19_

Key structures 关键句型

Where did he go? He went to the cinema. (Compare **KS9**) (对比第9课关键句型)

Read these sentences carefully. Pay close attention to the words in italics. We can often use phrases like these to answer questions beginning with *Where*, or *Which direction*.
细读以下句子, 特别注意斜体印出的词组。我们经常可以用这些词组来回答用 Where 或 Which direction 开头的问题。

a   Phrases with *to* and *from*. 带 to 和 from 的短语
    He flew *to Washington* last night. He will be flying *from Washington to Chicago* on Wednesday. 昨晚他飞到了华盛顿, 星期三他将从华盛顿飞往芝加哥。

b   Phrases with *into* and *out of*. 带 into 和 out of 的短语
    Where is Carol? She has just gone *into the kitchen*. 卡罗尔在哪里? 她刚刚到厨房去了。
    Where did you throw that piece of paper? I threw it *out of the* window. 你把那张纸扔到哪儿去了? 我把它扔到了窗外。

c   Phrases with *for*. 带 for 的短语
    We set out *for the village* at six o'clock next morning. 第二天早上 6 点我们出发去那个村子。
    George has left *for Scotland*. 乔治已动身去苏格兰。

d   Phrases with *towards*. 带 towards 的短语
    The car came *towards me*. 汽车向我开来。
    She swam *towards the shore*. 她向岸边游去。

e   Phrases with *at*. 带 at 的短语
    The boy threw a stone *at a dog*. 男孩用石头打狗。
    It is rude to point *at people*. 用手指人不礼貌。

155

Exercises 练习

A Answer these questions about the passage:
  回答有关课文的问题：

  1 Where did the girl set out from?

  2 Where did she jump?

  3 Where did she swim?

B Supply the missing words in the following sentences:
  用恰当的词填空：

1 Tell him to come _____ my office. I want to speak to him.

2 The ship sailed _____ the harbour and disappeared from sight.

3 We climbed _____ the top of the mountain.

4 The team set out _____ Australia yesterday.

5 This ship sails _____ Venice _____ London once a week.

6 He aimed _____ the bird, fired, and missed.

7 Please bring these things _____ the kitchen for me.

8 Have you received a letter _____ Alan yet?

C Write sentences using the following:
  用以下词和词组组成完整的句子：

1 bird/flew/the room.   2 parachutist/jumped/aeroplane.

3 child/pointed/fat lady.   4 put/milk/refrigerator.

Special difficulties 难点

Words often confused and misused 经常容易混淆和误用的词

Study these examples:

细读以下例句：

a *Passed* and *Past*. Nearly a week *passed* ... (l.1)

  He *passed* my house this morning. ('Passed' is a verb.) 他今天上午路过我家。

  He walked *past* my house. ('Past' is a preposition.) 他从我家旁边走过。

  He told me about his *past* experiences. ('Past' is an adjective.) 他告诉我他过去的经历。

  He seems to live in the *past*. ('Past' is a noun.) 他好像生活在过去的时代里。

b *Next* and *other*.

  Early *next* morning she saw a light ahead. (ll.6-7) 第二天凌晨，她看到前面有灯光。

  We arrived in Paris on Tuesday evening. The *next* day we went sightseeing. (The day after.) 星期二晚上我们到达巴黎。第二天我们去观光。

  I saw Mary the *other* day. (A few days ago.) 日前我见到了玛丽。

Exercise 练习

Choose the correct expressions in the following:

选择正确的表达方式：

1 I tried to telephone you (the other day) (the next day). You must have been out.

2 Have you (past) (passed) your driving test?

3 On the first day all went well. But on the (next) (other) day there was a storm.

4 The crowd cheered as the soldiers marched (past) (passed).

Multiple choice questions 选择题

Comprehension 理解

1 The girl was in the boat _____ .

(a) all day   (b) all night   (c) for about ten hours   (d) for about four hours

2 The girl woke up in hospital a day later _____ .

(a) and explained what had happened to her

(b) but some time passed before she could explain what had happened to her

(c) and at once remembered what had happened to her

(d) but never remembered what had happened to her

Structure 句型

3 What _____ to her?

(a) happen   (b) was happened   (c) happening   (d) happened

4 She swam to the shore _____ the night in the water.

(a) having spent   (b) having spending   (c) when spending   (d) had spent

5 How _____ was the shore? Eight miles.

(a) away far   (b) far from   (c) far away   (d) long

6 That was all she remembered. She couldn't remember _____ .

(a) some more   (b) anymore   (c) no more   (d) none more

7 She was taken _____ hospital.

(a) at the   (b) to   (c) in   (d) in the

Vocabulary 词汇

8 She was caught in a storm. The weather was _____ .

(a) fine   (b) warm and sunny   (c) very rough   (d) wet

9 She saw a light ahead. The light was _____ her.

(a) behind   (b) beside   (c) in front of   (d) above

10 Cliffs are usually _____ .

(a) narrow   (b) wide   (c) steep   (d) sharp

11 She struggled up the cliff. It wasn't _____ .

(a) easy   (b) hard   (c) difficult   (d) long

12 That was all she remembered. She couldn't _____ very much.

(a) remind   (b) memorise   (c) recollect   (d) mind

Sentence structure 句子结构

Rewrite this sentence, then check your answer against the text.

改写以下句子, 然后对照课文第 8-9 行, 核对你的答案。

When she arrived at the shore, the girl struggled up the cliff.

On _____ .

157

Lesson 34　Quick work　破案"神速"

First listen and then answer the question.

听录音，然后回答以下问题。

How long had the police taken to find his bicycle?

Dan Robinson has been worried all week. Last Tuesday he received
a letter from the local police. In the letter he was asked to call at the
station. Dan wondered why he was wanted by the police, but he
went to the station yesterday and now he is not worried anymore.

5　At the station, he was told by a smiling policeman that his bicycle
had been found. Five days ago, the policeman told him, the bicycle
was picked up in a small village four hundred miles away. It is now
being sent to his home by train. Dan was most surprised when he

heard the news. He was amused too, because he never expected the bicycle to be found. It was stolen twenty

10　years ago when Dan was a boy of fifteen!

a letter from the local police

New words and expressions 生词和短语

station (l.3) /'steɪʃən/ n. （警察）局

most (l.8) /məʊst/ adv. 相当，非常

Notes on the text 课文注释

1　the local police, 当地警察（局）。

2　call at, 拜访。

3　he is not worried anymore, 他不再担心了。

4　the policeman told him, 警察告诉他。这是插入成分，在讲故事时常用这种方式。

5　the bicycle was picked up in a small village four hundred miles away, 那辆自行车在 400 英里以外的一个小
村里被发现。pick up 有"意外地找到"的意思。

6　It is now being sent to his home by train. 现在正用火车给他运回家来。当被动语态用于现在进行时中，要在
助动词 be 后面加上 ing，再加上过去分词。

7　most surprised 中的 most 有 very 的意思，常常与起形容词作用的过去分词连用。

参考译文

　　丹·鲁宾逊焦虑了整整一个星期。上星期二他收到当地警察局的一封信，要他到警察局去一趟。丹奇怪
警察为什么找他，但昨天还是去了，现在他不再担心了。在警察局里，一位面带笑容的警察告诉他，他的自行车
找到了。那位警察对他说，那辆自行车是 5 天前在 400 英里外的一个小村里发现的，现在正用火车给他运回家
来。丹听到这个消息后，惊奇万分，但又感到非常好笑，因为他从未指望那辆自行车还能找到。这是 20 年前丹
还是一个 15 岁的孩子时被人偷走的！

Summary writing 摘要写作

Answer these questions *in not more than 55 words.*
回答以下问题, 将答案组成一个段落, 不要超过 55 个词。

 1 Was Dan Robinson worried or not?

 2 Whom had he received a letter from?

 3 Where did he go yesterday?

 4 Is he worried anymore or not?

 5 What have the police found?

 6 Was Dan surprised or not? Was he amused or not? (*not only ... but ... as well*)

 7 When was his bicycle stolen?

 8 How old was he then?

Composition 作文

Rewrite these sentences using the correct verbs and joining words:
用正确的动词和连词改写以下句子:

The man was (not only) (neither) tired (nor) (but) hungry (as well) (either). (However) (Therefore) all the hotels in the town (existed) (were) full, (but) (so) he went to the police station. The police (put) (gave) him a meal (and) (but) a bed for the night.

Letter writing 书信写作

In the address we usually write 'St.' for 'Street'; 'Rd.' for 'Road'; 'Sq.' for 'Square'; 'Ave.' for 'Avenue'; 'Pl.' for 'Place'. We write words like 'Lane' and 'Drive' in full.
在地址中我们通常使用缩略形式, 如: "St." (Street); "Rd." (Road); "Sq." (Square); "Ave." (Avenue); "Pl." (Place), 而有些词则不用缩略形式, 如 "Lane" 和 "Drive"。

Exercise 练习

Write these words in the way shown above:
写出以下词的缩略形式:

Place, Avenue, Street, Road, Square.

Key structures 关键句型

He was asked to call at the station.

Do you remember these sentences? **(KS10)**
你还记得这些句子吗? (参见第 10 课关键句型)

Prisoners of war built this bridge in 1942. (Who)

This bridge was built (by prisoners of war) in 1942. (What)

Now study these sentences:
仔细阅读以下句子:

They asked me to make a speech. (Who) 他们叫我作一次讲演。

I was asked to make a speech. (Who) 我应邀作一次讲演。

Unit 2 Lesson 34

You will notice that the form of the verb depends on the person or thing we mention first. We mention the most important person or thing first.

可以注意到, 句子使用的语态取决于我们首先提及的人或东西, 我们总是首先提到最重要的人或东西。

Instead of saying:	*We can say*:
除了这种表述方式外:	还可以说:
They are sending *him* abroad.	*He* is being sent abroad.
The police were questioning *the man*.	*The man* was being questioned (by the police).
He told *me* to wait for him.	*I* was told to wait for him.
They have found *your wallet*.	*Your wallet* has been found.
He never expected them to find *the bicycle*.	He never expected *the bicycle* to be found.

Exercises 练习

A Answer these questions on the passage. Write a complete sentence in answer to each question:
用完整的句子回答以下针对课文的问题:

1 Who has been worried all the week?

2 What was Dan asked to do?

3 What did Dan wonder?

4 What was Dan told at the station?

5 Where was Dan's bicycle picked up?

6 Where is the bicycle being sent?

7 What did Dan feel when he heard the news?

8 Why was Dan amused?

9 How long ago was the bicycle stolen?

B Change the form of the phrases in italics. Do not refer to the passage until you finish the exercise:
改变斜体部分的语态, 完成练习后再对照课文, 核对你的答案:

1 *Something has worried Dan* all the week.

2 In the letter *they asked him to* call at the station.

3 Dan wondered why *the police wanted him*.

4 At the station, *a smiling policeman told him* that *they had found his bicycle*.

5 *They picked up the bicycle* in a small village.

6 *They are sending it* to his home by train.

7 *This amused him* because he never expected *them to find the bicycle. Someone stole it* twenty years ago.

Special difficulties 难点

Read these sentences. Each sentence contains the verb *call*. The verb has a different meaning in each sentence:

细读以下句子, 每句中均有动词 call, 但词义不同:

He was asked to *call at* the station. (ll.2-3)。

He *called out* to me but I did not hear him. 他朝我大声叫喊, 但我没听见。

I *called on* George yesterday. (I paid him a short visit.) 我昨天去拜访乔治。

She'll *call you up* tomorrow. (She will telephone you.) 她将在明天给你打电话。

It began to rain so we *called off* the match. (We cancelled it.) 天开始下雨, 所以我们取消了这场比赛。

Exercise 练习

Supply the missing words in the following sentences:
用恰当的词填空:

1 I called _____ you five times yesterday. Were you out?

2 It's too late to go to the pictures. Why don't we call the whole thing _____?

3 We called _____ to him but he could not hear us.

4 I called _____ the post office on my way to work.

Multiple choice questions 选择题
Comprehension 理解

1 Dan was worried because _____ .

(*a*) he received a letter

(*b*) the police wanted him

(*c*) he went to the station yesterday

(*d*) he didn't know why the police wanted him

2 Dan _____ .

(*a*) had probably forgotten all about his bicycle

(*b*) probably expected to find his bicycle again

(*c*) probably expected to get a letter from the police

(*d*) was probably sorry to learn that his bicycle had been found

Structure 句型

3 Dan has been worried all week and he's _____ worried.

(*a*) even   (*b*) still   (*c*) yet   (*d*) anymore

4 The police _____ Dan's bicycle.

(*a*) had been finding   (*b*) had been found   (*c*) had found   (*d*) have been finding

5 _____ was the bicycle picked up? In a small village.

(*a*) Where   (*b*) Why   (*c*) What   (*d*) When

6 He never expected that _____ find the bicycle.

(*a*) to   (*b*) to be   (*c*) they   (*d*) they would

7 Someone _____ it twenty years ago.

(*a*) stolen   (*b*) has stolen   (*c*) stole   (*d*) was stolen

Vocabulary 词汇

8 All the police at the station are _____ men.

(*a*) topical   (*b*) local   (*c*) native   (*d*) neighbourly

9 The police wanted Dan to call at the station. They wanted him to call _____ them.

(*a*) at   (*b*) in   (*c*) on   (*d*) up

10 The bicycle was picked up four hundred miles away. It was _____ by a policeman.

(*a*) picked   (*b*) found   (*c*) dropped   (*d*) lifted

11 Dan was amused. He must have _____ .

(*a*) shouted   (*b*) cried   (*c*) laughed   (*d*) clapped

12 The bicycle was stolen. Dan was _____ .

(*a*) robbed   (*b*) stolen   (*c*) taken   (*d*) stealing

Sentence structure 句子结构

Rewrite this sentence, then check your answer against the text.

改写下列句子, 然后对照课文第 7-8 行, 核对你的答案。

They are now sending it to his home by train.

It _____ .

Lesson 35 Stop thief! 捉贼！

How did Roy stop the thieves?

He is finding his new work far more exciting

Roy Trenton used to drive a taxi. A short while ago, however, he became a bus driver and he has not regretted it. He is finding his new work far more exciting. When he was driving along Catford Street recently, he saw two thieves rush out of a shop and run towards
5 a waiting car. One of them was carrying a bag full of money. Roy acted quickly and drove the bus straight at the thieves. The one with the money got such a fright that he dropped the bag. As the thieves were trying to get away in their car, Roy drove his bus into the back of it. While the battered car was moving away, Roy stopped his bus and telephoned the police. The thieves'
10 car was badly damaged and easy to recognize. Shortly afterwards, the police stopped the car and both men were arrested.

New words and expressions 生词和短语

while (l.1) /waɪl/ *n.* 一段时间
regret (l.2) /rɪˈgret/ *v.* 后悔
far (l.3) /fɑː/ *adv.* 非常
rush (l.4) /rʌʃ/ *v.* 冲
act (l.6) /ækt/ *v.* 行动

straight (l.6) /streɪt/ *adv.* 径直
fright (l.7) /fraɪt/ *n.* 害怕
battered (l.9) /ˈbætəd/ *adj.* 撞坏的
shortly (l.10) /ˈʃɔːtli/ *adv.* 很快，不久
afterwards (l.10) /ˈɑːftəwədz/ *adv.* 以后

Notes on the text 课文注释

1 a short while ago, 不久前。
2 far more exciting, 令人兴奋得多。far 是副词，放在比较级的形容词前，表示程度，可译作"很"、"大大地"。
3 he saw two thieves rush out of a shop and run towards a waiting car, 他看到两个小偷从一家商店里冲出来，奔向等在那里的一辆汽车。在动词 see 后面接不定式时，不定式要省去 to, 如本句中的 rush 和 run 两个不定式。
4 a bag full of money, 一只装满钞票的提包。full of ... 是形容词短语，此处作定语，相当于一个定语从句 which was full of money。
5 The one with the money got such a fright that he dropped the bag. 拿钱的那个小偷吓得把提包都扔了。句中such ... that ... 的结构有"如此……以至于……"的意思，such 后面要跟名词。
6 shortly afterwards, 没过多久。

参考译文

　　罗伊·特雷顿原是开出租汽车的，然而就在前不久，他开上了公共汽车，也并不为此而感到后悔。他发觉自己的新工作令人兴奋得多。最近，当他正开车在凯特福德街上行驶时，看到有两个小偷从一家商店里冲出来，奔向等在那里的一辆汽车，其中一个提着一只装满钞票的提包。罗伊行动迅速，开车直冲窃贼而去。拿钱的

那个小偷吓得把提包都扔了。当那两个小偷企图乘车逃跑时，罗伊驾驶他的公共汽车撞在了那辆车的后尾上。当那辆被撞坏的车开走后，罗伊停下车，给警察挂了电话。小偷的车损坏严重，很容易辨认。没过多久，警察就截住了那辆车，两个小偷都被抓住了。

Summary writing 摘要写作

Answer these questions *in not more than 70 words.*
回答下列问题, 将答案组成一个段落, 不要超过 70 个单词。

1 Is Roy finding his new job as a bus driver exciting or not?

2 In which street did he see two thieves recently?

3 Were they running out of a shop, or were they running out of a bank? Where did Roy drive his bus? Did they drop the stolen money or not? Did they get into a car, or did they run away? (*and ... so ... and*)

4 Where did Roy drive his bus then? Did he damage their car or not? (*and*)

5 Whom did he telephone after this?

6 Were both men arrested later or did they get away?

Composition 作文

Rewrite these sentences using the correct verbs and joining words:
用正确的动词和连词改写以下句子:

The politician tried to (do) (make) a speech in the park (so) (but) no one (listened to) (heard) him. The audience shouted (and) (or) threw things (so) (but) the speaker got into his car and (drove) (ran) away.

Letter writing 书信写作

Supply commas or full stops where necessary in this heading:
在必要时为下列信头加上逗号或句号:

20 Crawford Ave

Cranley

Dorset

England

October 4th 19__

Key structures 关键句型

Review **KS26-34** 复习第 26-34 课的关键句型

These things always happen. **(KS26)** (第 26 课)

What happened? **(KS27)** (第 27 课)

What has happened? **(KS28)** (第 28 课)

He used to work fourteen hours a day. **(KS31)** (第 31 课)

He was asked to call at the station. **(KS34)** (第 34 课)

Exercises 练习

A Underline all the verbs in the passage.
   在课文所有动词的下面画上横线。

B Give the correct form of the verbs in parentheses. Do not refer to the passage until you finish the exercise.

用括号中动词的正确形式填空, 完成练习后再对照课文, 核对你的答案。

Roy Trenton _____ (drive) a taxi. A short while ago, however, he _____ (become) a bus driver and he _____ (not regret) it. He _____ (find) his new work far more exciting. When he _____ (drive) along Catford Street recently, he _____ (see) two thieves rush out of a shop and run towards a waiting car. One of them _____ (carry) a bag full of money. Roy _____ (act) quickly and _____ (drive) the bus straight at the thieves. The one with the money (get) _____ such a fright that he _____ (drop) the bag. As the thieves _____ (try) to get away in their car, Roy _____ (drive) his bus into the back of it. While the battered car _____ (move) away, Roy _____ (stop) his bus and _____ (telephone) the police. The thieves' car badly _____ (damage) and easy to recognize. Shortly afterwards, the police _____ (stop) the car and both men _____ (arrest).

C Give the correct form of the verbs in parentheses:

用括号中动词的正确形式填空:

1 This is what I _____ (mean). _____ (you understand) me?

2 Years ago, he _____ (smoke) but he _____ (not smoke) anymore.

3 The new Town Hall _____ (complete) last week.

4 I _____ (not see) him since 1995.

5 She _____ (drop) her handkerchief as she _____ (cross) the road.

Special difficulties 难点

So and Such

Study these examples:

细读以下例句:

The one with the money got *such* a fright that he dropped the bag. (ll.6-7)

He was *so* tired that he could not wake up. 他是这样困乏, 连醒都醒不过来。

You should not speak to *such* people. (People of this sort.) 你不应该和这样的人讲话。

You mustn't be *so* impatient. 你不能这样没耐心。

Exercise 练习

Supply *so*, *such* or *such a/an* in these sentences:

用 so, such 或 such a/an 填空:

1 He ran _____ quickly that I could not catch him.

2 Whoever told you _____ thing?

3 You should not make _____ many mistakes.

4 You should not say _____ things.

5 This picture is _____ beautiful that I shall hang it in my room.

6 It was _____ good book that it was bought by a film company.

7 It was _____ extraordinary exhibition that I went twice.

8 He is _____ lazy boy that he never does anything.

Multiple choice questions 选择题

Comprehension 理解

1 Roy Trenton _____ .

　(a) prefers driving a bus to driving a taxi　(b) prefers driving a taxi to driving a bus

　(c) is sorry he isn't a taxi driver　(d) is glad he didn't change his job

2 Because of Roy's action _____ .

　(a) the thieves were never caught

　(b) the thieves' car was damaged, but they were never caught

　(c) it was impossible for the police to catch the thieves

　(d) it was easy for the police to catch the thieves

Structure 句型

3 Roy Trenton used to drive a taxi. This means he _____ a taxi.

　(a) has stopped driving　(b) is used to driving　(c) got used to driving　(d) still drives

4 He noticed two thieves _____ out of a shop.

　(a) to come　(b) are coming　(c) in coming　(d) come

5 Which thief got a fright? _____ with the money.

　(a) He　(b) Him　(c) That　(d) The one

6 He got such a fright. He was _____ frightened.

　(a) so　(b) such　(c) such a　(d) a so

7 The car was easy to recognize, so it wasn't _____ difficult for the police to catch the thieves.

　(a) much　(b) very　(c) many　(d) too

Vocabulary 词汇

8 He hasn't regretted it. He _____ it.

　(a) isn't sorry about　(b) doesn't pity　(c) isn't pleased with　(d) doesn't laugh about

9 It's very _____ to drive a bus.

　(a) excited　(b) exciting　(c) excite　(d) excitedly

10 Roy drove the bus _____ at the thieves.

　(a) directly　(b) immediately　(c) at once　(d) soon

11 The thief dropped the bag. He _____ .

　(a) let it　(b) left it　(c) fell it　(d) let it fall

12 The thieves' car was battered because Roy _____ .

　(a) saw it　(b) rang the police　(c) recognized it　(d) hit it

Sentence structure 句子结构

Join these sentences, then check your answer against the text.

连接以下句子, 然后对照课文第 3-5 行, 核对你的答案。

He was driving along Catford Street recently. He saw two thieves. They rushed out of a shop. They ran towards a waiting car.

Lesson 36　Across the Channel　横渡英吉利海峡

![cassette icon] **First listen and then answer the question.**

听录音，然后回答以下问题。

What is Debbie going to try to do?

short rests every two hours

Debbie Hart is going to swim across the English Channel tomorrow. She is going to set out from the French coast at five o'clock in the morning. Debbie is only eleven years old and she hopes to set up a new world record. She is a strong swimmer and many people feel
5　that she is sure to succeed. Debbie's father will set out with her in a small boat. Mr. Hart has trained his daughter for years. Tomorrow he will be watching her anxiously as she swims the long distance to England. Debbie intends to take short rests every two hours. She will have something to drink but she will not eat any solid food. Most of Debbie's school friends will be
10　waiting for her on the English coast. Among them will be Debbie's mother, who swam the Channel herself when she was a girl.

New words and expressions　生词和短语

record (l.4) /ˈrekɔːd/ *n.* 纪录

strong (l.4) /strɒŋ/ *adj.* 强壮的

swimmer (l.4) /ˈswɪmə/ *n.* 游泳运动员

succeed (l.5) /səkˈsiːd/ *v.* 成功

train (l.6) /treɪn/ *v.* 训练

anxiously (l.7) /ˈæŋkʃəsli/ *adv.* 焦急地

intend (l.8) /ɪnˈtend/ *v.* 打算

solid (l.9) /ˈsɒlɪd/ *adj.* 固体的，硬的

Notes on the text　课文注释

1　set out, 出发。

2　set up, 创立，建立。

3　many people feel that she is sure to succeed, 许多人都认为她肯定成功。

4　every two hours, 每两小时。

5　Among them will be Debbie's mother, 他们当中还会有黛比的母亲。这是个倒装句，为的是与后面的定语从句相连。正常的语序应为 Debbie's mother will be among them.

参考译文

　　黛比·哈特准备明天横渡英吉利海峡。她打算早上 5 点钟从法国海岸出发。黛比只有 11 岁，她希望创一项新的世界纪录。她是一个游泳能手，很多人认为她一定能成功。黛比的父亲将乘一条小船同她一道出发。哈特先生训练她的女儿已经多年了，明天他将焦急地注视着女儿游过这段漫长的距离到达英国。黛比计划每两小时休息一下。她将喝些饮料，但不吃固体食物。黛比的大部分同学将在英国海岸等候她。他们当中还会有黛比的母亲，她本人还是个姑娘时，也曾横渡过英吉利海峡。

Summary writing 摘要写作

Answer these questions *in not more than 55 words*.

回答下列问题, 将答案组成一个段落, 不要超过 55 个单词:

1 Who is going to swim across the English Channel tomorrow?

2 How old is she? Is she a strong swimmer or not? (*and*)

3 Whom has Debbie been trained by?

4 Will he follow her in a small boat or not?

5 Where will Debbie's mother be waiting?

6 What did she do as a girl?

Composition 作文

Rewrite these sentences using the correct verbs and joining words:

用正确的动词和连词改写下列句子:

The man on the raft saw the boat (so) (but) he tried to send a signal. He (took off) (put out) his shirt (or) (and) (waved) (shook) it (but) (so) the men on the boat (neither) (either) saw (or) (nor) (heard) (listened to) him.

Letter writing 书信写作

We do not always write the names of areas or postal districts in full when writing the address. Sometimes we write part of a name or only capital letters. For instance: 'Berks.' stands for 'Berkshire'; 'Calif.' for 'California'; 'N.W.3' for 'North West 3'; 'N.Y.' for 'New York'.

当我们书写地址时, 常常不写地区或邮区的全称。有时只写名称的一部分或只用大写字母。如: Berkshire 写成 Berks., California 写成 Calif., North West 3 缩写成 N.W.3, New York 缩写成 N.Y.。

Exercise 练习

Write these words again in the way they might appear in an address:

用同样的方法重写下列可能在地址中出现的词语:

Street, Road, Avenue, Square, Place, New York, West 8, South West 3.

Key structure 关键句型

She is going to swim across the Channel tomorrow. 将来时 (KS12) (参见第 12 课关键句型)

Instead of saying:	*We can say*:
除了这种表述方法外:	还可以说:
I shall travel by air.	I am going to travel by air.
He will sell his car.	He is going to sell his car.
They will move to a new house.	They are going to move to a new house.
I intend to write to him.	I am going to write to him.
She means to ask for an explanation.	She is going to ask for an explanation.

We can often use *going to* in place of *shall* or *will* in simple statements and questions. We cannot use *going to* in sentences like this one:

在陈述句和疑问句中, 我们常常可用 going to 来替代 shall 或 will。在类似下列的句子中我们不能用 going to:

You will enjoy yourself if you travel by sea. 如果你乘船旅游, 你会玩得很开心的。

Exercises 练习

A Underline the verbs in the passage which tell us *what will happen*, *what is going to happen*, and *what will be happening* (KS13).
在课文中画出表示一般将来时和将来进行时的动词：（将来进行时参见第 13 课关键句型）

B Give the correct form of the verbs in parentheses. Do not refer to the passage until you finish the exercise:
用括号中动词的正确形式填空，完成练习后对照课文，核对你的答案：

Debbie Hart _____ (swim) across the English Channel tomorrow. She _____ (set out) from the French coast at five o'clock in the morning. Debbie is only eleven years old and she hopes to set up a new world record. ... Debbie's father _____ (set out) with her in a small boat. Mr. Hart has trained his daughter for years. Tomorrow he _____ (watch) her anxiously as she swims the long distance to England. Debbie intends to take short rests every two hours. She _____ (have) something to drink but she _____ (not eat) any solid food. Most of Debbie's school friends _____ (wait) for her on the English coast. Among them _____ (be) Debbie's mother, who swam the Channel herself when she was a girl.

C Write these sentences again. Use *going to* in place of the verbs in italics:
改写下列句子，用 going to 来替代斜体印出的动词：

1 We *intend to* leave at six o'clock.

2 I *intend to* pay these bills tomorrow.

3 *Do you intend to* write to him?

4 She *does not intend to* look for a new job.

5 When *do you intend to* buy a new car?

Special difficulties 难点

Words often confused 经常容易混淆的词

a *Watch, Look at, Follow.*

   Watch (something happening) 观看（正在发生的事情）：Tomorrow he *will be watching* her anxiously. (ll.6-7)

   Look at 看：*Look at* the blackboard. *Look at* your book. *Look at* this picture. 看黑板。看你的书。看这幅画。

   Follow (go after) 跟随（走在后面）：I *followed* my mother into the kitchen. 我跟着母亲走进厨房。

b *Solid, Firm, Stable.*

   Solid (not liquid) 固体的（非流体的）：She will not eat any *solid* food. (l.9)

   Firm (not loose) 稳固的（不松动的）：I've fixed that hook. It is *firm* now. 我把鱼钩固定好了，现在它很牢固。

   (not doubtful) 无疑的：He gave me a *firm* refusal. 他断然拒绝了我。

   (not lenient) 严格的：You must be very *firm* with that child. 对那个孩子你一定要非常严格。

   Stable (often describing character) 坚定的（常用来形容性格）：He is a very *stable* person. 他是一个性格坚定的人。

Exercise 练习

Use any of the above words in the following sentences:
用上面的词填空：

1 I came to a _____ decision and I will not change my mind.

2 I stood on the bridge and _____ the boats passing by.

3 May I _____ your photograph album?

4 The ice in the pond is so _____ that you can walk on it.

5 I tried to persuade him but he remained _____ .

Multiple choice questions 选择题

Comprehension 理解

1 One of these statements is true. Which one?

(a) Both Debbie's parents are very interested in their daughter's attempt to swim the Channel.

(b) Only Debbie's father is interested in his daughter's attempt.

(c) Only Debbie's mother is interested in her daughter's attempt.

(d) Debbie's mother and father aren't interested in their daughter's attempt to swim the Channel.

2 Debbie _____ .

(a) will only eat solid food during the swim   (b) will not drink anything during the swim

(c) will swim across the Channel without stopping   (d) will stop at intervals during the swim

Structure 句型

3 She is sure to succeed. Many people feel sure _____ it.

(a) to   (b) for   (c) in   (d) of

4 He will be watching her anxiously _____ she swims the long distance to England.

(a) though meanwhile   (b) meanwhile   (c) while   (d) during

5 _____ does she intend to take short rests? Every two hours.

(a) Since when   (b) How long   (c) How much   (d) How often

6 Debbie's friends will be on the coast. That's where _____ of them will be.

(a) more   (b) the most   (c) most   (d) the more

7 Debbie's mother will be _____ the crowd.

(a) between   (b) beside   (c) among   (d) around

Vocabulary 词汇

8 Debbie hopes to _____ a new world record.

(a) do   (b) make   (c) build   (d) fix

9 She is sure to succeed. She's sure to be _____ .

(a) successful   (b) success   (c) succession   (d) a succession

10 Mr. Hart has trained her. He's her _____ .

(a) leader   (b) guide   (c) trainee   (d) instructor

11 He'll be watching anxiously. He'll feel _____ .

(a) sad   (b) unhappy   (c) worried   (d) thoughtful

12 She'll take short rests every two hours. She will _____ every two hours.

(a) stay   (b) remain   (c) relax   (d) sleep

Sentence structure 句子结构

Arrange these groups of words in the right order, then check your answer against the text.

按正确的语序排列以下词和词组，完成练习后对照课文第 2-3 行，核对你的答案。

from the French coast/she/in the morning/is going to/at five o'clock/set out

Lesson 37　The Olympic Games　奥林匹克运动会

🔲 **First listen and then answer the question.**

听录音，然后回答以下问题。

When was the last time this country hosted the Olympic Games?

looking forward to the Olympic Games

The Olympic Games will be held in our country in four years' time. As a great many people will be visiting the country, the government will be building new hotels, an immense stadium, and a new Olympic-standard swimming pool. They will also be building new
5 roads and a special railway line. The Games will be held just outside the capital and the whole area will be called 'Olympic City'. Workers will have completed the new roads by the end of this year. By the end of next year, they will have finished work on the new stadium. The fantastic modern buildings have been designed by Kurt Gunter. Everybody will be watching anxiously as the new buildings go up. We are all very
10 excited and are looking forward to the Olympic Games because they have never been held before in this country.

New words and expressions　生词和短语

Olympic (title) /əˈlɪmpɪk/ *adj.* 奥林匹克的
hold (l.1) /həʊld/ (held /held/, held) *v.* 召开
government (l.2) /ˈɡʌvənmənt/ *n.* 政府
immense (l.3) /ɪˈmens/ *adj.* 巨大的
stadium (l.3) /ˈsteɪdiəm/ *n.* 露天体育场

standard (l.4) /ˈstændəd/ *n.* 标准
capital (l.6) /ˈkæpɪtl/ *n.* 首都
fantastic (l.8) /fænˈtæstɪk/ *adj.* 巨大的
design (l.9) /dɪˈzaɪn/ *v.* 设计

Notes on the text　课文注释

1　the Olympic Games, 奥林匹克运动会。

2　in four years' time, 4 年之后。

3　As a great many people ...，as 是连词，当"因为"讲，引出原因状语从句。

4　Olympic-standard swimming pool, 奥运会标准游泳池。

5　Workers will have completed the new roads by the end of this year. 今年年底前工人们将把新路铺好。句中用了将来完成时，这个时态用来表示到将来某一时刻已经完成的动作。

6　as the new buildings go up, as 是连词，当"当"、"正值"讲，引出时间状语从句。

7　look forward to ...，盼望、期待……。to 是介词，后可接名词、代词或动名词。

参考译文

　　4 年以后，奥林匹克运动会将在我们国家举行。由于将有大批的人到我们国家来，所以政府准备建造一些新的饭店、一个大型体育场和一个新的奥运会标准游泳池。他们还将修筑一些新的道路和一条铁路专线。奥运会就在首都市郊举办，整个地区将被称作"奥林匹克城"。工人们将在今年年底前把新路铺好；到明年年底，他们将把新体育场建成。这些巨大的现代化建筑是由库尔特·冈特设计的。大家都将急切地注视着新建筑的建成。我们都非常激动，盼望着奥运会的到来，因为在这个国家里还从未举办过奥运会。

Summary writing 摘要写作

Answer these questions *in not more than 70 words*.

回答下列问题, 将答案组成一个段落, 不要超过 70 个单词。

1 When will the Olympic Games be held in our country? Where will the government be putting up new buildings? (*so*)

2 Who has designed the buildings? When will workers have completed the new stadium? (*and*)

3 Will the Games be held in this country for the first time or not? Are we looking forward to them or not? (*and*)

Composition 作文

Rewrite the following sentences using the joining words in parentheses:

用括号中的连词来改写以下句子:

1 My brother is going to the Olympic Games. I am going to the Olympic Games. (*Both ... and*)

2 We bought tickets a long time ago. We shall be leaving soon. (*and*)

3 We shall see the Games. We shall visit many parts of the country. (*not only ... but ... as well*)

Letter writing 书信写作

We must write the date in full under the address. We can write the date in two ways: e.g. 17th April, 19__, April 17th, 19__. Numbers are written as follows: 1st (the first); 2nd (the second); 3rd (the third); 4th (the fourth), etc.

在信的地址下面必须写上完整的日期。日期有两种写法, 如 17th April, 19__, April 17th, 19__。数字写法如下: 1st (1 日); 2nd (2 日); 3rd (3 日); 4th (4 日) 等。

Exercise 练习

Write these dates as they would appear in a letter:

按书信的方式写出以下日期:

May 6; June 21; July 30; March 3; April 22; July 1.

Key structures 关键句型

Workers will have completed the new roads by the end of this year. 将来完成时

a Do you remember these sentences? (**KS13**)

你还记得下列句子吗? (参见第 13 课关键句型)

Now

I am writing letters now.

I'll see you tomorrow.

Tomorrow

I shall be writing letters all day tomorrow.

I'll be seeing you tomorrow.

b Compare these two questions and answers:

对比以下两个问题和回答:

When will they finish this bridge? 他们将于何时建成这座桥?

They will finish it next year. 他们将于明年建成它。

When will they have finished this bridge? 到什么时候他们将完成这座桥?

They will have finished this bridge in a year's time. 他们将于一年后完成这座桥。

Study these examples:

仔细阅读以下句子：

I shall have completed this novel by next June. 明年 6 月份之前我将完成这本小说。

He will have moved to a new flat in two months' time. 两个月以后他将搬进一套新的公寓。

You will have learnt the results of the examination by then. 到那个时候，你就会知道考试结果了。

I shall have received a reply by this time tomorrow. 明天的这个时候，我将会得到一个答复。

Exercises 练习

A Underline the verbs in the passage which tell us *what will happen, what will be happening,* and *what will have happened.*

画出课文中一般将来时、将来进行时和将来完成时的例子。

B Give the correct form of the verbs in parentheses. Do not refer to the passage until you finish the exercise:

用括号中动词的正确形式填空，完成练习后再对照课文，核对你的答案：

The Olympic Games _____ (hold) in our country in four years' time. As a great many people _____ (visit) the country, the government _____ (build) new hotels, an immense stadium, and a new Olympic-standard swimming pool. They also _____ (build) new roads and a special railway line. The Games _____ (hold) just outside the capital and the whole area _____ (call) 'Olympic City'. Workers _____ (complete) the new roads by the end of this year. By the end of next year, they _____ (finish) work on the new stadium. The fantastic modern buildings have been designed by Kurt Gunter. Everybody _____ (watch) anxiously as the new buildings go up.

Special difficulties 难点

Study these sentences:

细读以下的例句：

a *Hold.* The Olympic Games will be *held* in our country. (l.1)

This verb may be used in the sense of 'conduct', 'observe' or 'celebrate'.

这个动词可以用来表示"进行"、"纪念"或"庆祝"的意思。

A festival is *held* at Edinburgh every year. 节日庆典每年在爱丁堡举行一次。

We are going to *hold* a meeting tomorrow to discuss the subject. 明天我们准备开一次会来讨论这个议题。

The next conference will be *held* in Geneva. 下次会议将在日内瓦举行。

b *Look.*

The verb *look* has a different meaning in each sentence:

动词 look 在每句话中有不同的含义：

Look forward to (expect with pleasure) 盼望（高兴地期待）：I am *looking forward* to the summer holidays. 我正盼望暑假的到来。

Look out (be careful) 当心（注意）：*Look out!* A bus is coming. 当心点! 公共汽车来了。

Look up (get information from a reference book) 查阅（从参考书中获取资料）：I don't understand this word. I shall *look* it *up* in a dictionary. 我不懂这个词的词义，我要查一下字典。

(visit) 拜访：Don't forget to *look* me *up* when you return. 回来时别忘了来看我。

Exercise 练习

Supply the correct form of *hold* or *look* in these sentences:

用 hold 或 look 的正确形式填空：

1 We shall be _____ a party tomorrow. I am _____ it very much.

2 _____! You nearly knocked that jug over!

3 They say he is very famous. I shall _____ him _____ in 'Who's Who'.

4 The students' union _____ all interesting debate on capital punishment yesterday.

5 My friend Ingrid lives in Stockholm. Why don't you _____ her _____ when you're there?

6 Examinations will be _____ next week. I'm not _____ them.

Multiple choice questions 选择题

Comprehension 理解

1 Because of the Olympic Games _____ .

(a) there has been a lot of new building

(b) a lot of new building was completed

(c) a lot of new building has been planned

(d) there was a lot of new building

2 The Olympic Games _____ .

(a) have just been held in this country

(b) have never been held before in this country

(c) are held in this country every four years

(d) were held in this country four years ago

Structure 句型

3 Workers will have completed the new roads by the end of this year. They _____ .

(a) have already finished

(b) haven't finished yet

(c) finished a long time ago

(d) are finishing now

4 By the end of next year they will have finished the new stadium. This means they will finish it _____ the end of next year.

(a) at   (b) before   (c) after   (d) long before

5 The buildings have been designed by Kurt Gunter. So the designs _____ .

(a) are not complete yet

(b) are now complete

(c) will be completed soon

(d) haven't been completed yet

6 We are all very excited. _____ are very excited.

(a) All we   (b) Us all   (c) All us   (d) All of us

7 We are looking forward to the Olympic Games, _____ they have never been held before in this country.

(a) for   (b) why   (c) because of   (d) due to

Vocabulary 词汇

8 How often do we _____ the Olympic Games?

(a) make   (b) do   (c) have   (d) play

9 It will be an immense stadium. It will be _____ .

(a) tall   (b) wide   (c) high   (d) huge

10 A motorway is a _____ .

(a) street   (b) road   (c) avenue   (d) high street

11 Kurt Gunter designed the buildings. He is probably _____ .

(a) an engineer   (b) an architect   (c) a builder   (d) a mechanic

12 We are looking forward to the Games. So we will be _____ when they begin.

(a) pleased   (b) unhappy   (c) sorry   (d) impatient

Lesson 38　Everything except the weather　唯独没有考虑到天气

First listen and then answer the question.

听录音，然后回答以下问题。

Why did Harrison sell his house so quickly?

My old friend, Harrison, had lived in the Mediterranean for many years before he returned to England. He had often dreamed of retiring in England and had planned to settle down in the country. He had no sooner returned than he bought a house and went to live there. Almost
5　immediately he began to complain about the weather, for even though it was still summer, it rained continually and it was often bitterly cold. After so many years of sunshine, Harrison got a shock. He acted as if he had never lived in England before. In the end, it was more than he could bear. He had hardly had time to settle down when he sold the house and left the country.
10　The dream he had had for so many years ended there. Harrison had thought of everything except the weather.

He dreamed of retiring in England

New words and expressions　生词和短语

except (title) /ɪkˈsept/ *prep.* 除了
Mediterranean (l.1) /ˌmedɪtəˈreɪnɪən/ *n.* (the ~)
　地中海
complain (l.5) /kəmˈpleɪn/ *v.* 抱怨

continually (l.6) /kənˈtɪnjuəli/ *adv.* 不断地
bitterly (l.6) /ˈbɪtəli/ *adv.* 刺骨地
sunshine (l.7) /ˈsʌnʃaɪn/ *n.* 阳光

Notes on the text　课文注释

1　dreamed of, 梦想、幻想、向往。
2　settle down in the country, 在乡下定居。
3　He had no sooner returned than he bought a house and went to live there. 他刚回到英国就买了一幢房子住了进去。no sooner ... than ... 表示"一……就……"。这个句型用来引导时间状语从句。主句里常用过去完成时, than 后面的从句用一般过去时。
4　even though, 即使, 这一结构引出让步状语从句。
5　He acted as if he had never lived in England before. 他的举动就好像他从未在英国生活过一样。as if 常用来引导表示方式的状语从句。
6　more than he could bear, 超过他所能忍受的程度。
7　He had hardly had time to settle down when he sold the house and left the country. 他还没有来得及安顿下来就卖掉了房子, 离开了这个国家。

参考译文

　我的老朋友哈里森在回到英国以前曾多年居住在地中海地区。过去他常幻想退休后到英国，并计划在乡间安顿下来。他刚一回到英国便买下了一幢房子住了进去。但紧接着他就开始抱怨那里的天气了。因为即使那时仍为夏季，但雨总是下个不停，而且常常冷得厉害。在阳光下生活了那么多年的哈里森对此感到惊奇。他的举动就好像他从未在英国生活过一样。最后，他再也忍受不住，还没等安顿下来就卖掉了房子，离开了这个国家。他多年来的幻想从此破灭。哈里森把每件事情都考虑到了，唯独没想到天气。

Summary writing 摘要写作

Answer these questions *in not more than 60 words*.

回答下列问题，将答案组成一个段落，不要超过 60 个单词。

1　Where had the writer's friend, Harrison, spent many years? What did he want to do? What did he buy? (*but ... so ...*)

2　Was the summer that year very good, or was it very bad? What did he complain about? (*and*)

3　Did Harrison sell the house in the end or not? Did he leave the country or not? (*Harrison not only ... but also*)

Composition 作文

Rewrite the following sentences using the joining words in parentheses:

用括号中的连词改写以下句子:

1　He bought an old car. It was in a very bad state. (*but*)

2　The engine was worn out. The gearbox was full of sawdust. (*The engine ... not only ... but ... as well*)

3　He could not drive it. He could not sell it. He could not even give it away. (*neither ... nor ... nor*)

Letter writing 书信写作

The Date: The following months of the year are usually written in full: March, April, May, June and July. The remaining months are often written as follows: 'Jan.', 'Feb.', 'Aug.', 'Sept.', 'Oct.', 'Nov.', and 'Dec.'.

日期: 每年下列月份写出全称: 3 月, 4 月, 5 月, 6 月和 7 月。剩余的月份写成: Jan.（1 月）; Feb.（2 月）; Aug.（8 月）; Sept.（9 月）; Oct.（10 月）; Nov.（11 月）和 Dec.（12 月）。

Exercise 练习

Write today's date in the way it should appear on a letter.

按书信的要求写出今天的日期。

Key structures 关键句型

He acted as if he had never lived in England before. 过去完成时

a　Do you remember these sentences? (**KS14**)

你还记得这些句子吗?（参见第 14 课关键句型）

The children ran away *after they had broken* the window.

As soon as the sun had set we returned to our hotel.

When he had finished lunch he asked for a glass of water.

I did not understand the problem *until he had explained it*.

b　Now study these sentences. They tell us *what happened some time ago* and *what had happened some time before*.

仔细阅读以下句子, 它们告诉我们过去某一时间发生的事情和过去某一时刻之前发生的事情。

He *lived* in Scotland fifteen years ago. 15 年前他住在苏格兰。

He *had lived* in Scotland for fifteen years *before* he came to England. 在他来到英格兰之前, 他曾在苏格兰住了 15 年。

The police *found* Billy Wilkins *last night*. He *had run away* from home five days *before*. 昨天夜里警察找到了比利·威尔金斯。在 5 天之前他离家出走。

He *had spent* the last two nights near a farmhouse. The police *took* him home at once. 在过去的两个晚上, 他待在

Unit 2   Lesson 38

一农场附近。警察立即把他带回了家。

When she *saw* him, his mother *burst* into tears. She *said* he *had never run away before*. 当他的母亲见到他时，不禁失声痛哭起来。她说他以前从未出走过。

Exercises 练习

A Underline the verbs in the passage which tell us *what happened some time ago* and *what had happened some time before*.
画出课文中一般过去时和过去完成时的例子。

B Give the correct form of the verbs in parentheses. Do not refer to the passage until you finish your exercise.
用括号中动词的正确形式填空，完成练习后再对照课文，核对你的答案。

My old friend, Harrison, _____ (live) in the Mediterranean for many years before he _____ (return) to England. He often _____ (dream) of retiring in England and _____ (plan) to settle down in the country. He no sooner _____ (return) than he _____ (buy) a house and _____ (go) to live there. Almost immediately he _____ (begin) to complain about the weather, for even though it _____ (be) still summer, it _____ (rain) continually and it _____ (be) often bitterly cold. After so many years of sunshine, Harrison _____ (get) a shock. He _____ (act) as if he never _____ (live) in England before. In the end, it _____ (be) more than he could bear. He hardly _____ (have) time to settle down when he _____ (sell) the house and _____ (leave) the country. The dream he _____ (have) for so many years _____ (end) there. Harrison _____ (think) of everything except the weather.

Special difficulties 难点

Words often confused and misused 经常容易混淆和误用的词

Study these sentences:
细读以下的例句：

a *No sooner... than*（一……就）；*hardly ... when*（几乎未来得及……就……）.

He had *no sooner* returned *than* he bought a house. (ll.3-4)

He had *hardly* had time to settle down *when* he sold the house. (l.9)

b *Country*（国家，乡间）and *Countryside*（农村）.

He had planned to settle down in the *country*. (l.3)

He sold the house and left the *country*. (l.9)

The *countryside* around Vienna is very beautiful. 维也纳周围的乡村非常漂亮。

c *Continuously*（连续不断地）and *Continually*（频繁地）.

It rained *continually*. (l.6) (i.e. At frequent intervals.) 天频繁地下雨。

The river flows under this bridge *continuously*. (i.e. It does not stop at all.) 河水不停地从桥下流过。

Exercises 练习

A Join these sentences using *no sooner... than*:
用 no sooner ... than 连接下列句子：

1 I had left the house. It began to rain.

2 We had hung the picture on the wall. It fell down.

B Choose the correct words in the following sentences:

选用适当的词填空：

1 The sea moves (continuously) (continually).

2 He borrows money from people (continuously) (continually).

3 The Robertsons do not live here anymore. They now live in the (countryside) (country).

Multiple choice questions 选择题

Comprehension 理解

1 What was Harrison looking forward to doing?

(a) Complaining about the weather.

(b) Spending his old age in England.

(c) Buying a house somewhere.

(d) Living in the Mediterranean.

2 Harrison probably couldn't stand the English climate because _____ .

(a) it never stopped raining

(b) it was always cold

(c) he had spent so long in the Mediterranean, he had forgotten what it was like

(d) he had never lived in England before

Structure 句型

3 Harrison had made plans _____ he returned to England.

(a) before   (b) when   (c) as soon as   (d) after

4 He acted _____ he had never lived in England before.

(a) as though   (b) like   (c) as   (d) even if

5 It was more than he could bear. He couldn't bear it _____ .

(a) more   (b) longer   (c) any longer   (d) no more

6 He had hardly had time to settle down _____ he sold the house and left the country.

(a) than   (b) when   (c) as soon as   (d) after

7 When did he _____? He left immediately.

(a) live   (b) left   (c) leaves   (d) leave

Vocabulary 词汇

8 Harrison retired in England. So _____ a job.

(a) he was going to get (b) he had   (c) he would have   (d) he didn't have

9 He wanted to settle down in the country. He wanted to _____ .

(a) rest there   (b) live there permanently (c) live there for a while (d) go there for a visit

10 It rained continually. It _____ .

(a) stopped occasionally

(b) never stopped

(c) hardly rained at all

(d) never rained

11 He _____ as if he had never lived in England before.

(a) made   (b) did   (c) conducted   (d) behaved

12 It was more than he could bear. He couldn't _____ it.

(a) suffer   (b) put up   (c) carry   (d) stand

Lesson 39 Am I all right? 我是否痊愈?

First listen and then answer the question.

听录音，然后回答以下问题。

Why did Mr. Gilbert telephone Dr. Millington?

While John Gilbert was in hospital, he asked his doctor to tell him
whether his operation had been successful, but the doctor refused to
do so. The following day, the patient asked for a bedside telephone.
When he was alone, he telephoned the hospital exchange and asked
5 for Doctor Millington. When the doctor answered the phone, Mr.
Gilbert said he was inquiring about a certain patient, a Mr. John
Gilbert. He asked if Mr. Gilbert's operation had been successful
and the doctor told him that it had been. He then asked when Mr.
Gilbert would be allowed to go home and the doctor told him that he would have to stay in hospital for another
10 two weeks. Then Dr. Millington asked the caller if he was a relative of the patient. 'No,' the patient answered,
'I am Mr. John Gilbert.'

asked for a bedside telephone

New words and expressions 生词和短语

operation (l.2) /ˌɒpəˈreɪʃən/ n. 手术
successful (l.2) /səkˈsesfəl/ adj. 成功的
following (l.3) /ˈfɒləʊɪŋ/ adj. 下一个
patient (l.3) /ˈpeɪʃnt/ n. 病人
alone (l.4) /əˈləʊn/ adj. 独自的

exchange (l.4) /ɪksˈtʃeɪndʒ/ n. （电话的）交换台
inquire (l.6) /ɪnˈkwaɪə/ v. 询问，打听
certain (l.6) /ˈsɜːtn/ adj. 某个
caller (l.10) /ˈkɔːlə/ n. 打电话的人
relative (l.10) /ˈrelətɪv/ n. 亲戚

Notes on the text 课文注释

1 While John Gilbert was in hospital, 当约翰·吉尔伯特住院的时候。

2 ask for, 请求，索要。

3 a bedside telephone, 床头电话。

4 a Mr. John Gilbert, 一位名叫约翰·吉尔伯特的先生。

参考译文

　　当约翰·吉尔伯特住院的时候，他问医生他的手术是否成功，但医生拒绝告诉他。第二天，这位病人要了一
部床头电话。当房里只剩他一个人时，他挂通了医院的交换台，要求与米灵顿医生讲话。当这位医生接过电话
时，吉尔伯特先生说他想询问一个病人的情况，是一位名叫约翰·吉尔伯特的先生。他问吉尔伯特先生的手术
是否成功，医生告诉他手术很成功。然后他又问吉尔伯特先生什么时候可以回家，医生说他在医院还必须再住
上两个星期。之后，米灵顿医生问打电话的人是否是病人的亲属。"不是，"病人回答说，"我就是约翰·吉尔
伯特先生。"

Summary writing 摘要写作

Answer these questions *in not more than 60 words*.
回答下列问题，将答案组成一个段落，不要超过 60 个单词。

1 What did Dr. Millington refuse to tell his patient, John Gilbert?

2 Whom did the patient telephone next day? Whom did he inquire about? (*and*)

3 Did the doctor answer a number of questions about the patient or not? Did he ask whether the caller was a relative or not? (*and … then*)

4 Did the caller then tell him who he was or not?

Composition 作文

Rewrite the following sentences using the joining words in parentheses:
用括号内的连词改写下列句子：

1 After the telephone call, Dr. Millington was angry. He went to Gilbert's room. (*so*)

2 Gilbert was telephoning the nurses. He was asking questions about himself. (*and*)

3 Then the doctor burst out laughing. The patient burst out laughing. (*both … and*)

Letter writing 书信写作

Write the following dates in the way they might appear on a letter:
按书信要求写出以下日期：

3 January; February 28; 20 August; 13 September; October 22.

Key structures 关键句型

He said that … He told me … He asked … 直接引语和间接引语 **(KS15)** (参见第 15 课关键句型)

'I am very tired,' he said. "我非常疲劳" 他说。

What did he say? 他说了什么？

He *said that* he was very tired. 他说他非常累。

He told *me that* he was very tired. 他告诉我他非常累。

'Are you tired?' she asked. "你累吗？" 她问道。

What did she ask? 她问了什么？

She *asked if* (or *whether*) you were tired. 她问你是否感到疲劳。

'Will Jack arrive tomorrow?' Tom asked. "杰克明天能到吗？" 汤姆问道。

What did Tom ask? 汤姆问了什么？

Tom *asked if* (or *whether*) Jack would arrive the next day. 汤姆问杰克第二天是否能到。

'When will Jack arrive?' Tom asked. "杰克什么时候到？" 汤姆问道。

What did Tom ask? 汤姆问了什么？

Tom *asked when* Jack would arrive. 汤姆问杰克什么时候到。

'Have you ever been abroad?' Catherine asked. "你出过国吗？" 凯瑟琳问道。

What did Catherine ask? 凯瑟琳问了什么？

Catherine *asked if* (or *whether*) you had ever been abroad. 凯瑟琳问你是否出过国。

'Why didn't you write to me?' Jane asked. "你为什么不给我写信？" 简问道。

What did Jane ask? 简问了什么？

Jane *asked why* I hadn't written to her. 简问为什么我不给她写信。

Unit 2   Lesson 39

Exercise 练习

Here is part of the conversation between Mr. Gilbert and Dr. Millington:

下面是吉尔伯特先生与米灵顿医生之间谈话的片断:

1 'I am inquiring about a certain patient,' Mr. Gilbert said.

2 'Was Mr. Gilbert's operation successful?' he asked.

3 'Yes, it was,' the doctor told him.

4 'When will Mr. Gilbert be allowed to go home?' he asked.

5 'He will have to stay in hospital for another two weeks,' the doctor told him. 'Are you a relative of the patient?' Dr. Millington asked the caller.

6 'No,' the patient answered, 'I am Mr. John Gilbert.'

Now answer these questions. Do not refer to the passage until you finish the exercise.

回答以下问题, 完成练习后再对照课文核对你的答案。

1 What did Mr. Gilbert say?

2 What did he ask?

3 What did the doctor tell him?

4 What did he (Mr. Gilbert) ask?

5 What did the doctor tell him? What did Dr. Millington ask the caller?

6 What did the patient answer?

Special difficulties 难点

Speech marks 引号 (SD26) (参见第 26 课难点)

Exercise 练习

Write this piece of conversation again using speech marks. Refer to the dialogue in the exercise above when you have finished:

为下面的对话加上引号, 完成练习后对照关键句型的练习部分:

I am inquiring about a certain patient, Mr. Gilbert said. Was Mr. Gilbert's operation successful? he asked. Yes, it was, the doctor told him. When will Mr. Gilbert be allowed to go home? he asked. He will have to stay in hospital for another two weeks, the doctor told him. Are you a relative of the patient? Dr. Millington asked the caller. No, the patient answered, I am Mr. John Gilbert.

Multiple choice questions 选择题

Comprehension 理解

1 John Gilbert wanted a bedside telephone _____ .

   (a) to telephone the nurses   (b) to ring the hospital exchange

   (c) to make outside calls   (d) to find out about his operation

2 Dr. Millington answered the questions on the phone because he probably thought the caller _____ .

   (a) was a relative of John Gilbert   (b) was the patient

   (c) was the patient's father   (d) was another doctor

Structure 句型

3 John Gilbert was in hospital. He was taken _____ hospital last week.

(*a*) at   (*b*) in   (*c*) to   (*d*) on

4 The doctor refused to _____ about his operation.

(*a*) say him   (*b*) tell to him   (*c*) speak him   (*d*) speak to him

5 _____? A bedside telephone.

(*a*) For what did he ask   (*b*) What did he ask

(*c*) For what did he ask for   (*d*) What did he ask for

6 When will he be allowed to go home? When will they _____?

(*a*) let him go   (*b*) let him to go   (*c*) leave him to go   (*d*) leave him

7 He will have to stay in hospital. That's what he _____ .

(*a*) has done   (*b*) must do   (*c*) must be doing   (*d*) must have done

Vocabulary 词汇

8 A _____ usually performs operations.

(*a*) surgeon   (*b*) doctor   (*c*) nurse   (*d*) matron

9 The following day he asked for a telephone. He did this the _____ day.

(*a*) other   (*b*) followed   (*c*) next   (*d*) after

10 John Gilbert was a patient. He was _____ .

(*a*) a sick   (*b*) an ill   (*c*) a sick man   (*d*) not in a hurry

11 He was alone. He was _____ .

(*a*) on his own   (*b*) lonely   (*c*) with himself   (*d*) unique

12 He inquired about a patient. He wanted _____ .

(*a*) informations   (*b*) information   (*c*) knowledges   (*d*) knowledge

Sentence structure 句子结构

Join the following sentences. Make any changes you like, but do not alter the sense. Then check your answer against the text.

连接以下句子，可以作适当的调整，但不要改变原句的意思，然后对照课文第 1-3 行，核对你的答案。

John Gilbert was in hospital. Had his operation been successful? He asked his doctor. The doctor refused to tell him.

While _____ .

Lesson 40 Food and talk 进餐与交谈

First listen and then answer the question.

听录音，然后回答以下问题。

Was Mrs. Rumbold a good companion at dinner?

a large, unsmiling lady

Last week at a dinner party, the hostess asked me to sit next to Mrs.
Rumbold. Mrs. Rumbold was a large, unsmiling lady in a tight black
dress. She did not even look up when I took my seat beside her.
Her eyes were fixed on her plate and in a short time, she was busy
5 eating. I tried to make conversation.

   'A new play is coming to "The Globe" soon,' I said. 'Will you
be seeing it?'

   'No,' she answered.

   'Will you be spending your holidays abroad this year?' I asked.
10   'No,' she answered.

   'Will you be staying in England?' I asked.

   'No,' she answered.

   In despair, I asked her whether she was enjoying her dinner.

   'Young man,' she answered, 'if you ate more and talked less, we would both enjoy our dinner!'

New words and expressions 生词和短语

hostess (l.1) /ˈhəʊstɪs/ *n.* 女主人
unsmiling (l.2) /ʌnˈsmaɪlɪŋ/ *adj.* 不笑的，严肃的
tight (l.2) /taɪt/ *adj.* 紧身的

fix (l.4) /fɪks/ *v.* 凝视
globe (l.6) /gləʊb/ *n.* 地球
despair (l.13) /dɪˈspeə/ *n.* 绝望

Notes on the text 课文注释

1 next to, 挨着。

2 She did not even look up when I took my seat beside her. 当我在她身旁坐下来的时候，她甚至连头都没有抬一下。

3 she was busy eating, 她忙着吃饭。be busy doing sth. 是"忙于做某事"的意思。

4 The Globe, 环球剧场，伦敦著名的剧场之一。

5 Will you be seeing it? 用将来进行时来提问，尤其是提出问题但又不想迫使对方作出明确答复时，将来进行时可以显得比一般将来时 will 更委婉客气。

参考译文

  在上星期的一次宴会上，女主人安排我坐在兰伯尔德夫人的身旁。兰伯尔德夫人是一位身材高大、表情严肃的女人，穿一件紧身的黑衣服。当我在她身旁坐下来的时候，她甚至连头都没有抬一下。她的眼睛盯着自己的盘子，不一会儿就忙着吃起来了。我试图找个话题和她聊聊。

  "一出新剧要来'环球剧场'上演了，"我说，"您去看吗?"

  "不，"她回答。

"您今年去国外度假吗?"我又问。

"不,"她回答。

"您就待在英国吗?"我问。

"不,"她回答。

失望之中我问她饭是否吃得满意。

"年轻人,"她回答说,"如果你多吃点,少说点,我们两个都会吃得好的!"

Summary writing 摘要写作

Answer these questions *in not more than 70 words*.

回答下列问题,将答案组成一个段落,不要超过 70 个单词。

1 Where did the writer sit at the dinner party?

2 Did he try to make conversation or not? Was she busy eating or not? (*but*)

3 Did he talk about the new play at 'The Globe' or not? Did he talk about the holidays or not? (*and*)

4 Did she answer his questions briefly or not?

5 Did he ask her if she was enjoying her dinner or not? What did she answer? (*Then ... and*)

Composition 作文

Rewrite the following sentences using the joining words in parentheses:

用括号中的连词改写以下句子:

1 She refused to answer any questions. She did not ask any questions. (*not only ... but ... either*)

2 She was not interested in the theatre. She was not interested in travel. (*neither ... nor*)

3 She liked eating good food. She did not like talking about it. (*but*)

Letter writing 书信写作

Rewrite the following dates in the way they would appear on a letter:

按照书信形式改写以下日期:

2/3/95;   21/9/54;   13/8/76;   1/12/67;   22/1/86;   11/11/90.

Key structures 关键句型

If you ate more and talked less, we would both enjoy our dinner!

a   Do you remember these sentences? **(KS16)**

你还记得这些句子吗?(参见第 16 课关键句型)

在以下条件句中,主句中用将来时或祈使句,而从句中则用现在时。

If he is out, I'll call tomorrow.

You'll miss the train *if you don't hurry*.

If he is working I'll not disturb him.

If I have time, I'll be writing to him tomorrow.

Please don't disturb him *if he is busy*.

b   Now study these sentences carefully:

细读以下句子:

在这一类条件句中,if 从句谈论想象的情况,主句则推测想象的结果。在从句中要用动词的过去时,这并不表明过去的某一特定时间或过去某一动作,因此常被称作"非真实的过去",整个条件句也被称作非真实条件句。如果 if 从句中的动词是 be,那么应该在第一和第三人称单数名词之后用 were。

If you went to the exhibition you would enjoy it. 假如你去看展览,你会喜欢的。

If you saw him now you wouldn't recognize him. 假如你现在见到他，你会认不出来的。

Would he get annoyed *if I told* him about it? 假如我把此事告诉他，他会烦恼吗？

If I were in your position, I would act differently. 假如我处于你的位置，我会采取不同的做法。

He would help you *if he were* here. 假如他在这儿，他会帮你的。

If you could make him change his mind, you would save him a lot of trouble. 假如你能使他改变主意，你会使他免了许多麻烦。

Exercise 练习

Give the correct form of the verbs in parentheses:
用括号中动词的正确形式填空：

1 He would enjoy this if he _____ (be) present.

2 She can do better if she _____ (try).

3 If you play with matches, you _____ (burn) your fingers.

4 If you broke this window, you _____ (have to) pay for it.

5 If you _____ (lose) your way, you would have to ask a policeman.

6 If you _____ (not apologize), he will never speak to you again.

7 If he _____ (be) clever, he would not have any difficulty.

8 What would you do if you _____ (win) a lot of money?

9 If I were you, I _____ (not be) so confident.

10 If you _____ (can) help me, I would be grateful.

Special difficulties 难点

Make and Do

Study these phrases:
细读以下短语：

a *Make*.

I tried to *make conversation*. (l.5)

When she had *made the beds* she went downstairs. 她整理好床铺之后就下楼去了。

You mustn't *make so much noise*. 你们不应该这样喧闹。

I *made a promise* never to see him again. 我发誓永不见他。

He's the sort of person who always *makes trouble*. 他是那种总爱闹事的人。

He is learning English but he hasn't *made much progress*. 他正在学英语，但进步不大。

He *made a lot of money* in South America. 他在南美洲发了大财。

I was asked to *make a speech*. 我应邀发表一次演说。

I'll never *make the same mistake* again. 我再也不会犯同类错误了。

I found it difficult to *make up my mind*. 我发现很难下决心。

b *Do*.

He always *does his best*. 他总是尽力而为。

When did you *do your homework*? 你什么时候做作业？

Do me a favour please. 请帮帮忙。

I *did a few jobs* about the house. 我干了点家务活。

I can't *do any more work* today. 我今天干不了更多的工作了。

I want you to *do Exercise 24* on page 16. 我要你做第 16 页上的练习 24。

I *did a lot of shopping* yesterday. 我昨天买了许多东西。

That shop *does very good business*. 那家商店的生意很好。

Exercise 练习

Supply the correct form of *make* or *do* in the following:

用 make 或 do 的正确形式填空：

1 He _____ a mistake and I told him to _____ the exercise again.

2 He _____ business in Australia and _____ a lot of money.

3 I know you are _____ your best but you are not _____ very much progress.

4 After I had _____ the beds, I went out and _____ some shopping.

Multiple choice questions 选择题

Comprehension 理解

1 The writer asked questions because _____ .

  (*a*) he wanted to find out about Mrs. Rumbold

  (*b*) he wanted to know if Mrs. Rumbold was going abroad

  (*c*) he wanted to be sociable

  (*d*) he always talks too much

2 Which word best describes Mrs. Rumbold? She was _____ .

  (*a*) hungry　　　　(*b*) polite　　　　(*c*) rude　　　　(*d*) talkative

Structure 句型

3 The writer sat next to Mrs. Rumbold _____ the dinner party.

  (*a*) on　　　　(*b*) during　　　　(*c*) in　　　　(*d*) along

4 She asked me to sit next to Mrs. Rumbold. '_____ next to her,' she said.

  (*a*) Please to sit　　(*b*) To sit　　(*c*) Please sit　　(*d*) Please sitting

5 I took my seat beside her. I _____ beside her.

  (*a*) sat　　　　(*b*) seated　　　　(*c*) was sitted　　　　(*d*) was seating

6 A new play is coming to 'The Globe' soon. It _____ .

  (*a*) hasn't come yet　(*b*) is here　(*c*) has already come　(*d*) came

7 I asked her _____ she was enjoying her dinner.

  (*a*) weather　　(*b*) in case　　(*c*) if　　(*d*) unless

Vocabulary 词汇

8 The opposite of 'tight' is _____ .

  (*a*) lose　　(*b*) loose　　(*c*) loses　　(*d*) loosen

9 Her eyes were fixed on the plate. She _____ it.

  (*a*) was glancing at　(*b*) was staring at　(*c*) was thinking about　(*d*) was stuck to

10 'The Globe' must be a _____ .

  (*a*) circus　　(*b*) theatre　　(*c*) play　　(*d*) nightclub

11 Mrs. Rumbold won't go abroad. She rarely goes _____ .

  (*a*) outside　　(*b*) overseas　　(*c*) over　　(*d*) foreign

12 Are you enjoying your dinner? Is it _____?

  (*a*) enjoying you　(*b*) amusing you　(*c*) entertaining you　(*d*) giving you pleasure

Lesson 41 Do you call that a hat? 你把那个叫帽子吗?

a hat like a lighthouse

First listen and then answer the question.

听录音,然后回答以下问题。

What kind of shopping does the writer enjoy, do you think?

'Do you call that a hat?' I said to my wife.

'You needn't be so rude about it,' my wife answered as she looked at herself in the mirror.

I sat down on one of those modern chairs with holes in it and
5 waited. We had been in the hat shop for half an hour and my wife was still in front of the mirror.

'We mustn't buy things we don't need,' I remarked suddenly. I regretted saying it almost at once.

'You needn't have said that,' my wife answered. 'I needn't remind you of that terrible tie you bought
10 yesterday.'

'I find it beautiful,' I said. 'A man can never have too many ties.'

'And a woman can't have too many hats,' she answered.

Ten minutes later we walked out of the shop together. My wife was wearing a hat that looked like a lighthouse!

New words and expressions 生词和短语

rude (l.2) /ruːd/ *adj.* 无礼的
mirror (l.3) /'mɪrə/ *n.* 镜子
hole (l.4) /həʊl/ *n.* 孔

remark (l.7) /rɪ'mɑːk/ *v.* 评说
remind (l.9) /rɪ'maɪnd/ *v.* 提醒
lighthouse (l.14) /'laɪthaʊs/ *n.* 灯塔

Notes on the text 课文注释

1 ... needn't be so rude ..., 英语中实际上有两个 need。一个是普通动词 need; 另一个是情态动词 need。情态动词的 need 和 can, may 等情态动词一样, 后接动词原形, 但只用于否定和疑问句; 肯定句用 must, have to, ought to 或 should。

2 I regretted saying ..., regret 后接动名词表示对做过的事感到遗憾。

3 We mustn't buy things we don't need. 我们不应该买我们不需要的东西。句中的 need 是普通动词, 当"需要"讲。

4 You needn't have said that ...
needn't have done 表示本来用不着做某事, 而实际上已经做了。

5 I needn't remind you of that terrible tie you bought yesterday. 我也不必提醒你昨天买的那条糟糕透了的领带。remind sb. of sth. 是"提醒某人想起某事"的意思。

6 I find it beautiful, 我觉得它好看。句中的 beautiful 用来补充说明宾语 it, 在语法上称作宾语补足语。

7 A man can never have too many ties. 男人有多少领带也不会嫌多。

参考译文

"你把那个叫帽子吗？"我对妻子说。

"你说话没必要这样不客气，"我的妻子边回答边照着镜子。

我坐在一个新式的满是网眼儿的椅子上，等待着。我们在这家帽店已经待了半个小时了，而我的妻子仍在镜子面前。

"我们不应该买我们不需要的东西，"我突然发表意见说，但马上又后悔说了这话。

"你没必要这么说，"我妻子回答说，"我也不必提醒你昨天买的那条糟糕透了的领带。"

"我觉得它好看，"我说，"男人有多少领带也不会嫌多。"

"女人有多少帽子也不嫌多。"她回答。

10 分钟以后，我们一道走出了商店。我妻子戴着一顶像灯塔一样的帽子！

Summary writing 摘要写作

Answer these questions *in not more than 70 words*.

回答下列问题，将答案组成一个段落，不要超过 70 个单词。

1　Was the writer's wife trying on a hat or not? Did he like it or not? (*but*)

2　Did he sit down or not? Did he wait for her or did he leave the shop? (*and*)

3　Did they begin arguing again or not? (*Then*)

4　What had he bought the day before? Did his wife like it or not? (*but*)

5　Did he say, 'A man can never have too many ties,' or did he say, 'A man can never have too many hats.'?

6　Did his wife use exactly the same argument or not? Did she buy the hat or not? (*and*)

7　What did it look like?

Composition 作文

Rewrite the following sentences using the joining words in parentheses:

用括号中的连词改写以下句子：

1　My wife has too many hats. She has too many dresses. (*not only ... but ... as well*)

2　We have been invited to a party this evening. She does not want to go. (*but*)

3　She keeps looking at all those dresses. She keeps saying, 'I haven't got anything to wear!' (*and*)

Letter writing 书信写作

Rewrite the following dates in the way they would appear on a letter:

按照书信格式改写以下日期：

7/5/95; 1/10/78; 31/1/67; 18/2/83; 23/6/70; 17/4/ 27.

Key structures 关键句型

Must, Have to and Need

a　Do you remember these sentences? **(KS17)**

你还记得这些句子吗？（参见第 17 课关键句型）

I *must* leave now. I *have* (got) to leave now. He *must* be a fool.

b　Now study these sentences:

仔细阅读以下句子：

I *need* a new hat. I *must* buy one. 我需要一顶新帽子。我必须买一顶。

He *needs* a haircut. He *must* have one. 他需要理发。他一定要理发。

I won't buy that. I don't *need* it. 我不会买那个，我不需要它。

c *Instead of saying*:　　　　　　　　　　　　　*We can say*:

除了这种表述方法外：　　　　　　　　　　还可以说：

You *needn't* wait for me.　　　　　　　　You *don't have to* wait for me.

You *needn't have* waited for me.　　　　You *didn't have to* wait for me.

d Now compare *mustn't* and *needn't* in these sentences:

对比以下句子中的 mustn't 和 needn't：

You *mustn't* make a noise. The children are asleep. 你不应吵闹，孩子们都睡了。

You *needn't* drive so quickly; we have plenty of time. 你不必开得那么快，我们有足够的时间。

Or: You *don't have to* (*haven't got to*) drive so quickly; we have plenty of time.

You *mustn't* smoke in a theatre. It is forbidden. 你不应该在剧场里抽烟，这是不允许的。

You *needn't* come with us if you don't want to. 如果你不想去，你不必和我们一道去。

Or: You *don't have to* (*haven't got to*) come with us if you don't want to.

Exercises 练习

A Study the use of *need, needn't* and *mustn't* in the passage.

研究一下课文中 need, needn't 和 musn't 的用法。

B Supply *need, needn't* and *mustn't* in the following. Do not refer to the passage until you finish the exercise:

用 need, needn't 和 mustn't 填空，完成练习后再对照课文，核对你的答案：

1 'You _____ be so rude about it,' my wife answered as she looked at herself in the mirror.

2 'We _____ buy things we don't _____,' I remarked suddenly.

3 'You _____ have said that,' my wife answered. 'I _____ not remind you of that terrible tie you bought yesterday.'

C Supply *mustn't* or *needn't* in these sentences:

用 mustn't 或 needn't 填空：

1 You _____ leave your car here. Can't you see the 'No Parking' sign?

2 I _____ go to bed late tonight. I have to get up early tomorrow.

3 You _____ finish your soup if you don't like it.

4 You _____ push. There's plenty of room on the bus.

5 You _____ read in bed. It's bad for your eyes.

Special difficulties 难点

Words often confused 经常容易混淆的词

Remark, *Observe*, and *Notice*.

Study these examples:

细读以下例句：

'We mustn't buy things we don't need,' I *remarked*. (l.7)

'We mustn't buy things we don't need,' I *observed*. "我们不应该买我们不需要的东西，" 我评论说。

He *observed* me carefully. (He looked at me.) 他仔细地看着我。

Did you *notice* how she was dressed? 你注意到她的穿戴了吗？

Exercise 练习

Supply the correct form of *remark* or *notice* in the following:

用 remark 或 notice 的正确形式填空：

1 'That's a nice picture,' he _____ .

2 No one _____ me when I entered the room.

3 He made a lot of rude _____ about the hat she was wearing.

4 He failed to _____ that I had changed the furniture round.

Multiple choice questions 选择题

Comprehension 理解

1 The writer probably _____ .

(a) didn't like the hat his wife had chosen (b) liked the hat his wife had chosen

(c) chose a hat for his wife (d) chose the hat that looked like a lighthouse

2 The writer was sorry he made rude remarks because _____ .

(a) his wife reminded him that he had bought a terrible tie

(b) he has a lot of ties

(c) his wife has a lot of hats

(d) his wife got annoyed with him

Structure 句型

3 Do you have to buy this hat? No, I _____ . It isn't necessary.

(a) mustn't (b) won't (c) needn't (d) don't need

4 She is still in front of the mirror. She hasn't moved _____ .

(a) still (b) even (c) also (d) yet

5 We mustn't buy things we _____ .

(a) needn't (b) need not (c) don't need (d) haven't need

6 _____ do you find it? Beautiful.

(a) What (b) How (c) How much (d) Where

7 A man can never have too many ties. It's _____ .

(a) unable (b) impossible (c) improbable (d) incapable

Vocabulary 词汇

8 She looked in the mirror and saw her _____ .

(a) reflection (b) idol (c) imagination (d) picture

9 I needn't remind you of that terrible tie. You don't want me to _____ that terrible tie.

(a) recall you (b) remember you (c) memorise you (d) make you remember

10 They walked out together _____ walked out.

(a) They both (b) They all (c) Some of them (d) Neither of them

11 His wife was wearing a hat. She _____ .

(a) was dressing it (b) was putting it on (c) had it on (d) was carrying it

12 It looked like a lighthouse. It _____ a lighthouse.

(a) appeared similar (b) resembled (c) matched (d) likened

Lesson 42　Not very musical　并非很懂音乐

First listen and then answer the question.

听录音，然后回答以下问题。

What happened when the snake charmer began to play jazz?

As we had had a long walk through one of the markets of Old Delhi, we stopped at a square to have a rest. After a time, we noticed a snake charmer with two large baskets at the other side of the square, so we went to have a look at him. As soon as he saw us, he picked
5　up a long pipe which was covered with coins and opened one of the baskets. When he began to play a tune, we had our first glimpse of the snake. It rose out of the basket and began to follow the movements of the pipe. We were very much surprised when the snake charmer suddenly began to play jazz and modern pop songs. The snake, however, continued to 'dance' slowly. It
10　obviously could not tell the difference between Indian music and jazz!

began to play jazz

New words and expressions　生词和短语

musical (title) /'mjuːzɪkəl/ *adj.* 精通音乐的
market (l.1) /'mɑːkɪt/ *n.* 市场，集市
snake charmer (l.3) /'sneɪk-ˌtʃɑːmə/ 玩蛇者
　（通常借音乐控制）
pipe (l.5) /paɪp/ *n.* （吹奏的）管乐器
tune (l.6) /tjuːn/ *n.* 曲调
glimpse (l.6) /glɪmps/ *n.* 一瞥

snake (l.7) /sneɪk/ *n.* 蛇
movement (l.7) /'muːvmənt/ *n.* 动作
continue (l.9) /kən'tɪnjuː/ *v.* 继续
dance (l.9) /dɑːns/ *v.* 跳舞
obviously (l.10) /'ɒbvɪəsli/ *adv.* 显然
difference (l.10) /'dɪfərəns/ *n.* 差别
Indian (l.10) /'ɪndiən/ *adj.* 印度的

Notes on the text　课文注释

1　Not very musical 是指蛇并不那样"懂"音乐。

2　It obviously could not tell the difference between Indian music and jazz! 显然，它分辨不出印度音乐和爵士乐！
　tell the difference between ... , 辨别……之间的不同。

参考译文

　　当我们穿过旧德里的一个市场时走了很长一段路，我们在一个广场上停下来休息。过了一会儿，我们注意到广场的那一边有一个带着两个大筐的耍蛇人，于是就走过去看看。他一见我们，就拿起了一个长长的上面镶有硬币的管乐器，并掀开了一个筐的盖子。当他开始吹奏一支曲子时，我们才第一次看到那条蛇。它从筐里探出身子，随着乐器的摆动而扭动。当耍蛇人突然又吹奏起爵士乐和现代流行乐曲时，我们感到非常惊奇。然而那蛇却还是缓慢地"舞动"着。显然，它分辨不出印度音乐和爵士乐！

Summary writing 摘要写作

Answer these questions *in not more than 70 words*.

回答下列问题，将答案组成一个段落，不要超过 70 个单词。

1　What did we watch in a square in Old Delhi?

2　Did he have a long pipe and two large baskets or not?

3　Did he play a tune or not? What did the snake in one of the baskets do? (*and*)

4　Did the snake charmer play modern tunes or not? Did the snake continue to dance slowly, or did it dance quickly?
　　(*Then … but*)

5　Did it know the difference between Indian music and jazz or not?

Composition 作文

Rewrite the following sentences using the joining words in parentheses:

用括号中的连词改写以下句子：

1　The snake charmer opened his basket. He started to play a tune. The snake refused to move. (*and … but*)

2　The snake charmer shook the basket. The snake obeyed him. (*Then … and*)

3　Everybody was frightened. These snakes are not dangerous. (*but*)

Letter writing 书信写作

Arrange the following headings in the correct order. Supply full stops and commas; make any other changes you consider necessary:

按书信的要求排列以下信头，必要时加上句号、逗号，并作一些改动：

1　84 Wiley Drive/Buxton/England/Derbyshire/8 January 19__

2　May 21 19__/New York/844 West 54th Street/N.Y./U.S.A.

Key structures 关键句型

Have

a　Do you remember these sentences? (**KS18**)
　　你记得这些句子吗？（参见第 18 课关键句型）

Instead of saying:	*We can say*:
除了这种表述方法外：	还可以说：
He owns a new house.	He *has* a new house.
	Or: He *has got* a new house.
He possesses a lot of money.	He *has* a lot of money.
	Or: He *has got* a lot of money.
I took a bath before dinner.	I *had* a bath before dinner.
I enjoyed myself at the party.	I *had* a good time at the party.

b　Sometimes we can use *have* + noun in place of an ordinary verb.
　　有时我们可以用 have + 名词来代替普通动词。

　　Study these examples:
　　仔细阅读以下例句：

Unit 2　Lesson 42

Instead of saying:	*We can say*:
除了这种表述方法:	还可以说:
I *walked* in the garden.	I *had a walk* in the garden.
He wanted to *drink* a glass of water.	He wanted to *have a drink* of water.
We *will talk* about the problem tomorrow.	We *will have a talk* about the problem tomorrow.
Look at this.	*Have a look* at this.

Exercises 练习

A　Find four examples in the passage where *have* is used in place of an ordinary verb.
在课文中找出 have 替代普通动词的 4 个例子。

B　Write these sentences again using *have* + noun in place of the verbs in italics:
用 have + 名词来替代用斜体印出的动词:

1　Yesterday I *rode* on a horse for the first time in my life.

2　I *was looking* at those old photographs last night.

3　He *washed* before going out.

4　I *swam* in the sea this morning.

5　Those two sailors *fought* in the bar last night.

6　Dan and Caroline have been *quarrelling*.

7　He *tried* again. (Use 'another' in place of 'again').

8　She is *resting*.

9　I wanted to *smoke*.

10　Did you *sleep well* last night? (Use 'a good' in place of 'well'.)

Special difficulties 难点

参见第 6、7 两课的难点 (SD6, SD7)

Study these sentences. Each sentence contains the verb *pick*. This verb has a different meaning in each sentence:
细读以下句子, 每句中均有动词 pick, 但词义各不相同。

He *picked up* a long pipe which was covered with coins. (ll.4-5)

I'll *pick* you *up* in the car this evening. 今晚我开车来接你。

I *picked up* a lot of English while I was in England. (I learnt.) 在英国的时候, 我学到了不少英语。

There are so many beautiful cards on display, I can't *pick out* the ones I like best. (I can't choose.) 陈列着那么多漂亮的明信片, 我挑不出最喜欢的。

Exercise 练习

Use the correct form of the verb *pick* in place of the verbs in italics:
用 pick 来代替用斜体印出的动词:

1　That book has fallen on the floor. Please *get* it for me.

2　I'll *collect* the parcel on my way to work.

3　I can't *select* the material I want.

4　Where did you *learn* those tricks?

Multiple choice questions 选择题

Comprehension 理解

1 They stopped at a square because _____ .

　(*a*) they noticed a snake charmer　　　(*b*) there was a market

　(*c*) a snake charmer was playing a pipe　(*d*) they were tired

2 The snake probably 'danced' _____ .

　(*a*) by listening to the Indian music

　(*b*) by listening to the jazz

　(*c*) by looking at the snake charmer

　(*d*) by following the movements of the snake charmer's pipe

Structure 句型

3 We stopped at a square _____ have a rest.

　(*a*) so to　　　(*b*) in order　　　(*c*) in order that　　　(*d*) in order to

4 We went to have a look at him. We wanted to _____ him.

　(*a*) have　　　(*b*) see　　　(*c*) look　　　(*d*) have seen

5 Did it _____ out of the basket?

　(*a*) rose　　　(*b*) rise　　　(*c*) raise　　　(*d*) risen

6 We were very much surprised. We were _____ surprised.

　(*a*) more　　　(*b*) many　　　(*c*) most　　　(*d*) the most

7 It could not tell the difference between Indian music and jazz. It _____ .

　(*a*) might not　　　(*b*) may not　　　(*c*) must not　　　(*d*) wasn't able to

Vocabulary 词汇

8 It was covered with coins. There were coins _____ it.

　(*a*) in　　　(*b*) over　　　(*c*) under　　　(*d*) all over

9 He began to play a tune. It was a nice _____ .

　(*a*) melody　　　(*b*) music　　　(*c*) echo　　　(*d*) harmony

10 We had our first glimpse of the snake. We _____ .

　(*a*) saw it　　　(*b*) looked at it　　　(*c*) saw it for a moment　　　(*d*) stared at it

11 The songs are popular. _____ like them.

　(*a*) The people　　　(*b*) The country people　　　(*c*) The folk　　　(*d*) Many people

12 The snake, however, continued to dance. _____ the snake continued to dance.

　(*a*) But　　　(*b*) So　　　(*c*) Though　　　(*d*) Even

Sentence structure 句子结构

Join these sentences, then check your answer against the text.

连接以下句子, 然后对照课文第 4-6 行, 核对你的答案。

He saw us. He picked up a long pipe. It was covered with coins. He opened one of the baskets.

　As _____ .

Lesson 43 Over the South Pole 飞越南极

flew over the South Pole

🔊 **First listen and then answer the question.**

听录音, 然后回答以下问题。

How was the plane able to clear the mountains?

In 1929, three years after his flight over the North Pole, the American explorer, R.E. Byrd, successfully flew over the South Pole for the first time. Though, at first, Byrd and his men were able to take a great many photographs of the mountains that lay below, they soon
5 ran into serious trouble. At one point, it seemed certain that their plane would crash. It could only get over the mountains if it rose to 10,000 feet. Byrd at once ordered his men to throw out two heavy food sacks. The plane was then able to rise and it cleared the mountains by 400 feet. Byrd now knew that he would be able to reach the South Pole which was 300 miles
10 away, for there were no more mountains in sight. The aircraft was able to fly over the endless white plains without difficulty.

New words and expressions 生词和短语

pole (title) /pəʊl/ n. （地球的）极
flight (l.1) /'flaɪt/ n. 飞行
explorer (l.2) /ɪk'splɔːrə/ n. 探险家
lie (l.4) /laɪ/ (lay /leɪ/, lain /leɪn/)
    v. 处于
serious (l.5) /'sɪəriəs/ adj. 严重的
point (l.5) /pɔɪnt/ n. 地点

seem (l.5) /siːm/ v. 似乎, 好像
crash (l.6) /kræʃ/ v. 坠毁
sack (l.8) /sæk/ n. 袋子
clear (l.8) /klɪə/ v. 越过
aircraft (l.10) /'eəkrɑːft/ n. 飞机
endless (l.10) /'endləs/ adj. 无尽的
plain (l.10) /pleɪn/ n. 平原

Notes on the text 课文注释

1 the North Pole, 北极; the South Pole, 南极。
2 a great many photographs, 大量照片。
3 they soon ran into serious trouble, 他们很快陷入了困境里。run into trouble 是 "遇到麻烦" 的意思。
4 at one point, 在某一地方。
5 it seemed certain, 看起来肯定。
6 get over the mountains, 越过山头。
7 it cleared the mountains by 400 feet, 飞机在离山头 400 英尺的高度飞越了过去。by 表示 "相差" 的意思。

参考译文

    美国探险家 R. E. 伯德在飞越北极 3 年之后, 于 1929 年第一次成功地飞越了南极。虽然开始时伯德和他的助手们拍下了飞机下面连绵群山的大量照片, 但他们很快就陷入了困境。在有个地方, 飞机似乎肯定要坠毁了。只有在飞至 10,000 英尺的高度时, 它才能飞过这些山头。伯德马上命令他的助手们把两个沉重的食物袋扔掉, 于是飞机可以上升了, 它在离山头 400 英尺的高度飞越了过去。伯德这时知道他能够顺利飞抵 300 英里以外的南极了, 因为前面再没有山了。飞机可以毫无困难地飞过这片茫茫无际的白色原野!

Summary writing 摘要写作

Answer these questions *in not more than 65 words*.

回答下列问题，将答案组成一个段落，不要超过 65 个单词。

1 When did the American explorer, R.E. Byrd become the first man to fly over the South Pole?

2 Did he take a lot of photographs during the flight or not? Did he run into difficulties or not? (*but then*)

3 Could his plane get over the mountains or not? What did he order his men to do? (*so*)

4 Did the plane then fly over the mountains or did it crash? Did it continue without further trouble or not? (*and*)

Composition 作文

Rewrite the following sentences using the joining words (conjunctions) in parentheses.

用括号中的连词改写以下句子：

1 Byrd stayed in the Antarctic for a year. He made many more flights. (*and*)

2 He went back to America in 1930. He returned to the Antarctic in 1946. (*but*)

3 This time he had 4,000 men with him. He had thirteen ships and seventeen aeroplanes. (*not only … but … as well*)

Letter writing 书信写作

1 Write your home address and the date in the way they would appear in a letter to a friend in your own country.

按照给你本国的一个朋友写信的要求，写出你家的地址和日期。

2 Write the address of a person who lives abroad.

写出一位居住在国外的人士的地址。

Key structures 关键句型

Can and Be able to

a   Do you remember these sentences? **(KS19)**

你记得这些句子吗？（参见第 19 课关键句型）

Can I use your telephone?

Could I use your telephone?

b   Study these examples carefully:

仔细阅读下面的例子：

Instead of saying:	*We can say*:
除了这种表述方式外：	还可以说：
He will come if he *can*.	He will come if he *is able to*.
I *can* see you tomorrow.	I'*ll be able to* see you tomorrow.
I *couldn't* understand him.	I *wasn't able to* understand him.
He said he *could* see me next week.	He said he *would be able to* see me next week.

c   We must use *was able to* when we want to show that an action has been completed successfully. We cannot use *could* in these sentences:

当我们要表明一个动作已经成功地完成的时候，我们必须用 was able to。在以下句子中不能用 could：

He *was able to* go to London yesterday and he enjoyed himself very much.

他昨天去了伦敦，玩得非常高兴。

He didn't agree with me at first but I *was able to* persuade him.

他开始不同意我的观点，但我最终说服了他。

He *was able to* leave Europe before the war began.

他在战争开始之前得以离开欧洲。

Exercises 练习

A   Underline the verbs *can* and *be able to* in the passage.

画出课文中 can 和 be able to 的例子。

B   Give the correct form of *can* and *be able to* in this paragraph. Do not refer to the passage until you finish the exercise.

用 can 和 be able to 的正确形式填空，完成练习后再对照课文，核对你的答案。

Though, at first, Byrd and his men _____ take a great many photographs of the mountains that lay below, they soon ran into serious trouble. At one point, it seemed certain that their plane would crash. It _____ only get over the mountains if it rose to 10,000 feet. Byrd at once ordered his men to throw out two heavy food sacks. The plane then _____ rise and it cleared the mountains by 400 feet. Byrd now knew that he _____ reach the South Pole which was 300 miles away, for there were no more mountains in sight. The aircraft _____ fly over the endless white plains without difficulty.

Special difficulties 难点

Phrases with *At* 含有 at 的词组

Study these examples:

细读以下例句：

At first Byrd and his men were able to take photographs. (ll.3-4)

Byrd *at once* ordered his men to throw out two food sacks. (ll.7-8)

Billy is not *at home at present*. He's *at school*. 比利现在不在家，他在学校。

After walking for several hours, we arrived at the village *at last*. 步行几个小时后，我们最后抵达了那个村庄。

It's a pity you can't come to the concert. *At any rate* you'll be able to hear it on the radio. 你不能来听音乐会真令人感到遗憾。不管怎么说，你可以在收音机里听到。

I know he's often rude to people, but he's a very pleasant person *at heart*. 我知道他经常对人粗暴，但从本质上来讲，他是个非常好的人。

I didn't know you wouldn't be coming. *At least* you could have telephoned me. 我不知道你不能来，你至少可以给我来个电话。

He behaves very strangely *at times*. 有时他的举止非常古怪。

I don't know what I can do about it. I'm completely *at a loss*. 我不知道能为此事做点什么，我一点儿主意也没有了。

Exercise 练习

Use a phrase with *at* in place of the words in italics. Make any other necessary changes:

用带有 at 的词组来替代句中用斜体印出的部分，如有必要可作些改动：

1   We found our way home *in the end*.

2   He stayed *in the house* all day yesterday.

3   You must write to him *immediately*.

4   He cannot see you *now* as he is busy.

5 He annoys me *sometimes*.

6 When I saw that the house was on fire I *didn't know what to do*.

7 *When it began* I thought it would be a good film but I was wrong.

Multiple choice questions 选择题

Comprehension 理解

1 R. E. Byrd was the first man _____ .

   (*a*) to go to the South Pole   (*b*) to fly over the South Pole

   (*c*) to go to the North Pole   (*d*) to take photographs of the South Pole

2 Byrd succeeded in flying over the mountains _____ .

   (*a*) because his plane rose 400 feet   (*b*) by making his plane lighter

   (*c*) because there were heavy sacks in the plane   (*d*) because they were under 10,000 feet high

Structure 句型

3 Did the mountains _____ far below?

   (*a*) lie   (*b*) lay   (*c*) laid   (*d*) lain

4 It could only get over the mountains if it rose to 10,000 feet. This means it _____ over the mountains.

   (*a*) would succeed in getting   (*b*) got   (*c*) was able to get   (*d*) had got

5 The plane was then able to rise. This means it _____ .

   (*a*) could rise   (*b*) might rise   (*c*) might succeed in rising   (*d*) rose

6 Byrd knew that he would be able to reach the South Pole. It would be _____ .

   (*a*) impossible   (*b*) necessary   (*c*) able   (*d*) possible

7 He would be able to reach the Pole _____ was 300 miles away.

   (*a*) which   (*b*) who   (*c*) it   (*d*) which it

Vocabulary 词汇

8 They soon _____ serious trouble.

   (*a*) ran after   (*b*) followed   (*c*) had   (*d*) ran

9 Byrd at once ordered them to do this. He ordered them to do this _____ .

   (*a*) once   (*b*) soon   (*c*) immediately   (*d*) quickly

10 The plane cleared the mountains. It _____ them.

   (*a*) covered   (*b*) cleaned   (*c*) emptied   (*d*) flew over

11 Byrd now knew he would be able to _____ the South Pole.

   (*a*) arrive at   (*b*) arrive   (*c*) reach at   (*d*) reach in

12 There were no more mountains in sight. They _____ .

   (*a*) were blind   (*b*) couldn't see   (*c*) couldn't be seen   (*d*) were sightless

Sentence structure 句子结构

Rewrite this sentence, then check your answer against the text.

改写以下句子, 然后对照课文第 7-8 行, 核对你的答案。

'Throw out two heavy food sacks at once!' Byrd told his men.

Byrd at once ordered _____ .

197

Lesson 44 Through the forest 穿过森林

First listen and then answer the question.

听录音，然后回答以下问题。

How did Mrs. Sterling get her bag back?

The men got a fright

Mrs. Anne Sterling did not think of the risk she was taking when she ran through a forest after two men. They had rushed up to her while she was having a picnic at the edge of a forest with her children and tried to steal her handbag. In the struggle, the strap broke and,

5 with the bag in their possession, both men started running through the trees. Mrs. Sterling got so angry that she ran after them. She was soon out of breath, but she continued to run. When she caught up with them, she saw that they had sat down and were going through the contents of the bag, so she ran straight at them. The men got such a fright that they dropped the bag and ran

10 away. 'The strap needs mending,' said Mrs. Sterling later, 'but they did not steal anything.'

New words and expressions 生词和短语

forest (title) /ˈfɒrəst/ *n.* 森林
risk (l.1) /rɪsk/ *n.* 危险，冒险
picnic (l.3) /ˈpɪknɪk/ *n.* 野餐
edge (l.3) /edʒ/ *n.* 边缘
strap (l.4) /stræp/ *n.* 带，皮带

possession (l.5) /pəˈzeʃən/ *n.* 所有
breath (l.7) /breθ/ *n.* 呼吸
content (l.9) /ˈkɒntent/ *n.*（常用复数）内有的物品
mend (l.10) /mend/ *v.* 修理

Notes on the text 课文注释

1 the risk she was taking, 她所冒的风险，take the risk 有"冒险"的意思。

2 when she ran through a forest after two men, 当她穿过森林追赶两个男人时。run after, 追赶。

3 with the bag in their possession, 包落到他们手里。in one's possession, 为……所有。

4 Mrs. Sterling got so angry that she ran after them. 斯特林夫人非常气愤，向着他们追了过去。句中含有 so ... that ... 的句型，意思是"如此……以至于……"。

5 out of breath, 喘不上气，上气不接下气。

6 When she caught up with them, 当她追上他们时。catch up with, 赶上，追上。

7 going through, 翻看。

8 The strap needs mending, 背带需要修理。当 need 作"需要"讲时，后面接的动名词有被动的含义。

参考译文

安·斯特林夫人在穿过森林追赶两个男人时，她并没有考虑到所冒的风险。刚才，当她和孩子们正在森林边上野餐的时候，这两个人冲到她跟前，企图抢走她的手提包。在争抢中，手提包的带断了，包落入这两个人手里，他们拔腿跑进了树林。斯特林夫人非常气愤，向着他们追了过去。只追了一会儿便上气不接下气了，但她还是继续追赶。当她赶上他们时，发现他们已经坐了下来，正翻着包里的东西。于是她直冲过去。这两个人吓了一跳，扔下提包逃跑了。"这提包带需要修理，"斯特林夫人事后说道，"不过他们什么也没偷走。"

Summary writing 摘要写作

Answer these questions *in not more than 70 words*.

回答下列问题，将答案组成一个段落，不要超过 70 个单词。

1　How many men tried to steal Mrs. Sterling's handbag?

2　What was she doing at the time?

3　Did they take the bag after a struggle or not? Where did they run? (*and*)

4　Did she run after them or not? Did she catch up with them or not? (*and*)

5　Had the men sat down or not? What were they doing? (*and*)

6　What did Mrs. Sterling do? What did they do? (*so*)

Composition 作文

Rewrite the following sentences using the joining words in parentheses:

用括号内的连词改写以下句子：

1　Thieves can be very daring. They can be very timid. (*either ... or*)

2　A thief once broke into a house. He stole some money. The lady of the house caught him. (*and ... but*)

3　The thief gave back the money. He paid for the window he had broken. (*not only ... but*)

Letter writing 书信写作

Addressing the envelope: The name and address must appear in the middle of the envelope. Titles are always used with names. Study these examples:

信封上的地址的书写方式：收信人的姓名和地址必须在信封的中央，称呼总是和姓名连在一起的。研究以下例子：

Mr. James Thompson, James Thompson Esq.,

Miss H. Thompson, Mrs. D. Thompson,

Mr. and Mrs. J. Thompson,

Exercise 练习

Address an envelope to a friend who lives abroad.

给国外的一位朋友准备一个信封，上面写上他的地址。

Key structures 关键句型

Both men started running through the trees.

a　Do you remember these sentences? **(KS20)**

你记得这些句子吗？（参见第 20 课关键句型）

Eating is always a pleasure. 吃总是一种享受。

I am very keen on *cycling*. 我很热衷骑自行车。

He sat there without *saying* anything. 他坐在那里，一言不发。

I must apologize for *not letting* you know earlier. 没有让你早点知道，我必须向你道歉。

Unit 2   Lesson 44

b Now study these examples:

仔细阅读以下例子：

I am looking forward to *seeing* him tomorrow. **(SD37)** 我期待着明天与他会面。(第 37 课难点)

I am accustomed to *getting* up early. 我习惯早起。

I am used to *getting* up early. 我习惯早起。

(Compare: I used to get up early but I don't anymore. **[KS31]**) (对比：我过去常早起，但现在不再早起了。

〔参见第 31 课关键句型〕)

c *Instead of saying*:

除了这种表述方法外：

The men started *to run* through the trees.

They began *to run*.

They continued *to run*.

We can say:

还可以说：

The men started *running* through the trees.

They began *running*.

They continued *running*.

d Compare these sentences:

比较下面句子：

Now

I hate *to disturb* you, but can I come in for a moment please? 我不愿意打扰你，但我可以进来一会儿吗？

I'd love (or like) *to sit* in the garden. 我喜欢坐在花园里。

Always

I hate *disturbing* people when they are busy. 人们忙的时候，我不愿意打扰。

I love (or like) *sitting* in the garden when it's fine. 天气好的时候，我喜欢在花园里坐坐。

e Study these expressions:

研究以下表达方式：

My shirt is torn. It needs *mending*. 我的衬衫撕破了，需要缝补。

Those windows are dirty. They want *washing*. 那些窗户很脏，需要洗刷。

Exercises 练习

A There are some verbs in the passage which are similar in form to the examples given above. Can you find them?

在课文中有些动词的形式与以上讨论的句型相似，找出这些动词。

B Give the correct form of the verbs in parentheses:

用括号中动词的正确形式填空：

1 I'd love _____ (see) that film. Will it be on tomorrow?

2 He's accustomed to _____ (work) very hard.

3 These shirts need _____ (iron).

4 I hate _____ (leave) so early, but I'm afraid I have to.

5 They continued _____ (argue) till after midnight.

6 Would you like _____ (come) with me?

7 I shall be looking forward to _____ (see) you soon.

8 You must never come into this room without _____ (knock) first.

9 I got tired of _____ (wait) so I left.

10 It began _____ (rain) just as I was going out.

11 I don't believe in _____ (work) too hard.

12 He accused me of _____ (take) his umbrella.

Special difficulties 难点

Study these uses of the verbs *catch* and *run*:

研究 catch 和 run 的用法：

When she *caught up with* them, she saw that they had sat down. (ll.8-9) (When she reached them ...)

They dropped the bag and *ran away*. (ll.9-10)

Exercise 练习

Write two sentences using each of the verbs given above.

用例句中所给的动词短语各造一个句子。

Multiple choice questions 选择题

Comprehension 理解

1 The thieves _____ .

(*a*) found it easy to steal Mrs. Sterling's bag   (*b*) found a bag

(*c*) found it hard to steal the bag   (*d*) didn't steal the bag

2 Mrs. Sterling _____ .

(*a*) caught the thieves   (*b*) followed the thieves and got her handbag back

(*c*) never got her handbag back   (*d*) stayed with her children

Structure 句型

3 She was soon out of breath, but she continued _____ .

(*a*) run   (*b*) ran   (*c*) running   (*d*) in running

4 They were going through the contents of the bag. _____ she ran straight at them.

(*a*) For this   (*b*) That's because   (*c*) That's why   (*d*) That's so

5 They got such a fright. They were _____ .

(*a*) so frightful   (*b*) such frightened   (*c*) so frightened   (*d*) such fright

6 The strap needs mending. It _____ .

(*a*) has mended   (*b*) has to be mended   (*c*) has been mended   (*d*) has been mending

7 They didn't steal anything. They stole _____ .

(*a*) anything   (*b*) not anything   (*c*) not nothing   (*d*) nothing

Vocabulary 词汇

8 She took a risk. What she did was _____ .

(*a*) dangerous   (*b*) brave   (*c*) clever   (*d*) stupid

9 She was at the edge of the forest. She was _____ the forest.

(*a*) inside   (*b*) near   (*c*) among   (*d*) at the tip of

10 They tried to steal her handbag. They tried to _____ her of her handbag.

(*a*) rob   (*b*) steal   (*c*) be robbed   (*d*) be stolen

11 She was out of breath. She _____ .

(*a*) wasn't breathing   (*b*) was breathing with difficulty

(*c*) couldn't breathe   (*d*) stopped breathing

12 The bag contains money. Let me see the _____ of the bag.

(*a*) contains   (*b*) containing   (*c*) contenting   (*d*) contents

Lesson 45   A clear conscience   问心无愧

First listen and then answer the question.

听录音，然后回答以下问题。

How did Sam get his money back?

The whole village soon learnt that a large sum of money had been
lost. Sam Benton, the local butcher, had lost his wallet while taking
his savings to the post office. Sam was sure that the wallet must
have been found by one of the villagers, but it was not returned to
5 him. Three months passed, and then one morning, Sam found his
wallet outside his front door. It had been wrapped up in newspaper
and it contained half the money he had lost, together with a note
which said: 'A thief, yes, but only 50 per cent a thief!' Two months
later, some more money was sent to Sam with another note: 'Only 25 per cent a thief now!' In time, all Sam's
10 money was paid back in this way. The last note said: 'I am 100 per cent honest now!'

*the local butcher lost
his wallet*

New words and expressions 生词和短语

clear (title) /klɪə/ *adj.* 无罪的，不亏心的
conscience (title) /ˈkɒnʃəns/ *n.* 良心，道德心
wallet (l.2) /ˈwɒlɪt/ *n.* 皮夹，钱夹

savings (l.3) /ˈseɪvɪŋz/ *n.* 存款
villager (l.4) /ˈvɪlɪdʒə/ *n.* 村民
per cent (l.8) /pəˈsent/ 百分之……

Notes on the text 课文注释

1　Sam Benton, the local butcher, had lost his wallet while taking his savings to the post office. 当地的屠户萨姆·本顿在把存款送往邮局的途中把钱包丢了。其中的 while taking his savings 是现在分词用于连词之后，与表示时间的状语从句 while he was taking his savings 作用是一致的。

2　the wallet must have been found by one of the villagers, 钱包肯定是被某个村民捡到了。must 在这里表示推测，由于是对过去的推测，因此 must 之后的动词要用完成形式。

3　in time, 最后，终于。

参考译文

　　整个村子很快知道，有一大笔钱丢失了。当地的屠户萨姆·本顿在把存款送往邮局的途中把钱包丢了。萨姆确信那钱包一定是被某个村民捡到了，可是却不见有人来送还给他。3 个月过去了，后来在一天早晨，萨姆在自己的大门外发现了他的钱包。钱包是用报纸包着的，里面有他丢失的钱的一半，而且还附着一张纸条，上面写着："一个小偷，是的，但只是一个 50% 的小偷！"又过了两个月，又有一些钱送还给了萨姆，又附了一张字条："这回只是 25% 的小偷了！"最后，萨姆全部的钱都用同样的方式还了回来。最后的那张字条上写道："我现在是一个 100% 的诚实人了！"

Summary writing 摘要写作

Answer these questions *in not more than 70 words*.
回答下列问题，将答案组成一个段落，不要超过 70 个单词。

1 Where was the local butcher, Sam Benton, taking his savings? What did he lose? (*but*)

2 Did Sam receive half his money three months later, or did he receive all his money? Did he receive a note or not? (*not only ... but ... as well*)

3 What did the note say?

4 Did the thief include a note every time he sent Sam more money or not?

5 What did the last note say?

Composition 作文

Rewrite the following sentences using the joining words in parentheses:
用括号内的连词改写以下句子：

1 Sam told everybody about the wallet. He did not try to find the thief. (*but*)

2 The man was not really a thief. He needed money badly. (*but*)

3 He paid back the money. He bought himself a clear conscience. (*not only ... but also*)

Letter writing 书信写作

Address an envelope to a married lady who lives abroad.
为写给居住在国外的一位已婚女士的信配一个信封。

Key structures 关键句型

Review **KS10, KS21, KS34** 复习第 10，21，34 课关键句型：被动语态

a   Do you remember these sentences?
你还记得这些句子吗？

This bridge was built in 1942. **(KS10)** （第 10 课）

The thief was arrested by the police. **(KS10)** （第 10 课）

I can't find my bag. It must have been stolen. **(KS21)** （第 21 课）

I must be paid for this. **(KS21)** （第 21 课）

I was told to wait for him. **(KS34)** （第 34 课）

He never expected the bicycle to be found. **(KS34)** （第 34 课）

b   Now study these examples:
仔细阅读以下例子：

Instead of saying:	*We can say*:
除了这种表述方式外：	还可以说：
I found out that *someone had sent the parcel* to the wrong address.	I found out that *the parcel had been sent* to the wrong address.
He told me *the police had arrested the thief*.	He told me *the thief had been arrested* (*by the police*).

Exercises 练习

A There are some verbs in the passage which are similar in form to the examples given above. Can you find them?
课文中有一些动词的形式与上述的动词形式类似，找出课文中被动语态的动词。

B Change the form of the expressions in italics. Do not refer to the passage until you finish the exercise:
将斜体印出的动词改成被动语态，完成练习后再对照课文，核对你的答案：

The whole village soon learnt that *someone had lost a large sum of money*. Sam Benton, the local butcher, had lost his wallet while taking his savings to the post office. Sam was sure that *one of the villagers must have found the wallet*, but *no one returned it to him*. Three months passed, and then one morning, Sam found his wallet outside his front door. *Someone had wrapped it up* in newspaper and it contained half the money he had lost, together with a note which said: 'A thief, yes, but only 50 per cent a thief!' Two months later, *someone sent more money* to Sam with another note: 'Only 25 per cent a thief now!' In time, *someone paid back all Sam*'s *money* in this way.

C Change the form of the verbs in italics. Omit the word *someone* from each sentence:
将以下句子中用斜体印出的动词改成被动语态，省略 someone：

1 Someone *has prepared* a meal for you.

2 Someone *will translate* the book into English.

3 Someone *must send* a telegram to him.

4 Someone *had put out* the fire before the fire brigade arrived.

5 Someone *gave* the cat some milk to drink.

Special difficulties 难点

Words often confused 经常容易混淆的词

a *Steal and Rob*.

Steal (something from someone or somewhere) 偷（从某人或某处）：A thief broke into the building last night and *stole* some money from the safe. 昨天夜里一个窃贼闯入大楼，从保险箱中偷走了一些钱。

Rob (someone of something) 抢（某人的某物）：Two thieves attacked him last night and *robbed* him of all his money. 昨天夜里两个窃贼袭击了他，抢走了他的全部钱财。

(a building, a bank, a house, etc.) （大楼、银行、房子等等）The police have caught the men who *robbed* the bank. 警察已抓住抢劫银行的那伙人。

b *Pay back*.

Study these examples:
仔细阅读以下例子：

All Sam's money was *paid back*. (ll.9-10) (It was repaid).

I'll *pay* you *back* for what you did to me. (I'll get my revenge on you for what you did to me.) 你对我这样，我一定会报仇的。

Exercise 练习

Supply *steal*, *rob* or *back* in the following sentences:
用 steal, rob 或 back 填空：

1 Please lend me £25. I'll pay you _____ next week.

2 His house was _____ last night. Thieves broke in and _____ several valuable pictures.

3 He threatened to pay me _____ but he hasn't done so yet.

4 The bank clerk _____ some money from the safe.

5 A stranger attacked an old man in the train and _____ him of all his money.

Multiple choice questions 选择题

Comprehension 理解

1 Someone _____ .

(a) had stolen Sam's wallet

(b) had found Sam's wallet and kept it

(c) had lost Sam's wallet

(d) had taken the wallet from Sam's pocket.

2 The thief _____ in the end.

(a) kept Sam's money

(b) returned 50 per cent of the money

(c) returned 75 per cent of the money

(d) returned all the money

Structure 句型

3 Sam was taking his savings to the post office _____ he lost his wallet.

(a) when   (b) while   (c) as   (d) just as

4 He was taking his savings to the post office. He keeps his savings _____ the post office.

(a) to   (b) in   (c) on   (d) into

5 The wallet was found _____ one of the villagers.

(a) from   (b) by   (c) out of   (d) of

6 _____ had it been wrapped up in? A newspaper.

(a) Where   (b) Who   (c) How   (d) What

7 Some more money was sent to Sam. Sam _____ some more money.

(a) sent   (b) has sent   (c) was sent   (d) had sent

Vocabulary 词汇

8 We usually keep _____ in a wallet.

(a) coins   (b) notes   (c) cheques   (d) photographs

9 The thief had _____ the wallet in newspaper.

(a) wound   (b) rolled   (c) wrapped   (d) bound

10 How much did it contain? How much _____ ?

(a) did it consist   (b) was there in it   (c) did it include   (d) had it

11 Sam read the thief's note. In this sentence, 'note' means _____ .

(a) money   (b) a coin   (c) a cheque   (d) a message

12 _____ , all Sam's money was returned.

(a) At times   (b) After a time   (c) With the times   (d) A long time

Sentence structure 句子结构

Join these sentences, then check your answer against the text.

连接以下句子, 然后对照课文第 3-5 行, 核对你的答案。

The wallet must have been found by one of the villagers. Sam Was sure of it. It was not returned to him.

Sam was sure _____ .

Lesson 46 Expensive and uncomfortable 既昂贵又受罪

First listen and then answer the question.

听录音，然后回答以下问题。

What did the man in this story do?

When a plane from London arrived at Sydney airport, workers began to unload a number of wooden boxes which contained clothing. No one could account for the fact that one of the boxes was extremely heavy. It suddenly occurred to one of the workers to open up the
5 box. He was astonished at what he found. A man was lying in the box on top of a pile of woollen goods. He was so surprised at being discovered that he did not even try to run away. After he was arrested, the man admitted hiding in the box before the plane left London. He had had a long and uncomfortable trip, for he had been confined to the wooden box for over eighteen hours.
10 The man was ordered to pay £3,500 for the cost of the trip. The normal price of a ticket is £2,000!

he did not try to run away

New words and expressions 生词和短语

unload (l.2) /ʌnˈləʊd/ v. 卸（货）

wooden (l.2) /ˈwʊdn/ adj. 木制的

extremely (l.3) /ɪkˈstriːmli/ adv. 非常，极其

occur (l.4) /əˈkɜː/ v. 发生

astonish (l.5) /əˈstɒnɪʃ/ v. 使惊讶

pile (l.6) /paɪl/ n. 堆

woollen (l.6) /ˈwʊlən/ adj. 羊毛的

goods (l.6) /ɡʊds/ n.（常用复数）货物，商品

discover (l.7) /dɪsˈkʌvə/ v. 发现

admit (l.8) /ədˈmɪt/ v. 承认

confine (l.9) /kənˈfaɪn/ v. 关在（一个狭小的空间里）

normal (l.10) /ˈnɔːməl/ adj. 正常的，通常的

Notes on the text 课文注释

1 a number of, 许多。

2 No one could account for the fact that ...,谁也弄不清……这样一个事实。account for 有"说明原因"的意思；that 后面的从句用来进一步说明这个"事实"本身，在语法上称作同位语。

3 It suddenly occurred to one of the workers to open up the box. 突然一个工人想到打开箱子看看。occur to 可译作"想起"。在这句话中，it 是先行词，主语是动词不定式 to open up the box。

4 He was astonished at what he found. 看到的情景使他吃惊。在这句话中 what 引导的名词性从句作介词 at 的宾语，其中 what 相当于 the thing which。

5 on top of, 在……之上。

6 He was so surprised at being discovered that he did not even try to run away. 他由于被发现而感到非常吃惊，甚至都没有企图逃跑。这句话的主要句型仍为 so ... that ...。动名词短语 being discovered 是介词 at 的宾语，由于是被动语态，因此要用动词 be 加上 ing 的形式。

7 the man admitted hiding in the box, 这个人承认藏在箱子里。在这句话中动名词 hiding 作动词 admit 的宾语。

参考译文

当一架来自伦敦的飞机抵达悉尼机场时，工人们开始卸下装有服装的一批木箱。其中有只箱子特别重，可谁也弄不清是怎么回事。突然一个工人想到打开箱子看看。看到的情景使他吃惊，箱内有一个人正躺在一堆毛织品之上。他由于被人发现而感到非常吃惊，甚至都没有企图逃跑。此人被逮捕后，承认他是在飞机离开伦敦前躲进箱里的。他经历了一次漫长而又难受的旅程，因为他在那木箱里闷了 18 个多小时。此人被责令交付旅费 3,500 英镑，而正常票价是 2,000 英镑！

Summary writing　摘要写作

Answer these questions *in not more than 70 words*.
回答下列问题，将答案组成一个段落，不要超过 70 个单词。

1 Where did the plane from London arrive? What did workers unload from it? (*and*)
2 What did they contain?
3 Was one of the boxes extremely heavy or not? What did a worker do? (*so*)
4 What did he find on top of a pile of woollen goods?
5 Was the man arrested or not?
6 Had he travelled in the box from London or from Sydney?
7 How much did he have to pay?
8 How much does an ordinary ticket cost?

Composition　作文

Rewrite the following sentences using the joining words in parentheses:
用括号中的连词改写以下句子：

1 The man had had an uncomfortable trip. He was very hungry. (*not only ... but ... as well*)
2 He had not eaten anything for thirteen hours. He had not drunk anything for thirteen hours. (*neither ... nor*)
3 Woollen goods cannot be eaten. At least they are soft. The man had had a few hours' sleep. (*but ... so*)

Letter writing　书信写作

1 Write your home address and the date in the way they would appear in a letter to a friend who lives abroad.
按照书信的要求，在一封寄给国外朋友的信上写上你自己的家庭住址和日期。
2 Write the address of a friend who lives abroad in the way it would appear in a letter to you.
按照书信的要求，在国外朋友给你的一封信上写上对方的地址。

Key structures　关键句型

Verbs followed by *to, at, for* and *with* (Compare **KS22**)
与 to, at, for 和 with 连用的动词（对比第 22 课关键句型）
We can put *to*, *at*, *for* and *with* after certain verbs.
在一部分动词的后面可加上 to, at, for 和 with。
Compare:
对比：
I saw Tom yesterday. 昨天我见到了汤姆。
I shall see *to* the dinner tonight. (I shall prepare it.) 今晚我做晚饭。

Use this list for reference:

请参考下表:

a TO: accustom(ed), amount, appeal, apply (or for), attach(ed), attend, belong, challenge, compare (or with), condemn(ed), confess, confine, consent, convert, entitle(d), listen, mention, object, occur, prefer, react (or against), reply, respond, see, submit, surrender, turn, yield.

与 to 连用的动词: 习惯于; 达到; 呼吁; 适用于; 附属于; 参加; 属于; 向……提出挑战; 比较; 判刑; 承认; 限制; 同意; 改信 (某宗教); 享有权利; 听; 提到; 反对; 想到; 更喜欢; 对……反应; 回答; 响应; 注意; 服从于; 向……投降; 转向; 屈服。

b AT: amuse(d) (or by), arrive (or in), astonish(ed) (or by), exclaim, glance, guess, knock **(SD6)**, look **(SD37b)**, point (or to), shock(ed) (or by), stare, surprise(d) (or by), wonder (or about), work (or on).

与 at 连用的动词: 对……感到有趣; 到达; 感到惊愕; 惊叫; 对……看一眼; 猜测; 敲 (第 6 课难点); 看 (第 37 课难点 b); 指向; 感到震惊; 盯……看; 感到惊讶; 感到惊异; 钻研。

c FOR: account, ask (or of), act (or on), apologize, blame, beg, call **(SD34)**, charge, exchange, hope, look, mistake, mourn, pay **(SD 45b)**, prepare, provide, search, thank, vote (or on) **(KS22d)**, wait (or on).

与 for 连用的动词: 说明 (原因); 请求; 代表; 因……而道歉; 责备; 乞求; 需要 (第 34 课难点); 收费; 交换; 希望; 寻找; 误认为; 哀悼; 为……付款 (第 45 课难点 b); 准备; 提供; 寻求; 感谢; 投票支持 (第 22 课关键句型 d); 等候。

d WITH: agree, begin, communicate, compare (or to), compete (or against), comply, confuse, contrast (or to), cope, correspond, disgust(ed), finish, help (or in), interfere (or in), mix, occupy(ied), part, please(d), quarrel (or about), reason, satisfy(fied) (or by), threaten(ed).

与 with 连用的动词: 同意; 以……开始; 与……联络; 与……比较; 同……竞争; 同意; 误作; 形成对照; 对付; 与……一致; 使……讨厌; 完成; 帮助; 干扰; 混合; 从事于; 放弃; 对……满意; 争论; 规劝; 感到满足; 威胁。

Exercises 练习

A Point out verbs in the passage which are followed by to, at, or for.
找出课文中与 to, at, for 连用的动词。

B Supply the missing words (to, at, for and with) without referring to the above lists as far as possible:
用 to, at, for 或 with 填空, 尽可能不查以上动词表:

1 I don't agree _____ you.

2 She preferred _____ wait _____ him.

3 We have been corresponding _____ each other for years.

4 How do you account _____ this?

5 Do you object _____ my smoking?

6 I'm surprised _____ you!

7 You must reply _____ his letter.

8 He has some important business to attend _____ .

9 Do you mean to say you exchanged that lovely car _____ this?

10 Has it occurred _____ you that she must have arrived _____ London Airport by now?

11 I was shocked _____ his indifference!

12 You must comply _____ the rules of the game.

13 Poor Mary! She has so much to cope _____ !

14 Please don't mention it _____ my husband, but I paid £50 _____ this hat.

15 She was quite unprepared _____ the news.

16 Don't blame me _____ the accident!

17 I'm disgusted _____ your behaviour!

18 You forgot to thank Aunt Jane _____ her present.

19 It is rude to stare _____ people.

20 I'm not satisfied _____ your work.

21 His debt now amounts _____ £100.

22 Mix the contents of this packet _____ a little water.

23 I knocked _____ the door.

24 Whom does this book belong _____ ?

25 I reasoned _____ him, but he would not listen _____ me.

26 She's accustomed _____ living in comfort.

She'll never part _____ her precious possessions.

27 At what time will you call _____ me?

28 The spy surrendered himself _____ the enemy and was condemned _____ death.

29 I've looked _____ it everywhere, but I can't find it.

30 I'll see _____ the cooking tonight.

31 I must apologize _____ keeping you waiting.

32 The class failed to respond _____ the teacher's new methods.

33 He turned _____ me for help, even after

I had quarrelled _____ him.

34 Like Micawber, I hope _____ something better.

35 Please apply _____ the secretary for information.

36 There was a note attached _____ the parcel.

37 Just guess _____ the price of this carpet.

38 How long have you been working _____ this exercise?

39 The concert began _____ a piece by an unknown composer.

40 How much did they charge you _____ that?

Multiple choice questions 选择题

Comprehension 理解

1 The man was discovered because _____ .

(a) a worker opened the box

(b) the box was heavy

(c) the box contained woollen goods, but was very heavy

(d) he had hidden in the box

2 The man had hidden in the box _____ .

(a) to get to Sydney

(b) because it contained woollen goods

(c) to avoid paying the fare from London to Sydney

(d) because no one would find him

Structure 句型

3 Workers began _____ a number of wooden boxes.

(a) unload   (b) to unloading   (c) unloaded   (d) unloading

4 Which boxes contained clothing? _____ .

(a) The wooden   (b) The wood   (c) The woody ones   (d) The wooden ones

5 It occurred to him to open it. He thought _____ it.

(a) of opening   (b) to open   (c) to have opened   (d) opening

6 What did he find? He was surprised at what _____ .

(a) did he find   (b) he did find   (c) he found   (d) he has found

7 _____ a ticket to Sydney? £2,000.

(a) How many is   (b) How much is   (c) How much has   (d) How much costs

Vocabulary 词汇

8 The boxes contained clothing. They contained _____ .

(a) cloths   (b) cloth   (c) clothes   (d) dresses

9 No one could account for it. They couldn't _____ it.

(a) explain   (b) estimate   (c) interpret   (d) describe

10 The man was lying on top of a _____ of woollen goods.

(a) carpet   (b) column   (c) bag   (d) heap

11 He admitted hiding in the box. He _____ it.

(a) announced   (b) described   (c) confessed   (d) declared

12 He had been confined to the box, so he _____ .

(a) couldn't move   (b) could move   (c) couldn't sleep   (d) couldn't run away

Lesson 47　A thirsty ghost　嗜酒的鬼魂

First listen and then answer the question.

听录音，然后回答以下问题。

What evidence is there of a ghost?

five empty bottles which the ghost must have drunk

A public house which was recently bought by Mr. Ian Thompson is up for sale. Mr. Thompson is going to sell it because it is haunted. He told me that he could not go to sleep one night because he heard a strange noise coming from the bar. The next morning, he found
5 that the doors had been blocked by chairs and the furniture had been moved. Though Mr. Thompson had turned the lights off before he went to bed, they were on in the morning. He also said that he had found five empty whisky bottles which the ghost must have drunk the night before. When I suggested that some villagers must have come in for a free drink, Mr.
10 Thompson shook his head. The villagers have told him that they will not accept the pub even if he gives it away.

New words and expressions 生词和短语

thirsty (title) /ˈθɜːsti/ *adj.* 贪杯的
ghost (title) /gəʊst/ *n.* 鬼魂
haunt (l.2) /hɔːnt/ *v.* （鬼）来访，闹鬼
block (l.5) /blɒk/ *v.* 堵
furniture (l.5) /ˈfɜːnɪtʃə/ *n.* 家具

whisky (l.8) /ˈwɪski/ *n.* 威士忌酒
suggest (l.9) /səˈdʒest/ *v.* 暗示
shake (l.10) /ʃeɪk/ (shook /ʃʊk/, shaken /ˈʃeɪkən/) *v.* 摇动
accept (l.10) /əkˈsept/ *v.* 接受

Notes on the text 课文注释

1　up for sale, 供出售, to be up for 是 "为了某一目的" 的意思。

2　he heard a strange noise coming from the bar, 他听到酒吧里传来了一阵奇怪的声音。coming 是现在分词，用来进一步说明宾语 noise, 在语法上称作宾语补足语。

3　He also said that he had found five empty whisky bottles which the ghost must have drunk the night before. 他还说他发现了 5 只空的威士忌酒瓶子，这肯定是鬼魂头天晚上喝的。which 引导的从句用来修饰 five empty whisky bottles, 由于鬼魂喝的是酒，因此句中的 5 个瓶子指的是 5 瓶酒。这是一种借喻的修饰方法。句中的 must 用来表示推测。

4　a free drink, 免费饮料。

5　even if he gives it away, 即使他白送人。

6　shake one's head, 摇头，表示异议。

参考译文

　　伊恩·汤普森先生最近才买的一个小酒店现在又要卖出去。汤普森先生之所以想卖它，是因为那里常闹鬼。他告诉我有天夜里他怎么也睡不着，因为他听到酒吧里传来一阵奇怪的响声。第二天早上，他发现酒吧间的门被椅子堵上了，家具也被挪动过。虽然汤普森临睡觉时把灯关了，但早晨灯却都亮着。他还说他发现了 5 只空

的威士忌酒瓶子, 这肯定是鬼魂昨天晚上喝的。当我暗示说一定是村里有些人来喝不花钱的酒时, 汤普森先生摇了摇头。村里的人已经告诉他, 即使他把小酒店白送人, 他们也不要。

Summary writing 摘要写作

Answer these questions *in not more than 70 words.*
回答下列问题, 将答案组成一个段落, 不要超过 70 个单词。

1　What did Mr. Ian Thompson buy recently? Is it haunted or not? What is he going to do with it? (*but ... so*)

2　Was there a strange noise in the bar one night or not? Was the room in disorder next morning or not? (*and*)

3　What else did Mr. Thompson find?

4　Does he believe that some villagers broke into the bar and had a drink or not?

5　Does anybody in the village want to buy the pub?

Composition 写作

Rewrite the following sentences using the joining words in parentheses:
用括号中的连词改写以下句子:

1　One night Mr. Thompson heard a noise. He went downstairs. (*and*)

2　In the bar, five men were drinking whisky. They did not see him. (*but*)

3　Mr. Thompson put a sheet over his head. He went into the bar. (*and*)

4　The villagers ran away in fear. They never came back again. (*and*)

Letter writing 书信写作

Write your name and home address in the way they would appear on an envelope.
按照书信要求, 将你的姓名和地址写到信封上。

Key structures 关键句型

Review KS36-45 复习第 36-45 课的关键句型

She is going to swim across the Channel tomorrow. (**KS36**)（第 36 课）

Workers will have completed the new roads by the end of this year. (**KS37**)（第 37 课）

He acted as if he had never lived in England before. (**KS38**)（第 38 课）

He said that ... He told me ... He asked ... (**KS39**)（第 39 课）

If you ate more and talked less, we would both enjoy our dinner. (**KS40**)（第 40 课）

Must, Have to and Need. (**KS41**)（第 41 课）

Have. (**KS42**)（第 42 课）

Can and Be able to. (**KS43**)（第 43 课）

A large sum of money had been lost. (**KS45**)（第 45 课）

Exercises 练习

A　Underline all the verbs in the passage. Revise any Key structures you have forgotten.
　　在课文中所有的动词下面画上横线, 复习已经遗忘的关键句型。

B Give the correct form of the verbs in parentheses. Do not refer to the passage until you finish the
exercise:

用括号中动词的正确形式填空，完成练习后对照课文，核对你的答案：

A public house which recently _____ (buy) by Mr. Ian Thompson is up for sale. Mr. Thompson _____
(sell) it because it _____ (haunt). He told me that he _____ (can) not go to sleep one night because he
_____ (hear) a strange noise coming from the bar. The next morning, he _____ (find) that the doors
_____ (block) by chairs and the furniture _____ (move). Though Mr. Thompson _____ (turn) the
lights off before he _____ (go) to bed, they _____ (be) on in the morning. He also _____ (say)
that he _____ (find) five empty whisky bottles which the ghost _____ (must drink) the night before.
When I _____ (suggest) that some villagers _____ (must come) in for a free drink, Mr. Thompson
_____ (shake) his head. The villagers _____ (tell) him that they _____ (not accept) the pub even if
he _____ (give) it away.

C Give the correct form of the verbs in parentheses:

用括号中动词的正确形式填空：

1 By the end of next year they _____ (finish) work on the new stadium.

2 If you _____ (break) this window, you would have to pay for it.

3 He would enjoy the concert if he _____ (be) present.

4 If you _____ (can) help me, I would be grateful.

D Supply *mustn't* or *needn't* in these sentences:

用 mustn't 或 needn't 填空：

1 I _____ go to bed late tonight. I have to get up early tomorrow.

2 You _____ finish your soup if you don't like it.

E Read this paragraph, then answer the questions below:

阅读以下课文，然后回答问题：

1 'What are these people looking at?' I asked George.

2 'I don't know,' George answered. 'I think a new road is being built. It will be finished soon.'

3 George and I joined the crowd. 'All these people are very silly,' I whispered to George. 'They are looking into an
empty hole.'

4 'Some people enjoy watching others work,' George said.

5 Half an hour passed. Suddenly George said to me, 'Hurry up! We've been here for half an hour.' Then he added,
'There is nothing to see in an empty hole.'

6 'I don't want to go yet.' I answered. 'It's very interesting.'

Questions

1 What did I ask George?

2 What did George answer? What did he think?

3 Why did I tell George that all those people were very silly?

4 What did George say?

5 How much time passed? What did George tell me to do? How long had we been there? What did he add?

6 What did I answer?

Multiple choice questions 选择题

Comprehension 理解

1 Mr. Thompson wants to sell his pub because _____ .

  (a) he heard a strange noise coming from the bar

  (b) he found the doors had been blocked by chairs

  (c) he found five empty whisky bottles

  (d) he thinks it's visited by a ghost

2 Mr. Thompson _____ .

  (a) believes in ghosts

  (b) thinks the villagers are playing a trick

  (c) thinks the villagers drank the whisky

  (d) wants to give the pub away

Structure 句型

3 Mr. Ian Thompson _____ a public house a short time ago.

  (a) has bought   (b) bought   (c) was bought   (d) is bought

4 He's going to sell it. That's what he _____ to do.

  (a) intends   (b) will   (c) shall   (d) going

5 He told me he couldn't go to sleep. That's what he _____ .

  (a) said me   (b) talked to me   (c) told to me   (d) said to me

6 He heard a noise _____ coming from the bar.

  (a) which was   (b) who was   (c) that is   (d) which is

7 The ghost must have drunk the whisky. In Mr. Thompson's opinion, the ghost _____ whisky.

  (a) must drink   (b) has got to drink   (c) has to drink   (d) should drink

Vocabulary 词汇

8 Mr. Thompson is selling his pub. His pub is _____ .

  (a) sold   (b) to let   (c) for selling   (d) for sale

9 Before he went to bed, Mr. Thompson _____ the lights.

  (a) closed   (b) turned on   (c) closed up   (d) switched off

10 The lights were _____ in the morning.

  (a) open   (b) alight   (c) on   (d) on fire

11 Mr. Thompson shook his head. This meant _____ .

  (a) no   (b) perhaps   (c) yes   (d) I don't know

12 They will not _____ the pub even if he gives it away.

  (a) receive   (b) agree to   (c) agree to take   (d) allow

Sentence structure 句子结构

Rewrite this sentence, then check your answer against the text.

改写以下句子, 然后对照课文第 6-7 行, 核对你的答案。

Mr. Thompson had turned the lights off before he went to bed, but they were on in the morning.

Though _____ .

Lesson 48　Did you want to tell me something?
你想对我说什么吗？

I suddenly felt very worried

First listen and then answer the question.

听录音, 然后回答以下问题。

Why did the writer become very worried?

Dentists always ask questions when it is impossible for you to answer. My dentist had just pulled out one of my teeth and had told me to rest for a while. I tried to say something, but my mouth was full of cotton wool. He knew I collected match boxes and asked me whether
5 my collection was growing. He then asked me how my brother was and whether I liked my new job in London. In answer to these questions I either nodded or made strange noises. Meanwhile, my tongue was busy searching out the hole where the tooth had been. I suddenly felt very worried, but could not say anything. When the dentist at last removed the cotton wool from my mouth, I was able to tell him that he
10 had pulled out the wrong tooth.

New words and expressions　生词和短语

pull (l.2) /pʊl/ v. 拔

cotton wool (l.4) /ˌkɒtn-ˈwʊl/ 药棉

collect (l.4) /kəˈlekt/ v. 搜集

collection (l.5) /kəˈlekʃən/ n. 收藏品, 收集品

nod (l.7) /nɒd/ v. 点头

meanwhile (l.7) /ˈmiːnwaɪl/ adv. 同时

Notes on the text　课文注释

1　for a while, 一会儿, 片刻。

2　He then ask me how my brother was and whether I liked my new job in London. 接着他问我的兄弟近来如何, 问我是否喜欢伦敦的新工作。在这句话中, 以 how 和 whether 引导的从句都是作动词 asked 的宾语。

3　In answer to these questions, 作为对这些问题的答复。

4　search out, 搜寻。

5　the hole where the tooth had been, 刚拔掉的那颗牙的伤口。

参考译文

　　牙科医生们总是在你无法作出回答的时候向你提出问题。我的牙科医生刚刚给我拔掉了一颗牙, 叫我休息一会儿。我想说点什么, 但我嘴里塞满了药棉。他知道我收集火柴盒, 于是问我收藏的火柴盒是否在增加。接着他又问我的兄弟近来如何, 问我是否喜欢伦敦的新工作。作为对这些问题的回答, 我不是点头, 就是发出奇怪的声音。与此同时, 我的舌头正在忙着寻找刚拔掉的那颗牙的伤口。我突然非常着急起来, 但却什么也说不出来。当那位牙医最后将药棉从我嘴中取出时, 我总算有可能告诉他, 他拔错了牙。

Summary writing 摘要写作

Answer these questions *in not more than 75 words*.

回答下列问题, 将答案组成一个段落, 不要超过 75 个单词。

1 Had the dentist in the story pulled out one of the writer's teeth or not? What had he told him to do? (*and*)

2 Did he ask several questions or not? Could the writer answer them or not? (*but*)

3 What was his mouth full of?

4 Did he suddenly discover something wrong or not? Could he say anything or not? (*but*)

5 What did the dentist eventually remove from his mouth? What did the writer tell him? (*and*)

Composition 作文

Rewrite the following sentences using the joining words in parentheses:

用括号中的连词改写以下句子:

1 The dentist smiled. He showed me the tooth. (*and*)

2 He had pulled out the right one. I had not realized it. (*but*)

3 I had made a mistake. I had criticized his work. (*not only ... but ... as well*)

Letter writing 书信写作

Arrange the following heading in the correct order. Supply full stops and commas; make any other changes you consider necessary.

按书信的要求排列以下信头, 加上句号或逗号, 如果需要可作改动。

England/Seaview Hotel/Princes' Avenue/23 September 19__/Brighton.

Special difficulties 难点

Review **SD 26-45** 复习第 26-45 课的难点

Exercises 练习

A Words often confused 经常容易混淆的词

Choose the correct words in the following sentences:

选择正确的词:

1 The new school, (which) (who) has just been completed, is a fine building. **(SD28)** (第 28 课)

2 He (denied) (refused) that he had taken it. **(SD29)** (第 29 课)

3 The waiter (took) (fetched) me a clean glass. **(SD29)** (第 29 课)

4 He is (too) (very) ill to do any work. **(SD29)** (第 29 课)

5 I had a few (works) (jobs) to do in town this morning. **(SD31c)** (第 31 课 c)

6 (A) (One) day I spoke to (one) (a) man (who) (whom) had won the Nobel Prize. **(SD28, 32)** (第 28, 32 课)

7 A bird flew (past) (passed) my window. **(SD33b)** (第 33 课 b)

8 We spent the first day of our holidays in Geneva. The (next) (other) day we went to Basle. **(SD33b)** (第 33 课 b)

9 I spent the afternoon (watching) (following) the match. **(SD36a)** (第 36 课 a)

10 Ships (continuously) (continually) cross the sea. **(SD38c)** (第 38 课 c)

11 'Did you take that book from the shelf?' he (remarked) (noticed) suddenly. **(SD41)** (第 41 课)

12 The bank has been (stolen) (robbed). **(SD45a)** (第 45 课 a)

B   Write sentences using *so, such,* or *such a* with the following words: trouble, beautiful, nice day, tired. **(SD35)**

用 so, such 或 such a 与 trouble, beautiful, nice day, tired 等词一起造句。（参见第 35 课难点）

C   Join these sentences using *no sooner ... than*. **(SD38a)**

用 no sooner ... than 将以下句子连在一起。（参见第 38 课难点 a）

1   He had come home. They rang him up from the office.

2   The plane had taken off. It returned to the airport.

D   Supply the correct form of *make* or *do* in the following sentences: **(SD40)**

用 make 或 do 动词的正确形式填空：（参见第 40 课难点）

1   He has _____ progress.

2   You never _____ a job properly.

3   Why can't you _____ up your mind?

4   I have to go out now. I must _____ some shopping.

5   _____ me a favour, will you?

6   Don't _____ such a noise.

7   You have just _____ a mistake.

8   He always _____ his best.

E   *Put* **(SD27)**; *call* **(SD34)**; *look* **(SD37b)**; *pick* **(SD42)**; *catch* **(SD44)**; *pay* **(SD45b)**.

    Complete these sentences by adding any of the following words: *up with, up, off, out, away, back.*

用 up with, up, off, out, away, back 填空：

1   Have they put _____ that forest fire?

2   Haven't you learnt how to look _____ a word in the dictionary?

3   I tried to call her _____ but her phone was out of order.

4   Pick _____ all those toys and put them _____ .

5   If you can't find a room at the hotel. I can put you _____ .

6   Look _____ ! That bus nearly hit you!

7   I'll pay _____ the money I borrowed as soon as I can.

8   I can't put _____ _____ those children any longer.

9   He's so far ahead of you, you'll never catch _____ _____ him.

F   Phrases with *at*. **(SD43)**

含有 at 的短语（参见第 43 课难点）

Use each of the following phrases in sentences:

用以下短语造句：

at once, at a loss, at last, at present, at home.

Multiple choice questions 选择题

Comprehension 理解

1   The writer couldn't speak because _____ .

    (*a*) the dentist had just pulled one of his teeth out

    (*b*) the dentist was talking all the time

    (*c*) there was something in his mouth

    (*d*) he had a toothache

2 Why was the writer worried?

   (*a*) He thought the dentist had pulled out more than one tooth.

   (*b*) He thought the dentist had pulled out the wrong tooth.

   (*c*) He had had a tooth out.

   (*d*) His tongue was busy searching out the hole where the tooth had been.

Structure 句型

3 It is impossible for him to answer. He _____ answer.

   (*a*) might not   (*b*) could not   (*c*) cannot   (*d*) may not

4 He told me to rest for a while. '_____ for a while,' he said.

   (*a*) To rest   (*b*) Rest   (*c*) Do you rest   (*d*) Resting

5 He asked me how my brother was. 'How _____?' he asked.

   (*a*) is your brother   (*b*) your brother was   (*c*) your brother is   (*d*) was your brother

6 _____ your new job in London?

   (*a*) It likes you   (*b*) Does it like you   (*c*) Do you like   (*d*) Like you

7 He answered these questions by _____ his head.

   (*a*) to nod   (*b*) nodding   (*c*) nod   (*d*) to nodding

Vocabulary 词汇

8 He told me to rest for a while. He told me to rest _____ .

   (*a*) quietly   (*b*) for a short time   (*c*) while he spoke to me   (*d*) for a long time

9 I have a very good _____ of match boxes.

   (*a*) assembly   (*b*) gathering   (*c*) congregation   (*d*) collection

10 I nodded. This means I _____ .

   (*a*) agreed   (*b*) said no   (*c*) shouted   (*d*) whispered

11 Meanwhile my tongue was busy ... _____ my tongue was busy ...

   (*a*) However   (*b*) In the mean time   (*c*) Nevertheless   (*d*) Although

12 He removed the cotton wool from my mouth. He _____ .

   (*a*) took it off   (*b*) took it in   (*c*) took it out   (*d*) took it up

Sentence structure 句子结构

Rewrite this sentence, then check your answer against the text.

改写以下句子, 然后对照课文第 1 行, 核对你的答案。

Dentists always ask questions when you are unable to answer.

Dentists always ask questions when it _____ .

PRE-UNIT TEST 3
测试 3

IF YOU CAN DO THIS TEST GO ON TO UNIT 3

如果你能完成以下测验，请开始第3单元的学习

Key structures 关键句型

A Word order in compound statements 并列句中的语序

Join these pairs of sentences. Use the joining words in parentheses.

用括号中的连词连接以下各对句子。

1 He read the book. He returned it to the library. (*and*)

2 The boy climbed the tree. He picked some apples. (*and*)

3 I opened the door. He came into the hall. (*and*)

4 He looked for his pen. He could not find it. (*but*)

5 She called to him. He did not answer her. (*but*)

6 Everyone was out. I left a message. (*so*)

7 He plays soccer. He plays rugby. (*both ... and*)

8 Children enjoy holidays. Adults enjoy holidays. (*both ... and*)

9 He must be very clever. He must be very foolish. (*either ... or*)

10 George does not play football. Dave does not play football. (*neither ... nor*)

11 George does not play soccer. He does not play rugby. (*neither ... nor*)

12 He does not know. He does not care. (*neither ... nor*)

13 He forgot to take his umbrella. He forgot to take his briefcase. (*not only ... but ... as well*)

B Verbs 动词

a These things always happen. 一般现在时

What is happening? What always happens? 现在进行时和一般现在时

Give the correct form of the verbs in parentheses.

用括号中动词的正确形式填空。

'Some people still _____ (believe) the world is flat,' he said.

'You _____ (joke),' I replied. 'I _____ (not know) anyone who does.'

'Well, you _____ (know) me,' he replied. 'I _____ (believe) that the earth is flat. I met a man the other day. I _____ (forget) his name now. He said that the earth _____ (look) like a flat dish.'

'... you _____ (try) to tell me that you _____ (believe) him?' I asked.

'I certainly do,' he answered. 'I _____ (think) that he is right.'

'And which side of the dish ... you _____ (live) on?'

'Oh, I _____ (not know). He didn't tell me that!'

b What happened? 一般过去时

The verbs in parentheses tell us *what happened*. Give the correct form of each verb.

括号中的动词表示过去发生的动作，用正确的形式填空。

Late in the afternoon, the boys _____ (put) up their tent in the middle of a field. ... they _____ (cook) a meal over an open fire. They were all hungry and the food _____ (smell) good. After a wonderful meal, they _____ (tell) stories and _____ (sing) songs by the campfire. But some time later it _____ (begin) to rain. The boys _____ (feel) tired so they _____ (put) out the fire and _____ (creep) into their tent.

c What happened? What has happened? 一般过去时和现在完成时

The verbs in parentheses tell us *what happened* and *what has happened*. Give the correct form of each verb.

括号中的动词表示过去发生的动作和现在已经完成的动作，用正确的形式填空。

Captain Ben Fawcett has bought an unusual taxi and _____ (begin) a new service. The 'taxi' is a small Swiss aeroplane called a 'Pilatus Porter'. This wonderful plane can carry seven passengers. Captain Fawcett's first passenger _____ (be) a doctor who _____ (fly) from Birmingham to a lonely village in the Welsh mountains. Since then, Captain Fawcett _____ (fly) passengers to many unusual places. Once he _____ (land) on the roof of a block of flats and on another occasion, he _____ (land) in a deserted car park. Captain Fawcett just _____ (refuse) a strange request from a business man. The man _____ (want) to fly to Rockall, but Captain Fawcett _____ (not take) him because the trip _____ (be) too dangerous.

d What was happening? What happened? What used to happen? 过去进行时、一般过去时和表示过去习惯性的动作

The verbs in parentheses tell us *what was happening, what happened,* and *what used to happen*. Give the correct form of each verb.

括号中的动词表示过去某一时刻正在进行的动作、过去的动作和过去习惯性的动作，用正确的形式填空。

Yesterday afternoon Frank Hawkins _____ (tell) me about his experiences as a young man. Before he retired, Frank was the head of a very large business company, but as a boy he _____ (work) in a small shop. It _____ (be) his job to repair bicycles and at that time he _____ (work) fourteen hours a day. He _____ (save) money for years and in 1958 he _____ (buy) a small workshop of his own. In his twenties Frank _____ (make) spare parts for aeroplanes. At that time he _____ (have) two helpers. In a few years, the small workshop had become a large factory which _____ (employ) seven hundred and twenty-eight people. Frank _____ (smile) when he _____ (remember) his hard early years. He still _____ (smile) when the door _____ (open) and his wife _____ (come) in. She _____ (want) him to repair their grandson's bicycle!

e Going to 将来时

Write these sentences again. Use *going to* in place of the verbs in italics.

改写以下句子，用 going to 来代替用斜体印出的动词。

1 We *intend to* leave at six o'clock.

2 I *intend to* pay these bills tomorrow.

3 Do you *intend to* write to him?

4 She does not *intend to* look for a new job.

5 When do you *intend to* buy a new car?

f What will happen? What will be happening? What will have happened? 一般将来时、将来进行时和将来完成时

The verbs in parentheses tell us *what will happen, what will be happening,* and *what will have happened*. Give the correct form of each verb.

括号中的动词表示一般将来时、将来进行时和将来完成时，用正确的形式填空。

The Olympic Games _____ (hold) in our country in four years' time. As a great many people _____ (visit) the country, the government _____ (build) new hotels, an immense stadium, and an Olympic-standard swimming pool. They also _____ (build) new roads and a special railway line. The Games _____ (hold)

221

just outside the capital and the whole area _____ (call) 'Olympic City'. Workers _____ (complete) the new roads by the end of this year. By the end of next year, they _____ (finish) work on the new stadium.

g What happened some time ago? What had happened some time before? 一般过去时和过去完成时

The verbs in parentheses tell us *what happened some time ago* and *what had happened some time before*. Give the correct form of each verb.

括号中的动词表示一段时间前发生的动作和过去某一时刻前已完成的动作。用正确的形式填空。

The police _____ (find) Billy Wilkins last night. He _____ (run) away from home five days before. He _____ (spend) the last two nights near a farmhouse. The police _____ (take) him home at once. When she _____ (see) him, his mother _____ (burst) into tears. She _____ (say) he never _____ (run) away before.

h He was asked to call at the station.

Supply the correct form of the verbs in parentheses.

用括号中动词的正确形式填空。

Last Tuesday Dan received a letter from the local police. He _____ (ask) to call at the station. Dan wondered why he _____ (want) by the police, but he went to the station. There he _____ (tell) by a smiling policeman that his bicycle _____ (pick) up in a small village four hundred miles away. It now _____ (send) to his home by train. Dan never expected his bicycle to _____ (find). It _____ (steal) twenty years ago when Dan was a boy of fifteen!

i Answer the questions after each statement and question.

根据直接引语的内容回答下列问题。

1 'I am very tired,' he said.

What did he say? (He said that ...)

2 'Are you tired?' she asked.

What did she ask? (She asked if ...)

3 'Will Jack arrive tomorrow?' Tom asked.

What did Tom ask?

4 'When will Jack arrive?' Tom asked.

What did Tom ask?

5 'Have you ever been abroad?' Catherine asked.

What did Catherine ask?

6 'Why didn't you write to me?' Jane asked.

What did Jane ask?

j If 条件句

Give the correct form of the verbs in parentheses.

给出括号中动词的正确形式。

1 If he (be) out, I'll call tomorrow.

2 You'll miss the train if you (not hurry).

3 If you went to the exhibition, you (enjoy) it.

4 If I (be) in your position, I would act differently.

k Give the correct form of the verbs in parentheses.
   给出括号中动词的正确形式。

1 I'd love (see) that film. Will it be on tomorrow?

2 These shirts need (iron).

3 I hate (leave) so early, but I'm afraid I have to.

4 They continued (argue) till after midnight.

5 I shall be looking forward to (see) you tomorrow.

6 I got tired of (wait) so I left.

7 I don't believe in (work) too hard.

8 I did some shopping before (go) home.

C Must, Need, Have to, Can and Be able to

a Supply *mustn't* or *needn't* in these sentences.
   用 mustn't 或 needn't 填空。

1 You _____ make a noise. The children are asleep.

2 You _____ drive so quickly; we have plenty of time.

3 You _____ come with us if you don't want to.

4 You _____ smoke in a theatre. It is forbidden.

b Write these sentences again using constructions with *have* in place of the verbs in italics.
   改写以下句子，用含有 have 的结构来代替用斜体印出的动词。

1 *Look* at this.

2 He *washed* before going out.

3 I *swam* in the sea this morning.

4 She is *resting*.

c Supply *could* or *was able to* in the following sentences.
   用 could 或 was able to 填空。

1 _____ I use your telephone please?

2 He _____ leave Europe before the war began.

3 He said he _____ see me tomorrow.

4 He didn't agree with me at first but I _____ persuade him.

D A, The, Some and Any

Put in *a, the, some* or *any* where necessary.
在需要的地方填上 a, the, some 或 any。

_____ Wayle is _____ small river that cuts across _____ park near my home. I like sitting by _____ Wayle on fine afternoons. It was warm last Sunday, so I went and sat on _____ river bank as usual. _____ children were playing _____ games on _____ bank and there were _____ people rowing on _____ river. Suddenly, one of _____ children kicked _____ ball very hard and it went towards _____ passing boat. _____ people on _____ bank called out to _____ man in _____ boat, but he did not hear them. _____ ball struck him so hard that he nearly fell into _____ water. I turned to look at _____ children, but there weren't _____ in sight.

223

Pre-Unit Test 3

E Little and Few

Write these sentences again using *little*, *less than*, *few*, *fewer than*, *a little* and *a few* in place of the words in italics. Make any other necessary changes.

改写以下句子,用 little, less than, few, fewer than, a little 和 a few 来代替用斜体印出的词,可对句子作必要的调整。

1 There *isn't much* I can do to help him.

2 There aren't many apples on the tree, but you can pick *some* if you want to.

3 He *hasn't* got as *much* work to do *as* I have.

4 There isn't much whisky in this bottle, but you can have *some* if you want it.

5 He *hasn't as* many books *as* I have.

6 There *weren't many* people in the shop.

F Where did he go? He went to the cinema.

Supply the missing words in the following.
填空。

1 Tell him to come _____ my office. I want to speak to him.

2 The ship sailed _____ the harbour and disappeared from sight.

3 We climbed _____ the top of the mountain.

4 He aimed _____ the bird, fired, and missed.

5 Please bring the tea things _____ the kitchen for me.

G Verbs followed by *to*, *at*, *for* and *with*. 带有 to, at, for 和 with 的动词

Supply the missing words in the following sentences.
填空。

1 I agree _____ you. He never listens _____ anybody.

2 Don't blame me _____ that!

3 We must prepare _____ the coming year.

4 He has quarrelled _____ nearly all his old friends.

5 He came into the room without knocking _____ the door.

Special difficulties 难点

A Words often confused 经常容易混淆的词

Choose the correct words in the following sentences.
选择正确的词或短语。

1 I can't drink this coffee. It is (too) (very) hot.

2 He (denied) (refused) the accusation.

3 He often does (jobs) (works) about the house.

4 The train (passed) (past) at a terrific speed.

5 Have you seen Frank lately? I met him by accident the (next) (other) day.

6 He (looked at) (watched) the newspaper for a few minutes before going out.

7 I feel (such) (so) sleepy, I shall go to bed at once.

8 He is (so) (such a) difficult child. He objects to everything.

9 This water has been boiling (continuously) (continually) for over an hour.

10 He knocked me down and (stole) (robbed) me of all my money.

11 In the end, I bought (one) (a) tie instead of two.

12 I'm surprised you didn't (remark) (notice) my new hat.

B Speech Marks 引号

White this piece of conversation again using speech marks.

改写以下段落, 加上引号。

Haven't you finished this book yet? he asked. I haven't even started it, I answered. Why not? he asked. It's an exciting story. Perhaps it is, I answered, but it's too difficult for me. I spend more time referring to the dictionary than reading the book.

C Complete these sentences by adding any of the following words: *back, out, with, up.*

用 back, out, with, up 等词完成以下句子。

1 The firemen found it difficult to put _____ the fire.

2 I'll have to look that _____ in the encyclopaedia.

3 He ran so fast I couldn't catch up _____ him.

4 All his friends are Americans. He has picked _____ an American accent.

5 I haven't any money now. Can I pay you _____ next week?

D Make and Do

Supply the correct form of *make* and *do* in the following.

用 make 和 do 的正确形式填空。

1 I _____ a promise never to see him again.

2 I was asked to _____ a speech.

3 That shop _____ very good business.

4 Do you think it will _____ any difference?

5 When did you _____ your homework?

6 He's the sort of person who always _____ trouble.

Unit 3

第 3 单元

Unit 3　第3单元

INSTRUCTIONS TO THE STUDENT 致学生

In Unit 2 you learned how to join simple statements with words like 'and', 'but' and 'so' to make compound statements. In this unit you will learn how to join simple statements with words like 'when', 'as' and 'while' to make complex statements. You will learn how to write sentences which contain several ideas.
在第 2 单元, 你学会了如何用 "and", "but" 和 "so" 来连接简单句, 组成并列句。在这一单元, 你将学习如何用 "when", "as" 和 "while" 等词连接简单句以组成复合句。你将学会组成表达多层意思的句子。

Before you begin each exercise, read these instructions carefully. Read them *each time* you begin a new piece. They are very important.
在开始每项练习之前, 要细读这些指令。它们很重要, 每次开始新课前都要读读指令。

How to work — Summary writing 如何写摘要

Unit 3 contains twenty-four short passages. There are questions under each piece. Your answers to these questions will often take the form of complex statements. Put your answers together to make a short paragraph.
第 3 单元共有 24 篇短文。每篇课文下面都有问题。你的回答常常是复合句。把你的答案组成一个小的段落。

1　Read the passage carefully two or three times. Make sure you understand it.
　细读课文 2 至 3 遍, 一定要理解课文。

2　Write a full answer to each question. When several questions are given together, join your answers with the joining words or phrases given in parentheses. Each answer you write must be *a complete sentence*.
　给每个问题一个完整的答案。当几个问题相关联时, 用括号中的词或词组把它们连接起来。你的每一个答案必须是完整的句子。

3　Your answers to the questions must follow each other so that all your sentences will form *a complete paragraph*.
　你的答案必须句句相连, 组成一个完整的段落。

4　Read through your work and correct your mistakes.
　从头至尾读一遍你的答案, 纠正其中的错误。

5　Count the number of words in your paragraph. Do not go over the word limit. Words like 'the', 'a', etc. count as single words. Words which are joined by a hyphen also count as single words. At the end of your paragraph write the number of words that you have used.
　数一下段落中的字数, 不要超过字数的限制。冠词和用连字符连起来的复合词均为一个词。在段落的后面注明全段的字数。

Example 范例

Work through this example carefully and then try to do the exercises in Unit 3 in the same way.
仔细研究以下例题, 然后用同样的方式完成第 3 单元的练习。

The last and longest journey

Even ships grow old and have to be destroyed. The last journey of a ship, which people have worked in and grown to love, is always a sad occasion. The *F.S. 949* had not been a great liner, or even a remarkable merchant ship. She was a U-boat and had sunk more ships during the war than any other submarine. In one famous battle, she had sunk six ships in twenty-four hours. Alone, she had gone out to meet a convoy of merchant ships. Though these ships were protected by destroyers, the *F.S. 949* had sunk four of them before she was located. During the long battle that followed, two of the destroyers were sunk and the little submarine was only slightly damaged. Now, under a cold, grey sky, people were watching silently as she came into the harbour. She would soon make her last journey out to sea before resting for ever in the depths she knew so well.

Summary writing 摘要写作

Answer these questions *in not more than 75 words*.
回答以下问题, 将答案组成一个段落, 不要超过 75 个单词。

1 Was the *F.S. 949* an old U-boat or a new one? Would she soon be destroyed or not? (*which*)

2 What had she done during the war?

3 How many ships had she sunk in twenty-four hours in one famous battle?

4 How many merchant ships and destroyers had she sunk on that occasion? Was she slightly damaged or not? (*Though*)

5 What were people doing as the *F.S. 949* now came into the harbour? Would she make her last journey out to sea or not? (*before*)

Answer 答案

The *F.S. 949* was an old U-boat *which* would soon be destroyed. During the war, she had sunk more ships than any other submarine. In one famous battle, she had sunk six ships in twenty-four hours. *Though* on that occasion she had sunk four merchant ships and two destroyers, she was only slightly damaged. People were watching silently as the *F.S. 949* now came into the harbour *before* she made her last journey out to sea.

(74 words)

Composition 作文

Unit 3 contains two types of composition exercise based on ideas suggested by each passage:
第 3 单元的作文练习有两种形式, 都是根据课文引申出来的思路为基础的:

1 Writing two or three sentences of your own, using the information which has been given in note form.
根据笔记提供的信息写出 2 至 3 句话。

2 Joining sentences together to make complex statements.
连接句子, 组成复合句。

Examples 范例

Work through these examples carefully and then try to do the composition exercises in the same way.
仔细研究以下例题, 然后用同样的方式完成作文练习。

1 Sample composition 作文范例 1

Write two or three sentences using the ideas given below.
根据以下词组写出 2 至 3 句话来。

Nuclear submarines — may replace ordinary submarines — can travel long distances — *Nautilus* — North Pole — under ice — four days.

A possible answer 参考答案

Nuclear submarines may one day replace ordinary submarines, for they can travel under water over long distances. The American nuclear submarine, *Nautilus*, which sailed across the North Pole, remained under ice for four days.

2 Sample composition 作文范例 2

Rewrite the following sentences using the joining words in parentheses.
用括号中的连词改写以下句子。

1 The *F.S. 949* failed to return home after a long sea battle. It was feared that she had been sunk. (*Because*)

2 Everyone was surprised. The submarine suddenly arrived three weeks later. (*when*)

3 She had not been badly damaged. Her radio had been put out of action. (*Although*)

Answer 答案

Because the *F.S. 949* failed to return home after a long sea battle, it was feared that she had been sunk. Everyone was surprised *when* the submarine arrived three weeks later. *Although* she had not been badly damaged, her radio had been put out of action.

Letter writing 书信写作

Follow the instructions given under each passage.
遵循每课书后的指令。

Key structures and Special difficulties 关键句型和难点

When you finish the **Letter writing** exercise, go on to the language exercises that follow. The **Key structures** deal with exactly the same problems that were considered in Units 1 and 2. You may refer back if you have forgotten anything. A little more new information about the **Key structures** is added here. **Special difficulties** are dealt with after the **Key structures**. The work you do in grammar is based on material contained in the passages. Refer to the passages frequently. They will help you to understand the grammar and to do the exercises.

当你结束"书信写作"后，就可以开始紧随其后的语言练习。"关键句型"的问题与第1, 2 单元相同。如果有遗忘的地方，可以在前两个单元找到。这里增加了有关句型的一点新内容。"关键句型"之后是"难点"。其中的语法练习是以课文中的语言点为基础的。经常查找课文可以帮助你理解语法并完成练习。

Lesson 49   The end of a dream   美梦告终

First listen and then answer the question.

听录音，然后回答以下问题。

How did the dream end?

miraculously unhurt

Tired of sleeping on the floor, a young man in Teheran saved up for years to buy a real bed. For the first time in his life, he became the proud owner of a bed which had springs and a mattress. Because the weather was very hot, he carried the bed on to the roof of his house.
5 He slept very well for the first two nights, but on the third night, a storm blew up. A gust of wind swept the bed off the roof and sent it crashing into the courtyard below. The young man did not wake up until the bed had struck the ground. Although the bed was smashed to pieces, the man was miraculously unhurt. When he woke up, he was still on the mattress. Glancing at the
10 bits of wood and metal that lay around him, the man sadly picked up the mattress and carried it into his house. After he had put it on the floor, he promptly went to sleep again.

New words and expressions   生词和短语

tired (l.1) /taɪəd/ *adj.* 厌烦的
real (l.2) /riːl/ *adj.* 真正的
owner (l.3) /'əʊnə/ *n.* 主人
spring (l.3) /sprɪŋ/ *n.* 弹簧
mattress (l.3) /'mætrəs/ *n.* 床垫
gust (l.6) /gʌst/ *n.* 一阵狂风
sweep (l.6) /swiːp/ (swept /swept/, swept) *v.* 扫, 刮

courtyard (l.7) /'kɔːtjɑːd/ *n.* 院子
smash (l.8) /smæʃ/ *v.* 碰碎, 摔碎
miraculously (l.9) /mɪ'rækjʊləsli/ *adv.* 奇迹般地
unhurt (l.9) /ʌn'hɜːt/ *adj.* 没有受伤的
glance (l.9) /glɑːns/ *v.* 扫视
promptly (l.11) /'prɒmptli/ *adv.* 迅速地

Notes on the text   课文注释

1 Tired of sleeping on the floor, 由于对睡地板感到厌倦。be tired of 是"对……感到厌倦"的意思。在这句话里省略了现在分词 being, 这个短语表示原因状语。
2 save up, 攒钱。
3 blow up,（指暴风雨）出现并加剧；刮起。
4 A gust of wind swept the bed off the roof and sent it crashing into the courtyard below. 一阵大风把床从屋顶上刮了下来, 把它摔碎在下面的院子里。crashing into the courtyard below 是现在分词短语, 作宾语补足语。
5 The young man did not wake up until the bed had struck the ground. 那年轻人直到床撞到地上才醒了过来。
   not ... until 有"直到……才……"的意思。

参考译文

德黑兰的一个年轻人由于对睡地板感到厌倦, 于是积蓄多年买了一张真正的床。他平生第一次自豪地拥有了一张既有弹簧又带床垫的床。由于天气很热, 他便把床搬到了他的屋顶上。头两天晚上, 他睡得非常好。但第三天晚上起了风暴。一阵狂风把床从屋顶上刮了下来, 把它摔碎在下面的院子里。那年轻人直到床撞到地上

才醒了过来。尽管床摔成了碎片，但年轻人却奇迹般地没有受伤。他醒来时，仍然躺在床垫上。年轻人看了一眼周围的碎木片和碎金属片，伤心地捡起了床垫，把它拿进了屋。他把床垫往地板上一放，很快又睡着了。

Summary writing 摘要写作

Answer these questions *in not more than 80 words*.

回答下列问题，将答案组成一个段落，不要超过 80 个单词。

1 What did a young man in Teheran buy for the first time in his life?

2 Was the weather hot or cold? Did he sleep on the roof of his house or not? (*Because*)

3 Was the bed swept off the roof during a storm three nights later or not?

4 Was the man unhurt, or was he seriously injured? Was he still on his mattress or not? (*not only ... but*)

5 Was the bed in pieces or not? Did he carry the mattress indoors or not? Where did he put it? Did he go back to sleep or did he stay awake? (*As ... and*)

Letter writing 书信写作

Most letters begin with the word 'Dear' followed by a name. The word 'Dear' should be placed against the left-hand margin:

大多数书信都以"亲爱的"开头，后接姓名。"亲爱的"这个词一定要在信纸的左手边顶格：

	24 Clayton Ave., St. Albans, Herts. England. 17th June, 19__
Dear Tom,	

Exercise 练习

Write your address, the date and the beginning of a letter to a friend in the way shown above.

按照以上格式，写下你的地址、日期和给朋友的一封信的开头。

Key structures 关键句型

Word order in complex statements 复合句的语序 (Compare **KS1, 25**) (对比第 1，25 课关键句型)

We can join simple statements together to make *complex statements*. Here are some of the joining words we use:

我们可以把一些简单句连在一起组成复合句，以下是我们常用的一些连词：

when, until, after, as soon as, while, before, because, as, since, to, in order to, although, who, which and that.

Study these simple statements carefully. Pay close attention to the way they have been joined:

仔细阅读以下句子，特别注意这些句子的连接方式：

He missed the train. He did not hurry. 他误了火车。他没有赶紧离开。

He missed the train *because* he did not hurry. 因为没有赶紧离开，他误了火车。

He ran fast. He failed to win the race. 他跑得很快。他没有赢得比赛。

Although he ran fast, he failed to win the race. 虽然他跑得很快，但他没能在比赛中获胜。

Unit 3   Lesson 49

I was tired. I went to sleep immediately. 我很累。我立刻睡着了。

I was *so* tired *that* I went to sleep immediately. 我感到如此之疲倦以至马上就入睡了。

My neighbour went to Tokyo for a holiday. He could not return home. He did not have enough money. 我的邻居去东京度假。他回不来。他的钱不够了。

My neighbour, *who* went to Tokyo for a holiday, could not return home *because* he did not have enough money. 我那位去东京度假的邻居, 由于钱不够了回不来。

I went into the garden. I wanted to pick some flowers. 我进了花园。我想摘些花。

I went into the garden *to* pick some flowers. 我走进花园去摘些花。

I found the door unlocked. I went into the kitchen. 我发现门打开了。我走进了厨房。

Finding the door unlocked, I went into the kitchen. 发现门打开了, 我走进了厨房。

The city was destroyed during the war. It has now been completely rebuilt. 城市在战争中被摧毁了。它已被彻底重建了。

Destroyed during the war, the city has now been completely rebuilt. 在战争中被毁后, 这座城市现在已彻底重建了。

Exercises 练习

A   How many joining words can you find in the passage? Underline as many as you can.
在课文中所有连词的下面画上横线。

B   Rewrite these simple statements using the joining words in parentheses. Do not refer to the passage until you finish the exercise.
用括号中的连词改写以下简单句, 完成练习后再对照课文, 核对你的答案。

1   A young man in Teheran was tired of sleeping on the floor. He saved up for years to buy a real bed.
(*Tired of sleeping*)

2   He became the proud owner of a bed. It had springs and a mattress. (*which*)

3   The weather was very hot. He carried the bed on to the roof of his house. (*Because*)

4   The young man did not wake up. The bed had struck the ground. (*until*)

5   The bed was smashed to pieces. The man was unhurt. (*Although*)

6   He woke up. He was still on the mattress. (*When*)

7   He glanced at the bits of wood and metal. They lay around him. He sadly picked up the mattress. He carried it into his house. (*Glancing ... that ... and*)

8   He put it on the floor. He went to sleep again. (*After*)

Composition 作文

Write two or three sentences using the ideas given below:
用以下词组写出 2 至 3 个句子来:

The man gathered the pieces next morning — repaired the bed — put it on the roof — tied it down — enjoyed many comfortable nights' sleep.

Multiple choice questions 选择题

Comprehension 理解

1   Which statement best describes what happened?

(*a*) The bed was blown off the roof.

(*b*) The man was not hurt.

(c) The bed was smashed to pieces.

(d) The bed was blown off the roof, but the man was not hurt.

2 When the man discovered that his bed had been smashed _____ .

(a) he went back to sleep soon afterwards

(b) he couldn't sleep at all that night

(c) he tried to fix the bed

(d) he stayed where he was and immediately went back to sleep

Structure 句型

3 _____ the hot weather, he couldn't sleep indoors.

(a) Because   (b) Because of   (c) As   (d) For

4 Where did he _____ his bed?

(a) carry   (b) carries   (c) carried   (d) carrying

5 How _____ did he sleep?

(a) good   (b) well   (c) goodly   (d) nice

6 Where was the courtyard?

(a) Down.   (b) Under.   (c) Below.   (d) Bottom.

7 He looked at the bits of wood and metal _____ around him.

(a) laying   (b) laid   (c) lying   (d) lied

Vocabulary 词汇

8 A gust of wind swept the bed off the roof. The wind blew very _____ .

(a) hard   (b) fast   (c) quickly   (d) soon

9 The bed crashed into the courtyard. It _____ the courtyard.

(a) smashed   (b) knocked   (c) struck   (d) exploded

10 It was smashed to pieces. It _____ .

(a) was struck   (b) was cracked   (c) was destroyed   (d) was damaged

11 He glanced at the bits of wood and metal. He _____ the bits of wood and metal.

(a) looked quickly at   (b) had a glimpse of   (c) stared at   (d) watched

12 He promptly went to sleep again. He went to sleep _____ .

(a) straight away   (b) after a while   (c) after a time   (d) late

Sentence structure 句子结构

Rewrite this sentence, then check your answer against the text.

改写以下句子，然后对照课文第6行，核对你的答案。

The bed was swept off the roof by a gust of wind.

A gust of wind _____ .

Lesson 50　Taken for a ride　乘车兜风

First listen and then answer the question.

听录音,然后回答以下问题。

Why did the writer not get off the bus at Woodford Green?

I love travelling in the country, but I don't like losing my way.
I went on an excursion recently, but my trip took me longer than
I expected.

'This is as far as we go'

　　'I'm going to Woodford Green,' I said to the conductor as I got on
5 the bus, 'but I don't know where it is.'
　　'I'll tell you where to get off,' answered the conductor.
　　I sat in the front of the bus to get a good view of the countryside.
After some time, the bus stopped. Looking round, I realized with a
shock that I was the only passenger left on the bus.
10　　'You'll have to get off here,' the conductor said. 'This is as far as we go.'
　　'Is this Woodford Green?' I asked.
　　'Oh dear,' said the conductor suddenly. 'I forgot to put you off.'
　　'It doesn't matter,' I said. 'I'll get off here.'
　　'We're going back now,' said the conductor.
15　　'Well, in that case, I prefer to stay on the bus,' I answered.

New words and expressions　生词和短语

ride (title) /raɪd/ n. 旅行
excursion (l.2) /ɪk'skɜːʃən/ n. 远足

conductor (l.4) /kən'dʌktə/ n. 售票员
view (l.7) /vjuː/ n. 景色

Notes on the text　课文注释

1　标题 "Taken for a ride" 中 take ... for ... 是 "把……当作……" 的意思。taken for a ride 意思是 "就当作是一次乘车兜风"; take sb. for a ride 又作 "欺骗" 讲, 因此 taken for 也有 "上当了" 的含义。

2　lose one's way, 迷路。

3　go on an excursion, 作一次短距离的旅行。

4　get on the bus, 上公共汽车。

5　I'll tell you where to get off. 我告诉你哪里下车。在这个句子中, 副词 where 加上动词不定式 to get off 组成一个名词性结构, 作动词 tell 的直接宾语。

6　I sat in the front of the bus to get a good view of the countryside. 我坐在汽车的前部, 以便饱览农村风光。in the front of 作 "在……的前部" 讲; to get a good view 动词不定式短语作状语, 表示目的。

参考译文

　　我喜欢在乡间旅行, 但却不愿意迷路。最近我作了一次短途旅行, 但这次旅行所花费的时间比我预计的要长。
　　"我要去伍德福德草地," 我一上车就对售票员说, "但我不知道它在哪儿。"
　　"我会告诉您在哪儿下车," 售票员回答说。

我坐在汽车的前部，以便饱览农村风光。过了一些时候，车停了。我环视了一下身旁，惊奇地发现车里就只剩我一个乘客了。

"您得在这里下车，"售票员说，"我们的车到此为止了。"

"这里是伍德福德草地吗？"我问道。

"哎呀，"售票员突然说，"我忘了让您下车了。"

"没关系，"我说，"我就在这儿下吧。"

"我们现在要返回去，"售票员说。

"好吧，既然如此，我还是留在车上吧。"我回答说。

Summary writing 摘要写作

Answer these questions *in not more than 65 words*.
回答下列问题，将答案组成一个段落，不要超过 65 个单词。

1 Where did the writer want to go? Did he know the way or not? What did the conductor promise to do? (*but as*)

2 Did they arrive at the bus terminus or not? What did the writer ask? (*When*)

3 What did the conductor realize then? (*... that*)

4 Why did the writer stay on the bus? (*because*)

Composition 作文

Rewrite the following sentences using the joining words in parentheses:
用括号中的连词改写以下句子：

1 I went into the kitchen. I turned on the light. It was dark. (*On going ... because*)

2 My brother shouted angrily. The lights went on. (*when*)

3 I spoilt a film. He was developing it. (*which*)

Letter writing 书信写作

How to begin a letter
写信如何开头

a   Friends should be addressed by their first names: e.g. 'Dear Fred'. Never begin a letter with the words 'Dear Friend'.
给朋友写信要称呼他们的名字，如："亲爱的弗雷德"，决不要以"亲爱的朋友"之类的词语开头。

b   When writing to relations you may begin: Dear Mother, Dear Father, Dear Uncle Fred, Dear Aunt Alice, but never 'Dear Cousin', or 'Dear Cousin Fred'.
给亲戚写信，则可以这样开头：亲爱的妈妈，亲爱的爸爸，亲爱的弗雷德叔叔，亲爱的艾丽丝姨妈；但决不可以称"亲爱的表兄"或"亲爱的弗雷德表兄"。

Exercise 练习

How would you begin letters to: your grandmother, your cousin Elizabeth, your friend Jack, your uncle Tom?
给下列人写信你应如何开头：你的祖母，你的表姐伊丽莎白，你的朋友杰克，你的叔叔汤姆。

Key structures 关键句型

These things always happen. 表示习惯性动作 (**KS26**)（参见第 26 课关键句型）

Unit 3   Lesson 50

Here are some more verbs that tell us what always happens:

下面是一些表示习惯性动作的动词：

belong to, consist of, contain, desire, detest, dislike, hate, hope, love, matter, mean, mind, need, want, wish.

This box *contains* 48 matches. 盒子里有 48 根火柴。   Those papers *belong to* me. 这些报纸是我的。

He *needs* a new pair of shoes. 他需要一双新鞋。   I *hate* writing letters. 我讨厌写信。

Exercises 练习

A How many verbs in the passage tell us what always happens?
课文中有哪些表示习惯性动作的动词？

B What is happening? What always happens? 现在进行时和一般现在时

Give the correct form of the verbs in parentheses. Supply speech marks and commas where necessary and arrange the passage into paragraphs: **(SD26)**

用括号中动词的正确形式填空；需要时可加上引号和逗号，并划分段落（参见第 26 课难点）：

Let's eat here I said to my wife. I _____ (prefer) to have a drink first she answered. That's a good idea I said. I picked up the menu. I _____ (not understand) a thing I said. It's all in Spanish. It _____ (not matter) said my wife. What _____ that word _____ (mean) I asked. I _____ (not know) she answered. We called the waiter and pointed to the word on the menu. Two I said, holding up two fingers. After some time, my wife said suddenly Look! He _____ (bring) us two boiled eggs!

Special difficulties 难点

Words often confused 经常容易混淆的词

Study these examples:
仔细阅读以下例子：

a *Lose, Loose, Miss.*

I don't like *losing* my way. (1.1)

Take care not to *lose* your passport. 注意不要把护照丢了。

Several screws have come *loose*. I'll have to tighten them. 几个螺丝松了，我不得不把它们拧紧。

We haven't seen you for a long time. We have *missed* you. 我们好久没有见到你了，我们想念你。

We must hurry or we'll *miss* the train. 我们必须快一点，不然会误了火车的。

b *Expect* and *Wait for.*

My trip took me longer than I *expected*. (11.2-3)

I am *expecting* Jack to arrive at six o'clock, but I shall not *wait for* him if he is not here by 6.15. 我期待着杰克能在 6 点钟到达，但如果他 6 点 15 分还不到的话，我就不等他了。

Exercise 练习

Choose the correct words in these sentences:
选择正确的词或短语：

1 Hurry up! You'll (lose) (miss) the bus.

2 That doorknob has come (lose) (loose). It will fall off soon.

3 Do you (expect) (wait for) him to change his mind?

4 If you bet on that horse you will (loose) (lose) your money.

5 He (waited) (expected) at the street corner for over half an hour before his girlfriend arrived.

c   My trip took me longer than I expected. (ll.2-3)

Study these examples:

仔细阅读以下例子：

I did the trip in two hours. 我在两小时里完成了这次旅行。

The trip took me two hours. 这次旅行用了我两个小时的时间。

Exercise 练习

Rewrite these sentences so that they begin with *It takes* or *It took*.

改写以下句子，用 It takes 或 It took 来开头。

1 I get to the office in an hour.　　2 I reached Tokyo in fifteen hours.　　3 He wrote the book in six months.

Multiple choice questions 选择题

Comprehension 理解

1 Why did the writer ask the conductor to help him?

(*a*) He didn't know where he was going.　　(*b*) He didn't know where to get off.

(*c*) He had lost his way.　　(*d*) He was the only passenger on the bus.

2 Which word best describes the conductor? He was _____ .

(*a*) helpful　　(*b*) lazy　　(*c*) rude　　(*d*) forgetful

Structure 句型

3 _____ in the country is something he loves.

(*a*) Travelling　　(*b*) Travel　　(*c*) The travelling　　(*d*) To travelling

4 The trip took him longer than he expected. He didn't expect it to last _____ .

(*a*) longer　　(*b*) as long　　(*c*) so long　　(*d*) such a long

5 'Where _____ get off?' I asked. 'I'll tell you where to get off,' answered the conductor.

(*a*) to　　(*b*) for　　(*c*) shall I　　(*d*) in order to

6 I was the only passenger. There weren't _____ more.

(*a*) any　　(*b*) many　　(*c*) lots　　(*d*) a few

7 This is as far as we go. We don't go _____ .

(*a*) any further　　(*b*) more far　　(*c*) further more　　(*d*) so far

Vocabulary 词汇

8 A bus conductor usually _____ .

(*a*) drives a bus　　(*b*) inspects the tickets　　(*c*) buys tickets　　(*d*) collects fares

9 The writer got on the bus, but he didn't know where to _____ .

(*a*) get down　　(*b*) get off　　(*c*) get out of　　(*d*) get over

10 There was a good _____ of the countryside from the front of the bus.

(*a*) sight　　(*b*) view　　(*c*) scene　　(*d*) scenery

11 'It doesn't matter,' I said. I _____ .

(*a*) don't remember　　(*b*) don't know　　(*c*) don't mind　　(*d*) don't matter

12 I prefer to stay on the bus. That's _____ .

(*a*) my favourite　　(*b*) my best　　(*c*) beloved　　(*d*) what I'd like to do best

Lesson 51   Reward for virtue   对美德的奖赏

First listen and then answer the question.

听录音，然后回答以下问题。

Why did Hugh's diet not work?

My friend, Hugh, has always been fat, but things got so bad recently that he decided to go on a diet. He began his diet a week ago. First of all, he wrote out a long list of all the foods which were forbidden. The list included most of the things Hugh loves: butter, potatoes,
5 rice, beer, milk, chocolate, and sweets. Yesterday I paid him a visit. I rang the bell and was not surprised to see that Hugh was still as fat as ever. He led me into his room and hurriedly hid a large parcel under his desk. It was obvious that he was very embarrassed. When I asked him what he was doing, he smiled guiltily and then put the parcel on the desk. He explained that his
10 diet was so strict that he had to reward himself occasionally. Then he showed me the contents of the parcel. It contained five large bars of chocolate and three bags of sweets!

The list included the things Hugh loves

New words and expressions 生词和短语

reward (title) /rɪˈwɔːd/ *n.* 报偿
virtue (title) /ˈvɜːtʃuː/ *n.* 美德
diet (l.2) /ˈdaɪət/ *n.* 节食
forbid (l.3) /fəˈbɪd/ (forbade /fəˈbæd/, forbidden /fəˈbɪdn/ *v.* 禁止
hurriedly (l.7) /ˈhʌrɪdli/ *adv.* 匆忙地

embarrass (l.8) /ɪmˈbærəs/ *v.* 使尴尬
guiltily (l.9) /ˈgɪltɪli/ *adv.* 内疚地
strict (l.10) /strɪkt/ *adj.* 严格的
reward (l.10) /rɪˈwɔːd/ *v.* 给奖赏
occasionally (l.10) /əˈkeɪʒənəli/ *adv.* 偶尔地

Notes on the text 课文注释

1 Reward for virtue, virtue 作 "美德" 讲, 此处指 "节食" 一事。

2 but things got so bad, 但是情况变得如此糟糕。动词 get 作 "变得","成为" 讲。

3 go on a diet（= be on a diet），实行节食。

4 first of all, 首先。

5 I paid him a visit. 我去拜访他。

6 as fat as ever, 像以往一样胖, 其中的 as ever 实际上是状语从句 as he ever was 的省略形式。

7 It was obvious that he was very embarrassed. 显然他感到很尴尬。that 引导的从句是一个名词性从句, 在句子中作主语, it 是先行主语。

参考译文

　　我的朋友休一直很胖, 但是近来情况变得越发糟糕, 以致他决定节食。他是一星期前开始节食的。首先, 他开列了一张长长的单子, 上面列了所有禁吃的食物。这张单子上的大多数食物都是休喜欢吃的: 黄油、土豆、米饭、啤酒、牛奶、巧克力和糖果。昨天我去看望了他。我按响了门铃, 当看到休仍和往常一样胖时, 我并不感到惊奇。他把我领进屋, 慌忙把一个大包藏到了桌子下面。显然他感到很尴尬。当我问他正干什么时, 他内疚地笑了，然后把那个大包拿到了桌上。他解释说，他的饮食控制得太严格了，以致不得不偶尔奖赏自己一下。接着他给我看了包里的东西。里面装了5大块巧克力和3袋糖果!

Summary writing 摘要写作

Answer these questions *in not more than 65 words*.

回答下列问题，将答案组成一个段落，不要超过65个单词。

1 Is Hugh fat or not? Has he gone on a diet or not? (*so ... that*)

2 Has he forbidden himself all the foods he likes, or has he forbidden himself all the foods he does not like? Has he lost weight or not? (*but*)

3 What did he hide under his desk when the writer visited him yesterday?

4 Did the parcel contain chocolate and sweets, or did it contain biscuits?

5 Why did Hugh say that he had to reward himself occasionally? (*because*)

Composition 作文

Write two or three sentences using the ideas given below.

用以下词组写出2至3个句子来。

I invited a friend to dinner — expensive restaurant — good meal — asked for the bill — not enough money — borrowed some from my guest.

Letter writing 书信写作

How to begin a letter: If you are writing to a person you do not know very well, you should begin as follows: Dear Mr. Brown, Dear Miss Williams, Dear Mrs. Smith. Always put a comma after the name.

写信如何开头： 如果你给一个不很熟悉的人写信，应按如下方式开头：亲爱的布朗先生，亲爱的威廉斯小姐，亲爱的史密斯夫人。在姓名之后总要加上一个逗号。

Exercise 练习

How would you begin a letter to: your sister, your friend Bill, your employer, your old headmaster?

给下列人写信应如何开头：你的姐姐，你的朋友比尔，你的老板，你的老校长。

Key structures 关键句型

What happened? 一般过去时 (KS27)（参见第27课关键句型）

Study these sentences carefully. The verbs in italics tell us what happened:

仔细阅读以下句子，用斜体印出的动词表示过去发生的动作：

I *got on* the bus and *sat* down. 我上了公共汽车并坐了下来。

The magazine I *ordered was sent* to the wrong address. 我订的杂志送错了地址。

A fire *broke out* in our town recently and a large factory *was burnt* to the ground. 最近我们的城里起了一场大火，一家大工厂被彻底烧毁了。

Exercises 练习

A Underline the verbs in the passage that tell us *what happened*.

画出课文中所有表示过去发生的动作的动词。

B Give the correct form of the verbs in parentheses. Do not refer to the passage until you finish the exercise:

用括号中动词的正确形式填空, 完成练习后再对照课文, 核对你的答案:

My friend, Hugh, has always been fat, but things _____ (get) so bad recently that he _____ (decide) to go on a diet. He _____ (begin) his diet a week ago. First of all, he _____ (write) out a long list of all the foods which were forbidden. The list _____ (include) most of the things Hugh loves. Yesterday I _____ (pay) him a visit. I _____ (ring) the bell and _____ (not surprise) to see that Hugh was still as fat as ever. He _____ (lead) me into his room and hurriedly _____ (hide) a large parcel under his desk. It was obvious that he _____ (embarrass). When I _____ (ask) him what he was doing, he _____ (smile) guiltily and then _____ (put) the parcel on the desk. He _____ (explain) that his diet _____ (be) so strict that he _____ (have to) reward himself occasionally. Then he _____ (show) me the contents of the parcel. It _____ (contain) five large bars of chocolate and three bags of sweets!

Special difficulties 难点

Verbs often confused 经常容易混淆的动词

Study these examples:

仔细阅读以下例子:

a *Raise* and *Rise*.

That boy always *raises* his hand when I ask a question. 当我提问时, 那个男孩总举手。

That shelf was too low so we *raised* it a few inches. 那个架子太低了, 因此我们把它架高了几英寸。

Heavy rains *have raised* the level of the river this year. 大雨使今年河水的水位上升了。

I always *rise* at six o'clock. 我总是 6 点起床。

After the concert, evrybody *rose* and clapped. 音乐会之后, 大家起立鼓掌。

The sun *has* just risen. 太阳刚刚升起。

b *Lay* and *Lie*.

Lay those parcels on the floor, please. 请把那些包放在地板上。

Where's my book? I *laid* it on that shelf a moment ago. 我的书在什么地方? 刚才我把它放在那个书架上了。

Haven't you *laid* the table yet? 你还没有把桌子摆好吗?

It's nice to get up in the morning, but it's nicer to *lie* in bed. 早上起床固然不错, 但躺在床上更好。

I *lay* in bed till 10 o'clock last Sunday morning. 上星期日早晨, 我一直躺到 10 点才起床。

The children are playing a game. They've all just *lain* on the grass. 孩子们正在玩游戏, 刚才他们都躺到草地上了。

c *Beat* and *Win*.

Arsenal *beat* Manchester United last Saturday. 上星期六阿森纳队战胜了曼彻斯特联队。

Arsenal *won* the game. 阿森纳队赢了这场比赛。

Exercise 练习

Choose the correct verbs in the following sentences:

选择正确的动词:

1 Everybody (raised) (rose) when he entered the room.

2 I have been (laying) (lying) here for half an hour.

3 Mrs. Jones (laid) (lay) the table before breakfast.

4 The aeroplane (raised) (rose) into the air.

5 I'm not very good at chess. He always (wins) (beats) me.

6 'Did you (win) (beat) or lose?' I asked.

Multiple choice questions 选择题

Comprehension 理解

1 The writer's friend, Hugh, decided to go on a diet _____ .

(a) and he lost a little weight   (b) but he didn't lose any weight at all

(c) but he didn't lose much weight   (d) and he lost a lot of weight

2 Hugh _____ .

(a) has avoided eating chocolate and sweets   (b) has kept to a strict diet

(c) hasn't kept to a strict diet   (d) has been very strict with himself

Structure 句型

3 My friend, Hugh, has always been fat. He still _____ fat.

(a) was   (b) has   (c) has been   (d) is

4 How long ago _____ his diet?

(a) will he begin   (b) has he begun   (c) was he beginning   (d) did he begin

5 Most of the things he loves were included _____ the list.

(a) into   (b) on   (c) with   (d) in

6 Where did he _____ the parcel?

(a) hide   (b) hidden   (c) hid   (d) hiding

7 He smiled guiltily. He felt _____ .

(a) guilt   (b) guiltily   (c) guiltless   (d) guilty

Vocabulary 词汇

8 The foods were forbidden. He wasn't _____ to eat them.

(a) left   (b) let   (c) allowed   (d) aloud

9 I paid him a visit. I _____ .

(a) visited him   (b) made him visit   (c) did him a visit   (d) paid for a visit

10 He led me into his room. He _____ me into his room.

(a) steered   (b) pulled   (c) drove   (d) showed

11 He was very embarrassed. He felt _____ .

(a) shy   (b) shameful   (c) hot   (d) uncomfortable

12 He had to reward himself occasionally. He had to reward himself _____ .

(a) again and again   (b) now and again   (c) once again   (d) over and over again

Sentence structure 句子结构

Join these sentences, then check your answer against the text.

连接以下句子，然后对照课文第 8-9 行，核对你的答案。

I asked him what he was doing. He smiled guiltily. Then he put the parcel on the desk.

Lesson 52   A pretty carpet   漂亮的地毯

First listen and then answer the question.

听录音，然后回答以下问题。

What is the writer's carpet made of?

We have just moved into a new house and I have been working hard all morning. I have been trying to get my new room in order. This has not been easy because I own over a thousand books. To make matters worse, the room is rather small, so I have tempo-
5   rarily put my books on the floor. At the moment, they cover every inch of floor space and I actually have to walk on them to get in or out of the room. A short while ago, my sister helped me to carry one of my old bookcases up the stairs. She went into my room and got a big surprise when she saw all those books on the floor. 'This is the prettiest carpet I have ever seen,'
10   she said. She gazed at it for some time then added, 'You don't need bookcases at all. You can sit here in your spare time and read the carpet!'

You can sit here and read the carpet

New words and expressions   生词和短语

temporarily (11.4-5) /'tempərərɪli/ *adv.* 暂时地

inch (1.6) /ɪntʃ/ *n.* 英寸（度量单位）

space (1.6) /speɪs/ *n.* 空间

actually (1.6) /'æktʃuəli/ *adv.* 实际上

Notes on the text   课文注释

1   I have been working hard all morning. 我辛辛苦苦地干了整整一个上午。句中用了现在完成进行时，用来强调动作在某一段时间内一直在进行，而且动作有现在的结果。

2   get ... in order, 把……整理好。

3   to make matters worse, 更糟糕的是。

4   in your spare time, 你空闲的时候。

参考译文

我们刚刚搬进一所新房子，我辛辛苦苦地干了整整一个上午。我试图把我的新房间收拾整齐，但这并不容易，因为我有1,000多本书。更糟糕的是房间还非常小，所以我暂时把书放在了地板上。这会儿，书把地板的每一点空隙都占据了，我实际上是踩着这些书进出房间的。几分钟前，我妹妹帮我把一个旧书橱抬上了楼。她走进我的房间，当她看到地板上的那些书时，大吃一惊。"这是我见过的最漂亮的地毯，"她说。她盯着"地毯"看了一会儿，又说："你根本用不着书橱，空闲时你可以坐在这儿读地毯！"

Summary writing 摘要写作

Answer these questions *in not more than 75 words*.

回答下列问题, 将答案组成一个段落, 不要超过 75 个单词。

1 Has the writer been trying to get his new room in order all morning or not?

2 Why has this proved difficult? Do they cover every inch of floor space at the moment or not? (*because ... which*)

3 What did his sister help him to do a short while ago?

4 Did she get a surprise when she saw his room or not? Did she think that the books made a pretty carpet, or did she find the room untidy? (*but*)

Composition 作文

Rewrite the following sentences using the joining words in parentheses:

用括号中的连词改写以下句子:

1 I moved into a new room. Three workmen brought my things upstairs. (*When*)

2 There were several cases of clothes. There were hundreds of books. (*not only ... but ... as well*)

3 The pile was as high as the ceiling. I could not get into my room. (*Since*)

Letter writing 书信写作

How would you begin letters to: your cousin Ted, your bank manager, your friend Mary, your grandfather?

给下列人写信时你如何开头: 你的表弟特德, 你的银行经理, 你的朋友玛丽, 你的祖父?

Key structures 关键句型

What has happened? What has been happening? 现在完成时和现在完成进行时
(KS28) (参见第28课关键句型)

Compare these pairs of sentences:

比较以下各对句子:

It *hasn't rained* for six weeks. 已经 6 个星期没有下雨了。

It *has been raining* hard since yesterday and it is still raining. 昨天以来一直下雨, 而且现在还在下着。

He *has rung* me up five times since 12 o'clock. 从 12 点以来他已经给我打了 5 次电话了。

He *has been ringing* me up all morning. 整个上午他一直在给我打电话。

He *has never stayed* at this hotel before. 他从未在这家酒店住过。

He *has been staying* at this hotel for the last three weeks. 过去的 3 个星期他一直住在这家酒店。

I *have read* Oliver Twist five times. 《雾都孤儿》我已读了 5 遍。

I *have been reading* all afternoon. 整个下午我一直在看书。

Exercises 练习

A Underline the verbs in the passage that tell us *what has happened* and *what has been happening*.

画出课文中表示现在完成时和现在完成进行时的动词。

B Give the correct form of the verbs in parentheses. Do not refer to the passage until you finish the exercise:

用括号中动词的正确形式填空, 完成练习后再对照课文, 核对你的答案:

We have just _____ (move) into a new house and I _____ (work) hard all morning. I _____ (try) to get my new room in order. This _____ (not be) easy because I own over a thousand books. The room is rather small, so I have temporarily _____ (put) my books on the floor. My sister got a big surprise when she saw all those books on the floor. 'This is the prettiest carpet I ever _____ (see),' she said.

C What has happened? What has been happening? Give the correct form of the verbs in parentheses:
现在完成时和现在完成进行时。用括号中动词的正确形式填空：

    'I _____ (explain) this to you several times already,' said the teacher. 'I hope you _____ (understand) it now.' Then he looked at a little boy at the back of the class. '_____ you _____ (listen), Jones?' he asked. 'Here is a simple problem: "Sally _____ (work) in an office for thirty-four weeks. In that time, she _____ (earn) £300 a week. How much _____ she _____ (earn) so far?" '

    'Please, sir,' Jones answered, 'I can only answer your first question. I _____ (not listen).'

Special difficulties 难点

I have been working hard all morning. (ll.1-2) 形容词和相应的副词

Compare these pairs of sentences:
对比以下例句：

She has a beautiful voice. She sings beautifully. 她的嗓音很好。她唱歌很动听。

He is a slow worker. He works slowly. 他是一个迟钝的人。他工作很慢。

He is a hard worker. He works hard. 他是一个勤奋的人。他工作很努力。

He is a fast driver. He drives fast. 他是一个开快车的人。他开车很快。

Now compare these pairs of sentences:
对比以下例句：

The train arrived very late. 这列火车到得很晚。

Have you travelled by train lately? 最近你有没有乘火车旅行？

He worked very hard. 他工作非常努力。

He hardly ever does any work. 他几乎从不工作。

The plane flew very high. 飞机飞得很高。

He thinks very highly of me. 他对我的评价很好。

He made sure it was safe before he went near. 他确信是安全的以后才走近。

He was nearly run over by a car. 他差一点儿被一辆汽车撞倒。

Exercise 练习

Choose the correct words in the following sentences:
选择正确的词：

1 She dusted the furniture very (careful) (carefully).

2 I hit him very (hardly) (hard).

3 This exercise is not (hard) (hardly).

4 I got home from work very (lately) (late) last night.

5 I (near) (nearly) missed the bus this morning.

6 He ran so (fastly) (fast) no one could keep up with him.

7 I can't jump so (highly) (high).

Multiple choice questions 选择题

Comprehension 理解

1 The writer owns over a thousand books so _____ .

   (*a*) he can't get in and out of his room   (*b*) he is finding it difficult to get his room in order

   (*c*) his sister can't get into his room   (*d*) he can't get them on to his bookcases

2 The writer's sister thinks _____ .

   (*a*) the books look untidy   (*b*) the bookcases aren't big enough

   (*c*) the books make a nice carpet   (*d*) he needs more bookcases than he has

Structure 句型

3 He has been working all morning and he _____ hard.

   (*a*) still works   (*b*) has still worked   (*c*) is still working   (*d*) still worked

4 He's been trying to get his room in order. He wants to _____ .

   (*a*) make it tidy   (*b*) keep it tidy   (*c*) made order   (*d*) keep order

5 His room is rather small. It's _____ room.

   (*a*) a small enough   (*b*) a fairly small   (*c*) terribly small   (*d*) a much smaller

6 She helped him _____ one of his old bookcases up the stairs.

   (*a*) carrying   (*b*) to carrying   (*c*) for carrying   (*d*) carry

7 The writer _____ bookcases.

   (*a*) needn't   (*b*) needs not   (*c*) doesn't need   (*d*) isn't needing

Vocabulary 词汇

8 He has temporarily put his books on the floor. They won't be there _____ .

   (*a*) for a short time   (*b*) long   (*c*) for a few days   (*d*) for a few hours

9 The books cover every inch of floor space. They take up a lot of _____ .

   (*a*) room   (*b*) place   (*c*) area   (*d*) spaces

10 He actually has to walk on them. He can't do _____ .

   (*a*) else   (*b*) different   (*c*) otherwise   (*d*) other

11 She gazed at the carpet for some time. She _____ it.

   (*a*) watched   (*b*) stared at   (*c*) glanced at   (*d*) had a glimpse of

12 You can sit here in your spare time. You can sit here when you're _____ .

   (*a*) working   (*b*) studying   (*c*) not working   (*d*) reading

Sentence structure 句子结构

Rewrite this sentence, then check your answer against the text.

改写以下句子, 完成后对照课文第 3-4 行, 核对你的答案。

What makes matters worse is that the room is rather small.

To _____ .

Lesson 53   Hot snake   触电的蛇

The explanation was very unusual . . .

First listen and then answer the question.

听录音，然后回答以下问题。

What caused the fire?

At last firemen have put out a big forest fire in California. Since then, they have been trying to find out how the fire began. Forest fires are often caused by broken glass or by cigarette ends which people carelessly throw away. Yesterday the firemen examined the
5 ground carefully, but were not able to find any broken glass. They were also quite sure that a cigarette end did not start the fire. This morning, however, a fireman accidentally discovered the cause. He noticed the remains of a snake which was wound round the electric wires of a 16,000-volt power line. In this way, he was able to solve the mystery. The explanation
10 was simple but very unusual. A bird had snatched up the snake from the ground and then dropped it on to the wires. The snake then wound itself round the wires. When it did so, it sent sparks down to the ground and these immediately started a fire.

New words and expressions   生词和短语

hot (title) /hɒt/ *adj.* 带电的，充电的
fireman (l.1) /'faɪəmən/ *n.* 消防队员
cause (l.3) /kɔːz/ *v.* 引起；*n.* 原因
examine (l.4) /ɪg'zæmɪn/ *v.* 检查
accidentally (l.7) /ˌæksɪ'dentli/ *adv.* 意外地，
　　偶然地
remains (l.8) /rɪ'meɪnz/ *n.* 尸体，残骸

wire (l.9) /waɪə/ *n.* 电线
volt (l.9) /vəʊlt/ *n.* 伏特（电压单位）
power line (l.9) /'paʊə-laɪn/ 电力线
solve (l.9) /sɒlv/ *v.* 解决
mystery (l.9) /'mɪstəri/ *n.* 谜
snatch (l.10) /snætʃ/ *v.* 抓住
spark (l.11) /spɑːk/ *n.* 电火花

Notes on the text   课文注释

1   at last, 最后，终于。

2   they have been trying to find out how the fire began, 他们一直试图找出起火的原因。句中短语动词 find out 的宾语是一个从句 how the fire began。

3   broken glass, 碎玻璃。

4   cigarette ends, 烟头。

5   in this way, 就这样。

参考译文

　　消防队员们终于扑灭了加利福尼亚的一场森林大火。从那时起，他们一直试图找出起火的原因。森林火灾时常由破碎的玻璃或人们随手扔掉的香烟头引起。昨天，消防队员仔细查看了地面，但未能发现碎玻璃。他们还十分肯定火灾也不是由烟头引起的。然而今天上午，一个消防队员偶然发现了起火的原因。他发现了缠绕在16,000伏高压线上的一条死蛇。就这样，他解开了起火之谜。解释很简单，却异乎寻常。一只鸟把蛇从地上抓

起来，然后把它扔到了电线上。于是蛇就缠住了几根电线。当它这样做时，把火花送到了地面，这些火花立刻引起了一场大火。

Summary writing　摘要写作

Answer these questions *in not more than 85 words*.
回答下列问题，将答案组成一个段落，不要超过 85 个单词。

1　Have firemen put out a big forest fire in California or not? Have they been trying to discover its cause? (*Now that …*)
2　Was there any evidence that it was started by broken glass or by a cigarette end or not?
3　Who has just solved the mystery? (*However*)
4　What did he notice? Had it been dropped by a bird on to the electric wires or not? (*which*)
5　Where did the snake wind itself? What had it sent to the ground? Did this cause the fire or not? (*In winding … and*)

Composition　作文

Write two or three sentences using the ideas given below:
用以下词组写出 2 至 3 个句子来：
I was smoking in bed — went to sleep — suddenly woke up — the sheet was burning — I jumped up — put the fire out — a big hole in the sheet.

Letter writing　书信写作

Write your home address, the date and the beginning of a letter to a married woman you do not know well.
你给一位不很熟悉的已婚女士写信，写出你家的地址、日期和信的开头。

Key structures　关键句型

What happened? What has happened? (KS29) What has been happening? (KS52) 一般过去时、现在完成时和现在完成进行时（参见第 29，52 课关键句型）

Study these examples:
仔细阅读以下例子：
I stayed at this hotel five years ago. 5 年前我在这家酒店住过。
Have you ever stayed at this hotel? 你曾在这家酒店住过吗？
I have been staying at this hotel for three weeks. 我已在这家酒店住了 3 个星期了。

Exercises　练习

A　Underline the verbs in the passage which tell us *what happened, what has happened,* and *what has been happening*.
　　画出课文中表示一般过去时、现在完成时和现在完成进行时的动词。

B　Give the correct form of the verbs in parentheses. Do not refer to the passage until you finish the exercise:
　　用括号中动词的正确形式填空，完成练习后再对照课文，核对你的答案：
　　At last firemen _____ (put) out a big forest fire in California. Since then, they _____ (try) to find out how the fire _____ (begin). Yesterday the firemen _____ (examine) the ground carefully, but _____ (not be) able to find any broken glass. They _____ (be) also quite sure that a cigarette end _____ (not start) the fire.

C What happened? What has happened? What has been happening? Give the correct form of the verbs in parentheses. Supply speech marks and commas where necessary and arrange the passage into paragraphs. **(KS26)**

一般过去时、现在完成时和现在完成进行时。用括号中动词的正确形式填空，必要时加上引号和逗号，并分段。（参见第 26 课关键句型）

Jack _____ (look) at his watch for the twentieth time. Suddenly Jill _____ (arrive). I _____ (wait) for over an hour he said angrily. You never come on time. Oh, is that so? Jill _____ (answer). _____ (Be) you here at 2.30? Jack _____ (go) red. Well he _____ (say) I _____ (get) here five minutes late myself, but you _____ (not be) here. I _____ (come) here at exactly 2.30 Jill _____ (say) and I _____ (wait) for five minutes, but you _____ (not come). What you _____ (do) since then? Jack _____ (ask). I just _____ (be) to the hairdresser's Jill _____ (answer) brightly.

Special difficulties 难点

Words often confused 经常容易混淆的词

Study these examples:

仔细阅读以下例子：

a *Throw to, Throw at,* and *Throw away.*

Forest fires are often caused by cigarette ends which people carelessly *throw away.* (ll.2-4)

He *threw* the ball *to* me and I caught it. 他把球扔给我，我接住了。

The boy *threw* a stone *at* the window and broke it. 男孩向窗户扔了一块石头把玻璃打碎了。

b *Quite* and *Quiet.*

They were also *quite* sure that a cigarette end did not start the fire. (ll.5-6)

The class kept very *quiet* during the lesson. 上课时全班都很安静。

c *Cause* and *Reason.*

A fireman discovered the *cause* of the fire. (l.7)

What *caused* the fire? 什么原因引起了这场大火？

That is the *reason* why he left. 那是他离开的缘由。

I *reasoned* with him for hours, but I couldn't persuade him to change his mind. 我劝了他几个小时，但我没能说服他改变主意。

d *Drop* and *Fall*

A bird *had dropped* the snake on to the wires. (ll.10-11)

He *fell* down the stairs and broke his leg. 他从楼梯上摔下来，断了一条腿。

Exercise 练习

Use each of the words given above in sentences of your own.

用以上词和词组造句。

Multiple choice questions 选择题

Comprehension 理解

1 Firemen examined the ground carefully because they _____ .

   (*a*) were looking for cigarette ends

   (*b*) were looking for broken glass

(c) wanted to find out what had caused the fire

(d) were looking for a snake

2 The fire had been caused by _____ .

(a) a bird which flew on to the wires

(b) a snake which climbed on to the wires

(c) a bird which was eating a snake

(d) a snake which had been dropped on to the wires by a bird

Structure 句型

3 The firemen have been examining the ground _____ yesterday.

(a) since   (b) for   (c) ago   (d) by

4 Broken glass often _____ fires.

(a) is causing   (b) has caused   (c) causes   (d) is caused by

5 They were quite sure it wasn't a cigarette end. They were _____ .

(a) almost certain   (b) fairly certain   (c) completely certain   (d) nearly certain

6 He was able to solve the mystery. He _____ .

(a) could if he wanted to   (b) could but he didn't want to

(c) succeeded in solving it   (d) didn't succeed in solving it

7 The bird had snatched the snake from the ground. The snake had been _____ the ground.

(a) at   (b) from   (c) over   (d) on

Vocabulary 词汇

8 Firemen have put out the fire. They have _____ .

(a) controlled it   (b) checked it   (c) extinguished it   (d) turned it off

9 Firemen discovered the cause _____ .

(a) today morning   (b) today in the morning

(c) in the morning today   (d) this morning

10 They discovered the cause of the fire accidentally. They discovered it _____ .

(a) by chance   (b) chancily   (c) fortunately   (d) luckily

11 In this way he was able to solve the mystery. _____ he did it.

(a) That's so   (b) Like this   (c) That's how   (d) So

12 The bird had snatched up the snake from the ground. It had _____ it.

(a) taken   (b) pulled   (c) seized   (d) carried

Sentence structure 句子结构

Rewrite this sentence, then check your answer against the text.

改写以下句子, 然后对照课文第11行, 核对你的答案。

In doing so, it sent sparks down to the ground.

When _____ .

Lesson 54 Sticky fingers 黏糊的手指

First listen and then answer the question.

听录音，然后回答以下问题。

What two interruptions did the writer have?

What a mess!

After breakfast, I sent the children to school and then I went to the
shops. It was still early when I returned home. The children were at
school, my husband was at work and the house was quiet. So I
decided to make some meat pies. In a short time I was busy mixing
5 butter and flour and my hands were soon covered with sticky pastry.
At exactly that moment, the telephone rang. Nothing could have
been more annoying. I picked up the receiver between two sticky
fingers and was dismayed when I recognized the voice of Helen
Bates. It took me ten minutes to persuade her to ring back later. At last I hung up the receiver. What a mess!
10 There was pastry on my fingers, on the telephone, and on the doorknobs. I had no sooner got back to the
kitchen than the doorbell rang loud enough to wake the dead. This time it was the postman and he wanted me
to sign for a registered letter!

New words and expressions 生词和短语

sticky (title) /'stɪki/ *adj.* 黏的
finger (title) /'fɪŋgə/ *n.* 手指
pie (l.4) /paɪ/ *n.* 馅饼
mix (l.4) /mɪks/ *v.*（使）混合，拌和
pastry (l.5) /'peɪstri/ *n.* 面糊
annoying (l.7) /ə'nɔɪ-ɪŋ/ *adj.* 恼人的
receiver (l.7) /rɪ'siːvə/ *n.* 电话的话筒

dismay (l.8) /dɪs'meɪ/ *v.* 使失望，使泄气
recognize (l.8) /'rekəgnaɪz/ *v.* 认出，听出
persuade (l.9) /pə'sweɪd/ *v.* 说服，劝说
mess (l.9) /mes/ *n.* 乱七八糟
doorknob (l.10) /'dɔːnɒb/ *n.* 门把手
sign (l.12) /saɪn/ *v.* 签字
register (l.12) /'redʒɪstə/ *v.* 挂号邮寄

Notes on the text 课文注释

1 The children were at school, my husband was at work. 孩子在上学，我丈夫在上班。
2 at exactly that moment, 恰恰在此时。
3 I picked up the receiver between two sticky fingers. 我用两个沾满面糊的手指捏起话筒。
4 ring back later, 晚一点再来电话。
5 What a mess! 真是糟糕透了，真狼狈。
6 I had no sooner got back to the kitchen than the doorbell rang loud enough to wake the dead. 我刚回厨房，门
铃又响了起来，响声足以把死人唤醒。no sooner ... than ... 的句型有 "刚……就……" 的意思。短语 loud
enough to wake the dead 用来作状语，修饰 rang。注意 enough 作为副词要用在形容词或副词之后。
7 a registered letter, 挂号信。

参考译文

早饭后，我送孩子们上学，然后就去了商店。我回到家时，时间还早。孩子们在上学，我丈夫在上班，家里

清静得很。于是我决定做些肉馅饼。不一会儿我就忙着调拌起了黄油和面粉，很快我的手上就沾满了黏黏的面糊。恰恰在此时，电话铃响了。没有什么能比这更烦人了。我用两个沾满面糊的手指捏起了话筒。当我听出是海伦·贝茨的声音时，非常丧气。我用了 10 分钟的时间才说服她过会儿再来电话。我终于挂上了话筒。真是糟糕透了！我的手指上、电话机上以及门的把手上，都沾上了面糊。我刚回到厨房，门铃又响了起来，响声足以把死人唤醒。这次是邮递员，他要我签收一封挂号信！

Summary writing 摘要写作

Answer these questions *in not more than 75 words.*
回答下列问题，将答案组成一个段落，不要超过 75 个单词。

1 Did the writer return home from the shops or not? What did she begin to make? (*As soon as*)

2 Did the telephone ring soon afterwards or not? Were her fingers very sticky or not? (*When*)

3 How long did she spend talking to Helen Bates on the telephone?

4 Did she look at the mess she had made or not? (*After that*)

5 What was covered with pastry?

6 Who rang the doorbell? (*Just then*)

7 What did he want her to do?

Composition 作文

Rewrite the following sentences using the joining words in parentheses:
用括号中的连词改写以下句子：

1 I put the cake in the oven. I forgot all about it. (*After putting*)

2 Two hours had passed. I smelled something burning. (*When*)

3 I went into the kitchen. I found it full of smoke. (*On going*)

Letter writing 书信写作

In the first paragraph of your letter you should refer either to a letter you have received or to an event which has prompted you to write. Look at the example below. Note where the first paragraph begins:
在信的第一段里，你应该提及你已经收到的一封信或促使你回信的某一事件。请看下面的实例，注意第一段开头处：

Dear Fred,

I was very pleased to learn that you are well.

Exercise 练习

Write your address, the date and the first sentence of a letter to a friend beginning: 'Thank you for ...'.
写上你的地址、日期和给朋友的一封信的第一句话，用 "Thank you for" 开头。

Key structures 关键句型

A, The, Some and Any (KS30)（参见第 30 课关键句型）

a *Some* and *Any.* **(KS30a, SD9)**（参见第 30 课关键句型 a 和第 9 课难点）

Study the use of *some* and *any* in these sentences:
研究 some 和 any 在以下句子中的用法：

Did you get *any* information? I want *some* information. 你有任何消息吗？我想知道点消息。

Is there *any* news in the paper? There is *some* interesting news in the paper. 报上有什么消息吗? 报上有些有趣的消息。

Did the storm do *any* damage? The storm did *some* damage to the crops. 风暴是否造成损失? 风暴给庄稼带来了一些损失。

Did you do *any* work yesterday? I did *some* work before breakfast. 昨天你干活了吗? 我在早饭前干了点活。

Did you bring *any* luggage? I have *some* luggage in the car. 你带行李了吗? 我在汽车里有行李。

b   Compare these pairs of sentences:
在英文中, 部分形容词前加定冠词 the, 用来表示一个群体。对比以下各对句子:

He was very *poor* years ago, but now he is *a rich man*. 几年前他很穷, 但现在他成了一个富人。

The rich should help *the* poor. 富人应该帮助穷人。

She was born *deaf* and *blind*. 她生下来就失聪、失明。

There are many organizations to help *the* deaf and *the* blind. 有许多组织帮助聋人和盲人。

c   Compare these pairs of sentences:
对比以下各对句子:

The school in our village was built last year. 我们村的那所学校是去年建的。

The children went *to school* early this morning. 孩子们一早去上学了。

We need *a new cinema* and *a new theatre*. 我们需要一座新的电影院, 一座新的剧场。

I often go to *the cinema* and *the theatre*. 我经常光顾电影院和剧场。

d   Compare these sentences:
对比以下句子:

It is *the most interesting* exhibition I have ever seen. 这是我参观过的最有趣的展览。

Most people enjoyed it. 大多数人都欣赏它。

It is *the biggest* shop in London. 这是伦敦最大的商店。

Most shops are closed on Saturday afternoons. 大多数商店星期六下午不营业。

Exercises 练习

A   Underline the words *a, the* and *some* in the passage.
画出课文中的 a, the 和 some。

B   Put in the words *a, the* and *some* where necessary. Do not refer to the passage until you finish the exercise:
在需要的地方填上 a, the 或 some, 完成练习后再对照课文, 核对你的答案:

After _____ breakfast, I sent _____ children to school and then l went to _____ shops. It was still early when I returned home. _____ children were at _____ school, my husband was at _____ work, and _____ house was quiet. So I decided to make _____ meat pies. In _____ short time I was busy mixing _____ butter and _____ flour and my hands were soon covered with _____ sticky pastry. At exactly that moment, _____ telephone rang. Nothing could have been more annoying. I picked up _____ receiver between _____ two sticky fingers and was dismayed when I recognized _____ voice of Helen Bates. It took me ten minutes to persuade her to ring back later. At last I hung up _____ receiver. What _____ mess! There was _____ pastry on my fingers, on _____ telephone, and on _____ doorknobs. I had no sooner got back to _____ kitchen than _____ doorbell rang loud enough to wake _____ dead. This time it was _____ postman and he wanted me to sign for _____ registered letter!

Multiple choice questions 选择题

Comprehension 理解

1 The telephone rang _____ .

  (*a*) at a convenient time   (*b*) when the house was empty

  (*c*) when the tarts were in the oven   (*d*) at an inconvenient time

2 Everything got into a mess because _____ .

  (*a*) the writer was making meat pies

  (*b*) the writer was interrupted several times while making meat pies

  (*c*) the writer answered the telephone

  (*d*) the writer opened the front door

Structure 句型

3 _____ breakfast is the first meal of the day.

  (*a*) The   (*b*) A   (*c*) This   (*d*) –

4 She returned home. She was _____ home all morning.

  (*a*) to   (*b*) at   (*c*) in   (*d*) on

5 Nothing could have been more annoying. It was _____ annoying thing that could have happened.

  (*a*) the more   (*b*) more   (*c*) most   (*d*) the most

6 Whose voice did she recognize? Helen _____ .

  (*a*) Bate's   (*b*) Bates'   (*c*) Bates   (*d*) Bate

7 She had hardly got back to the kitchen _____ the doorbell rang.

  (*a*) when   (*b*) than   (*c*) as   (*d*) as soon as

Vocabulary 词汇

8 She was busy mixing butter and flour. She was _____ .

  (*a*) joining them   (*b*) uniting them   (*c*) unifying them   (*d*) putting them together

9 Pastry is as sticky as _____ .

  (*a*) ink   (*b*) water   (*c*) glue   (*d*) flour

10 She was dismayed when she heard Helen Bates. She felt _____ .

  (*a*) pity   (*b*) sorry   (*c*) ill   (*d*) tired

11 She hung up the receiver. This means she _____ .

  (*a*) let it hang   (*b*) didn't put it back   (*c*) held it   (*d*) put it back in its place

12 She has just _____ up the receiver.

  (*a*) hanged   (*b*) hang   (*c*) hanging   (*d*) hung

Sentence structure 句子结构

Join these sentences, then check your answer against the text.

连接以下句子, 然后对照课文第 7-9 行, 核对你的答案。

I picked up the receiver between two sticky fingers. I was dismayed. I recognized the voice of Helen Bates.

Lesson 55 Not a gold mine 并非金矿

First listen and then answer the question.

听录音，然后回答以下问题。

What did the team find?

Dreams of finding lost treasure almost came true recently. A new machine called 'The Revealer' has been invented and it has been used to detect gold which has been buried in the ground. The machine was used in a cave near the seashore where — it is said — pirates
5 used to hide gold. The pirates would often bury gold in the cave and then fail to collect it. Armed with the new machine, a search party went into the cave hoping to find buried treasure. The leader of the party was examining the soil near the entrance to the cave when the machine showed that there was gold under the ground. Very excited, the party dug a hole two feet deep. They
10 finally found a small gold coin which was almost worthless. The party then searched the whole cave thoroughly but did not find anything except an empty tin trunk. In spite of this, many people are confident that 'The Revealer' may reveal something of value fairly soon.

almost worthless

New words and expressions 生词和短语

gold (title) /gəʊld/ n. 金子

mine (title) /maɪn/ n. 矿

treasure (l.1) /'treʒə/ n. 财宝

revealer (l.2) /rɪ'viːlə/ n. 探测器

invent (l.2) /ɪn'vent/ v. 发明

detect (l.3) /dɪ'tekt/ v. 探测

bury (l.3) /'beri/ v. 埋藏

cave (l.4) /keɪv/ n. 山洞

seashore (l.4) /'siːʃɔː/ n. 海岸

pirate (l.5) /'paɪərət/ n. 海盗

arm (l.6) /ɑːm/ v. 武装

soil (l.8) /sɔɪl/ n. 泥土

entrance (l.8) /'entrəns/ n. 入口

finally (l.10) /'faɪnəli/ adv. 最后

worthless (l.10) /'wɜːθləs/ adj. 毫无价值的

thoroughly (l.10) /'θʌrəli/ adv. 彻底地

trunk (l.11) /trʌŋk/ n. 行李箱

confident (l.11) /'kɒnfɪdənt/ adj. 有信心的

value (l.12) /'væljuː/ n. 价值

Notes on the text 课文注释

1 Dreams of finding lost treasure almost came true recently. 最近，找到失踪宝藏的梦想差一点儿变成了现实。come true, 变成现实。

2 it is said 是插入语，当"据说"讲。课文中用破折号把插入语与正文隔开，给人以临时插入的感觉。

3 The pirates would often bury gold in the cave and then fail to collect it. 海盗们过去常把金子埋藏在洞里，但后来却没能取走。would 表示过去的习惯性动作，fail 后面接动词不定式表示否定。

4 armed with the new machine, 由于装备着这台新机器。这里过去分词短语作状语，表示伴随状态。

5 hoping to find buried treasure, 希望能找到埋藏的金子。现在分词短语作状语，表示目的。

6 a hole two feet deep, 两英尺深的坑。

参考译文

最近，找到失踪宝藏的梦想差一点儿变成现实。一种叫"探宝器"的新机器已经发明出来，并被人们用来探测地下埋藏的金子。在靠近海边的一个据说过去海盗常在里面藏金子的岩洞里，这种机器被派上了用场。海盗们过去常把金子埋藏在那个洞里，可后来却没能取走。一支用这种新机器装备起来的探宝队进入了这个岩洞，希望找到埋藏着的金子。当这个队的队长正在检查洞口附近的土壤时，那台机器显示出地下埋有金子。队员们异常激动，就地挖了一个两英尺深的坑，但最后找到的是一枚几乎一钱不值的小金币。队员们接着又把整个洞彻底搜寻了一遍，但除了一只空铁皮箱外什么也没找到。尽管如此，很多人仍然相信"探宝器"很快就会探出值钱的东西来。

Summary writing 摘要写作

Answer these questions *in not more than 65 words*.
回答下列问题，将答案组成一个段落，不要超过 65 个单词。

1 Is 'The Revealer' a new machine or an old machine? Is it used for detecting buried gold or not? (*which*)

2 Did a search party use this machine or not? Where did they try to find gold recently? (*Using this machine …*)

3 Did they examine the cave thoroughly or not? Did they only find a small gold coin? Was it valuable or was it practically worthless? (*Although … which*)

4 Do many people believe that the machine may reveal something of value soon or not? (*However*)

Composition 写作

Write two or three sentences using the ideas given below:
用以下词组写出 2 至 3 个句子来：
I was digging in the garden — lost a gold ring — searched everywhere — dug up the garden — did not find it — found a valuable old coin instead.

Letter writing 书信写作

Arrange this heading in the correct order:
按书信要求排列以下信头：
Sevenoaks, 17 Bunyan St., England, Kent, 27th March, 19__ .

Now write the first sentence of a letter to a friend beginning: 'I was very pleased to ...'
写出给朋友的信的第一句话，用"I was very pleased to ..."开头。

Key structures 关键句型

Pirates would often bury gold in the cave and then fail to collect it. 表示过去习惯性动作

A　Study these sentences carefully:
仔细阅读以下句子：
I dropped my briefcase as I was getting off the bus. (**KS7**)（参见第 7 课关键句型）
I *used to* go to work by bus. Now I go by car. (**KS31**)（参见第 31 课关键句型）
I have given up smoking. I *used to* smoke very heavily. 我已戒了烟。过去我抽得很厉害。(**KS31**)（参见第 31 课关键句型）

B When we refer to a definite time in the past, we can sometimes use *would* in place of *used to*. We cannot, for instance, use *would* in this sentence:

当我们提到过去某一特定时间时，我们有时可用 would 来代替 used to。但是，我们不能在下面这个句子中使用 would：

This sort of novel *used to* be very popular. 这种小说过去很流行。

But note the use of *would* in these sentences: 请注意 would 在下列句子中的用法：

When I was young I used to have a lot more free time than I do now. I used to live near my work and *would* always get home early. Sometimes I *would* do a bit of gardening or go for a long walk. Now I never have time for anything like that. 当我年轻的时候，我常有比现在多很多的空闲时间。我过去住得离工作的地方很近，总是很早回家。有时我在花园里干点园艺，或散散步。现在我从来没有时间去做这些事了。

Exercises 练习

A Underline the verbs in the passage which tell us *what happened, what was happening* and *what used to/would happen*.

画出课文中表示一般过去时、过去进行时和过去习惯性动作的动词。

B Give the correct form of the verbs in parentheses. Do not refer to the passage until you finish the exercise:

用括号中动词的正确形式填空，完成练习后再对照课文，核对你的答案：

The machine _____ (use) in a cave near the seashore where — it is said — pirates _____ (hide) gold. The pirates often _____ (bury) gold in the cave and then _____ (fail) to collect it. Armed with the new machine, a search party _____ (go) into the cave hoping to find buried treasure. The leader of the party _____ (examine) the soil near the entrance to the cave when the machine _____ (show) that there _____ (be) gold under the ground. Very excited, the party _____ (dig) a hole two feet deep. They finally _____ (find) a small gold coin which was almost worthless.

Special difficulties 难点

Words often confused 经常容易混淆的词

a *I use, I am used to, I used to.*

Study these examples:

细读以下例句：

The machine has been *used* to detect gold which has been buried in the ground. The machine was *used* in a cave near the seashore where — it is said — pirates *used to* hide gold. (11.3-5）

I am *used to* staying up late. **(KS44)** （参见第 44 课关键句型）

I am *used to* looking after myself. 我习惯于自己照料自己。

She didn't like this district at first, but she is *used to* it now. 她开始时不喜欢这个地区，但现在已经习惯了。

Exercise 练习

Choose the correct form of the verbs given in parentheses:

选择正确的动词：

1 He (is used to) (used to) work sixteen hours a day.

2 I (use to) (used to) see him often.

3 He always (uses) (used to) scented soap.

4 He (used to) (is used to) buy two bars of chocolate a day.

5 I couldn't stand the noise at first but I (am used to) (used to) it now.

6 I (am used to) (used to) swimming in cold water.

b *Gold* and *Golden*.

Study these examples:

细读以下例句：

It has been used to detect *gold*. (11.2-3)

He has a *gold* watch. 他有一块金表。

He missed a *golden* opportunity. 他错过了一次绝好的机会。

Exercise 练习

Supply *gold* or *golden*:

用 gold 或 golden 填空：

1 All that glitters is not _____ .

2 Silence is _____ .

Multiple choice questions 选择题

Comprehension 理解

1 The search party was looking for _____ .

(*a*) gold   (*b*) a gold mine   (*c*) pirates   (*d*) a tin trunk

2 The search for gold proved that 'The Revealer' _____ .

(*a*) works very well   (*b*) doesn't work well   (*c*) is quite useless   (*d*) isn't very good

Structure 句型

3 'The Revealer' has been used for _____ gold.

(*a*) to detect   (*b*) detecting   (*c*) detect   (*d*) detected

4 Pirates used to hide gold there, _____ .

(*a*) and they always do   (*b*) and they still do

(*c*) and they still do sometimes   (*d*) that's what they would do

5 They hoped to find buried treasure. They hoped they _____ it.

(*a*) would find   (*b*) had found   (*c*) will find   (*d*) are going to find

6 Where did they _____ the hole?

(*a*) dig   (*b*) digging   (*c*) dug   (*d*) have dug

7 How _____ was the hole?

(*a*) deeply   (*b*) depth   (*c*) deep   (*d*) down

Vocabulary 词汇

8 'The Revealer' is a very good _____ .

(*a*) machine   (*b*) engine   (*c*) machinery   (*d*) mechanic

9 The leader of the party was examining the soil. He was _____ .

(*a*) testing it   (*b*) looking at it carefully (*c*) watching it   (*d*) trying it

10 The coin was almost worthless. So it was of small _____ .

(*a*) worthy   (*b*) honour   (*c*) price   (*d*) value

11 They searched the cave thoroughly. They searched it _____ .

(*a*) completely   (*b*) across   (*c*) inside   (*d*) finally

12 Some people are confident. They _____ the machine will be useful.

(*a*) confide   (*b*) believe   (*c*) confuse   (*d*) confess

Lesson 56　Faster than sound!　比声音还快

First listen and then answer the question.

听录音，然后回答以下问题。

How fast did the winning car go?

Once a year, a race is held for old cars. A lot of cars entered for this race last year and there was a great deal of excitement just before it began. One of the most handsome cars was a Rolls-Royce Silver Ghost. The most unusual car was a Benz which had only three
5　wheels. Built in 1885, it was the oldest car taking part. After a great many loud explosions, the race began. Many of the cars broke down on the course and some drivers spent more time *under* their cars than *in* them! A few cars, however, completed the race. The winning car reached a speed of forty miles an hour — much faster than any of its rivals. It sped downhill at the
10　end of the race and its driver had a lot of trouble trying to stop it. The race gave everyone a great deal of pleasure. It was very different from modern car races but no less exciting.

It was different from modern car races

New words and expressions　生词和短语

sound (title) /saʊnd/ n. 声音
excitement (l.2) /ɪk'saɪtmənt/ n. 激动，兴奋
handsome (l.3) /'hænsəm/ adj. 漂亮的；美观的
Rolls-Royce (l.3) /ˌrəʊlz-'rɔɪs/ 劳斯莱斯
Benz (l.4) /benz/ n. 奔驰
wheel (l.5) /wiːl/ n. 轮子

explosion (l.6) /ɪk'spləʊʒən/ n. 爆炸，轰响
course (l.7) /kɔːs/ n. 跑道；行程
rival (l.9) /'raɪvəl/ n. 对手
speed (l.9) /spiːd/ (sped /sped/, sped) v. 疾驶
downhill (l.9) /ˌdaʊn'hɪl/ adv. 下坡

Notes on the text　课文注释

1　once a year, 每年一次。

2　A lot of cars entered for this race last year. 去年许多车参加了这项比赛。

3　a great deal of, 大量的，后面接不可数名词。

4　break down, 抛锚，出故障。

5　some drivers spent more time *under* their cars than *in* them! 有些驾驶员花在汽车底下的时间比坐在车子里面的时间还长。under the car 是指在车下面修理，in the car 是指正常驾驶。句中的 under 和 in 都是斜体，主要是用来对比，有强调的意味，要重读。

6　its driver had a lot of trouble trying to stop it, 驾驶员费了很大劲才把车停了下来。

7　but no less exciting, 但激动人心的程度并不亚于现代汽车大赛。这是一句省略句，完整的句子应是 but it was no less exciting than modern car races。

参考译文

　　旧式汽车的比赛每年举行一次。去年有很多汽车参加了这项比赛。比赛开始之前，人们异常激动。最漂亮的汽车之一是劳斯莱斯银灵系列的车，而最不寻常的一辆则要属只有 3 只轮子的奔驰牌汽车了。该车造于

1885 年, 是参赛车中最老的一辆。在好一阵喧闹的爆炸声之后, 比赛开始了。很多汽车在途中就抛了锚, 而有些驾驶员花在车汽车底下的时间比坐在汽车里面的时间还长。然而还是有几辆汽车跑完了全程。获胜的那辆车达到了时速 40 英里——远远超过任何对手。它在接近终点时, 冲下了山坡, 驾驶员费了好大劲才把车停下来。这次比赛使每个人都挺开心。它虽然与现代汽车比赛大不相同, 但激动人心的程度并不亚于现代汽车大赛。

Summary writing 摘要写作

Answer these questions *in not more than 70 words.*

回答下列问题, 将答案组成一个段落, 不要超过 70 个单词。

1 Did a lot of old cars enter for the race or not? How often is it held? (*which*)

2 What could be heard when they set off? Did many cars break down during the race or not? Did a few manage to complete the course or not? (*and though*)

3 Did the winning car go downhill quickly or slowly? When did its driver have a lot of difficulty trying to stop it? (*so quickly ... that*)

Composition 作文

Rewrite the following sentences using the joining words in parentheses. Where necessary omit the words in italics.

用括号中的连词改写以下句子, 必要时可以省略用斜体印出的词。

1 There was a loud explosion. My old car stopped. (*and*)

2 I got out. *I wanted to* have a look at the engine. (*to*)

3 Then a man passed me. *He was* driving a large modern car. (*a man who*)

4 I waved to him. He did not stop. (*but*)

5 I passed the large car later. Its driver was changing a wheel. (*When*)

Letter writing 书信写作

Learn the following opening phrases by heart:

熟记以下两个开头语:

I am sorry it has taken me so long to write, but ...

I was glad to hear from you at last and to learn that ...

Exercise 练习

Write two short paragraphs (of not more than two sentences each) completing the above phrases.

用以上两个开头语写两小段话, 每段不超过两句。

Key structures 关键句型

A lot of cars entered for this race.

a Do you remember these sentences? (**KS32**)

你记得这些表示比较关系的句型吗? (参见第 32 课关键句型)

He is *as* old *as* I am. 他与我同龄。

She is *not as* intelligent *as* we think. 她并不像我们想象的那样聪明。

There is *little* I can do to help him. 我帮不了他多少忙。

There were *few* people in the shop. 商店里几乎没有人。

There isn't much whisky, but you can have *a little*. 威士忌酒不多, 但你可以喝一点。

There aren't many apples, but you can pick *a few*. 苹果不多了, 但你可以摘一些。

b   Now study these sentences:
细读以下句子：

Instead of saying:
除了这种表述方式外：

There isn't *much* I can do to help him.

Many of our products are sold overseas.

We can say:
还可以说：

There isn't *a lot* I can do to help him.

Or: There isn't *a great deal* I can do to help him.

A lot of our products are sold overseas.

Or: *A great many of* our products are sold overseas.

Or: *A great number of* our products are sold overseas.

c   Study these sentences:
细读以下句子：

Instead of saying:
除了这种表述方式外：

My jacket is *like* yours.

My jacket *isn't like* yours.

We can say:
还可以说：

My jacket is *the same as* yours.

My jacket is *differet from* yours.

Exercises 练习

A   How many comparisons can you find in the passage? Underline them. Note the use of the following:
画出课文中表示比较的用法，注意以下这些词组的用法：
a lot of, a great deal of, a great many, a few and *different from*.

B   Supply the missing words in the following. Do not refer to the passage until you finish the exercise.
补上遗漏的词，完成练习后再对照课文，核对你的答案。

Once a year a race is held for old cars. A _____ _____ cars entered for this race last year and there was a great _____ of excitement just before it began. One of the _____ handsome cars was a Rolls-Royce Silver Ghost. The _____ unusual car was a Benz which had only three wheels. Built in 1885, it was the _____ (old) car taking part. After a great _____ loud explosions, the race began. _____ of the cars broke down on the course and some drivers spent _____ time *under* their cars than *in* them! A _____ cars, however, completed the race. The winning car reached a speed of forty miles an hour — much faster _____ any of its rivals. It sped downhill at the end of the race and its driver had a _____ _____ trouble trying to stop it. The race gave everyone a great _____ of pleasure. It was very different _____ modern car races but no _____ exciting.

Special difficulties 难点

Words often confused and misused 经常容易混淆和误用的词

Study the examples given under each heading:
细读每组词的例句：

a   *Handsome* (1.3), *Beautiful, Pretty, Good-looking.*

He is a very *handsome* young man. 他是一个非常清秀的年青人。

She used to be very *pretty* as a child. She is now a *beautiful* woman. 孩提时她很好看。现在是个漂亮的女子。

She's a very g*ood-looking* girl, and her boyfriend's *good-looking* too. 她是个很好看的女孩，她的男朋友也很好看。

b   *Reach* and *Arrive in/at.*

The winning car *reached* a speed of forty miles an hour. (11.8-9)

Will you pass me that book please? I can't *reach* it. 你能把那本书递给我吗？我够不着。

We *arrived in* New York yesterday. We *arrived at* the station in good time. 我们昨天到达纽约。我们及时到站。

c *Take Part* and *Take Place*.

It was the oldest car *taking part*. (1.5)

The next race will *take place* in a year's time. 下一次比赛会在一年后举行。

Exercise 练习

Write eight sentences using each of the above words.

用以上 8 个词各造一个句子。

Multiple choice questions 选择题

Comprehension 理解

1 What was unusual about the car race?

(*a*) The Rolls-Royce Silver Ghost.

(*b*) The Benz which was built in 1885.

(*c*) All the cars were old.

(*d*) There were many loud explosions.

2 A lot of cars took part in the race, _____ .

(*a*) but only a few completed the course

(*b*) and they all completed the course

(*c*) and most of them completed the course

(*d*) but only one of them completed the course

Structure 句型

3 A lot of cars entered for this race. There were _____ cars in it.

(*a*) much   (*b*) lot of   (*c*) lots of   (*d*) plenty

4 _____ in 1885, so it was the oldest car in the race.

(*a*) It built   (*b*) Built   (*c*) It was built   (*d*) Having built

5 It was the oldest car taking part. There wasn't _____ one.

(*a*) an older   (*b*) the oldest   (*c*) an elder   (*d*) the eldest

6 It reached a speed of forty miles an hour. It _____ forty miles an hour.

(*a*) ran   (*b*) ran with   (*c*) went at   (*d*) drove with

7 It was different from modern cars. It wasn't _____ modern cars.

(*a*) the same as   (*b*) the same with   (*c*) same with   (*d*) same as

Vocabulary 词汇

8 One of the most handsome cars was a Rolls-Royce. It was a _____ car.

(*a*) pretty   (*b*) beautiful   (*c*) seemly   (*d*) nice

9 The most unusual car was a Benz. It wasn't a _____ car.

(*a*) used   (*b*) common   (*c*) vulgar   (*d*) accustomed

10 There were many loud explosions. There were many loud _____ .

(*a*) knocks   (*b*) hits   (*c*) bangs   (*d*) thumps

11 Many of the cars broke down. They _____ .

(*a*) were in pieces   (*b*) were broken up   (*c*) couldn't go   (*d*) were spoilt

12 It went faster than any of its rivals. It went faster than its _____ .

(*a*) opponents   (*b*) enemies   (*c*) competitors   (*d*) partners

Lesson 57   Can I help you, madam?   您要买什么，夫人？

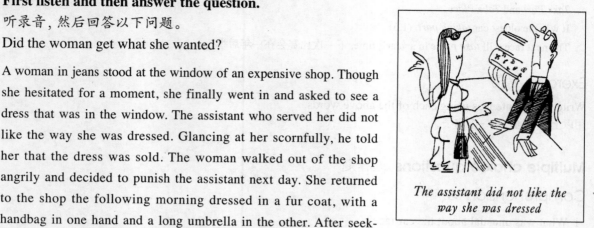

First listen and then answer the question.

听录音，然后回答以下问题。

Did the woman get what she wanted?

A woman in jeans stood at the window of an expensive shop. Though she hesitated for a moment, she finally went in and asked to see a dress that was in the window. The assistant who served her did not like the way she was dressed. Glancing at her scornfully, he told
5 her that the dress was sold. The woman walked out of the shop angrily and decided to punish the assistant next day. She returned to the shop the following morning dressed in a fur coat, with a handbag in one hand and a long umbrella in the other. After seeking out the rude assistant, she asked for the same dress. Not realizing who she was, the assistant was eager to
10 serve her this time. With great difficulty, he climbed into the shop window to get the dress. As soon as she saw it, the woman said she did not like it. She enjoyed herself making the assistant bring almost everything in the window before finally buying the dress she had first asked for.

The assistant did not like the way she was dressed

New words and expressions 生词和短语

madam (title) /ˈmædəm/ n. (对妇女的尊称)
太太，夫人
jeans (1.1) /dʒiːnz/ n. 牛仔裤
hesitate (1.2) /ˈhezɪteɪt/ v. 犹豫，迟疑
serve (1.3) /sɜːv/ v. 接待 (顾客)

scornfully (1.4) /ˈskɔːnfəli/ adv. 轻蔑地
punish (1.6) /ˈpʌnɪʃ/ v. 惩罚
fur (1.7) /fɜː/ n. 裘皮
eager (1.9) /ˈiːgə/ adj. 热切的，热情的

Notes on the text 课文注释

1 Can I help you, madam? 您要买什么，夫人？这是售货员的常用语。

2 A woman in jeans, 一位穿着牛仔裤的妇女。

3 She returned to the shop the following morning dressed in a fur coat, with a handbag in one hand and a long umbrella in the other. 第二天上午，她又来到这家商店，穿着一件裘皮大衣，一手拎着一只手提包，另一只手拿着一把长柄伞。dressed in a fur coat 是过去分词短语作状语，表示伴随状态。

4 seek out, 找出，找到。

5 Not realizing who she was, 没有认出她是谁。这是现在分词短语的否定形式。

6 She enjoyed herself making the assistant bring almost everything in the window. 她开心地迫使那位售货员把橱窗里几乎所有的东西都拿了出来。enjoy oneself, 开心。

参考译文

一位穿着牛仔裤的妇女站在一家高档商店的橱窗前。她虽然犹豫了片刻，但终于还是走进了商店，要求把陈列在橱窗里的一件衣服拿给她看。接待她的售货员不喜欢她的那副打扮，轻蔑地看了她一眼后，便告诉她那

件衣服已经卖出去了。这位妇女怒气冲冲地走出了商店，决定第二天教训一下那个售货员。第二天上午，她又来到这家商店，穿着一件裘皮大衣，一只手拎着一只手提包，另一只手拿着一把长柄伞。找到那个无礼的售货员后，她还要看昨天的那件衣服。那个售货员没有认出她是谁，这一回接待她的态度非常殷勤。费了好大劲儿，他爬进橱窗去取那件衣服。这位妇女对那件衣服只看一眼，就说不喜欢。她开心地让那位售货员把橱窗里几乎所有的东西都拿了出来，最后才买下了她最先要看的那一件。

Summary writing 摘要写作

Answer these questions *in not more than 80 words.*
回答下列问题，将答案组成一个段落，不要超过 80 个单词。

1 Did the woman in jeans hesitate for a moment or not? Did she enter an expensive shop or not? What did she ask to see? (*Though ... and*)

2 What did an assistant tell her? When did the woman return? Was she dressed in a fur coat or not? (*On being told by*)

3 What was the assistant eager to do this time?

4 What did she make him bring her? What did the woman finally buy? (*After making*)

Composition 作文

Write two or three sentences using the ideas given below:
用以下词组写出 2 至 3 个句子来：
The owner of a shop wanted to see how polite his assistants were — dressed as a tramp — went into his shop — asked to see a suit — was thrown out

Letter writing 书信写作

Learn the following opening phrases by heart:
熟记以下两个开头语：
What a surprise it was to ...
Forgive me for not writing earlier, but ...

Exercise 练习

Write two short paragraphs (of not more than two sentences each) completing the above phrases.
用以上两个开头语写出两小段文字，每段不超过两句话。

Key structures 关键句型

At, In, Off and With (Compare **KS9, KS33**) （对比第 9，33 课关键句型）

a Study these sentences carefully. Pay close attention to the words in italics.
仔细阅读以下句子，特别注意用斜体印出的词。
Phrases with *at.* 带 at 的短语
He lives *at 27 West Street.* 他住在西大街 27 号。
A large crowd was waiting *at the bus stop.* 一大群人在公共汽车站等候。
I'll see you *at the station.* 我将到车站送你。
On the way home, we stopped *at a small village called Puddleton.* 在回家的路上，我们在一个叫普都顿的小村逗留。
Someone is *at the door.* 有人敲门。

Phrases with *in*. 带有 in 的短语

There were a lot of people *in the street*. 街上有许多人。

I would like to live *in a warm country*. 我喜欢住在一个气候温暖的国家。

He lives *in Berlin*. 他住在柏林。

Let's go for a walk *in the park*. 让我们到公园去散散步。

Where's Tom? He's *in his room*. 汤姆在哪里？他在自己的房间里。

Phrases with *off*. 带有 off 的短语

The lid came *off* easily. 这个盖子很容易掉。

Take your coat *off*. 把你的外套脱下来。

The pencil rolled *off* the table. 铅笔滚到桌子下面去了。

b Now study these phrases with *in* and *with*:

仔细阅读以下含有 in 和 with 的短语：

Can you see that woman *in the blue coat*? 你能看见那个穿蓝外套的女士吗？

He was dressed *in a black suit*. 他穿着一套黑衣服。

That man *with long hair* is supposed to be a poet. 那个留着长发的男人应该是个诗人。

The police are looking for a man *with a scar* on his face. 警察正在搜寻一个脸上有疤的男人。

The woman *with the brown handbag* and long umbrella is a famous novelist. 那个手上拿着棕色手提包和长柄伞的女士是一位著名的小说家。

Exercises 练习

A Study the use in the passage of the following words: *in, at, out of, to, with* and *into*.

仔细阅读课文中 in, at, out of, to, with 和 into 的用法。

B Supply the missing words in the following sentences. Do not refer to the passage until you finish the exercise.

填上遗漏的词，完成练习后再对照课文，核对你的答案。

1 A woman _____ jeans stood _____ the window of an expensive shop. Though she hesitated for a moment, she finally went _____ and asked to see a dress that was _____ the window.

2 Glancing _____ her scornfully, he told her that the dress was sold. The woman walked _____ the shop angrily.

3 She returned _____ the shop the following morning dressed _____ a fur coat, _____ a handbag _____ one hand and a long umbrella _____ the other.

4 _____ great difficulty, he climed _____ the shop window.

5 She enjoyed herself making the assistant bring almost everything _____ the window.

Special difficulties 难点

Make and Let

Study these examples:

细读以下例句：

She enjoyed herself making the assistant *bring* almost everything in the window. (11.11-12)

I can't make him *change* his mind. 我无法使他改变主意。

The teacher made the boy *write* the exercise again. 教师叫那男孩把练习重做一遍。

Don't let him *persuade* you. 不要让他把你说服了。

Let me *try*. 让我试一试。

Don't let the children *touch* anything in this room please. 请别让孩子们动这个房间里的任何东西。

Exercise 练习

Complete these sentences:

完成以下句子：

1 Don't let him _____ .

2 Why don't you make him _____ ?

3 No one call make me _____ .

4 Will your parents let you _____ ?

5 Let's _____ .

Multiple choice questions 选择题

Comprehension 理解

1 The assistant refused to help the woman because he _____ .

(*a*) didn't approve of the way she was dressed

(*b*) approved of the way she was dressed

(*c*) liked the way she was dressed

(*d*) noticed the way she was dressed

2 The woman got her revenge by _____ .

(*a*) buying a dress

(*b*) putting the assistant to a lot of trouble

(*c*) complaining to the manager

(*d*) asking for something in the window

Structure 句型

3 The woman stood at the window. She stood _____ it.

(*a*) in front

(*b*) in front of

(*c*) front

(*d*) ahead of

4 The assistant _____ her did not like the way she was dressed.

(*a*) served

(*b*) serving

(*c*) who serving

(*d*) was serving

5 After _____ out the rude assistant she asked for the same dress.

(*a*) she was seeking

(*b*) she had sought

(*c*) sought

(*d*) when she sought

6 _____ who she was, the assistant was eager to serve her this time.

(*a*) Not to realize

(*b*) Without to realize

(*c*) Except realizing

(*d*) Without realizing

7 She bought the dress _____ she had first asked for.

(*a*) who

(*b*) what

(*c*) that

(*d*) whom

Vocabulary 词汇

8 He glanced at her scornfully. He _____ her.

(*a*) mocked

(*b*) teased

(*c*) laughed at

(*d*) despised

9 She returned the following day. She returned the day _____ .

(*a*) other

(*b*) next

(*c*) after

(*d*) else

10 She sought out the rude assistant. He had been _____ polite.

(*a*) un-

(*b*) im-

(*c*) in-

(*d*) dis-

11 He was eager to serve her. He was _____ to serve her.

(*a*) prompt

(*b*) fast

(*c*) nervous

(*d*) anxious

12 He brought almost everything in the window. He brought _____ everything.

(*a*) nearly

(*b*) scarcely

(*c*) hardly

(*d*) already

Lesson 58　A blessing in disguise?　是因祸得福吗？

First listen and then answer the question.

听录音，然后回答以下问题。

Why does the vicar refuse to cut down the tree?

not one has been struck down

The tiny village of Frinley is said to possess a 'cursed tree'. Because the tree was mentioned in a newspaper, the number of visitors to Frinley has now increased. The tree was planted near the church fifty years ago, but it is only in recent years that it

5　has gained an evil reputation. It is said that if anyone touches the tree, he will have bad luck; if he picks a leaf, he will die. Many villagers believe that the tree has already claimed a number of victims. The vicar has been asked to have the tree cut down, but so far he has refused. He has pointed out that the tree is a useful source of income, as tourists have been

10　coming from all parts of the country to see it. In spite of all that has been said, the tourists have been picking leaves and cutting their names on the tree-trunk. So far, not one of them has been struck down by sudden death!

New words and expressions 生词和短语

blessing (title) /ˈblesɪŋ/ *n.* 福分，福气
disguise (title) /dɪsˈɡaɪz/ *n.* 伪装
tiny (l.1) /ˈtaɪni/ *adj.* 极小的
possess (l.1) /pəˈzes/ *v.* 拥有
cursed (l.1) /kɜːst/ *adj.* 可恨的
increase (l.3) /ɪnˈkriːs/ *v.* 增加
plant (l.3) /plɑːnt/ *v.* 种植
church (l.4) /tʃɜːtʃ/ *n.* 教堂

evil (l.5) /ˈiːvəl/ *adj.* 坏的
reputation (l.5) /ˌrepjuˈteɪʃən/ *n.* 名声
claim (l.7) /kleɪm/ *v.* 夺走（生命）
victim (l.8) /ˈvɪktɪm/ *n.* 受害者，牺牲品
vicar (l.8) /ˈvɪkə/ *n.* 教区牧师
source (l.9) /sɔːs/ *n.* 来源
income (l.9) /ˈɪnkʌm/ *n.* 收入
trunk (l.11) /trʌŋk/ *n.* 树干

Notes on the text 课文注释

1　a blessing in disguise, 坏事变好事, 因祸得福。

2　The tiny village of Frinley, 弗林利这个小村庄。介词 of 这里表示的是同位关系。

3　but it is only in recent years that it has gained an evil reputation, 但是只是近年来才得到了一个坏名声。句中的 it 是强调句型, 结构是 it is (was) + 被强调的部分 + that (who) 从句。

4　to have the tree cut down, 把这棵树砍掉。在这个短语中 cut down 是动词 have 的宾语 the tree 的补足语, 常用来表示叫别人完成的动作。

5　In spite of all that has been said 是介词短语, 在句中作让步状语。that has been said 是定语从句, 修饰 all, 关系代词 that 在从句中作主语, 不能省略。

参考译文

　　据说弗林利这个小村里有一棵"被诅咒的树"。就因为报上提到过这棵树, 所以现在来弗林利参观的人越

来越多。该树是 50 年前栽在教堂附近的，但只是近几年才得到了一个坏名声。据说，谁要是触摸了这棵树，谁就会交上恶运；如果谁摘了一片树叶，谁就会死去。很多村民相信此树已经害了不少人。人们曾请求教区的牧师叫人把树砍掉，但他直到现在也没有同意。他指出，由于人们从全国各地纷纷前来参观这棵树，它成了一个有用的财源。尽管有上述种种说法，但游客们还是照常摘树叶和把他们的名字刻在树干上。然而到目前为止，还没有一个人暴死呢!

Summary writing 摘要写作

Answer the questions *in not more than 85 words*.
回答下列问题，将答案组成一个段落，不要超过 85 个单词。

1 Has the number of visitors to the village of Frinley increased or not? Is there said to be a 'cursed tree' near a church or not? (*because*)

2 Do the villagers believe that if anyone picks a leaf he will die? What have they asked the vicar to do? (*Since*)

3 Is the tree a useful source of income or not? Has the vicar agreed to have the tree cut down, or has he refused to do so? (*As*)

4 Have tourists been picking leaves or not? Has any of them come to harm or not? (*Meanwhile, though* ...)

Composition 作文

Rewrite the following sentences using the joining words in parentheses:
用括号内的连词改写以下句子：

1 A village well was said to be cursed. It was bought by a man. (*which*)

2 Tourists came to see it. There was not even any water in it. (*though*)

3 The tourists could look into the well. They had to throw a coin in first. (*Before*)

Letter writing 书信写作

Learn the following opening phrases by heart:
熟记以下两个开头语：

You will be glad to hear that ...

Thank you for letting me know that ...

Exercise 练习

Write two short paragraphs (of not more than two sentences each) completing the above phrases.
用以上两个开头语写出两小段文字，每段不要超过两句话。

Key structures 关键句型

Frinley is said to possess a 'cursed tree'. 被动语态

a   Do you remember these sentences? **(KS34)**
你记得这些句子吗?（参见第 34 课关键句型）

He *is being sent* abroad. 他正被送出国。

I *was told to* wait for him. 我被通知等等他。

Your wallet *has been found*. 你的钱包被找到了。

269

b   Now study these sentences:

细读以下句子:

Instead of saying:

除了这种表述方式外:

People say he is a genius.

People say that there is oil under the North Sea.

She gave me a pen.

The manager offered the vacant post to him.

We can say:

还可以说:

He is said to be a genius.

Or: *It is said that* he is a genius.

There is said to be oil under the North Sea.

Or: *It is said that* there is oil under the North Sea.

I was given a pen.

Or: *A pen was given* to me.

He was offered the vacant post.

Or: *The vacant post was offered* to him.

Exercises   练习

A   There are some verbs in the passage which are similar in form to the examples given above. Can you find them?

找出课文中与以上例句类似的用法。

B   Give the correct form of the verbs in parentheses. Do not refer to the passage until you finish the exercise.

用括号中动词的正确形式填空, 完成练习后再对照课文, 核对你的答案。

1   The tiny village of Frinley _____ (say) to possess a 'cursed tree'. Because the tree _____ (mention) in a newspaper, the number of visitors to Frinley has now increased. The tree _____ (plant) near the church fifty years ago, but it is only in recent years that it has gained an evil reputation. It _____ (say) that if anyone touches the tree, he will have bad luck.

2   The vicar _____ (ask) to have the tree cut down, but so far he has refused.

3   In spite of all that _____ (say), the tourists have been picking leaves and cutting their names on the tree-trunk. So far, not one of them _____ (strike) down by sudden death!

Special difficulties   难点

Verbs often confused 经常容易混淆的动词

Study these examples:

细读以下例子:

a   *Increase* and *Grow*

The number of visitors to Frinley has now *increased/grown*. (ll.2-3)

She has *grown* so much. She is nearly as tall as I am. 她长了这么多, 都快和我一样高了。

b   *Gain* and *Earn*.

It has *gained/earned* an evil reputation. (ll.4-5)

He has gone abroad and I hear he is *earning* a lot of money. 他已经出国, 我听说他赚了许多钱。

c   *Pick* and *Cut*.

The tourists have been *picking* the leaves and cutting their names on the tree-trunk. (ll.10-11)

She has *picked* a lot of flowers. 她摘了许多花。

She *cut* the apple in two. 她把苹果切成两块。

Exercise　练习

Choose the correct words in these sentences:

选择正确的词：

1　This fruit is fresh. I have just (cut) (picked) it.

2　If you travel by air, you will (earn) (gain) time.

3　He (earns) (gains) £300 a week.

4　Judy has (increased) (grown) so much I can hardly recognize her.

Multiple choice questions　选择题

Comprehension　理解

1　The vicar has refused to have the tree cut down because _____ .

　(a) it is cursed　　　　(b) it earns money　　　(c) he is afraid　　　　(d) he is superstitious

2　One of these statements is true. Which one?

　(a) Tourists are afraid to pick leaves off the tree.

　(b) Tourists are afraid to cut their names on the tree-trunk.

　(c) Tourists who have picked leaves have died.

　(d) Tourists who have picked leaves haven't died.

Structure　句型

3　_____ that Frinley has a cursed tree.

　(a) They say　　　　　(b) It said　　　　　(c) Said　　　　　　(d) It is saying

4　If anyone picked the leaves, he _____ die.

　(a) would　　　　　　(b) will　　　　　　(c) shall　　　　　(d) would have

5　Tourists have been coming from all parts of the country. They haven't stopped coming _____ .

　(a) still　　　　　　　(b) even　　　　　　(c) yet　　　　　　(d) more

6　_____ all that has been said, the tourists have been picking leaves.

　(a) In spite　　　　　(b) Despite　　　　　(c) Even　　　　　(d) Even so

7　So far _____ of them has been struck down by sudden death.

　(a) no one　　　　　　(b) nobody　　　　　(c) not any　　　　(d) none

Vocabulary　词汇

8　Frinley is a tiny village. It is very _____ .

　(a) big　　　　　　　(b) great　　　　　　(c) small　　　　　(d) famous

9　The number of visitors has increased. The number has _____ .

　(a) grown　　　　　　(b) grown up　　　　(c) overgrown　　　(d) grown old

10　It has _____ an evil reputation.

　(a) won　　　　　　　(b) beaten　　　　　(c) profited　　　　(d) earned

11　It has gained an evil reputation. It has a bad _____ .

　(a) fame　　　　　　　(b) name　　　　　　(c) rumour　　　　(d) report

12　He has pointed out that it's a source of income. He's _____ this to the villagers.

　(a) shown　　　　　　(b) pointed　　　　　(c) noted　　　　　(d) explained

Lesson 59 In or out? 进来还是出去？

🔊 **First listen and then answer the question.**

听录音，然后回答以下问题。

Why did Rex run away?

Our dog, Rex, used to sit outside our front gate and bark. Every time he wanted to come into the garden he would bark until someone opened the gate. As the neighbours complained of the noise, my husband spent weeks training him to press his paw on the latch to
5 let himself in. Rex soon became an expert at opening the gate. However, when I was going out shopping last week, I noticed him in the garden near the gate. This time he was barking so that someone would let him out! Since then, he has developed another bad habit.

My husband spent weeks training him

As soon as he opens the gate from the outside, he comes into the garden and waits until the gate
10 shuts. Then he sits and barks until someone lets him out. After this he immediately lets himself in and begins barking again. Yesterday my husband removed the gate and Rex got so annoyed we have not seen him since.

New words and expressions 生词和短语

bark (l.1) /bɑːk/ v. 狗叫
press (l.4) /pres/ v. 按，压
paw (l.4) /pɔː/ n. 脚爪
latch (l.4) /lætʃ/ n. 门闩

expert (l.5) /'ekspɜːt/ n. 专家
develop (l.8) /dɪ'veləp/ v. 养成
habit (l.8) /'hæbɪt/ n. 习惯
remove (l.11) /rɪ'muːv/ v. 拆掉，取下

Notes on the text 课文注释

1 every time 此处是连词，作 "每当"、"无论何时" 讲，引出时间状语从句。

2 Rex soon became an expert at opening the gate. 很快雷克斯成了开门的专家。become an expert at 作 "成了……能手" 讲。

3 This time he was barking so that someone would let him out! 这次它叫着让人把它放出去。so that 是连词，作 "为的是" 讲，引导状语从句。

4 Rex got so annoyed we have not seen him since. 雷克斯很生气，此后我们便再也没有见到它。句中含有一个 so annoyed that ... 的状语从句，表示结果，但 that 被省略了。

参考译文

　　我家的狗雷克斯，过去常坐在大门外面叫。每当它想到花园里来时，便汪汪叫个不停，直到有人把门打开。由于邻居们对狗叫很有意见，所以我丈夫花了几个星期的时间训练它用脚爪按住门闩把自己放进来。雷克斯很快成了开门的专家。然而上星期我正要出去买东西时，发现它正待在花园里边靠门的地方。这次它叫着让人把它放出去! 从那以后，它养成了另外一种坏习惯。它从外面把门一打开，就走进花园，等着门自动关上。这之后它就坐下汪汪叫起来，直到有人来把它放出去。出去之后，它又马上把自己放进来，接着再开始叫。昨天，我丈夫把大门卸了下来，雷克斯很生气，此后我们便再也没有见到它。

Summary writing 摘要写作

Answer these questions *in not more than 80 words.*

回答下列问题, 将答案组成一个段落, 不要超过 80 个单词。

1 Why did our dog, Rex, use to sit outside the front gate and bark? (*so that*)

2 Did my husband train him to open the gate himself or not? Has Rex developed another bad habit or not? (*Ever since*)

3 Why does he bark when he is in the garden? (*so that*)

4 Does he let himself in after this or not? Does he bark until someone opens the gate again or not? (*and*)

5 Has my husband removed the gate or not? Has Rex disappeared or not? (*Now that*)

Composition 作文

Write two or three sentences using the ideas given below:

用以下词组写出 2 至 3 个句子来:

My husband put the gate back — kept it locked — Rex returned — delighted at first — could not open the gate — dissatisfied — disappeared.

Letter writing 书信写作

How would the following appear in a letter:

按书信的格式, 重新排列以下日期、地址, 并给出几个词的缩略形式:

August the first; the third of December; July the second; Avenue; Place; Street; London, East Central 4.

Key structures 关键句型

Review KS50-58 复习第 50-58 课的关键句型

These things always happen. (**KS50**)（第 50 课）

What happened? (**KS51**)（第 51 课）

What has happened? What has been happening? (**KS52**)（第 52 课）

Pirates would often bury gold in the cave ... (**KS55**)（第 55 课）

Frinley is said to possess a 'cursed tree'. (**KS58**)（第 58 课）

Exercises 练习

A Which verbs in the passage tell us *a* what is happening now; *b* what always happens; *c* what happened; *d* what has happened; *e* what was happening.

从课文中选出表示以下动作的动词: a 现在正正在进行的动作; b 经常发生的动作; c 过去发生的动作; d 已经完成的动作; e 过去正在进行的动作。

B Give the correct form of the verbs in parentheses. Do not refer to the passage until you finish the exercise:

用括号中动词的正确形式填空, 完成练习后再对照课文, 核对你的答案:

Our dog, Rex, _____ (sit) outside our front gate and bark. Every time he _____ (want) to come into the garden he _____ (bark) until someone opened the gate. As the neighbours _____ (complain) of the noise, my husband _____ (spend) weeks training him to press his paw on the latch to let himself in. Rex soon _____ (become) an expert at opening the gate. However, when I _____ (go) out shopping last week, I

_____ (notice) him in the garden near the gate. This time he _____ (bark) so that someone would let him out! Since then, he _____ (develop) another bad habit. As soon as he opens the gate from the outside, he _____ (come) into the garden and _____ (wait) 'until the gate shuts. Then he _____ (sit) and _____ (bark) until someone lets him out. After this he immediately lets himself in and _____ (begin) barking again. Yesterday my husband _____ (remove) the gate and Rex _____ (get) so annoyed we _____ (not see) him since.'

C Write these sentences again changing the form of the words in italics. Omit any words that are not necessary.

改变以下句子中用斜体印出的词组，可以省略不必要的词语。

1 *People say that he* is very rich.

2 *People say that there is* a hold-up on the roads.

3 She *gave me* a pen.

4 They *gave her* a prize.

5 They *promised us* a new office.

Special difficulties 难点

To, in order to, so as to, so that, in order that 表示目的的几种方式

Note the way these pairs of sentences have been joined:

注意下面各对句子连接的方法:

He ran to the station. He wanted to catch the train. 他跑到车站。他想赶上火车。

He ran to the station *to* catch the train. 他跑到车站，想赶上火车。

I told him about it. I wanted to help you. 我把这事告诉了他。我想帮助你。

I told him about it *in order to* help you. 我把这事告诉了他，以便帮助你。

I opened the door quietly. I did not want to disturb him. 我轻轻地把门打开。我不想打搅他。

I opened the door quietly *so as not to* disturb him. 我轻轻把门打开，为的是不打搅他。

He works hard. He wants to pass his exams. 他学习很刻苦。他想通过考试。

He works hard *in order that he may* pass his exams. 他学习刻苦，为的是通过考试。

He left the letter on the table. He wanted me to see it. 他把信留在桌子上。他希望我看见。

He left the letter on the table *in order that I might (should)* see it. 他把信留在桌子上，以便我能看见。

He was barking. He wanted someone to let him out. 它正在叫。它希望有人放它出去。

He was barking *so that someone would* let him out. (ll.7-8) 它在叫，以便有人把它放出去。

He was barking *for someone to* let him out. 它在叫着，为的是让人放它出去。

He sent a fax. He wanted his mother to learn the good news. 他发了一份传真，他希望他的母亲知道这个好消息。

He sent a fax *in order that his mother might (should)* learn the good news. 他发了一份传真，以便他的母亲能知道这个好消息。

He sent a fax *for his mother to* learn the good news. 他发了一份传真，为的是让他的母亲能知道这个好消息。

Exercise 练习

Join the following sentences leaving out the verb *to want*.

连接以下句子，用括号中的词组来替代动词 want。

1 He left early. He did not want to see me. (*so as to*)

2 The secretary asked me into the office. The manager wanted to speak to me. (*so that*)

3 I ran to the station. I did not want to be late. (*so as to*)

4 He worked hard. He wanted to learn English. (*in order to*)

5 He has not sent me his address. He does not want me to write to him. (*so that*)

6 I went to see him. I wanted to find out what had happened. (*to*)

Multiple choice questions 选择题

Comprehension 理解

1 The writer's husband trained Rex to open the gate because _____ .

(a) Rex couldn't get in   (b) Rex needed help

(c) Rex enjoyed opening the gate   (d) Rex barked a lot and disturbed the neighbours

2 One of these statements is true. Which one?

(a) Rex only learnt to open the gate from the inside.

(b) Rex only learnt to open the gate from the outside.

(c) Rex never learnt to open the gate.

(d) Rex doesn't like opening the gate.

Structure 句型

3 He would bark until someone opened the gate. That's what he _____ .

(a) is used to doing   (b) used   (c) is used to   (d) used to do

4 The neighbours complained _____ the noise.

(a) for   (b) to   (c) concerning   (d) about

5 The writer went _____ last week.

(a) for shopping   (b) for shop   (c) to shopping   (d) shopping

6 He was barking _____ let him in.

(a) for someone to   (b) in case someone   (c) so someone to   (d) so that someone

7 As soon as he _____ the gate from the outside he comes into the garden.

(a) will open   (b) opens   (c) is opening   (d) has been opening

Vocabulary 词汇

8 My husband spent weeks _____ him to press his paw on the latch.

(a) teaching   (b) guiding   (c) leading   (d) conducting

9 Rex became an expert. He was very _____ .

(a) crafty   (b) sly   (c) cunning   (d) skilful

10 I _____ him in the garden.

(a) observed   (b) looked   (c) remarked   (d) took care of

11 He has developed another bad _____ .

(a) habit   (b) custom   (c) use   (d) usefulness

12 My husband removed the gate. He _____ .

(a) took it in   (b) took it away (c) took it on   (d) took it up

Sentence structure 句子结构

Join these sentences, then check your answer against the text.

连接以下句子, 然后对照课文第 10 行, 核对你的答案。

Then he sits. He barks. Someone lets him out.

Lesson 60   The future   卜算未来

First listen and then answer the question.
听录音，然后回答以下问题。

Does what Madam Bellinsky said come true?

At a village fair, I decided to visit a fortune-teller called Madam
Bellinsky. I went into her tent and she told me to sit down. After I
had given her some money, she looked into a crystal ball and said:
'A relation of yours is coming to see you. She will be arriving this
5 evening and intends to stay for a few days. The moment you leave
this tent, you will get a big surprise. A woman you know well will
rush towards you. She will speak to you and then she will lead you
away from this place. That is all.'

A woman will rush towards you

As soon as I went outside, I forgot all about Madam Bellinsky because my wife hurried towards
10 me. 'Where have you been hiding?' she asked impatiently. 'Your sister will be here in less than an hour and
we must be at the station to meet her. We are late already.' As she walked away, I followed her out of the
fair.

New words and expressions 生词和短语

future (title) /'fjuːtʃə/ *n.* 未来，前途

fair (l.1) /feə/ *n.* 集市

fortune-teller (l.1) /'fɔːtʃən-ˌtelə/ *n.* 算命人

crystal (l.3) /'krɪstl/ *n.* 水晶

relation (l.4) /rɪ'leɪʃən/ *n.* 亲属

impatiently (l.10) /ɪm'peɪʃəntli/ *adv.* 不耐烦地

Notes on the text 课文注释

1 a relation of yours, 您的一个亲戚，这是名词双重所有格的又一个例子。

2 The moment you leave the tent, 您一走出帐篷。the moment 起连词作用，相当于 as soon as。

3 A woman you know well, 一个您很熟悉的女人。you know well 作名词 woman 的定语，引导词（whom 或
that）被省略了。

4 That is all. 就这些。

参考译文

在一个乡村集市上，我决定去拜访一位称作别林斯基夫人的算命人。我走进她的帐篷，她叫我坐下。我给
了她一些钱后，她便察看着一个水晶球说道："您的一个亲戚就要来看您了。她将于今天傍晚到达，并准备住上
几天。您一走出这个帐篷，就会大吃一惊。一位您很熟悉的女人将向您冲来。她会对您说点什么，然后带您离
开这个地方。就是这些。"

我一走出帐篷，就把别林斯基夫人给我算卦的事忘得一干二净了，因为我的妻子正匆匆向我跑来。"你躲
到哪儿去了？"她不耐烦地问，"再有不到一个小时你姐姐就要到这儿了，我们得去车站接她。现在就已经晚
了。"当她走开时，我也跟着她出了集市。

Summary writing 摘要写作

Answer these questions *in not more than 80 words*.
回答下列问题, 将答案组成一个段落, 不要超过 80 个单词。

1 Whom did the writer visit at a village fair? Did she tell him that a relation was coming to see him or not? (*who*)
2 Who would speak to him when he left the tent? Would he follow her out of the fair or not? (*She added that ... and*)
3 Did this come true or not? Did his wife speak to him when he went outside, or did a strange woman speak to him? (*because*)
4 Whom did she tell him they had to meet at the station? Did she lead him out of the fair or not? (*and*)

Composition 作文

Rewrite the following sentences using the joining words in parentheses.
用括号中的连词改写以下句子。

1 Fortune-tellers always tell the truth. They speak in general terms. (*because*)
2 They say you will go on a journey. You will meet a friend. They are right. We often do these things. (*If ... or ... because*)

Letter writing 书信写作

Address an envelope to a married couple who live abroad.
写出寄给居住在国外的一对已婚夫妇的信封上的地址。

Key structures 关键句型

The moment you leave this tent, you will get a big surprise. 表示将要发生的事情

a　Do you remember these sentences? **(KS36)**
你还记得这些句子吗? (参见第 36 课关键句型)
I am going to travel by air. 我将乘飞机旅游。
You will enjoy yourself if you travel by sea. 如果你乘船旅游, 你会玩得很开心的。

b　Now study these sentences carefully:
仔细阅读以下句子, 英文中可用现在进行时来表示为将来安排好的活动和事件:

Instead of saying:
除了这种表述方法外:
He will arrive tomorrow.
He will come at four o'clock.
She will leave in two days' time.

We can say:
还可以说:
He is arriving tomorrow.
He is coming at four o'clock.
She is leaving in two days' time.

c　Study these sentences. Pay close attention to the words in italics:
细读以下句子, 特别注意用斜体印出的词语:
If it rains tomorrow we shall stay at home. **(KS16)** (参见第 16 课关键句型)
The moment he arrives, I shall let you know. 他一到我就告诉你。
I shall wait here *until he comes*. 我要在这里等他来。
As soon as the rain stops, we shall go out. 雨一停我们就要出去。
You must finish your dinner *before you leave the table*. 你必须把饭吃完后才能离开桌子。
We'll go into the living room *after we finish dinner*. 吃完饭后我们去起居室。
I'll give him the message *when he returns*. 他回来时我就把这个口信给他。

Exercises 练习

A Underline all the verbs in the passage which tell us what will happen in the future.
画出课文中表示将要发生的动作的动词。

B This is what Madam Bellinsky told the writer. Give the correct form of the verbs in parentheses. Note that more than one form can be used for some of these verbs. Do not refer to the passage until you finish the exercise:

以下是别林斯基夫人对作者说的话。用括号中动词的正确形式填空。注意其中的有些动词可以有多种形式。完成练习后再对照课文，核对你的答案。

A relation of yours _____ (come) to see you. She _____ (arrive) this evening and intends to stay for a few days. The moment you _____ (leave) this tent, you _____ (get) a big surprise. A woman you know well _____ (rush) towards you. She _____ (speak) to you and then she _____ (lead) you away from this place.

C What will happen tonight? Give the correct form of the verbs in parentheses:
一般将来时。用括号中动词的正确形式填空：

A lifeboat _____ (set) out tonight to search for the shipwreck. The crew _____ (send) radio messages to the wreck until they _____ (receive) a signal from the men on board. As soon as they _____ (receive) a signal, they _____ (try) and find the wreck with powerful searchlights. The moment the crew _____ (locate) the wreck, they _____ (fire) a special gun which _____ (carry) a rope from the life boat to the sinking ship. If the sea is rough, they _____ (pour) oil on the water. They are sure to succeed, but if they fail, a helicopter _____ (send) out tomorrow morning. Helicopters are very useful for rescue work, but they cannot be used at night.

Special difficulties 难点

At a village fair, I decided to visit a fortune-teller. (Compare SD13)

（对比第 13 课难点）

Instead of saying:	*It is better to say*:
除了这种表述之外：	这样说更合适：
We went to the fair in the village.	We went to the *village fair*.

Exercise 练习

Write these sentences again. Express the phrases in italics in a different way:
改写以下句子中用斜体印出的部分：

1 *The dining room in our school* is very large.

2 He told us *a story about ghosts*.

3 She gave me *a present for my birthday*.

4 We stopped at *a pub in the village*.

5 *The leader of the party* made a speech.

6 I have lost the *key to the front door*.

7 He sent me a *card for Christmas*.

8 We are painting the *gate in our garden*.

Multiple choice questions 选择题

Comprehension 理解

1 Madam Bellinsky could only tell the writer's future when _____ .

   (a) he asked her   (b) he paid her

   (c) she looked into the crystal ball   (d) he showed her his palm

2 Madam Bellinsky _____ .

   (a) foretold the future correctly   (b) told him a lot of nonsense

   (c) was a bad fortune-teller   (d) was a liar

Structure 句型

3 A relation of yours is coming to see you. She _____ soon.

   (a) comes   (b) came   (c) will be coming   (d) will have come

4 She intends to stay for a few days. That's what she _____ to do.

   (a) is about   (b) plans   (c) is due   (d) hopes

5 When he _____ this tent he will get a surprise.

   (a) will leave   (b) leave   (c) leaves   (d) is leaving

6 You will get a surprise. You _____ .

   (a) will surprise   (b) will be surprised   (c) surprise   (d) will be surprising

7 'Where have you been hiding?' she asked. She asked me where _____ hiding.

   (a) I had been   (b) had I been   (c) had been I   (d) had I being

Vocabulary 词汇

8 I decided to visit a fortune-teller. That's what I _____ to do.

   (a) made up   (b) made up my mind   (c) minded   (d) cared

9 Crystal is a kind of _____ .

   (a) glass   (b) metal   (c) wood   (d) plastic

10 A relation of yours is coming. A _____ is coming.

   (a) friend   (b) colleague   (c) relative   (d) acquaintance

11 A woman you know well will rush towards you. She will _____ .

   (a) be in a hurry   (b) be slow   (c) be tired   (d) be angry

12 She was impatient. She _____ .

   (a) was angry   (b) was cross   (c) didn't speak   (d) didn't like waiting

Sentence structure 句子结构

Join these sentences, then check your answer against the text.

连接以下句子, 然后对照课文第 2-3 行, 核对你的答案。

First I gave her some money. Then she looked into a crystal ball.

After I _____ .

Lesson 61 Trouble with the Hubble 哈勃望远镜的困境

First listen and then answer the question.

听录音,然后回答以下问题。

What is the special importance of a telescope in space?

astronauts

The Hubble telescope was launched into space by NASA on April 20, 1990 at a cost of over a billion dollars. Right from the start there was trouble with the Hubble. The pictures it sent us were very disappointing because its main mirror was faulty! NASA is now
5 going to put the telescope right, so it will soon be sending up four astronauts to repair it. The shuttle *Endeavour* will be taking the astronauts to the Hubble. A robot-arm from the *Endeavour* will grab the telescope and hold it while the astronauts make the necessary repairs. Of course, the Hubble is above the earth's atmosphere, so it will soon be sending us the clearest
10 pictures of the stars and distant galaxies that we have ever seen. The Hubble will tell us a great deal about the age and size of the universe. By the time you read this, the Hubble's eagle eye will have sent us thousands and thousands of wonderful pictures.

New words and expressions 生词和短语

Hubble (title) /'hʌbl/ *n.* 哈勃
telescope (l.1) /'telɪskəʊp/ *n.* 望远镜
launch (l.1) /lɔːntʃ/ *v.* 发射
space (l.1) /speɪs/ *n.* 空间
NASA (l.1) /'næsə/ *n.* (National Aeronautics and Space Administration) 国家航空和航天局
billion (l.2) /'bɪljən/ *n.* 10亿
faulty (l.4) /'fɔːlti/ *adj.* 有错误的
astronaut (l.6) /'æstrənɔːt/ *n.* 宇航员

shuttle (l.6) /'ʃʌtl/ *n.* 航天飞机
Endeavour (l.6) /'ɪndevə/ *n.* "奋进" 号
robot-arm (l.7) /'rəʊbɒt-,ɑːm/ *n.* 机器手
grab (l.8) /græb/ *v.* 抓
atmosphere (l.9) /'ætməsfɪə/ *n.* 大气层
distant (l.10) /'dɪstənt/ *adj.* 遥远的
galaxy (l.10) /'gæləksi/ *n.* 星系
universe (l.11) /'juːnɪvɜːs/ *n.* 宇宙
eagle eye (l.11) /'iːgəl-'aɪ/ 鹰眼

Notes on the text 课文注释

1 the Hubble telescope, 哈勃望远镜。
2 at a cost of, 造价为……。
3 right from the start, 从最开始。

参考译文

哈勃望远镜于1990年4月20日由国家航空和航天局发射升空,耗资10多亿美元。从最开始哈勃望远镜就有问题。它传送给我们的图像很令人失望,因为它的主要镜子有误差。国家航空和航天局准备纠正这一错误,为此将把4名宇航员送入太空修复望远镜。"奋进"号航天飞机将把宇航员送上哈勃。当宇航员进行必要的修复工作时,"奋进"号上的一只机器手将抓住望远镜并托住它。当然,哈勃位于地球的大气层之外,因此,它很

快就会给我们传送我们所见到过的、有关恒星和远距离星系的最清晰的照片。哈勃将告诉我们有关宇宙的年龄和大小的许多事情。等到你读到这篇文章时，敏锐的哈勃望远镜已经为我们送来了成千上万张精彩的照片。

Summary writing 摘要写作

Answer these questions *in not more than 60 words*.
回答下列问题, 将答案组成一个段落, 不要超过 60 个单词。

1 When was the Hubble telescope launched into space? What were the pictures it sent us like? Why? (*When the Hubble ..., the pictures ..., because ...*)

2 What will the four astronauts from the shuttle *Endeavour* be doing? What will the pictures from the Hubble tell us? (*and eventually*)

Composition 作文

Write three or four sentences using the ideas given below.
用以下词组写出 3 至 4 个句子来。

There was trouble with the Hubble — the main mirror — faulty — the pictures — disappointing — now the shuttle *Endeavour* — four astronauts — make the necessary repairs — the Hubble — soon send — the clearest pictures — ever seen.

Letter writing 书信写作

Learn the following opening phrases by heart:
熟记以下两个开头语:

I have not heard from you for some time, so ...

It was very kind of you to ...

Exercise 练习

Write two short paragraphs (of not more than two sentences each) completing the above phrases.
用以上两个开头语写出两小段话, 每段不超过两句。

Key structures 关键句型

By the time you read this, the Hubble's eagle eye will have sent us thousands and thousands of wonderful pictures. 将来完成时、将来进行时和将来完成进行时

a Study these sentences. (**KS37**)
   细读以下句子。(参见第 37 课关键句型)
   I will be writing letters all day tomorrow. 明天我一天都将写信。
   Soon the astronauts will have repaired the telescope. 宇航员很快会把望远镜修好。

b Compare these two sentences:
   对比将来完成时和将来完成进行时:
   Soon the astronauts will have repaired the telescope. 宇航员很快会把望远镜修好。
   By Friday midday, they will have been working on it for seven days. 到星期五中午, 他们就在这个工程上干了 7 天了。

c Compare these pairs of sentences. Pay close attention to the words in italics. (**KS60c**)
   对比以下各组句子, 特别注意用斜体印出的部分。(参见第 60 课关键句型 c)
   He will have arrived by this time tomorrow. 明天的这个时候他已经到了。

Unit 3　Lesson 61

The moment he has arrived, I will let you know. 他一来我就会告诉你。

You can go home at five o'clock. 你可以在 5 点钟的时候回家。

Now that you have finished work, you can go home. 你既然已经做完工作, 你就可以回家了。

He will phone us later today. He will have received his exam results by then. 今天晚些时候他会给我们打电话, 那时他已经接到考试成绩了。

As soon as he has received his exam results, he will phone us. 他一接到考试成绩就会给我们打电话的。

Exercises 练习

A　Underline all the verbs in the passage which tell us what will happen in the future.
画出课文中所有表示将来发生事情的动词。

B　Give the correct form of the verbs in parentheses. Do not refer to the passage until you have finished the exercise.
用括号中动词的正确形式填空, 完成练习后再对照课文, 核对你的答案。

The Hubble telescope _____ (launch) into space by NASA on April 20, 1990 at a cost of over a billion dollars. Right from the start there _____ (be) trouble with the Hubble. The pictures it _____ (send) us _____ (be) very disappointing because its main mirror _____ (be) faulty! NASA now _____ (put) the telescope right, so it soon _____ (send up) four astronauts to repair it. The shuttle *Endeavour* _____ (take) the astronauts to the Hubble. A robot-arm from the *Endeavour* _____ (grab) the telescope and _____ (hold) it while the astronauts _____ (make) the necessary repairs. Of course, the Hubble _____ (be) above the earth's atmosphere, so it soon _____ (send) us the clearest pictures of the stars and distant galaxies that we ever _____ (see). The Hubble _____ (tell) us a great deal about the age and size of the universe. By the time you _____ (read) this, the Hubble's eagle eye _____ (send) us thousands and thousands of wonderful pictures.

Special difficulties 难点

Words often confused 经常容易混淆的词

Study these examples:
细读以下例子:

a　Nouns: *Cost, Price, Value*

The Hubble was launched at a *cost* of over a billion dollars. 哈勃望远镜发射升空, 耗资 10 多亿美元。

How much is that blouse? Let's ask the *price*. 这件衬衣多少钱? 让我们来问一下价钱。

The stolen items were of sentimental, rather than financial *value*. 被盗物品更具有情感上的含义, 而不是经济上的价值。

b　Verbs: *Cost, Price, Value.*

What does this blouse *cost*, please? 请问, 这件衬衣多少钱?

I want to *price* the bed linen in a few other shops before I buy any. 我想在买床单之前打听几家商店的价格。

I *value* your advice a great deal. 我非常尊重你的建议。

Exercise 练习

Choose the correct words in the following sentences.
选择正确的词。

1 There has been a sharp rise in the (price) (cost) (value) of living.

2 Whenever I buy anything new, my father always asks me the (value) (cost) (price).

3 If you have to work for something you will (value) (price) (cost) it more.

4 That house (valued) (cost) (priced) a fortune to build.

5 Dr. James's work is of enormous (value) (cost) (price) to the community.

6 Jane has (valued) (cost) (priced) the alternative products and she recommends this one.

7 So far, ten countries have given money towards the (value) (price) (cost) of rebuilding after the earthquake.

Multiple choice questions 选择题

Comprehension 理解

1 The Hubble failed to send us satisfactory pictures because _____ .

(a) the cost of sending satisfactory pictures was terrible

(b) there was a problem with its main mirror

(c) it was a long time since it was launched into space

(d) it was high above the earth's atmosphere

2 The Hubble telescope _____ .

(a) will tell us a great deal about the universe

(b) cost a lot but was almost worthless

(c) will measure the size of the earth

(d) requires constant care from the astronauts

Structure 句型

3 NASA is now going to put the telescope right. NASA _____ it.

(a) is repairing   (b) has already repaired   (c) will be repairing   (d) to repair

4 Four astronauts _____ to the Hubble.

(a) will take   (b) will send up   (c) will be taken   (d) will be sending up

5 A robot-arm will hold the telescope _____ the astronauts to repair it.

(a) for   (b) so that   (c) so long as   (d) which

6 The Hubble will be sending us clear pictures _____ it is above the earth's atmosphere.

(a) when   (b) and   (c) while   (d) because

7 _____ you read this, thousands of pictures will have been sent to us.

(a) As soon as   (b) The moment   (c) Before   (d) When

Vocabulary 词汇

8 The Hubble was launched by NASA. It was _____ .

(a) sent into space   (b) carried away   (c) put up   (d) taken up

9 There was trouble with the Hubble _____ .

(a) then   (b) from the beginning   (c) a few years ago   (d) before

10 The pictures the Hubble sent us were _____ .

(a) wonderful   (b) unsatisfactory   (c) the clearest   (d) disappointed

11 The main mirror of the Hubble _____ .

(a) had problems   (b) was distant   (c) was the clearest   (d) requires repairs

12 The Hubble is _____ the earth's atmosphere.

(a) below

(c) within

(b) over

(d) outside

Lesson 62   After the fire   大火之后

The seed was sprayed by aeroplanes

First listen and then answer the question.
听录音，然后回答以下问题。
What was the danger to the villages after the fire?

Firemen had been fighting the forest fire for nearly three weeks before they could get it under control. A short time before, great trees had covered the countryside for miles around. Now, smoke still rose up from the warm ground over the desolate hills. Winter was coming
5 on and the hills threatened the surrounding villages with destruction, for heavy rain would not only wash away the soil but would cause serious floods as well. When the fire had at last been put out, the forest authorities ordered several tons of a special type of grass-seed which would grow quickly. The seed was sprayed over the ground in huge quantities by aeroplanes. The
10 planes had been planting seed for nearly a month when it began to rain. By then, however, in many places the grass had already taken root. In place of the great trees which had been growing there for centuries, patches of green had begun to appear in the blackened soil.

New words and expressions 生词和短语

control (l.2) /kən'trəʊl/ n. 控制
smoke (l.3) /sməʊk/ n. 烟
desolate (l.4) /'desələt/ adj. 荒凉的
threaten (l.5) /'θretn/ v. 威胁
surrounding (l.5) /sə'raʊndɪŋ/ adj. 周围的
destruction (l.5) /dɪ'strʌkʃən/ n. 破坏，毁灭
flood (l.7) /flʌd/ n. 洪水，水灾
authority (l.8) /ɔː'θɒrɪti/ n. (常用复数) 当局

grass-seed (ll.8-9) /'grɑːs-ˌsiːd/ n. 草籽
spray (l.9) /spreɪ/ v. 喷撒
quantity (l.9) /'kwɒntɪti/ n. 量
root (l.11) /ruːt/ n. 根
century (l.11) /'sentʃəri/ n. 世纪
patch (l.11) /pætʃ/ n. 小片
blacken (l.12) /'blækən/ v. (使) 变黑，(使) 发暗

Notes on the text 课文注释

1 had been fighting 是过去完成进行时，表示过去某一时刻之前一直进行的动作。
2 before they could get it under control, 在他们控制住火势之前。
   under control, 受到控制。
3 for miles around, 方圆数英里。
4 Winter was coming on, 冬季即将来临，come on 这里作 "开始"、"来临" 讲，用于指时间、季节等自然条件情况的出现。
5 for heavy rain would not only wash away the soil but would cause serious floods as well, 因为大雨不仅会冲走土壤，而且还会引起严重的水灾。for 是一个并列连词，用于陈述原因；wash away 是 "冲刷" 的意思。
6 in huge quantities, 大量地。
7 take root, 生根。
8 in place of, 代替。

参考译文

　　消防队员们同那场森林大火搏斗了将近 3 个星期才最后把火势控制住。就在不久之前，参天大树还覆盖方圆数英里的土地。而现在，发热的地面上仍然升腾着烟雾，弥漫在荒凉的山丘上。冬季即将来临，这些山丘对周围的村庄具有毁灭性的威胁，因为大雨不仅会冲走土壤，而且还会引起严重的水灾。在大火最后被扑灭后，森林管理当局订购了好几吨一种生长迅速的特殊类型的草籽。飞机把这种草籽大量地撒播在地上。飞机撒播近一个月后，开始下起雨来。然而到那时，很多地方的草已经生了根。一片片的绿草开始出现在这片烧焦的土地上，代替了多少世纪以来一直生长在那里的参天大树。

Summary writing 摘要写作

Answer these questions *in not more than 75 words*.
回答下列问题，将答案组成一个段落，不要超过 75 个单词。

1 How long did it take the firemen to get the forest fire under control?

2 Had all the great trees been burnt or not? Was there danger that heavy rain would cause serious floods or not? Would the floods destroy the surrounding villages or not? (*Now that … which*)

3 Did the forest authorities order grass-seed to prevent this or not? For how long was it sprayed over the ground by planes? (*To prevent this … which …*)

4 Did it begin to rain or not? Where had the grass taken root? (*By the time that …*)

Composition 作文

Rewrite the following sentences using the joining words in parentheses:
用括号中的连词改写以下句子：

1 The firemen cut down trees. They prevented the fire from spreading. (*in order to*)

2 The fire raged for two weeks. It caused millions of pounds' worth of damage. (*which*)

3 Forest workers planted young trees quickly. The whole area would become a desert. (*so that … not*)

Letter writing 书信写作

Write six sentences beginning with each of the following phrases:
完成用以下短语开头的句子：

I am sorry ...; Forgive me for ...; I was so glad ...; I have not heard ...; What a surprise ...; It was very kind ... .

Key structures 关键句型

The planes had been planting seed for nearly a month when it began to rain. 过去完成时和过去完成进行时

a Do you remember these sentences? **(KS38)**
你还记得以下句子吗？（参见第 38 课关键句型）

He *lived in* Scotland fifteen years *ago*.　　　　He *had lived in* Scotland for fifteen years *before* he came to England.

b Now compare these pairs of sentences:
对比以下句子：

He had already finished work before I arrived. 我到达之前他已经完成了工作。　　.

He had been working in a factory for years before he got this job. 在得到这个工作前，他已在一个工厂干了多年。

I asked him what he had lost. 我问他丢了什么。

I asked him what he had been doing all afternoon. 我问他整个下午在干什么。

Exercises 练习

A Underline the verbs in the passage which tell us *what had happened* and *what had been happening*.
画出课文中过去完成时和过去完成进行时的句子。

B Give the correct form of the verbs in parentheses. Do not refer to the passage until you finish the exercise:
用括号中动词的正确形式填空，完成练习后再对照课文，核对你的答案：

1 Firemen _____ (fight) the forest fire for nearly three weeks before they could get it under control. A short time before, great trees _____ (cover) the countryside for miles around.

2 The planes _____ (plant) seed for nearly a month when it began to rain. By then, however, in many places the grass already _____ (take) root. In place of the great trees which _____ (grow) there for centuries, patches of green _____ (begin) to appear in the blackened soil.

C What happened? What had happened? What had been happening?
Give the correct form of the verbs in parentheses:
一般过去时、过去完成时和过去完成进行时。用括号中动词的正确形式填空：

After Howard Carter _____ (discover) Tutankhamen's tomb, strange reports _____ (appear) in the newspapers. Three of the people who _____ (take) part in the discovery _____ (die) soon afterwards. Though nothing _____ (happen) to Carter himself, newspapers _____ (claim) that these people _____ (die) because of the 'curse of the Pharaohs'. These absurd stories have been forgotten, but Carter's great discovery remains. Archaeologists _____ (search) the Valley of Kings for years, but until 1922 nothing _____ (find).

Special difficulties 难点

Words often confused 经常容易混淆的词

Study these examples:
细读以下例子：

a *Control* (1.2) and *Check*.
He *controls* a large business company. 他掌控着一个很大的商业公司。
A mechanic *checked* my car engine. 一位机械师检查了我汽车的发动机。

b *Great* (1.2) and *Big*.
The Parthenon is a *great* building. (An important building.) 帕台农神庙是一座重要的建筑。
Skyscrapers are *big* buildings. 摩天大楼是高大的楼房。

c *Soil* (1.6) and *Ground* (1.4).
Olive trees can grow in poor *soil*. 橄榄树能在贫瘠的土壤里生长。
The ball fell to the *ground*. 球落到地面上。

Exercise 练习

Choose the correct words in the following sentences:
选择正确的词：

1 The inspector (checked) (controlled) my ticket.

2 Nothing can grow in this poor (soil) (ground).

3 Have you (checked) (controlled) those figures?

4 Beethoven was a (big) (great) composer.

Multiple choice questions 选择题

Comprehension 理解

1 Grass-seed had to be planted quickly _____ .

(*a*) to prevent flooding

(*b*) because it was late in the season

(*c*) to save the trees

(*d*) because the trees had been growing for centuries

2 Planes were used because _____ .

(*a*) there had been a fire

(*b*) the hills were bare

(*c*) there weren't any trees

(*d*) this was the quickest way to plant huge quantities of seed

Structure 句型

3 _____ had they been fighting the forest fire? For nearly three weeks.

(*a*) How much   (*b*) How often   (*c*) What time   (*d*) How long

4 The hills threatened the surrounding villages with destruction. The villages _____ .

(*a*) were destroyed   (*b*) had destroyed   (*c*) might be destroyed   (*d*) could destroy

5 If it rained heavily there _____ floods.

(*a*) will be   (*b*) can be   (*c*) had been   (*d*) would be

6 The planes _____ nearly a month to plant the seed.

(*a*) did   (*b*) made   (*c*) took   (*d*) had

7 The trees had been there _____ .

(*a*) since centuries   (*b*) before centuries   (*c*) for centuries   (*d*) centuries long

Vocabulary 词汇

8 Heavy rain would wash away the soil. It would _____ .

(*a*) clean it   (*b*) carry it away   (*c*) wash it   (*d*) wet it

9 Large _____ of seed were used.

(*a*) weights   (*b*) measures   (*c*) tons   (*d*) amounts

10 The seed had already taken root. It had begun to _____ .

(*a*) grow   (*b*) root   (*c*) grow up   (*d*) increase

11 Patches of green had begun to appear. There was green grass _____ .

(*a*) everywhere   (*b*) only in one or two places

(*c*) in one place   (*d*) here and there

12 The grass had begun to appear in the soil. It had begun to _____ .

(*a*) point   (*b*) show   (*c*) seem   (*d*) point out

Lesson 63　She was not amused　她并不觉得好笑

First listen and then answer the question.

听录音，然后回答以下问题。

Why did Jenny want to leave the wedding reception?

his great sense of humour

Jeremy Hampden has a large circle of friends and is very popular at parties. Everybody admires him for his great sense of humour — everybody, that is, except his six-year-old daughter, Jenny. Recently, one of Jeremy's closest friends asked him to make a speech at a
5 wedding reception. This is the sort of thing that Jeremy loves. He prepared the speech carefully and went to the wedding with Jenny. He had included a large number of funny stories in the speech and, of course, it was a great success. As soon as he had finished, Jenny told him she wanted to go home. Jeremy was a little disappointed by this but he did as his daughter asked. On
10 the way home, he asked Jenny if she had enjoyed the speech. To his surprise, she said she hadn't. Jeremy asked her why this was so and she told him that she did not like to see so many people laughing at him!

New words and expressions　生词和短语

circle (l.1) /'sɜːkəl/ n. 圈子
admire (l.2) /əd'maɪə/ v. 赞美，钦佩
close (l.4) /kləʊs/ adj. 亲密的

wedding (l.5) /'wedɪŋ/ n. 婚礼
reception (l.5) /rɪ'sepʃən/ n. 招待会
sort (l.5) /sɔːt/ n. 种类

Notes on the text　课文注释

1　has a large circle of friends, 交际很广。

2　Everybody admires him for his great sense of humour. 人人都钦佩他那绝妙的幽默感。admire ... for ..., 钦佩……的…… ; sense of humour, 幽默感。

3　but he did as his daughter asked, 但他还是按照女儿的要求做了。as 是连词，引导出状语从句，表示方式。
　　did 是指前一句话中的 go home。

4　To his surprise, 使他吃惊的是。

5　she did not like to see so many people laughing at him, 她不愿意看到那么多人嘲笑他。句中的 laughing at him 是现在分词短语，作 see 的宾语补足语。

参考译文

　　杰里米·汉普登交际甚广，是各种聚会上深受大家欢迎的人。人人都钦佩他那绝妙的幽默感——人人，就是说，除他 6 岁的女儿珍妮之外的每一个人。最近，杰里米的一个最亲密的朋友请他在一个婚礼上致祝词。这正是杰里米喜欢做的事情。他认真准备了讲稿，带着珍妮一道去参加婚礼。他的祝词里面加进了大量逗人的故事，自然大获成功。他刚一讲完，珍妮就对他说她要回家。这不免使杰里米有点扫兴，但他还是按照女儿的要求做了。在回家的路上，他问珍妮是否喜欢他的祝词。使他吃惊的是，她说她不喜欢。杰里米问她为何不喜欢，她说她不愿意看到那么多人嘲笑他！

Summary writing 摘要写作

Answer these questions *in not more than 80 words*.

回答下列问题，将答案组成一个段落，不要超过 80 个单词。

1 Is Jeremy Hampden greatly admired for his great sense of humour or not? What was he invited to do? Did he immediately agree to do so or not? (*When Jeremy ... who is ...*)

2 Did the speech contain a lot of funny stories or not? Was it a great success or not? (*Since*)

3 What did his six-year-old daughter, Jenny, want to do after his speech? Was Jeremy disappointed or not? (*When*)

4 Why had she not enjoyed it? (*because*)

Composition 作文

White two or three sentences using the ideas given below.

用以下词组写出 2 至 3 个句子来。

Jeremy was amused by Jenny's answer — he explained why everybody laughed — there was another reception some time later — Jeremy made a speech — not very funny — Jenny asked why no one laughed.

Letter writing 书信写作

Learn the following opening phrases by heart.

熟记以下两个开头语。

You must be very annoyed with me for ...

I have just heard that ...

Exercise 练习

Write two short paragraphs (of not more than two sentences each) completing the above phrases.

用以上两个开头语写两小段话，每段不超过两句。

Key structures 关键句型

He said that ... He told me ... He asked ... 间接引语 **(KS15, KS39)**

（参见第 15，39 课关键句型）

Study these sentences carefully:

仔细阅读以下句子：

'Open the door for me please,' she said to me. "请给我开门，" 她对我说。

What did she ask me to do? 她让我干什么？

She asked me to open the door for her. 她让我给她把门打开

'Don't make so much noise,' she said to the children. "别弄出这么大的噪音，" 她对孩子们说。

What did she tell the children? 她告诉孩子们什么？

She told them not to make so much noise. 她告诉他们不要弄出这么大的噪音。

'Stay to lunch,' he insisted. "留下来吃午饭，" 他坚持说。

What did he do? 他干了什么？

He insisted that I should stay to lunch. 他坚持我要留下来吃午饭。

'Come with me,' he suggested. "跟我来，" 他建议说。

What did he suggest? 他建议了什么？

He suggested that I should go with him. 他建议我一定要跟他去。

Exercises 练习

A This is the conversation which took place between Jenny and her father. Supply speech marks, commas and question marks where necessary.

下面是珍妮和她父亲的一段对话, 在需要的地方添上引号、逗号和问号。**(SD26)**（参见第 26 课难点）

1 I want to go home Jenny told him.

2 Did you enjoy the speech Jenny Jeremy asked.

3 No she said.

4 Why didn't you enjoy it Jeremy asked.

5 I do not like to see so many people laughing at you she told him.

B Now answer these questions. Do not refer to the passage until you finish the exercise:

回答以下问题, 完成练习后再对照课文, 核对你的答案:

1 What did Jenny tell him?

2 What did Jeremy ask Jenny?

3 What did she answer?

4 What did Jeremy ask her?

5 What did she tell him?

C Answer these questions:

回答以下问题:

1 'Keep quiet!' he said. What did he tell me to do?

2 'Send him a fax,' he suggested. What did he suggest?

3 'Don't worry about it,' he told me. What did he tell me?

4 'Ask him about it,' he insisted. What did he do?

D Study these examples:

仔细阅读以下句子:

Will it rain tomorrow? 明天会下雨吗?

I wonder if it will rain tomorrow. 我不知道明天是否会下雨。

Why didn't he mention this to me? 他为什么不向我提这件事?

I wonder why he didn't mention this to me. 我不知道他为什么不向我提这件事。

Write the following sentences again, beginning each one with 'I wonder'.

用 I wonder 开头来改写以下句子。

1 Can he wait a few minutes longer? I wonder if ...

2 When will he arrive? I wonder when ...

3 Has he passed his examination?

4 Where is he?

5 Why didn't she telephone?

6 When shall we see him again?

7 Did she catch the wrong bus?

8 Could you spare me a moment?

Multiple choice questions 选择题
Comprehension 理解

1 Jeremy is very popular because _____ .

  (a) he makes speeches   (b) he tells stories

  (c) he loves wedding receptions   (d) he's an amusing person

2 Jeremy's daughter, Jenny, failed to realize that _____ .

  (a) the wedding reception hadn't finished

  (b) everyone had been laughing at Jeremy's stories, not at Jeremy

  (c) it was a party

  (d) Jeremy had finished his speech

Structure 句型

3 Everybody admires him because _____ a great sense of humour

  (a) he's got   (b) he is   (c) he got   (d) has he

4 _____ Jenny, everyone admires him for his great sense of humour.

  (a) Except for   (b) Apart   (c) Except   (d) Unless

5 Jeremy _____ making speeches.

  (a) is loving   (b) loves   (c) has been loving   (d) was loving

6 It was a great success. He succeeded _____ everyone laugh.

  (a) to make   (b) for making   (c) in make   (d) in making

7 Jeremy was a little disappointed. He was _____ disappointed.

  (a) little   (b) somehow   (c) enough   (d) somewhat

Vocabulary 词汇

8 Everyone admires him. They _____ him.

  (a) think highly of   (b) laugh at   (c) estimate   (d) esteem

9 Recently he was invited to a reception. He was invited to a reception _____ .

  (a) lastly   (b) at last   (c) lately   (d) at least

10 He made a speech at a wedding reception. He spoke during the _____ .

  (a) wedding   (b) marriage   (c) ceremony   (d) party

11 This is the sort of thing he loves. It's the _____ of thing he loves.

  (a) species   (b) category   (c) kind   (d) class

12 He included some funny stories. He _____ .

  (a) put them in   (b) consisted of them   (c) contained them   (d) comprised them

Sentence structure 句子结构

Rewrite this sentence, then check your answer against the text.

改写以下句子, 完成练习后再对照课文第 5-6 行, 核对你的答案。

After preparing the speech carefully, he went to the wedding with Jenny.

He _____ .

Lesson 64 The Channel Tunnel 英吉利海峡隧道

First listen and then answer the question.

听录音，然后回答以下问题。

Why was the first tunnel not completed?

connecting Britain to the European continent

In 1858, a French engineer, Aimé Thomé de Gamond, arrived in England with a plan for a twenty-one-mile tunnel under the English Channel. He said that it would be possible to build a platform in the centre of the Channel. This platform would serve as a port and a
5 railway station. The tunnel would be well-ventilated if tall chimneys were built above sea level. In 1860, a better plan was put forward by an Englishman, William Low. He suggested that a double railway-tunnel should be built. This would solve the problem of ventilation, for if a train entered this tunnel, it would draw in fresh air behind it. Forty-two years later a tunnel was actually
10 begun. If, at the time, the British had not feared invasion, it would have been completed. The world had to wait almost another 100 years for the Channel Tunnel. It was officially opened on March 7, 1994, finally connecting Britain to the European continent.

New words and expressions 生词和短语

tunnel (title) /'tʌnl/ *n.* 隧道
port (l.4) /pɔːt/ *n.* 港口
ventilate (l.5) /'ventɪleɪt/ *v.* 通风
chimney (l.6) /'tʃɪmni/ *n.* 烟囱
sea level (l. 6) /'siː-ˌlevəl/ 海平面
double (l.7) /'dʌbəl/ *adj.* 双的
ventilation (l.8) /ˌventɪ'leɪʃən/ *n.* 通风

fear (l.10) /fɪə/ *v.* 害怕
invasion (l.10) /ɪn'veɪʒən/ *n.* 入侵，侵略
officially (l.11) /ə'fɪʃəli/ *adv.* 正式地
connect (l.12) /kə'nekt/ *v.* 连接
European (l.12) /ˌjʊərə'piːən/ *adj.* 欧洲的
continent (l.12) /'kɒntɪnənt/ *n.* 大陆

Notes on the text 课文注释

1 a plan for a twenty-one-mile tunnel under the English Channel, 建造一条长 21 英里、穿越英吉利海峡的隧道计划, for a ... Channel 是介词短语, 作定语, 修饰名词 plan。

2 serve as ..., 用作……, 充当……, 与 serve for 同义。

3 a better plan was put forward, 提出了一项更好的计划, put forward 提出（计划、建议等）。

4 He suggested that a double railway-tunnel should be built. 他提议建造双轨隧道。在英文中, 动词 suggest, demand, recommend 等后面所接的 that 宾语从句中, 谓语动词要用 should +动词原形, 而 should 又常常省略, 这是一种虚拟语气的结构。

5 If, at the time, the British had not feared invasion, it would have been completed. 如果不是因为那时英国人害怕入侵, 隧道早就建成了。这是英语中的虚拟语气。虚拟语气所表述的不是一个事实, 而只是一种假设或愿望, 常伴有 if 引导的非真实条件句。以上的这句话是对大战期间所发生的事情的一种假设, 而这种假设与事实不符。因此, 在条件句中要用过去完成时 had not feared, 而主句中则要用 would + have +过去分词。

参考译文

1858 年，一位名叫埃梅·托梅·德·干蒙的法国工程师带着建造一条长 21 英里、穿越英吉利海峡的隧道计划到了英国。他说，可以在隧道中央建造一座平台，这座平台将用作港口和火车站。如果再建些伸出海面的高大的烟囱状通风管，隧道就具备了良好的通风条件。1860 年，一位名叫威廉·洛的英国人提出了一项更好的计划。他提议建一条双轨隧道，这样就解决了通风问题。因为如果有一列火车开进隧道，它就把新鲜空气随之抽进了隧道。42 年以后，隧道实际已经开始建了。如果不是因为那时英国人害怕入侵，隧道早已建成了。世界不得不再等将近 100 年才看到海峡隧道竣工。它于 1994 年 3 月 7 日正式开通，将英国与欧洲大陆连到了一起。

Summary writing 摘要写作

Answer these questions *in not more than 85 words.*
回答下列问题，将答案组成一个段落，不要超过 85 个单词。

1 Who planned to build a tunnel under the English Channel in 1858? How would it be ventilated? (*The tunnel, which ...*)

2 Who suggested a better plan two years later?

3 How would passing trains solve the problem of ventilation in his proposed double railway-tunnel? (*because they would*)

4 Did work begin forty-two years later or not? Why was it stopped? (*Though ... because*)

5 When was the Channel Tunnel officially opened? (*However*)

Composition 作文

Rewrite the following sentences using the joining words in parentheses:
用括号中的连词改写以下句子：

1 The English Channel separates Britain from Europe. The country has not been invaded since 1066. (*Thanks to ... which*)

2 Modern warfare is far more complex. Such fears no longer exist. (*However, now that ...*)

3 Britain benefits enormously from a Channel Tunnel. Europe benefits enormously from a Channel Tunnel. (*Both ... and*)

Letter writing 书信写作

Write opening sentences which would be suitable for letters to the following:
为以下书信写出恰当的开头语：

1 A former teacher who has just got engaged.

2 A friend who has sent you a telegram on your birthday.

3 A librarian who has sent you information you wanted.

4 An aunt you failed to meet for an appointment.

Key structures 关键句型

If the British had not feared invasion, it would have been completed.

a   Do you remember these sentences?
你还记得以下句子吗？
If he is out, I'll call tomorrow. **(KS16)**（参见第 16 课关键句型）
You'll miss the train *if you don't hurry.* **(KS16)**（参见第 16 课关键句型）

If you went to the exhibition, you would enjoy it. **(KS40)**（参见第 40 课关键句型）

If I were in your position, I would act differently. **(KS40)**（参见第 40 课关键句型）

b　Now study these sentences carefully:

仔细阅读以下句子：

You would have missed the train *if you had not hurried*. 如果你当时不赶紧的话，你就会赶不上火车的。

If you had gone to the exhibition, you would have enjoyed it. 如果你去过那个展览的话，你就会享受到它的乐趣的。

If I had been in your position, I would have acted differently. 如果我当时处在你的位置上，我会采用不同的做法的。

If you could have made him change his mind, you would have saved him a lot of trouble. 如果你当时能使他改变想法，你就会使他免遭许多麻烦。

Exercises　练习

A　How many sentences in the passage contain the word *if*? Study the form of the verbs in these sentences.

课文中有几个包含 if 的句子？注意其中动词的时态。

B　Give the correct form of the verbs in parentheses. Do not refer to the passage until you finish the exercise:

用括号中动词的正确形式填空，完成练习后再对照课文，核对你的答案：

1　The tunnel would be well-ventilated if tall chimneys ＿＿＿＿＿＿ (be) built above sea level.

2　If a train entered this tunnel, it ＿＿＿＿＿＿ (draw) in fresh air behind it.

3　If, at the time, the British had not feared invasion, it ＿＿＿＿＿＿ (complete).

C　Give the correct form of the verbs in parentheses:

用括号中动词的正确形式填空：

1　If you had told me about it earlier, I ＿＿＿＿＿＿ (be able) to help you.

2　If you ＿＿＿＿＿＿ (can/come) with us, we would have been pleased.

3　You ＿＿＿＿＿＿ (not make) such a mistake if you had been more careful.

4　If father ＿＿＿＿＿＿ (be) alive, he would be horrified.

5　If it ＿＿＿＿＿＿ (be) fine tomorrow, we shall go for a swim.

Special difficulties　难点

The verb *draw* has a different meaning in each of these sentences. Study them carefully:

动词 draw 在以下句子中的含义各不相同。仔细阅读以下例句：

If a train entered this tunnel, it would *draw in* fresh air behind it. (1.9)

The dog *drew back* in terror when it saw the snake. 当那条狗看见蛇时，它就恐惧地退了回来。

A taxi *drew up* outside the bank. (It stopped.) Two men got out and then the taxi *drew off*. (It went away.) 一辆出租车停在银行外面，两个男人下了车，然后车开走了。

A new trading agreement was *drawn up* between Holland and Denmark. (A new agreement was made.) 荷兰和丹麦签署了一项新的贸易协定。

Exercise　练习

Choose the correct words in the following sentences:

选择正确的词：

1　We shall have to draw (in) (up) a new plan.

2　When I recognized who he was I drew (back) (up) in horror.

3　The car drew (back) (up) outside the cinema.

Multiple choice questions 选择题

Comprehension 理解

1 William Low's idea was better than de Gamond's because _____ .

(*a*) it was cheaper

(*b*) there were no chimneys in his plan

(*c*) his tunnel would be better ventilated

(*d*) it wouldn't be necessary to build a platform in the centre of the Channel

2 Work on the Channel Tunnel _____ .

(*a*) began immediately after William Low outlined his plan

(*b*) never began

(*c*) began a long time after William Low put up his plan

(*d*) began recently when William Low put up his plan

Structure 句型

3 It would be possible to build a platform. A platform _____ .

(*a*) could build　　(*b*) would be built　　(*c*) could be built　　(*d*) would build

4 He suggested _____ a double railway tunnel.

(*a*) to build　　(*b*) build　　(*c*) building　　(*d*) that building

5 This would solve the problem. That's how the problem _____ solved.

(*a*) would been　　(*b*) would be　　(*c*) would have been　　(*d*) had been

6 If a train _____ this tunnel, it would draw in fresh air behind it.

(*a*) would enter　　(*b*) entered　　(*c*) will enter　　(*d*) enters

7 People were _____ the idea of a Channel Tunnel.

(*a*) interesting in　　(*b*) interested for　　(*c*) interested in　　(*d*) interesting for

Vocabulary 词汇

8 The tunnel would be well ventilated. It would have good _____ .

(*a*) air　　(*b*) airing　　(*c*) ventilation　　(*d*) circulation

9 A plan was put forward by William Low. He _____ it.

(*a*) suggested　　(*b*) intended　　(*c*) aimed at　　(*d*) planned

10 The British feared invasion. They were _____ it.

(*a*) in favour of　　(*b*) afraid of　　(*c*) prevented　　(*d*) ended

11 It finally connects Britain and Europe. Britain and Europe are finally _____ .

(*a*) mixed　　(*b*) joined together　　(*c*) rejoined　　(*d*) combined

12 The tunnel has now been completed. It has been _____ .

(*a*) ended　　(*b*) finished　　(*c*) prevented　　(*d*) stopped

Sentence structure 句子结构

Make two sentences of the following, then check your answer against the text.

将下列句子改写成两句话，然后对照课文第 6-8 行，核对你的答案。

In 1860, a better plan was put forward by an Englishman, William Low, who suggested that a double railway-tunnel should be built.

Lesson 65   Jumbo versus the police   小象对警察

First listen and then answer the question.

听录音, 然后回答以下问题。

Why did the police have to push Jumbo off the main street?

The police had a difficult time

Last Christmas, the circus owner, Jimmy Gates, decided to take some presents to a children's hospital. Dressed up as Father Christmas and accompanied by a 'guard of honour' of six pretty girls, he set off down the main street of the city riding a baby
5 elephant called Jumbo. He should have known that the police would never allow this sort of thing. A policeman approached Jimmy and told him he ought to have gone along a side street as Jumbo was holding up the traffic. Though Jimmy agreed to go at once, Jumbo refused to move. Fifteen policemen had to push very hard to get him off the main street. The police had a
10 difficult time, but they were most amused. 'Jumbo must weigh a few tons,' said a policeman afterwards, 'so it was fortunate that we didn't have to carry him. Of course, we should arrest him, but as he has a good record, we shall let him off this time. '

New words and expressions   生词和短语

versus (title) /'vɜːsəs/ *prep.* 对
Christmas (l.1) /'krɪsməs/ *n.* 圣诞节
circus (l.1) /'sɜːkəs/ *n.* 马戏团
present (l.2) /'prezənt/ *n.* 礼物
accompany (l.3) /ə'kʌmpəni/ *v.* 陪伴

approach (l.6) /ə'prəʊtʃ/ *v.* 走近
ought (l.7) /ɔːt/ *modal verb* 应该
weigh (l.10) /weɪ/ *v.* 重
fortunate (l.11) /'fɔːtʃənət/ *adj.* 幸运的

Notes on the text   课文注释

1 Dressed up as Father Christmas and accompanied by a 'guard of honour' of six pretty girls, 打扮成圣诞老人, 在由 6 位漂亮姑娘组成的 "仪仗队" 的陪同下。过去分词短语 dressed up ... 和 accompanied by 作状语, 说明伴随状态。

2 He should have known, 他本应知道。这里 "should + have + 过去分词" 表示本应发生但实际上并未发生的事情。

3 he ought to have gone along a side street, 他本应该走一条小路。ought 是助动词, "ought + have + 过去分词" 表示过去该做而没有做的事情。

4 hold up the traffic, 阻碍交通。

5 get him off the main street, 把它推离主要街道。

6 he has a good record, 它表现一贯很好, 这里的 record 是指履历, 特别是警察局的档案。

7 let him off, 饶恕他。

参考译文

去年圣诞节, 马戏团老板吉米·盖茨决定送些礼物给儿童医院。他打扮成圣诞老人, 在由 6 个漂亮姑娘组成的"仪仗队"的陪同下,骑上一头名叫江伯的小象,沿着城里的主要街道出发了。他本该知道警察决不会允许这类事情发生。一个警察走过来告诉吉米,他应该走一条小路,因为江伯阻碍了交通。虽然吉米同意马上就走,但江伯却拒绝移动。15 个警察不得不用很大的力气把它推离主要街道。警察虽然吃了苦头,但他们还是感到很有趣。"江伯一定有好几吨重,"一个警察事后这样说,"值得庆幸的是它没让我们抬它走。当然,我们应该逮捕它,但由于它一贯表现很好,这次我们饶了它。"

Summary writing 摘要写作

Answer these questions *in not more than 80 words.*

回答下列问题,将答案组成一个段落,不要超过 80 个单词。

1 What did he decide to take to a children's hospital? How did the circus owner, Jimmy Gates, dress up? Did he set off down the main street of the city, or did he go down a side street? Was he riding an elephant called Jumbo or not? (*After having ... and ... riding*)

2 Was he told that he was holding up the traffic or not? Did Jimmy agree to go at once, or not? Did Jumbo agree to go, or did he refuse to move? How many policemen had to push him off the main street? (*On being ... but ... so ...*)

3 Did he have a good record or not? Was Jumbo arrested or not? (*As ... however, ...*)

Composition 作文

Write three or four sentences using the ideas given below:

用以下词组写出 3 至 4 个句子来:

The children were waiting at the hospital — Jimmy and the guard of honour arrived — a great welcome — Jimmy gave presents to the children — they rode on Jumbo — time to leave — Jumbo refused to move.

Letter writing 书信写作

Learn the following opening phrases by heart:

熟记以下两个开头语:

I really hate to complain, but ... Some time ago, I ...

Exercise 练习

Write two short paragraphs (of not more than two sentences each) completing the above phrases.

用以上两个开头语各写一小段话,每段不要超过两句。

Key structures 关键句型

Must, Have to, Should and Ought to

a Do you remember these sentences?

你还记得以下句子吗?

I must leave now. I have got to leave now. **(KS17)**(参见第 17 课关键句型)

She had to go shopping yesterday. **(KS17)**(参见第 17 课关键句型)

b Now compare these pairs of sentences:

对比以下各组句子:

I can't go to the cinema tonight; I must (or have to) write some letters. 今晚我不能去看电影,我必须写信。

I should (or ought to) do some work tonight, but I think I shall go to the cinema instead. 我今晚应该做点事,但我想我会去看电影。

Unit 3   Lesson 65

I missed the train, so I had to take a taxi. 我误了火车，因此不得不搭个出租车。

I'm sorry I'm late. I should have taken (or ought to have taken) a taxi. 很遗憾我迟到了。我应该搭个出租车。

Exercises 练习

A Study the use in the passage of *have to, should* and *ought*.

认真学习课文中 have to, should 和 ought 的用法。

B Give the correct form of the verbs in parentheses. Do not refer to the passage until you finish the exercise:

用括号中动词的正确形式填空，完成练习后再对照课文，核对你的答案：

1 He _____ (should/know) that the police would never allow this sort of thing. A policeman approached Jimmy and told him he _____ (ought/go) along a side street as Jumbo was holding up the traffic.

2 Fifteen policemen _____ (have to) push very hard.

3 It was fortunate that we _____ (not have to) carry him. Of course, we _____ (should/arrest) him, but we shall let him off this time.

C Supply the correct form of *should, ought to* or *have to* in these sentences:

用 should, ought to 或 have to 的正确形式填空：

1 He _____ (come) at 4 o'clock if the plane arrives on time.

2 I didn't go shopping this morning as I _____ (do) the housework.

3 She _____ (come) to see me yesterday, but she forgot.

4 You _____ (ask) for permission before you left the table.

5 As they didn't understand, I _____ (explain) everything again.

Special difficulties 难点

a The verb *let* has a different meaning in each of these sentences. Study them carefully:

动词 let 在以下句子中含义各不相同，仔细阅读以下例句：

As he has a good record, we shall *let him off* this time. (ll.11-12) (We shall not punish him.)

I expected him to help me, but he *let me down*. (He failed to do what I expected him to do.) 我期待着他来帮我，但他使我感到失望。

If anyone knocks at the door when I am out, don't *let him in*. 我不在时如有人敲门，不要让他进来。

Who *let the dog out*? 谁把狗放出去了？

b Words often confused 经常容易混淆的词

Study these examples:

仔细阅读以下例句：

Agree and *Accept*.

Though Jimmy *agreed* to go at once, Jumbo refused to move. (ll.8-9)

We are not allowed to *accept* presents from customers. 不允许我们接受顾客的礼物。

c *Dress up* and *Dress*.

Dressed up as Father Christmas ... (ll.2-3) (Wearing fancy dress.) 打扮成圣诞老人……

I got up at 6 o'clock, washed, shaved, *dressed* and had breakfast. 我 6 点钟起床、洗脸、刮胡子、穿衣、吃早饭。

Exercise 练习

Choose the correct words in the following sentences:

选择正确的词或短语：

1 The teacher (agreed) (accepted) the boy's apology and let him (off) (down).

2 He was going to lend me a policeman's uniform so that I could (dress) (dress up) for the party, but he let me (in) (down).

Multiple choice questions 选择题

Comprehension 理解

1 Jimmy wouldn't have been stopped if _____ .

   (a) he had gone down a side street

   (b) he hadn't ridden an elephant

   (c) he had gone down the main street

   (d) he hadn't dressed up as Father Christmas

2 One of these statements is true. Which one?

   (a) Jumbo was arrested.

   (b) Jimmy was arrested.

   (c) The police were not amused by what had happened.

   (d) The police had a difficult time getting Jumbo off the main street.

Structure 句型

3 Jimmy _____ Father Christmas.

   (a) seemed as   (b) looked like   (c) looked as   (d) seemed

4 He should have known the police wouldn't allow it _____ .

   (a) and he did   (b) but he didn't   (c) but he couldn't   (d) but he had

5 He ought to have gone along a side street. That's what he _____ .

   (a) should do   (b) should be doing   (c) should have done   (d) should

6 Jumbo must weigh a few tons. Jumbo _____ a few tons.

   (a) probably weighs (b) has to weigh   (c) ought to weigh   (d) should weigh

7 _____ to carry him?

   (a) Did they have   (b) Had they   (c) Must they   (d) Have they

Vocabulary 词汇

8 He set off down the main street. He _____ .

   (a) ran   (b) walked   (c) rode   (d) started his journey

9 Jumbo was holding up the traffic. He had _____ cars.

   (a) picked up some   (b) sat on some   (c) stopped the   (d) held on to the

10 Jimmy agreed to go at once, but Jumbo _____ to move.

   (a) denied   (b) resisted   (c) refused   (d) negated

11 It was fortunate we didn't have to carry him. It was our _____ .

   (a) good chance   (b) good luck   (c) fortune   (d) fate

12 The police let him off. They _____ him.

   (a) allowed   (b) permitted   (c) didn't forbid   (d) didn't punish

Lesson 66　Sweet as honey!　像蜜一样甜！

🔊 **First listen and then answer the question.**

听录音，然后回答以下问题。

What was 'sweet as honey' and why?

In 1963 a Lancaster bomber crashed on Wallis Island, a remote place in the South Pacific, a long way west of Samoa. The plane wasn't too badly damaged, but over the years, the crash was forgotten and the wreck remained undisturbed. Then in 1989, twenty-six years

5　after the crash, the plane was accidentally rediscovered in an aerial survey of the island. By this time, a Lancaster bomber in reasonable condition was rare and worth rescuing. The French authorities had the plane packaged and moved in parts back to France. Now a group of enthusiasts are going to have the plane restored. It has four Rolls-Royce Merlin engines, but the group will

10　need to have only three of them rebuilt. Imagine their surprise and delight when they broke open the packing cases and found that the fourth engine was sweet as honey — still in perfect condition. A colony of bees had turned the engine into a hive and it was totally preserved in beeswax!

sweet as honey

New words and expressions　生词和短语

Lancaster (l.1) /ˈlæŋkəstə/ *n.* 兰开斯特
bomber (l.1) /ˈbɒmə/ *n.* 轰炸机
remote (l.1) /rɪˈməut/ *adj.* 偏僻的
Pacific (l.2) /pəˈsɪfɪk/ *n.* 太平洋
damage (l.3) /ˈdæmɪdʒ/ *v.* 毁坏
wreck (l.4) /rek/ *n.* 残骸
rediscover (l.5) /riːdɪsˈkʌvə/ *v.* 重新发现
aerial (l.5) /ˈeərɪəl/ *adj.* 航空的
survey (l.6) /ˈsɜːveɪ/ *n.* 调查
rescue (l.7) /ˈreskjuː/ *v.* 营救

package (l.8) /ˈpækɪdʒ/ *v.* 把……打包
enthusiast (l.9) /ɪnˈθjuːzɪæst/ *n.* 热心人
restore (l.9) /rɪˈstɔː/ *v.* 修复
imagine (l.10) /ɪˈmædʒɪn/ *v.* 想象
packing case (ll.10-11) /ˈpækɪŋ-keɪs/ 包装箱
colony (l.11) /ˈkɒləni/ *n.* 群
bee (l.11) /biː/ *n.* 蜂
hive (l.12) /haɪv/ *n.* 蜂房
preserve (l.12) /prɪˈzɜːv/ *v.* 保护
beeswax (l.12) /ˈbiːzwæks/ *n.* 蜂蜡

Notes on the text　课文注释

1　west of Samoa, 萨摩亚群岛以西。

2　worth rescuing, 有抢救的价值。

3　The French authorities had the plane packaged and moved in parts back to France. 法国政府让人把飞机包装起来，一部分一部分地搬回法国。句子中的动词 have 被称为使役动词，结构是 have +名词或代词+过去分词。在使用这种结构时，我们可能不知道或认为不必指明为我们服务的人是谁，然而，这种结构比被动语态更强调"使"别人为我们服务这一事实。

参考译文

　　1963 年，一架兰开斯特轰炸机在瓦立斯岛坠毁。那是南太平洋中一个很偏僻的小岛，位于萨摩亚群岛以西，距离群岛还有很长一段距离。飞机损坏的程度并不严重，但是，多年来这起飞机失事已被遗忘，飞机残骸也没受到破环。于是，到了 1989 年，飞机失事 26 年后，在对小岛的一次航空勘查中那架飞机被意外地发现了。到了那个时候，状况良好的兰开斯特轰炸机实属罕见，值得抢救。法国政府让人把飞机包装起来，一部分一部分地搬回法国。一群热心人计划修复这架飞机。该飞机装配有 4 台劳斯莱斯的默林发动机，但是他们只需要修复其中的 3 台。想一想他们所感受到的惊奇和兴奋——当他们拆开包装箱时，他们发现第 4 台发动机就像蜂蜜一样甜——发动机完好无损。一群蜜蜂把发动机变成了蜂房，发动机在蜂蜡中被完整地保存了下来。

Summary writing 摘要写作

Answer these questions *in not more than 100 words*.
回答下列问题，将答案组成一个段落，不要超过 100 个单词。

1　Was the Lancaster bomber badly damaged when it crashed on a remote island in the south Pacific?
2　How long did the wreck remain undisturbed? How was it rediscovered? (*Then ... until ...*)
3　What did the French authorities do with the plane? Who will be having it restored? (*..., where ...*)
4　How many engines will they have to have rebuilt? Why is the fourth engine still in perfect condition? (..., *but ... because ...*)

Composition 作文

Rewrite the sentences below using the joining words in parentheses. Make any necessary changes:
用括号中的连词改写以下句子，必要时可作改动：

1　The Lancaster bomber crashed. It was not too badly damaged. The island was very remote. The wreck remained undisturbed for more than twenty years. (*When..., but ... so ... that*)
2　Now some enthusiasts in France plan to have the plane restored. They are absolutely delighted. (*who*)
3　They will only need to have three of the engines rebuilt. The fourth engine was preserved in beeswax. It is still as sweet as honey. (*because ... and*)

Letter writing 书信写作

Write a short opening paragraph of a letter to a friend who has invited you to go to the circus with him.
一位朋友邀请你和他一起去看马戏表演，写出一小段话作为给他的信的开头部分。

Key structures 关键句型

Have (KS18, KS42)（参见第 18，42 课的关键句型）

Study these sentences carefully.
细读以下句子：

I washed my car. (I washed it myself.) 我洗了车。
I *had* my car *washed*. (Someone else washed it for me.) 我让人洗了车。
I'm going to clean my suit. (I'm going to clean it by myself.) 我将洗一洗我的西服。
I'm going to *have* my suit *cleaned*. (Someone else will do it for me.) 我将把我的西服送出去洗一洗。
He *had* his hair *cut* yesterday. 他昨天理了发。
I will have to *have* my watch *repaired*. 我将不得不去修表。
Did you *have* your watch *repaired*? 你把你的表修好了吗？
I didn't *have* my watch *repaired*. 我没有把表修好。

Unit 3   Lesson 66

Exercises 练习

A Find four examples in the passage of *have* + object + past participle: *have something done*.
从课文中找出 4 个使役动词的例子，即 have + 宾语 + 过去分词。

B Write these sentences again using *have* with the verbs in italics. Do not refer to the passage until you have finished the exercise.
将以下句子改成使役结构，保留用斜体印出的动词。完成练习后再对照课文，核对你的答案。

1 The French authorities took charge of the plane. It was *packaged* and moved in parts back to France.

2 The plane is going to be *restored* by a group of enthusiasts.

3 The group are delighted. Only three of the engines will need to be *rebuilt*.

C Rewrite these sentences using *have* with the verb in italics and making any necessary changes.
用 have 和斜体印出的动词改写以下句子，必要时可作改动。

1 He *is building* a new house.

2 She *will make* a new dress.

3 I *did not decorate* the house.

4 They *repaired* the washing machine.

5 We *must cut* this dangerous tree down.

6 We have *to install* this new television set.

Special difficulties 难点

A group of enthusiasts are going to have the plane repaired.

Collective noun + singular or plural verb.
集合名词与连用动词的单数或复数形式。当我们把这个名词当作一种非人格的东西看待时，即当作一个整体，连用的动词应为单数。当我们把这个名词人格化时，即看作组成整体的若干人时，连用的动词应为复数。

Study these sentences:
细读以下句子：

The national team is travelling to London tomorrow. 国家代表队将于明天去伦敦。

The team are all highly talented young people. 全队人员都是天赋极高的年轻人。

The audience is made up of school children. 观众是由学校的学生组成的。

The audience were spellbound by the magic of the performance. 观众们被表演的魅力迷住了。

Exercise 练习

Choose the correct verb in these sentences:
选择正确的动词：

1 The Government (has) (have) taken strong measures against inflation.

2 The shipwrecked crew (was) (were) rescued from the water by helicopter.

3 (Has) (Have) the staff been informed about the meeting?

4 This class (is) (are) a pleasure to teach.

Multiple choice questions 选择题

Comprehension 理解

1 People are interested in restoring the Lancaster bomber because _____ .

   (a) it had crashed over twenty years ago

   (b) the crash took place in a remote island in the South Pacific

   (c) it was a rare model

   (d) it was discovered accidentally

2 What had preserved one of the four engines all these years?

   (a) The kind efforts of the French government.   (b) A colony of bees.

   (c) The interest of a group of enthusiasts.   (d) The remote island west of Samoa.

Structure 句型

3 Wallis Island is west of Samoa. Wallis is _____ .

   (a) to the west of Samoa   (b) to the east of Samoa

   (c) in the west of Samoa   (d) in the east of Samoa

4 The wreck remained undisturbed. It was not _____ .

   (a) moved   (b) damaged   (c) packaged   (d) restored

5 By 1989, a Lancaster bomber was rare and worth _____ .

   (a) to be saved   (b) to save   (c) saved   (d) saving

6 Only three of the four Rolls-Royce Merlin engines _____ rebuilt.

   (a) will have to be   (b) need have been   (c) are being   (d) had to be

Vocabulary 词汇

7 A group of enthusiasts are planning to have the plane _____ .

   (a) repaired   (b) repairing   (c) reparation   (d) being repaired

8 The plane was moved back to France in parts. It was sent _____ .

   (a) as a whole   (b) bit by bit   (c) completely   (d) totally

9 Wallis Island is a remote place in the South Pacific. It is _____ .

   (a) far away   (b) well-known

   (c) popular   (d) close to the European continent

10 _____ the years that followed, the crash was forgotten.

   (a) Between   (b) During   (c) While   (d) Among

11 A Lancaster bomber was rare by 1989. It was _____ .

   (a) common   (b) uncommon   (c) popular   (d) well-known

12 The bomber was in _____ condition.

   (a) fair   (b) bad   (c) perfect   (d) terrible

Sentence structure 句子结构

Join the following sentences, then check your answer against the text.
连接以下句子, 完成练习后对照课文第 1-2 行, 核对你的答案。

A Lancaster bomber crashed on Wallis Island. The island is a remote place in the South Pacific. It is west of Samoa. It is a long way from Samoa.

Lesson 67　Volcanoes　火山

First listen and then answer the question.

听录音，然后回答以下问题。

Why does Tazieff risk his life like this?

Haroun Tazieff, the Polish scientist, has spent his lifetime studying active volcanoes and deep caves in all parts of the world. In 1948, he went to Lake Kivu in the Congo to observe a new volcano which he later named Kituro. Tazieff was able to set up his camp very
5　close to the volcano while it was erupting violently. Though he managed to take a number of brilliant photographs, he could not stay near the volcano for very long. He noticed that a river of liquid rock was coming towards him. It threatened to surround him

he could not stay for very long

completely, but Tazieff managed to escape just in time. He waited until the volcano became quiet and he was
10　able to return two days later. This time, he managed to climb into the mouth of Kituro so that he could take photographs and measure temperatures. Tazieff has often risked his life in this way. He has been able to tell us more about active volcanoes than any man alive.

New words and expressions　生词和短语

volcano (title) /vɒl'keɪnəʊ/ *n.* 火山
active (l.2) /'æktɪv/ *adj.* 活动的
Kivu (l.3) /'kɪvuː/ *n.* 基伍湖
Congo (l.3) /'kɒŋɡəʊ/ *n.* (the ~)刚果
Kituro (l.4) /kɪ'tuːrəʊ/ *n.* 基图罗
erupt (l.5) /ɪ'rʌpt/ *v.*（火山）喷发

violently (l.5) /'vaɪələntli/ *adv.* 猛烈地，剧烈地
manage (l.6) /'mænɪdʒ/ *v.* 设法
brilliant (l.6) /'brɪljənt/ *adj.* 精彩的
liquid (l.7) /'lɪkwɪd/ *adj.* 液态的
escape (l.9) /ɪ'skeɪp/ *v.* 逃脱
alive (l.12) /ə'laɪv/ *adj.* 活着的

Notes on the text　课文注释

1　has spent his lifetime studying, 把毕生的精力都用于研究。动词 spend 后面常加 in doing sth., 其中 in 可以省略。

2　in all parts of the world, 这个介词短语用来修饰前面两个名词, 意思是 "世界各地的（活火山和深洞）"。

3　a river of liquid rock, 一股岩浆, 这是一种修辞方法, 被称为暗喻。

4　in time, 及时地。

5　risked his life, 冒着生命危险。

6　any man alive 中, alive 作定语, 意思是 "在世的人"、"活人"。

参考译文

　　波兰科学家哈罗恩·塔捷耶夫花了毕生的精力来研究世界各地的活火山和深洞。1948 年他去了刚果的基伍湖, 对一座后来被他命名为基图罗的新火山进行观察。当火山正在猛烈地喷发时, 塔捷耶夫有办法把帐篷搭在离它非常近的地方。尽管他设法拍了一些十分精彩的照片, 但他却不能在火山附近停留太长的时间。他发现有一股岩浆正向他流过来, 眼看就要将他团团围住, 但塔捷耶夫还是设法及时逃离了。他等到火山平静下来, 两

天以后又返回去。这次他设法爬进了基图罗火山口, 以便能拍摄照片和测试温度。塔捷耶夫经常冒这样的生命危险。他能告诉我们的有关活火山的情况比任何在世的人都要多。

Summary writing 摘要写作

Answer these questions *in not more than 80 words*.
回答下列问题, 将答案组成一个段落, 不要超过 80 个单词。

1　Where did Tazieff, the Polish scientist, go in 1948? Why did he go there? What did he call it? (*to ... which*)
2　Did he take photographs or not? Did he have to leave almost at once or not? Did a river of liquid rock threaten to surround him or not? (*After taking ... because*)
3　Did he escape just in time or not? When did he return? Had the volcano become quiet, or was it still active? (*but ... when*)
4　Where did he climb this time? Why did he do so? (*in order to*)

Composition 作文

Write three or four sentences using the ideas given below:
用以下词组写出 3 至 4 个句子来:
Tazieff went into the mouth of Kituro — saw the boiling red centre — ash — lumps of rock shooting up — in great danger — took photographs — returned to camp.

Letter writing 书信写作

White six sentences beginning with each of the following:
用以下词组写出 6 封信的开头语:
Thank you ...; What a ...; Forgive ...; I have not ...; I am sorry ...; It was very ... .

Key structures 关键句型

Can, Be able to and Manage to

a　Do you remember these sentences? (**KS43b, c**)
你还记得以下句子吗? (参见第 43 课关键句型 b, c)
I couldn't understand him.
I wasn't able to understand him.
He was able to leave Europe before the war began. 在战争爆发之前, 他离开了欧洲。

b　*Managed to* can be used like *was able to* to show that an action has been completed successfully. (**KS43c**)
managed to 可以像 was able to 表示一个成功地完成了的动作。(参见第 43 课关键句型 c)

Instead of saying: 除了这种表述方法外:	*We can say*: 还可以说:
He didn't agree with me at first but I *was able to* persuade him.	He didn't agree with me at first but I *managed to* persuade him.
He *was able to* leave Europe before the war began.	He *managed to* leave Europe before the war began.

Exercises 练习

A　Underline the verbs *could, was able to* and *managed to* in the passage. Note how they have been used.
画出课文中 could, was able to 和 managed to, 并注意它们的用法。

Unit 3　Lesson 67

B　Supply *could, was able to* or *managed to* in this paragraph. Do not refer to the passage until you finish the exercise.

用 could, was able to 或 managed to 填空，完成练习后再对照课文，核对你的答案。

Tazieff _____ set up his camp very close to the volcano while it was erupting violently. Though he _____ take a number of brilliant photographs, he _____ not stay near the volcano for very long. He noticed that a river of liquid rock was coming towards him. It threatened to surround him completely, but Tazieff escaped just in time. He waited until the volcano became quiet and he _____ return two days later. This time, he _____ climb into the mouth of Kituro so that he _____ take photographs and measure temperatures.

C　Rewrite these sentences using *managed to* in place of *could not*.

改写以下句子，用 managed to 来代替 could not。

1　I could not get into town this morning.

2　They could not find the boy who had run away.

3　He could not find a new job.

4　I could not translate the passage into English.

5　They could not swim to the other side of the river.

Special difficulties　难点

Phrases with *say* and *tell* (KS15) 带 say 与 tell 的短语（参见第15课关键句型）

Study these sentences:

细读以下句子：

a　*Say.*

Did he say *anything* to you about it? No, he *said nothing.* 他有没有告诉你有关的任何事情？没有，他什么也没有说。

He knelt down and s*aid his prayers.* 他跪了下来作祷告。

If you want some more cake, please *say so.* 如果你还想要蛋糕的话，请说一声。

I'm sure it would help if you could s*ay a good word* for him. 如果你能为他说句好话，我相信肯定是有帮助的。

He *said goodbye* and left. 他告辞后离开了。

Please *say no more* about it. 请不要再说这件事了。

b　*Tell.*

He has been able to *tell* us more about volcanoes ... (ll.11-12)

Can you *tell me* anything about it? 你能告诉我有关的任何事情吗？

Please *tell us a story.* 请给我们讲个故事。

Can you *tell the time* in English? 你能用英语报时吗？

I want you to *tell me the truth.* 我要你讲真话。

He often *tells lies.* 他经常说谎。

If you promise not to tell anyone, I'll *tell you a secret.* 如果你发誓不告诉任何人，我要告诉你一个秘密。

Can't you *tell the difference* between an Austin and a Morris? 你能区分奥斯丁舞和莫利斯舞吗？

Exercise　练习

Supply the correct form of *say* or *tell* in the following sentence:

用 say 或 tell 的正确形式填空：

1　He is only five, but he can already _____ the time.

2　They asked the prisoner several questions, but he _____ nothing.

3　If you _____ so, I suppose it's true. I don't think you would _____ me a lie.

4　They are so alike, I can't _____ the difference between them.

5 He _____ me about his experiences in the Navy.

6 If you could _____ a good word for him, he might get the job.

Multiple choice questions 选择题

Comprehension 理解

1 Tazieff went to the Congo _____ .

(a) to observe Lake Kivu

(b) to take photographs

(c) to name a new volcano

(d) to investigate a new volcano

2 Kituro erupted violently _____ .

(a) and Tazieff had to leave but he returned later

(b) so Tazieff had to leave and couldn't return

(c) so Tazieff couldn't take photographs

(d) so Tazieff couldn't measure temperatures

Structure 结构

3 He managed to take a number of photographs. This means he _____ them.

(a) might have taken   (b) could have taken   (c) should have taken   (d) succeeded in taking

4 He escaped just in time. He _____ escaped.

(a) just only   (b) only   (c) soon   (d) only just

5 He waited until the volcano became quiet. He waited _____ quiet.

(a) to the volcano to become   (b) the volcano to become

(c) the volcano became   (d) for the volcano to become

6 He was able to return. This means he _____ .

(a) could if he wanted to   (b) might   (c) could have   (d) did

7 He has been able to tell us a lot _____ volcanoes.

(a) considering   (b) on the subject of   (c) in relation   (d) referring

Vocabulary 词汇

8 Tazieff is a Polish scientist. He comes from _____ .

(a) Pole   (b) Poland   (c) Polish   (d) the Pole

9 He named it Kituro. That's what he _____ it.

(a) called   (b) shouted   (c) cried   (d) screamed

10 The rock was in a liquid state. It wasn't _____ .

(a) firm   (b) stable   (c) whole   (d) solid

11 He wanted to measure temperatures. He wanted to _____ them.

(a) count   (b) make   (c) do   (d) take

12 He has told us more than any _____ person.

(a) alive   (b) lively   (c) live   (d) living

Sentence structure 句子结构

Make two sentences of the following, then check your answer against the text.

将下面的句子改写成两句话, 完成练习后, 再对照课文第 7-9 行, 核对你的答案。

Tazieff noticed that a river of liquid rock, which threatened to surround him completely, was coming towards him, but he managed to escape just in time.

Lesson 68   Persistent   纠缠不休

First listen and then answer the question.

听录音, 然后回答以下问题。

Why did Elizabeth tell Nigel that she was going to the dentist?

I crossed the street to avoid meeting him, but he saw me and came running towards me. It was no use pretending that I had not seen him, so I waved to him. I never enjoy meeting Nigel Dykes. He never has anything to do. No matter how busy you are, he always
5 insists on coming with you. I had to think of a way of preventing him from following me around all morning.

'Hello, Nigel,' I said. 'Fancy meeting you here!'

'Hi, Elizabeth,' Nigel answered. 'I was just wondering how to spend the morning — until I saw you. You're not busy doing anything, are you?'
10 'No, not at all,' I answered. 'I'm going to ...'

'Would you mind my coming with you?' he asked, before I had finished speaking.

'Not at all,' I lied, 'but I'm going to the dentist.'

'Then I'll come with you,' he answered. 'There's always plenty to read in the waiting room!'

There's always plenty to read

New words and expressions 生词和短语

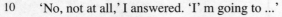

persistent (title) /pə'sɪstənt/ *adj.* 坚持的, 固执的   insist (l.5) /ɪn'sɪst/ *v.* 坚持做
avoid (l.1) /ə'vɔɪd/ *v.* 避开

Notes on the text 课文注释

1 to avoid meeting him, 避免碰上他, 这是动词后面用动名词作宾语的结构。本课下文中出现的 enjoy, fancy, mind, finish 等动词, 也是只接动名词作宾语的动词。
2 came running towards me, 向我跑来。running 是现在分词, 作状语, 表示状况。
3 It was no use pretending, 装作……是没有用了。在这句话中, it 是先行词, 实际上主语是动名词短语 pretending that I had not seen him。
4 No matter how busy you are, 不管你有多忙。这是一个让步状语从句, no matter 常与 how, when, where, what, who 等引导的从句相连, 可译成"无论"。
5 prevent sb. from doing sth. 是"阻止某人做某事", 介词 from 可以省略。
6 Fancy meeting you here! 想不到在这里见到你! fancy + ing 表示对后面的 ing 所表示的动作感到惊奇。
7 You're not busy doing anything, are you? 你不忙, 是吧? 这是一个附加疑问句, 也称反意疑问句。它是由陈述句加上简略疑问句构成的。如果陈述句是肯定的, 那么疑问句用否定形式; 反之, 陈述句是否定的, 疑问句用肯定形式。
8 Would you mind my coming with you? 我跟你一道去行吗? 这是一个表示客气请求的结构, my 是动名词 coming 的逻辑主语。
9 the waiting room, 候诊室。

参考译文

　　我穿过马路以便避开他，但他看到我并朝我跑过来。若再装作没看见他已是没有用了，我只好向他招手。我就怕遇到奈杰尔·戴克斯。他从来都是无事可做，不管你多忙，他总是坚持要跟着你。我得想办法不让他整个上午缠着我。

　　"你好，奈杰尔，想不到在这儿见到你。"我说。

　　"你好，伊丽莎白，"奈杰尔回答说，"我正不知道怎么消磨这一上午呢，正好见到你。你不忙，是吗？"

　　"是的，不忙，我打算去……"我回答。

　　"我跟你一道去行吗？"没等我说完话他就问道。

　　"没关系，但我准备去牙医那里。"我说了个谎。

　　"那我也跟你去，候诊室里总有很多东西可供阅读！"他回答。

Summary writing 摘要写作

Answer these questions *in not more than 70 words.*
回答下列问题，将答案组成一个段落，不要超过 70 个单词。

1　Did Elizabeth try to avoid meeting Nigel Dykes or not? Was she able to do so or not? (*Even though*)
2　Did he always insist on accompanying her or not? What did she have to do? (*As*)
3　Where did she tell him she was going? Why did he say he would come with her? (*When ... because*)

Composition 作文

Rewrite the sentences below using the joining words in parentheses:
用括号中的连词改写以下句子：

1　There was a dentist nearby. She knew him well. Elizabeth decided to go there. She would explain what had happened. (*As ... whom ... in order to*)
2　Nigel was in the waiting room. Elizabeth spoke to the dentist. He told her to leave at once through another door. (*While ... and*)
3　Elizabeth left. The dentist went into the waiting room. 'Do you want to have your teeth examined?' he asked Nigel. (*After ... and asked Nigel if ...*)

Letter writing 书信写作

Write four sentences beginning with each of the following:
完成以下开头语：

You must be very annoyed with me for ...
I have just heard that ...
I really hate to complain, but ...
Sometime ago, I ...

Key structures 关键句型

I crossed the street to avoid meeting him. (Compare **KS20, KS44**)

（对比第 20，44 课的关键句型）

a　Study these sentences carefully. Pay close attention to the words in italics:
　　细读以下句子，特别注意用斜体印出的词或词组：
　　I always *avoid travelling* during rush hour. 我总是避免在高峰时间乘车。
　　He *enjoys playing* football. 他喜欢踢足球。

He completely *denies taking* it. 他完全否认把它拿走了。

Fancy meeting you here! 真想不到在这里见到你。

It's no use crying about it. 为它而哭是没有用的

It's not worth worrying about. 这不值得忧虑。

I can't *stand* people *shouting and pushing*. 我不能容忍人们大声吵嚷和乱冲乱撞。

Can't you see *I'm busy writing*? 你难道看不见我正忙着写作吗？

Would you mind opening the window? 麻烦你把窗子打开好吗？

I don't mind waiting. 我不在乎等候。

b   Compare these sentences:

对比以下句子，注意动名词的逻辑主语的表达形式：

Would you mind opening the window? 你介意把窗户打开吗？

Would you mind my opening the window? 你介意我把窗户打开吗？

Fancy writing a letter like that! 真想不到写了那样一封信。

Fancy her writing a letter like that! 真想不到她写了那样一封信。

c   *See, Hear* and *Smell*.

Study these sentences:

细读以下例句：

I *saw him coming*. 我看见他来了。

He *heard me opening* the door. 他听见我开门。

I can *smell something burning*. 我闻见什么东西烧焦了。

d   *Go* and *Come*.

Study these sentences:

细读以下例句：

Let's *go dancing*. 让我们去跳舞。

I *went shopping* this morning. 今天上午我去买东西了。

Come swimming with me tomorrow. 明天和我一起去游泳。

Exercises 练习

A   Underline all the verbs in the passage that end in *ing*.

画出课文中所有以 ing 结尾的动词。

B   Give the correct form of the verbs in parentheses. Do not refer to the passage until you finish the exercise:

用括号中动词的正确形式填空，完成练习后再对照课文，核对你的答案：

I crossed the street to avoid _____ (meet) him, but he saw me and came _____ (run) towards me. It was no use _____ (pretend) that I had not seen him, so I waved to him. I never enjoy _____ (meet) Nigel Dykes. No matter how busy you are, he always insists on _____ (come) with you. I had to think of a way of _____ (prevent) him from _____ (follow) me around all morning.

'Hello, Nigel,' I said. 'Fancy _____ (meet) you here!'

'Hi, Elizabeth,' Nigel answered. 'I was just wondering how to spend the morning — until I saw you. You're not busy _____ (do) anything, are you?'

'No, not at all,' I answered. 'I'm going to ...'

'Would you mind my _____ (come) with you?' he asked, before I had finished _____ (speak).

C Write sentences beginning with each of the following:
用以下短语造句：

1 It's no use ...   3 Forgive my ...   5 He came ...   7 I always enjoy ...
2 Let's go ...   4 Do you deny ...   6 I'm busy ...   8 Would you mind ...

Multiple choice questions 选择题

Comprehension 理解

1 Elizabeth greeted Nigel Dykes _____ .

(*a*) because she likes him   (*b*) out of politeness

(*c*) because she likes his company   (*d*) because he waved to her

2 Which word best describes Nigel Dykes? He is _____ .

(*a*) funny   (*b*) insensitive   (*c*) nuisance   (*d*) cruel

Structure 句型

3 He came running towards her. He went _____ after her.

(*a*) run   (*b*) to running   (*c*) running   (*d*) ran

4 It was no use pretending that she had not seen him. It wasn't worth _____ .

(*a*) to do   (*b*) do   (*c*) done   (*d*) doing

5 Nigel Dykes never has anything to do. He always _____ .

(*a*) has to do nothing   (*b*) has nothing to do   (*c*) nothing has to do   (*d*) to do nothing has

6 He insisted _____ with her.

(*a*) to go   (*b*) that he should go   (*c*) to going   (*d*) in going

7 She said she didn't mind _____ going with her.

(*a*) –   (*b*) his   (*c*) he   (*d*) himself

Vocabulary 词汇

8 Elizabeth wanted to _____ meeting him.

(*a*) prevent   (*b*) prevent from   (*c*) avoid   (*d*) escape from

9 She didn't pretend she hadn't seen him. She didn't _____ she hadn't.

(*a*) make as if   (*b*) do as if   (*c*) act as if   (*d*) conduct as if

10 She waved to him. She _____ him.

(*a*) shook   (*b*) saluted   (*c*) greeted   (*d*) called

11 Fancy meeting you here! _____ !

(*a*) Imagine   (*b*) Think   (*c*) Consider   (*d*) Contemplate

12 She lied to him. What she said was _____ .

(*a*) false   (*b*) true   (*c*) lie   (*d*) wrong

Sentence structure 句子结构

Rewrite this sentence, then check your answer against the text.
改写以下句子，然后对照课文第 4-5 行，核对你的答案。

It doesn't matter whether you are busy or not, he always insists on coming with you.

No _____ .

Lesson 69   But not murder!   并非谋杀！

The examiner must have been pleased

First listen and then answer the question.

听录音, 然后回答以下问题。

Do you think that the writer passed his driving test? Why?

I was being tested for a driving licence for the third time. I had been asked to drive in heavy traffic and had done so successfully. After having been instructed to drive out of town, I began to acquire confidence. Sure that I had passed, I was almost beginning to enjoy
5 my test. The examiner must have been pleased with my performance, for he smiled and said, 'Just one more thing, Mr. Eames. Let us suppose that a child suddenly crosses the road in front of you. As soon as I tap on the window, you must stop within five feet.' I continued driving and after some time, the examiner tapped loudly. Though the sound could be heard clearly,
10 it took me a long time to react. I suddenly pressed the brake pedal hard and we were both thrown forward. The examiner looked at me sadly. 'Mr. Eames,' he said, in a mournful voice, 'you have just killed that child!'

New words and expressions 生词和短语

murder (title) /ˈmɜːdə/ n. 谋杀
instruct (l.3) /ɪnˈstrʌkt/ v. 命令, 指示
acquire (l.3) /əˈkwaɪə/ v. 取得, 获得
confidence (l.4) /ˈkɒnfɪdəns/ n. 信心
examiner (l.5) /ɪgˈzæmɪnə/ n. 主考人
suppose (l.7) /səˈpəʊz/ v. 假设

tap (l.8) /tæp/ v. 轻敲
react (l.10) /rɪˈækt/ v. 反应
brake (l.10) /breɪk/ n. 刹车
pedal (l.10) /ˈpedl/ n. 踏板
mournful (l.11) /ˈmɔːnfəl/ adj. 悲哀的

Notes on the text 课文注释

1 driving licence, 驾驶执照。

2 After having been instructed to drive out of town, 在接到把车开出城的指令后。介词 after 后面接动名词完成式的被动结构, 整个介词短语作时间状语, 相当于一个时间状语从句 After I had been instructed to ... 。

3 Sure that I had passed, 确信我已通过考试。sure 的前面省略了 Being。

4 The examiner must have been pleased, 主考人对我的驾驶想必是满意的。这里用 must + have + 过去分词来对过去的事情表示推测。

5 in a mournful voice, 用悲伤的声调。

参考译文

　　我第3次接受驾驶执照考试。按照要求在车辆拥挤的路上驾驶, 我圆满地完成了。在接到把车开出城的指令后, 我开始有了信心。确信我已通过考试, 所以我几乎开始喜欢起这次考试。主考人对我的驾驶想必是满意的, 因为他微笑着说: "埃姆斯先生, 只剩1项了。让我们假设一个小孩子突然在你前面穿过马路。你必须把车停在5英尺之内。"我继续往前开着。过了一会儿, 主考人砰砰地敲了起来。虽然声音听得很清

楚；但我过了好一会儿才作出反应。我突然用力踩紧刹车踏板，结果我俩的身体都向前冲去。主考人伤心地看着我。"埃姆斯先生，"他以悲伤的口吻说，"你刚刚把那个小孩轧死了！"

Summary writing 摘要写作

Answer these questions *in not more than 80 words*.
回答下列问题，将答案组成一个段落，不要超过 80 个单词。

1 Had Mr. Eames driven successfully in heavy traffic during his third driving test or not? What did the examiner instruct him to do? (*when*)

2 What did he tell him to suppose? (*that ... would*)

3 What would Mr. Eames have to do when the examiner tapped on the window?

4 Did he tap loudly or not? Did Mr. Eames react quickly enough or not? What was he told? (*Though ... and*)

Composition 作文

Write two or three sentences using the ideas given below:
用以下词组写出 2 至 3 个句子来：

Three months later Eames appeared for his fourth test — again told to stop — the examiner was thrown forward, but the child's life was saved — Eames passed his test, but the examiner said, 'You nearly killed me this time!'

Letter writing 书信写作

Write five opening phrases which could be used in letters to friends or relations.
为给朋友和亲戚的信写出 5 句开头语。

Key structures 关键句型

After having been instructed to drive out of town, I began to acquire confidence.
被动语态

a You have learnt to write sentences like these:
你已经学习了写这样的句子：

It was made in Germany in 1681. **(KS10)**（第 10 课关键句型）

I told you it could be done. **(KS21)**（第 21 课关键句型）

I can't find my bag. It must have been stolen. **(KS21)**（第 21 课关键句型）

The man was being questioned by the police. **(KS34)**（第 34 课关键句型）

He never expected the bicycle to be found. **(KS34)**（第 34 课关键句型）

I found the parcel had been sent to the wrong address. **(KS45)**（第 45 课关键句型）

b Now study these sentences:
仔细阅读以下句子：

Instead of saying:　　　　　　　　　　　*We can say*:
除了这种表达方法外：　　　　　　　　　还可以说：

After he was arrested, the man confessed that he had stolen the money.　　　*After being arrested,* the man confessed that he had stolen the money.

After he had been instructed to drive out of town, he began to acquire confidence.　　　*After having been instructed* to drive out of town, he began to acquire confidence.

Unit 3   Lesson 69

Exercises 练习

A Underline the verbs in the passage which are similar in form to the examples given above.
在课文中画出与以上例子相似的动词。

B Give the correct form of the verbs in parentheses. Do not refer to the passage until you finish the exercise.
用括号中动词的正确形式填空，完成练习后再对照课文，核对你的答案。

I _____ (test) for my driving licence for the third time. I _____ (ask) to drive in heavy traffic and had done so successfully. After _____ (have/instruct) to drive out of town, I began to acquire confidence. Sure that I had passed, I was almost beginning to enjoy my test. The examiner _____ (must/please) with my performance, for he smiled and said, 'Just one more thing, Mr. Eames. Let us suppose that a child suddenly crosses the road in front of you. As soon as I tap on the window, you must _____ (stop) within five feet.' I continued driving and after some time, the examiner tapped loudly. Though the sound _____ (could/hear) clearly, it took me a long time to react. I suddenly pressed the brake pedal hard and we both _____ (throw) forward.

Special difficulties 难点

Words often confused 经常容易混淆的词

a   *Practice, Advice.*

Study these pairs of sentences:
细读以下各对句子：

He still *needs* a lot of *practice*. 他仍需大量的练习。

He *practises* the piano every day. 他每天练习弹钢琴。

I want to give you some *advice*. 我想给你提点建议。

What do you *advise* me to do? 你想建议我干什么？

b   *Enjoy, Entertain* and *Amuse.*

Study these examples:
细读以下各对句子：

I was almost beginning to *enjoy* my test. (ll.4-5)

We *enjoyed* ourselves at the party. 在聚会上我们玩得很痛快。

He *entertained* me to dinner. 他请我吃饭。

He *entertained* everybody with his clever tricks. 他精彩的戏法使大家都很高兴。

The children were *amused* by the circus clown. (They laughed.) 孩子们被马戏团的小丑逗乐了。

His funny stories *amused* us all. (They made us laugh.) 他那些稀奇古怪的故事把我们大家都逗乐了。

That child can *amuse* himself for hours playing in the sand. (He can pass his time happily.) 那个孩子可以一个人在沙堆里玩上几个小时。

Exercise 练习

Choose the correct words in the following sentences:
选择正确的词：

1 I never (amuse) (enjoy) (practicing) (practising) the piano.

2 We were all (amused) (enjoyed) by the jokes he told us.

3 He (advised) (adviced) me to get a (license) (licence).

4 We rarely (entertain) (amuse) these days.

5 We (entertained) (enjoyed) some friends to dinner last night.

6 The magician (amused) (enjoyed) the audience very much.

Multiple choice questions 选择题

Comprehension 理解

1 Mr. Eames felt confident because _____ .

  (*a*) he was sure he hadn't failed this time   (*b*) he had driven in heavy traffic

  (*c*) he had driven out of town   (*d*) the examiner smiled

2 Mr. Eames probably failed his test because _____ .

  (*a*) he ran over a child   (*b*) he didn't stop quickly enough

  (*c*) he pressed the brake pedal too hard   (*d*) he and the examiner were thrown forward

Structure 句型

3 Mr. Eames was taking the driving test. The examiner _____ him.

  (*a*) was being testing   (*b*) was been testing   (*c*) was testing   (*d*) was tested

4 The examiner must have been pleased. He _____ pleased.

  (*a*) had to be   (*b*) was probably   (*c*) was certainly   (*d*) should be

5 Let us suppose that a child suddenly crosses the road. Imagine it _____ .

  (*a*) would happen   (*b*) happening   (*c*) had been happening   (*d*) will have happened

6 Mr. Eames continued _____ .

  (*a*) to driving   (*b*) drive   (*c*) to drive   (*d*) to have been driving

7 I want the car to be stopped. I _____ the car.

  (*a*) want to stop   (*b*) want stop   (*c*) want you stop   (*d*) want you to stop

Vocabulary 词汇

8 When you have passed a driving test, you are allowed to _____ .

  (*a*) drive a car   (*b*) buy a car   (*c*) sell a car   (*d*) keep a car

9 He began to acquire confidence. He gradually _____ confident.

  (*a*) became   (*b*) came   (*c*) obtained   (*d*) took

10 He was instructed by the examiner to drive out of town. He was _____ to do this.

  (*a*) taught   (*b*) told   (*c*) trained   (*d*) prepared

11 The examiner must have been pleased with my performance. He was pleased with my _____ .

  (*a*) act   (*b*) behaviour   (*c*) efforts   (*d*) doings

12 The examiner spoke in a mournful voice. His voice was _____ .

  (*a*) lamentable   (*b*) sorry   (*c*) pitiful   (*d*) sorrowful

Sentence structure 句子结构

Rewrite this sentence, then check your answer against the text.

改写以下句子, 然后对照课文第 2-4 行, 核对你的答案。

I had been instructed to drive out of town and I began to acquire confidence.

After _____ .

Lesson 70   Red for danger   危险的红色

🔊 **First listen and then answer the question.**

听录音, 然后回答以下问题。

How was the drunk removed from the ring?

Apparently sensitive to criticism

During a bullfight, a drunk suddenly wandered into the middle of the ring. The crowd began to shout, but the drunk was unaware of the danger. The bull was busy with the matador at the time, but it suddenly caught sight of the drunk who was shouting rude remarks
5 and waving a red cap. Apparently sensitive to criticism, the bull forgot all about the matador and charged at the drunk. The crowd suddenly grew quiet. The drunk, however, seemed quite sure of himself. When the bull got close to him, he clumsily stepped aside to let it pass. The crowd broke into cheers and the drunk bowed. By this time, however, three men had come
10 into the ring and they quickly dragged the drunk to safety. Even the bull seemed to feel sorry for him, for it looked on sympathetically until the drunk was out of the way before once more turning its attention to the matador.

New words and expressions 生词和短语

bullfight (l.1) /ˈbʊlfaɪt/ *n.* 斗牛
drunk (l.1) /drʌŋk/ *n.* 醉汉
wander (l.1) /ˈwɒndə/ *v.* 溜达, 乱走
ring (l.2) /rɪŋ/ *n.* 圆形竞技场地
unaware (l.2) /ˌʌnəˈweə/ *adj.* 不知道的, 未觉察的
bull (l.3) /bʊl/ *n.* 公牛
matador (l.3) /ˈmætədɔː/ *n.* 斗牛士
remark (l.4) /rɪˈmɑːk/ *n.* 评论; 言语

apparently (l.5) /əˈpærəntli/ *adv.* 明显地
sensitive (l.5) /ˈsensɪtɪv/ *adj.* 敏感的
criticism (l.5) /ˈkrɪtɪsɪzəm/ *n.* 批评
charge (l.6) /tʃɑːdʒ/ *v.* 冲上去
clumsily (l.8) /ˈklʌmzɪli/ *adv.* 笨拙地
bow (l.9) /baʊ/ *v.* 鞠躬
safety (l.10) /ˈseɪfti/ *n.* 安全地带
sympathetically (l.11) /ˌsɪmpəˈθetɪkli/ *adv.* 同情地

Notes on the text 课文注释

1 be unaware of ..., 不知道, 没有觉察……。
2 catch sight of ..., 突然看到……。
3 Apparently sensitive to criticism, 可以看作是省略了 being 的现在分词短语, 作状语, 说明原因。
4 charge at ..., 向……攻击。
5 break into cheers, 突然喝起彩来, break into ... 作 "突然发出", "突然……起来" 讲。
6 look on, 旁观。
7 out of the way, 不碍事; 不挡路。

参考译文

　　在一次斗牛时, 一个醉汉突然溜达到斗牛场中间, 人们开始大叫起来, 但醉汉却没有意识到危险。当时那公牛正忙于对付斗牛士, 但突然它看见了醉汉, 只见他正大声说着粗鲁的话, 手里挥动着一顶红帽子。对挑衅显然

316

非常敏感的公牛完全撇开斗牛士，直奔醉汉而来。观众突然静了下来，可这醉汉像是很有把握似的。当公牛逼近他时，他跟跄跄地往旁边一闪，牛扑空了。观众欢呼起来，醉汉向人们鞠躬致谢。然而，此时已有 3 个人进入斗牛场，迅速把醉汉拉到安全的地方。好像连牛也在为他感到遗憾，因为它一直同情地看着醉汉，直到他的背影消逝，才重新将注意力转向斗牛士。

Summary writing 摘要写作

Answer these questions *in not more than 75 words*.
回答下列问题，将答案组成一个段落，不要超过 75 个单词。

1 Did a drunk suddenly wander into the middle of the ring during a bullfight or not? What did he do? (*and*)

2 Did the bull ignore the matador or not? What did it do? Why did he step aside? (*Ignoring ... but*)

3 Did the crowd cheer or not? What did the drunk do? (*and*)

4 Did three men drag the drunk to safety just after this or not? Did the bull look on sympathetically or not? Did it once more turn its attention to the matador or not? (*Just after this ... while ... before it ...*)

Composition 作文

Rewrite the following sentences using the joining words in parentheses:
用括号中的连词改写以下句子：

1 The man became sober. It was possible to discover his identity. (*When*)

2 He was Domingo Cordova. He had been a great matador in his youth. He had failed in the ring. He had taken to drinking. (*... a man who ... but having ...*)

3 He had changed. No one recognized him. (*so much that*)

Letter writing 书信写作

Learn the following opening phrases by heart:
熟记以下 3 个开头语：

I have not forgotten that ...   You will find it hard to believe, but ...   I am afraid I ...

Exercise 练习

Write sentences completing each of the above phrases.
用以上 3 个开头语写出完整的句子。

Key structures 关键句型

Words followed by *for, with, of, to, at, from, in, on* and *about* (Compare **KS22, KS46**)

与 for, with, of, to, at, from, in, on 和 about 连用的词（对比第 22，46 课的关键句型）

Use this list for reference:
请参考下表：

a FOR: eager, enough, famous, fit, grateful (or to), qualified (or in), ready (or to), responsible, sorry, sufficient, thankful (or to), valid.
与 for 连用的形容词：渴望的；足够的；以……而闻名；适合的；因……而感激；能胜任的；准备好的；对……负责；对……感到遗憾；充足的；感谢的；有效期为……。

b WITH: angry (with someone; at something), busy (or at), consistent, content, familiar (or to), patient, popular.
与 with 连用的形容词：（因某人或某事）生气的；忙于……；与……一致；对……满足；与……熟悉；有耐心的；为……所喜爱。

c   OF: afraid, ahead, aware, capable, careful (or with), certain, conscious, envious, fond, guilty, ignorant, independent, jealous, kind (or to), north/south/east/west, short, shy, sure, worthy.

与 of 连用的形容词：害怕的；在……前面；知道的；有能力的；小心的；确信的；意识到的；妒忌的；爱好的；有……罪的；不了解的；独立的；妒忌的；对……和蔼；在……的北/南/东/西面；缺乏的；顾虑的；肯定的；值得的。

d   TO: close, contrary, cruel, dear, equal, faithful, fatal, harmful, identical, indifferent, inferior, liable, new, obedient, obvious, polite, previous, rude, sensitive, similar, useful.

与 to 连用的形容词：接近的；与……相反；对……残忍；对……很重要；与……相等；忠于……；对……致命；对……有害；与……相同；对……不关心；劣于……；对……有义务；对……没有经验；对……服从；对……清楚；对……有礼貌；先于……；对……粗暴无礼；对……敏感；与……相似；对……有用。

e   AT: bad, clever, efficient, expert (or in), good, indignant, quick, sad (or about), slow, skillful (or in).

与 at 连用的形容词：不善于……；擅长的；能胜任的；能熟练做……；善于……；对……感到愤慨；很快的；因……而悲伤；对……迟钝；熟练的。

f   FROM: away, different, far, safe.

与 from 连用的形容词：距……远；与……不同；远离的；无危险的。

g   IN: deficient, fortunate, honest, weak.

与 in 连用的形容词：缺少的；在……很幸运；对……很诚实；在……薄弱。

h   ON: dependent, intent, keen.

与 on 连用的形容词：依赖于……；专心于……；热心于……。

i   ABOUT: curious, doubtful (or of), enthusiastic, reluctant (or to), right (or in), uneasy.

与 about 连用的形容词：对……好奇；对……有疑问；对……热心；勉强的；在……正确；对……感到不安。

Exercises 练习

A   There are some words in the passage which are included in the above list. These words are followed by *for, with, of* and *to*. Can you find them?

课文中有些词包括在上面搭配表中。这些词后面跟着 for, with, of 和 to。你能找出这些词吗？

B   Supply the missing words (*for, with, of, to, at, from, in, on* or *about*) without referring to the above list as far as possible.

用 for, with, of, to, at, from, in, on 或 about 填空。

1 George is jealous _____ his younger sister.

2 She is well-qualified _____ languages and very efficient _____ her work.

3 We are fortunate _____ having sufficient supplies of fuel _____ the winter.

4 Contrary _____ my expectations, there was no need to be uneasy _____ the results of the match.

5 I am not familiar _____ his novels and not very keen _____ reading them.

6 I know he is slow _____ understanding, but you have to be patient _____ him.

7 It is obvious _____ everyone that he is not responsible _____ this mistake.

8 I think he's quite honest _____ his intentions.

9 He is not only indifferent _____ other people; he is often extremely rude _____ them as well.

10 I'm not very fond _____ dancing.

11 Children remain dependent _____ their parents for a long time.

12 I should be grateful _____ any advice you can give.

13 He is not different _____ anyone else.

14 He may be quick _____ understanding, but he's not capable _____ remembering anything.

15 He is intent _____ passing the examination, but I'm doubtful _____ his chances.

16 He says he's sorry _____ what he did, so don't get angry _____ him.

17 I've never been good _____ arithmetic.

18 That boy is far ahead _____ everyone else in the class.

19 Even though he was often cruel _____ his dog, it remained faithful _____ him.

20 Your conclusions are not consistent _____ the facts.

21 This diary will prove useful _____ you.

22 I'm not sure _____ the exact date, but I think he arrived here in 1993.

23 He was found guilty _____ a great many crimes.

24 You should not be so sensitive _____ criticism.

25 This passport is valid _____ all countries.

Multiple choice questions 选择题

Comprehension 理解

1 The drunk went into the ring _____ .

   (*a*) but the bull didn't notice him   (*b*) and the matador asked him to leave

   (*c*) and threw something at the bull   (*d*) and attracted the bull's attention

2 The drunk spent some time in the ring _____ .

   (*a*) but the bull didn't notice him   (*b*) before he was removed

   (*c*) and was badly hurt   (*d*) and annoyed the crowd

Structure 句型

3 The bull charged at the drunk. It ran straight _____ him.

   (*a*) to   (*b*) against   (*c*) at   (*d*) for

4 The drunk was sure of himself. He was sure _____ be all right.

   (*a*) he will   (*b*) that he will   (*c*) he would   (*d*) he may

5 The drunk stepped aside and let the bull _____ .

   (*a*) passing   (*b*) to pass   (*c*) in passing   (*d*) pass

6 _____ , however, three men had come into the ring.

   (*a*) Up till that time   (*b*) By then   (*c*) So far   (*d*) Until then

7 It looked on before _____ its attention to the matador.

   (*a*) turn   (*b*) to turn   (*c*) it turned   (*d*) it was turning

Vocabulary 词汇

8 The drunk was unaware of the danger. He wasn't _____ it.

   (*a*) conscious of   (*b*) sensitive to

   (*c*) knowledgeable about   (*d*) sensible about

9 The crowd suddenly grew quiet. It _____ quiet.

   (*a*) increased   (*b*) began   (*c*) became   (*d*) behaved

10 He stepped aside. He got _____ the way.

   (*a*) in   (*b*) on   (*c*) this   (*d*) out of

11 It looked on sympathetically. It _____ him.

   (*a*) liked   (*b*) loved   (*c*) sympathised   (*d*) felt sorry for

12 The bull had been _____ the drunk.

   (*a*) taking care of   (*b*) looking after   (*c*) paying attention to   (*d*) minding

Lesson 71 A famous clock 一个著名的大钟

A painter slowed it down

First listen and then answer the question.

听录音，然后回答以下问题。

Has Big Ben ever gone wrong?

When you visit London, one of the first things you will see is Big Ben, the famous clock which can be heard all over the world on the B.B.C. If the Houses of Parliament had not been burned down in 1834, the great clock would never have been erected. Big Ben takes
5 its name from Sir Benjamin Hall who was responsible for the making of the clock when the new Houses of Parliament were being built. It is not only of immense size, but is extremely accurate as well. Officials from Greenwich Observatory have the clock checked twice a day. On the B.B.C. you can hear the clock when it is actually striking because microphones are connected to
10 the clock tower. Big Ben has rarely gone wrong. Once, however, it failed to give the correct time. A painter who had been working on the tower hung a pot of paint on one of the hands and slowed it down!

New words and expressions 生词和短语

parliament (1.3) /'pɑːləmənt/ *n.* 议会，国会
erect (1.4) /ɪ'rekt/ *v.* 建起
accurate (1.7) /'ækjʊrət/ *adj.* 准确的
official (1.8) /ə'fɪʃəl/ *n.* 官员，行政人员
Greenwich (1.8) /'grenɪtʃ/ *n.* 格林尼治

observatory (1.8) /əb'zɜːvətəri/ *n.* 天文台
check (1.8) /tʃek/ *v.* 检查
microphone (1.9) /'maɪkrəfəʊn/ *n.* 扩音器，麦克风
tower (1.10) /'taʊə/ *n.* 塔

Notes on the text 课文注释

1 Big Ben, 大钟的名字，译成"大本"。

2 the B.B.C. 是英国广播公司（British Broadcasting Corporation）的缩写。

3 If the Houses of Parliament had not been burned down in 1834, the great clock would never have been erected. 如果不是国会大厦在 1834 年被焚毁的话，这座大钟永远也不会建造。这是一个表示与过去事实不相符的虚拟语气结构。

4 take its name from, 以……命名。

5 when the new Houses of Parliament were being built, 注意这个从句中过去进行时的被动结构。

6 It is not only of immense size, 它不仅外型巨大，"to be of＋名词"用来表示人或物的特征。

7 Big Ben has rarely gone wrong. "大本"钟很少出差错。

参考译文

当你游览伦敦时，首先看到的东西之一就是"大本"钟，即那座从英国广播公司的广播中全世界都可以听到它的声音的著名大钟。如果不是国会大厦在 1834 年被焚毁的话，这座大钟永远也不会建造。"大本"钟得名于本杰明·霍尔爵士，因为当建造新的国会大厦时，他负责建造大钟。此钟不仅外型巨大，而且走时也非常准确。格林尼治天文台的官员们每天两次派人矫正此钟。当大钟打点的时候，你可以从英国广播公司的广播中听

到，因为钟塔上接了麦克风。"大本"钟很少出差错。然而有一次，它却把时间报错了。在钟塔上干活的一位油漆工把一只油漆桶挂在了一根指针上，把钟弄慢了!

Summary writing 摘要写作

Answer these questions *in not more than 75 words*.
回答下列问题，将答案组成一个段落，不要超过 75 个单词。

1　When were the Houses of Parliament burnt down? Who was made responsible for the construction of a huge clock? Did it become known as Big Ben or not? (*After ... which ...*)

2　Why is it very accurate despite its immense size? (*for*)

3　Has this clock often gone wrong, or has it rarely gone wrong? Why can it be heard on the B.B.C. when it is striking? (*This clock which ... because ...*)

Composition 作文

Write two or three sentences using the ideas given below:
用以下词组写出 2 至 3 个句子来:

Big Ben tells correct time — it also tells us when Parliament is in session — there is a light in the clock tower — it is kept on until the House closes — sometimes it is on all night.

Letter writing 书信写作

Learn the following phrases by heart:
熟记以下两个开头语:

I wonder how you learnt that ...
You will never guess who/what ...

Exercise 练习

Write two short paragraphs (of not more than two sentences each) completing the above phrases.
用以上开头语写出两小段话，每段不要超过两句。

Key structures 关键句型

Review **KS60-69** 复习第 60-69 课关键句型

The moment you leave this tent, you will get a big surprise. **(KS60)**（第 60 课）

By the time you read this, the Hubble's eagle eye will have sent us thousands of wonderful pictures. **(KS61)**（第 61 课）

The planes had been planting seed for nearly a month when it began to rain. **(KS62)**（第 62 课）

If the British had not feared invasion, it would have been completed. **(KS64)**（第 64 课）

Must, Have to, Should and Ought to **(KS65)**（第 65 课）

Have **(KS66)**（第 66 课）

After having been instructed to drive out of town, I began to acquire confidence. **(KS69)**（第 69 课）

Exercises 练习

A　Underline the verbs in the passage. Revise any Key structures you have forgotten.
画出课文中所有动词，复习已遗忘的句型。

Unit 3   Lesson 71

B Give the correct form of the verbs in parentheses. Do not refer to the passage until you finish the exercise.

用括号中动词的正确形式填空，完成练习后再对照课文，核对你的答案。

1 When you _____ (visit) London, one of the first things you will see is Big Ben, the famous clock which _____ (can/hear) all over the world on the B.B.C. If the Houses of Parliament _____ (not burn) down in 1834, the great clock would never have been erected.

2 Officials from Greenwich Observatory have the clock _____ (check) twice a day. On the B.B.C. you can hear the clock when it actually _____ (strike) because microphones _____ (connect) to the clock tower.

3 Once, however, it failed to give the correct time. A painter who _____ (work) on the tower hung a pot of paint on one of the hands.

C Give the correct form of the verbs in parentheses:

用括号中动词的正确形式填空：

1 I shall have completed this novel by December. By then I _____ (work) on it for ten months.

2 Now that you _____ (finish) work you can go home.

D Supply the correct form of *should, ought to* or *have to* in these sentences:

用 should, ought to 或 have to 的正确形式填空：

1 I couldn't go shopping yesterday afternoon. I _____ (go) to the dentist.

2 I really _____ (buy) a new car but I can't afford to.

3 I didn't know you would be late. You _____ (telephone).

Special difficulties 难点

Words often confused 经常容易混淆的词

Study these examples:

细读以下例子：

a *Official, Employee, Shop assistant.*

  Officials from Greenwich Observatory have the clock checked twice a day. (11.8-9)

  The Customs *official* asked me several questions. 那个海关官员问了我好几个问题。

  Over a thousand factory *employees* went on strike. 上千的工厂工人罢工了。

  She works as a *shop assistant* in a clothing store. 她在一家服装商店当店员。

b *Hang/Hung* and *Hang/Hanged.*

  A painter *hung* a pot of paint on one of the hands. (11.11-12)

  When the sun came out, she *hung* the washing on the line. 当太阳出来的时候，她把洗好的衣服晾在绳子上。

  The murderer was *hanged*. 杀人犯被绞死了。

Exercise 练习

Choose the correct words in the following sentences:

选择正确的词：

1 The (clerk) (shop assistant) who served me was very helpful.

2 I (hanged) (hung) my coat in the hall.

3 Capital punishment has been abolished. Murderers will not be (hung) (hanged) in future.

322

Multiple choice questions 选择题

Comprehension 理解

1 Big Ben was built _____ .

(a) for the B.B.C.   (b) after a fire

(c) in honour of Sir Benjamin Hall   (d) long before 1834

2 Accuracy is maintained _____ .

(a) by microphones in the clock tower

(b) by workmen

(c) because the clock is at Greenwich Observatory

(d) by officials who check the clock frequently

Structure 句型

3 Big Ben is one of the first sights you will see when you _____ London.

(a) will visit   (b) visit   (c) have visited   (d) will be visiting

4 Big Ben is the _____ clock in London.

(a) famousest   (b) most famous   (c) more famous   (d) famouser

5 It is _____ very big and very accurate.

(a) and   (b) also   (c) both   (d) together

6 How often _____ checked?

(a) have they it   (b) they have it   (c) do they have it (d) they do have it

7 A painter _____ working on the tower hung a pot of paint on one of the hands.

(a) who   (b) had been   (c) had   (d) –

Vocabulary 词汇

8 The clock was erected after 1834. That's when it was put _____ .

(a) in   (b) up   (c) off   (d) down

9 Sir Benjamin Hall was responsible. It was his _____ to see to it.

(a) responsible   (b) duty   (c) charge   (d) control

10 It is of immense size. It is _____ .

(a) great   (b) large   (c) huge   (d) big

11 You can hear it when it is actually striking. You can hear it _____ it is striking.

(a) the hour   (b) the moment   (c) really   (d) indeed

12 The clock slowed down. It _____ .

(a) was slow   (b) was behind   (c) went back   (d) went slowly

Sentence structure 句子结构

Rewrite this sentence with *if ... not,* then check your answer against the text.
用 if ... not 来改写以下句子, 然后对照课文第 3-4 行, 核对你的答案。

The Houses of Parliament had been burned down and that's why the great clock was erected.

Lesson 72   A car called *Bluebird*   "蓝鸟"汽车

First listen and then answer the question.

听录音，然后回答以下问题。

What mistake was made?

301 miles per hour

The great racing driver, Sir Malcolm Campbell, was the first man to drive at over 300 miles per hour. He set up a new world record in September 1935 at Bonneville Salt Flats, Utah. *Bluebird,* the car he was driving, had been specially built for him. It was over 30 feet in
5 length and had a 2,500-horsepower engine. Although Campbell reached a speed of over 304 miles per hour, he had great difficulty in controlling the car because a tyre burst during the first run. After his attempt, Campbell was disappointed to learn that his average speed had been 299 miles per hour. However, a few days later, he was told that a mistake had been made. His
10 average speed had been 301 miles per hour. Since that time, racing drivers have reached speeds over 600 miles an hour. Following in his father's footsteps many years later, Sir Malcolm's son, Donald, also set up a world record. Like his father, he was driving a car called *Bluebird*.

New words and expressions 生词和短语

racing (l.1) /'reɪsɪŋ/ *n.* 竞赛
per (l.2) /pɜː/ *prep.* 每
Utah (l.3) /'juːtɑː/ *n.* 犹他（美国州名）
horsepower (l.5) /'hɔːs,paʊə/ *n.* 马力

burst (l.7) /bɜːst/ (burst, burst) *v.* 爆裂
average (l.8) /'ævərɪdʒ/ *adj.* 平均的
footstep (l.11) /'fʊtstep/ *n.* 足迹

Notes on the text 课文注释

1   drive at over 300 miles per hour, 以每小时 300 多英里的速度驾车。
2   30 feet in length, 30 英尺长。
3   the first run, 开始的行程。
4   Following in his father's footsteps, 踩着父亲的足迹。

参考译文

　　杰出的赛车选手马尔科姆·坎贝尔爵士是第一个以每小时超过 300 英里的速度驾车的人。他于 1935 年 9 月在犹他州的邦纳维尔盐滩创造了一项新的世界纪录。他驾驶的"蓝鸟"牌汽车是专门为他制造的。它的车身长 30 英尺，有一个 2,500 马力的发动机。尽管坎贝尔达到了每小时超过 304 英里的速度，但因为在开始的行程中爆了一只轮胎，所以他很难把汽车控制住。比赛结束后，坎贝尔非常失望地得知他的平均时速是 299 英里。然而，几天之后，有人告诉他说弄错了。他的平均时速实际是 301 英里。从那时以来，赛车选手已达到每小时超过 600 英里的速度。很多年之后，马尔科姆爵士的儿子唐纳德踩着父亲的足迹，也创造了一项世界纪录。同他父亲一样，他也驾驶着一辆名叫"蓝鸟"的汽车。

Summary writing 摘要写作

Answer these questions *in not more than 75 words.*

回答下列问题, 将答案组成一个段落, 不要超过 75 个单词。

1 Who set up a land-speed record in 1935? What was his car called? Had it been specially built for him or not? (*driving a car ... which*)

2 Was his average speed incorrectly declared to be 299 miles per hour or 289 miles per hour? Was this mistake corrected later or not? (*but*)

3 How many miles an hour had he averaged?

4 Is Sir Malcolm's son, Donald, one of the racing drivers who have exceeded the old record? What was his car called? (*Among them is ... whose*)

Composition 作文

Write two or three sentences using the ideas given below:

用以下词组写出 2 至 3 个句子来:

During a car race — leading car skidded — overturned — the driver was not hurt — got his car back on to the course — won the race.

Letter writing 书信写作

Write sentences completing each of the following phrases:

将以下书信的开头语写成完整的句子:

I have not forgotten that ...

You will find it hard to believe, but ...

I am afraid I ...

I wonder how you learnt that ...

You will never guess who/what ...

Special difficulties 难点

Review SD50-71 复习第 50-71 课难点

Exercises 练习

A Words often confused 经常容易混淆的词

Choose the correct words in the following sentences:

选择正确的词:

1 Hurry up or you will (lose) (miss) (loose) the train. **(SD50a)**（第 50 课 a）

2 I'm (expecting) (waiting) to receive a letter soon. **(SD50b)**（第 50 课 b）

3 You should (raise) (rise) that picture a few inches. **(SD51a)**（第 51 课 a）

4 I love (lying) (laying) in bed. **(SD51b)**（第 51 课 b）

5 He always (beats) (wins) me at chess. **(SD51c)**（第 51 课 c）

6 Are you (quiet) (quite) ready? **(SD53b)**（第 53 课 b）

7 I dislike getting up early, but I (am used to) (use to) it now. **(SD55a)**（第 55 课 a）

8 People often come into our garden and (pick) (cut) flowers. **(SD58c)**（第 58 课 c）

9 Whenever I buy anything new, my father always asks me the (value) (cost) (price). **(SD61a)** （第 61 课 a）

10 That house (valued) (cost) (priced) a fortune to build. **(SD61b)** （第 61 课 b）

11 I (value) (price) (cost) your advice a great deal. **(SD61b)** （第 61 课 b）

12 The oil level in the engine must be (checked) (controlled). **(SD62a)** （第 62 课 a）

13 I could not (accept) (agree) his offer. **(SD65b)** （第 65 课 b）

14 Who is going to (dress) (dress up) as Father Christmas? **(SD65c)** （第 65 课 c）

15 How many hours a day do you (practise) (practice)? **(SD69a)** （第 69 课 a）

16 We were (enjoyed) (amused) by his stories. **(SD69b)** （第 69 课 b）

17 She (hung) (hanged) the clothes on the line. **(SD71b)** （第 71 课 b）

18 The train arrived (late) (lately) as usual. **(SD52)** （第 52 课）

19 He has been working too (hardly) (hard). **(SD52)** （第 52 课）

20 He was (near) (nearly) run over by a car. **(SD52)** （第 52 课）

B Join the following sentences leaving out the verb *want to*. **(SD59)**
连接以下各组句子, 省略动词 want to。(参见第 59 课难点)

1 I told him about it. I wanted to help you. (*in order to*)

2 I opened the door quietly. I did not want to disturb him. (*so as to*)

3 He left the letter on the table. He wanted me to see it. (*in order that*)

C Draw **(SD64)**; Let **(SD65a)**
Complete these sentences by adding any of the following words: *out, down, up, off*.
用 out, down, up, off 填空：

1 A big car drew _____ outside our house.

2 You can't rely on him. He is sure to let you _____ .

3 Don't let the children _____ of the garden.

4 We shall have to draw _____ a new agreement.

5 He was going to punish the boy, but he let him _____ .

D Supply the correct form of *say* or *tell* in the following sentences: **(SD67)**
用 say 或 tell 的正确形式填空：(参见第 67 课难点)

1 I can _____ no more. He _____ me a secret and I have to keep it.

2 Why don't you _____ him the truth?

3 If you didn't want it, why didn't you _____ so?

4 He knelt down and _____ a prayer.

5 I can't prevent him from _____ lies.

Multiple choice questions 选择题

Comprehension 理解

1 One of these statements is true. Which one?

(*a*) There was some doubt whether Sir Malcolm had maintained an average speed of 301 miles per hour.

(*b*) Sir Malcolm set up a new world record recently.

(*c*) Sir Malcolm's average speed was 299 miles per hour.

(*d*) Sir Malcolm's car had a 250-horsepower engine.

2 One of these statements is true. Which one?

(*a*) No one has ever driven faster than Sir Malcolm Campbell.

(*b*) Donald Campbell couldn't beat his father's record.

(*c*) More than one racing driver has driven faster than 300 miles per hour since Sir Malcolm set up his record.

(*d*) Donald Campbell drove at 400 miles an hour.

Structure 句型

3 He was the first man to drive at over 300 miles an hour. No one had done this _____ .

(*a*) before   (*b*) ago   (*c*) since   (*d*) again

4 _____ was it? 30 feet.

(*a*) How long ago   (*b*) Which length   (*c*) How length   (*d*) How long

5 _____ to control the car.

(*a*) It was difficulty for him   (*b*) It was difficult for him

(*c*) It was difficulty   (*d*) He was difficult

6 How fast did he drive? _____ 301 miles an hour.

(*a*) At   (*b*) With   (*c*) To   (*d*) By

7 Donald Campbell was driving a car _____ *Bluebird*.

(*a*) to call   (*b*) calling   (*c*) called   (*d*) calls

Vocabulary 词汇

8 He set up a new world record. He _____ a new record.

(*a*) did   (*b*) played   (*c*) created   (*d*) found

9 It was over 30 feet in length. That's how _____ it was.

(*a*) length   (*b*) tall   (*c*) large   (*d*) long

10 It reached a speed of over 301 miles per hour. That's how _____ it went.

(*a*) speed   (*b*) fast   (*c*) soon   (*d*) rapid

11 He was disappointed to learn this. He felt _____ .

(*a*) sorry   (*b*) hopeless   (*c*) despair   (*d*) desperate

12 They had made a mistake. They had been _____ .

(*a*) mistake   (*b*) correct   (*c*) right   (*d*) wrong

Sentence structure 句子结构

Rewrite this sentence, then check your answer against the text.

改写以下句子, 然后对照课文第 11-12 行, 核对你的答案。

Sir Malcolm's son, Donald, followed in his father's footsteps many years later and also set up a world record.

Following _____ .

PRE-UNIT TEST 4
测试 4

IF YOU CAN DO THIS TEST GO ON TO UNIT 4
如果你能完成以下测验，请开始第4单元的学习

Key structures 关键句型

A Word order in complex statements 复合句中的语序

Rewrite these sentences using the joining words in parentheses.
用括号中的连词改写以下句子。

1 He missed the train. He did not hurry. (*because*)

2 He ran fast. He failed to win the race. (*Although*)

3 I was tired. I went to sleep immediately. (*so … that*)

4 My neighbour went to Tokyo for a holiday. He could not return home. He did not have enough money. (*who … because*)

5 I found the door unlocked. I went into the kitchen. (*Finding*)

6 I bought a picture. It was very valuable. (*which*)

7 He walked quietly down the corridor. He did not want anyone to hear him. (*so … that*)

8 They cleared the ground. They wanted to build a house. (*to*)

B Composition 作文

Write two or three sentences using the ideas given below.
用以下词组写出 2 至 3 句话。

A workman was digging in a field — struck a 6,000-volt electricity cable with his spade — was thrown twenty feet — unhurt — town was in darkness — no one knew what had happened.

C Verbs 动词

a These things always happen. 经常发生的事情

What is happening? What always happens? 现在进行时和一般现在时

Give the correct form of the verbs in parentheses.
用括号中动词的正确形式填空。

'Let's eat here,' I said to my wife.

'I _____ (prefer) to have a drink first,' she answered.

'That's a good idea,' I said. I picked up the menu. 'I _____ (not understand) a thing,' I said. 'It's all in Spanish.'

'It _____ (not matter),' said my wife.

'What _____ that word _____ (mean)?' I asked.

'I _____ (not know),' she answered.

We called the waiter and pointed to the word on the menu.

'Two,' I said, holding up two fingers.

After some time, my wife said suddenly, 'Look! He _____ (bring) us two boiled eggs!'

b   What happened? 一般过去时

The verbs in parentheses tell us *what happened*. Give the correct form of each verb.

括号中的动词告诉我们过去发生的动作。给出动词的正确形式。

My friend, Hugh, has always been fat, but things _____ (get) so bad recently that he _____ (decide) to go on a diet. He _____ (begin) his diet a week ago. First of all, he _____ (write) out a long list of all the foods which were forbidden. The list _____ (include) most of the things Hugh loves. Yesterday I _____ (pay) him a visit. I _____ (ring) the bell and _____ (not surprise) to see that Hugh was still as fat as ever. He _____ (lead) me into his room and hurriedly _____ (hide) a large parcel under his desk. It was obvious that he _____ (embarrass).

c   What happened? What has happened? What has been happening? 一般过去时、现在完成时和现在完成进行时

Give the correct form of the verbs in parentheses.

用括号中动词的正确形式填空。

Jack _____ (look) at his watch for the twentieth time. Suddenly Jill _____ (arrive). 'I _____ (wait) for over an hour,' he _____ (say) angrily. 'You never come on time.'

   'Oh, is that so?' Jill _____ (answer). '_____ (Be) you here at 2.30?' Jack _____ (go) red. 'Well,' he _____ (say), 'I _____ (get) here five minutes late myself, but you _____ (not be) here.'

   'I _____ (come) here at exactly 2.30,' Jill _____ (say) and I _____ (wait) for five minutes, but you _____ (not come).'

   'What you _____ (do) since then?' Jack _____ (ask).

   'I just _____ (be) to the hairdresser's,' Jill _____ (answer) brightly.

d   What was happening? What happened? What used to happen? 过去进行时、一般过去时和表示过去的习惯性动作

Give the correct form of the verbs in parentheses. Use *would* in place of *used to* where possible.

用括号中动词的正确形式填空。可能情况下用would来代替used to。

Dreams of finding lost treasure almost _____ (come) true recently. A new machine called 'The Revealer' has been invented and it has been used to detect gold which has been buried in the ground. The machine _____ (use) in a cave near the seashore where — it is said — pirates _____ (hide) gold. The pirates often _____ (bury) gold in the cave and then _____ (fail) to collect it. Armed with the new machine, a search party _____ (go) into the cave hoping to find buried treasure. The leader of the party _____ (examine) the soil near the entrance to the cave when the machine _____ (show) that there _____ (be) gold under the ground. Very excited, the party _____ (dig) a hole two feet deep. They finally _____ (find) a small gold coin which was almost worthless.

e   What will happen tonight? 一般将来时

Give the correct form of the verbs in parentheses.

用括号中动词的正确形式填空。

A lifeboat _____ (set) out tonight to search for the shipwreck. The crew _____ (send) radio messages to the wreck until they _____ (receive) a signal from the men on board. As soon as they _____ (receive) a signal, they _____ (try) and find the wreck with powerful searchlights. The moment the crew _____ (locate) the wreck, they _____ (fire) a special gun which _____ (carry) a rope from the lifeboat to the sinking ship. If the sea is rough, they _____ (pour) oil on the water. They are sure to succeed, but if they fail, a helicopter _____ (send) out tomorrow morning. Helicopters are very useful for rescue work, but they cannot be used at night.

f   What will happen? What will be happening? What will have happened? What will have been happening?
一般将来时、将来进行时、将来完成时和将来完成进行时
Give the correct form of the verbs in parentheses.
用括号中动词的正确形式填空。

NASA is now going to put the telescope right, so it _____ (soon/send) up four astronauts to repair it. The
shuttle *Endeavour* _____ (take) the astronauts to the Hubble. A robot-arm from the *Endeavour* _____
(grab) the telescope and hold it while the astronauts make the necessary repairs. Of course, the Hubble is above the
earth's atmosphere, so it _____ (soon/send) us the clearest pictures of the stars and distant galaxies that we
have ever seen. The Hubble _____ (tell) us a great deal about the age and size of the universe. By the time
you read this, the Hubble's eagle eye _____ (send) us thousands and thousands of wonderful pictures.

g   What happened? What had happened? What had been happening? 一般过去时、过去完成时和过去完成
进行时
Give the correct form of the verbs in parentheses.
用括号中动词的正确形式填空。

After Howard Carter _____ (discover) Tutankhamen's tomb, strange reports _____ (appear) in the newspapers. Three of the people who _____ (take) part in the discovery _____ (die) soon afterwards. Though
nothing _____ (happen) to Carter himself, newspapers _____ (claim) that these people _____ (die)
because of the 'curse of the Pharaohs'. These absurd stories have been forgotten, but Carter's great discovery
remains. Archaeologists _____ (search) the Valley of Kings for years, but until 1922 nothing _____ (find).

h   Give the correct form of the verbs in parentheses.
用括号中动词的正确形式填空。

I _____ (take) my driving test for the third time. I _____ (ask) to drive in heavy traffic and had done so
successfully. After _____ (have/instruct) to drive out of town, I began to acquire confidence. Sure that I had
passed, I was almost beginning to enjoy my test. The examiner _____ (must/please) with my performance, for
he smiled and said, 'Just one more thing, Mr. Eames. Let us suppose that a child suddenly crosses the road in front
of you. As soon as I tap on the window, I want the car to _____ (stop) immediately.' I continued driving and
after some time, the examiner tapped loudly. Though the sound _____ (could/hear) clearly, it took me a long
time to react. I suddenly pressed the brake pedal hard and we both _____ (throw) forward.

i   Answer the questions after each statement.
直接引语和间接引语。

1 'Keep quiet!' he said.
   What did he tell me to do?

2 'Send him a telegram,' he suggested.
   What did he suggest?

3 'Ask him about it,' he insisted.
   What did he do?

4 'Don't worry about it,' he told me.
   What did he tell me?

j   Write the following sentences again beginning each one with 'I wonder'.
　　用 I wonder 开头来改写以下句子。

1 Can he wait a few minutes longer?

2 When will he arrive?

3 Has he passed his examination?

4 Where is he?

k   If 条件句
　　Give the correct form of the verbs in parentheses.
　　用括号中动词的正确形式填空。

1 If you _____ (listen) to me you would not have lost all that money.

2 I could have saved you a lot of trouble if you _____ (write) to me.

3 If you had applied earlier, you _____ (have) your passport by now.

l   Give the correct form of the verbs in parentheses.
　　用括号中动词的正确形式填空。

I crossed the street to avoid _____ (meet) him, but he saw me and came _____ (run) towards me. It was no use _____ (pretend) that I had not seen him, so I waved to him. I never enjoy _____ (meet) Nigel Dykes. No matter how busy you are, he always insists on _____ (come) with you. I had to think of a way of _____ (prevent) him from _____ (follow) me around all morning.

'Hello, Nigel,' I said. 'Fancy _____ (meet) you here!'

'Hi, Elizabeth,' Nigel answered. 'I was just wondering how to spend the morning — until I saw you. You're not busy _____ (do) anything, are you?'

'No, not at all,' I answered. 'I'm going to …'

'Would you mind my _____ (come) with you?' he asked, before I had finished _____ (speak).

D Other verbs 其他动词

a   Supply the correct form of *should, ought to*, or *have to* in these sentences.
　　用 should, ought to 或 have to 的正确形式填空。

1 He _____ (come) at four o'clock if the plane arrives on time.

2 I didn't go shopping this morning as I _____ (do) the housework.

3 She _____ (come) to see me yesterday, but she forgot.

4 You _____ (ask) for permission before you left the table.

b   Rewrite these sentences using *have* with the verbs in italics.
　　改写以下句子，将使役动词 have 与以下用斜体印出的动词连用。

1 He *is building* a new house.

2 She *will make* a new dress.

3 I *cut* my hair yesterday.

4 We *must cut* this tree down.

c   Rewrite these sentences using *managed to* in place of *could not*.
　　改写以下句子，用 managed to 来代替 could not。

1 I could not get into town this morning.

2 They could not find the boy who had run away.

3 He could not find a new job.

4 I could not translate the passage into English.

E A, The and Some

Put in *a*, *the* and *some* where necessary.
在需要的地方填上 a, the 和 some。

After _____ breakfast, I sent _____ children to _____ school and then I went to _____ market. It was still early when I returned home. _____ children were at _____ school, my husband was at _____ work, and _____ house was quiet. So I decided to make _____ tarts for _____ tea. In _____ short time I was busy mixing _____ butter and _____ flour and my hands were soon covered with _____ sticky pastry. At exactly that moment, _____ telephone rang. Nothing could have been more annoying. I picked up _____ receiver between _____ two sticky fingers and was dismayed when I recognized _____ voice of Helen Bates. It took me ten minutes to persuade her to ring back later. At last I hung up _____ receiver. What _____ mess! There was _____ pastry on my fingers, on _____ telephone, and on _____ doorknobs. I had no sooner got back to _____ kitchen than _____ doorbell rang loud enough to wake _____ dead. This time it was _____ postman and he wanted me to sign for _____ registered letter!

F A lot of cars entered for the race.

Supply the missing words in the following.
填空。

Once a year a race is held for old cars. A lot _____ cars entered for this race last year and there was a great _____ of excitement just before it began. One of the _____ handsome cars was a Rolls-Royce Silver Ghost. The _____ unusual car was a Benz which had only three wheels. Built in 1885, it was the _____ (old) car taking part. After a great _____ loud explosions, the race began. _____ of the cars broke down on the course and some drivers spent _____ time *under* their cars than *in* them! A _____ cars, however, completed the race. The winning car reached a speed of forty miles an hour — much faster _____ any of its rivals. It sped downhill at the end of the race and its driver had a _____ trouble trying to stop it. The race gave everyone a great _____ of pleasure. It was very different _____ modern car races but no _____ exciting.

G Supply the missing words in the following sentences.

填空。

1 A woman _____ blue jeans stood _____ the window of an expensive shop. Though she hesitated for a moment, she finally went _____ and asked to see a dress that was _____ the window.

2 Glancing _____ her scornfully, the assistant told her that the dress was sold. The woman walked _____ the shop angrily.

3 She returned _____ the shop the following morning dressed _____ a fur coat, _____ a handbag _____ one hand and a long umbrella _____ the other.

H Words followed by *for, with, of, to* and *at* 与 *for, with, of, to, at* 连用的词

Supply the missing words in the following sentences.
填空。

1 You shouldn't get so angry _____ him.
2 He is very good _____ finding excuses.
3 I'm not very fond _____ ice cream.
4 I would be thankful _____ any advice you can give me.

5 He remained faithful _____ the firm even after he had been dismissed.

6 I cannot be held responsible _____ other people's mistakes.

7 Don't be so sure _____ yourself.

8 His excellent progress should be obvious _____ everyone.

Special difficulties 难点

A Words often confused 经常容易混淆的词

Choose the correct words in the following sentences.
选择合适的词完成以下句子。

1 This screw is (loose) (lose).

2 I always (rise) (raise) at six o'clock.

3 He (laid) (lay) the book on the table.

4 He works very (hard) (hardly).

5 Who (won) (beat) the match?

6 Please keep (quiet) (quite).

7 I (used to) (am used to) smoke a lot once.

8 The waitress (fell) (dropped) her tray.

9 The teacher got angry and threw a book (to) (at) the boy.

10 We went into the orchard to help him (pick) (cut) some apples.

11 Your son has (increased) (grown) since I last saw him.

12 Sir Frank Whittle (discovered) (invented) the jet engine.

13 Please (leave) (let) him come with me.

14 Would you like to take (part) (place) in the contest?

15 No one knows the (reason) (cause) for his disappearance.

16 We were (amused) (enjoyed) by the circus clown.

17 They are now (controlling) (checking) our passports.

18 What do you (advice) (advise) me to do?

B Say and Tell

Write sentences using either *say* or *tell* with the following.
用动词 say 或 tell 与以下短语造句。

a secret, your prayers, a lie, nothing, a story, so.

C Write these sentences again. Express the phrases in italics in a different way.

改写以下句子，用另一种方式来表达用斜体印出的短语。

1 *The dining room in our school* is very large.

2 He told us a *story about ghosts*.

3 She gave me a *present for my birthday*.

4 We stopped at *a pub in the village*.

5 *The leader of the party* made a speech.

Unit 4
第 4 单元

Unit 4   第 4 单元

INSTRUCTIONS TO THE STUDENT   致学生

In Unit 4 you will be expected to write simple, compound and complex statements. You will have less help than you had in the previous units.

在第 4 单元, 要求你会写简单句、并列句和复合句。和前几个单元相比, 你所能得到的帮助更少。

Before you begin each exercise, read these instructions carefully. Read them each time you begin a new piece. They are very important.

在开始每项练习之前, 要细读这些指令。它们都很重要, 每次开始新课前都要读读指令。

How to work — Summary writing 如何写摘要

Unit 4 contains twenty-four short passages. There are no Comprehension questions under these passages. Instead, you will find the answers to imaginary questions. These 'answers' have been written in note form and are, in fact, the main points of a summary.

第 4 单元共有 24 篇短文。课文之后没有针对课文理解的问题。你会发现针对假设的问题的答案。这些答案是用笔记的形式列出的, 事实上也组成了一篇摘要的要点。

1 Read the passage carefully two or three times. Make sure you understand it.

   细读课文 2 至 3 遍, 一定要理解课文。

2 Read the general instructions immediately below each passage. They will tell you what you have to do.

   读一读每课之后的指令。

3 Under the titles CONNECTIONS, you will find two sets of joining words which have been given with each list of POINTS.

   在 "连接词" 的下面有两组词, 是与 "要点" 相对应的。

4 Using the first set of connections, join up the points to make sentences. The number of points which each sentence will contain is given in parentheses. All your sentences together should form *a complete paragraph*. When joining up the points, you may refer to the passage as much as you like.

   用第 1 组 "连接词" 将要点连成句子。每句话所含的要点数目列在括号中。你所写的句子应组成一个完整的段落, 在连接过程中可以随意看课文。

5 Read through your work and correct your mistakes.

   从头至尾读一遍你的答案, 纠正其中的错误。

6 Count the number of words in your paragraph. Do not go over the word limit. Words like 'the', 'a', etc. count as single words. Words which are joined by a hyphen also count as single words. At the end of your paragraph, write the number of words that you have used.

   数一下段落的总字数, 不要超过字数的限制。冠词和用连字符组成的复合词均为一个词。在段落后面注明全段的字数。

7 Now, using the second set of connections, write *another* composition of the passage in exactly the same way.

   然后, 用第 2 组 "连接词" 按同样方式写出另一篇作文。

Example 范例

Work through this example carefully and then try to do the exercises in Unit 4 in the same way.

仔细研究以下例题, 然后用同样的方式完成第 4 单元的练习。

The sacred tree

In the nineteenth century, Mugo Kibiru, a famous prophet of the Kikuyu tribe, foretold that a fig tree at Thika, twenty-six miles north of Nairobi, would wither and die on the day that Kenya gained independence. Kibiru also prophesied that Kenya would become a white man's colony, but that one day the white man would return the land to the Africans. He foresaw the coming of the railway which he described as 'an iron snake with many legs, like an earthworm'. Kibiru's prophecies proved to be so accurate that for many years the tree at Thika was regarded as sacred. Even the white men took the prophecy seriously, for they built the tree up with earth and put a concrete wall around it so that it would not fall. These measures were doomed to fail. Shortly before Kenya gained independence, the tree was struck by lightning and it began to wither rapidly. By the day Kenya officially became independent, it had decayed completely, fulfilling the prophecy made over seventy years before by Kibiru.

Summary writing 摘要写作

In not more than 80 words write an account of the tree at Thika. Write two different paragraphs using the points and connections given below.

用不到 80 个单词的篇幅，描述一下塞卡的那棵树，用以下要点和连词写出两段不同的文字。

CONNECTIONS	POINTS	CONNECTIONS
that	1 19th century — Kibiru foretold.	*According to*
when	2 Fig tree — wither — Kenya independent.	*on the day that*
As	3 Other prophecies accurate.	
	4 Tree sacred.	*so*
Though	5 White men — wall.	
	6 Prevent it falling.	*to*
for	7 Prophecy true.	*but*
	8 Tree — lightning — before independence.	*After having been*
and	9 Decayed.	

1 A possible answer (First set of connections) 参考答案 1

In the nineteenth century, Kibiru, a famous prophet of the Kikuyu tribe, foretold *that* a fig tree at Thika would wither *when* Kenya became independent. *As* many of Kibiru's prophecies proved to be accurate, the tree was considered sacred. *Though* white men built a wall round the tree, they could not prevent it from falling. Kibiru's prophecy came true, *for* the tree was struck by lightning just before Kenya gained her independence *and* it decayed completely.

(76 words)

2 A possible answer (Second set of connections) 参考答案 2

According to a prophecy made in the nineteenth century by the Kikuyu prophet, Kibiru, a fig tree at Thika would wither *on the day that* Kenya gained independence. Other prophecies made by Kibiru proved to be accurate *so* the tree was regarded as sacred. The white men even built a wall round it *to* prevent it from falling, *but* the prophecy came true. *After having been* struck by lightning just before Kenya became independent, the tree decayed completely.

(78 words)

Composition 作文

In Unit 4 Composition exercises are based on ideas suggested by each passage. You will be asked to write *two* paragraphs of about 150 words using ideas which have been given in note form. You may, of course, add to these ideas if you wish or change them to make them suit your purposes. 第 4 单元的作文练习是以课文引申出来的思路为基础的。要求你写出两篇 150 词左右的作文，使用所列的词组。你当然可以作出增补，以便使它们实现你的目标。

Example 范例

Work through this example carefully and then try to do the Composition exercises in the same way.
仔细研究以下例题，然后用同样方式完成作文练习。

Sample composition 作文范例

Write an imaginary account of what happened to the tree from the time it was struck by lightning to when Kenya gained her independence. Write two paragraphs of about 150 words using the ideas given below. 根据想象写出从这棵树遭雷击到肯尼亚获得独立所发生的事情。用以下短语写出 150 词左右的两个段落。

1 Shortly before independence — storm — tree struck — news to Nairobi — whole of Kenya — Kibiru's prophecy true.

2 Visitors from all parts of Kenya — excitement — tree decayed — completely by independence day — high wall remained — life to a new country.

A possible answer 参考答案

Shortly before Kenya gained her independence, there was a terrible storm. The next morning, the inhabitants of Thika were astonished to find that the sacred tree had been struck by lightning. Its trunk was split in the middle and blackened branches lay everywhere. The news travelled quickly to Nairobi. Soon everybody in Kenya heard that the sacred tree had begun to wither. It now seemed certain that Kibiru's prophecy would come true.

During the next few weeks, people came from all parts of Kenya to see the sacred tree. The tree decayed before their eyes. Everybody was excited and a little frightened by what was happening. Day by day, branches fell, until only part of the trunk remained. By independence day, the trunk had decayed completely. Only the high wall, which had been built by the white men, was still standing. The dead tree had given its life to a new country.

(About 150 words)

Letter writing 书信写作

Follow the instructions given under each passage.
遵循每课书后的指令。

Key structures and Special difficulties 关键句型和难点

When you finish the **Letter writing** exercise, go on to the language exercises that follow. The **Key structures** deal with exactly the same problems that were considered in Units 1, 2 and 3. In this unit you will revise what you have learnt so far. You may refer back if you have forgotten anything. **Special difficulties** are dealt with after the **Key structures.** The work you do in grammar is based on material contained in the passages. Refer to the passages frequently. They will help you to understand the grammar and to do the exercises.

当你完成"书信写作"后，就可以开始紧随其后的语言练习。"关键句型"的问题与第 1、2、3 单元相同。在这个单元你将复习前面的知识。如有遗忘，可以在前几个单元查找。"关键句型"之后是"难点"。其中的语法练习是以课文中的语言点为基础的。经常查找课文可以帮助你理解语法并完成练习。

Lesson 73   The record-holder   纪录保持者

First listen and then answer the question.

听录音，然后回答以下问题。

Did the boy go where he wanted to?

Children who play truant from school are unimaginative. A quiet
day's fishing, or eight hours in a cinema seeing the same film over
and over again, is usually as far as they get. They have all been put
to shame by a boy who, while playing truant, travelled 1,600 miles.
5 He hitchhiked to Dover and, towards evening, went into a boat to
find somewhere to sleep. When he woke up next morning, he
discovered that the boat had, in the meantime, travelled to Calais.
No one noticed the boy as he crept off. From there, he hitchhiked to
Paris in a lorry. The driver gave him a few biscuits and a cup of coffee and left him just outside the city. The
10 next car the boy stopped did not take him into the centre of Paris as he hoped it would, but to Perpignan on the
French-Spanish border. There he was picked up by a policeman and sent back to England by the local authorities.
He has surely set up a record for the thousands of children who dream of evading school.

He was picked up by a policeman

New words and expressions   生词和短语

record-holder (title) /'rekɔːd-'həʊldə/ 纪录保持者
truant (1.1) /'truːənt/ n. 逃学的孩子
unimaginative (1.1) /ˌʌnɪ'mædʒɪnətɪv/ adj. 缺乏想象力的
shame (1.4) /ʃeɪm/ n. 惭愧，羞耻
hitchhike (1.5) /'hɪtʃhaɪk/ v. 搭便车旅行

meantime (1.7) /'miːntaɪm/ n. 其间
lorry (1.9) /'lɒri/ n. 卡车
border (1.11) /'bɔːdə/ n. 边界
evade (1.12) /ɪ'veɪd/ v. 逃避，逃离

Notes on the text   课文注释

1   play truant from school, 逃学, 也可以说 play truant。
2   as far as they get, 他们顶多到这种程度而已。as far as 作 "到……程度" 解。
3   They have all been put to shame …, 这是被动语态; put sb. to shame, 使某人感到羞愧, 使……黯然失色。
4   while playing truant 是分词短语作状语, 相当于一个状语从句 while he was playing truant。
5   in the meantime, 在此期间。
6   did not take him into the centre of Paris as he hoped it would, 没有像他希望的那样把他带到巴黎市中心。
    as he hoped it would 是一个方式状语从句, 作 "像……那样" 解, would 后面省略了和前文相同的谓语 take
    him into the centre of Paris。

参考译文

　　逃学的孩子们都缺乏想象力。他们通常能够做到的, 至多也就是安静地钓上一天鱼, 或在电影院里坐上 8
个小时, 一遍遍地看同一部电影。而有那么一个小男孩, 他在逃学期间旅行了 1,600 英里, 从而使上述所有逃
学的孩子们都相形见绌了。他搭便车到了多佛, 天快黑时钻进了一条船, 想找个地方睡觉。第二天早上他醒来

时，发现船在这段时间已经到了加来。当男孩从船里爬出来时，谁也没有发现他。从那里他又搭上卡车到了巴黎。司机给了他几块饼干和一杯咖啡，就把他丢在了城外。男孩截住的下一辆车，没有像他希望的那样把他带到巴黎市中心，而是把他带到了法国和西班牙界上的佩皮尼昂。他在那儿被一个警察抓住了，之后被当局送回了英国。他无疑为成千上万梦想逃避上学的孩子们创造了一项纪录。

Summary writing 摘要写作

In not more than 80 words, describe the boy's experiences. Write two different paragraphs using the points and connections given below.

用不超过 80 个单词的篇幅描述这个孩子的经历。用以下要点和连词写出两个不同的段落。

CONNECTIONS		POINTS		CONNECTIONS
who		1	Boy played truant.	
		2	Travelled 1,600 miles.	*and*
		3	Hitchhiked — Dover.	*After*
where		4	Slept — boat.	
only to find		5	Found himself — Calais — morning.	
		6	Lorry driver: lift and something to eat.	*where*
and		7	Boy got off near Paris.	*On getting off*
but, instead		8	Stopped another car.	*which … not to …*
of being		9	Not taken Paris — Perpignan.	*but to …*
After		10	Picked up — policeman.	*There*
		11	Sent home — authorities.	*and*

Composition 作文

Write two paragraphs in about 150 words using the ideas given below:

按以下思路写出两段文字，字数为 150 个词左右：

1 The boy returned — sick, cold and hungry — his parents were worried — met him at the harbour — their reactions.

2 The boy returned to school — he was afraid he would be punished — the boys gave him a hero's welcome — asked questions — the headmaster punished him by making him give a talk to the whole school about his experiences abroad.

Letter writing 书信写作

A letter contains three main parts: the Introduction, the Purpose and the Conclusion. The most important part is the Purpose. Here you must explain why you are writing.

每封信包含 3 个主要部分：引言、目的和结束语。其中最重要的部分是目的。在这部分中你必须说明为什么要写此信。

Exercise 练习

Write a short Introduction of a letter to a friend beginning:

用以下句子写出给朋友的一封信的引言。

'You will never guess what …'

Key structures 关键句型

Simple, Compound and Complex Statements (**KS1, 25, 49**) 简单句、并列句和复合句
(复习第 1，25，49 课的关键句型)

Exercises 练习

A How many joining words can you find in the passage? Underline as many as you can.
画出课文中的连词。

B Rewrite these simple statements using the joining words in parentheses. Do not refer to the passage until you finish the exercise.
用括号中的连词改写以下句子，完成练习后再对照课文，核对你的答案。

1 Children play truant from school. They are unimaginative. (*who*)

2 They have all been put to shame by a boy. He played truant. He travelled 1,600 miles. (*a boy who, while* …)

3 He hitchhiked to Dover. Towards evening, he went into a boat. He wanted to find somewhere to sleep. (*and … to*)

4 He woke up next morning. He discovered that the boat had, in the meantime, travelled to Calais. (*When*)

5 No one noticed the boy. He crept off. (*as*)

6 The driver gave him a few biscuits. He gave him a cup of coffee. He left him outside the city. (*and … and*)

C Rewrite the following sentences using the joining words in parentheses:
用括号中的连词改写以下句子：

1 The climbers reached the top of the mountain. They spent the night there. (*not only … but … as well*)

2 A fire broke out in a cinema. Several hundred people tried to leave the building. A number of them were injured. (*When … and*)

3 James Sullivan will give a lecture at the local library next week. His book on the Antarctic was published recently. (*whose*)

4 The police searched everywhere. The missing boy could not be found. His dog could not be found. (*Although … neither … nor*)

5 Fares have increased. The railway company is still losing money. The employees have demanded higher wages. (*In spite of the fact that … because*)

6 He gave me a fright. I knocked the teapot over. (*such … that*)

7 I made sure. The alarm clock worked. I set it. It would ring at six o'clock. (*After making … that … so that*)

8 I hid the Christmas presents under the desk quickly. My young daughter would not see them. She entered the room. (*so that … when*)

9 I refused the offer. I explained. I had already been offered a job by another company. (*Refusing … that …*)

10 He fought the wolves off for three hours. Help arrived. (*before*)

Multiple choice questions 选择题

Comprehension 理解

1 How did the boy get to Dover?
(*a*) He walked.   (*b*) He went by train.
(*c*) Someone gave him a lift.   (*d*) He went in a lorry.

2 The boy _____ .

    (a) didn't expect to be taken to Perpignan   (b) decided to go to Perpignan

    (c) went to Paris   (d) wanted to go to Spain

Structure 句型

3 _____ did he travel? 1,600 miles.

    (a) How long   (b) How long ago   (c) How much further   (d) How far

4 How did he get to Dover?

    (a) By hitchhiking.   (b) With hitchhike.   (c) Hitchhiking.   (d) With hitchhiking.

5 He wasn't noticed by _____ as he crept off the boat.

    (a) no one   (b) none   (c) anyone   (d) not one

6 The driver gave him a few biscuits. _____ was given a few biscuits.

    (a) To him   (b) Him   (c) For him   (d) He

7 After _____ by a policeman, he was sent back to England.

    (a) being picked up   (b) he picked up   (c) been picked up   (d) picking up

Vocabulary 词汇

8 Little boys who play truant don't go to school _____ .

    (a) because they are ill   (b) because they have left

    (c) because they are not allowed to   (d) on purpose

9 They are unimaginative. They haven't much _____ .

    (a) imagination   (b) fantasy   (c) imaginary   (d) fantasia

10 They have been put to shame by a boy. They should feel _____ .

    (a) ashamed   (b) shy   (c) shyness   (d) shameful

11 He was picked up by a policeman. A policeman _____ him.

    (a) gathered   (b) collected   (c) assembled   (d) found

12 Thousands of boys dream of evading school. They dream of _____ it.

    (a) escaping   (b) avoiding   (c) preventing   (d) running away

Sentence structure 句子结构

Rewrite this sentence, then check your answer against the text.

改写以下句子, 然后对照课文第 6-7 行, 核对你的答案。

On waking up next morning, he discovered that the boat had, in the meantime, travelled to Calais.

When _____ .

Lesson 74　Out of the limelight　舞台之外

First listen and then answer the question.

听录音, 然后回答以下问题。

Why was their disguise 'too perfect'?

'I'm sheriff here'

An ancient bus stopped by a dry river bed and a party of famous actors and actresses got off. Dressed in dark glasses and old clothes, they had taken special precautions so that no one should recognize them. But as they soon discovered, disguises can sometimes be too
5　perfect.

　　'This is a wonderful place for a picnic,' said Gloria Gleam.

　　'It couldn't be better, Gloria,' Brinksley Meers agreed. 'No newspaper men, no film fans! Why don't we come more often?'

　　Meanwhile, two other actors, Rockwall Slinger and Merlin Greeves, had carried two large food baskets
10　to a shady spot under some trees. When they had all made themselves comfortable, a stranger appeared. He looked very angry. 'Now you get out of here, all of you!' he shouted. 'I'm sheriff here. Do you see that notice? It says "No Camping" — in case you can't read!'

　　'Look, sheriff,' said Rockwall, 'don't be too hard on us. I'm Rockwall Slinger and this is Merlin Greeves.'

　　'Oh, is it?' said the sheriff with a sneer. 'Well, I'm Brinksley Meers, and my other name is Gloria Gleam.
15　Now you get out of here fast!'

New words and expressions　生词和短语

limelight (title) /'laɪmlaɪt/ n. 舞台灯光
precaution (1.3) /prɪ'kɔːʃən/ n. 预防措施
fan (1.8) /fæn/ n. 狂热者, 迷
shady (1.10) /'ʃeɪdi/ adj. 遮荫的

sheriff (1.11) /'ʃerɪf/ n. 司法长官
notice (1.12) /'nəʊtɪs/ n. 告示
sneer (1.14) /snɪə/ n. 冷笑

Notes on the text　课文注释

1　Out of the limelight, 这里的limelight是指舞台。

2　as they soon discovered 中的as是关系代词, 代替后面的整个主句disguises can sometimes be too perfect, 作动词discovered的宾语。

3　Why don't we come more often? 我们为什么不经常来这里呢? 这是一个否定的特殊疑问句, 表示一种建议。

4　get out of here, 从这里走开。

5　in case you can't read, 除非你们不识字。

6　be hard on us, 使我们难堪, 对我们过于严厉。

参考译文

　　一辆古旧的汽车停在一条干涸的河床边, 一群著名男女演员下了车。他们戴着墨镜, 穿着旧衣裳, 特别小心以防别人认出他们。但他们很快就发觉, 化装的效果有时过分完美了。

　　"在这个地方野餐简直是太妙了," 格洛里亚·格利姆说。

"是再好不过的了，格洛利亚。"布林克斯利·米尔斯表示同意，"没有记者，没有影迷! 我们为什么不经常来这里呢?"

此时，另外两位演员，罗克沃尔·斯林格和默林·格里夫斯，已经把两个大食品篮子提到了一片树阴下。当他们都已安排舒适时，一个陌生人出现了。他看上去非常气愤。"你们都从这里走开，全都走开!"他大叫着，"我是这里的司法长官。你们看到那个布告牌了吗? 上面写着'禁止野营'——除非你们不识字!"

"好了，好了，司法长官，"罗克沃尔说，"别使我们难堪。我是罗克沃尔·斯林格，这位是默林·格里夫斯。"

"噢，是吗?"那位司法长官冷笑一声说道，"那么，我就是布林克斯利·米尔斯。我还有一个名字叫格洛利亚·格利姆。现在你们赶快滚吧!"

Summary writing 摘要写作

In not more than 80 words describe what happened. Write two different paragraphs using the points and connections given below.

用不超过 80 个单词的篇幅描述一下所发生的事情。用以下要点和连词写出两段不同的文字。

CONNECTIONS		POINTS		CONNECTIONS
After		1	But stopped — river bed.	
		2	Film stars descended.	*A party of*
		3	Dressed — glasses, clothes.	
so as not to		4	Recognize.	*in order that*
		5	Picnic things, shady spot.	
and		6	Sat down.	*Everyone had*
Just then		7	Sheriff, rudely — must leave.	*when*
because		8	Camping not allowed.	*as*
Even when		9	Told him who they were.	
		10	Did not believe them.	*but*

Composition 作文

Write two paragraphs in about 150 words using the ideas given below:

按以下思路写出两段文字，字数为 150 个词左右:

1 A fine day — we prepared for a picnic — drove into the country — found a quiet spot — unpacked our hampers.

2 There were a few wasps — then a great many — our efforts to drive them away — saw a wasp nest in a tree nearby — seized our things — returned to car pursued by wasps — drove away.

Key structures 关键句型

What is happening? What always happens? (KS2, 26, 50) 现在进行时和一般现在时

(复习第 2，26，50 课的关键句型)

Exercises 练习

A Give the correct form of the verbs in parentheses. Do not refer to the passage until you finish the exercise:

用括号中动词的正确形式填空，完成练习后再对照课文，核对你的答案:

1 'It couldn't be better, Gloria,' Brinksley Meers agreed. 'No newspaper men, no film fans! Why we _____ (not come) more often?'

2 'I'm sheriff here. _____ you (see) that notice? It _____ (say) "No Camping" — in case you can't read!'

B What happens? What is happening?

Give the correct form of the verbs in parentheses:

一般现在时和现在进行时。用括号中动词的正确形式填空：

1 The police now _____ (investigate) the matter.

2 Light _____ (travel) at a speed of 186,000 miles a second.

3 He _____ (resemble) his father.

4 The postman who _____ (deliver) my letters is on holiday.

5 It _____ (look) as if it will rain.

6 Caroline still _____ (love) him even though he has behaved so badly.

7 Hurry up! The bus _____ (come).

8 Which _____ you _____ (prefer)? The red one or the white one?

C Write sentences using the following verbs:

用以下动词造句：

contain, mean, believe, understand, want, matter.

Special difficulties 难点

a The verb *get* has a different meaning in each of these sentences. Study them carefully:

在以下句子中，动词get有各种不同的词义。细读以下例句：

Now you *get out of* here, all of you! (1.11)

The door is locked. I can't *get out*. 门是锁着的，我出不去。

I've lost my key. I can't *get into* the house. 我把钥匙丢了，我进不了屋子。

How is he *getting on* in his new job? (How is he progressing?) 他的这份新工作干得怎么样？

Get on with your work. (Continue ...) 继续你的工作。

He's so difficult, I can't *get on with* him. (We are not on good terms.) 他这个人这么别扭，我无法和他相处。

Tom was punished, but Jim *got off* lightly. (He escaped punishment.) 汤姆受到了惩罚，但吉姆逃脱了。

I can't *get* the cap of this pen *off*. (I can't remove it.) 我无法取下这支笔的笔帽。

He has now *got over* his illness. (He has recovered.) 他已从病中恢复过来了。

I want to *get* this interview *over* as quickly as possible. (I want to finish it.) 我想尽快地结束这次会见。

He *got through* his exams. (He succeeded in passing his exams.) 他通过了考试。

He *got through* a huge amount of food. (He succeeded in eating ...) 他吃完了一大堆食品。

Exercise 练习

Supply the missing words in the following sentences:

填空：

1 He has never got _____ his wife's death.

2 How did the thief manage to get _____ the house?

3 Did you get _____ your driving test?

4 The lid is stuck. I can't get it _____ .

5 He gets _____ very well _____ all his new colleagues.

6 'Please stop talking and get _____ your work,' she said.

b   No Camping (l.12)

On public notices we write *No Camping* instead of *Do not camp*.

在公告牌上我们不用Do not camp, 而用No Camping。

Exercise 练习

How would these appear on public notices:

下列词语应如何写到公告牌上：

1 Do not smoke in this compartment.　　2 Do not park.　　3 Do not wait on this side of the street today.

Multiple choice questions 选择题
Comprehension 理解

1 The actors disguised themselves _____ .

(*a*) to have a picnic

(*b*) so that no one would know who they were

(*c*) so that the sheriff wouldn't recognize them

(*d*) because they were famous

2 The sheriff _____ .

(*a*) knew that they were famous actors

(*b*) believed that they were famous actors

(*c*) was an actor himself

(*d*) didn't believe that they were famous actors

Structure 句型

3 Disguises can be too perfect. This means they can be _____ .

(*a*) perfect

(*b*) quite perfect

(*c*) more perfect than is convenient

(*d*) almost perfect

4 This is a wonderful place. _____ wonderful place!

(*a*) How　　(*b*) What　　(*c*) What a　　(*d*) How a

5 Why don't we come more often? We _____ come more often.

(*a*) could　　(*b*) would　　(*c*) might　　(*d*) should

6 'No Camping' means _____ .

(*a*) there isn't any

(*b*) it's without camping

(*c*) you aren't allowed to camp

(*d*) you needn't camp

7 _____ you look at the notice, you'll see it says 'No Camping'.

(*a*) If　　(*b*) Providing that　　(*c*) Whether　　(*d*) In the situation

Vocabulary 词汇

8 They were dressed in old clothes. They were wearing old _____ .

(*a*) cloth　　(*b*) cloths　　(*c*) clothing　　(*d*) dresses

9 Which of these objects would make a good disguise? A _____ .

(*a*) computer　　(*b*) mask　　(*c*) bus　　(*d*) train

10 A film fan is a person who _____ films.

(*a*) makes　　(*b*) sees　　(*c*) enjoys seeing　　(*d*) possesses

11 Do you see that notice? Do you see that _____ ?

(*a*) sign　　(*b*) label　　(*c*) signal　　(*d*) board

12 'Oh, is it?' said the sheriff with a sneer. He was _____ .

(*a*) pleased　　(*b*) scornful　　(*c*) teasing them　　(*d*) mocking them

Lesson 75 SOS 呼救信号

First listen and then answer the question.

听录音，然后回答以下问题。

How did the woman get help?

When a light passenger plane flew off course some time ago, it crashed in the mountains and its pilot was killed. The only passengers, a young woman and her two baby daughters, were unhurt. It was the middle of winter. Snow lay thick on the ground. The
5 woman knew that the nearest village was miles away. When it grew dark, she turned a suitcase into a bed and put the children inside it, covering them with all the clothes she could find. During the night, it got terribly cold. The woman kept as near as she could to the children and even tried to get into the case herself, but it was too small. Early next morning, she heard planes
10 passing overhead and wondered how she could send a signal. Then she had an idea. She stamped out the letters 'SOS' in the snow. Fortunately, a pilot saw the signal and sent a message by radio to the nearest town. It was not long before a helicopter arrived on the scene to rescue the survivors of the plane crash.

She turned a suitcase into a bed

New words and expressions 生词和短语

thick (1.4) /θɪk/ *adj.* 厚的
signal (1.10) /'sɪgnəl/ *n.* 信号
stamp (1.10) /stæmp/ *v.* 踩，踩

helicopter (1.12) /'helɪkɒptə/ *n.* 直升机
scene (1.12) /siːn/ *n.* 现场
survivor (1.12) /sə'vaɪvə/ *n.* 幸存者

Notes on the text 课文注释

1 SOS = "Save Our Souls"，国际通用的呼救信号。
2 fly off course，飞行偏离航线。
3 Snow lay thick on the ground. 地上积着厚厚的雪。lay是系动词，thick是表语，表示主语的状态或性质。
4 she heard planes passing overhead，她听见头顶上有飞机飞过。passing overhead是现在分词短语，作宾语planes的补足语。
5 stamp out，踩出。其中out是一个副词，out与一些动词连用时常常有"看得见"、"听得见"的意思，如 write out, tap out, ring out等。
6 It was not long before a helicopter arrived on the scene to rescue the survivors of the plane crash. 不久，一架直升机飞抵失事现场，来搭救这几个幸存者。注意这句话中的before是连词，引导的是时间状语从句，long是形容词，是主句的表语。不要把这句话中的long和before的用法同long before或before long词组的用法混淆。

参考译文

不久前，一架轻型客机偏离了航线，在山区坠毁，飞行员丧生。机上仅有的乘客，一位年轻的妇女和她的两个女婴却平安无事。此时正值隆冬季节，地上积着厚厚的雪。这位妇女知道，即使最近的村庄也有数英里远。

天黑下来的时候，她把提箱当作小床，把两个孩子放了进去，又把所有能找到的衣服都盖在了孩子们身上。夜里，天冷得厉害。这位妇女尽可能地靠近孩子，甚至自己也想钻进箱子里去，只是箱子太小了。第二天一大早，她听到头顶上有飞机飞过，但不知道怎样才能发个信号。后来她有了一个主意。她在雪地上踩出了"SOS"这3个字母。幸运得很，一位飞行员看到了这个信号，并用无线电给最近的城镇发了报。不久，一架直升机飞抵飞机失事现场，来搭救这几个幸存者。

Summary writing 摘要写作

In not more than 80 words, describe what happened. Write two different paragraphs using the points and connections given below.

用不超过 80 个单词的篇幅来描述所发生的事情。用以下要点和连词写出两个不同的段落。

CONNECTIONS	POINTS	CONNECTIONS
	1　Plane crashed — mountains.	*When*
but	2　Only passengers — woman, baby daughters not hurt.	
and	3　Mid-winter — extremely cold.	*However, and*
so	4　Put children in case.	*After putting*
	5　Covered them — clothes.	*However, and*
and	6　Kept close all night.	*the woman*
When	7　Planes — next morning.	*On hearing*
	8　Stamped 'SOS' — snow.	*the woman*
This	9　Seen by pilot.	*which*
who	10　Message sent.	
and	11　Rescued — helicopter.	*and*

Composition 作文

Write two paragraphs in about 150 words using the ideas given below:

按以下思路写出两段文字，字数为 150 个词左右：

1　A light aeroplane with a heavy cargo — sudden storm — high winds — the pilot made a crash — landing in the snow.

2　The pilot was unhurt — roped the plane to a rock — spent the night in a tent — next morning — found that the plane had been swept away by the wind — smashed to pieces — cargo and wreckage in the snow.

Letter writing 书信写作

Write a suitable *Purpose* in about 50 words to follow this introductory paragraph:

按照以下引言的思路，用 50 个左右的单词写出一段"目的"：

Forgive me for not writing earlier to thank you for the lovely scarf you sent me for my birthday, but I have been in bed with flu.

Key structures 关键句型

What happened? 一般过去时 **(KS3, 27, 51)**（复习第 3，27，51 课的关键句型）

Unit 4   Lesson 75

Exercises 练习

A Underline all the verbs in the passage that tell us *what happened*.
画出课文中所有一般过去时的动词。

B Give the correct form of the verbs in parentheses. Do not refer to the passage until you finish the exercise.
用括号中动词的正确形式填空, 完成练习后再对照课文, 核对你的答案。

When a light passenger plane _____ (fly) off course some time ago, it _____ (crash) in the mountains and its pilot _____ (kill). The only passengers, a young woman and her two baby daughters, _____ (be) unhurt. It _____ (be) the middle of winter. Snow _____ (lie) thick on the ground. The woman _____ (know) that the nearest village _____ (be) miles away. When it _____ (grow) dark, she _____ (turn) a suitcase into a bed and _____ (put) the children inside it, covering them with all the clothes she _____ (can) find. During the night, it _____ (get) terribly cold. The woman _____ (keep) as near as she could to the children and even _____ (try) to get into the case herself, but it _____ (be) too small. Early next morning, she _____ (hear) planes passing overhead and _____ (wonder) how she _____ (can) send a signal. Then she _____ (have) an idea. She _____ (stamp) out the letters 'SOS' in the snow. Fortunately, a pilot _____ (see) the signal and _____ (send) a message by radio to the nearest town. It _____ (not be) long before a helicopter _____ (arrive) on the scene to rescue the survivors of the plane crash.

Special difficulties 难点

When it grew dark ... (l.5)

Study the verbs in italics. They are all used in the sense of the verb *become*.
注意用斜体印出的动词, 它们均有 "变成" 的意思。

He *grew* (or *got*) angry when I told him about it. 当我告诉他这件事时, 他变得非常生气。

The leaves are *turning* (or *getting*) yellow. 树叶正在变黄。

This apple *has gone* bad. 这个苹果坏了。

Coal *got* scarce last winter. 去年冬天煤变得很缺乏。

Everything you said *came* true. 你说过的每一件事都成了现实。

She *fell* ill while she was on holiday. 她在度假时生病了。

Exercise 练习

Supply the correct verbs in the following sentences:
用正确的动词填空:

1 During the night it _____ terribly cold.

2 He was so tired, he _____ asleep.

3 When the teacher left the classroom, the children _____ noisy.

4 If you do not put the milk in the refrigerator, it will _____ sour.

5 This knob has _____ loose.

6 The children _____ quiet when he entered the room.

7 Even though I am _____ older, I am not _____ wiser.

8 She's _____ so fat you won't recognize her.

9 This post _____ vacant last year.

10 Don't worry, everything will _____ right in the end.

Multiple choice questions 选择题

Comprehension 理解

1 The plane crashed because _____ .

   (*a*) it was a light passenger plane   (*b*) the pilot was killed

   (*c*) it wasn't flying in the right direction   (*d*) it was the middle of winter

2 The next morning a pilot flying overhead _____ .

   (*a*) must have seen the letters 'SOS' in the snow   (*b*) must have seen the woman

   (*c*) must have seen the wrecked plane   (*d*) must have seen the children

Structure 句型

3 She was a young woman. The woman was _____ .

   (*a*) a youth   (*b*) young   (*c*) a young   (*d*) youth

4 Did the snow _____ thick on the ground?

   (*a*) lay   (*b*) laid   (*c*) lain   (*d*) lie

5 It was too small. It wasn't _____ .

   (*a*) enough big   (*b*) big enough   (*c*) fairly big   (*d*) rather big

6 She heard planes _____ overhead.

   (*a*) pass   (*b*) to pass   (*c*) to passing   (*d*) in passing

7 It was not long before a helicopter arrived. It arrived _____ .

   (*a*) after   (*b*) soon afterwards   (*c*) behind   (*d*) much later

Vocabulary 词汇

8 It was a light plane. It wasn't _____ .

   (*a*) dark   (*b*) heavy   (*c*) black   (*d*) deep

9 It got terribly cold. The cold was _____ .

   (*a*) frightening   (*b*) horrifying   (*c*) shocking   (*d*) frightful

10 She wondered how she could send a signal. She wanted to send _____ .

   (*a*) a letter   (*b*) a sign   (*c*) a signature   (*d*) a message

11 She probably stamped out the letters 'SOS' with her _____ .

   (*a*) hands   (*b*) head   (*c*) feet   (*d*) knees

12 The survivors were _____ .

   (*a*) live   (*b*) lively   (*c*) alive   (*d*) in life

Sentence structure 句子结构

Join these sentences, then check your answer against the text.

连接以下句子, 然后对照课文第 5-7 行, 核对你的答案。

It grew dark. She turned a suitcase into a bed. She put the children inside it. She covered them with all the clothes she could find.

When _____ .

Lesson 76 April Fools' Day 愚人节

First listen and then answer the question.

听录音，然后回答以下问题。

What was the joke?

golden brown macaroni stalks

'To end our special news bulletin,' said the voice of the television announcer, 'we're going over to the macaroni fields of Calabria. Macaroni has been grown in this area for over six hundred years. Two of the leading growers, Giuseppe Moldova and Riccardo 5 Brabante, tell me that they have been expecting a splendid crop this year and harvesting has begun earlier than usual. Here you can see two workers who, between them, have just finished cutting three cartloads of golden brown macaroni stalks. The whole village has been working day and night gathering and threshing this year's crop before the September rains. On the 10 right, you can see Mrs. Brabante herself. She has been helping her husband for thirty years now. Mrs. Brabante is talking to the manager of the local factory where the crop is processed. This last scene shows you what will happen at the end of the harvest: the famous Calabrian macaroni-eating competition! Signor Fratelli, the present champion, has won it every year since 1991. And that ends our special bulletin for today, Thursday, April 1st. We're now going back to the studio.'

New words and expressions 生词和短语

fool (title) /fuːl/ *n.* 傻瓜
bulletin (1.1) /'bʊlətɪn/ *n.* 新闻简报
announcer (1.2) /ə'naʊnsə/ *n.* （电视、电台）播音员
macaroni (1.3) /mækə'rəʊni/ *n.* 通心面, 空心面条
leading (1.4) /'liːdɪŋ/ *adj.* 主要的
grower (1.4) /'grəʊə/ *n.* 种植者
splendid (1.5) /'splendɪd/ *adj.* 极好的
stalk (1.8) /stɔːk/ *n.* 梗

gather (1.9) /'gæðə/ *v.* 收（庄稼）
thresh (1.9) /θreʃ/ *v.* 打（庄稼）
process (1.11) /'prəʊses/ *v.* 加工
Signor (1.13) /'siːnjɔː/ *n.* （意大利语）先生
present (1.13) /'prezənt/ *adj.* 目前的
champion (1.13) /'tʃæmpɪən/ *n.* 冠军
studio (1.14) /'stjuːdɪəʊ/ *n.* 播音室

Notes on the text 课文注释

1 April Fools' Day, 愚人节，4 月 1 日。根据西方国家的风俗，这一天人们往往以愚弄别人作为乐事，本文所述的通心粉长在地里便是一个例子。

2 between them 是 "由于他们共同努力的结果" 的意思。

3 the September rains, 9 月雨季。

参考译文

"作为我们专题新闻节目的结尾，"电视广播员说，"我们现在到卡拉布里亚的通心粉田里。通心粉在这个地区已经种植了 600 多年了。两个主要种植者，朱塞皮·莫尔道瓦和里卡多·布拉班特告诉我，他们一直期待着今年获得一个大丰收，收割工作比往年开始得要早些。这里您可以看到两个工人，他们协力割下了 3 车金黄色的通心粉梗。全村的人都日夜奋战，要赶在 9 月的雨季之前把今年的庄稼收割上来，打完场。在屏幕的右侧，您可以看到布拉班特太太本人，她已经帮了她的丈夫 30 年了。布拉班特太太现在正和负责通心粉加工的当地加工厂的经理交谈。这最后一个镜头向您展示了收获之后将发生的事情：著名的卡拉布利亚人吃通心粉大赛！目前的冠军弗拉特里先生，自 1991 年以来，年年获胜。今天——4 月 1 日，星期四——的专题新闻节目到此结束。现在我们回到电视演播室。"

Summary writing 摘要写作

In not more than 85 words write an account of the television programme. Write two different paragraphs using the points and connections given below.

用不超过 85 个单词的篇幅叙述一下电视节目。用以下要点和连词写出两段不同的文字。

CONNECTIONS		POINTS		CONNECTIONS
		1	End of news bulletin.	
		2	Television announcer showed viewers fields — Calabria.	
where		3	Grown — six hundred years.	*Here*
		4	Harvesting earlier this year.	*This year*
and		5	Whole village working hard.	
before		6	September rains.	*before*
		7	Crop: processed — factory.	*so that the crop*
		8	After harvest — famous competition.	
which		9	Signor Fratelli — since 1991.	*This*
That		10	End of bulletin — April 1st.	*With that*

Composition 作文

Write an imaginary account of a macaroni-eating competition. Write two paragraphs in about 150 words using the ideas given below:

按以下思路写出一个想象中的吃通心粉大赛的场面，写两段文字，字数为 150 个词左右：

1   The appearance of the six competitors — all very fat — their past achievements — huge quantity of macaroni prepared, weighed and served.

2   Quantity, not speed was the important thing — competitors eating for three hours — only one man left — he asked for more!

Letter writing 书信写作

Write a suitable *Purpose* of about 50 words to follow this introductory paragraph:

按照以下引言的思路，用 50 个左右的单词写出一段"目的"：

I have just heard that Tom Blake will be staying with you for a week. I would love to meet him again as I haven't seen him for years.

Key structures 关键句型

What has happened? What has been happening? **(KS4, 28, 52)** 现在完成时与现在完成进行时

（复习第 4，28，52 课关键句型）

Unit 4   Lesson 76

Exercises 练习

A Underline all the verbs in the passage which tell us *what has happened* and *what has been happening*.
画出课文中所有现在完成时和现在完成进行时的动词。

B Give the correct form of the verbs in parentheses. Do not refer to the passage until you finish the exercise:
用括号中动词的正确形式填空，完成练习后再对照课文，核对你的答案：

Macaroni _____ (grow) in this area for over six hundred years. Two of the leading growers, Giuseppe Moldova and Riccardo Brabante, tell me that they _____ (expect) a splendid crop this year and harvesting _____ (begin) earlier than usual. Here you can see two workers who, between them, just _____ (finish) cutting three cartloads of golden brown macaroni stalks. The whole village _____ (work) day and night gathering and threshing this year's crop before the September rains. On the right, you can see Mrs. Brabante herself. She _____ (help) her husband for thirty years now. This last scene shows you what will happen at the end of the harvest: the famous Calabrian macaroni-eating competition! Signor Fratelli, the present champion, _____ (win) it every year since 1991.

Special diffculties 难点

Words often confused 经常容易混淆的词

Study these examples:
细读以下例子：

a *Usual* and *Usually*.
Harvesting has begun earlier than *usual*. (1.6)
He *usually* gets up at six o'clock. 他通常在 6 点起床。

b *Between*（在 [两者] 之间）and *Among*（在 [三者或三者以上] 之中）.
Here you can see two workers who, *between* them, have just finished cutting three cartloads of macaroni. (11.6-8)
Tom sat *between* Jill and Jennifer. 汤姆坐在吉尔和詹妮弗之间。
The Prime Minister was *among* those present. 首相在出席者之中。
You'll find it somewhere *among* those newspapers. 你会在那些报纸中找到它。

c *Manager*（经理）, *Director*（主任）, *Headmaster*（校长）.
Mrs. Brabante is talking to the *manager* of the local factory. (11.10-11) 布拉本特太太正在和当地一个工厂经理谈话。
Mr. Jones is the *director* of several companies. 琼斯先生是几个公司的主管。
Who is the *headmaster* of this school? 这所学校的校长是谁？

Exercise 练习

Supply any of the above words in the following sentences:
用以上词填空：

1 I found your pipe. It was _____ those things on the table.

2 As _____, he asked the same silly questions.

3 The lady in the shop asked to see the _____ .

4 He has been _____ of this school for seventeen years.

5 It seems to be warmer than _____ this month.

6 Everybody dreams of living like a company _____ with a large expense account.

7 She stuck the flower _____ the pages of a book.

8 He _____ returns from work about this time, but he is late today.

Multiple choice questions 选择题

Comprehension 理解

1 Macaroni _____ .

   (*a*) grows in Calabria

   (*b*) grows in fields

   (*c*) must be harvested before the September rains

   (*d*) is man-made

2 What was the intention behind the television broadcast?

   (*a*) To show viewers how macaroni is grown.

   (*b*) To play a trick on viewers.

   (*c*) To provide useful information about macaroni.

   (*d*) To introduce viewers to conditions in Calabria.

Structure 句型

3 Giuseppe Moldova and Riccardo Brabante _____ they have been expecting a splendid crop.

   (*a*) tell   (*b*) tell that   (*c*) say to me   (*d*) say

4 Harvesting has begun earlier than usual. It _____ yet.

   (*a*) hasn't finished   (*b*) didn't finish   (*c*) hadn't finished   (*d*) isn't finishing

5 They must gather the crop before it rains _____ September.

   (*a*) in   (*b*) on   (*c*) the   (*d*) at

6 How long has she been helping her husband? _____ she was a young woman.

   (*a*) From then   (*b*) Since   (*c*) For   (*d*) By then

7 Where _____ ?

   (*a*) the crop is processed   (*b*) is the crop processed

   (*c*) is processed the crop   (*d*) processed is the crop

Vocabulary 词汇

8 To end our bulletin ... To _____ our bulletin ...

   (*a*) conclude   (*b*) stop   (*c*) prevent   (*d*) halt

9 It has been grown for over six hundred years. That's more than six _____ .

   (*a*) sentries   (*b*) ages   (*c*) centuries   (*d*) eras

10 They've been expecting a splendid crop. That's what they've been _____ .

   (*a*) waiting   (*b*) waiting for   (*c*) waiting to   (*d*) waiting on

11 They have been gathering this year's crop. They have been _____ .

   (*a*) assembling it   (*b*) picking it up   (*c*) collecting it   (*d*) bringing it in

12 He is the manager of the factory. He's _____ it.

   (*a*) charged with   (*b*) in the charge of   (*c*) charged   (*d*) in charge of

Lesson 77　A successful operation　一例成功的手术

🔊 **First listen and then answer the question.**

听录音，然后回答以下问题。

Did the doctors find out how the woman died?

The mummy of an Egyptian woman who died in 800 B.C. has just had an operation. The mummy is that of Shepenmut who was once a singer in the Temple of Thebes. As there were strange marks on the X-ray plates taken of the mummy, doctors have been trying to
5 find out whether the woman died of a rare disease. The only way to do this was to operate. The operation, which lasted for over four hours, proved to be very difficult because of the hard resin which covered the skin. The doctors removed a section of the mummy and
sent it to a laboratory. They also found something which the X-ray plates did not show: a small wax figure of
10 the god Duamutef. This god which has the head of a cow was normally placed inside a mummy. The doctors have not yet decided how the woman died. They feared that the mummy would fall to pieces when they cut it open, but fortunately this has not happened. The mummy successfully survived the operation.

The operation proved to be very difficult

New words and expressions　生词和短语

mummy (1.1) /'mʌmi/ n. 木乃伊
Egyptian (1.1) /ɪ'dʒɪpʃən/ adj. 埃及的
temple (1.3) /'tempəl/ n. 庙
mark (1.3) /mɑːk/ n. 斑点
plate (1.4) /pleɪt/ n. (照相)底片
disease (1.5) /dɪ'ziːz/ n. 疾病
last (1.6) /lɑːst/ v. 持续

prove (1.7) /pruːv/ v. 显示出
resin (1.7) /'rezɪn/ n. 树脂
skin (1.8) /skɪn/ n. 皮, 皮肤
section (1.8) /'sekʃən/ n. 切片
figure (1.9) /'fɪgə/ n. (人的)体形; 人像
normally (1.10) /'nɔːməli/ adv. 通常地
survive (1.12) /sə'vaɪv/ v. 幸免于

Notes on the text　课文注释

1　800 B.C., 公元前 800 年。B.C. 是 Before Christ 的缩略语。
2　… plates taken of the mummy, taken 是过去分词作定语修饰 plates, take the plates of … 作 "给……拍片子" 讲。
3　die of …, 因 (患) ……而死。
4　The operation, which lasted for over four hours, proved to be very difficult. 手术持续了 4 个多小时，非常难做。在这句话中 which 引导的从句是一个定语从句，用来修饰前面的名词 operation。但这是一个非限定性定语从句，它与主句用两个逗号隔开，它所提供的仅是补充信息，可以略去而不影响主句所表达的意思。
5　fall to pieces, 散掉, 成为碎片。

参考译文

　　死于公元前 800 年的一位埃及妇女的木乃伊刚刚接受了一次手术。这是曾在底比斯神殿里当过歌手的赛潘姆特的木乃伊。由于在给这个木乃伊拍摄的X光片子上有奇怪的斑点，所以，医生们一直试图搞清这位妇女是否死于一种罕见的疾病。搞清的唯一办法就是手术。手术持续了 4 个多小时，非常难做，因为皮肤上覆盖着一层硬硬的树脂。医生们从木乃伊身上取下一个切片，送去化验。他们还发现了 X 光片所没有显示的东西：一个蜡制的杜瓦木特夫神小塑像。这种牛头人身的神像通常被放在木乃伊体内。医生们至今还未确定这位妇女的死因。他们曾担心在把木乃伊切开后，它会散成碎片，但幸运得很，这种情况并未发生。这具木乃伊成功地经受了这次手术。

Summary writing 摘要写作

Write a summary of the passage *in not more than 70 words*. Write two different paragraphs using the points and connections given below.

用不超过 70 个单词的篇幅写出课文的摘要。用以下要点和连词写出两段不同的文字。

CONNECTIONS	POINTS		CONNECTIONS
	1 Doctors operated — mummy: Egyptian woman.		
who	2 Died 800 B.C.		*who*
whether	3 Wanted to find out — died rare disease.		*in order ... if*
After removing	4 Removed section.		
	5 Sent it to laboratory.		*which*
During the operation	6 Unexpectedly found figure — god.		*Inside the mummy*
Though	7 Afraid mummy fall to pieces.		
	8 Survived operation.		*but*

Composition 作文

Write two paragraphs in about 150 words using the ideas given below:

按以下思路写出两段文字，字数为 150 个词左右：

1 A mummy disappeared from a museum — newspaper reports — strange stories about the mummy — the public got alarmed.
2 An official announcement was issued from the museum — scientists were studying the mummy — it would be back in its place soon.

Key structures 关键句型

What happened? What has happened? What has been happening? (KS5, 29, 53) 一般过去时、现在完成时和现在完成进行时（复习第 5，29，53 课关键句型）

Exercises 练习

A Underline all the verbs in the passage *which tell us what happened, what has happened*, and *what has been happening*.

画出课文中所有一般过去时、现在完成时和现在完成进行时的动词。

B Give the correct form of the verbs in parentheses. Do not rear to the passage until you finish the exercise:

用括号中动词的正确形式填空，完成练习后再对照课文，核对你的答案：

The mummy of an Egyptian woman who _____ (die) in 800 B.C. just _____ (have) an operation. As there _____ (be) strange marks on the X-ray plates taken of the mummy, doctors _____ (try) to find out whether the woman _____ (die) of a rare disease. The only way to do this _____ (be) to operate. The operation, which _____ (last) for over four hours, _____ (prove) to be very difficult. The doctors _____ (remove) a section of the mummy and _____ (send) it to a laboratory. They also _____ (find) something which the X-ray plates not _____ (show). The doctors not _____ (decide) yet how the woman _____ (die). They _____ (fear) that the mummy would fall to pieces when they _____ (cut) it open, but fortunately this not _____ (happen). The mummy successfully _____ (survive) the operation.

C Supply *since, for* or *ago* in the following sentences:

用 since, for 或 ago 填空：

1 He stayed with us _____ two weeks.

2 She arrived two weeks _____ .

3 I have not seen him _____ Monday.

4 He has been ringing up continually _____ lunchtime.

5 We waited _____ ages.

6 He left a month _____ and I have not seen him _____ then.

7 It has not rained _____ March.

8 My grandparents lived here a long time _____ .

9 I have not heard from him _____ 1993.

10 We have been working on this new plane _____ over a year now.

Special difficulties 难点

Words often confused 经常容易混淆的词

Study these examples:

细读以下例子：

a   *B.C.* and *A.D.*

The mummy of an Egyptian woman who died in 800 B.C. ... (1.1)

Julius Caesar died in 44 B.C. 朱利叶斯·凯撒死于公元前 44 年。

William the Conqueror invaded Britain in 1066 A.D. 威廉征服者于公元 1066 年入侵英国。

b   *Skin*（皮肤）, *Leather*（皮革）, *Complexion*（肤色）.

Hard resin covered the *skin*. (11.7-8)

This briefcase is made of *leather*. 这个公文包是皮做的。

Look at her rosy cheeks. She has a lovely *complexion*. 看看她那玫瑰色的面颊。她的肤色太美了。

c   *Wax*（蜡）and *Candle*（蜡烛）.

a small *wax* figure of the god Duamutef (11.9-10)

The lights went out so we lit *candles*. 灯灭了，所以我们点燃了蜡烛。

Exercise 练习

Choose the correct words in the following sentences: 选择正确的词：

1 Even though she is old, she still has a good (skin) (complexion).

2 These seat covers are made of (skin) (leather).

3 A baby's (skin) (leather) is very soft.

4 It is pleasant to have a meal by (candle) (wax) light.

5 Homer lived around 800 (A.D.) (B.C.)

Multiple choice questions 选择题

Comprehension 理解

1 Doctors operated on the mummy _____ .

   (*a*) to find out what the woman had died of

   (*b*) to find out what was inside it

   (*c*) to remove a small wax figure of the god, Duamutef

   (*d*) because the woman died of a rare disease

2 The doctors _____ .

   (*a*) found out what they were looking for

   (*b*) couldn't prevent the mummy from falling to pieces

   (*c*) haven't yet found out what they were looking for

   (*d*) expected to find the small wax figure inside the mummy

Structure 句型

3 What did the woman die of? _____ did the woman die?

   (*a*)How   (*b*) Where   (*c*) What   (*d*) When

4 The only way to do this … There was only one way _____ doing this.

   (*a*) in   (*b*) of   (*c*) by   (*d*) to

5 The operation proved to be very difficult. It proved to be _____ operation.

   (*a*) difficult   (*b*) the difficult   (*c*) a difficult   (*d*) difficult the

6 It was difficult because of the hard resin _____ the skin.

   (*a*) covered   (*b*) which covering (*c*) in covering   (*d*) covering

7 They haven't decided yet. They are _____ undecided.

   (*a*) even   (*b*) yet   (*c*) more   (*d*) still

Vocabulary 词汇

8 An operation is usually performed by a _____ .

   (*a*) doctor   (*b*) dentist   (*c*) scientist   (*d*) surgeon

9 There were strange _____ on the X-ray plates.

   (*a*) markings   (*b*) notes   (*c*) signs   (*d*) messages

10 They wanted to know if the woman had died of a rare _____ .

   (*a*) illness   (*b*) pain   (*c*) ache   (*d*) hurt

11 The operation lasted for over four hours. That's how long it _____ .

   (*a*) went   (*b*) went on   (*c*) went over   (*d*) went off

12 There was a small wax figure in it. It was _____ .

   (*a*) a carving   (*b*) a shape   (*c*) a number   (*d*) a body

Lesson 78   The last one?   最后一支吗?

First listen and then answer the question.
听录音, 然后回答以下问题。
For how long did the writer give up smoking?

After reading an article entitled 'Cigarette Smoking and Your Health'
I lit a cigarette to calm my nerves. I smoked with concentration and
pleasure as I was sure that this would be my last cigarette. For a
whole week I did not smoke at all and during this time, my wife
5 suffered terribly. I had all the usual symptoms of someone giving
up smoking: a bad temper and an enormous appetite. My friends
kept on offering me cigarettes and cigars. They made no effort to
hide their amusement whenever I produced a packet of sweets from
my pocket. After seven days of this I went to a party. Everybody around me was smoking and I felt extremely
10 uncomfortable. When my old friend Brian urged me to accept a cigarette, it was more than I could bear. I took
one guiltily, lit it and smoked with satisfaction. My wife was delighted that things had returned to normal
once more. Anyway, as Brian pointed out, it is the easiest thing in the world to give up smoking. He himself
has done it lots of times!

*My friends kept on offering
me cigarettes*

New words and expressions 生词和短语

entitle (1.1) /ɪnˈtaɪtl/ v. 以……为名
calm (1.2) /kɑːm/ v. 使镇定
nerve (1.2) /nɜːv/ n. 神经
concentration (1.2) /ˌkɒnsənˈtreɪʃən/ n. 集中, 专心
suffer (1.5) /ˈsʌfə/ v. 受苦, 受害
symptom (1.5) /ˈsɪmptəm/ n. 症状

temper (1.6) /ˈtempə/ n. 脾气
appetite (1.6) /ˈæpɪtaɪt/ n. 胃口, 食欲
produce (1.8) /prəˈdjuːs/ v. 拿出
urge (1.10) /ɜːdʒ/ v. 力劝, 怂恿
satisfaction (1.11) /ˌsætɪsˈfækʃən/ n. 满意, 满足
delighted (1.11) /dɪˈlaɪtɪd/ adj. 欣喜的

Notes on the text 课文注释

1   an article entitled …, 题名为……的文章。
2   as I was sure that this would be my last cigarette, 因为我确信这是我最后一支烟。as 是 "因为" 的意思。
3   I had all the usual symptoms of someone giving up smoking …, 戒烟的人通常表现的一切征兆, 我都有……。
    someone giving up smoking 是独立主格结构, 作 of 的宾语。someone 是逻辑主语, giving up smoking 是逻辑
    谓语。
4   kept on offering me cigarettes and cigars, 不断给我递香烟和雪茄。keep on doing 是 "持续不断做" 的意思。
5   They made no effort to hide, 他们毫不掩饰。make no effort, 根本不作努力。
6   seven days of this, 其中 this 是指戒烟后的情况。
7   as Brian pointed out, 正如布赖恩指出的。as 是关系代词, 作 pointed out 的宾语, 代替后面整个句子。

362

参考译文

　　读完一篇题为《吸烟与健康》的文章之后，我点上了一支香烟，来镇定一下自己紧张的神经。我聚精会神而又愉快地吸着这支烟。因为我确信这是我最后一支烟了。整整一个星期我根本没有吸烟。在此期间，我妻子吃尽了苦头。我具备了戒烟者通常表现出来的所有症状：脾气暴躁和食欲旺盛。我的朋友们不断地向我递香烟和雪茄。每当我从口袋里掏出一包糖果时，他们都毫不掩饰地表现出他们对此感到非常好笑。这样过了 7 天以后，我去参加一次聚会。我周围的每个人都在吸烟，我感到非常不自在。当我的老朋友布赖恩极力劝我接受一支香烟时，我再也忍不住了。我内疚地接过一支点上，心满意足地抽起来。一切又都恢复了正常，为此我妻子十分高兴。不管怎么说，正如布赖恩指出的那样，戒烟是世界上最容易的事情，他自己就已戒了很多次了！

Summary writing 摘要写作

In not more than 80 words describe the writer's experiences. Write two different paragraphs using the points and connections given below.
用不超过 80 个单词的篇幅来描述一下作者的经历。用下列要点和连词写出两段不同的文字。

CONNECTIONS	POINTS		CONNECTIONS
Having read	1	Read article — smoking.	*The writer*
	2	Writer smoked last cigarette.	*and*
	3	Did not smoke — week.	
and	4	Wife suffered.	*and*
because	5	Bad temper — large appetite.	*because of her husband's*
Meanwhile	6	Friends offered cigarettes.	*Whenever*
and … to see	7	Amused — sweets.	*because*
When	8	Went to party.	
	9	Accepted cigarette.	*However, at a …*
which	10	Offered by friend.	*from*
and since then	11	Returned to normal.	*Now*

Composition 作文

Write two paragraphs in about 150 words using the ideas given below:
按以下思路写出两段文字，字数为 150 个词左右：

1 Two young boys wanted to smoke — took two cigarettes from father's packet — went and hid in the garage.
2 They lit the cigarettes — smoke and coughing — father saw smoke coming from garage — rushed down — smiled when he saw boys — offered them cigars — the boys accepted them — both very sick.

Letter writing 书信写作

Arrange the following heading in the correct order. Put in full stops and commas where necessary:
按书信要求排列以下信头，需要时可加上句号和逗号：
Brisbane/15 Gower St/24th April 19__ /Australia/Queensland

Key structures 关键句型

A and The 冠词 (KS6, 30, 54)（复习第 6，30，54 课关键句型）

Exercises 练习

A Put in *a(n)* or *the* where necessary. Do not refer to the passage until you finish the exercise:

在需要的地方填上 a(n) 或 the, 完成练习后再对照课文, 核对你的答案:

After reading _____ article entitled '_____ Cigarette Smoking and Your Health' I lit _____ ciga-rette to calm my nerves. I smoked with _____ concentration and _____ pleasure as I was sure that this would be my last cigarette. For _____ whole week I did not smoke at all and during this time my wife suf-fered terribly. I had all _____ usual symptoms of someone giving up _____ smoking: _____ bad temper and _____ enormous appetite. My friends kept on offering me _____ cigarettes and _____ cigars. They made no effort to hide their amusement whenever I produced _____ packet of _____ sweets from my pocket. After seven days of this I went to _____ party.

B Write sentences using *a, the, some* or *any* with the following:

用以下短语与 a, the, some 或 any 造句:

1 Making coffee. Do you want …?
2 Exports/increase/this year.
3 Afraid/thunder/lightning.
4 Boy/sent/school/deaf.
5 Tax laws/help/rich.
6 Spend evening/listen/music.
7 Crime/not pay.
8 Like/apple or orange?
9 Are you/artist or musician?
10 Take/sugar/tea?

Special difficulties 难点

The verb *keep* has a different meaning in each of these sentences. Study them carefully:

在下列句子中 keep 有不同的含义:

My friends *kept on* offering me cigarettes. (1.7) (Continued.)

Please *keep off* the grass. (Do not walk on it.) 请勿践踏草坪。

He *kept away from* the party. (He did not come.) 他避开了那次聚会。

Under my essay, the teacher wrote, 'Good work! *Keep it up*!' (Continue making an effort.) 在我的文章下面, 老师写道: "写得好! 继续努力!"

He ran so fast, I could not *keep up with* him. (I could not remain beside him.) 他跑得很快, 我跟不上他。

A big notice on the door said, '*Keep out*!' (Do not come in.) 门上贴着一张醒目的告示: "切勿入内!"

The cat *was kept in* during the fireworks. (It was made to stay indoors.) 放烟火的时候, 猫被关到了屋里。

Exercise 练习

Supply the missing words in the following sentences:

填空:

1 I think he kept _____ _____ the meeting on purpose.
2 Keep _____ the floor. I have just finished scrubbing it.
3 He has just begun a diary. I wonder how long he will keep it _____ .
4 He kept _____ making the same mistake.

5 We keep Tim _____ of the room because Betty has measles.
6 Most people spend their lives trying to keep _____ _____ their neighbours.
7 Three children were kept _____ after school for being noisy in class.

Multiple choice questions 选择题
Comprehension 理解

1 What prompted the writer to give up smoking?

(a) Something he had read.   (b) His health.

(c) Something he had heard.   (d) Something his wife said.

2 The writer _____ .

(a) succeeded in giving up smoking for good

(b) began smoking again to please his wife

(c) only gave up smoking for a short time

(d) started smoking again because he didn't like sweets

Structure 句型

3 Did he _____ a cigarette?

(a) lit   (b) light   (c) lighted   (d) lighting

4 He smoked with concentration. He concentrated _____ it.

(a) with   (b) on   (c) in   (d) for

5 He had an enormous appetite. He _____ .

(a) had hungry   (b) had hunger   (c) was hungry   (d) hungered

6 They kept on offering him cigarettes. They _____ .

(a) continued to do this (b) did so   (c) kept them   (d) held them

7 Everybody around him was smoking. _____ smoking.

(a) They was all   (b) They all was   (c) They were all   (d) All of them was

Vocabulary 词汇

8 He had a bad temper. He was in a bad _____ .

(a) spirit   (b) mood   (c) feeling   (d) disposition

9 They made no effort to hide their amusement. They _____ .

(a) didn't try to   (b) didn't afford to   (c) couldn't afford to   (d) didn't have a trial

10 I produced a packet of sweets from my pocket. I took one _____ .

(a) off   (b) out   (c) out of   (d) from

11 Brian urged me to accept a cigarette. He tried to _____ me to have one.

(a) make   (b) pursue   (c) persuade   (d) do

12 He urged me to accept a cigarette. He wanted me to _____ one.

(a) take   (b) agree to   (c) receive   (d) undertake

Sentence structure 句子结构

Join these sentences, then check your answer against the text.
连接以下句子, 然后对照课文第 7-9 行, 核对你的答案。

They made no effort to hide their amusement. I produced a packet of sweets from my pocket.

Lesson 79 By air 乘飞机

I used to travel by air a great deal

First listen and then answer the question.

听录音，然后回答以下问题。

Why did the plane turn back?

I used to travel by air a great deal when I was a boy. My parents used to live in South America and I used to fly there from Europe in the holidays. A flight attendant would take charge of me and I never had an unpleasant experience. I am used to travelling by air

5 and only on one occasion have I ever felt frightened. After taking off, we were flying low over the city and slowly gaining height, when the plane suddenly turned round and flew back to the airport. While we were waiting to land, a flight attendant told us to keep calm and to get off the plane quietly as soon as it had touched down. Everybody on board was worried and

10 we were curious to find out what had happened. Later we learnt that there was a very important person on board. The police had been told that a bomb had been planted on the plane. After we had landed, the plane was searched thoroughly. Fortunately, nothing was found and five hours later we were able to take off again.

New words and expressions 生词和短语

parent (1.1) /'peərənt/ n. 父（母）亲

flight attendant (1.3) /'flaɪt-ə,tendənt/ 空中乘务员

frightened (1.5) /'fraɪtnd/ adj. 害怕的，担惊的

curious (1.10) /'kjʊərɪəs/ adj. 急于了解的，好奇的

bomb (1.11) /bɒm/ n. 炸弹

plant (1.11) /plɑːnt/ v. 安放

Notes on the text 课文注释

1 take charge of me, 照顾我。

2 I am used to travelling by air, 我习惯了乘飞机旅行。

be used to doing sth. 是"习惯于做某事"，后接名词、代词、动名词。

3 only on one occasion have I ever felt frightened, 只有一次把我吓坏了。这是一句倒装句，即have放在主语之前。如果only加上一个状语放在句首，那么就要用倒装语序。

4 take off, 起飞。

5 gain height,（飞机）爬高。

6 touch down,（飞机）着陆。

7 on board, 在……（如飞机）上。

参考译文

我在幼年的时候，曾多次乘飞机旅行。我的父母曾经住在南美洲，所以假期里我常从欧洲乘飞机到他们那里。我总是由一位空中乘务员照管，从未遇到过不愉快的经历。我习惯了乘飞机旅行，只是有一次把我吓坏了。起飞之后，我们在城市上空低低地飞行，然后慢慢爬高。这时飞机突然调转头来，飞回了机场。在我们等待降落时，一位空中乘务员告诉我们要保持镇静，待飞机一着陆，就安静地离开飞机。飞机上的人都很着急，

大家都急于想知道究竟出了什么事。后来我们才得知，飞机上坐了一位非常重要的人物。有人报告警察，说飞机上安放了一枚炸弹。我们降落之后，飞机被彻底搜查了一遍。幸运的是，什么也没有找到。5 个小时后，我们又起飞了。

Summary writing 摘要写作

In not more than 80 words describe what happened from the moment the plane took off. Write two different paragraphs using the points and connections given below.

用不超过 80 个单词的篇幅描述一下飞机起飞后发生的事情。用以下要点和连词写出两段不同的文字。

CONNECTIONS		POINTS		CONNECTIONS
		1　Plane took off.		*After having*
and	[	2　Flew low — city.		
When	[	3　Gaining height.		*Although*
		4　Had to return — airport.	]	
Meanwhile	[	5　Told to keep calm.		*During this time*
After	[	6　Disembarked.		*until*
		7　Learnt — important person.	]	
Someone had told		8　Police — bomb.		*Because*
but though		9　Searched.		
	[	10　Found nothing.		*However*
	[	11　Five hours later took off.		*so*

Composition 作文

Write two paragraphs in about 150 words using the ideas given below:

按以下思路写出两段文字，字数为 150 个词左右：

1　Plane took off — a passenger threw a lighted cigarette into an air vent — he thought it was an ash tray.

2　Smoke — panic — the plane returned to the airport — fire engines, ambulances — no one was hurt — the fire was put out — the plane took off again.

Letter writing 书信写作

Write a suitable *Purpose* of about 50 words to follow this introductory paragraph:

按照以下引言的思路，写出一段 50 个词左右的"目的"：

You will be surprised to hear that your uncle Peter has unexpectedly returned from South America. He is staying with us at present and I know that he would very much like to see you.

Key structures 关键句型

What happened? What was happening? What used to happen? **(KS7, 31, 55)** 表示过去发生、过去正在发生和过去经常发生的动作（复习第 7，31，55 课关键句型）

Exercises 练习

A　Underline all the verbs in the passage that tell us *what happened, what was happening*, and *what used to/would happen.*

画出课文中所有说明过去发生、过去正在发生、过去经常或将要发生的情况的动词。

B Give the correct form of the verbs in parentheses. Use *would* in place of *used to* where possible. Do not refer to the passage until you finish the exercise:

用括号中动词的正确形式填空，可能情况下用would来替代used to，完成练习后再对照课文，核对你的答案：

I _____ (travel) by air a great deal when I _____ (be) a boy. My parents _____ (live) in South America and I _____ (fly) there from Europe in the holidays. A flight attendant _____ (take) charge of me and I never _____ (have) an unpleasant experience. I am used to travelling by air and only on one occasion have I ever felt frightened. After taking off, we _____ (fly) low over the city and slowly _____ (gain) height, when the plane suddenly _____ (turn) round and _____ (fly) back to the airport. While we _____ (wait) to land, a flight attendant _____ (tell) us to keep calm and to get off the plane quietly as soon as it had touched down.

C Explain the difference in meaning between these two sentences:

解释以下两个句子在词义上的不同点：

1 I *used to* fly there from Europe in the holidays. (11.2-3)

2 I *am used to* travelling by air. (1.4)

Special difficulties 难点

The verb *take* has a different meaning in each of these sentences. Study them carefully:

动词take在以下句子中有不同的含义。细读这些例句：

After *taking off*, we were flying over the city … (11.5-6)

He *took off* his coat. 他脱下外套。

He is always taking his teacher *off*. (He is always making fun of him by imitating him.) 他总是模仿他的老师。

Young Tom *takes after* his father. (He resembles his father.) 年轻的汤姆长得像他的父亲。

That wardrobe *takes up* a lot of space. (It occupies a lot of space.) 那个衣柜很占地方。

He has *taken up* French. (He has begun to learn French.) 他开始学法语。

When his wife died, he *took to* drinking. (He started drinking and it became a habit.) 妻子死后他染上酗酒的习惯。

He was so persuasive that I *was taken in*. (I was deceived.) 他真能说，结果我被骗了。

The reporter *took down* everything I said. (The reporter wrote …) 记者记下了我说的每件事情。

That business was doing very badly until Jones *took over*. (He became in charge of it.) 琼斯接管公司之前，公司的经营很差。

Exercise 练习

Supply the missing words in the following sentences:

填空：

1 Who will take _____ when the present director leaves?

2 As soon as he got into the lift he took his hat _____ .

3 You shouldn't be taken _____ by stories like that.

4 Last year he took _____ Russian; now he's taking _____ Chinese.

5 None of my children takes _____ me.

6 The new rocket will take _____ from Cape Canaveral.

7 'Please take _____ this letter for me, Pamela,' the manager said.

8 He takes people _____ so well he ought to go on the stage.

Multiple choice questions 选择题

Comprehension 理解

1 The aeroplane had to return _____ .

   (*a*) a long time after it had taken off   (*b*) shortly after it had taken off

   (*c*) just before landing   (*d*) the next day

2 The plane had to return because _____ .

   (*a*) there was a very important person on board   (*b*) everyone was worried

   (*c*) the flight attendant said so   (*d*) there was fear of an explosion

Structure 句型

3 I used to travel a great deal when I was a boy. I still _____ a great deal today.

   (*a*) use to travel   (*b*) used to travel   (*c*) travel   (*d*) am used to travelling

4 I used to travel a great deal. I used to travel _____ .

   (*a*) very many   (*b*) a great number   (*c*) a lot   (*d*) lots

5 _____ have you been travelling? Since I was a boy.

   (*a*) Since when   (*b*) When   (*c*) For when   (*d*) How much

6 I used to fly to South America _____ the holidays.

   (*a*) on   (*b*) to   (*c*) at   (*d*) during

7 I felt frightened. It was _____ experience.

   (*a*) frightening   (*b*) a frightening   (*c*) the frightening   (*d*) one frightening

Vocabulary 词汇

8 I used to travel by air. I always went on a long _____ .

   (*a*) trip   (*b*) travel   (*c*) way   (*d*) distance

9 She would take charge of me. She was _____ .

   (*a*) dutiful   (*b*) commanding   (*c*) charging   (*d*) responsible

10 I am used to travelling by air. I am _____ to it.

   (*a*) accustomed   (*b*) habitual   (*c*) customary   (*d*) inhabited

11 She told us to keep calm. She told us not to be _____ .

   (*a*) nervous   (*b*) angry   (*c*) irritated   (*d*) annoyed

12 We were curious to find out. We _____ .

   (*a*) were strange   (*b*) were odd   (*c*) wanted to know   (*d*) were peculiar

Sentence structure 句子结构

Rewrite this sentence, then check your answer against the text.

改写以下句子, 然后对照课文第 5 行, 核对你的答案。

I have only ever felt frightened on one occasion.

Only on one occasion _____ .

369

Lesson 80   The Crystal Palace   水晶宫

First listen and then answer the question.

听录音，然后回答以下问题。

How many people visited the Great Exhibition of 1851?

Perhaps the most extraordinary building of the nineteenth century
was the Crystal Palace, which was built in Hyde Park for the Great
Exhibition of 1851. The Crystal Palace was different from all other
buildings in the world, for it was made of iron and glass. It was one
5   of the biggest buildings of all time and a lot of people from many
countries came to see it. A great many goods were sent to the
exhibition from various parts of the world. There was also a great
deal of machinery on display. The most wonderful piece of
machinery on show was Nasmyth's steam hammer. Though in those days, travelling was not as easy as it is
10 today, steam boats carried thousands of visitors across the Channel from Europe. On arriving in England, they
were taken to the Crystal Palace by train. There were six million visitors in all, and the profits from the
exhibition were used to build museums and colleges. Later, the Crystal Palace was moved to South London.
It remained one of the most famous buildings in the world until it was burnt down in 1936.

*The most wonderful piece
of machinery*

New words and expressions   生词和短语

palace (title) /'pælɪs/ *n.* 宫殿
extraordinary (1.1) /ɪk'strɔːdənəri/ *adj.* 不平常的，
　　非凡的
exhibition (1.3) /ˌeksɪ'bɪʃən/ *n.* 展览
iron (1.4) /'aɪən/ *n.* 铁
various (1.7) /'veərɪəs/ *adj.* 各种各样的

machinery (1.8) /mə'ʃiːnəri/ *n.* 机器
display (1.8) /dɪ'spleɪ/ *n.* 展览
steam (1.9) /stiːm/ *n.* 蒸汽
profit (1.11) /'prɒfɪt/ *n.* 利润
college (1.12) /'kɒlɪdʒ/ *n.* 学院

Notes on the text   课文注释

1   which was built in Hyde Park, 是一个非限定性定语从句, 修饰 the Crystal Palace。
2   the Great Exhibition, 世界博览会。
3   it was made of iron and glass, 它是用钢和玻璃建成的。be made of ..., 用……制造（指原材料没有发生化学
　　上的变化）。
4   of all time, 空前的。
5   on display = on show, 展出。
6   on arriving in England, 一到英国。
7   in all, 总共。

参考译文

　　19 世纪最不寻常的建筑也许要数水晶宫了，它是为 1851 年的"世界博览会"而建在海德公园的。这座水

晶宫不同于世界上所有的其他建筑，因为它是用钢和玻璃建成的。它是有史以来最高大的建筑物之一，因此，人们从各个国家纷纷前来参观。大量的商品从世界各地运送到了博览会，参展的还有很多机器，其中最奇妙的是内史密斯的蒸汽锤。尽管在当时旅行不像现在这么容易，但汽船还是把成千上万的参观者从欧洲大陆送过了英吉利海峡。一到英国，火车就把他们送到了水晶宫。参观的人数总共是 600 万。博览会的盈利用来建造博物馆和高等学校。后来，"水晶宫" 被移到了伦敦南部。在 1936 年被焚毁之前，它一直是世界上最著名的建筑物之一。

Summary writing 摘要写作

Give an account of the history of the Crystal Palace *in not more than 85 words*. Write two different paragraphs using the points and connections given below.
用不超过 85 个单词的篇幅来讲述一下水晶宫的历史。用以下要点和连词写出两段不同的文字。

CONNECTIONS	POINTS	CONNECTIONS
	1 The Crystal Palace.	
which	2 Built — exhibition.	
	3 Different — others.	*Made of … it*
because	4 Iron and glass.	
	5 Goods — world.	*… not only …*
as well as	6 Machinery.	*but … as well*
So many	7 Visitors: boat, train.	*This attracted … who*
that it was possible	8 Colleges — museums.	*Later*
from	9 Profits.	*from*
After the exhibition	10 Moved — South London.	*The Crystal Palace*
where	11 Remained.	*and … until*
until	12 Burnt down 1936.	*when*

Composition 作文

Write two paragraphs in about 150 words using the ideas given below:
按以下思路写出两段文字，字数为 150 个词左右：

1 A visit to a modern exhibition — how I got there — the exhibition attracted large crowds.
2 My first impressions — the things on display — a walk round the exhibition hall — the exhibits that I liked best — tired at the end of the day.

Letter writing 书信写作

Write a suitable *Purpose* of about 50 words to follow this introductory paragraph:
按照以下引言的思路，写出一段 50 个词的 "目的"：

I have some wonderful news for you. I have at last managed to get two tickets for the Cup Final.

Key structures 关键句型

The best and the worst 形容词和副词的比较级和最高级 **(KS8, 32, 56)**（复习第 8，32，56 课关键句型）

Exercises 练习

A How many comparisons can you find in the passage? Underline as many as you can.
画出课文中的比较级和最高级。

B Supply the missing words in the following. Do not refer to the passage until you finish the exercise:
填空，完成练习后再对照课文，核对你的答案：

Perhaps the _____ extraordinary building of the nineteenth century was the Crystal Palace, which was built in Hyde Park for the Great Exhibition of 1851. The Crystal Palace was different _____ all other buildings _____ the world, for it was made of iron and glass. It was one of the _____ (big) buildings _____ all time and a _____ of people from _____ countries came to see it. A great _____ goods were sent to the exhibition from various parts of the world. There was also a great _____ of machinery on display. The _____ wonderful piece of machinery on show was Nasmyth's steam hammer. Though in those days, travelling was not _____ easy _____ it is today, steam boats carried thousands of visitors across the Channel from Europe. The Crystal Palace remained one of the _____ famous buildings _____ the world until it was burnt down in 1936.

Special difficulties 难点

Phrases with *on* (Compare SD43) 带 on 的短语（对比第 43 课难点）

Study these examples:
仔细阅读以下例句：

There was also a great deal of machinery *on display*. (ll.7-8)

The most wonderful piece of machinery *on show* … (ll.8-9)

He has gone to Frankfurt *on business*. 他因公去法兰克福。

I didn't catch the bus. I came here *on foot*. 我没赶上公共汽车，我是走的。

I asked to see the officer *on duty*. 我请求见值班官员。

On the whole, it has been a very successful year. 总的来说，这是成功的一年。

Look at that smoke. That building must be *on fire*. 看那股烟，那座大楼肯定着火了。

I don't think it was an accident. He did it *on purpose*. 我认为那不是个意外事故，他是故意的。

On the average, I make six telephone calls a day. 我每天平均打 6 个电话。

You mustn't *on any account* sign the contract before you read it. 你一定要读完合同后再签字。

I know I had agreed to let you go to the cinema, but *on second thoughts*, you should stay at home and finish your homework. 我知道我曾同意你去看电影，但经过重新考虑，你应该待在家里完成你的作业。

Exercise 练习

Supply phrases with *on* in the following sentences:
用带有 on 的短语填空：

1 While the guard was _____, he heard a shot.

2 I've changed my mind. _____ I'll go by plane instead.

3 I think you dropped your handkerchief _____, so that he could pick it up.

4 You must be exhausted! Did you come all that way _____? You should have taken a taxi.

5 I'm not always pleased with his work, but _____ it is satisfactory.

6 You must not, _____, leave this room.

7 _____, 250,000 tourists visit this town each year.

Multiple choice questions 选择题

Comprehension 理解

1 The Crystal Palace differed from all other buildings at the time because _____ .

   (*a*) it was very big   (*b*) it was in an exhibition

   (*c*) it was made of unusual materials   (*d*) it was in Hyde Park

2 The Great Exhibition of 1851 was _____ .

   (*a*) a failure   (*b*) highly successful   (*c*) not very profitable   (*d*) spoilt by a fire

Structure 句型

3 When was the Great Exhibition? _____ 1851.

   (*a*) Of   (*b*) On   (*c*) At   (*d*) In

4 A great many goods were sent. There were _____ .

   (*a*) quite a few   (*b*) quite a little   (*c*) not too many   (*d*) very much

5 Travelling was not as easy as it is today. It wasn't so easy _____ in those days.

   (*a*) for travelling   (*b*) in travelling   (*c*) in order to travel   (*d*) to travel

6 On arriving in England … _____ they arrived in England …

   (*a*) On   (*b*) Why   (*c*) When   (*d*) Where

7 It was one of the most famous buildings in the world. It was one of the most famous _____ all buildings.

   (*a*) of   (*b*) from   (*c*) by   (*d*) than

Vocabulary 词汇

8 It was an extraordinary building. It was quite _____ .

   (*a*) extreme   (*b*) funny   (*c*) big   (*d*) exceptional

9 Goods were sent from various parts of the world. They came from _____ parts.

   (*a*) mixed   (*b*) assorted   (*c*) different   (*d*) mixed up

10 There was a great deal of machinery. This means there _____ .

   (*a*) was one big machine   (*b*) was one big engine

   (*c*) were many machines   (*d*) was one powerful machine

11 There were six million visitors in all. That was the _____ .

   (*a*) all   (*b*) whole   (*c*) result   (*d*) total

12 Museums were built with the profits. They were built with the _____ .

   (*a*) benefits   (*b*) earnings   (*c*) winnings   (*d*) excesses

Sentence structure 句子结构

Join these sentences, then check your answer against the text.
连接以下句子, 然后对照课文第 3-4 行, 核对你的答案。

The Crystal Palace was different from all other buildings in the world. It was made of iron and glass.

Lesson 81 Escape 脱逃

🔊 **First listen and then answer the question.**

听录音，然后回答以下问题。

Why did the prisoner attack the driver?

The prisoner marched boldly up and down

When he had killed the guard, the prisoner of war quickly dragged him into the bushes. Working rapidly in the darkness, he soon changed into the dead man's clothes. Now, dressed in a blue uniform and with a rifle over his shoulder, the prisoner marched boldly up
5 and down in front of the camp. He could hear shouting in the camp itself. Lights were blazing and men were running here and there: they had just discovered that a prisoner had escaped. At that moment, a large black car with four officers inside it, stopped at the camp gates. The officers got out and the prisoner stood to attention and saluted as they passed. When they had gone,
10 the driver of the car came towards him. The man obviously wanted to talk. He was rather elderly with grey hair and clear blue eyes. The prisoner felt sorry for him, but there was nothing else he could do. As the man came near, the prisoner knocked him to the ground with a sharp blow. Then, jumping into the car, he drove off as quickly as he could.

New words and expressions 生词和短语

prisoner (1.1) /'prɪzənə/ n. 囚犯
bush (1.2) /bʊʃ/ n. 灌木丛
rapidly (1.2) /'ræpɪdli/ adv. 迅速地
uniform (1.3) /'juːnɪfɔːm/ n. 制服
rifle (1.4) /'raɪfəl/ n. 来福枪，步枪
shoulder (1.4) /'ʃəʊldə/ n. 肩
march (1.4) /mɑːtʃ/ v. 行进

boldly (1.4) /'bəʊldli/ adv. 大胆地
blaze (1.6) /bleɪz/ v. 闪耀
salute (1.9) /səˈluːt/ v. 行礼
elderly (1.10) /'eldəli/ adj. 上了年纪的
grey (1.10) /greɪ/ adj. 灰白的
sharp (1.12) /ʃɑːp/ adj. 猛烈的
blow (1.12) /bləʊ/ n. 打击

Notes on the text 课文注释

1 When he had killed the guard, the prisoner of war quickly dragged him into the bushes. 那个战俘杀死卫兵之后,（他）迅速地将（那个卫兵的）尸体拖进灌木丛。这是一个含有时间状语从句的复合句，根据英语的习惯，人称代词要放在从句中，所代的名词要放在主句当中。
2 the prisoner of war（常缩写成POW），战俘。
3 up and down, 来回，前后。
4 here and there, 到处。
5 stand to attention, 立正。

参考译文

那个战俘杀死卫兵以后，迅速地把尸体拖进了灌木丛。他在黑暗中忙活了一阵儿，很快就换上了死者的衣

服。现在他身穿蓝军装，肩扛步枪，在军营门前大胆地来回走着。他听得见军营里面的喧闹声。那里灯火通明，人们在东奔西跑：他们刚刚发现有一个俘房跑了。正在此时，一辆黑色大轿车在军营门口停了下来，里面坐了4个军官。军官们下了车，战俘立正站好，并在他们从他面前经过时敬了礼。他们走后，汽车司机向他走来，这人显然是想聊天。他上了年纪，有着灰白的头发和明亮的蓝眼睛。战俘为他感到惋惜，但却没有别的选择。当这个人走近时，战俘一拳把他打倒在地，然后跳进车里，以最快的速度把车开走了。

Summary writing 摘要写作

In not more than 85 words describe what the prisoner did. Write two different paragraphs using the points and connections given below.

用不超过 85 个单词的篇幅描述一下这个战俘脱逃的经过，用以下要点和连词写出两段不同的文字。

CONNECTIONS	POINTS		CONNECTIONS
After having	1 Prisoner of war killed guard.		*As soon as he*
	2 Dragged bushes.		*and*
and	3 Changed into clothes.		*the prisoner of war*
Then he	4 Rifle over shoulder.		*With*
and	5 Marched — camp.		
A short time afterwards	6 Four officers — car.		*when*
so ... and	7 Attention — saluted.		*and*
When they had gone	8 Driver — towards him.		*When the driver*
and after	9 Knocked out.		
	10 Jumped into car.		*Then, jumping*
and	11 Drove away.		

Composition 作文

Write two paragraphs in about 150 words using the ideas given below:

按以下思路写出两段文字，字数为 150 个词左右：

1 Dark night — a prisoner of war who had escaped was dressed as a guard — he was still in the camp — took part in the search for the 'missing' prisoner.

2 He went out in a lorry with the other guards — into the countryside — the guards went into the forest — the prisoner escaped.

Letter writing 书信写作

The Conclusion. The last paragraph of a letter should take the form of a polite wish. Learn the following phrases by heart:

结束语。书信的最后一段应是有礼貌的问候。熟记以下短语：

Please give my love/regards to ...

I hope you feel better soon.

Exercise 练习

Write five opening sentences which could be used in letters to friends or relations.

写出 5 句给朋友或亲属的信的开头语。

Key structures 关键句型

At, In, To, With, etc. **(KS9, 33, 57)** (复习第 9，33，57 课关键句型)

Exercise 练习

A Underline the words *into, in, with, at* and *to* in the passage. Note how they have been used.
画出课文中的 into, in, with, at 和 to。注意它们的用法。

B Supply the missing words in the following. Do not refer to the passage until you finish the exercise:
填空，完成练习后再对照课文，核对你的答案：

1 When he had killed the guard, the prisoner of war quickly dragged him _____ the bushes. Working rapidly _____ the darkness, he soon changed _____ the dead man's clothes. Now, dressed _____ a blue uniform and _____ a rifle over his shoulder, the prisoner marched boldly up and down in front of the camp. He could hear shouting _____ the camp itself.

2 _____ that moment, a large black car _____ four officers inside it, stopped _____ the camp gates. The officers got out and the prisoner stood _____ attention.

3 He was rather elderly _____ grey hair and clear blue eyes.

4 As the man came near, the prisoner knocked him _____ the ground _____ a sharp blow. Then, jumping _____ the car, he drove off as quickly as he could.

Special difficulties 难点

Words often confused 经常容易混淆的词

Study these examples:
细读以下例子：

a *Cloth, Clothing, Clothes.*

He soon changed into the dead man's *clothes.* (ll.2-3)

I wanted to have a suit made so I bought three and a half yards of *cloth.* 我想做套西服，因此我买了 3 码半布料。

You should give all this old *clothing* away. 你应该把旧衣物送人。

b *Salute, Greet.*

He stood to attention and *saluted* as they passed. (l.9)

He went to the station to *greet* his friend. 他去车站迎接他的朋友。

c *Clear, Clean.*

He was rather elderly with *clear* blue eyes. (ll.10-11)

The water in the stream was very *clear.* 小河的水很清澈。

His instructions were very *clear.* (They were easy to understand.) 他讲授的条理非常清楚。

We can cross now. The road is *clear.* 我们可以过马路了，路上没车。

She keeps her house very *clean.* 她把她的房子收拾得干干净净。

Exercise 练习

Supply any of the above words in the following sentences:
用以上词填空：

1 The guard _____ the general.

2 When the canal was _____ the ship went through.

3 I bought a piece of _____ to make a dress.

4 I haven't bought any new _____ for years.

5 The soldier _____ his mother with a kiss.

Multiple choice questions 选择题

Comprehension 理解

1 The prisoner's escape _____ .

(a) had not attracted any attention in the camp　　(b) had passed unnoticed

(c) was never discovered　　(d) was soon discovered in the camp

2 The four officers must have thought the man was _____ .

(a) a guard　　(b) a driver　　(c) a prisoner　　(d) an officer

Structure 句型

3 When he had killed the guard, he dragged him into the bushes. _____ the guard he dragged him into the bushes.

(a) On having killed　　(b) When killing　　(c) When having killed　　(d) On having been killed

4 A black car stopped at the gates. _____ officers inside it.

(a) They had　　(b) There had　　(c) There was　　(d) There were

5 He saluted as they passed. He saluted _____ .

(a) while they had passed　　(b) while they were passing

(c) though they were passing　　(d) because they had passed

6 He was rather elderly. He was _____ .

(a) very old　　(b) quite old　　(c) too old　　(d) old enough

7 There was nothing else he could do. That was _____ .

(a) the whole　　(b) complete　　(c) every　　(d) all

Vocabulary 词汇

8 He dragged him into the bushes. He _____ .

(a) carried him　　(b) lifted him

(c) pulled him along the ground　　(d) took him

9 He changed into the dead man's clothes. He _____ them.

(a) changed　　(b) wore　　(c) dressed　　(d) put

10 He marched boldly. He was _____ .

(a) timid　　(b) bald　　(c) strong　　(d) brave

11 Lights were blazing. They were _____ .

(a) gleaming　　(b) shining　　(c) reflecting　　(d) being burnt

12 He knocked him down with a sharp blow. He _____ .

(a) beat him　　(b) blew him over　　(c) knocked him　　(d) struck him

Sentence structure 句子结构

Join these sentences, then check your answer against the text.

连接以下句子, 然后对照课文第 9 行, 核对你的答案。

The officers got out. The prisoner stood to attention. He saluted. They passed.

Lesson 82　Monster or fish?　是妖还是鱼？

📼 **First listen and then answer the question.**

听录音，然后回答以下问题。

What was the monster called?

Fishermen and sailors sometimes claim to have seen monsters in
the sea. Though people have often laughed at stories told by seamen, it is now known that many of these 'monsters' which have at
times been sighted are simply strange fish. Occasionally, unusual
5　creatures are washed to the shore, but they are rarely caught out at
sea. Some time ago, however, a peculiar fish was caught near Madagascar. A small fishing boat was carried miles out to sea by the
powerful fish as it pulled on the line. Realizing that this was no
ordinary fish, the fisherman made every effort not to damage it in any way. When it was eventually brought
10　to shore, it was found to be over thirteen feet long. It had a head like a horse, big blue eyes, shining silver
skin, and a bright red tail. The fish, which has since been sent to a museum where it is being examined by a
scientist, is called an oarfish. Such creatures have rarely been seen alive by man as they live at a depth of six
hundred feet.

rarely been seen alive by man

New words and expressions　生词和短语

monster (title) /'mɒnstə/ *n.* 怪物

sailor (1.1) /'seɪlə/ *n.* 海员

sight (1.4) /saɪt/ *v.* 见到

creature (1.5) /'kriːtʃə/ *n.* 动物，生物

peculiar (1.6) /pɪ'kjuːliə/ *adj.* 奇怪的，不寻常的

shining (1.10) /'ʃaɪnɪŋ/ *adj.* 闪闪发光的

oarfish (1.12) /'ɔːfɪʃ/ *n.* 桨鱼

Notes on the text　课文注释

1　Fishermen and sailors sometimes claim to have seen monsters in the sea. 渔夫和水手有时声称看到过海里的妖
怪。句中的动词不定式 to have seen 是不定式的完成时结构，作动词 claim 的宾语。

2　at times, 有时。

3　out at sea, 在远海。

4　no ordinary fish, 根本不是一条普通的鱼。no 比 not 否定的意味更重。

5　made every effort, 尽一切努力。

参考译文

　　渔夫和水手们有时声称自己看到过海里的妖怪。虽然人们常常对水手们讲的故事付诸一笑，但现在看来，
人们有时看到的这些"妖怪"很多不过是些奇怪的鱼。一些异常的生物偶尔会被冲到岸上来，但它们在海上却
极少能被捕到。然而不久前，在马达加斯加附近的海里却捕到了一条奇怪的鱼。一条小渔船被一条咬住钩的强
壮的大鱼拖到了几英里以外的海面上。那位渔民意识到这根本不是一条普通的鱼，于是千方百计不让它受到丝
毫伤害。当终于把它弄上岸后，人们发现它身长超过了 13 英尺。它长着一个像马一样的头，有着一双蓝色的大

眼睛和闪闪发光的银色皮肤，还有一条鲜红色的尾巴。此鱼叫桨鱼，被送进了博物馆，现正接受一位科学家的检查。人们很少能看到活着的这类动物，因为它们生活在 600 英尺深的水下。

Summary writing 摘要写作

Give an account of what happened *in not more than 80 words*. Write two different paragraphs using the points and connections given below.

用不超过 80 个单词的篇幅描述一下所发生的事情，用以下要点和连词写出两段不同的文字。

CONNECTIONS	POINTS		CONNECTIONS
	1 Strange fish caught — Madagascar.		
after having pulled	2 Fishing boat — out to sea.		*Though*
Making	3 Effort — damage.		
	4 Fisherman — brought it to shore.		*On being brought*
The fish, which	5 Thirteen feet.		*the fish*
with	6 Head like horse.		*and*
	7 Sent museum.		*Now that*
It … who said	8 Examined — scientist.		
	9 Oarfish.		*It*
and	10 Six hundred feet.		*and*

Composition 作文

Write two paragraphs in about 150 words using the ideas given below:

按以下思路写出两段文字，字数为 150 个词左右：

1 A man in a bar — explaining to others how he caught a big fish — rough seas — great difficulty — boat carried out to sea.

2 After several hours he pulled the fish up — never seen before — its size, appearance and colours — but it got away.

Letter writing 书信写作

The Conclusion. Learn the following phrases by heart:

结束语。熟记以下结束语：

I shall be looking forward to hearing from/seeing you soon.

I hope you will soon settle down in your (new job, school, etc.).

Exercise 练习

Write a suitable *Purpose* for a letter in about 50 words.

The letter has as its conclusion:

根据这封信的结束语，写出 50 个词左右的"目的"。其结束语为：

'I hope you feel better soon.'

Unit 4　Lesson 82

Key structures 关键句型

A peculiar fish was caught near Madagascar. **(KS10, 34, 58)** (复习第 10, 34, 58 课关键句型)

Exercises 练习

A Underline the verbs in the passage and study their form.
画出课文中的动词并学习它们的用法。

B Give the correct form of the verbs in parentheses. Do not refer to the passage until you finish the exercise.
用括号中动词的正确形式填空，完成练习后再对照课文，核对你的答案。

Though people have often laughed at stories told by seamen, it _____ now _____ (know) that many of these 'monsters' which _____ at times _____ (sight) are simply strange fish. Occasionally, unusual creatures _____ (wash) to the shore, but they _____ rarely _____ (catch) out at sea. Some time ago, however, a peculiar fish _____ (catch) near Madagascar. A small fishing boat _____ (carry) miles out to sea by the powerful fish as it pulled on the line. When it _____ eventually _____ (bring) to shore, it _____ (find) to be over thirteen feet long. The fish, which _____ since _____ (send) to a museum where it _____ (examine) by a scientist, _____ (call) an oarfish. Such creatures _____ rarely _____ (see) alive by man as they live at a depth of six hundred feet.

Special difficulties 难点

Words often confused 经常容易混淆的词

Study these examples:
细读以下例子：

a　*Laugh* and *Laugh at*.

Though people have often *laughed at* stories told by seamen … (11.2-4) (People have made fun of …)

Everybody *laughed* when the circus clown made his appearance. 马戏团的小丑出现时大家都笑了。

b　*Wash* and *Wash up*.

Unusual creatures are *washed* to the shore. (11.4-5) (They are carried to the shore by water.)

I must *wash* my hands. They are very dirty. 我必须洗手，它们很脏。

Have you ever seen a cat *washing* itself? 你见过猫给自己洗澡吗？

The man was *washed* overboard by a big wave. 那个男的被一个大浪从船上卷入水中。

I'll *wash up* tonight. (I'll *wash* the dishes.) 今晚我洗碗。

Exercise 练习

Supply any of the above words in the following sentences:
用以上词和词组填空：

1 What a lot of dirty plates! Who is going to _____?

2 Don't wear that hat. People will _____ you.

3 The bridge was _____ away by the river.

4 We all _____ when he told us a funny story.

5 The boy was told to _____ his hands before sitting at table.

Multiple choice questions 选择题

Comprehension 理解

1 The monsters which fishermen sometimes claim to have seen _____ .

  (*a*) are probably unusual fish　　　　　(*b*) are not fish at all

  (*c*) exist in deep water　　　　　　　　(*d*) are often washed up on the shore

2 The creature that was caught in Madagascar by a fisherman was _____ .

  (*a*) a monster　　　　　　　　　　　　(*b*) an unusual fish

  (*c*) half horse, half fish　　　　　　　　(*d*) a common fish

Structure 句型

3 They claim _____ monsters in the sea.

  (*a*) that they have seen　(*b*) have seen　　(*c*) to be seen　　　(*d*) to being seen

4 People often laugh at stories _____ told by seamen.

  (*a*) which　　　　(*b*) which have　　(*c*) which have being　(*d*) which have been

5 When _____ that this was no ordinary fish, he tried not to damage it.

  (*a*) realizing　　　(*b*) having realized　(*c*) he realized　　(*d*) he has realized

6 _____ eventually brought to the shore, it was found to be very long.

  (*a*) Been　　　　(*b*) When being　　(*c*) On being　　(*d*) When it was being

7 It had a head like a horse. _____ head was like that of a horse.

  (*a*) It　　　　　(*b*) It's　　　　　(*c*) Its'　　　　(*d*) Its

Vocabulary 词汇

8 Fishermen claim to have seen monsters. They _____ that they have.

  (*a*) state　　　　(*b*) own　　　　　(*c*) owe　　　　(*d*) persist

9 People have often laughed at these stories. They _____ .

  (*a*) haven't taken them seriously　　　　(*b*) enjoyed them

  (*c*) teased them　　　　　　　　　　　(*d*) mocked them

10 'Monsters' have at times been sighted. They have been _____ .

  (*a*) viewed　　　　(*b*) glanced at　　(*c*) seen　　　(*d*) caught

11 The fish was powerful. It was _____ .

  (*a*) dynamic　　　(*b*) strong　　　　(*c*) forceful　　(*d*) wilful

12 Such creatures have rarely been seen. They have _____ been seen.

  (*a*) never　　　　(*b*) unusually　　　(*c*) always　　(*d*) seldom

Sentence structure 句子结构

Join these two sentences, then check your answer against the text.

连接以下句子, 然后对照课文第 11-12 行, 核对你的答案。

The fish is called an oarfish. It has since been sent to a museum. It is being examined by a scientist.

Lesson 83 After the elections 大选之后

First listen and then answer the question.

听录音，然后回答以下问题。

Why did Patrick keep on asking the same question?

The former Prime Minister, Mr. Wentworth Lane, was defeated in
the recent elections. He is now retiring from political life and has
gone abroad. My friend, Patrick, has always been a fanatical opponent of Mr. Lane's Radical Progressive Party. After the elections,
5 Patrick went to the former Prime Minister's house. When he asked
if Mr. Lane lived there, the policeman on duty told him that since
his defeat, the ex-Prime Minister had gone abroad. On the following day, Patrick went to the house again. The same policeman was

retiring from political life

just walking slowly past the entrance, when Patrick asked the same question. Though a little suspicious this
10 time, the policeman gave him the same answer. The day after, Patrick went to the house once more and
asked exactly the same question. This time, the policeman lost his temper. 'I told you yesterday and the day
before yesterday,' he shouted, 'Mr. Lane was defeated in the elections. He has retired from political life and
gone to live abroad!'

'I know,' answered Patrick, 'but I love to hear you say it!'

New words and expressions 生词和短语

election (title) /ɪˈlekʃən/ n. 选举
former (1.1) /ˈfɔːmə/ adj. 从前的
defeat (1.1) /dɪˈfiːt/ v. 打败
fanatical (1.3) /fəˈnætɪkəl/ adj. 狂热的
opponent (11.3-4) /əˈpəʊnənt/ n. 反对者，对手

radical (1.4) /ˈrædɪkəl/ adj. 激进的
progressive (1.4) /prəˈgresɪv/ adj. 进步的
ex- (1.7) /eks/ prefix（前缀，用于名词前）前……
suspicious (1.9) /səˈspɪʃəs/ adj. 怀疑的

Notes on the text 课文注释

1 the elections, 大选。在英文中 election 常用复数形式，后接表示复数的动词，用来指全国性的选举。
2 Prime Minister, 首相。
3 He is now retiring from political life, 他现在退出了政界。
4 Though a little suspicious this time, 虽然这次有点疑心。这是一个让步状语从句，其中的主语和谓语动词都
   省略了，完整的从句应是 Though the policeman was a little suspicious this time。
5 lost his temper, 发脾气。

参考译文

　　前首相温特沃兹·莱恩先生在最近的大选中被击败。他现在退出了政界，到国外去了。我的朋友帕特里克
一直是莱恩先生的激进党的强烈反对者。大选结束后，帕特里克来到了前首相的住处。当他询问莱恩先生是否
住在那里时，值班的警察告诉他这位前首相落选后出国去了。第二天，帕特里克再次来到前首相的住处。昨天
的那位警察正从门口慢慢走过，帕特里克上前问了和昨天同样的问题。虽然那位警察这次有点疑心，但还是对

他作了同样的回答。第三天，帕特里克又去了，提出了同前两天完全一样的问题。这一次警察火了。"我昨天和前天都告诉过您了，"他大叫，"莱恩先生在大选中被击败了，他已经退出了政界去国外了!"

　　"这我都知道，"帕特里克说，"可我就是喜欢听你说出这些!"

Summary writing 摘要写作

Give an account of what happened *in not more than 80 words*. Write two different paragraphs using the points and connections given below.

用不超过 80 个单词的篇幅描述一下所发生的事情，用以下要点和连词写出两段不同的文字。

CONNECTIONS	POINTS	CONNECTIONS
After having	1　Defeated — elections.	*Since*
	2　Prime Minister retired — abroad.	
who	3　Patrick — fanatical opponent. — Party.	*As*
	4　Went — house — three times.	
and	5　Asked policeman.	*Each time*
whether	6　Mr. Lane's house.	*if*
When	7　Third time — angry policeman.	
	8　Told — defeat, retirement.	*he was told*
	9　Patrick said — something he loved to hear.	*but*

Composition 作文

Write two paragraphs in about 150 words using the ideas given below:

按以下思路写出两段文字，字数为 150 个词左右：

1　A politician was giving a pre-election speech: big promises: more houses, schools, etc. — better foreign policy.

2　Members of the audience asked rude questions — the politician lost his temper — said that the audience did not deserve more houses, etc. — walked off angrily — defeated in the election.

Letter writing 书信写作

The Conclusion. Learn the following phrases by heart:

结束语。熟记以下结束语：

I am very sorry for all the trouble this has caused you. I wish you good luck/every success in …

Exercise 练习

In about 50 words write the *Purpose* for a letter which has one of the above phrases as its conclusion. 写出一段 50 个词左右的"目的"，而你的信可以使用以上一句话作为结束语。

Key structures 关键句型

Review **KS74-82** 复习第 74-82 课关键句型

What is happening? What always happens? **(KS74)** （第 74 课）

Unit 4　Lesson 83

What happened? **(KS75)** （第 75 课）

What has happened? What has been happening? **(KS76)** （第 76 课）

What was happening? **(KS79)** （第 79 课）

A peculiar fish was caught near Madagascar. **(KS82)** （第 82 课）

Exercises 练习

A　Underline all the verbs in the passage noting carefully how they have been used. Revise any Key structures you have forgotten.

画出课文中所有动词, 并注意它们的用法, 复习忘记的关键句型。

B　Give the correct form of the verbs in parentheses. Do not refer to the passage until you finish the exercise:

用括号中动词的正确形式填空, 完成练习后再对照课文, 核对你的答案:

The former Prime Minister, Mr. Wentworth Lane, _____ (defeat) in the recent elections. He now _____ (retire) from political life and _____ (go) abroad. My friend, Patrick, always _____ (be) a fanatical opponent of Mr. Lane's Radical Progressive Party. After the elections, Patrick _____ (go) to the former Prime Minister's house. When he _____ (ask) if Mr. Lane _____ (live) there, the policeman on duty _____ (tell) him that since his defeat, the ex-Prime Minister had gone abroad. On the following day, Patrick _____ (go) to the house again. The same policeman just _____ (walk) slowly past the entrance, when Patrick _____ (ask) the same question. Though a little suspicious this time, the policeman _____ (give) him the same answer. The day after, Patrick _____ (go) to the house once more and _____ (ask) exactly the same question. This time, the policeman _____ (lose) his temper. I _____ (tell) you yesterday and the day before yesterday,' he _____ (shout), 'Mr. Lane _____ (defeat) in the elections. He _____ (retire) from political life and _____ (go) to live abroad!'

　'I _____ (know),' _____ (answer) Patrick, 'but I _____ (love) to hear you say it!'

Special difficulties 难点

Words often confused 经常容易混淆的词

Temper and *Mood*.

Study these examples:

细读以下例子:

This time, the policeman *lost his temper.* (1.11) (He got angry.)

Keep your temper! (Don't get angry!) 不要发火!

After what happened last night, I was surprised to find that he was *in* such a *good temper* this morning. (He was not angry.) 在昨晚发生的事情之后, 我惊奇地发现他今天早上的情绪很好。

You should apologize to him. He's *in a very bad temper.* (He is angry.) 你应该向他道歉, 他非常生气。

I enjoyed myself at the party. I was *in a very good mood.* (I was cheerful.) 我在聚会上玩得很开心, 心情非常好。

Don't disturb him. He's *in a very bad mood.* (He is not cheerful, but not necessarily angry.) 别打扰他, 他心情不好。

I'm *in the mood for* a drive into the country. (I would very much like to go for a drive into the country.) 我很想开车去乡下兜兜风。

Exercise 练习

Use each of the above italicized phrases in sentences of your own.

用以上斜体印出的短语各造一个句。

Multiple choice questions 选择题

Comprehension 理解

1 If Mr. Wentworth Lane had won the recent election _____ .

   (*a*) he would probably have gone abroad

   (*b*) he would probably have been Prime Minister again

   (*c*) he would probably have returned from abroad

   (*d*) he would probably have given up politics

2 Patrick kept asking about the former Prime Minister _____ .

   (*a*) because he was so pleased that Mr. Lane had been defeated

   (*b*) because he wanted information

   (*c*) because he wanted to annoy the policeman

   (*d*) because he didn't understand what the policeman had told him

Structure 句型

3 He has always been a fanatical opponent and he still _____ .

   (*a*) has been   (*b*) was   (*c*) is   (*d*) has

4 He has been an opponent. He has been opposed _____ it.

   (*a*) against   (*b*) for   (*c*) to   (*d*) from

5 He asked if Mr. Lane lived there. He didn't know _____ Mr. Lane lived there.

   (*a*) whether   (*b*) that   (*c*) unless   (*d*) providing that

6 The policeman was suspicious _____ Patrick.

   (*a*) to   (*b*) of   (*c*) for   (*d*) from

7 He has gone to live abroad. He _____ abroad for some time now.

   (*a*) has gone   (*b*) went   (*c*) has been   (*d*) did go

Vocabulary 词汇

8 Mr. Lane was the former Prime Minister. He was the _____ one.

   (*a*) first   (*b*) previous   (*c*) latter   (*d*) before

9 He was defeated in the elections. He was _____ .

   (*a*) conquered   (*b*) won   (*c*) beaten   (*d*) destroyed

10 Patrick has always been a fanatical opponent. He is _____ him.

   (*a*) opposite   (*b*) anti   (*c*) at   (*d*) against

11 The policeman lost his temper. He _____ .

   (*a*) got angry   (*b*) was in a bad mood   (*c*) lost his nerve   (*d*) was in a bad humour

12 Mr. Lane was defeated in the elections. He didn't get enough _____ .

   (*a*) marks   (*b*) votes   (*c*) points   (*d*) grades

Sentence structure 句子结构

Rewrite this sentence, then check your answer against the text.

改写以下句子, 然后对照课文第 8-9 行, 核对你的答案。

Just as the same policeman was walking slowly past the entrance, Patrick asked the same question.

The same policeman _____ .

Lesson 84 On strike 罢工

First listen and then answer the question.

听录音，然后回答以下问题。

Who will be driving the buses next week?

... *people on their way to work*

Busmen have decided to go on strike next week. The strike is due to begin on Tuesday. No one knows how long it will last. The busmen have stated that the strike will continue until general agreement is reached about pay and working conditions. Most people
5 believe that the strike will last for at least a week. Many owners of private cars are going to offer 'free rides' to people on their way to work. This will relieve pressure on the trains to some extent. Meanwhile, a number of university students have volunteered to drive buses while the strike lasts. All the students are expert drivers, but before they drive any of the buses, they
10 will have to pass a special test. The students are going to take the test in two days' time. Even so, people are going to find it difficult to get to work. But so far, the public has expressed its gratitude to the students in letters to the Press. Only one or two people have objected that the students will drive too fast!

New words and expressions 生词和短语

strike (title) /straɪk/ n. 罢工
busman (1.1) /'bʌsmən/ n. 公共汽车司机
state (1.3) /steɪt/ v. 正式提出，宣布
agreement (11.3-4) /ə'griːmənt/ n. 协议
relieve (1.7) /rɪ'liːv/ v. 减轻
pressure (1.7) /'preʃə/ n. 压力，麻烦

extent (1.7) /ɪk'stent/ n. 程度
volunteer (1.8) /ˌvɒlən'tɪə/ v. 自动提出，自愿
gratitude (1.11) /'ɡrætɪtjuːd/ n. 感激
Press (1.12) /pres/ n. 新闻界
object (1.12) /əb'dʒekt/ v. 不赞成，反对

Notes on the text 课文注释

1 go on strike, 举行罢工。
2 ... is due to begin 中的 due 有 "定于（某时做某事）" 的意思，后接不定式。
3 free ride, 免费乘车。
4 to some extent, 在某种程度上。
5 Only one or two people have objected that ... 本句中 only 在句首，因为是修饰主语，因此句子的谓语并不用倒装语序。

参考译文

　　公共汽车司机决定下星期罢工。罢工定于星期二开始，谁也不知道会持续多久。司机们声称此次罢工将一直持续到就工资和工作条件问题达成全面协议的时候为止。多数人认为此次罢工至少会持续一个星期。很多私人汽车的车主正准备为乘车上班的人们提供 "免费乘车" 的服务，这将在某种程度上减轻对火车的压力。与此同时，有一部分大学生自愿在罢工期间驾驶公共汽车。所有的学生都是开车的能手，但在驾驶公共汽车之

前，他们必须通过一项专门测验。学生们准备在两天后就接受测验。即使这样，人们仍会感到上班有困难。但到目前为止，公众已经向新闻界写信表达他们对学生们的感激之情了。只有一两个人提出反对意见，说学生们会把车开得太快！

Summary writing 摘要写作

In not more than 80 words describe what will happen next week. Write two different paragraphs using the points and connections given below.
用不超过 80 个单词的篇幅描述下周将会发生的事情，用下列要点和连词写出两段不同的文字。

CONNECTIONS		POINTS		CONNECTIONS
which		1	Busmen's strike begins Tuesday.	*Because ... which*
		2	May last a week.	
Because of this		3	Car owners — rides.	
		4	People going — work.	
, too,		5	University students — volunteered — buses.	*who*
but		6	Pass special test.	
Though		7	Difficult to get to work.	*Despite the fact that*
		8	Public grateful.	
Only		9	One or two objected.	*except for ... who*
that		10	Too fast.	*that*

Composition 作文

Write two paragraphs in about 150 words using the ideas given below:
按以下思路写出两段文字，字数为 150 个词左右：

1　The strike began — the students drove badly — the buses were seldom on time — often crowded — the public complained — the busmen were pleased.

2　The students threatened to go on strike — they did so — this angered the busmen who returned to work.

Letter writing 书信写作

The Conclusion. Complete the following sentences:
结束语。完成以下结束语：

1 I shall be looking …

2 I am very sorry for …

3 I hope you will …

4 I wish you …

5 Please give my …

Key structures 关键句型

What will happen? 一般将来时 **(KS12, 36, 60)** （复习第 12，36，60 课关键句型）

Unit 4   Lesson 84

Exercises 练习

A Underline all the verbs in the passage which tell us what will happen.
画出课文中所有表示将要发生事件的动词。

B Give the correct form of the verbs in parentheses. Do not refer to the passage until you finish the exercise:
用括号中动词的正确形式填空，完成练习后再对照课文，核对你的答案：

Busmen have decided to go on strike next week. The strike is due to begin on Tuesday. No one knows how long it _____ (last). The busmen have stated that the strike _____ (continue) until general agreement _____ (reach) about pay and working conditions. Most people believe that the strike _____ (last) for a week. Many owners of private cars _____ (offer) 'free rides' to people on their way to work. This _____ (relieve) pressure on the trains to some extent. Meanwhile, a number of university students have volunteered to drive buses while the strike _____ (last). All the students are expert drivers, but before they _____ (drive) any of the buses, they _____ (have to) pass a special test. The students _____ (take) the test in two days' time. Even so, people _____ (find) it difficult to get to work. But so far, the public has expressed its gratitude to the students in letters to the Press. Only one or two people have objected that the students _____ (drive) too fast!

Special difficulties 难点

Study the word order in the following sentences:
注意以下句子中的语序：

People are going to find it difficult to get to work. (ll.10-11)

He thought it easy to pass the examination. 他以为通过考试很容易。

He considered it wrong that she should have to wait. 他认为她不得不等待是不对的。

I feel it right that he should be punished. 我认为他应该受到惩罚。

I think it wrong for people to behave like that. 我认为人们这样做是错误的。

Exercise 练习

Supply the missing parts in the following sentences. Your sentences must be similar in form to those given above.
完成以下句子，你的句子必须与以上例句类似。

1 He thought it _____ .

2 He finds it unnecessary _____ .

3 _____ to find a job.

4 She thinks it important _____ .

5 _____ for him to wait so long.

6 _____ a good thing that _____ .

Multiple choice questions 选择题

Comprehension 理解

1 The busmen say they won't go back to work _____ .

   (a) until next Tuesday

   (b) until they agree about their holidays

(c) until they have solved their problems

(d) until the students stop driving the buses

2 What will be the main effect of the strike?

(a) There won't be any buses on the road.

(b) Students will have to take a test.

(c) The trains will be crowded.

(d) There won't be many private cars on the road.

Structure 句型

3 The strike is due to begin on Tuesday. That's when it _____ .

(a) is going to begin   (b) began   (c) has begun   (d) will have begun

4 How _____? No one knows.

(a) long it will last   (b) long will it last   (c) it will last   (d) it lasts

5 The strike will last for a week. That's what _____ people believe.

(a) most of   (b) the most of   (c) the more   (d) most

6 Before _____ any buses, they will have to take a special test.

(a) to drive   (b) drive   (c) driving   (d) they will drive

7 one or two people have objected _____ the students.

(a) at   (b) for   (c) to   (d) against

Vocabulary 词汇

8 They will go on strike. So they _____ .

(a) will be fighting   (b) will be arguing   (c) won't be working   (d) won't be talking

9 No one knows how long it will last. They don't know how long it will _____ .

(a) keep   (b) hold   (c) carry   (d) continue

10 It will last for at least a week. So it might be _____ than a week.

(a) more   (b) less   (c) much less   (d) a good deal less

11 They've volunteered to drive buses. That's what they're _____ to do.

(a) eager   (b) anxious   (c) willing   (d) impatient

12 The public has expressed its gratitude. People are _____ .

(a) annoyed   (b) thankless   (c) surprised   (d) thankful

Sentence structure 句子结构

Rewrite this sentence, then check your answer against the text.

改写以下句子，然后对照课文第 8-9 行，核对你的答案。

University students have volunteered to drive buses during the strike.

University students have volunteered to drive buses while _____ .

Lesson 85   Never too old to learn   活到老学到老

First listen and then answer the question.

听录音，然后回答以下问题。

How long has Mr. Page been teaching?

I have just received a letter from my old school, informing me that
my former headmaster, Mr. Stuart Page, will be retiring next week.
Pupils of the school, old and new, will be sending him a present to
mark the occasion. All those who have contributed towards the gift
5 will sign their names in a large album which will be sent to the
headmaster's home. We shall all remember Mr. Page for his patience
and understanding and for the kindly encouragement he gave us
when we went so unwillingly to school. A great many former pupils

will be attending a farewell dinner in his honour next Thursday. It is a curious coincidence that the day before
10 his retirement, Mr. Page will have been teaching for a total of forty years. After he has retired, he will devote
himself to gardening. For him, this will be an entirely new hobby. But this does not matter, for, as he has often
remarked, one is never too old to learn.

one is never too old to learn

New words and expressions 生词和短语

inform (1.1) /ɪnˈfɔːm/ v. 告诉, 通知
headmaster (1.2) /ˈhedmɑːstə/ n. 校长
contribute (1.4) /kənˈtrɪbjuːt/ v. 捐助, 援助
gift (1.4) /gɪft/ n. 礼物, 赠品
album (1.5) /ˈælbəm/ n. 签名簿, 相册
patience (1.6) /ˈpeɪʃəns/ n. 耐心
encouragement (1.7) /ɪnˈkʌrɪdʒmənt/ n. 鼓励

farewell (1.9) /ˈfeəwel/ n. 告别
honour (1.9) /ˈɒnə/ n. 敬意
coincidence (1.9) /kəʊˈɪnsɪdəns/ n. 巧合
total (1.10) /ˈtəʊtl/ n. 总数
devote (1.10) /dɪˈvəʊt/ v. 致力于
gardening (1.11) /ˈgɑːdnɪŋ/ n. 园艺
hobby (1.11) /ˈhɒbi/ n. 爱好, 嗜好

Notes on the text 课文注释

1 old and new 是 pupils of the school 的同位语。由并列连词连接的两个形容词作定语时, 要放在所修饰的词的后面。
2 All those who have contributed towards the gift, 所有凑钱买此礼品的人。contribute towards 是 "为……捐款" 的意思。
3 remember … for …, 记住……的……。
4 a farewell dinner in his honour, 为他举行的告别宴会。in one's honour 是 "为向……表示敬意" 的意思。
5 It is a curious coincidence that …, ……真是奇妙的巧合。that 引导主语从句。
6 a total of, 总共。
7 devote oneself to …, 致力于……。to 这里是介词, 后接名词、动名词。

参考译文

我刚刚收到母校的一封信, 通知我说以前的校长斯图亚特·佩奇先生下星期就要退休了。为了纪念这个日

子，学校的学生——无论老同学还是新同学——将送他一件礼物。所有凑钱买此礼品的人都将把自己的名字签在一本大签名簿上，签名簿将被送到校长的家里。我们不会忘记佩奇先生对我们既有耐心又充满理解，也不会忘记在我们不愿去上学时他给予我们的亲切鼓励。很多老同学都准备参加下星期四为他举行的告别宴会。佩奇先生退休的前一天正好是他执教满 40 年的日子，这真是奇妙的巧合。他退休后，将致力于园艺。对于他来说，这将是一种全新的爱好。但这没有关系，因为正如他常说的那样，人要活到老学到老。

Summary writing 摘要写作

Make a summary of the passage *in not more than 80 words*. Write two different paragraphs using the points and connections given below.

用不超过 80 个单词的篇幅写一篇本课课文的摘要，用以下要点和连词写出两段不同的文字。

CONNECTIONS	POINTS	CONNECTIONS
Now that	1　Former headmaster, Mr. Page, retiring.	*After twenty-eight years as*
and with	2　Pupils — gift.	*not only*
	3　Album — signatures.	*but also*
	4　Attending farewell dinner in honour.	
After having	5　Completed forty years as teacher.	*of a man who*
	6　Devote — gardening.	*Now*
which for him	7　New hobby.	*Though*
but	8　Never too old.	*because*

Composition 作文

Write two paragraphs in about 150 words using the ideas given below:

按以下思路写出两段文字，字数为 150 个词左右：

1　The headmaster's speech — he thanked the pupils — he remembered pupils past and present — many successful careers — humorous incidents.

2　His own future — memories — old pupils welcome to come and visit him — how he would spend his time — it would take him forty years to put his garden in order.

Letter writing 书信写作

How to end a letter. Study this example:

如何结束一封信。细读以下例子：

I am looking forward to seeing you soon.

　　　　　　Best regards,

　　　　　　　　Tom

This is how we usually end letters to friends. We may end 'Best wishes,' 'Yours,' or 'Love,'.

这是我们通常给朋友的书信的结束方法。我们可以用 "Best wishes,"、"Yours," 或 "Love," 结尾。

Exercise 练习

How would you end letters to each of the following?

你将如何结束给以下各位的信：

Your mother; your best friend; an acquaintance.

Key structures 关键句型

What will happen? What will be happening? What will have been happening?
一般将来时、将来进行时和将来完成进行时 **(KS13, 37, 61)**（复习第 13，37，61 课关键句型）

Exercises 练习

A Study the use in the passage of all the verbs which express the future.
注意课文中表示将来的动词的用法。

B Give the correct form of the verbs in parentheses. Do not refer to the passage until you finish the exercise.
用括号中动词的正确形式填空，完成练习后再对照课文，核对你的答案：

I have just received a letter from my old school, informing me that my former headmaster, Mr. Stuart Page, _____ (retire) next week. Pupils of the school, old and new, _____ (send) him a present to mark the occasion. All those who have contributed towards the gift _____ (sign) their names in a large album which _____ (send) to the headmaster's home. We all _____ (remember) Mr. Page for his patience and under-standing and for the kindly encouragement he gave us when we went so unwillingly to school. A great many for-mer pupils _____ (attend) a farewell dinner in his honour next Thursday. It is a curious coincidence that the day before his retirement, Mr. Page _____ (teach) for a total of forty years. After he _____ (retire)，he _____ (devote) himself to gardening. For him, this _____ (be) an entirely new hobby.

Special difficulties 难点

Words often confused 经常容易混淆的词
Too（太，过分）and *Enough*（足够，十分）.
Study the following sentences:
细读以下句子：
One is never *too* old to learn. (1.12)
It is *too* difficult for me to understand. 它太难了，我理解不了。
It is easy *enough* for me to understand. 它十分容易，我能理解。

Exercise 练习

Join the sentences below in the way shown in these examples:
按例句连接以下句子：

a The wall is high. I cannot climb it. (too)
   The wall is too high to climb.
   The wall is too high for me to climb.

b The wall is low. I can climb it. (enough)
   The wall is low enough to climb.
   The wall is low enough for me to climb.

1 This car is expensive. I cannot buy it. (too)
2 This car is cheap. I can buy it. (enough)
3 The tea is hot. I cannot drink it. (too)
4 This piece of music is difficult. I cannot play it. (too)
5 This piece is easy. I can play it. (enough)

Multiple choice questions 选择题

Comprehension 理解

1 The pupils who will be signing their names in the album are those who _____ .

   (*a*) are at the school now

   (*b*) used to go to the school

   (*c*) will attend the farewell dinner

   (*d*) have given money to buy the headmaster a present

2 The headmaster _____ .

   (*a*) believes it's too late to take up gardening

   (*b*) thinks that only young people should take up gardening

   (*c*) has no intention of taking up gardening

   (*d*) doesn't believe it's too late to take up gardening

Structure 句型

3 He will be retiring next week. He _____ be retiring next year.

   (*a*) willn't   (*b*) won't   (*c*) shall not   (*d*) shan't

4 We went so unwillingly to school. We were _____ unwilling pupils.

   (*a*) such   (*b*) so   (*c*) so much   (*d*) such an

5 The farewell dinner will be _____ Thursday.

   (*a*) in   (*b*) on   (*c*) the   (*d*) at

6 How long _____ teaching? Forty years.

   (*a*) will he have been   (*b*) he will have been   (*c*) will have he been   (*d*) will have been he

7 One is never too old to learn. _____ are never too old to learn.

   (*a*) We   (*b*) You   (*c*) They   (*d*) Everyone

Vocabulary 词汇

8 They informed me about it. That's the _____ I received.

   (*a*) inform   (*b*) informs   (*c*) informations   (*d*) information

9 They will put their _____ in an album.

   (*a*) signs   (*b*) signatures   (*c*) signals   (*d*) marks

10 He gave us encouragement. He was always _____ .

   (*a*) courageous   (*b*) helpful   (*c*) helpless   (*d*) thankful

11 We shall attend a farewell dinner to say _____ to him.

   (*a*) hello   (*b*) something   (*c*) our good wishes   (*d*) goodbye

12 It's entirely new to him. It's _____ new to him.

   (*a*) eventually   (*b*) finally   (*c*) completely   (*d*) fully

Sentence structure 句子结构

Join these sentences, then check your answer against the text.

连接以下句子, 然后对照课文第4-6行, 核对你的答案。

They have contributed towards the gift. They will sign their names in a large album. It will be sent to the headmaster's home.

All those _____ .

Lesson 86   Out of control   失控

First listen and then answer the question.

听录音，然后回答以下问题。

What was the danger?

... *swam on quickly*

As the man tried to swing the speedboat round, the steering wheel came away in his hands. He waved desperately to his companion, who had been water skiing for the last fifteen minutes. Both men had hardly had time to realize what was happening when they were
5 thrown violently into the sea. The speedboat had struck a buoy, but it continued to move very quickly across the water. Both men had just begun to swim towards the shore, when they noticed with dismay that the speedboat was moving in a circle. It now came straight towards them at tremendous speed. In less than a minute, it roared past them only a few feet away. After it had
10 passed, they swam on as quickly as they could because they knew that the boat would soon return. They had just had enough time to swim out of danger when the boat again completed a circle. On this occasion, however, it had slowed down considerably. The petrol had nearly all been used up. Before long, the noise dropped completely and the boat began to drift gently across the water.

New words and expressions   生词和短语

swing (1.1) /swɪŋ/ (swung /swʌŋ/, swung) v. 转向
speedboat (1.1) /'spiːdbəut/ n. 快艇
desperately (1.2) /'despərɪtli/ adv. 绝望地
companion (1.2) /kəm'pænjən/ n. 同伙，伙伴
water ski (1.3) /'wɔːtə-ˌskiː/（由快艇牵引水橇）滑水
buoy (1.5) /bɔɪ/ n. 浮标

dismay (1.7) /dɪs'meɪ/ n. 沮丧
tremendous (1.9) /trɪ'mendəs/ adj. 巨大的
petrol (1.12) /'petrəl/ n. 汽油
drift (1.13) /drɪft/ v. 漂动，漂流
gently (1.13) /'dʒentli/ adv. 缓慢地，轻轻地

Notes on the text   课文注释

1 came away, 脱落，离开。

2 Both men had hardly had time to realize what was happening when they were thrown violently into the sea.
他们两个还没有来得及意识到究竟发生了什么事情，就被猛地抛入海里。hardly ... when ... 表示"刚……就……"。

3 on this occasion, 这一次。

4 use up, 耗尽，用光。

参考译文

　　当那人试图让快艇转弯时，方向盘脱手了。他绝望地向他的伙伴挥手，他的伙伴在过去的 15 分钟里一直在滑水。他们两个还没来得及意识到究竟发生了什么事情，就被猛地抛入了海里。快艇撞上了一个浮标，但它仍在水面上快速行驶着。两个人刚开始向岸边游去，就突然惊愕地发现快艇正在转着圈行驶，它现在正以惊人的

速度直冲他们驶来。不到 1 分钟的工夫，它从离他们只有几英尺远的地方呼啸着驶了过去。快艇过去之后，他们以最快的速度向前游去，因为他们知道快艇马上就要转回来。他们刚刚来得及游出危险区，快艇就又转完了一圈。然而这一次它的速度慢多了。汽油几乎已经用光。没过多久，噪音便彻底消失，快艇开始在水面上慢悠悠地漂流。

Summary writing 摘要写作

In not more than 80 words describe what happened from the moment the men were thrown into the sea. Write two different paragraphs using the points and connections given below.

用不超过 80 个词的篇幅描述一下从两个人被抛入水中起所发生的事情，用以下要点和连词写两段不同的文字。

CONNECTIONS	POINTS	CONNECTIONS
The moment	1 Speedboat struck buoy.	*Because*
	2 Both men — water.	
As	3 It moved off.	
	4 Men — shore.	*and while*
Turning	5 Circle — towards them.	
After	6 Just missed them.	*and only just*
until	7 Swam — out of danger.	*no sooner ... than*
When	8 Boat returned.	
	9 Lost speed.	*This time, however*
Soon ... and	10 Petrol used up — floated.	*because ... and*

Composition 作文

Write two paragraphs in about 150 words using the ideas given below:

按以下思路写出两段文字，字数为 150 个词左右：

1 A speedboat was out of control — no one was in it — it was moving towards a small fishing boat — the fishermen tried to row away.

2 The speedboat came nearer — the fishermen dived into the sea — the speedboat ran out of petrol — stopped just before it reached the fishermen.

Letter writing 书信写作

Which of the following endings are correct?

以下哪几个结束语是正确的？

Yours sincerely, Your's sincerely, yours sincerely, Yours Sincerely, Your's, Yours, Yours Very Sincerely.

Key structures 关键句型

What had happened? What had been happening? 过去完成时与过去完成进行时

KS14, 38, 62（复习第 14，38，62 课关键句型）

Unit 4   Lesson 86

Exercises 练习

A Underline the verbs in the passage which tell us *what happened, what had happened* and *what had been happening*.

画出课文中所有表示过去时、过去完成时和过去完成进行时的动词。

B Give the correct form of the verbs in parentheses. Do not refer to the passage until you finish the exercise:

用括号中动词的正确形式填空，完成练习后再对照课文，核对你的答案：

As the man tried to swing the speedboat round, the steering wheel came away in his hands. He _____ (wave) desperately to his companion, who _____ (water ski) for the last fifteen minutes. Both men hardly _____ (have) time to realize what was happening when they _____ (throw) violently into the sea. The speedboat _____ (strike) a buoy, but it _____ (continue) to move very quickly across the water. Both men just _____ (begin) to swim towards the shore, when they _____ (notice) with dismay that the speedboat was moving in a circle. It now _____ (come) towards them at tremendous speed. In less than a minute, it _____ (roar) past them only a few feet away. After it _____ (pass), they _____ (swim) on as quickly as they could because they _____ (know) that the boat would soon return. They just _____ (have) enough time to swim out of danger when the boat again _____ (complete) a circle. On this occasion, however, it _____ (slow) down considerably. The petrol nearly all _____ (use) up. Before long, the noise _____ (drop) completely and the boat _____ (begin) to drift gently across the water.

Special difficulties 难点

Words often confused 经常容易混淆的词

Study these examples:

细读以下例句：

Enough and *Fairly*.

They had just had *enough* time to swim out of danger. (11.10-11)

Your work is not good *enough*. 你的工作不够好。**(SD85)**（对比第 85 课难点）

I missed the train this morning. I didn't get up early *enough*. 今天早上我没赶上火车，我起得不够早。

I didn't buy *enough* sugar. 我没买足够的糖。

There are *enough* flowers in that vase. 花瓶里的花够多的了。

George is a *fairly* tall person but still not tall enough to get into the police force. 乔治的身材相当高，但要加入警察部队还不够高。

I knew he's a *fairly* good player, but he doesn't play well enough to get into the team. 我知道他是一个相当好的队员，但他的球打得还不够好，还不能参加球队。

Exercise 练习

Supply the missing words in the following sentences:

填空：

1 It's _____ cold today, but not really cold _____ to light a fire.

2 This book was _____ interesting, but I didn't enjoy it as much as I expected to.

3 This class has given me _____ trouble so far.

4 You haven't put _____ flowers in that vase.

5 Is that suitcase large _____ to take all these clothes?

Multiple choice questions 选择题

Comprehension 理解

1 The men were thrown into the water _____ .

   (*a*) when the steering wheel came away

   (*b*) when the boat struck the buoy

   (*c*) when the man tried to swing the speedboat round

   (*d*) because they had been water skiing

2 While they were in the water the men thought that _____ .

   (*a*) the speedboat was moving in a circle   (*b*) the speedboat was going out to sea

   (*c*) the speedboat was going to hit them   (*d*) the speedboat was going to stop

Structure 句型

3 _____ did he wave to? His companion.

   (*a*) Who   (*b*) Whose   (*c*) Which   (*d*) What

4 Both men realized what was happening. _____ could do anything about it.

   (*a*) They neither   (*b*) Neither of them   (*c*) Neither they   (*d*) Either of them

5 They had hardly begun to swim towards the shore _____ they noticed the boat.

   (*a*) than   (*b*) when   (*c*) as   (*d*) so

6 How fast did it go? _____ tremendous speed.

   (*a*) With   (*b*) At   (*c*) In   (*d*) From

7 It had slowed down considerably. It had slowed down _____ .

   (*a*) much   (*b*) many   (*c*) very   (*d*) a lot

Vocabulary 词汇

8 The man tried to swing the boat round. He tried to _____ .

   (*a*) circle it   (*b*) twist it   (*c*) make it turn   (*d*) wind it

9 He waved desperately. He waved _____ .

   (*a*) in despair   (*b*) helplessly   (*c*) desperate   (*d*) with despair

10 It roared past them. It _____ them.

   (*a*) past   (*b*) passed   (*c*) pasted   (*d*) passing

11 It came straight towards them. It came _____ towards them.

   (*a*) in direction   (*b*) directly   (*c*) in the way   (*d*) on the way

12 The boat drifted across the water. It _____ across the water.

   (*a*) stopped   (*b*) ran   (*c*) floated slowly   (*d*) wondered

Sentence structure 句子结构

Join these sentences, then check your answer against the text.
连接以下句子, 然后对照课文第 9-10 行, 核对你的答案。
It had passed. They swam on as quickly as they could. They knew that the boat would soon return.

Lesson 87　A perfect alibi　极好的不在犯罪现场的证据

First listen and then answer the question.

听录音，然后回答以下问题。

What was wrong with the man's story?

'At the time the murder was committed, I was travelling on the 8 o'clock train to London,' said the man.

'Do you always catch such an early train?' asked the inspector.

'Of course I do,' answered the man. 'I must be at work at 10
5 o'clock. My employer will confirm that I was there on time.'

'Would a later train get you to work on time?' asked the inspec-tor.

'I suppose it would, but I never catch a later train.'

'At what time did you arrive at the station?'

10 'At ten to eight. I bought a paper and waited for the train.'

'And you didn't notice anything unusual?'

'Of course not.'

'I suggest,' said the inspector, 'that you are not telling the truth. I suggest that you did not catch the 8 o'clock train, but that you caught the 8.25 which would still get you to work on time. You see, on the
15 morning of the murder, the 8 o'clock train did not run at all. It broke down at Ferngreen station and was taken off the line.'

'I suggest you are not telling the truth'

New words and expressions　生词和短语

alibi (title) /ˈælɪbaɪ/ *n.* 不在犯罪现场
commit (1.1) /kəˈmɪt/ *v.* 犯（罪、错）
inspector (1.3) /ɪnˈspektə/ *n.* 探长
employer (1.5) /ɪmˈplɔɪə/ *n.* 雇主

confirm (1.5) /kənˈfɜːm/ *v.* 确认，证实
suggest (1.13) /səˈdʒest/ *v.* 提醒
truth (1.13) /truːθ/ *n.* 真相

Notes on the text　课文注释

1　At the time the murder was committed, the murder was committed 可以看作是定语从句修饰 time。at the time 意为 at the moment when something happened。

2　on time, 准时。

3　And you didn't notice anything unusual? 难道你没有注意到有什么异常情况？
这是由陈述句后加问号表示的问句。

4　the 8.25 是指 8 点 25 分的火车。

参考译文

"在凶杀发生的时候，我正坐在 8 点钟开往伦敦的火车上。"那人说。
"您总是赶这样早的火车吗？"探长问。

"当然是的，"那人回答。"我必须在 10 点钟上班，我的雇主会证明我是按时到了那儿的。"

"晚一点儿的车也能送您按时上班吗？"探长问。

"我认为可以，但我从来不乘晚一点儿的车。"

"您几点钟到的火车站？"

"7 点 50 分。我买了张报纸，等着车来。"

"您没有注意到有什么异常情况发生吗？"

"当然没有。"

"我提醒您，"探长说，"您讲的不是实话。您乘的不是 8 点钟的火车，而是 8 点 25 分的，这次车同样能使您按时上班。您看，在凶杀发生的那天早晨，8 点钟的那次车根本没有发。它在芬格林车站出了故障而被取消了。"

Summary writing 摘要写作

In not more than 80 words show how the inspector proved that the man's alibi was false. Write two different paragraphs using the points and connections given below.

用不超过 80 个单词的篇幅，描述探长是如何证明该人提供的不在现场证据是假的，用下列要点和连词写两段不同的文字。

CONNECTIONS		POINTS	CONNECTIONS
At		1 Time of murder.	*When the murder*
that		2 Man claimed — travelling.	*that*
		3 8 o'clock train, London.	
and		4 Arrived work on time.	*He said that*
When		5 Inspector asked — later train, work on time.	*Then*
		6 Man agreed it would.	*Though*
but		7 Always travelled early.	
		8 Inspector suggested: lying.	*In reply*
because		9 8 o'clock train — broke down.	*as*
so		10 Man caught 8.25.	*and therefore*

Composition 作文

Continue the conversation begun in the passage. Write about 150 words using the ideas given below:

继续课文的对话，按以下思路写出 150 个词左右的对话：

The man suddenly 'remembered' that he had caught the later train — didn't he notice anything unusual? — not unusual for a train to be late — how did he spend the time? — waited on the platform for 25 minutes — read a newspaper — the inspector suggested that the man was lying — a neighbour saw him leave the house at 8.15, just after the murder — the man was arrested.

Letter writing 书信写作

The Signature. How you sign your name depends on how well you know the person you are writing to. You may use your full name, your first name, or even a nickname. Your signature must be readable. It must come under the letter-ending.

签名。你如何签名取决于你和收信人的熟悉程度。你可以用全名、你的名字甚至绰号。你的签名必须清楚，必须落在信末尾的下面。

Unit 4   Lesson 87

Exercise 练习

Write suitable letter-endings and signatures to the following:

为以下几封信写出信尾结束语并签名：

Your sister; your wife or husband; your employer; a close friend.

Key structures 关键句型

He said that ... He told me ... He asked ... 间接引语 (KS15, 39, 63) (复习第 15，39，63 课关键句型)

Exercises 练习

A Imagine that you are writing a newspaper report of the conversation that took place between the man and the inspector. Answer these questions on the passage. Where necessary, use the words given in parentheses:

设想一下你正在为报纸写一篇有关探长和嫌疑犯对话的报道。回答以下问题，必要时可用括号内的短语：

Lines 1-2	What did the man say he was doing at the time the murder was committed?
Line 3	What did the inspector ask him?
Lines 4-5	Did the man say that he did or that he didn't? At what time did he have to be at work? (*because*) What would his employer confirm?
Lines 6-7	What did the inspector ask him then?
Line 8	What did the man suppose? Did he ever catch a later train? (*but*)
Line 9	What did the inspector ask?
Line 10	At what time did the man say he had arrived at the station? What did he do there? (*He added that he ...*)
Lines 11-12	What did the inspector ask him? Did the man say that he had or that he hadn't? (*When the inspector asked him ... the man ...*)
Line 13	What did the inspector suggest?
Lines 13-16	What did the inspector point out?

B Here is part of a report that appeared in a newspaper. Write the actual conversation that took place between the man and the inspector. Do not refer to the passage until you finish the exercise. **(SD26)**

下面是登在报上有关那段对话的报道。写出探长和嫌疑犯实际的对话。完成练习后再对照课文，核对你的答案。(参见第 26 课难点)

At the time the murder was committed, the man said that he was travelling on the 8 o'clock train to London. The inspector asked if he always caught such an early train. The man answered that he did. He had to be at work at 10 o'clock. His employer would confirm that he was there on time. Then the inspector asked him if a later train would get him to work on time. The man supposed that a later train would get him to work on time but he never caught a later train. The inspector asked him what time he arrived at the station. The man said that he had arrived there at ten to eight. He added that he bought a paper and waited for the train. When the inspector asked him if he had noticed anything unusual, the man said that he had not.

Multiple choice questions 选择题

Comprehension 理解

1 The man thought his alibi was perfect because _____ .

(a) he caught the 8 o'clock train

(b) he was at the station at 7.50

(c) he arrived at work on time

(d) his employer knew he always caught the 8 o'clock train

2 The 8 o'clock train broke down that morning _____ .

(a) when the man was on it   (b) and it arrived late

(c) and the man knew this very well   (d) so the inspector knew the man was lying

Structure 句型

3 He was travelling to London. He works _____ London.

(a) at   (b) to   (c) in   (d) on

4 He catches an early train. He _____ every day.

(a) uses to   (b) used to   (c) is accustomed to   (d) always does

5 The man wasn't telling the truth. He was _____ a lie.

(a) telling   (b) saying   (c) talking   (d) speaking

6 He didn't catch the train that leaves _____ 8 o'clock.

(a) on   (b) –   (c) at   (d) in

7 It broke down so the man _____ it.

(a) can't catch   (b) mightn't catch

(c) couldn't have caught   (d) mightn't have caught

Vocabulary 词汇

8 'Of course I do,' _____ the man.

(a) replied   (b) responded   (c) returned   (d) told

9 My employer will _____ that I was there on time.

(a) assure   (b) be sure   (c) make sure   (d) certify

10 He didn't notice anything unusual. He didn't notice anything _____ .

(a) out of the ordinary   (b) unused   (c) unaccustomed   (d) inquisitive

11 'And you didn't notice anything unusual?' '_____ not.'

(a) Certainly   (b) Surely   (c) Doubtlessly   (d) Truly

12 He didn't catch the 8 o'clock train. He _____ it.

(a) lost   (b) didn't find   (c) escaped   (d) missed

Sentence structure 句子结构

Rewrite this sentence, then check your answer against the text.

改写以下句子, 然后对照课文第 13 行, 核对你的答案。

In my opinion you are not telling the truth.

I suggest _____ .

Lesson 88 Trapped in a mine 困在矿井里

📻 **First listen and then answer the question.**

听录音，然后回答以下问题。

Why is the rescue taking so long?

the men are cheerful

Six men have been trapped in a mine for seventeen hours. If they are not brought to the surface soon they may lose their lives. However, rescue operations are proving difficult. If explosives are used, vibrations will cause the roof of the mine to collapse. Rescue
5 workers are therefore drilling a hole on the north side of the mine. They intend to bring the men up in a special capsule. If there had not been a hard layer of rock beneath the soil, they would have completed the job in a few hours. As it is, they have been drilling for sixteen hours and they still have a long way to go. Meanwhile, a microphone, which was lowered into the
10 mine two hours ago, has enabled the men to keep in touch with their closest relatives. Though they are running out of food and drink, the men are cheerful and confident that they will get out soon. They have been told that rescue operations are progressing smoothly. If they knew how difficult it was to drill through the hard rock, they would lose heart.

New words and expressions 生词和短语

trap (title) /træp/ v. 陷入，使陷于困境
surface (1.2) /'sɜːfɪs/ n. 地面，表面
explosive (1.3) /ɪk'spləʊsɪv/ n. 炸药
vibration (1.4) /vaɪ'breɪʃən/ n. 震动
collapse (1.4) /kə'læps/ v. 坍塌
drill (1.5) /drɪl/ v. 钻（孔）

capsule (1.6) /'kæpsjuːl/ n. 容器
layer (1.7) /'leɪə/ n. 层
beneath (1.7) /bɪ'niːθ/ prep. 在……之下
lower (1.9) /'ləʊə/ v. 放下，降低
progress (1.11) /prəʊ'gres/ v. 进展，进行
smoothly (1.12) /'smuːðli/ adv. 顺利地

Notes on the text 课文注释

1 rescue operations, 营救工作。
2 If there had not been a hard layer of rock beneath the soil, they would have completed the job in a few hours.
   如果不是因为土壤下面有一层坚硬的岩石，他们的营救工作仅用几个小时就可以完成了。
3 As it is, 事实上，实际上。
4 they still have a long way to go, 他们离钻透还早着呢。
5 keep in touch with, 与……保持联系。
6 run out of, 用完，用尽。
7 lose heart, 失望，丧失信心。

参考译文

　　6个人被困在矿井里已有 17 个小时了。如果不把他们尽快救到地面上来，他们就有可能丧生。然而，事实证明营救工作非常困难。如果用炸药爆破，震动会引起矿顶塌落。因此，营救人员在矿井的北侧钻了一个洞。

他们准备用一种特制的容器把这 6 个人救上来。如果不是因为土壤下面有一层坚硬的岩石，他们的营救工作仅用几个小时就可以完成了。实际情况是，他们已连续钻了 16 个小时了，但离钻透还早着呢。与此同时，两个小时以前放到井下去的一只麦克风使井下的人可以与其亲属保持联系。虽然他们的食物和饮料都快消耗尽了，但这些人的心情很好，坚信他们很快就会出去。他们一直被告知营救工作进行得非常顺利。如果他们知道了钻透那坚硬的岩石有多么困难，他们会丧失信心的。

Summary writing 摘要写作

Make a summary of the passage *in not more than 80 words*. Write two different paragraphs using the points and connections given below.

用不超过 80 个词的篇幅写出故事的摘要，用以下要点和连词写出两段不同的文字。

CONNECTIONS		POINTS		CONNECTIONS
who		1	Six men — trapped — seventeen hours.	
		2	May lose lives.	and
because		3	Rescue difficult.	
Since		4	Explosives — collapse.	as
		5	Drilling — hard rock.	Because of this
but		6	Progress slow.	yet
Two hours ago		7	Microphone lowered.	Now that
and		8	In touch — relatives.	
		9	Running short — food.	Though
but		10	Good spirits.	

Composition 作文

Continue the above passage. Write two paragraphs in about 150 words using the ideas given below:

根据以下思路继续讲这个故事，字数为 150 个词左右：

1　During the rescue operations there was a loud noise — collapse of mine — microphone silent — the men's voices were heard an hour later — they were all right.

2　Drilling began again — the collapse had made things easier — the men were brought to the surface — the scene on their return.

Letter writing 书信写作

The Postscript. If you wish to add something to your letter after you have finished it, you may do so under your signature. Whatever you write must be preceded by the letters 'P.S.' which stand for 'Postscript'. Study this example:

又及。如果信写完后还想再作些补充，可以写在签名下面。在你所写的附言之前必须加上P.S. 两个字母，这是"又及"的意思。细读以下的例子：

Best regards,

Tom

P.S. I'll send you a copy of the book by separate post.

Exercise 练习

Write two letter-endings followed by postscripts.

写出两封信的结尾再加上附言。

Key structures 关键句型

If **(KS16, 40, 64)** (复习第 16，40，64 课关键句型)

Exercises 练习

A How many sentences in the passage contain the word *if*? Study the form of the verbs in these sentences.
课文中有几个含有 if 的句子？注意句中的动词形式。

B Give the correct form of the verbs in parentheses. Do not refer to the passage until you finish the exercise.
用括号中动词的正确形式填空，完成练习后再对照课文，核对你的答案。

1 If they _____ (not bring) to the surface soon they may lose their lives.

2 If explosives are used, vibrations _____ (cause) the roof of the mine to collapse.

3 If there had not been a hard layer of rock beneath the soil, they _____ (complete) the job in a few hours.

4 If they knew how difficult it was to drill through the hard rock, they _____ (lose) heart.

C Give the correct form of the verbs in parentheses:
用括号中动词的正确形式填空：

1 If he had fitted safety belts to his car, he _____ (not injure).

2 The man would have been saved if a helicopter _____ (be) available.

3 If you come home late, you _____ (find) the key under the mat.

4 I would have found the house easily if he _____ (give) me the correct address.

5 If smoking _____ (forbid), illnesses will be reduced.

Special difficulties 难点

The verb *run* has a different meaning in each of these sentences. Study them carefully:
在以下句子中动词 run 有不同的含义，细读以下例句：

They are *running out of* food. (1.10) (They have nearly used up all their supplies.)
他们的食物快吃光了。

A crowd of boys *ran after* the beggar. (They chased the beggar.) 一群男孩子在追那个乞丐。

That boy was nearly *run over* by a car. (The car nearly hit him.) 那个男孩差点儿被汽车轧着。

Don't drive so fast. This car hasn't been *run in* yet. (The car must be driven slowly so as not to damage the new engine.)
不要开得这么快，这辆车还未试过车。

I *ran into* Helga while I was in Sweden. (I met her by accident.) 我在瑞典的时候偶然遇到了海尔盖。

Exercise 练习

Supply the missing words in the following sentences:
填空：

1 I ran _____ an old friend of mine in a restaurant yesterday.

2 While driving to work yesterday, I ran _____ petrol and had to walk to a garage.

3 This car will have to be serviced as soon as it has been run _____ .

4 She's been taken to hospital. She was run _____ by a car.

5 I ran _____ him, but I could not catch him.

Multiple choice questions 选择题

Comprehension 理解

1 They are drilling through the hard rock. This is the _____ way to rescue the men.

  (*a*) easiest   (*b*) quickest   (*c*) safest   (*d*) most dangerous

2 Rescue operations are proving difficult _____ .

  (*a*) but it is certain the men will be saved

  (*b*) so it is not certain that the men will be saved

  (*c*) so it is certain the men will not be saved

  (*d*) so it is certain the men will die

Structure 句型

3 They have been trapped for seventeen hours. They tried to come up seventeen hours _____ .

  (*a*) since   (*b*) ago   (*c*) for   (*d*) since then

4 _____ they are brought to the surface soon they may lose their lives.

  (*a*) Except   (*b*) Without   (*c*) Unless   (*d*) Whether

5 It's proving difficult _____ the men.

  (*a*) for rescuing   (*b*) to rescuing   (*c*) to rescue   (*d*) in rescuing

6 Vibrations will cause the roof to collapse. They will _____ collapse.

  (*a*) make it   (*b*) make it to   (*c*) do it to   (*d*) do it

7 They would have completed the job in a few hours _____ the hard layer of rock.

  (*a*) except   (*b*) but for   (*c*) if not   (*d*) unless

Vocabulary 词汇

8 The roof might collapse. It might _____ .

  (*a*) explode   (*b*) fall down   (*c*) fall over   (*d*) blow up

9 The microphone enabled them to keep in touch. It made it _____ for them to keep in touch.

  (*a*) able   (*b*) capable   (*c*) possible   (*d*) probable

10 They are running out of food. They _____ .

  (*a*) have none   (*b*) have a lot   (*c*) haven't much   (*d*) can't eat it

11 The men are cheerful. They are in good _____ .

  (*a*) temper   (*b*) mood   (*c*) spirits   (*d*) disposition

12 They may lose heart. They may _____ in despair.

  (*a*) give   (*b*) give up   (*c*) give off   (*d*) give over

Sentence structure 句子结构

Rewrite this sentence, then check your answer against the text.

改写以下句子, 然后对照课文第 12-13 行, 核对你的答案。

They didn't know how difficult it was to drill through the hard rock, otherwise they would lose heart.

If _____ .

Lesson 89   A slip of the tongue   口误

First listen and then answer the question.

听录音，然后回答以下问题。

Who made the only funny joke that evening and why?

People will do anything to see a free show — even if it is a bad one. When the news got round that a comedy show would be presented at our local cinema by the P. and U. Bird Seed Company, we all rushed to see it. We had to queue for hours to get in and there must
5   have been several hundred people present just before the show began. Unfortunately, the show was one of the dullest we have ever seen. Those who failed to get in need not have felt disappointed, as many of the artistes who should have appeared did not come. The only funny things we heard that evening came from the advertiser at the beginning of the programme. He was
10   obviously very nervous and for some minutes stood awkwardly before the microphone. As soon as he opened his mouth, everyone burst out laughing. We all know what the poor man *should* have said, but what he *actually* said was: 'This is the Poo and Ee Seed Bird Company. Good ladies, evening and gentlemen!'

He was obviously very nervous

New words and expressions   生词和短语

slip (title) /slɪp/ n. 小错误
comedy (1.2) /ˈkɒmɪdi/ n. 喜剧
present (1.2) /prɪˈzent/ v. 演出；adj. 出席，到场的
queue (1.4) /kjuː/ v. 排队

dull (1.6) /dʌl/ adj. 枯燥的，无味的
artiste (1.8) /ɑːˈtiːst/ n. 艺人
advertiser (1.9) /ˈædvətaɪzə/ n. 报幕员

Notes on the text   课文注释

1   a slip of the tongue, 说走了嘴；失言。
2   do anything to see a free show, 想方设法看不花钱的戏。
3   when the news got round that …, 当……的消息一传开。这是一个时间状语从句。get round 作"四处传遍"讲。
4   need not have felt disappointed, 本来不必要感到失望。
    need 后接不定式的完成式表示不必做某事而实际已经做了。
5   who should have appeared 是定语从句，修饰 artistes。should + 不定式的完成式表示本来应该做而实际未做某事。
6   … what the poor man should have said, but what he actually said was …, 这个可怜的人本应说什么，但实际他所说的却是……。
    这里两个 what 都是连接代词，指所说的话（= the words which …）。should 和 actually 两词都用斜体印出，这是强调"应该"和"实际"，形成了对比，应重读。

参考译文

  人们总会想尽办法去看不花钱的演出——哪怕是拙劣的演出。当"皮尤"鸟食公司将在我们当地影院演出喜剧节目的消息传开后, 我们都赶紧跑去观看。我们不得不排了好几个小时才进得场去。在演出开始前场内肯定已有好几百人了。不幸的是, 这次演出是我们看过的最乏味的演出了。那些没能进到场内的人没有必要感到失望, 因为很多应该出场的专业演员都没有来。那天晚上唯一有趣的事情是节目开始时那个报幕员的开场白。他显然非常紧张, 局促不安地在麦克风前站了好几分钟。但他刚一开口说话, 人们便哄堂大笑起来。我们都明白那个可怜的人应该说些什么, 而他实际说的却是:"这是'浦伊'食鸟公司, 好女士们, 晚上和先生们!"

Summary writing 摘要写作

Make a summary of the passage *in not more than 80 words*. Write two different paragraphs using the points and connections given below.

用不超过 80 个单词的篇幅写一篇故事摘要, 用下面的要点和连词写出两段不同的文字。

CONNECTIONS	POINTS	CONNECTIONS
	1 Local cinema — packed.	
because	2 P. & U. Bird Seed Co.	
	3 Presenting free comedy show.	
As … who	4 Many artistes should …	*but … who*
	5 Failed to turn up.	
	6 Show very dull.	*Because of this*
	7 Funniest thing —	
who	8 Advertiser introduced programme saying:	*who at the beginning*
	9 'This … gentlemen.'	

Composition 作文

Write a newspaper report of the event described in the passage. Write two paragraphs in about 150 words using the ideas given below:

写一篇新闻报道, 报道一下演出的实况, 按以下思路写两段文字, 字数为 150 个词左右:

1   There was a long queue of people outside the cinema — many people failed to get in — they were the lucky ones.
2   A description of the stage — there was a large, ugly model of a yellow bird — free packets of bird seed for the audience — the advertiser's mistake — how the audience reacted — the rest of the show: a disappointment.

Letter writing 书信写作

Write three letter-endings followed by postscripts.

写出 3 封信的结束语再加上附言。

Key structures 关键句型

Must, Have to, Need, Should (**KS17, 41, 65**)(复习第 17, 41, 65 课关键句型)。

Exercises 练习

A Note how the verbs *have to*, *must*, *need* and *should* have been used in the passage.

注意课文中 have to, must, need 和 should 的用法。

B Supply the correct form of *have to, must, need* and *should* in the following. Do not refer to the passage until you finish the exercise:

用 have to, must, need 和 should 的正确形式填空，完成练习后再对照课文，核对你的答案：

1 We _____ queue for hours to get in and there _____ (be) several hundred people present just before the show began. Unfortunately, the show was one of the dullest we have ever seen. Those who failed to get in _____ not (feel) disappointed as many of the artistes who _____ (appear) did not come.

2 As soon as he opened his mouth, everyone burst out laughing. We all know what the poor man _____ (say), but what he *actually* said was: 'This is the Poo and Ee Seed Bird Company ...'

C Supply *must not* or *need not* in the following sentences:

用 must not 或 need not 填空：

1 You _____ open the door of the compartment until the train has stopped. It is very dangerous.

2 You _____ bother to post those letters for me. I'll be going out myself soon.

D Supply the correct form of *have to* or *should* in the following sentences:

用 have to 或 should 的正确形式填空：

1 I'm sorry I couldn't get here on time. I _____ (go) to the bank.

2 I _____ (go) to the dentist yesterday but I forgot all about it.

3 We _____ (begin) work at 9 o'clock but we never do.

Special difficulties 难点

Words often confused and misused 经常容易混淆和误用的词

Study these examples:

细读以下例子：

a *Free* and *Single*.

People will do anything to see a *free* show. (1.1)

The people are *free* to choose who will govern them. 人民有自由选举领导他们的人。

Is she still *single*? I thought she was going to get married last April. 她还是独身吗？我原以为她去年 4 月就已经结婚了。

b *Queue* and *Row*.

We had to *queue* for hours to get in. (1.4)

There was a long *queue* outside the cinema. 电影院外面排着长长的队。

I enjoyed the performance because I had a very good seat in the fifth *row*. 我喜欢这场演出，因为我坐在第 5 排一个好位子上。

c *Funny*.

The only *funny* things we heard that evening ... (11.8-9)

There's something *funny* about this house. (Something peculiar.) 这栋房子有点古怪的地方。

Exercises 练习

A Choose the correct words in the following sentences:

选择正确的词：

1 I joined the (queue) (row) at the bus stop.

2 He's still (free) (single) even though he's over forty. I don't think he'll ever get married.

B Write two sentences bringing out the meanings of the word *funny*.
写出两个能够说明funny的意思的句子。

Multiple choice questions 选择题

Comprehension 理解

1 There was a big demand for tickets because _____ .

  (*a*) they didn't cost any money

  (*b*) there were many famous artistes in the show

  (*c*) the show was presented by the P. and U. Bird Seed Company

  (*d*) the show was very funny

2 The audience _____ .

  (*a*) enjoyed the advertiser's opening remarks

  (*b*) enjoyed the show

  (*c*) enjoyed the advertisements

  (*d*) enjoyed the performance by the artistes

Structure 句型

3 People will do anything to see a free show — even if it is _____ .

  (*a*) badly   (*b*) bad one   (*c*) a bad   (*d*) bad

4 How long _____ queue?

  (*a*) did they have to   (*b*) they had to   (*c*) had they to   (*d*) they did have to

5 There must have been several hundred people present _____ …

  (*a*) There had to be   (*b*) There must be

  (*c*) It was necessary to be   (*d*) I think there were

6 Many of the artistes who _____ did not come.

  (*a*) ought to appear   (*b*) should appear   (*c*) had to appear   (*d*) ought to have appeared

7 He stood awkwardly _____ the microphone.

  (*a*) in front of   (*b*) ahead of   (*c*) on top of   (*d*) instead of

Vocabulary 词汇

8 A comedy show is usually very _____ .

  (*a*) serious   (*b*) different   (*c*) unusual   (*d*) light

9 We had to queue. We had to wait our _____ .

  (*a*) queue   (*b*) turn   (*c*) row   (*d*) line

10 The show was dull. It was _____ .

  (*a*) disinterested   (*b*) uninterested   (*c*) interesting   (*d*) uninteresting

11 He was nervous. He felt _____ .

  (*a*) angry   (*b*) bad-tempered   (*c*) annoyed   (*d*) anxious

12 Everyone burst out laughing. There was a lot of _____ .

  (*a*) laughs   (*b*) laughter   (*c*) laughings   (*d*) laugh

Lesson 90   What's for supper?   晚餐吃什么？

🎧 **First listen and then answer the question.**

听录音，然后回答以下问题。

What kind of fish are they?

Who eats who?

Fish and chips has always been a favourite dish in Britain, but as the oceans have been overfished, fish has become more and more expensive. So it comes as a surprise to learn that giant fish are terrifying the divers on North Sea oil rigs. Oil rigs have to be repaired
5 frequently and divers, who often have to work in darkness a hundred feet under water, have been frightened out of their wits by giant fish bumping into them as they work. Now they have had special cages made to protect them from these monsters. The fish are not sharks or killer whales, but favourite eating varieties like cod and skate which grow to unnatural sizes, sometimes as
10 much as twelve feet in length. Three factors have caused these fish to grow so large: the warm water round the hot oil pipes under the sea; the plentiful supply of food thrown overboard by the crews on the rigs; the total absence of fishing boats around the oil rigs. As a result, the fish just eat and eat and grow and grow in the lovely warm water. Who eats who?

New words and expressions 生词和短语

chip (1.1) /tʃɪp/ *n.* 炸土豆条
overfish (1.2) /ˌəʊvəˈfɪʃ/ *v.* 过度捕捞
giant (1.3) /ˈdʒaɪənt/ *adj.* 巨大的
terrify (1.4) /ˈterɪfaɪ/ *v.* 吓，使恐怖
diver (1.4) /ˈdaɪvə/ *n.* 潜水员
oil rig (1.4) /ˈɔɪl-rɪg/ 石油钻塔
wit (1.6) /wɪt/ *n.*（复数）理智，头脑
cage (1.7) /keɪdʒ/ *n.* 笼

shark (1.8) /ʃɑːk/ *n.* 鲨鱼
whale (1.9) /weɪl/ *n.* 鲸
variety (1.9) /vəˈraɪəti/ *n.* 品种
cod (1.9) /kɒd/ *n.* 鳕
skate (1.9) /skeɪt/ *n.* 鳐
factor (1.10) /ˈfæktə/ *n.* 因素
crew (1.11) /kruː/ *n.* 全体工作人员

Notes on the text 课文注释

1 fish and chips, 炸鱼加炸土豆条。这是英国的一种家常菜，被看作是一盘菜，因此要用单数动词。
2 North Sea, 北海。
3 who often have to work in darkness a hundred feet under water, 常常要在水面 100 英尺以下摸黑工作（的人员）。
   这是一个非限定性定语从句，对主句中的名词divers进行补充说明，因此这个从句与主句用逗号隔开。
4 be frightened out of their wits, 被吓昏了，被吓得惊慌失措。
5 favourite eating varieties, 深受人们喜爱的食用的品种。
6 as a result, 结果是。

410

参考译文

炸鱼加炸土豆条一直是英国人喜爱的一道菜, 但是随着海洋里的滥捕滥捞, 鱼已经变得越来越昂贵。因此, 听说北海石油钻井平台上的潜水员受到巨型鱼类的恐吓, 确实很让人吃惊。钻井平台需要经常修理, 潜水员常常要在水面 100 英尺以下摸黑工作, 他们曾在工作时被撞到他们身上的大鱼吓得惊慌失措。现在他们有了特制的笼子, 用来保护他们免受大鱼的侵袭。这些鱼并不是鲨鱼或逆戟鲸, 而是深受人们喜爱的食用鱼品种, 如鳕鱼和鳐鱼, 只不过它们长得出奇地大, 有时长达 12 英尺。这些鱼能长得这么大是由 3 个因素造成的: 海底热的输油管道附近的温暖的海水, 钻井平台工作人员抛到海里充足的食物, 钻井平台周围根本没有捕鱼船只。结果是, 这些鱼就在舒适温暖的水流中吃呀吃, 长呀长。究竟谁吃谁呢?

Summary writing 摘要写作

Make a summary of the passage *in not more than 80 words*. Write two different paragraphs using the points and connections given below.

用不超过 80 个单词的篇幅写出一篇摘要, 用以下要点和连词写出两段不同的文字。

CONNECTIONS		POINTS		CONNECTIONS
working	[	1 Divers — North Sea oil rigs.	]	*who*
		2 Terrified by giant fish.		
that bump		3 Bump into them.		*bumping*
when	[	4 Work in deep water.	]	*while*
	[	5 Fish not sharks or whales.		*but*
On the contrary,		6 Favourite eating varieties.		*which*
that	[	7 Grow to unnatural sizes.	]	
	[	8 Three factors:		
The first	[	9 Warmth from oil-pipes.		
The second	[	10 Plentiful food.		
The third	[	11 Absence of fishing.	]	*and*

Composition 作文

Imagine that you were visiting the oil rig when the divers reported what they had seen. Write two paragraphs of a letter to a friend, using the ideas given below:

假设你在参观钻井平台时, 潜水员对你讲了他们所看到的情景。按以下思路给你的朋友写一封由两段文字组成的信:

1 Strange story — diving team went down last week — work at a depth of sixty feet — work went well — one diver reported — nasty bump in the dark — sounded like a joke — the men on the rigs laughed — must be a monster.

2 Today — second team went down — came up immediately — cod eight feet in length — skate twelve feet across — refuse to go down again — managers had to promise to have special cages made.

Key structures 关键句型

Have (KS18, 42, 66)（复习第 18, 42 和 66 课关键句型）

Exercises 练习

A Study the various different uses of the verb *have* in the passage.
  仔细阅读课文中 have 的不同用法。

B   Study these two sentences:

细读下面两句话：

Oil rigs have to be repaired frequently.

They have had the oil rigs repaired continuously.

Write these sentences again choosing the appropriate *have* construction in place of the words in italics.

改写以下句子，用适当的have结构来替代句子中用斜体印出的部分。

1 Special cages *have been made* to protect the divers from these monsters.

2 The oil companies *make arrangements for the rigs to be repaired* frequently.

3 The divers *must* often work in total darkness.

4 He *has published* a book.

5 We *need to* protect fish stocks.

6 We *have not sent* the letter to his new address.

7 'I *will send* the package to you,' she promised.

8 *Must* you go so soon?

9 Are you going *to clean* this suit?

10 When will you *fix* this loose handle?

11 I must take this car in for new brakes *to be fitted*.

12 How long is it since you *needed* to see a doctor?

13 The doctor told me I *must* get more exercise.

Special difficulties 难点

Two nouns joined by 'and' + singular or plural verb 用and连接的两个名词以及后面的动词单数或复数形式

有些用and相连的名词常在一起连用。当我们把它们看成一个整体时，谓语动词用单数形式；如果我们把它们看成分开的东西，动词就用复数形式。

Study these sentences:

细读以下句子：

Fish *and* chips *has* always been a favourite dish in Britain. (1.1)

Jane *and* Keith *have* always been good friends of ours. 简和基思一直是我们的好朋友。

Exercise 练习

Choose the correct verb in the following sentences:

选择正确的动词：

1 Bread and butter (is) (are) fattening.

2 There (is) (are) a knife and fork missing.

3 There (is) (are) a light bulb and a screwdriver in the drawer.

4 (Is) (Are) there bacon and eggs for breakfast?

5 A chequebook and a purse (has) (have) been taken.

Multiple choice questions 选择题

Comprehension 理解

1 It is a surprise to hear the divers on North Sea oil rigs have been frightened by giant fish because _____ .

  (a) fish and chips has always been a favourite dish for the English

  (b) fish has become rare

  (c) it is not common for fish to grow very large

  (d) divers have been friendly with fish around the oil rigs

2 Divers are terrified because _____ .

  (a) they have to work in the dark   (b) they have to work a hundred feet under water

  (c) the fish are huge   (d) there are no fishing boats around the oil rigs

Structure 句型

3 These eating varieties are sometimes twelve feet _____ .

  (a) length   (b) depth   (c) long   (d) deep

4 There is a total absence of fishing boats around the oil rigs. There are _____ fishing boats.

  (a) few   (b) a few   (c) no   (d) not

5 Oil rigs have to be repaired frequently. They _____ repaired often.

  (a) ought to be   (b) need to   (c) have had   (d) require

6 Giant fish are, in fact, eating varieties _____ cod and skate.

  (a) as   (b) like   (c) similar   (d) resemble

7 These monsters are sometimes _____ twelve feet.

  (a) so much as   (b) longer   (c) as long as   (d) bigger

Vocabulary 词汇

8 Divers _____ those giant fish while working under water.

  (a) come over   (b) are hit by   (c) bump off   (d) are terrifying

9 The report comes as a surprise. It is _____ .

  (a) surprising   (b) surprised   (c) delightful   (d) shocked

10 Those fish grow to unnatural sizes. They are _____ .

  (a) expensive   (b) overfished   (c) lovely   (d) huge

11 Divers are terrified. They are _____ .

  (a) terrifying   (b) at their wits' end   (c) frightening   (d) frightened out of their wits

12 Special cages are made to _____ .

  (a) catch the fish   (b) attack sharks and killer whales

  (c) terrify divers   (d) keep the fish away

Sentence structure 句子结构

Join these sentences, then check your answer against the text.

连接以下句子, 然后对照课文第 5-7 行, 核对你的答案。

Divers often have to work in darkness a hundred feet under water. They have been frightened out of their wits by giant fish. Giant fish bump into divers as they work under water.

Lesson 91 Three men in a basket 三人同篮

First listen and then answer the question.

听录音，然后回答以下问题。

Where was the station's Commanding Officer?

A pilot noticed a balloon which seemed to be making for a Royal
Air Force Station nearby. He informed the station at once, but
no one there was able to explain the mystery. The officer in the control tower was very angry when he heard the news, because bal-
5 loons can be a great danger to aircraft. He said that someone might
be spying on the station and the pilot was ordered to keep track of
the strange object. The pilot managed to circle the balloon for some
time. He could make out three men in a basket under it and one of

someone might be spying

them was holding a pair of binoculars. When the balloon was over the station, the pilot saw one of the men
10 taking photographs. Soon afterwards, the balloon began to descend and it landed near an airfield. The police
were called in, but they could not arrest anyone, for the basket contained two Members of Parliament and the
Commanding Officer of the station! As the Commanding Officer explained later, one half of the station did
not know what the other half was doing!

New words and expressions 生词和短语

balloon (1.1) /bə'lu:n/ *n.* 气球
royal (1.1) /'rɔɪəl/ *adj.* 皇家的
spy (1.6) /spaɪ/ *v.* 侦察

track (1.6) /træk/ *n.* 轨迹，踪迹
binoculars (1.9) /bɪ'nɒkjʊləz/ *n.* 望远镜

Notes on the text 课文注释

1 which seemed to be making for a Royal Air Force Station nearby, 好像正朝着附近的一个皇家空军机场的方
向移动。这是定语从句。seem后接不定式的进行式，是 "似乎正在进行某事" 的意思。make for, 走向，飞向。

2 might be spying on ..., might＋不定式的进行时表示对正在进行的动作的推测。

3 keep track of, 是 "跟踪" 的意思。

4 make out, 看出，辨认出。

参考译文

　　一个飞行员发现了一只气球，它像是正飞往附近的一个皇家空军基地。他马上把情况报告了该基地，但那
里的人没有一个能解释这到底是怎么回事。控制塔上的官员得知这一消息后，非常气愤，因为气球有可能给飞
机造成极大的危险。他说可能有人正对基地进行侦察，因此命令那个飞行员跟踪那个奇怪的飞行物。飞行员设
法绕着气球飞了一阵。他看清了气球下面有 3 个人待在一只筐里，其中一个举着望远镜。当气球飞临基地上空
时，飞行员看见有一个人在拍照。不久，气球开始降落，在一个停机坪附近着了陆。警察被召来了，但他们却不
能逮捕任何人，因为筐里是两名国会议员和一名基地的指挥官！正如指挥官后来解释的那样，基地的这半边不知
道那半边正在干什么！

Summary writing 摘要写作

In not more than 85 words explain what happened from the time the pilot was ordered to keep track of the balloon. Write two different paragraphs using the points and connections given below.

用不超过 85 个单词的篇幅，描述一下从飞行员受命监视这个气球开始所发生的一切，用以下词组写出两段不同的文字。

CONNECTIONS		POINTS		CONNECTIONS
While circling		1	Pilot circled balloon.	*under which there was*
		2	Saw three men — basket.	*… containing*
one of whom		3	A pair of binoculars.	*one of whom*
When		4	Flew station.	*Before landing on*
		5	Took photographs.	*and*
Then		6	Landed — airfield.	
but		7	Police — arrest.	*As two of the men*
				were … and the
because		8	Two Members of Parliament and	*other was … the*
			Commanding Officer.	*police …*
Afterwards		9	One half — the other half.	*The mystery was*
				explained when

Composition 作文

Imagine that the police did not believe the three men and arrested them. Write two paragraphs in about 150 words using the ideas given below:

假设警察不相信这 3 个人，并逮捕了他们，按以下思路写出两段文字，字数为 150 个词左右：

1　The men struggled — they explained who they were — they were not believed — taken to the police station.
2　The police questioned the men — they refused to answer — the Commanding Officer telephoned the station — a senior officer arrived — he identified the C.O. — the police apologized.

Letter writing 书信写作

Write opening sentences which would be suitable for letters to the following:

按以下要求写出给下列 4 人的信的引言：

1 A friend who has not written to you for a long time.
2 A friend who has been expecting to hear from you for a long time.
3 An aunt who entertained you to dinner and a visit to the theatre.
4 A friend who has successfully passed a difficult examination.

Key structures 关键句型

Can, Be able to, Manage to (**KS19, 43, 67**)（复习第 19，43，67 课关键句型）

Exercises 练习

A　Underline the verbs *can, able to* and *manage to* in the passage. Note how they have been used.
　　画出课文中的 can, able to, manage to 并注意其用法。

B Supply the correct forms of *can, able to* and *manage to* in this paragraph. Do not refer to the passage until you finish the exercise:

用can, able to和manage to的正确形式填空，完成练习后再对照课文，核对你的答案：

He informed the station at once, but no one there _____ explain the mystery. The officer in the control tower was very angry when he heard the news, because balloons _____ be a great danger to aircraft. He said that someone might be spying on the station and the pilot was ordered to keep track of the strange object. The pilot _____ circle the balloon for some time. He _____ make out three men in a basket under it and one of them was holding a pair of binoculars.

C Supply the correct form of *can* or *be able to* in the following:

用can 或be able to的正确形式填空：

1 _____ you show me the way to the station please?

2 I gave him a few lessons and he _____ soon swim.

3 They _____ jump into the sea before the boat sank.

4 You _____ not leave this room until you get permission.

Special difficulties 难点

The verb *make* has a different meaning in each of the following sentences. Study them carefully.

在下面的句子，动词make有不同的含义。细读以下句子。

A balloon seemed to be *making for* a Royal Air Force Station. (11.1-2) (It seemed to be travelling towards …)

He could *make out* three men in a basket. (11.8-9) (He could see.)

I could not *make out* what he said. (I could not understand.) 我无法理解他说的话。

Please *make out* a fresh copy. (Write out another one.) 请重写一份。

He *made up* a story about two men and a horse. (He invented.) 他编造了一个有关两个人和一匹马的故事。

She spends hours *making up* in front of the mirror. (She uses cosmetics.) 她一连几个小时坐在镜子前化妆。

I must *make up for* the time I lost this morning. (I must compensate for …) 我必须把上午损失的时间补上。

Exercise 练习

Supply the missing words in the following sentences:

填空：

1 I lost my lecture notes and had to make _____ a new set.

2 I can't make _____ what you've written.

3 When it got dark we made _____ home.

4 My daughter often makes _____ stories of her own.

5 How can you make _____ all those lessons you missed?

Multiple choice questions 选择题

Comprehension 理解

1 The officer in the control tower was angry because _____ .

(*a*) he thought the men in the balloon were spies

(*b*) one of the men in the balloon was taking photographs

(*c*) the balloon was over the Royal Air Force Station

(*d*) he was worried about aircraft safety

Unit 4　Lesson 91

2 The officer in the control tower wouldn't have been angry _____ .

(a) if he had seen the balloon himself

(b) if he had known his Commanding Officer had arranged the trip

(c) if the balloon had gone away

(d) if the balloon had landed on an airfield

Structure 句型

3 A pilot noticed a balloon _____ for a Royal Air Force Station.

(a) make　(b) to make　(c) making　(d) in making

4 He informed the station _____ the balloon.

(a) for　(b) about　(c) of　(d) from

5 He was angry when he heard the news. He was angry _____ the news.

(a) with hearing　(b) in heating　(c) on hearing　(d) for heating

6 He heard the news. The news _____ bad.

(a) were　(b) are　(c) had　(d) was

7 The balloon contained two MPs. _____ two MPs in it.

(a) They were　(b) There were　(c) They had　(d) There had

Vocabulary 词汇

8 The Royal Air Force Station was nearby. It was _____ them.

(a) quite far　(b) quite close to　(c) beside　(d) rather far from

9 He was ordered to keep track of it. He was ordered to _____ it.

(a) record　(b) control　(c) follow　(d) check

10 He could make out three men. That's how many he could _____ .

(a) find　(b) see　(c) follow　(d) watch

11 Soon afterwards, the balloon began to descend. It began to come _____ .

(a) over　(b) off　(c) down　(d) away

12 The balloon landed near an airfield. It _____ .

(a) came along　(b) came down　(c) came over　(d) came off

Sentence structure 句子结构

Make two sentences from the following, then check your answer against the text.

把以下句子改写成两句话，然后对照课文第 1-3 行，核对你的答案。

The pilot who noticed a balloon which seemed to be making for a Royal Air Force Station nearby informed the station at once, but no one there was able to explain the mystery.

A pilot _____ .

417

Lesson 92   Asking for trouble   自找麻烦

First listen and then answer the question.
听录音，然后回答以下问题。

Why did the policeman ask the writer to come to the police station?

'I'd prefer to stay here'

It must have been about two in the morning when I returned home. I tried to wake up my wife by ringing the doorbell, but she was fast asleep, so I got a ladder from the shed in the garden, put it against the wall, and began climbing towards the bedroom window. I was
5 almost there when a sarcastic voice below said, 'I don't think the windows need cleaning at this time of the night.' I looked down and nearly fell off the ladder when I saw a policeman. I immediately regretted answering in the way I did, but I said, 'I enjoy cleaning windows at night.'

10   'So do I,' answered the policeman in the same tone. 'Excuse my interrupting you. I hate to interrupt a man when he's busy working, but would you mind coming with me to the station?'

'Well, I'd prefer to stay here,' I said. 'You see, I've forgotten my key.'

'Your what?' he called.

'My key,' I shouted.

15   Fortunately, the shouting woke up my wife who opened the window just as the policeman had started to climb towards me.

New words and expressions   生词和短语

fast (1.2) /fɑːst/ *adv.* 熟（睡）
ladder (1.3) /ˈlædə/ *n.* 梯子
shed (1.3) /ʃed/ *n.* 棚子

sarcastic (1.5) /sɑːˈkæstɪk/ *adj.* 讽刺的，讥笑的
tone (1.10) /təʊn/ *n.* 语气，腔调

Notes on the text   课文注释

1 I don't think, 当think后接表示否定意思的宾语从句时，通常在主句中使用否定形式，但译成汉语时否定意义仍在宾语从句中。

2 I immediately regretted answering in the way I did, 我立刻后悔不该那样回答。在regret后面可接动名词，也可接动词不定式，但表示的意思不一样。接动名词是对已发生的事情表示后悔，而接动词不定式则是对现在要发生的事表示抱歉。

3 So do I, 我也是的。这是接前面一句话 "I enjoy cleaning windows at night." 当前面一句话的谓语也适用于后一句时，可用so（肯定）或neither（否定）开头，然后接倒装语序。

参考译文

　　我回到家时，肯定已是凌晨两点左右了。我按响了门铃，试图唤醒我的妻子，但她睡得很熟。于是，我从花园的小棚里搬来了一个梯子，把它靠在墙边，开始向卧室的窗口爬去。快要爬到窗口时，下面一个人用讽刺的口

吻说:"我看不必在夜里这个时候擦窗子吧。"我向下面看去。当我看清是一个警察时,差一点儿从梯子上掉下去。我回答了他的话,但马上又后悔不该那样说,我是这样说的:"我喜欢在夜里擦窗子。"

"我也是的,"警察用同样的声调回答,"请原谅我打断了您。当一个人在忙着干活时,我是不愿意去打断他的,但请您跟我到警察局去一趟好吗?"

"可我更愿意待在这儿,"我说,"您瞧,我忘带钥匙了。"

"什么?"他大声问。

"钥匙!"我喊道。

幸运得很,这喊声惊醒了我的妻子。就在警察开始向我爬上来时,她打开了窗子。

Summary writing 摘要写作

In not more than 80 words describe what happened from the moment the writer returned home. Write two different paragraphs using the points and connections given below.

用不超过 80 个单词的篇幅描述一下作者回家后发生的事情,用以下要点和连词写出两段不同的文字。

CONNECTIONS	POINTS	CONNECTIONS
	1　The writer returned home — 2.0 a.m.	*On*
and	2　Rang doorbell.	
Having	3　Failed to wake wife.	*but*
	4　Put ladder — wall	*After having*
and	5　Climbed — bedroom window.	
Suddenly	6　Policeman called out.	*when*
but	7　Answered rudely.	*Answering*
	8　Told him — key.	
	9　Shouting woke wife.	
	10　Opened window.	*who*
just as	11　Policeman climbing ladder after him.	*at the moment when*

Composition 作文

Continue the above passage. Write two paragraphs in about 150 words using the ideas given below:

继续这个故事,用 150 个词左右写出两段文字:

1　At first my wife did not recognize me — thought l was a thief — saw the policeman — called for help.

2　The policeman pulled me down the ladder — my wife realized her mistake — she explained who I was — she apologized to the policeman — the policeman apologized to me.

Letter writing 书信写作

Address an envelope to a married woman who lives abroad.

你给一位居住在国外的已婚妇女写信,写出你的信封。

Key structures 关键句型

I don't think the windows need cleaning. **(KS20, 44, 68)**（复习第 20，44，68 课关键句型）

Unit 4 Lesson 92

Exercises 练习

A Give the correct form of the verbs in parentheses. Do not refer to the passage until you finish the exercise.

用括号中动词的正确形式填空,完成练习后再对照课文,核对你的答案:

I tried to wake up my wife by _____ (ring) the doorbell, but she was fast asleep, so I got a ladder from the shed in the garden, put it against the wall, and began _____ (climb) towards the bedroom window. I was almost there when a sarcastic voice below said, 'I don't think the windows need _____ (clean) at this time of the night.' I looked down and nearly fell off the ladder when I saw a policeman. I immediately regretted _____ (answer) in the way I did, but I said, 'I enjoy _____ (clean) windows at night.'

'So do I,' answered the policeman in the same tone. 'Excuse my _____ (interrupt) you. I hate _____ (interrupt) a man when he's busy _____ (work), but would you mind _____ (come) with me to the station?'

'Well, I'd prefer _____ (stay) here,' I said. 'You see, I've forgotten my key.'

'Your what?' he called.

'My key,' I shouted.

Fortunately, the _____ (shout) woke up my wife who opened the window just as the policeman had started _____ (climb) towards me.

B Complete the following sentences:

完成以下句子:

1 I am accustomed to _____ .

2 Fancy _____!

3 I always avoid _____ .

4 He accused me of _____ .

Special difficulties 难点

'I enjoy cleaning windows at night.'

'So do I,' answered the policeman. (ll.8-10)

Study these examples:

细读以下句子:

He reads a lot and *so do I*. 他书读得很多,我也是这样。

He doesn't read much and *neither do I*. 他很少读书,我也是这样。

He can swim and *so can I*. 他会游泳,我也会。

He can't swim and *neither can I*. 他不会游泳,我也不会。

Exercise 练习

Join each of these pairs of sentences using *so* or *neither*.

用so或neither连接以下各组句子。

1 He likes classical music. I like classical music.

2 He has had breakfast. I have had breakfast.

3 He doesn't like classical music. I don't like classical music.

4 She will buy a new dress. I will buy a new dress.

5 He hasn't had breakfast. I haven't had breakfast.

6 They ran quickly. We ran quickly.

7 She won't buy a new dress. I won't buy a new dress.

8 You are late. I am late.

9 They didn't run quickly. We didn't run quickly.

10 He could speak French. I could speak French.

11 He couldn't speak French. I couldn't speak French.

Multiple choice questions 选择题

Comprehension 理解

1 The policeman _____ .

  (a) believed the writer was going to clean the windows

  (b) suspected that the writer was a thief

  (c) arrested the writer

  (d) interrupted the writer when he was busy working

2 None of this would have happened if the writer _____ .

  (a) hadn't been rude

  (b) hadn't fallen off the ladder

  (c) had remembered his key

  (d) hadn't shouted at the policeman

Structure 句型

3 I don't think the windows need cleaning. They don't need _____ .

  (a) to clean   (b) to be clean   (c) to be cleaning   (d) to be cleaned

4 I regretted answering like that. I was sorry _____ so.

  (a) to do   (b) in doing   (c) to have done   (d) to be doing

5 Excuse my interrupting you. Excuse _____ you.

  (a) me to interrupt   (b) me for interrupting   (c) me for interrupt   (d) me in interrupting

6 Would you mind coming with me? I'd like _____ with me.

  (a) you to come   (b) to come   (c) coming   (d) you coming

7 I'd prefer to stay here. That's what I'd _____ .

  (a) do   (b) rather do   (c) have done   (d) do best

Vocabulary 词汇

8 She was fast asleep. She was _____ asleep.

  (a) deeply   (b) sound   (c) quick   (d) soon

9 I got a ladder from the shed. I _____ one.

  (a) fetched   (b) took   (c) brought   (d) carried

10 He spoke in a sarcastic voice. He spoke in a _____ voice.

  (a) funny   (b) laughing   (c) despicable   (d) mocking

11 I nearly fell off the ladder. I nearly _____ .

  (a) fell in   (b) fell over   (c) fell down   (d) fell away

12 Fortunately, the shouting woke my wife. _____ , it woke her up.

  (a) Luckily   (b) By chance   (c) By accident   (d) On purpose

Sentence structure 句子结构

Rewrite this sentence, then check your answer against the text.

改写以下句子, 然后对照课文第 1 行, 核对你的答案。

I think it was about two in the morning when I returned home.

It must _____ .

Lesson 93   A noble gift   崇高的礼物

First listen and then answer the question.

听录音，然后回答以下问题。

Where was the Statue of Liberty made?

One of the most famous monuments in the world, the Statue of
Liberty, was presented to the United States of America in the
nineteenth century by the people of France. The great statue, which
was designed by the sculptor Auguste Bartholdi, took ten years to
5   complete. The actual figure was made of copper supported by a
metal framework which had been especially constructed by Eiffel.
Before it could be transported to the United States, a site had to be
found for it and a pedestal had to be built. The site chosen was an
island at the entrance of New York Harbour. By 1884, a statue which was 151 feet tall had been erected in
10 Paris. The following year, it was taken to pieces and sent to America. By the end of October 1886, the statue
had been put together again and it was officially presented to the American people by Bartholdi. Ever since
then, the great monument has been a symbol of liberty for the millions of people who have passed through
New York Harbour to make their homes in America.

*One of the most
famous monuments*

New words and expressions   生词和短语

noble (title) /'nəʊbəl/ *adj.* 高尚的，壮丽的
monument (1.1) /'mɒnjʊmənt/ *n.* 纪念碑
statue (1.1) /'stætʃuː/ *n.* 雕像
liberty (1.2) /'lɪbəti/ *n.* 自由
present (1.2) /prɪ'zent/ *v.* 赠送
sculptor (1.4) /'skʌlptə/ *n.* 雕刻家
actual (1.5) /'æktʃuəl/ *adj.* 实际的，真实的

copper (1.5) /'kɒpə/ *n.* 铜
support (1.5) /sə'pɔːt/ *v.* 支持，支撑
framework (1.6) /'freɪmwɜːk/ *n.* 构架，框架
transport (1.7) /træ'spɔːt/ *v.* 运送
site (1.7) /saɪt/ *n.* 场地
pedestal (1.8) /'pedɪstəl/ *n.* 底座

Notes on the text   课文注释

1   the site chosen = the site which was chosen, 这里用过去分词作定语，与定语从句的作用相同。
2   take ... to pieces, 把……拆卸开。
3   put ... together, 把……装配起来。
4   make their homes in America, 在美国安家落户。

参考译文

　　世界上最著名的纪念碑之一的自由女神雕像是在 19 世纪时由法国人民赠送给美国的。这座由雕刻家奥古
斯特·巴索尔地设计的巨大雕像是用 10 年时间雕刻成的。这座雕像的主体是用铜制成的，由艾菲尔特制的金
属框架支撑着。在雕像被运往美国之前，必须为它选好一块场地，同时必须建造一个基座。场地选在了纽约港
入口处的一个岛上。到 1884 年，一座高度达 151 英尺的雕像在巴黎竖立起来了。第二年，它被拆成若干小块，
运到美国。到 1886 年 10 月底，这座雕像被重新组装起来，由巴索尔地正式赠送给美国人民。从那时起，这座

伟大的纪念碑对通过纽约港进入美国定居的千百万人来说就一直是自由的象征。

Summary writing 摘要写作

In not more than 80 words describe how the Statue of Liberty came to be built in New York Harbour. Write two different paragraphs using the points and connections given below.

用不超过 80 个单词的篇幅，描述一下自由女神像是如何建在纽约港的，用下面的要点和连词写出两段不同的文字。

CONNECTIONS		POINTS		CONNECTIONS
which		1 Statue — presented U.S.A.		
		2 French people — 19th century.		
		3 Designed — Bartholdi.		*Though*
and		4 Built on metal frame — Eiffel.		
where		5 Site chosen — island — New York Harbour.		
		6 Pedestal built.		*and*
		7 The statue erected Paris 1884.		*The statue was first*
and		8 Re-erected two years later — America.		*but*
		9 October 1886 — presented.		*and*

Composition 作文

Imagine you are entering New York Harbour by ship. Write two paragraphs in about 150 words using the ideas given below:

假设你正乘船进入纽约港，按下面的思路写出两段文字，字数为 150 个词左右：

1 Sailing into N.Y. Harbour between Long Island and Staten Island: the Statue of Liberty: first impressions.
2 A first glimpse of New York — Manhattan — skyscrapers: the Empire State building — the United Nations building — great ships in the harbour — bridges, traffic and people.

Letter writing 书信写作

Write five sentences which could be used to begin letters to friends. 写出 5 封给朋友的信的引言。

Key structures 关键句型

The Statue of Liberty was presented to the United States of America. **(KS21, 45, 69)**

（复习第 21，45，69 课关键句型）

Exercises 练习

A Underline the verbs in the passage and study their form.
  画出课文中所有动词，注意它们的形式。

B Give the correct form of the verbs in parentheses. Do not refer to the passage until you finish the exercise.
用括号中动词的正确形式填空，完成练习后再对照课文，核对你的答案。

One of the most famous monuments in the world, the Statue of Liberty, _____ (present) to the United States of America in the nineteenth century by the people of France. The great statue, which _____ (design) by the sculptor Auguste Bartholdi, took ten years to complete. The actual figure _____ (make) of copper _____ (support) by a metal framework which _____ especially _____ (construct) by Eiffel. Before it _____ (could/transport) to the United States, a site had _____ (to find) for it and a pedestal had _____ (to build). The site _____ (choose) was an island at the entrance of New York Harbour. By 1884, a statue which was 151 feet tall, _____ (erect) in Paris. The following year, it _____ (take) to pieces and _____ (send) to America. By the end of October 1886, the statue _____ (put) together again and it _____ officially _____ (present) to the American people by Bartholdi.

Special difficulties 难点
Stress 重音

Read these two sentences aloud:
大声朗读以下句子：

The Statue of Liberty was a present from the French people. 自由女神像是来自法国人民的一件礼物。

It was presented to the United States of America. 它被送给了美利坚合众国。

In the first sentence, *present* is a noun and the accent falls on the first syllable: /'prezənt/;

在第 1 个句子里，present 是一个名词，重音落在第 1 个音节上；

In the second sentence, *present* is a verb and the accent falls on the second syllable: /prɪ'zent/.

在第 2 个句子里，present 是一个动词，重音落在第 2 个音节上。

Here are some common words which are stressed in the same way:

以下词均有两种不同的重读方法 accent, conduct, contest, contrast, export, import, increase, insult, produce, protest, record, and transport.

Exercise 练习

Read these sentences aloud. Mark in the correct stress of the words in italics:
朗读以下句子，画出斜体字的重音：

1 This year we have *exported* more than we have *imported*.

2 Our *records* show that *exports* have gone up.

3 Everybody *protested* against the *increase* in income tax.

4 He was *insulted* when I criticized his *accent*.

5 Please *conduct* yourselves properly when you are in the museum.

6 He entered for the *contest* and broke a *record*.

Multiple choice questions 选择题
Comprehension 理解

1 The Statue of Liberty was first put up _____ .

(a) in 1886

(b) at the entrance of New York Harbour

(c) in Paris

(d) on a pedestal at the entrance of New York Harbour

2 The Statue of Liberty was presented to the American people _____ .

(a) by Eiffel who was the sculptor

(b) by Bartholdi who made the metal framework

(c) by the French Premier

(d) by the sculptor Bartholdi

Structure 句型

3 Who was the statue presented _____? The people of France.

(a) from   (b) by   (c) to   (d) at

4 It took him ten years to complete it. That's how long _____ to do it.

(a) he took   (b) him took   (c) took him   (d) he was taken

5 It was made _____ copper.

(a) by   (b) from   (c) of   (d) in

6 It was Eiffel _____ constructed the metal framework.

(a) whom   (b) which   (c) who   (d) whose

7 A site had to be found for it. It was necessary _____ for it.

(a) a site to be found   (b) for to be found a site

(c) for a site to be found   (d) to be found a site

Vocabulary 词汇

8 Copper is a kind of _____ .

(a) stone   (b) marble   (c) wood   (d) metal

9 It was especially constructed by Eiffel. It was constructed _____ .

(a) in particular   (b) particularly

(c) for a special purpose   (d) on purpose

10 A site had to be found for it. _____ had to be found.

(a) A land   (b) A plot of land   (c) A property   (d) An estate

11 It was erected in 1884. That's when it was _____ .

(a) put off   (b) put over   (c) put in   (d) put up

12 It's a symbol of liberty. It _____ liberty.

(a) replaces   (b) stands for

(c) is a representative of   (d) is an agent for

Sentence structure 句子结构

Join these sentences, then check your answer against the text.

连接以下句子, 然后对照课文第 1-3 行, 核对你的答案。

The Statue of Liberty is one of the most famous monuments in the world. It was presented to the United States of America in the nineteenth century by the people of France.

One _____ .

Lesson 94　Future champions　未来的冠军

🔊 **First listen and then answer the question.**

听录音，然后回答以下问题。

What kind of race do the children compete in?

Experiments have proved that children can be instructed in swimming at a very early age. At a special swimming pool in Los Angeles, children become expert at holding their breath under water even
before they can walk. Babies of two months old do not appear to be
5　reluctant to enter the water. It is not long before they are so accustomed to swimming that they can pick up weights from the floor of
the pool. A game that is very popular with these young swimmers
is the underwater tricycle race. Tricycles are lined up on the floor
of the pool seven feet under water. The children compete against each other to reach the other end of the
10　pool. Many pedal their tricycles, but most of them prefer to push or drag them. Some children can cover the
whole length of the pool without coming up for breath even once. Whether they will ever become future
Olympic champions, only time will tell. Meanwhile, they should encourage those among us who cannot
swim five yards before they are gasping for air.

future Olympic champions

New words and expressions　生词和短语

instruct (1.1) /ɪn'strʌkt/ v. 指导，传授
Los Angeles (11.2-3) /lɒs-'ændʒɪləs/ 洛杉矶
reluctant (1.5) /rɪ'lʌktənt/ adj. 勉强的，不愿意的
weight (1.6) /weɪt/ n. 重物
underwater (1.8) /ˌʌndə'wɔːtə/ adj. 水下的

tricycle (1.8) /'traɪsɪkəl/ n. 三轮车
compete (1.9) /kəm'piːt/ v. 比赛，对抗
yard (1.13) /jɑːd/ n. 码
gasp (1.13) /gɑːsp/ v. 喘气

Notes on the text　课文注释

1　hold their breath, 屏住呼吸。
2　be popular with …, 深受……的欢迎，为……所喜爱。
3　compete against, 与……竞争，与……抗衡。
4　come up for breath, 升上水面换气。
5　Whether they will ever become future Olympic champions, only time will tell. 他们将来是否能成为奥林匹克
的冠军，这只能由时间来作出回答。以 whether 引导的从句是 tell 的宾语，把宾语放在句首是为了强调。

参考译文

　　实验证明，儿童在很小的时候就可以开始学习游泳。在洛杉矶的一个特制的游泳池里，孩子们甚至在还没
有学会走路时就已经能熟练地在水下屏住呼吸了。两个月的婴儿并未显得不愿意入水。他们很快便适应了游
泳，以致能捡起池底的物品。这些幼小的游泳运动员非常喜爱的一种游戏是水下三轮车比赛。三轮车并排放在
7 英尺深的游泳池底上。孩子们比赛看谁先到达游泳池的另一端。很多孩子用脚蹬车，但多数孩子更愿意推或

是拉着三轮车。有些孩子能够跑完游泳池的全长而不用露出水面换气。他们将来是否能成为奥林匹克的冠军，这只能由时间来作出回答。与此同时，他们对我们中的那些游不了5码就已喘不过气来的人应该是种鼓舞。

Summary writing 摘要写作

In not more than 80 words describe what goes on at the children's swimming pool in Los Angeles. Write two different paragraphs using the points and connections given below.

用不超过 80 个单词的篇幅，描述一下在洛杉矶的儿童游泳池正在进行的试验，用以下要点和连词写出两段不同的文字。

CONNECTIONS	POINTS	CONNECTIONS
	1 Swimming pool — Los Angeles.	
	2 Children taught — hold breath — walk.	who
	3 Begin learning: two months old.	often begin
and, in time	4 Weights — bottom of pool.	Though
	5 Game they enjoy — race.	
which	6 Takes place seven feet under water.	This
Some … others	7 Pedal — push — pull.	and
and	8 A few get across — without coming up for air.	

Composition 作文

Imagine witnessing the sort of underwater tricycle race described in the passage. Write two paragraphs in about 150 words using the ideas given below:

假设你亲眼看见了课文中所讲的水下三轮车比赛。按以下思路写两段文字，字数为150个词左右：

1   The children dived into the water — found their tricycles — started off.
2   A child was pulling his tricycle — dropped it — hindered two others — got it out of the way — another child was pedalling hard — won the race — rose to surface dragging up his tricycle.

Letter writing 书信写作

Write suitable conclusions which could be used in letters to:

为给以下人写的信写出恰当的结束语：

1   A friend who has got a new job.
2   A friend you will be meeting soon.
3   A friend who has been ill.

Key Structures 关键句型

Review **KS22, 46, 70** 复习第 22，46，70 课关键句型

Exercise 练习

Study these examples:

细读以下例子：

Unit 4   Lesson 94

Children can be instructed *in* swimming … (11.1-2)

Children become expert *at* holding their breath … (11.3-4)

They do not appear to be reluctant *to* enter the water. (11.4-5)

They are so accustomed *to* swimming … (11.5-6)

The children compete *against* each other … (11.9-10)

Supply the missing words in the following sentences:

填空：

1 Many people do not approve _____ blood sports.

2 He was found guilty _____ murder and condemned _____ death.

3 Has it ever occurred _____ you that those twins are quite different _____ each other in many ways?

4 I consulted my lawyer _____ the matter and I shall act _____ his advice.

5 It is impossible to prevent them _____ quarrelling _____ each other.

6 He is responding _____ treatment and will soon be cured _____ his illness.

7 Even though he is thirty-five, he lives _____ his mother and is completely dependent _____ her.

8 I tried to reason _____ him, but he was very rude _____ me.

9 I am grateful _____ you for being so patient _____ him.

10 He might be good _____ his job, but you can't rely _____ him.

11 I am thinking _____ looking _____ a new job.

12 If you interfere _____ other people's affairs, you will regret it.

13 Do you believe _____ all that nonsense?

14 It should be obvious _____ you that if you persist _____ bothering him, he will get angry _____ you.

15 You demand too much _____ him; he is not really equal _____ the task.

16 Don't be so sure _____ yourself!

17 He has provided _____ every emergency.

18 I was afraid _____ mentioning it _____ him.

19 Don't blame him _____ this; I am responsible _____ what has happened.

20 He is so keen _____ learning, you should encourage him _____ his efforts.

21 Beware _____ people who appear to be enthusiastic _____ your success.

22 I appealed _____ him for help.

23 I am sorry _____ having asked him. I was shocked _____ his refusal.

24 Are you interested _____ opera?

25 Are you aware _____ the difficulties that lie ahead _____ you?

26 He's entitled _____ a pension, but he won't dream _____ retiring yet.

27 Who is going to pay _____ the damage?

28 This car is inferior _____ the one I bought last year.

29 I'm afraid I can't comment _____ your work just yet.

30 She may pride herself _____ her abilities, but she's not capable _____ bringing up children.

31 We are accustomed _____ bad weather.

32 How can you agree _____ such an idea when you are ignorant _____ the basic facts?

33 He confessed _____ me that he had just been converted _____ some strange religion.

34 She wanted to borrow the record _____ me but she was shy _____ asking.

35 If you fail _____ this attempt, don't count _____ me for help.

Multiple choice questions 选择题

Comprehension 理解

1 One of these statements is true. Which one?

(*a*) Children can learn to swim much earlier than is commonly supposed.

(*b*) Babies are unwilling to enter the water.

(*c*) All Los Angeles children learn to swim when they are very young.

(*d*) Children can only learn to swim after they have learnt to walk.

2 One of these statements is true. Which one?

(*a*) None of the children can cover the length of the pool without coming up for air.

(*b*) Not all the children ride their tricycles during the underwater race.

(*c*) The children don't like picking up weights.

(*d*) These children will certainly become Olympic champions one day.

Structure 句型

3 Children can be instructed in swimming. They can be _____ .

(*a*) learnt to swim   (*b*) learnt swimming   (*c*) taught how to swim   (*d*) learnt how to swim

4 They can be instructed in swimming _____ they are very young.

(*a*) in spite   (*b*) in spite of the fact that

(*c*) in spite of   (*d*) despite

5 They are accustomed to swimming. They _____ swimming.

(*a*) are used to   (*b*) are used   (*c*) used to   (*d*) used

6 _____ is the pool? Seven feet.

(*a*) How deeply   (*b*) How tall   (*c*) How high   (*d*) What depth

7 They compete _____ .

(*a*) against one another   (*b*) the one against the other

(*c*) each against the other   (*d*) against each one

Vocabulary 词汇

8 They are not reluctant to enter the water. They are _____ .

(*a*) unwilling to   (*b*) not ready to   (*c*) willing to   (*d*) slow to

9 The game is popular. _____ .

(*a*) It is common.   (*b*) It is well known.   (*c*) It is pleasing.   (*d*) They like it very much.

10 A tricycle has _____ .

(*a*) three wheels   (*b*) two wheels   (*c*) four wheels   (*d*) one wheel

11 Perhaps they will _____ future champions.

(*a*) begin as   (*b*) grow up to be   (*c*) get into   (*d*) happen to be

12 Some of us are gasping for air. We are soon _____ .

(*a*) without breath   (*b*) breathing   (*c*) out of breath   (*d*) coughing

Sentence structure 句子结构

Rewrite this sentence, then check your answer against the text.
改写以下句子, 然后对照课文第 5-6 行, 核对你的答案。

They are soon accustomed to swimming.

It is not long _____ .

Lesson 95   A fantasy   纯属虚构

 First listen and then answer the question.

听录音，然后回答以下问题。

Why was the Ambassador particularly lucky?

When the Ambassador of Escalopia returned home for lunch, his wife got a shock. He looked pale and his clothes were in a frightful state.

'What has happened?' she asked. 'How did your clothes get into
5 such a mess?'

'A fire extinguisher, my dear,' answered the Ambassador drily. 'University students set the Embassy on fire this morning.'

'Good heavens!' exclaimed his wife. 'And where were you at the time?'

10 'I was in my office as usual,' answered the Ambassador. 'The fire broke out in the basement. I went down immediately, of course, and that fool, Horst, aimed a fire extinguisher at me. He thought I was on fire. I must definitely get that fellow posted.'

The Ambassador's wife went on asking questions, when she suddenly noticed a big hole in her husband's hat.

15 'And how can you explain *that*?' she asked.

'Oh, that,' said the Ambassador. 'Someone fired a shot through my office window. Accurate, don't you think? Fortunately, I wasn't wearing it at the time. If I had been, I would not have been able to get home for lunch.'

*set the Embassy on fire
this morning*

New words and expressions 生词和短语

fantasy (title) /ˈfæntəsi/ *n.* 幻想故事
ambassador (1.1) /æmˈbæsədə/ *n.* 大使
Escalopia (1.1) /eskəˈləʊpɪə/ *n.* 艾斯卡罗比亚
　（虚构的国名）
frightful (1.2) /ˈfraɪtful/ *adj.* 可怕的，令人吃惊的
fire extinguisher (1.6) /ˈfaɪə-ˌɪkˈstɪŋgwɪʃə/ 灭火器
drily (1.6) /ˈdraɪli/ *adv.* 冷淡地，枯燥无味地

embassy (1.7) /ˈembəsi/ *n.* 大使馆
heaven (1.8) /ˈhevən/ *n.* 天，天堂
basement (1.10) /ˈbeɪsmənt/ *n.* 地下室
definitely (1.12) /ˈdefɪnɪtli/ *adv.* 肯定地
post (1.12) /pəʊst/ *v.* 派任
shot (1.16) /ʃɒt/ *n.* 子弹

Notes on the text 课文注释

1　get into such a mess, 搞得这样糟。
2　set on fire, 放火。
3　Good heavens! 天啊!
4　The fire broke out in the basement. 地下室突然着火。
5　aim ... at, 用……瞄准。
6　get that fellow posted, 把那个家伙派走。post可以与letter, parcel等名词连用，表示"寄"。如果把post与人连用时，仅指把人"派往"政府的一个新职位。

430

7　Accurate, don't you think? 很准, 是不是?

　　这个句子可以理解成: Don't you think it was accurate?

8　If I had been, I would not have been able to get home for lunch. 如果真戴着它, 我现在就不能回家来吃午饭了。

　　这是表示与过去的事实不相符合的虚拟语气结构。If I had been 后面省略了 wearing my hat。

参考译文

　　当艾斯卡罗比亚国的大使回到家吃午饭时, 把他的夫人吓了一跳。他面色苍白, 衣服也弄得不成样子。

　　"发生了什么事?"她问,"你的衣服怎么弄得一塌糊涂?"

　　"灭火器弄的, 亲爱的,"大使冷冷地回答,"今天上午大学生们放火烧了大使馆。"

　　"天啊!"他的夫人惊叫,"那你当时在什么地方?"

　　"我和往常一样, 在办公室里,"大使回答说。"地下室突然着火, 我当然马上下去了。但那个傻瓜霍斯特把灭火器对准了我。他认为是我着火了。我一定要把那个家伙打发走。"

　　大使夫人继续提出问题, 她突然又发现丈夫的帽子上有个洞。

　　"那么你对那又作何解释呢?"她问。

　　"那个嘛,"大使说,"有人向我办公室窗户开了一枪。真够准的, 是不是? 幸亏我当时没戴帽子。如果真戴着它, 我现在就不能回家来吃午饭了。"

Summary writing 摘要写作

In not more than 80 words write an account of what had happened at the Escalopian Embassy. Write two different paragraphs using the points and connections given below.

用不超过 80 个单词的篇幅, 描述一下艾斯卡罗比亚大使馆发生的事情, 用以下要点和连词写出两段不同的文字。

CONNECTIONS		POINTS		CONNECTIONS
While	[	1　Ambassador, Escalopia — in office.	]	
		2　Students — basement — fire.		*when*
When	[	3　Ambassador — went to investigate.		*After*
		4　Man called Horst — fire extinguisher	]	
because	[	5　Thought Ambassador on fire.		*under the impression*
Moreover	[	6　Hole — Ambassador's hat.		*In addition to this*
which		7　Made when someone fired shot — window.	]	*It*
	[	8　Ambassador lucky.		
for		9　Not wearing it.	]	*that*

Composition 作文

In about 150 words write an imaginary account of the scene in the basement when the Ambassador went down to investigate. Use the ideas given below:

按以下思路写出大使去地下室调查火情所发生的事情的想象性报道, 字数为 150 个词左右:

The Ambassador shouted — Horst explained: the Ambassador *was* on fire — the Ambassador denied it — Horst insisted — aimed the fire extinguisher at him — the Ambassador very angry — will send Horst to the South Pole — Horst explained that Escalopia has broken off diplomatic relations with the South Pole — the Ambassador went out angrily — Horst was pleased with himself.

Letter writing 书信写作

Write a letter to a friend inviting him or her to come to a party. Supply a suitable Introduction and Conclusion. Use the following ideas to write your *Purpose:*

给你的朋友写封信，邀请他（她）来参加一次聚会，写出恰当的引言和结束语，"目的"部分按以下思路写：the reason for the party — time and place — many old friends will be there.

Key structures 关键句型

Review of verb forms. 复习第 60，69 课的关键句型

Exercises 练习

A Imagine that you are writing a newspaper report of the conversation that took place between the Ambassador and his wife. Write the passage again using the notes given below:

假设你正为报社写一篇关于大使和他夫人对话的报道，用以下笔录写出这篇短文：

Lines 4-7   When she asked what … and how …, the Ambassador answered drily that a fire extinguisher had been responsible. He then told her that …

Lines 8-9   His wife was most surprised and asked him where …

Lines 10-11   The Ambassador answered that he … When the fire broke out … he … Omit: 'of course'.

Lines 11-12   Horst thought the Ambassador … The Ambassador said that he must …

Lines 13-14   … big hole in her husband's hat and asked him how …

Line 16   Omit: 'Oh, that,' The Ambassador said that someone had …

Lines 16-18   The shot was accurate, but fortunately he had not been wearing his hat at the time. If he …

B Give the correct form of the verbs in parentheses:

用括号中动词的正确形式填空：

'We just _____ (receive) a report,' _____ (say) the radio announcer, 'that rioting _____ (break) out in Umgolia. Students, who _____ (demonstrate) outside the Escalopian Embassy during the day, _____ (break) into the building last night and _____ (set) it on fire. The students _____ (protest) against the new tax on beer mugs which recently _____ (impose) by the Escalopian government. A spokesman _____ (say) that the beer mug industry in Umgolia seriously _____ (affect). The Escalopian Ambassador, who _____ (say) to have been slightly injured, bravely _____ (defend) by his servant, Mr. Flugel Horst. Mr. Horst _____ (keep) off the students with a fire extinguisher. The Premier of Umgolia _____ (announce) this evening that, in future, steps _____ (take) to prevent further incidents.'

C Give the correct form of the verbs in parentheses. Do not refer to the passage until you finish the exercise:

用括号中动词的正确形式填空，完成练习后再对照课文，核对你的答案：

1 'What _____ (happen)?' she asked. 'How _____ your clothes _____ (get) into such a mess?'

2 'Oh, that,' said the Ambassador. 'Someone _____ (fire) a shot through my office window. Accurate, _____ n't you think? Fortunately, I not _____ (wear) it at the time. If I had been, I not _____ (be able) to get home for lunch.'

Multiple choice questions 选择题

Comprehension 理解

1 The Ambassador got into a mess _____ .

  (*a*) while trying to put out the fire 　(*b*) while fighting the students

  (*c*) because he was on fire 　(*d*) because Horst thought he was on fire

2 Which word best describes the Ambassador? He was very _____ .

  (*a*) calm 　　(*b*) angry 　　(*c*) worried 　　(*d*) upset

Structure 句型

3 His wife got a shock. She _____ .

  (*a*) has shocked 　(*b*) was shocked 　(*c*) was shocking 　(*d*) shocked

4 They set the Embassy on fire. They tried _____ it.

  (*a*) to burn 　(*b*) burning 　(*c*) for burning 　(*d*) in burning

5 'Where were you?' His wife wanted to know where _____ .

  (*a*) he was 　(*b*) was 　(*c*) was he 　(*d*) he had been

6 I must get that fellow posted. I must _____ .

  (*a*) post him 　(*b*) have posted him 　(*c*) have him posted 　(*d*) have got him posted

7 Fortunately I wasn't wearing it. He was lucky _____ .

  (*a*) to be not 　(*b*) to not be 　(*c*) to don't be 　(*d*) not to be

Vocabulary 词汇

8 His clothes were in a mess, so they were _____ .

  (*a*) inside out 　(*b*) upside down 　(*c*) dirty 　(*d*) back to front

9 A fire extinguisher is used to put _____ a fire.

  (*a*) out 　(*b*) in 　(*c*) off 　(*d*) over

10 They tried to set the Embassy on fire. They tried to _____ .

  (*a*) fire it 　(*b*) shoot it 　(*c*) burn it down 　(*d*) light it up

11 The fire broke out in the basement. That's where it _____ .

  (*a*) burst 　(*b*) burst out 　(*c*) set out 　(*d*) began

12 Horst will be posted. He will be _____ .

  (*a*) dismissed 　　(*b*) sent by air

  (*c*) sent to another place 　(*d*) shot

Sentence structure 句子结构

This was the Ambassador's answer to his wife's question: 'A fire extinguisher, my dear.' Write the question, then consult the text.

写出大使夫人的问题, 然后对照课文第 4-5 行, 核对你的答案。

'How _____?'

Lesson 96   The dead return   亡灵返乡

First listen and then answer the question.

听录音, 然后回答以下问题。

What happens to the lanterns at the end of the festival?

a cheerful occasion

A Festival for the Dead is held once a year in Japan. This festival is a cheerful occasion, for on this day, the dead are said to return to their homes and they are welcomed by the living. As they are ex-pected to be hungry after their long journey, food is laid out for
5 them. Specially-made lanterns are hung outside each house to help the dead to find their way. All night long, people dance and sing. In the early morning, the food that had been laid out for the dead is thrown into a river or into the sea as it is considered unlucky for anyone living to eat it. In towns that are near the sea, the tiny lanterns which had been hung in the streets the
10 night before, are placed into the water when the festival is over. Thousands of lanterns slowly drift out to sea guiding the dead on their return journey to the other world. This is a moving spectacle, for crowds of people stand on the shore watching the lanterns drifting away until they can be seen no more.

New words and expressions 生词和短语

festival (1.1) /'festɪvəl/ n. 节日
lantern (1.5) /'læntən/ n. 灯笼

spectacle (1.11) /'spektəkəl/ n. 景象, 壮观, 场面

Notes on the text 课文注释

1 the dead are said to return to their homes, 据说死去的人要回到他们的家里来。the dead, 死人。定冠词用在某些形容词之前, 可以用来表示某类人。
2 lay out, 摆开, 展示, 摆设。
3 all night long, 整夜。
4 the other world, 另一个世界, 即阴间。

参考译文

　　日本每年过一次"亡灵节"。这个节日是个欢乐的日子, 因为在这一天, 据说死去的人要回到他们的家里来, 活着的人则对他们表示欢迎。因为预料到他们在经过长途旅行之后会感到饥饿, 所以为他们摆放好了食品。特制的灯笼挂在各家的门外, 为的是帮助亡灵看清道路。整个夜晚人们载歌载舞。一大早, 人们便把为死者摆放的食品扔进河中或海里, 因为人们认为活着的人吃了这些东西是不吉利的。在靠海的城镇中, 头天夜里挂在大街小巷的小灯笼在节后就放在了水里。成千上万只灯笼慢慢漂向大海, 指引着亡灵返回另一个世界。这是一个感人的场面, 人们成群地伫立在海岸上, 注视着灯笼远去, 直到再也看不见为止。

Summary writing 摘要写作

In not more than 80 words, give an account of the Festival for the Dead. Write two different paragraphs using the points and connections given below.
用不超过 80 个词的篇幅，描述一下亡灵节的景象，用以下要点和连词写出两段不同的文字。

CONNECTIONS		POINTS		CONNECTIONS
		1	Japanese annual festival — cheerful occasion.	
As		2	Dead return home.	*for*
		3	Food laid out.	*Food is not only*
and		4	Lanterns lit — guide them.	*but ... as well*
		5	People dance, sing all night.	*while*
and		6	Uneaten food — sea, river, next morning.	
		7	Some places: lanterns: sea.	
and		8	People watch — shore.	
until		9	Drift out of sight.	*as*

Composition 作文

Imagine witnessing the sort of festival described in the passage. Write two paragraphs in about 150 words using the ideas given below:
假设你亲眼看到了亡灵节的景象，按照以下思路写出两段文字，字数为 150 个词左右：

1　Preparations: the making of the lanterns; preparing food — description of the streets at night; people dancing and singing.
2　The following morning — food was thrown away — lanterns on the sea — people watching — the lanterns disappeared — the sun rose.

Letter writing 书信写作

Write a letter to a friend refusing an invitation to a party. Supply a suitable Introduction and Conclusion. Use the following ideas to write your *Purpose*:
朋友邀请你去参加一个聚会，写封信谢绝这一邀请。写出恰当的引言和结束语，"目的"部分按以下思路写：

you regret you cannot come — reason why — you bought tickets for a play a month ago — you have arranged to go with several friends.

Special difficulties 难点

Review **SD 74-91** 复习第 74-91 课的难点

Exercises 练习

A Words often confused 经常容易混淆的词

Choose the correct words in the following sentences:
选择正确的词：

435

Unit 4   Lesson 96

1 He came to see me yesterday as (usually) (usual). (第 76 课 a)

2 There was no one I knew (between) (among) those present. (第 76 课 b)

3 The (headmaster) (manager) of this store is kept very busy. (第 76 课 c)

4 Children's (cloths) (clothes) are difficult to choose. (第 81 课 a)

5 He never (greets) (salutes) anyone in the morning. (第 81 课 b)

6 Your hands are not very (clean) (clear), are they? (第 81 课 c)

7 Mary's in the kitchen. She's (washing) (washing up) the plates. (第 82 课 b)

8 If you lose your (temper) (mood) you will regret it. (第 83 课)

9 This problem is (enough) (too) difficult for me. (第 85 课)

10 He is (enough) (fairly) good at his work. (第 86 课 a)

11 He is trying hard but his work is still not good (enough) (fairly). (第 86 课 a)

12 Young people should remain (free) (single) for a few years before they marry. (第 89 课 a)

13 There was a long (row) (queue) at the bus stop. (第 89 课 b)

B   Get (第 74 课 a); keep (第 78 课); take (第 79 课); run (第 88 课); make (第 91 课).

Complete these sentences by adding any of the following words: *into, in, after, out, out of, down, up, away, for, over, from.*

选词填空, 完成句子。

1 His lies would not take ＿＿＿＿＿ anybody but a fool.

2 The explorers returned because they had run ＿＿＿＿＿ food.

3 He is very good at making ＿＿＿＿＿ stories for children.

4 It took him a long time to get ＿＿＿＿＿ his illness.

5 Mrs. Jones told her daughter to keep ＿＿＿＿＿ the stove.

6 During the storm, the ship made ＿＿＿＿＿ the nearest harbour.

7 Has this car been run ＿＿＿＿＿ yet?

8 The bird accidentally flew into the room and couldn't get ＿＿＿＿＿ .

9 He spoke so quickly, I didn't have time to take ＿＿＿＿＿ what he said.

10 Though we all ran ＿＿＿＿＿ the thief, we could not catch him.

11 I hadn't seen him for years and I accidentally ran ＿＿＿＿＿ him in the street this morning.

12 Ronald will take ＿＿＿＿＿ the family business now that his father has died.

13 Can you make ＿＿＿＿＿ the address on this envelope?

14 I've taken ＿＿＿＿＿ painting in my spare time.

Multiple choice questions 选择题

Comprehension 理解

1 The festival is a cheerful occasion because ＿＿＿＿＿ .

   (*a*) of the lanterns   (*b*) food is laid out for the dead

   (*c*) people stay up all night   (*d*) the dead are welcomed home by the living

2 What is the purpose of the lanterns?

   (*a*) They are nice decorations.

   (*b*) They can be thrown into the sea.

   (*c*) They are supposed to help the dead to find their way.

   (*d*) They help the living to find their way.

Structure 句型

3 _____ a year is the festival held? Only once a year.

  (*a*) How much   (*b*) How many   (*c*) How many times   (*d*) Which times

4 The dead are said to return. _____ they return to their homes.

  (*a*) It is saying   (*b*) People say   (*c*) People are said   (*d*) It said

5 All night long people dance and sing. They do this _____ .

  (*a*) during the whole night   (*b*) in all the night

  (*c*) the night long   (*d*) in the night

6 If anyone _____ the food he will be unlucky.

  (*a*) would eat   (*b*) will eat   (*c*) had eaten   (*d*) eats

7 Lanterns which had been hung in the streets _____ are placed into the water.

  (*a*) since the night   (*b*) a night ago   (*c*) the previous night   (*d*) before the night

Vocabulary 词汇

8 It's a cheerful occasion. It's a cheerful _____ .

  (*a*) situation   (*b*) condition   (*c*) place   (*d*) event

9 The food is thrown into the river. It is thrown _____ .

  (*a*) away   (*b*) off   (*c*) out   (*d*) down

10 The lanterns are placed into the water when the festival is over. This happens _____ the festival.

  (*a*) during   (*b*) after   (*c*) before   (*d*) at the same time as

11 The lanterns guide the dead to the other world. They _____ .

  (*a*) drive them   (*b*) steer them   (*c*) show them the way   (*d*) instruct them

12 It's a moving spectacle. It's a wonderful _____ .

  (*a*) view   (*b*) sight   (*c*) vision   (*d*) viewpoint

Sentence structure 句子结构

Rewrite this sentence, then check your answer against the text.

改写以下句子, 然后对照课文第 3-5 行, 核对你的答案。

It's expected that they will be hungry after their long journey, so food is laid out for them.

As they _____ .

Appendix 1: Personal names 附录 1： 人名中英文对照表

英文（课）	译文	英文（课）	译文
Aimé Thomé de Gamond (64)	埃梅·托梅·德·干蒙	Jasper White (28)	贾斯珀·怀特
		Jennifer (17)	詹尼弗
Anne Sterling (44)	安·斯特林	Jenny (63)	珍尼
Auguste Bartholdi (93)	奥古斯特·巴索尔地	Jeremy Hampden (63)	杰里米·汉普登
Bellinsky (60)	别林斯基（姓）	Jimmy Gates (65)	吉米·盖茨
Ben Fawcett (29)	本·弗西特	Joe Sanders (8)	乔·桑德斯
Benjamin Hall (71)	本杰明·霍尔	John Gilbert (39)	约翰·吉尔伯特
Bill Frith (8)	比尔·弗里斯	Kurt Gunter (37)	库尔特·冈特
Brian (78)	布赖恩	Lucy (2)	露西
Brinksley Meers (74)	布林克斯利·米尔斯	Malcolm Campbell (72)	马尔科姆·坎贝尔
Charles Alison (12)	查尔斯·艾利森	Merlin Greeves (74)	默林·格里夫斯
Dan Robinson (34)	丹·鲁宾逊	Millington (39)	米灵顿（姓）
Debbie Hart (36)	黛比·哈特	Nasmyth (80)	内史密斯（姓）
Donald (72)	唐纳德	Nigel Dykes (68)	奈杰尔·戴克斯
Eames (69)	埃姆斯（姓）	Patrick (83)	帕特里克
Eiffel (93)	艾菲尔（姓）	Percy Buttons (6)	珀西·巴顿斯
Elizabeth (68)	伊丽莎白	Rex (59)	雷克斯
Frank Hawkins (31)	弗兰克·霍金斯	R. E. Byrd (43)	R. E. 伯德
Fratelli (76)	弗拉特里（姓）	Riccardo Brabante (76)	里卡多·布拉班特
Giuseppe Moldova (76)	朱塞皮·莫尔道瓦	Rockwall Slinger (74)	罗克沃尔·斯林格
Gloria Gleam (74)	格洛里亚·格利姆	Roy Trenton (35)	罗伊·特雷顿
Harmsworth (15)	哈姆斯沃斯（姓）	Rumbold (40)	兰伯尔德（姓）
Haroun Tazieff (67)	哈罗恩·塔捷耶夫	Sam Benton (45)	萨姆·本顿
Harrison (38)	哈里森	Shepenmut (77)	塞潘姆特
Helen Bates (54)	海伦·贝茨	Stuart Page (55)	斯图亚特·佩奇
Horst (95)	霍斯特	Susan (19)	苏珊
Hugh (51)	休	Tim (3)	蒂姆
Ian Thompson (47)	伊恩·汤普森	Tony Steele (11)	托尼·斯蒂尔
James Scott (5)	詹姆斯·斯科特	Wentworth Lane (83)	温特沃兹·莱恩
Jane (22)	简	William Low (64)	威廉·洛

Appendix 2: Geographical names 附录2：地名中英文对照表

英文（课）	译文	英文（课）	译文
Alice Springs (4)	艾利斯斯普林斯	London (25)	伦敦
America (93)	美国	Los Angeles (94)	洛杉矶
Atlantic, the (12)	大西洋	Madagascar (82)	马达加斯加
Australia (4)	澳大利亚	Mediterranean, the (38)	地中海
Birmingham (29)	伯明翰	New York Harbour (93)	纽约港
Bonneville Salt Flats (72)	邦纳维尔盐滩	Nigeria (23)	尼日利亚
Britain (90)	英国	North Pole, the (43)	北极
Calabria (76)	卡拉布里亚	North Sea (90)	北海
Calais (73)	加来	Old Delhi (42)	旧德里
California (53)	加利福尼亚	Paris (73)	巴黎
Congo (67)	刚果	Perpignan (73)	佩皮尼昂
Crystal Palace, the (80)	水晶宫	Perth (4)	珀斯
Darwin (4)	达尔文	Pinhurst (5)	平赫斯特
Dover (73)	多佛	Portsmouth (12)	朴次茅斯
Escalopia (95)	艾斯卡罗比亚	Rockall (29)	罗卡尔
England (23)	英国	Samoa (66)	萨摩亚
English Channel, the (36)	英吉利海峡	Silbury (5)	锡尔伯里
Europe (79)	欧洲	South Africa (7)	南非
Ferngreen (87)	芬格林	South America (79)	南美洲
France (14)	法国	South Pacific (66)	南太平洋
Frinley (58)	弗林利	South Pole, the (43)	南极
Germany (10)	德国	Sweden (16)	瑞典
Greenwich Observatory (71)	格林尼治天文台	Sydney (46)	悉尼
Holland (22)	荷兰	Teheran (49)	德黑兰
Hyde Park (80)	海德公园	Temple of Thebes, the (77)	底比斯神庙
Italy (3)	意大利	Utah (72)	犹他
Japan (96)	日本	Wallis Island (66)	瓦立斯岛
Lake Kivu (67)	基伍湖	Woodford Green (50)	伍德福德草地

新概念英语系列·全套产品目录

教材及教学辅导用书	书号 *
新概念英语 1（另配录音带 2 盒）	1346-6 (01)
新概念英语 2（另配录音带 3 盒）	1347-3 (01)
新概念英语 3（另配录音带 3 盒）	1348-0 (01)
新概念英语 4（另配录音带 3 盒）	1349-7 (01)
新概念英语 教师用书 1（另配录音带 4 盒）	1350-3
新概念英语 教师用书 2（另配录音带 4 盒）	1351-0
新概念英语 教师用书 3（另配录音带 4 盒）	1771-6
新概念英语 教师用书 4（另配录音带 4 盒）	1841-6
新概念英语 练习册 1	1840-9
新概念英语 练习册 2	1723-5
新概念英语 练习册 3	2482-0
新概念英语 练习册 4	2775-3 (01)
新概念英语 自学导读 1	1799-0
新概念英语 自学导读 2	1733-4
新概念英语 自学导读 3	1940-6
新概念英语 自学导读 4	2512-4
新概念英语 练习详解 1	2225-3
新概念英语 练习详解 2	1812-6
新概念英语 练习详解 3	1873-7
新概念英语 练习详解 4	2329-8
新概念英语 词汇随身听速记手册 1（另配录音带 4 盒）	3063-0
新概念英语 词汇随身听速记手册 2（另配录音带 4 盒）	3150-7
新概念英语 词汇随身听速记手册 3（另配录音带 7 盒）	3151-X
新概念英语 词汇练习 1	4208-4
新概念英语 词汇练习 2	5632-6
新概念英语 词汇练习 3	4390-6 (01)
新概念英语 词汇练习 4	5633-4
新概念英语 语法练习 1	3304-4
新概念英语 语法练习 2	4591-X
新概念英语 语法练习 3	4308-1
新概念英语 口语练习 1	4391-3
新概念英语 口语练习 2	4573-3
新概念英语 口语练习 3	4752-2
新概念英语 口语练习 4	4792-8

教材及教学辅导用书	书号 *
新概念英语 词汇大全	1727-3
新概念英语 语法手册	4230-5
新概念英语（1）课本同步讲解辅导 VCD	
新概念英语（2）课本同步讲解辅导 VCD	
新概念英语（3）课本同步讲解辅导 VCD	
新概念英语（4）课本同步讲解辅导 VCD	
新概念英语（盒装版）	
新概念英语 1（含 CD 2 张）	6729-2
新概念英语 2（含 CD 3 张）	6730-8
新概念英语 3（含 CD 3 张）	6731-5
新概念英语 4（含 CD 3 张）	6732-2
新概念英语 1（含录音带 2 盒）	6725-4
新概念英语 2（含录音带 3 盒）	6726-1
新概念英语 3（含录音带 3 盒）	6727-8
新概念英语 4（含录音带 3 盒）	6728-5
新概念英语青少版	
新概念英语青少版 学生用书 1A（含 mp3 和动画 DVD）	7354-5
新概念英语青少版 学生用书 1B（含 mp3 和动画 DVD）	7356-9
新概念英语青少版 学生用书 2A（含 mp3 和动画 DVD）	7371-2
新概念英语青少版 学生用书 2B（含 mp3 和动画 DVD）	7372-9
新概念英语青少版 学生用书 3A（含 mp3 和动画 DVD）	7373-6
新概念英语青少版 学生用书 3B（含 mp3 和动画 DVD）	7374-3
新概念英语青少版 练习册 1A	7355-2
新概念英语青少版 练习册 1B	7357-6
新概念英语青少版 练习册 2A	7375-0
新概念英语青少版 练习册 2B	7376-7
新概念英语青少版 练习册 3A	7377-4
新概念英语青少版 练习册 3B	7378-1
新概念英语青少版 教师用书 1（含 mp3）（另配录音带）	7368-2
新概念英语青少版 教师用书 2（含 mp3）（另配录音带）	7369-9
新概念英语青少版 教师用书 3（含 mp3）（另配录音带）	7370-5

* 本产品目录中书号为完整书号的后 5 位；如订书，请在前面加 978-7-5600-。

上述图书和音像产品全国各大书店均有销售。欢迎登录新概念英语官方教学网站 **www.ncehome.com** 查询具体信息。